D1711525

# FIRST CORINTHIANS:

## An Exegetical and Explanatory Commentary

### A Somewhat Traditional Interpretation
### Plus Contemporary Application

Also by B Ward Powers

*A Brief Outline of the Books of the Bible*
*The Christian and his Church*
*The Christian and his Salvation*
*Divorce*
*Learn To Read the Greek New Testament*
*Marriage and Divorce: The New Testament Teaching*
*Notes and Comments on 1 Corinthians*
*Principles and Practice of Religious Accounting & Taxation*
*The Progressive Publication of Matthew's Gospel*
*Remarriage After Divorce — A Christian Perspective*
*The Ministry of Women in the Church: Which Way Forward?*
*The Sin That We Treat As a Virtue*
*This Fragile World: The Earth God Gave To Man*
*To Take It Upon Himself*
*The Writing of the Synoptic Gospels*

Contributor to

*Faith Active in Love* (Edited by J. Diesendorf)
*New Dictionary of Biblical Theology* (Edited by T. Alexander)


*Dedicated to all those diligent students of Scripture*
*who, down the years and still today, are*
*wrestling with the sometimes difficult -*
*and always important - question of*
*what Paul meant by what he said*

# FIRST CORINTHIANS:

# An Exegetical and Explanatory Commentary

*"Let the reader understand ..." (Matthew 25:15//Mark 13:14)*

**A Consideration of Some Views Ancient and Modern
in the Light of A Verse-by-Verse Look at
What the Text Actually Says**

**A Somewhat Traditional Interpretation
Plus Contemporary Application**

*by B Ward Powers*
B.A., B.D., B.Comm., Th.L., Dip.R.E., M.A., Ph.D.

2008

WIPF & STOCK · Eugene, Oregon

Wipf and Stock Publishers
199 W. 8th Avenue
Eugene OR 97401

Copyright © 2008, by I.M.P.A.C.T. Inc.,
259A Trafalgar Street, PETERSHAM NSW 2049 AUSTRALIA.

ISBN: 978-1-55635-933-0

Typeset in 11 pt Times Roman and printed in USA.

# CONTENTS

# EXPLANATIONS

Where reference is made to a commentator without a page number being given, the reference is to that commentator's commentary on the verse under consideration.

Bibliographical information about a book or article cited is given under the author's (editor's) name at the end of this volume. (There are no footnotes in the text.)

// is used between Gospel references to indicate parallel passages.

cf = compare; p., pp. = page(s); f., ff. = following (singular/plural)

The letter E after a verse reference indicates that that verse is the End of that chapter.

# INTRODUCTION

## CONSIDERING 1 CORINTHIANS

This book is one of Paul's major writings, not only because of its length but because of its subject matter. Indeed we can note that every major doctrine in the New Testament is given its most thorough consideration and exposition in either this Epistle or Romans (or both). And Romans was written from Corinth only about two years after 1 Corinthians.

There are, then, dozens of commentaries available on 1 Corinthians. Go into any Christian bookshop, and look at them all, large and small, older ones still in demand and recent ones just out. Why add another to the collection?

There are basically two reasons for writing this commentary. Firstly, because on numerous issues some of the great writers and exegetes of the past have shown wisdom and insight in their understanding of Paul's message in this Epistle, while many modern commentators have gone in a different direction. In quite a few of these cases, relating to numerous passages of this Epistle, I believe we need to recapture some of this wisdom and insight which may be in danger now of being lost or overlooked. In this commentary I wish to remind readers - students and scholars alike - of these "traditional" views, and draw attention to the basis and the reasons for them.

Additionally, though, it seems to me that there are also places in this Epistle where some further reflection upon the text is warranted. Translational traditions have developed which result in each new translation that is published following the same approach to a passage, when that approach and interpretation may validly be open to question. Related to this, there are places where most of the mainstream versions (or a significant number of them) have a very "interpretational" approach to the translation of a passage, and where I do not consider this interpretation to be quite so settled. Or at least the translation should be made more neutral where the Greek leaves the meaning more open, or certainly the issue should be aired and readers alerted to the fact that the matter is not as clearcut and definite as some versions imply - that in fact it warrants further consideration.

We can for example see numerous instances along these lines in a comparison of recent "committee" translations such as the ESV, NIV,

NKJV, REB, and NRSV with other and more "independent" translations like J B Phillips and Richmond Lattimore and those of particular scholars in their commentaries. (And I mention these in their appropriate contexts.)

Then in commentaries themselves, it is salutary to compare a major "new" commentary on *1 Corinthians* such as that by David Garland, in the Baker Exegetical Commentary series on the New Testament (published 2003) with an older "traditional" commentary like that of Charles Hodge, first published in 1857, but still in print. (It is, I think, instructive that Garland does not refer to Hodge at all, though he cites a very considerable number of other commentaries.)

When seeking to understand Paul's teaching, and ascertain his meaning, it is of course crucial to consider each passage in terms of what he wrote in Greek. Where interpretations differ, we must weigh the arguments for each position, and how they line up with what is found in the Greek. The aim will be to adopt that interpretation of the passage which we can see to be - to the best of our knowledge - most faithful to what the Greek text, as Paul wrote it, actually says. I therefore refer regularly to Greek words and expressions, but the transliteration and translation is given in each instance, so that a reader without Greek will be able to follow the discussion and see what is at issue, and how it points this way or that.

A comparison of any two commentaries, chosen pretty-well at random, will show examples of the differing ways in which 1 Corinthians can be interpreted. And where we do not feel that the evidence clearly supports one view rather than another, then we must hold our own view with a measure of caution and tentativity, ready to change if subsequently we receive more light upon the problem.

An awareness of this will encourage us to keep an open mind and to avoid becoming overdogmatic about our chosen interpretation of a particular passage. On the other hand, we must come to *some* conclusion, on the basis of the evidence, to the best of our respective abilities in understanding it. My goal has been to give more careful consideration to those passages where Christians differ in their viewpoints, drawing attention to those issues which seem significant for our understanding, so that readers will have a more informed basis for coming to their own conclusions in these matters.

The treatment of the biblical material in this commentary will focus primarily upon the meaning of the text, including its exegesis and practical and pastoral application for life in today's world - the commentary on a chapter therefore concludes with a section of reflection upon these considerations.

At controversial points, where differing views are held in the churches, I will aim to tell you about them and to explain fully my reasons for coming to my particular conclusions about the meaning of the text.

## A TRADITIONALIST APPROACH?

Does this Commentary take a traditionalist approach in interpretation? Well, yes and no. In a word: frequently. I am not intentionally seeking to adopt a traditionalist line in my approach to the Epistle, but rather to study it carefully on its own terms to understand what Paul means by what he says. But then, in comparing the outcome of my own examination of the text with that of others, I have found that frequently I have come to the same understanding of Paul's meaning as that of early church commentators. Of course there are many sections of the Epistle in which they did not seem especially interested or which they pass over lightly, saying no more than can be seen from a surface reading of the text, whereas current issues in our present century would cause us to examine more closely the meaning and application of Paul's teaching. On the other hand, on numbers of matters of contemporary relevance they do show views which are significant.

One of these in particular is the meaning of "tongues" in chapters 12 to 14, where this term is taken by early church fathers as referring to human languages as in Acts 2 - this is also the view of Calvin, Wesley, Hodge, and numbers of other commentators. I have come to the same conclusion: what Paul says in this section of the Epistle makes a great deal more sense and is self-consistent when seen in this way.

But there are other times when I would dissent from the views of the early commentators. This is especially so in relation to their views on sex and marriage and attendant issues ranging from virginity to divorce (chapters 6 and 7). As will be seen in the discussion of these chapters, there was in the early church a widespread negative attitude towards sex (which was frequently regarded as a necessary evil for the purpose of procreation, and not to be enjoyed), and marriage (which was considered much inferior to virginity and which prevented one from being fully devoted to the Lord). In my book *Marriage and Divorce - the New Testament Teaching* I have traced in some detail how and when this negative view of sex and marriage came to enter the church, and how its origins are Manicheanism and Platonism and not from Paul; in my discussion (below) of chapters 6 and 7 of the Epistle I present the case for seeing that the early church commentators missed Paul's meaning in relation to these issues.

One basic issue where I totally concur with their approach is in regard to the inspiration and authority of Paul's teaching in this Epistle. We may need to wrestle with the text and argue about its meaning, but once we have arrived at our understanding of what Paul is teaching, it is to be believed and acted upon. It is the Word of the Lord, given to us through Paul. In this Epistle it comes through very clearly that Paul had a high view of his authority, together with that of his fellow apostles. He claimed that they were inspired by the Holy Spirit, down to their very words (2:12-13). He differentiated carefully between what he could quote from the Lord's teaching and what he was saying upon his own authority (7:10, 12, 25) - but that authority was directly from the Lord through the Spirit (7:40; 11:23; 14:37) and is not to be lightly regarded.

A second issue that is related to this: the early church commentators saw Paul's teaching in this Epistle as being part of the inspired mosaic of God's revelation, and they brought to bear upon a given passage the other related teachings of Scripture (from elsewhere in Paul's writings or from anywhere else in Old Testament or New) which threw light on, or could add to, what 1 Corinthians taught.

Kovacs (in *1 Corinthians Interpreted by Early Christian Commentators*, pages xiv-xvi) tells us that:

> early Christian commentators believed that the Bible spoke with a single (though nuanced) voice, and they took apparent inconsistencies between biblical authors as an invitation to probe below the surface of the inspired words, that is, to penetrate the spiritual reality about which the text spoke ... When they listened to the Scripture read in divine worship or pondered its words in prayer, the early Christians heard the Word of God spoken to their communities and to their lives. [In his commentaries Origen of Alexandria] is interpreting Scripture by Scripture, an axiom accepted by all early Christian writers. 'The entire Scripture is one book and was spoken by the one Holy Spirit,' wrote Cyril of Alexandria, another prolific biblical commentator.

With these two basic attitudes I am in full agreement. Paul is quite clear in his claim to inspiration and authority. We cannot reject or qualify that claim and still accept his teaching (or some of it, being selective about what we take and what we reject). Unless we are going to entirely reject the historic Christian faith, we much assent fully to the authority with which Paul writes. And if we are going to accept his teaching, how important it then is to understand correctly his meaning. This is a task and a delight to which we now set our mind and our hand.

# OUTLINE OF 1 CORINTHIANS

**INTRODUCTION: GREETINGS AND THANKSGIVING (1:1-9)**
1. Greetings (1:1-3)
2. Thanksgiving (1:4-9)

**SECTION 1: DIVISIONS IN THE CHURCH (1:10-4:21E)**
1. The Right Relationship Between Brothers in Christ (1:10)
2. The Problem in the Church At Corinth (1:11-12)
3. Paul's Response To This Problem (1:13-2:16E)
        not baptism, but preaching the gospel (1:13-17a)
     Paul's Excursus: God's Message For Mankind (1:17b-2:16E)
     not eloquent wisdom, but the power of the cross (1:17b)
     (a) The Content of God's Message (1:18-20)
     (b) The Response to God's Message (1:21-25)
     (c) The Effectiveness of God's Message (1:26-2:10)
     (d) The Inspiration of God's Message (2:11-16E)
4. Consequences of the Division Amongst the Corinthians (3:1-4)
5. Paul's Response To This Situation (3:5-4:21E)

**SECTION 2: CONCERNING SEX AND MARRIAGE (5:1-7:40E)**
1. Dealing With A Case of Immorality (5:1-13E)
2. Christians and Lawsuits (6:1-8)
3. Sexual Fulfillment - Getting It Wrong (6:9-20E)
4. Sexual Fulfillment - Getting It Right (7:1-5)
5. Problems Concerning the Married (7:6-16)
    (a) Problems if a relationship has terminated (7:6-9)
    (b) Problems that split a marriage (7:10-11)
    (c) Problems of a divided marriage (7:12-16)
6. Leading the Life the Lord Assigns (7:17-24)
7. Problems Concerning the Unmarried (7:25-40E)

**SECTION 3(a): CONCERNING**
     **THINGS SACRIFICED TO IDOLS (8:1-11:1)**
1. The Issue Stated (8:1-13E)
2. The Nature of Freedom (9:1-27E)
3. The Example of the Fathers (10:1-22)
4. Summary: Principles of Action (10:23-11:1)

**SECTION 3(b): CONCERNING**
     **BEHAVIOR IN THE CHURCH OF GOD (11:2-34E)**
1. Women and a Covering (11:2-16)
2. The Lord's Supper (11:17-34E)

**SECTION 4: CONCERNING**
         **GIFTS AND MINISTRIES IN THE CHURCH (12:1-14:40E)**
1. The Nature of the Gifts and Ministries (12:1-11)
2. The Reason for the Gifts and Ministries (12:12-26)
3. The Allocation of the Gifts and Ministries (12:27-31E)
4. The Exercise of the Gifts and Ministries (13:1-13E)
5. The Role of Tongues and Prophecy (14:1-40E)

**SECTION 5: CONCERNING THE RESURRECTION (15:1-58E)**
1. The Message of the Gospel (15:1-11)
2. The Necessity of Christ's Resurrection (15:12-34)
3. The Nature of our Resurrection (15:35-58E)

**SECTION 6: FINAL MESSAGES AND GREETINGS (16:1-24E)**
1. The Collection For The Jerusalem Saints (16:1-4)
2. Plans, People, and Exhortations (16:5-24E)

# CHRONOLOGICALLY SPEAKING

A wise and valuable preliminary at this point, in preparation for studying this Epistle, is to anchor it in time and space. Therefore it would be helpful now to take your copy of a Bible Atlas and locate Corinth on it, on the isthmus connecting the Peloponnesus to the rest of Greece. Also note where Ephesus is, from which Paul wrote this letter, which letter was then taken to Corinth ("through Fortunatus, Stephanas and Achaicus", John Chrysostom tells us [Kovacs 10] - 16:15-18).

Hurd 138f. explains:

> Paul expected his letter to arrive in Corinth before Timothy, as 16:10 indicates: "*If* Timothy should come, see that you put him at ease among you. ..." The "if" (with the subjunctive verb) shows that the letter was not entrusted to Timothy, and that Paul was not sure whether Timothy would reach Corinth or not. Corinth, therefore, was not Timothy's principal destination. This fact suggests that Timothy had travelled north from Ephesus to visit the churches in Macedonia, and that the letter was to travel a faster route. It is possible, of course, that the bearers of the letter planned to use the overland route but did not intend to visit along the way. It is more probable, however, that the faster route was a shorter route, namely the route by sea.

Next, check out the Chronology of Paul's life and where his contacts with the Corinthians come in his ministry. There is some doubt, to a varying extent, about the different key dates in Paul's life, but we have a high level of certainty that Gallio was appointed to office (Acts 18:12) in AD 51.

Other dates tend to be calculated from this time, forwards and back. After consideration of the factors involved, and the views of others, this is the chronology at which I have arrived:

## CHRONOLOGY OF THE GOSPELS, ACTS, AND PAUL'S LIFE
*(Entries in bold italic type indicate events from Roman or Jewish history.)*

| | |
|---|---|
| 5/4 BC | Birth of Jesus Christ |
| 30 April 7-9 | Crucifixion/Resurrection |
| 32 or 33 | Paul's conversion (Acts 9:1-19a) |
| 32/33-35 | In Damascus (Acts 9:19b-25; Gal 1:15-17; 2 Cor 11:32-33) |
| 35 | Paul's First post-conversion visit to Jerusalem (Ac 9:26-30; Gal 1:18-24E) |
| 35-45 | In Syria and Cilicia (Acts 9:30) |
| 45 | Barnabas brings Paul back to Antioch (Acts 11:25-26) |
| 46 | Paul's Second (famine-relief) visit to Jerusalem (Acts 11:27-12:25E) |
| 47-48 | **First Missionary Jrny: Cyprus-Derbe-Syrian Antioch** (Ac 13:1-14:28E) |
| 48 | Judaizers come to Syrian Antioch & Galatia (Acts 15:1-2; Gal 1:7; 2:12) |
| 48 | *The Epistle to the Galatians* written (from Antioch) (Acts 15:2) |
| 48 | Council of Jerusalem (Paul's Third visit to Jerusalem) (Acts 15:3-35) |
| 49 early spring | **Commencement of Paul's Second Missionary Journey** (Acts 15:36-40) |
| 49 | Second Missionary Journey: Antioch to Troas (Acts 15:41-16:10) |
| *49* | ***Claudius expelled all the Jews from Rome*** (Acts 18:2) |
| 49 | First visit to Philippi (Acts 16:11-40E) |
| 49 | Thessalonica-Berea-Athens (Acts 17:1-34E) |
| 50 early | Arrival in Corinth; staying with Aquila & Priscilla (Acts 18:1-4) |
| 50-51 | In Corinth (Acts 18:1-11) |
| 50 | Silas and Timothy arrive from Macedonia (Acts 18:5) |
| 50 | *The Epistles to the Thessalonians* written (from Corinth) |
| *51-52* | ***Gallio proconsul of Achaia*** |
| 51 May/July | After 18 months, appearance before Gallio (Acts 18.11-17) |
| 51 autumn | Corinth-Jerusalem; Fourth visit to Jerusalem (Acts 18:18-22a) |
| 51 | Jerusalem-Antioch (Acts 18:22b) |
| 51 winter | In Antioch (Acts 18:23a) |
| *52* | ***Felix succeeded Cumanus as Procurator of Judea*** |
| 52 spring | **Commencement of Paul's Third Missionary Journey** (Acts 18:23b) |
| 52 late summer | Arrival in Ephesus (Acts 19:1-7) |
| 52-55 | At Ephesus (Acts 19:8-41E) |
| *54 Oct 13* | ***Nero proclaimed emperor in Rome after death of Claudius*** |
| 55 spring | *The First Epistle to the Corinthians written* (from Ephesus) |
| 55 | Second visit to Corinth (from Ephesus; 2 Cor 2:1; 12:14; 13:1) |
| 55 summer | From Ephesus to Troas (2 Cor 2:12) |
| 56 early | In Macedonia (2 Cor 2:13; Acts 20:1); Second visit to Philippi |

| | |
|---|---|
| 56 | *The Second Epistle to the Corinthians written* (from Macedonia) |
| 56 | Ministry in Macedonia and Illyricum (Romans 15:19-23) |
| 56 winter | In Achaia; Third visit to Corinth (Acts 20:2; 1 Cor 16:5-6) |
| 57 early | *The Epistle to the Romans* written (from Corinth) |
| 57 March/April | Left Corinth for Macedonia; Third visit to Philippi (Acts 20:3-6) |
| 57 March-May | Troas, Miletus, Tyre, Ptolemais, Caesarea (Acts 20:6b-21:14) |
| 57 May or June | Arrival in Jerusalem; Fifth visit to Jerusalem (Acts 21:15-23:22) |
| 57 June-59 July | Arrested; imprisonment in Caesarea (Acts 23:23-24:27E) |
| *59 July* | **Festus succeeded Felix as Procurator of Judea** (Ac 24:27) |
| 59 July & August | Hearings before Festus and Agrippa (Acts 25:1-26:32E) |
| 59 September | **The voyage to Rome:** Caesarea to Fair Havens (Acts 27:1-8) |
| *59 October 5* | *The Fast (The Day of Atonement)* (Acts 27:9) |
| 59 October (mid) | The storm voyage: Fair Havens to Malta (Acts 27:9-26) |
| 59 November (early) | Shipwreck on Malta (Acts 27:27-44E) |
| 60 February (early) | Departure from Malta "after three months" (Acts 28:1-11) |
| 60 February/March | Journey from Malta to Rome (Acts 28:12-16) |
| 60-62 | **Imprisonment in Rome For Two Years** (Acts 28:16-31E) |
| 60 | *Gospel of Luke* published |
| 61 July/September | *Asiatic Epistles (Philemon, Col, Eph)* written (from Rome) |
| *62 February* | *The Death of Burrus* |
| 62 Feb or March | Completion of the two years of Paul's "house arrest" in Rome |
| 62 March/June | Completion and publication of *The Acts of the Apostles* |
| 62 April/July | Commencement of the initial hearing of Paul's trial |
| 62 May/July | News of the trial and Epaphroditus's illness taken to Philippi |
| 62 June/August | News of the Philippians' reaction brought back to Paul |
| 62 July/September | In response, Paul writes his *Epistle to the Philippians* |
| 62 | Paul released shortly after; sends Timothy to them; visits them himself |
| *62* | ***Death of Festus; Sanhedrin kills James the Lord's brother*** |
| 63 ? | Paul visits Colosse (Philemon 22) |
| 64 ? | Paul visits Spain (Romans 15:22-29) |
| *64 July* | *The Fire of Rome; persecution of Christians begins* |
| 65 ? | Paul's evangelistic ministry in Crete; *Titus* and *1 Timothy* written |
| 65/67 ? | Paul in prison in Rome; *2 Timothy* written; Paul beheaded |
| 65/68 ? | Martyrdom of Peter |
| *68 June* | *Suicide of Nero* |
| *66-73* | *The Jewish War* |
| *70* | *Destruction of Jerusalem* |
| *73 April 21* | *The Jews' Last Stand, at Masada; mass suicide* |

# THE CORINTHIAN CORRESPONDENCE

## 1. Background: The City of Corinth

The city of Corinth had played a significant role in the affairs of classical Greece, until in 146 BC the Romans defeated the alliance of Greek states and destroyed Corinth and slaughtered its citizens or sold them into slavery. The site lay desolate for a century, until Julius Caesar refounded the city in 46 BC as a Roman colony, with settlers from all over the Empire, many of them being discharged soldiers. It became the capital of the Roman province of Achaia, and the residence of the Roman proconsul was located there (Acts 18:12).

When Paul arrived in Corinth, the city had a population of about half a million.

Ancient Corinth was situated on the south of the narrow isthmus which connects southern Greece (called the Peloponnesus) with northern Greece. The isthmus is only a few miles wide, and most of the east-west sea trade came across the Aegean Sea to Corinth, was unloaded at Cenchreae (Corinth's eastern port) and carried across the isthmus to Lechaeum, the port on the western side of the isthmus, on the Gulf of Corinth. And vice versa. Many of the ships were drawn up out of the water on one side of the isthmus and moved bodily across the isthmus on rollers to resume their journey in the gulf on the other side. This was much preferred to undertaking the risky journey around the stormswept and dangerous southern shores of the Peloponnesus.

Because of its location at a strategic crossroads of the ancient world, Corinth was a major maritime city and center for trade and commerce, and in consequence it was rich and prosperous. These factors also meant that the city had an itinerant population of seamen, traders and travellers from all parts of the ancient world, who brought to the city every kind of vice and sin that humanity had devised. Even the name became a word for debauchery - "to Corinthize" ("to act like a Corinthian") was a term meaning to be a whoremonger, or to practise immorality, and "Corinthian girl" meant a prostitute. From the Corinthian plain on the south side of the city rises up a steep hill almost two thousand feet (five hundred and seventy meters) high, dominating the city. This acropolis, the Acrocorinth, was the site of the renowned Temple of Aphrodite, where - so ancient writers inform us - adherents "worshipped" with the assistance of the services of a thousand temple prostitutes. Some scholars now doubt that this was still the case in Paul's time, but the city was notorious for its debauchery.

Corinth was only forty miles west of Athens, but was little influenced by the intellectual interests of that city. Corinth remained preoccupied with making and spending money - trade and commerce, indulgence and pleasure-seeking.

## 2. The Establishment of the Corinthian Church

This is the city into which Paul came on his Second Missionary Journey after his departure from Athens (Acts 18:1ff.). How would you go about evangelizing such a place? Acts 18:1-18 records the events of the founding of the church, and in 1 Corinthians chapters 1 and 2 Paul himself describes his message and ministry.

Paul was alone during the first part of this period. After the trouble in Berea, the Bereans had taken him on to Athens by himself, while Silas and Timothy had remained in Macedonia, and he had at first been waiting for them in Athens (see Acts 17:13-16). He had now moved on to Corinth on his own, and it appears that his funds were running low.

Luke tells us how in Corinth Paul found a Jew named Aquila, and Paul took employment with him - for they were both tentmakers - and he stayed with Aquila and his wife Priscilla. From the way in which Luke introduces Aquila into the narrative - as a Jew, not as a believer, a brother - it seems clear that he and Priscilla were not already Christians, but would have been converted as a result of Paul's ministry. (See also my comment, below, on 16:19.)

As was his practice, Paul began evangelism in the synagogue and argued the gospel there every sabbath with Jews and Greeks (Acts 18:4). Then Silas and Timothy arrived from Macedonia with news of the churches there. Shortly after this the opposition of the Jews forced Paul out of the synagogue, and he continued his ministry next door in the house of Titius Justus. Numbers of the Corinthians became believers, including Crispus, the ruler of the synagogue, and his family.

When Gallio became proconsul of Achaia (AD 51/52), the Jews brought Paul before him on charges of breaking the law, but Gallio dismissed these charges - in effect, a pronouncement permitting Christian evangelism: a very important decision, for it meant that the Roman administration declined to support the Jews in their opposition to the preaching of the gospel.

Acts 18:11 informs us that Paul stayed 18 months in Corinth, and this is followed by the Gallio incident, after which "Paul stayed many days longer" (Acts 18:18). It is uncertain whether the eighteen-month period was up till the Gallio incident, to which the "many days longer" is to be added, or whether it represents the total period of Paul's stay.

Then Paul, accompanied by Priscilla and Aquila, left Corinth. These two remained in Ephesus, while Paul returned to Antioch (Acts 18:22). From there subsequently he began his Third Missionary Journey, which brought him in due course to Ephesus (Acts 19:1-10; some say, this was in AD 53, whereas other scholars date this part of Paul's life one year earlier - they date his arrival in Corinth in AD 50, brought before Gallio in AD 51, and the beginning of his stay in Ephesus in AD 52: this is the view set out in the outline Chronology, above.)

## 3. The Corinthian Correspondence

Paul regularly kept in touch with his churches by personal visits where possible and by letter - most of his letters in the New Testament were written for this purpose. The most sustained of these contacts which Paul had was with the church at Corinth.

Either while he was on his travels or when he arrived in Ephesus, Paul apparently heard a report about the situation at Corinth which prompted him to write a letter to the church. He refers to this first letter (which we can call Corinthians A) in 1 Corinthians 5:9: "I wrote to you in my letter not to associate with immoral men . . ."

This first letter seems to have been misunderstood by the Corinthians or at any rate it did not have the intended result. Paul continued to receive disquietening news from Corinth - through Chloe's household (1 Corinthians 1:11) and through Stephanas, Fortunatus and Achaicus, who apparently came from the church to him in an official capacity (1 Corinthians 16:17-18) and who were thus, it would appear, the bearers of the letter that Paul received at this time from the Corinthian church (or at least, from some in the church) (1 Corinthians 7:1). Paul probably had also received news about Corinth from Apollos who had ministered there (Acts 18:24-28) - in fact, Paul encouraged Apollos to visit Corinth again, but Apollos declined (1 Corinthians 16:12).

Paul then wrote his second letter to the Corinthians (Corinthians B: our 1 Corinthians), this letter apparently being taken back to them by Stephanas and his companions (16:15-18).

But even after this letter, there were still problems and misunderstandings with the Corinthian church, and so Paul himself journeyed across to visit Corinth. The visit was not a success - he refers to it as a "painful visit" (2 Corinthians 2:1); this second visit by Paul to Corinth is also referred to or implied in 2 Corinthians 12:14, 21; 13:1. Back home again in Ephesus, Paul wrote them a third letter (Corinthians C) "out of much affliction and anguish of heart and with many tears" (2 Corinthians 2:4; also 7:8).

Then Paul sent Titus to them (or, Titus may have been the bearer of Corinthians C) to report back to him how this letter was received (2 Corinthians 12:18).

Paul himself then left Ephesus, moving towards Macedonia, and came to Troas, hoping to meet up with the returning Titus (2 Corinthians 2:12-13). Not finding him, Paul continued on to Macedonia, feeling much oppressed (2 Corinthians 2:13; 7:5). It was there in Macedonia that he met Titus, who brought him very encouraging news of a good response to his "sorrowful letter" (i.e., to Corinthians C - cf. 2 Corinthians 7:6-16).

Paul then sat down and wrote them, from Macedonia, his fourth letter (Corinthians D - our 2 Corinthians), in which he mentions his intention to visit them for the third time (2 Corinthians 12:14). He did subsequently pay them this planned third visit (Acts 20:1-3).

This sequence of events can be summarized thus:

1. Founding of the Corinthian Church, AD 50, during Paul's Second Missionary Journey (Acts 18:1-18).
2. Writing of Corinthians A - the letter about immoral men (1 Corinthians 5:9). [This letter is lost.]
3. Reports reach Paul, together with a letter from the Corinthians (1 Corinthians 1:11; 7:1; 16:17-18).
4. Writing of Corinthians B (our 1 Corinthians) in AD 55 from Ephesus during his Third Missionary Journey.
5. The "painful visit" (2 Corinthians 2:1).
6. Writing of Corinthians C - the "severe letter" or "sorrowful letter" (2 Corinthians 2:4; 7:8). [This letter is lost.]
7. Titus returns with a favorable report (2 Corinthians 7:5-16), meeting up with Paul in Macedonia.
8. Writing of Corinthians D (our 2 Corinthians) in AD 56 from Macedonia during his Third Missionary Journey.
9. Paul visits Corinth for the third time (Acts 20:1-3).

# THE MESSAGE OF 1 CORINTHIANS

Paul appears to have had three interrelated reasons for writing his second letter to the Corinthians, which we know as 1 Corinthians:

(a) As we noted earlier, his first letter concerning the attitude of Christians to immoral people appears to have been misunderstood or at least not followed as he intended; so he wanted to clarify this matter (see 1 Corinthians 5:9).

(b) More generally, he wished to respond to the disquietening reports which, as we have seen, had been reaching him concerning the situation at Corinth (1 Corinthians 1:11; 16:17-18). This he does primarily in chapters 1 to 6, but even in later chapters his comments reveal an awareness of what was being said and done by some at Corinth (see 8:1; 9:3; 10:23; 11:17-18; 15:12).

(c) He had received a letter from Corinth raising a number of issues to which he wanted to reply. Chapters 7 to 16 contain his reply - though we cannot be certain that all the questions which he deals with in these chapters had been asked by the Corinthians in their letter. Some may have also been matters that Paul wished to discuss on the basis of verbal reports which had reached him (see 11:17-18 and 15:12).

We are now ready to begin a detailed consideration of the message of Paul in 1 Corinthians. As we do so, we need, firstly, to see this letter in the context of Paul's total relationship and correspondence with the Corinthians at this time, and secondly, to note that reading this letter is rather like listening-in to one side of a telephone conversation - to understand fully what we can hear, we need to take account of what is being said by the other party in the conversation, as best we can judge this from the part of the conversation that we are able to listen to. In regard to 1 Corinthians, this is not very difficult as a rule, because Paul refers clearly to each issue raised by the Corinthians as he begins to discuss it, or he reports what he has heard about the situation at Corinth before commenting on it, and on a number of occasions he includes in his letter specific quotations of what the Corinthians were saying or had written. (Places where it appears that Paul is quoting the Corinthians include: 1:12; 3:4; 6:12-13; 7:1; 8:1, 4; 10:23, 28; 12:3; 15:12, 32, 35; plus some others that are discussed in the commentary.)

Numerous commentaries make a major break in the Epistle between chapters 6 and 7, because in 7:1 Paul indicates that he is now taking up a matter (about marriage) which the Corinthians raised in their letter. However, the issues discussed in chapter 7 are very closely related in content and sequence to those he has just been dealing with in chapter 6, and it does greater justice to the flow of Paul's thought to preserve the close connection between these two chapters which their common subject matter indicates. Questions about marriage are indeed raised in the letter from the Corinthians, and so Paul refers to their letter as he commences to deal with these issues. But before discussing the aspects of this overall matter that *they* raise, first of all he intends to take up an issue that still needs to be dealt with after his previous letter to them (1 Corinthians 5:9), and to discuss some questions of sexual morality at Corinth which are crying aloud for correction (6:9-20E; cf. especially verses 11-13).

Thus the major areas of concern covered in 1 Corinthians are, as may be seen from the detailed Outline above:

1.    Divisions in the Church (1-4)
2.    Sex and Marriage (5-7)
3(a)  Things Sacrificed to Idols (8-10)
3(b)  Behavior in the Church of God (11)
4.    Gifts and Ministries in the Church (12-14)
5.    The Resurrection (15)
6.    Final Messages and Greetings (16)

So I see in this Epistle an Introduction (in Paul's usual style), then four practical sections primarily focussing upon behavior, a doctrinal section, and then his concluding remarks as he draws his letter to a close. Others may divide it up marginally differently.

Thus for instance in his Commentary on 1 Corinthians, Godet notes that "Ten subjects, more or less extended and very heterogeneous, were present to the apostle's mind, when he set himself to compose this letter". This raises the question of how Paul will cover them all in the one letter - as Godet 27 puts it, "In other words, will the First Epistle to the Corinthians be a heap or a building?" Godet examines the structure of 1 Corinthians and concludes (29):

The subjects treated are thus classified, notwithstanding their profound diversity, in four natural groups, and these groups show a rational graduation:

i.    An *ecclesiastical* question: chapters 1:10-4:21E.

ii.   Five *moral* questions: foremost that of discipline, which still touches the ecclesiastical side: chapters 5-10.

iii.  Three questions which are *liturgical* or relative to public worship: chapters 11-14.

iv.   A *doctrinal* question: chapter 15.

Godet 20 concludes his analysis of the structure of this letter with the comment,

> Never, as it seems to us, was an intellectual edifice more admirably conceived and carried out than the First Epistle to the Corinthians, though with the most varied materials.

However it be that one may actually divide up the Epistle into topics, it is clear that it is indeed very carefully constructed, as Godet has said, and is unquestionably the result of painstaking and thorough thought. This we shall recognize more and more as we progress through it.

# CHAPTER ONE

## PAUL'S INTRODUCTION:
## GREETINGS AND THANKSGIVING (1:1-9)

### 1. Greetings (1:1-3)

**1:1** Paul begins by gently but specifically emphasizing his apostolic authority and his call to be an apostle by the will of God. "Sosthenes" is most likely the same man mentioned in Acts 18:17, who had been ruler of the synagogue in Corinth and was beaten by the mob at the conclusion of Paul's appearance before Gallio - and it would appear that Sosthenes was now Paul's fellow-worker in Ephesus. If so, this would make it particularly appropriate for Paul to join Sosthenes's name to his own in the initial greeting in this letter to the Corinthians. Paul customarily dictated his letters, adding a final greeting at the end in his own handwriting; this is true of 1 Corinthians also (see 16:21-24). It is reasonable to deduce that Sosthenes is the amanuensis who wrote out this letter for Paul: if this implication is valid, it would be an additional reason for his being mentioned in the greeting, and having his name joined with that of the actual author of this letter.

**1:2** Those at Corinth, in spite of their failings and shortcomings (which this letter makes clear), are nonetheless "sanctified in Christ Jesus" and "called holy" or "called saints" or "called as saints" (better than "called to be holy" or "called to be saints", which suggests that they are to "become holy" or "saints" in the future: but there is no "to be" in the Greek here). As Christians we *ARE* saints in Christ Jesus, for we have been sanctified in him: we are now to live as what we are. "Sanctified" and "saint" (most translations) are, in the Greek, cognate with the words for "holy" (NIV) and "holiness". The Corinthians are called to holiness, as indeed are "all those everywhere who call on the name of our Lord Jesus - their Lord and ours". "Everywhere" means "wherever Christians are found". Ambrosiaster (Kovacs 15) explains Paul's comments in this verse thus:

> And even though he reproves them in many respects, still he says, "to those sanctified in Christ Jesus". This is because they are sanctified by being reborn in Christ, though afterward they had begun to behave badly. Paul wanted to show that the whole church was sanctified in

Christ but that certain of them had turned aside from the tradition of the truth because of the evil teachings of the false apostles.

**1:3** Next Paul records his usual initial prayer for grace and peace for his readers. Note the emphasis upon the Lordship of Jesus Christ in verses 2 and 3, and indeed in this Epistle generally.

## 2. Thanksgiving (1:4-9)

**1:4** Paul is about to call the Corinthians to task over a number of serious matters. But first: there are many things about the Corinthians which are praiseworthy, and Paul commences by thanking God for all these things. (Here he has set an example for us to follow in similar situations.) Underlying everything praiseworthy in the Corinthian church is God's grace - which is, the fullness of the mighty power of God made available to each child of God to meet his need, whatever form that need may take (from our initial need of forgiveness and salvation, to our ongoing need for guidance and enabling strength in our daily Christian walk).

**1:5** Paul recognizes the many gifts of speech and knowledge which the Corinthian Christians possessed. This is a genuine tribute by Paul, not sarcasm or exaggeration - he takes up this thought again in chapters 12 and 13.

**1:6** Their acceptance of Paul's proclamation of Christ was itself a confirmation of that testimony.

**1:7** "Spiritual gift" occurs in the ESV, RSV, NRSV, and NIV translations of this verse - but the word "spiritual" is not in the Greek text, which has the word χαρισμα, *charisma*. Newman's Greek Dictionary translates this word as "gift as an expression of divine grace"; the Greenfield/Green Lexicon gives it as "a free favor, free gift, benefit, a divinely conferred endowment". The word "spiritual" is *not* added here by the AV, NASB, NEB, TEV, or Phillips. To insert the word "spiritual" here is misleading, as the gifts referred to are not said in context either to be related to the Holy Spirit nor concerned with the "spiritual" side of man as distinct from other aspects of man - there is no limitation of this kind in what Paul is saying here. Where a specific reference *IS* being made to a *spiritual* gift, then the Greek word for "spiritual" is actually used (as in Romans 1:11). Note that the Corinthians are waiting eagerly "for our Lord Jesus Christ to be revealed" (at his Second Coming).

**1:8-9** Paul assures the Corinthians that the Lord Jesus Christ will keep them strong to the end (i.e., the end of the present age, which ends with Christ's Return - see previous verse - or the end of the life of an individual upon Earth, as the case may be) so that they will be "guiltless on the day of our Lord Jesus Christ", i.e., the day of judgement. The basis of this is the truth that "God is faithful" (dependable, reliable, trustworthy) and he is the One who called us into fellowship (i.e., our saving relationship) with "his Son Jesus Christ our Lord". This word of reassurance and encouragement which Paul gives to the Corinthians is one which we can accept for ourselves today also.

Note the continuing emphasis upon Jesus Christ as Lord - mentioned three times in Paul's prayer (in verses 7, 8, and 9), three times in the initial greetings, and again in verse 10: seven references in the first ten verses of this Epistle! We can see behind this emphasis the basic underlying conviction of Paul that the foundation of true Christian living and the answer to all the problems in the Corinthian church (which he is just about to deal with in detail) is the acceptance of the Lordship of Jesus Christ in one's life.

Now, after this Introduction - and after laying this foundation - Paul is ready to talk to the Corinthians about the issues which are giving him cause for so much concern.

## SECTION 1: DIVISIONS IN THE CHURCH (1:10-4:21E)

### 1. A Right Relationship Between Brothers in Christ (1:10)

After his greetings and prayer of thanksgiving, Paul moves straight into his first subject, "divisions in the church", which occupies him for the first four chapters out of the sixteen of the Epistle.

**1:10** Right relationships between brothers in Christ imply, Paul says:

(a) that all of you agree with one another;

(b) that there be no divisions (dissensions) among you;

(c) that you be perfectly united in mind and purpose.

This is the ideal; it *IS* possible, but only by "the name of our Lord Jesus Christ". Paul has a large list of issues which he intends to take up with the Corinthians in this letter. Some of the other matters which are to follow may well appear to us to be of greater seriousness than the question of dissension and faction-fighting at Corinth. But the space which Paul devotes to this issue, the way in which he deals with it, and the fact that he deals with it ahead of anything else, combine to indicate the seriousness with which he views the matter. Satan is at work sowing discord amongst the brethren (Revelation 12:10). When we join in faction-fighting in the church, we are in fact doing the devil's work.

## 2. The Problem in the Church At Corinth (1:11-12)

**1:11** Paul was informed about the quarrels in the Corinthian church by members of Chloe's household. We do not know who Chloe was (she is not otherwise mentioned in the New Testament), nor even whether she herself was a Christian, nor where she lived, nor who the members of her household were (members of her family, slaves, or freedmen); but William Ramsey 31 points out one probability:

> "We cannot suppose that Paul quotes the statement of messengers sent by one of the factious Corinthians as trustworthy evidence about the factions. It is clear that 'the representative of Chloe' are quoted as being in themselves good and sufficient witnesses, and therefore they must have stood outside the factions as external observers. ... Chloe, therefore, was not a Corinthian. She was an outsider; and her representatives were unprejudiced witnesses in the matter. .. Probably, therefore, Chloe was a native of some city of Asia Minor, head of a business whose agents were passing to and fro between Corinth and Ephesus.

Or perhaps they came specifically in order to see Paul, out of concern for the situation in the Corinthian church.

**1:12** The church is dividing itself up into rival factions, claiming to follow particular leaders (Paul, Apollos, Peter) - and some claiming simply to follow Christ. Paul and Apollos had ministered in Corinth; it is *possible* but not *likely* that Peter (Cephas) had visited the city; the party claiming his name may have been the Jewish party at Corinth (as Peter was an acknowledged leader of the Jewish church) or the party which favored marriage (as Peter was married, and was accompanied by his wife in his Christian ministry, as Paul tells us in 1 Corinthians 9:5).

## 3. Paul's Response To This Problem (1:13-2:16E)

**1:13-17a** In response Paul shows

    **(a)** that Christ is not divided, and that this division within the Corinthian church is in fact "dividing up" Christ;

    **(b)** that he himself is not the foundation for their faith, which is Christ alone and his death on the cross for them;

    **(c)** that baptism is not into the followers of a particular leader nor into a particular group: baptism is into the whole church of Jesus Christ and is to symbolize *unity*, not *division* (this is an important truth for the Church of today also);

    **(d)** that our Christian standing does not derive from any particular human leader or from human wisdom, but directly from the power of God at work in us, through the preaching of the crucified Christ (see the whole of this section, and note especially 2:5).

John Chrystostom comments (Kovacs 20) on verse 13:

> "Is Christ divided?" What he means is, "You have dismembered
> Christ and divided up his body." Do you see his anger? Do you see the
> rebuke? Do you see how his speech is filled with indignation? For Paul
> does not mount an argument but only raises questions, whenever the
> point at issue is admittedly absurd.

In 1:13-17a Paul disclaims an emphasis upon baptism in his ministry
in a way which suggests that others (either other preachers at Corinth, or
leaders in the Christian movement by whom the Corinthians were being
influenced, or possibly some of the Corinthians themselves) were over-
emphasizing baptism. Possibly those who had been baptized by a particular Christian leader formed the core of the group calling themselves by
the name of that leader. Paul explicitly disowns the very suggestion of
this; his question (1:13c) "Were you baptized in the name of Paul?"
(apparently using himself as representative of any leaders who were
being regarded in this way), taken with "Is Christ divided?" (1:13a),
indicates that baptism was in the name of Jesus Christ (cf. Acts 2:38) or
at any rate if at this time in the name of the godhead (see Matthew
28:19) it was certainly into the unity of the whole body of Christ, not
into a factional party.

**1:14** Crispus was the ruler of the synagogue at Corinth when Paul
began teaching there (Acts 18:8). When he and his household were converted, this may well have been the factor that finally precipitated Paul's
split with the synagogue (Acts 18:6), as the two circumstances are mentioned in Acts in close relation to each other.

Gaius is a common Roman name, and at least three and possibly four
men of that name are mentioned in the New Testament (see Acts 19:29;
20:4; Romans 16:23; 3 John 1). Gaius of Corinth is not mentioned in
Acts (unless he is also to be identified with Gaius of Macedonia, Acts
19:29, or Gaius of Derbe, Acts 20:4 - but this is not very likely); he is
mentioned here as one whom Paul baptized at Corinth, and in Romans
16:23 he is Paul's host when Paul was later staying in Corinth and it was
in his house, it would seem, that the Epistle to the Romans was written.

**1:15** The wording of Paul's comment indicates that there were those
at Corinth who regarded themselves as linked in a special way with the
leader by whom they were baptized.

**1:16** Stephanas was Paul's first convert in Achaia (1 Corinthians
16:15) and visited him in Ephesus as a member of the group of three
who came from Corinth (16:16-18) and who (presumably) brought Paul
the Corinthians' letter (see 7:1).

The fact that Paul baptized Stephanas's household is sometimes used as a justification of the practice of infant baptism, on the basis of the assumption (taken by some to be self-evident) that the household would have (or at least, could have) included infants. However, 16:15 mentions explicitly that the members of the household of Stephanas were converts, and that "they have devoted themselves to the service of the saints": this would appear to exclude the use of the baptism of the household of Stephanas in support of the baptism of infants. The controversy over infant baptism must be argued on the basis of other passages.

**1:17a** In saying that Christ did not send him to baptize but to preach the gospel, Paul is not denigrating the practice of baptism. Rather, he is saying that this type of ministry is not the one to which Christ has called him. However, the wording of Paul's comment here makes it quite clear that the sacrament of baptism is not of the essence of the gospel, for Paul makes a very distinct differentiation between the two. This shows that any interpretation of Scripture which would make baptism a means to salvation or essential for salvation is mistaken. In these first two chapters of 1 Corinthians, and also in chapter 15:1-11, Paul explains the gospel by which we are saved. He states clearly that baptism is not part of the gospel, and thus not part of the way of salvation. Note however that Paul was baptized himself (Acts 9:28), practised baptism (even if of a few people only, as this was not his primary ministry), and accepted its role within the Church.

As part of Paul's response to this problem at Corinth, he includes a detailed discussion of the message of God for mankind, which he preached. This exposition of the message of God then becomes the basis of his rebuke to the Corinthians for their unspiritual divisions, and his call for them to be united in Christ. This section of Paul's letter is thus an excursus upon God's message, from which he then returns to the issue of the divisions within the Corinthian church.

## PAUL'S EXCURSUS:
## GOD'S MESSAGE FOR MANKIND (1:17b-2:16E)

**1:17b** This is the transition from the direct discussion of the divisions at Corinth to the exposition of God's message. Paul's ministry from Christ is to preach the gospel, but not in the wisdom of word, i.e., of what he said, for this would be to empty the cross of Christ of its power. Paul is not here speaking against wisdom - in what follows he vindicates God's wisdom (see especially 2:7) - but against *the wisdom of this* *world*, and in particular against a dependence in preaching upon the wisdom of one's own words and message, that is, upon purely human wisdom and eloquence. The differentiation between human wisdom and eloquence and the divine wisdom displayed in the cross of Christ is a significant aspect of Paul's theme in the Excursus which now follows.

## (a) The Content of God's Message (1:18-20)

**1:18** God's message to mankind centers upon the cross. Although Corinth was a city steeped in sin and idolatry, yet a church grew there: only the power of God could accomplish that. And God accomplished it through the preaching of the message of the cross. That is why Paul's preaching centered upon "Jesus Christ and him crucified" (2:2). 1:17-18 portrays the gospel as being the power of God at work in the lives of people to save them; and 2:5 shows that this is through faith. This is very similar to what Paul says in Romans 1:16-17 as he begins his letter to the Christians in that city (written shortly after the Corinthian letters, and from Corinth).

However, in this Excursus in 1 Corinthians Paul is emphasizing that the gospel consists of the exposition of the crucifixion of Christ, and its meaning.

The word "gospel" means "good news" and is used in Scripture in the widest sense referring to all that God is doing for mankind (for example, in Christ's so-called Nazareth manifesto, Luke 4:18-19, quoted from the Septuagint of Isaiah 60:1-2, in which this same word εὐαγγελίζομαι (*euangelizomai*), "preach the gospel", is used). The word can also be used in the more specific sense of the message of God concerning salvation, centering on the cross; this is its sense in 1 Corinthians (see also 15:1).

Those who do not accept this message of the cross "are perishing" - note the significance of the present continuous tense: these people are even now in the process of perishing; their lives and personalities are disintegrating (a process that will continue in the next world). For them, the message of the cross is "foolishness". In contrast, this message is the power of God for those who "are being saved".

Note again the present continuous tense: those who are in the process of being saved - salvation in Scripture is more than the act of God in a person's conversion; it is also the ongoing work of God's grace in that person's life: healing, restoring, and building that person into what God intends him to become. This is a familiar theme in the New Testament, especially in Paul's teaching.

**1:19** From Isaiah 29:14. Paul uses this quotation to show the weakness and folly of human wisdom before God. Paul frequently quotes the Old Testament in his teaching. Implicit in the way he does so, without explanation or justification, is the assumption that the Corinthian church (and others to whom he wrote) will recognize what he is doing, and that they acknowledge the authority of the Old Testament Scriptures. This presumes that in Paul's ministry to Gentiles he has taught them to accept and use the Scriptures, i.e., that the Jewish Scriptures are part of their heritage as Christians.

**1:20** In structure and thought this verse is similar to Isaiah 33:18 in the Septuagint. A characteristic of Paul's style in this letter is to make his point by the asking of questions. They challenge the hearer to think the issue through. These four questions show that no one - wise man, scholar, or eloquent philosopher and debater - is able to compare with the wisdom of God, for the highest flight of human wisdom is but folly in comparison with God's wisdom. This entire passage (1:18-2:16E) is a comparison of human and divine wisdom, showing how God's wisdom differs from human wisdom, and that we should receive God's wisdom when it is imparted to us (2:7, 13), so that we will have the mind of Christ (2:16).

## (b) The Response to God's Message (1:21-25)

**1:21** The world as a whole did not know God - its wisdom cannot bring anyone to a knowledge of God. God in *his* wisdom has ordained it thus. This is not in order to *prevent* man coming to God, but to *facilitate* it, so that knowing God is not restricted to the wise amongst mankind. Salvation does not come through any human attainment or ability, but through faith in the message preached. The Greek word translated "preaching" (AV), "what we preach" (ESV), or "what was preached" (NIV) is κηρυγμα (*kērygma*), the message of the gospel. The response of many to this message, Paul repeats (see 1:18), is to regard it as folly or foolishness. But foolish or simple-minded (Phillips's translation) though it may seem to them, it is through the preaching of this message that God is pleased to save those who believe.

"To save" here is aorist tense, referring to God's decisive once-for-all act in effecting the salvation of those who believe (i.e. believe in the message, and in the One of whom the message speaks). Paul thus indicates that there always will be those who will respond positively to the κηρυγμα (*kērygma*), for God is at work in the preaching, accomplishing his purpose of salvation.

We need to note that God in his wisdom has elected to make preaching the means by which the gospel brings salvation, through the response of faith. This underlines for today the importance of preaching the gospel so that people can hear it and come to faith. Paul writes in a similar way in Romans 10:8-17.

**1:22** When Jesus was upon earth, Jews demanded signs from him (e.g. Matthew 12:38, 16:1, and parallels). Paul's comment here may be the result of his own awareness of the attitudes of his fellowcountrymen, but very probably also indicates his knowledge of this response of the Jews to the ministry of Jesus. Paul's writings (not least among them this Epistle) frequently reveal a quite extensive knowledge on his part of the details of the life and teaching of Christ. He mentions also that it was a characteristic of the Greeks to make the attainment of wisdom their goal.

**1:23** The gospel is, in fact - if only they could see it as such - the answer to the aspirations of both Jews and Greeks. It is indeed a sign from heaven, and it is the ultimate height of wisdom. But the gospel that Paul and other preachers proclaimed was "Christ crucified" (i.e., "a Messiah who has been crucified").

A crucified Messiah was an offence to the Jews, a stumbling block, "an obstacle that they cannot get over" (Jerusalem Bible). The Gentiles saw a group of people whose leader had been executed proclaiming that the way to salvation - and wisdom - was through the death of that leader, and to them this was "sheer nonsense" (Phillips), even "madness" (Jerusalem Bible).

Modern attitudes still echo those of Paul's day.

**1:24** The wonder then is that anyone would accept this message. That there are those who do is due to the calling of God: and then those who are called, both Jews and Greeks, are able to see that "Christ crucified" is in fact "Christ the power of God and the wisdom of God".

**1:25** The foolishness of God - God at his most foolish (humanly speaking), or God acting in a way which appears foolish to human eyes - is wiser than the greatest wisdom of men. Human wisdom, in its most outrageous thoughts, would never have conceived of God defeating sin and providing salvation for mankind through himself becoming vulnerable man and dying the death of a criminal. God at his weakest - becoming man, and allowing his creatures to murder him - is stronger beyond comparison than the greatest strength to which man can attain.

## (c) The Effectiveness of God's Message (1:26-2:10)

**1:26** Salvation is the result of God's calling, God's choosing. It is not linked to intellectual ability or cleverness ("not many of you were wise"), nor to position or influence ("not many were influential") nor to racial descent or family connections ("not many were of noble birth"). However, the "not many", as opposed to "not any", shows that while such people were not *preferred*, nor were they *excluded* from God's call. After "wise", Paul has added, "according to worldly standards" (ESV; see its footnote: Greek: "according to the flesh", i.e. man in his absolute humanness) to guard the point that they *are* in fact the wisest of men, by the ultimate standards of God, because they have responded to God's call.

**1:27-28** In saying that God chose what is foolish and weak and lowly and despised in the world to shame and bring to nothing all that is valued by purely human standards of judgement, Paul is referring back to what he mentioned earlier: the message of a crucified Messiah, a God who let himself be executed. But in context of his reference to the lowly status of the Corinthians, we see that Paul is also referring to *them* in this passage - they are foolish, weak, lowly and despised, they are "those who are nothing at all" (Jerusalem Bible), and God chose them in order to destroy what the world thinks is important (TEV). Paul would similarly refer to himself in these terms, as one who is of no account apart from the grace of God.

**1:29** The reason for God choosing thus is in order that it shall be crystal clear to everyone that God's choice is not made on the basis of either ability or merit, and thus that no one shall ever have any ground for boasting that any goodness or virtue or attainment of his own was the reason why God chose him. ("Man" [NIV], "human being" [ESV - see its footnote] is translating σαρξ (*sarx*), "flesh".)

**1:30** The ESV/RSV/NRSV is not very accurate in this verse ("he is the source of your life in Christ Jesus"). The word "life" does not occur in the Greek; more accurately, "But by His doing you are in Christ Jesus" (NASB) or "It is because of him that you are in Christ Jesus" (NIV).

Similarly, "whom God made our wisdom" etc. is a loose rendering; it is better by far in the NIV: "who has become for us wisdom from God - that is, our righteousness, holiness and redemption". Having contrasted human wisdom and God's wisdom, Paul shows that because of God's choice of us we are "in Christ Jesus" (a favorite Pauline expression for the position and standing of the Christian), and that Christ himself became for us wisdom from God. When we have Christ we possess the true wisdom. This wisdom is then further explained as righteousness ("we are put right with God", TEV), holiness (conveying the idea of a separation *from* sin, *for* God) and redemption (we are delivered or "set free" from sin; TEV and NEB). These are the matters with which God's wisdom is concerned.

**1:31E** Again Paul quotes from the Old Testament (Jeremiah 9:24 - so also 2 Corinthians 10:17) to show that the only ground upon which the Christian can boast is "in the Lord" and what the Lord has done for him.


## SOME PRACTICAL AND PASTORAL REFLECTIONS

### Fracturing and Fragmenting the Church of God

In verses 10-12 Paul speaks, in some considerable concern, about how the Corinthians are plagued with divisions and quarrels. They are dividing themselves into factions clustered around the names of Paul, Apollos, Cephas (Peter), and Christ himself.

Commentators are agreed that the factions were neither started by nor supported by the men whose names they bore. We have no real knowledge now of the basis for these factions, nor do we know what they were differing about. Various conjectures have been made. For example, that the Jewish Christians laid claim to Cephas and probably Apollos, and the Gentiles to Paul. Or those who were (or wanted to be) married pointed to the marital status of Peter, while those who were unmarried elevated Paul and Christ himself as their exemplars (the married status of Apollos is not mentioned in 9:5-6, and remains unknown). Or the differences between the factions may have centered in differences of methods, of preaching, of behavior, or the like, which the Corinthians detected (or thought they detected) between the persons around whose names they gathered themselves. The fact is, we do not know.

But for the Corinthians - and for Paul - the matter was a serious one. Paul has many important issues to raise, requiring careful consideration and extensive change. But before discussing any of these, Paul feels obliged to tackle this issue of their disunity. It is dividing brother from brother in a destructive way (3:17). It must be faced. It must be dealt with. It must be stopped.

Paul's approach is, first, to reiterate the nature of the gospel, which is the major factor which unites them all; then, to emphasize that he and Apollos (and the others) are equally inspired and led by the Spirit, and are colaborers, even if their ministries may perhaps differ in some ways ("I planted, Apollos watered"). Christ is the foundation (3:11): all of us

(Paul indicates) are building upon that foundation - and we must be very careful just how we build (3:12-15).

As we shall see in subsequent chapters, there are various kinds of differences to be seen at Corinth. In addition to those indicated in this first chapter (whatever in fact they were), there are the different builders of chapter 3; the differences between the "libertarians" and the "ascetics" in the church in regard to their attitude to sex (chapters 6 and 7); between the "knowers" and the "weak" in relation to food offered to idols (chapters 8 to 10); between the "haves" and the "have nots" at the Lord's Supper (chapter 11); between those more obviously gifted by the Spirit and those less so (chapters 12 to 14); and between those with various views concerning the resurrection (chapter 15). Where there were moral or doctrinal errors involved, Paul pointed these out clearly and called for change. But, these apart, Paul did not ask them to become what they were not. His basic approach, which we can see exemplified in 7:20, was, "Stay as you are."

What he did ask was that there be no disunity, no quarreling, "but that you all be united in the same mind and the same judgement" (1:10).

Some churches of today, in seeking to put into practice the spirit of this teaching of Paul, have adopted as their policy not to make any changes to the status quo unless the whole church (or at least the whole body of the leadership of that church) are unanimously agreed. So till then they will continue to pray and to "wait upon God".

But there are so many issues which Scripture leaves open for our own determination (e.g. various aspects of how we conduct our worship of God), and so many ways in which we will differ (perfectly legitimately) from one another, that when this approach is followed rigorously it often happens that that church moves very slowly in any matter, or not at all. In some ways, some matters, this may be to the good; but overall it inhibits progress in adapting the eternal gospel to the circumstances of a changing world. Often this means that those people who are most vocal or have the strongest personalities (or who simply get in first to express their views) carry the day, because the less vocal, or the less pushy, or the more reticent, do not want to jeopardize the "unity of the Spirit" by expressing a different opinion.

Some have had, historically, a different approach: when (say) 75% want this and 25% want that, and they cannot agree or accommodate each other's differences, they split - often acrimoniously. Then in their separate enclaves they can each have their "unanimity" over the issue. And thus perhaps another denomination is created. Then because of our investment (both emotional and financial) in the whole situation, the divisions and the divergences become so totally entrenched that they continue long after the basic causes have been forgotten and the original antagonists have passed from the scene.

Sometimes God blesses them all in this situation, and good may result. It can happen. The most famous example in Scripture is the quarrel between Paul and Barnabas (Acts 15:36-41), which resulted in two missionary parties going out, each under an experienced leader. But more often, in modern times, this simply results in bad feelings, a more divided Christian witness to the world, the waste of precious resources through the doubling-up on church infrastructure, and the fact that the one group can no longer benefit from the gifts of ministry which the Lord has given to members of the other group.

Oftentimes the fact that a minority dissents over an issue will mean that the whole matter receives more careful consideration. Issues should still be decided by majority, but it will happen with an awareness of how often in history significant progress was made in any given field of endeavor only because a minority - or a single voice - dissented from the accepted outlook or the consensus of the majority or the status quo. It may indeed be that he or she is a voice in the wilderness, but they *could* be voicing prophetic insights from the Lord. Or not.

Paul's earnest plea in this section is not a call for uniformity. Or unanimity. We need to distinguish clearly between the danger of the factions forming in our church which was of so much concern to Paul, on the one hand, and on the other, the expressing in valuable robust discussion of differing points of view. Different people espousing differing views and opinions is no justification for fracturing the unity of the body of Christ in a given church.

## Athens, and The Nature of the Gospel Message

A question arises here: did Paul make a mistake at Athens?

Some scholars have seen in Paul's Excursus a deliberate repudiation by Paul of the policy which (on their view) he had followed in Athens, the city from which he had just come, where he preached philosophy and logic rather than the simple gospel (Acts 17:22-31). Paul's approach at Athens was a failure (these scholars say), and thus he changed his message for his ministry at Corinth to a simple gospel presentation, as he outlines in his Excursus.

But this is reading some rather far-reaching conclusions into the text on the basis of flimsy evidence. It is highly probable that Paul's comments on the Greeks seeking wisdom (1:22), and not being able to perceive the wisdom of God, are indeed made against a background of his recollection of his difficulties in proclaiming Christ at Athens. But what he did at Athens was, in accordance with his established policy (see 1 Corinthians 9:19-23), to seek for a bridge for the gospel to the thinking of his hearers. He began with their religious beliefs and practices (Acts 17:22-23) and quoted their poets (Acts 17:27-29) to gain their attention and goodwill, and to win a hearing for himself. In this he was successful - but in his sermon, just as soon as he reached the subject of the death and resurrection of Jesus (Acts 17:31), they laughed him to a standstill (Acts 17:32). He never got to finish his address: they sneered at him; they said, "We will hear you on this subject some other time" (NEB): but they would not let him continue his presentation of the gospel to them then, and he was forced to leave them (Acts 17:33 - note particularly the force of the word "so", ESV/RSV/TEV/NEB, "at that", NIV). There was a small response (Acts 17:34), but the attitude of the Athenians was such that Paul could see it would be pointless to persevere there, so "After this Paul left Athens and went to Corinth" (18:1).

The difference between Athens and Corinth was not that he preached an unsuccessful message at the one and had more success after changing his message for the other city, but that the Athenians were not prepared to grant him a hearing and he gave up the attempt as futile, whereas at Corinth there were significant numbers who were at least willing to listen to his message (Acts 18:4-11).

It would be interesting to learn what Paul would have said at Athens had he been permitted to finish his address. He had reached the presentation of the resurrection when the sophisticated Athenians stopped him in his tracks and said to him, "Some other time" (Acts 17:32). I suspect his message would have been very like his outline of the gospel that we find in 1 Corinthians 1 and 2: for, he says (1:23), "we preach Christ crucified - to both Jews and Gentiles." Note the "we" and the "preach". In context we can see that Paul is speaking of himself and his fellow apostles and evangelists. And "preach" is present tense: this is their universal and their habitual message: "Christ crucified". There is no other.

The full gospel message is found in here, in Paul's Excursus, plus 15:1-10. It has an objective and a subjective element.

Objectively, historically: Christ was crucified, dead and buried, and rose again. This is "the message ($\lambda$o$\gamma$o$\varsigma$, *logos*) of the cross", which is utter foolishness to those who are lost (1:18) - but which is the demonstration of the power of God to those who are being saved (1:18, 2:4).

Subjectively, personally: It was for our sins that Christ died (15:3);

and the gospel becomes effective in our individual lives when we encounter the resurrected Christ ourselves, as Paul did (15:8, 10), and experience the forgiveness of our sins that he died to accomplish for us.

This is what Paul and the others preach (15:11, again present tense), this is the gospel message in which the Corinthians had placed their faith (2:5; 15:11), and by which they are being saved (1:18; 15:3). This must continue to be the center of our own proclamation, and we can thus have confidence that, in demonstration of the Spirit and of power (2:4), we shall then see God at work saving those who believe (1:21).

# CHAPTER TWO

## SECTION 1: DIVISIONS IN THE CHURCH (continued)

## PAUL'S EXCURSUS:
## GOD'S MESSAGE FOR MANKIND (1:17b-2:16E)(cont.)

### (d) The Spirit's Role in God's Message (2:1-5)

**2:1-2** Paul refers here to the occasion when he first came to Corinth and won converts and founded the church through his ministry (Acts 18:1-8). The message of God was not proclaimed by means of high-sounding words and wisdom, but Paul avoided anything except the simple presentation of "Jesus Christ and him crucified".

**2:3** At Corinth he felt "in weakness and in fear and much trembling"; quite possibly as a result of the way in which he had been forced out of every town and city he had preached in in Europe since coming from Troas (Acts 16:11-17:15) - until he came to Athens, where he was met with mockery and outright rejection before he could even begin to expound his gospel fully. At the human level, this must have been very discouraging.

**2:4** He felt thrown back in utter dependence upon the Spirit and his power as he presented the message of God. The message itself and Paul's way of presenting it were simple and straight-forward - he did not practise the rhetorical flourishes and ornate style common to orators in his day. The implied comparison here is not with what Paul did at Athens, but with the eloquent preaching of others at Corinth, to which he makes reference in various ways on occasion (see for example 1:5-7; 12:8; 13:1). The fact that the Corinthians responded was "a demonstration of the Spirit's power" (i.e., the power of God - see verse 5 - through the Holy Spirit). "My speech and my message" (ὁ λογος μου και το κηρυγμα μου [*ho logos mou kai to kērygma mou*]) could be rendered as "my speech in my message", i.e. how I spoke my message.

**2:5** In consequence, when the Corinthians accepted the message, it plainly was not because of human wisdom (Paul's - or theirs) nor yet because of the persuasiveness of Paul's eloquence, but because of God's power at work in their lives. Thus it was upon this (and not in any way upon Paul himself) that their faith was established. That is to say, the effectiveness of God's message lies in the inherent power of God's Spirit in the message itself, and is not dependent upon the ability or eloquence of the messenger.

## (e) The Wisdom of God's Message (2:6-10)

**2:6-10** While Paul rejects human wisdom, he imparts divine wisdom. This does not mean a "wisdom" still concealed from the majority and revealed only to those initiated into an elite minority in the church, and still less does this passage justify the idea of a hidden teaching or tradition passed down orally and independently of Scripture. This passage shows that the revelation of this wisdom is intended for all God's people (2:8-12), but can only be understood by those who are spiritually mature Christians (2:6, 13-16E) because it is to be spiritually discerned (2:14). This wisdom has hitherto been hidden in the counsels of God (2:7) and has not been understood by the rulers of this age (2:8a).

It is, first, that Jesus of Nazareth is in fact the Lord of Glory whom the rulers, in their willful ignorance, have crucified (2:8b). Furthermore, this hidden wisdom of God includes his ultimate purpose for his people - the inconceivable glorification which God has prepared for those who love him (2:7b, 9). Note the connection between "our glorification", promised in 2:7b, and the description of Christ (2:8b) as "the Lord of Glory" - being the Lord of Glory, he is the source and the architect of our glory (the same Greek word δοξα [doxa], is used of us in 2:7b and of Christ in 2:8b): it was "his secret purpose framed from the very beginning to bring us to our full glory" (2:7b, NEB).

In witness to this Paul quotes (2:9) from the Septuagint version of Isaiah 64:4 which he combines loosely with Isaiah 65:17, with some interpretative rewording of a part of it. Lenski 102-103 says here,

> Paul often quotes freely and also combines Old Testament sayings. His reason is always evident: he wishes to stress certain expressions that are found in the passages which he quotes; these he conserves while the rest, about which he is unconcerned, is formulated to fit the general connection in which he writes. We ourselves exercise the same liberty.
>
> Bearing these facts in mind, we shall have no difficulty in this case. Paul uses Isa 64:4, and Isa 65:17 for the second line. When he uses expressions from these two passages Paul's evident object is to show the mystery character of the wisdom which he and others are preaching.

All this, God has now revealed "to us" (2:10) - meaning initially to Paul and the other apostles, and then through them to all believers who have spiritual discernment (as Paul explains more fully in the verses which follow).

### (f) The Inspiration of God's Message (2:11-16E)

**2:11-12** Having mentioned that God's revelation comes through the Spirit (2:10), Paul now explains the Spirit's role in more detail. As no one can really know a man as he knows himself (that is, within his own spirit), so by analogy Paul argues that no one knows the thoughts of God except God's Spirit (2:11). And we receive this Spirit from God, and thus we are enabled to understand the thoughts of God (2:12). In the first instance the "we" here refers to Paul and his fellow-apostles, and then, by extension through their ministry and their writings, to all Christians - see "Reflections", below.

The "spirit of the world" presumably means in this context not "Satan" but rather, "worldly wisdom", "human wisdom". The RSV and NRSV translations have "the gifts bestowed on us by God": but there is no word "gifts" in the Greek text, nor is this thought implied; this is better translated, "so that we may know all that God of his own grace has given us" (NEB), or, "that we might understand the things freely given us by God" (ESV). What is referred to here by "all that" or "the things" consists of "the entire sum of the divinely granted wisdom, all that God revealed to the apostles in the gospel" (Lenski).

**2:13** "We" - i.e., the apostles (see "Reflections", below) - impart this. "in words taught by human wisdom": i.e. "the best we can manage with our own abilities" - a very "humanistic" view of apostolic teaching, but the way their teaching is viewed by some, as a totally human endeavor. "Not so," says Paul.

The second part of this verse, translated literally, is "combining spiritual matters with (the) spirituals" (πνευματικοις, *pneumatikois*). The latter word is ambiguous. It could be masculine; in which case it could mean "with spiritual people". It could be neuter; in which case it will mean "with spiritual matters".

In the verses which follow (2:14-3:1) Paul is discussing "the spiritual man" and "the unspiritual man" and thus it would fit well with the context to take 2:13b as masculine, so that Paul is saying "combining spiritual truths with spiritual people", i.e. making spiritual truths known to spiritual people; or just possibly (though employing an unusual translation for the verb), "interpreting the things of the Spirit to people who have the Spirit" (taken thus by ESV, RSV, NRSV, Phillips, TEV, and NEB).

On the other hand, if the word is to be regarded as neuter, then this phrase would mean, "combining spiritual things with spiritual things", i.e. teaching spiritual things by spiritual methods (taken thus by AV and Jerusalem Bible).

However, there is a third alternative: that the word "spirituals" is indeed to be taken as masculine, but that it is referring to the word λογοις (*logois*), "words", which Paul has used a few words earlier, and that it is agreeing with the gender of λογοις (*logois*), which is masculine. The Greek of 2:13, rendered literally (and preserving the Greek word order) would be: "which things also we speak, not in taught-of-human-wisdom words, but in [those] taught-of-[the]-Spirit, expressing spiritual things with spiritual [words]"; i.e. expressing truths revealed by the Spirit by means of words themselves that are given by the Spirit. Johnson 69 sums it up:

> Paul certainly seems to be claiming that the divinely revealed wisdom of the gospel of the crucified Christ is shared with others by means of language taught to the teachers by the same Holy Spirit who gave the original revelation.

I completely concur. The apostles are not left to find their own words in which to express the truths revealed to them by the Spirit (2:10). Rather, even the words themselves in which these truths are to be expressed are given them by the Spirit.

I consider that this is the meaning which it would have been most readily understood to have by the first readers of the Epistle, and it is taken this way by the NASB and the NIV - which reads: "This is what we speak, not in words taught us by human wisdom but in words taught by the Spirit, expressing spiritual truths in spiritual words." I judge the NIV translation of this verse to be far and away the one that does the best justice to the Greek text in its context.

Paul's teaching in this passage is in accord with the teaching of Jesus about the inspiration of Scripture. Jesus confirms the Old Testament as God speaking to us (e.g., Matthew 22:29-31); Jesus claims that he always spoke only what God commanded him to say (John 12:48-50); Jesus promises that his apostles will be his true witnesses (Mark 3:14; Luke 24:44-48; John 14:26; 15:26-27; 16:12-15) - and the writing of the New Testament is part of the fulfillment of this promise. Therefore upon the authority of Christ we are to believe in the complete and total inspiration of Holy Scripture, which is the authoritative truth of God, and thus is infallible and inerrant in everything that it affirms. So here (2:13) Paul is saying, God's Holy Spirit guided even in the words that are used.

**2:14** The RSV and NRSV again here (as in 2:12) insert the word "gifts", which is not in the Epistle as Paul wrote it in the Greek. Inserting "gifts" into these verses in this way is going to mislead the reader into thinking of "spiritual gifts" - and this distorts Paul's meaning. As the verse goes on to speak of "understanding" these things, it is clear that what are being referred to are (as in the preceding verses) *the truths* imparted by the apostles through the Spirit. A better translation is as in the ESV: "The natural person does not accept the things of the Spirit of God." Similarly the NIV.

Or note the excellent Jerusalem Bible translation of the whole verse: "An unspiritual person is one who does not accept anything of the Spirit of God: he sees it all as nonsense; it is beyond his understanding because it can only be understood by means of the Spirit."

The word "unspiritual" is ψυχικος (*psychikos*), "worldly", "natural man", that is, unregenerate man in his "natural" state apart from the transforming and enlightening grace of God. Such a person cannot understand "anything of the Spirit of God" - this only becomes possible when first he receives the Spirit of God, and accepts the enlightenment that the Spirit makes possible. Now, this certainly is a description of the non-Christian: but can it also be true of a Christian? This is something upon which Paul is to comment in 3:1ff.

**2:15-16E** Paul has, in this Excursus, discussed the nature of God's message, showing that it is the divine wisdom centering in Jesus Christ and his crucifixion. This wisdom in all its ramifications is to be received through the Spirit. Paul and the other apostles (and in his use of "we" Paul intends to include, by implication, Apollos and Peter) impart the divine truths of God as the Spirit teaches them to do so. The unspiritual man does not (indeed, cannot) receive the things of the Spirit of God - they are so much nonsense to him! But the spiritual man does discern and receive everything that the Spirit is teaching him. To the extent that he receives and believes the things of God taught by the Spirit, he is beyond the judgement of others - for he has the mind of Christ.

How are we to view this question of judging and the mind of Christ? The word translated twice as "judge" in 2:15, ἀνακρινω (*anakrino*), is the same word rendered as "discern" in 2:14; Newman's Dictionary gives its meanings as "question, examine, judge, evaluate, sit in judgement on, call to account". The spiritual person judges or evaluates everything; but he himself is judged or called to account by no one. This word is used elsewhere in the New Testament only by Luke (once in his Gospel, five times in Acts) but occurs ten times in this letter; Barrett writes in his Commentary that:

it has been suggested (Weiss) that it was a word in common use in Corinth among Paul's adversaries, and that in response Paul plays on it in various shades of meaning.

Even so, Paul's teaching here is not easy to follow. How is it that the spiritual person (that is, the one who has the Spirit) is able to judge everything? And why is it that no one is able to judge him? It could be that "no one" means "no one without the Spirit", and that such a person is incapable of judging or understanding (or perhaps, sitting in judgement on) a Christian, as he lacks the discernment and does not have the true standard of judgement. It may be that this is an anticipation of what Paul says more fully in 4:3-5 - he does not accept or acknowledge human judgement because "It is the Lord who judges me".

Probably the best interpretation is to note the "for" (γαρ, *gar*) which introduces the next verse (2:16), and take this verse as giving the explanation of Paul's meaning. He quotes here from Isaiah 40:13 to show that no one knows the mind of the Lord so as to be able to instruct him. But we (i.e., initially, the apostles, and then, in context here, those who have the Spirit and embrace God's wisdom) have the mind of Christ (equivalent in meaning to "the mind of the Lord", 2:16a). Therefore no one is able to instruct us or call us to account.

We do not have **all** the mind of Christ - at times we shall fall far short of the implication of what it means to have the mind of Christ, and we remain in perpetual need of further instruction. But insofar as we are "spiritual", under the control of the Spirit, and receptive to his revelation of God, then those truths that we have received are Christ's mind, and are thus beyond challenge: for "What we think and what Christ thinks (in these cases) are identical" (Clark's Commentary). Godet says:

> Thus the minister of a sovereign could say, after an intimate conversation with his king, I am in full possession of my master's mind. From this moment, therefore, to criticize the servant is to criticize the Master.

The christological significance of 2:16 is worthy of note: in Isaiah 40:13, "the Lord" refers to Jehovah; in his use of this quotation in 2:16 Paul uses "the mind of Christ" as being synonymous with "the mind of the Lord": that is, he identifies the Lord (Jehovah) of the Old Testament as Jesus Christ, thus revealing his total acceptance of the deity of Christ.

However, we must be careful about giving too wide and too simplistic an interpretation to "We have the mind of Christ" - see "Reflections" below.

Paul is now ready to resume his interrupted discussion of the divisions at Corinth - but he bases his next comments to the Corinthians upon what he has just been explaining.

# SOME PRACTICAL AND PASTORAL REFLECTIONS

## Who Is "We"?

In 2:1-5 Paul writes in the singular - "I", "me", and "my", and he is writing autobiographically about himself; then from 2:6 to 2:16E he changes to the use of the plural: "we", "us", "our". To whom is he referring? Who is "we"? For who it is that Paul means when he writes "we" in this chapter is an important consideration.

Is he referring to himself here, using the "royal plural"? This is unlikely in view of his prior use of the singular, to which he returns once more in 3:1. Then is he referring to himself and his fellow apostles ("exclusive we"), or to himself and his readers ("inclusive we")?

At times one finds Christians today applying the words of this passage directly to themselves and their fellow-Christians as if what Paul says is referring to and directed to all believers. Which would imply that what Paul wrote here referred to the Corinthians. (There is no basis for interpreting Paul's words to apply to Christians generally today but *not* to the Corinthians.) Further reflection upon the passage should show that this is most certainly not the case.

Is he saying of the Corinthians in 2:16, "You have the mind of Christ", when in the very next verse (3:1) he tells them that he can't address them as spiritual, and when he then proceeds throughout the rest of this Epistle to correct their thinking (and their practice) in relation to one error after another? Nor is it the Corinthians who impart wisdom, a secret and hidden wisdom of God (2:6-7); nor has God revealed to the Corinthians God's secret truths (2:8); nor is it the Corinthians who are taught by the Spirit the very words in which to impart truths revealed by God through the Spirit (2:12-13).

The context of this passage is Paul's response to the factions at Corinth calling themselves after the names of Paul, Apollos, and Peter (1:12). First he sets out the gospel which "we preach" (1:21 and 22) - he is showing that they are not "competitors" with each other in the church, but united in the message preached. The same thing is seen in 3:4-9a, where Paul emphasizes that he and Apollos (who had both ministered in Corinth) had differing roles "as the Lord assigned to each" (3:5), but are "God's fellow workers" (3:9a). To the Corinthians, in contrast, he says, "You are God's field, God's building."

What Paul says here (2:13) is highly significant. When he imparts "this" (i.e. the matters which he has just mentioned in 2:12, which had been revealed through the Spirit - 2:10 - and which he had earlier referred to in 2:6-7), he does not do so "in words taught by human wisdom". This is to emphasize afresh the point that he had made earlier (see 2:4): "my speech and my message were not in plausible words of wisdom". Rather, he spoke "in words taught by the Spirit".

**Paul** is the one who has received the specific calling of God for the apostolic ministry of imparting spiritual truth to win people to faith and then to instruct them in the faith (to which ministry he alludes a few verses further on, in 3:5-6, and many times elsewhere in his writings).

Notice that 2:13 is a claim by Paul to be inspired by the Spirit in what he is teaching, and that this claim extends to the very words in which this teaching is framed. It is a claim to verbal inspiration.

What is said here by Paul to the Corinthians in reference to his teaching would apply to this letter written to them and also to the other Epistles of his which we have in the New Testament - there would be no valid grounds for reducing the scope of its applicability to its immediate Corinthian context, for the way in which he speaks shows that he is speaking more widely.

Note moreover the significance in this verse in particular of the plural "we". What Paul says here of himself he is saying also of the others whom the Holy Spirit has chosen similarly to receive the revelation of God's truth and teach it.

This is elucidated in further detail in Ephesians 2:20-3:12: those upon whom the church is built are the "apostles and prophets" (2:20) for "When you read this, you can perceive my insight into the mystery of Christ which was not made known to the sons of men in other generations as it has now been revealed to his holy apostles and prophets by the Spirit" (Ephesians 3:4-5).

In particular, Paul is now telling his readers that the apostles and their associates are imparting to them (the Corinthians) the truths taught by the Spirit, in words given by the Spirit (2:13). Things unimagined hitherto, that God has prepared for those who love him, have now been revealed to "us" (i.e., to the holy apostles and prophets) through the Spirit, and these things in turn are taught by them to the church (2:9-10).

The Corinthians received these things orally; and these truths revealed through the Spirit have been written down under the Spirit's guidance, and we now have them available to us: this teaching is now embodied in the New Testament. In the New Testament sense and use of the word "prophet" (as will be further elucidated in discussing chapter 14), the non-apostolic New Testament writers can be recognized as being New Testament prophets. The scope of 2:13 (and indeed of this whole section of the Epistle) may legitimately be taken to include in its span all the other writers of the New Testament.

In view of Paul's obvious knowledge of the life and ministry of Jesus, it is possible that he knows, and has in mind, the promise that Jesus gave in John 14:26 and 16:13: "But the Helper, the Holy Spirit, whom the Father will send in my name, he will teach you all things. ... When the Spirit of truth comes, he will guide you into all truth."

In any case, the teaching of Paul here and the teaching of these passages in John's Gospel are all in accord in stating explicitly the role of the Holy Spirit in teaching God's truth to the apostles after the Ascension. This is directly connected in John 15:26-27 with the apostles' ministry of testifying to Christ.

It is clear then that in 2:6-16 Paul is referring to the calling and ministry God has given, through the Spirit, to his chosen apostles and their associates. Thus he is not referring to all Christians, but just to himself and his fellow-apostles and the New Testament writers. These men impart the things given to them by God in words taught by the Spirit.

Can Christians in general (and Christians today) say, "We have the mind of Christ"? There is no basis for thinking of some kind of revelation direct to us today: God has given his revelation of divine truth through his holy apostles and prophets, and it is recorded as Scripture, and it is complete. And as for the "natural person" (a person on their own apart from the working of God's Spirit): No - these things are spiritually discerned (2:14). It remains true, as the Lord said through Isaiah (55:8-9), "For my thoughts are not your thoughts, neither are your ways my ways, declares the Lord. For as the heavens are higher than the earth, so are my ways higher than your ways, and my thoughts than your thoughts."

But God has revealed himself in Scripture. To the extent that the Spirit fills us (so that we become a "spiritual person", 2:15), and that we become immersed in the teaching of Scripture, and develop a "Christian world view", to that extent can it be true of us that we now have the mind of Christ.

## The Inspiration of Scripture - And Our Response

In some churches, at the end of the reading of the passage of Scripture in the worship service, the Bible reader concludes with "This is the Word of the Lord", and the congregation responds, "Thanks be to God!" I like that. I like that very much. It is a recognition by both reader and

congregation of what has just been happening: we have been listening to
the **Word of God** read to us.

The foundation of our faith in God is the teaching of Scripture. Thus
such a recognition by the worshipers in the service, that we have been
listening to the Word of God, is beneficial for us all.

There are so many ways in which our full confidence in the Scriptures can be called into question these days - sometimes overtly, and
sometimes much more subtly. Have you noticed the spate of "red letter
Bibles" churned out by respectable publishers? Bibles with the words of
Jesus printed in red type: an apparently innocuous device that highlights
and immediately enables us to identify what Jesus himself has said.

But to what purpose? we might ask. For convenience, and ease of
use, we are told. But how would this help us? we ask. So that we can distinguish what Jesus said from bare narrative and from what other people
said. And why might we want to do that? we may enquire. And at this
point we can generally go around in circles.

But red letter Bibles are indeed produced so that we can readily distinguish the words of Jesus. Which leads us to register in our minds a
difference between the two: the words in red and the words in black, and
then (the next step, so easily taken) to see a distinction between the two.
"These are the very words of Jesus (and these are just the words of
somebody else)" - and that concept of "just" slips in, and next we will be
likely to find ourselves regarding the "words of Jesus" differently from
the rest of Scripture (for are they not highlighted in red?). The stage
beyond that is imperceptively easy to reach: the words of Jesus are more
important, more inspired, more authoritative, than the rest.

We are thus insidiously being brought to the acceptance of the idea of
*two* levels of inspiration in the Scripture: the words of Jesus, and everything else.

So, Christians can end up thinking, "This is the teaching of Jesus",
and therefore accepting it as authoritative; and "This is just the opinion
of Paul (or some other writer)", and therefore it is able, in varying
degrees, to be treated just the same as anybody else's opinion, and dis-
regarded or disagreed with if we so choose.

Of course people can come to this kind of attitude without needing
the assistance of a red letter Bible, but it certainly helps.

And making this distinction between the words of Jesus and the rest
can result in undercutting the authority of the rest of Scripture by featur-
ing the words of Jesus in red as "special" and being somehow different
from all the rest. You preach on 2 Timothy 3:16, "All Scripture is
inspired by God ..." but your listeners have already qualified and inter-

preted this as "Yes, but the teaching of Jesus is different from the rest, isn't it?" because their red letter Bible is saying that to them loud and clear every time they open it.

If we recognize that the apostles and prophets - and all the writers of Scripture - spoke and wrote as the Holy Spirit guided and inspired them (Ephesians 3:4-5; 2 Peter 1:20-21), we need to act so as to underline and reinforce that truth. *Not* undercut it and call it into question with the use of a printed Bible that shrieks on every page "There's the red bit and the black bit, and they're different, as you can plainly see."

Paul clearly says (2:13) that he and his fellow servants of God impart the truths of God in words not taught by human wisdom but taught by the Spirit. The things that Paul writes are the commandment of the Lord (14:37). Which is true also of every one of the other authors whom the Spirit used in the writing of the Scriptures. Let us accept the full authority with which they write and not relegate their writings, *de facto*, to being some "type 2" subordinate kind of Scripture.

Recognizing these things does not in any way call into question the individuality of each biblical author. It does not imply some wrong-headed mechanistic "typewriter" idea of the Spirit's inspiration of Scripture, as if the "authors" were no more than "transcribers" of words dictated to them from heaven. Not at all: the Holy Spirit used the individual writers just as they were. That is why we can see difference between books written by different authors - differences of vocabulary and phraseology, of structure and ways of writing, of interests and emphases. And it can indeed be profitable to look at all these things and examine (for instance) "Pauline theology" compared with "Johannine theology", and so on.

But after we have fully recognized these things, we are to recognize also that "men spoke from God" in what they wrote, as "they were carried along by the Holy Spirit" (2 Peter 1:21), and that what they produced was exactly what God wanted said and conveyed his truth with complete accuracy.

Thus we can endorse what Cyril of Alexandria said early in the Christian era (Kovacs xvi), "The entire Scripture is one book and was spoken by the one Holy Spirit".

Ultimately, this is what Paul is telling us in 1 Corinthians 2:13.

# CHAPTER THREE

## SECTION 1: DIVISIONS IN THE CHURCH (continued)

### 4. The Consequences of the Corinthians' Divisions (3:1-4)

**3:1-4** Paul has just explained (2:15-16E) how the spiritual man (πνευματικος, *pneumatikos*) discerns or judges all things, for such a person can come to have the mind of Christ. Now he declares that the existence of the divisions amongst the Corinthians (3:3) is a clear demonstration of their own spiritual state:

**(a)** They are not spiritual people, but worldly ("of the flesh" - 3:1a and 3:3a);

**(b)** They show no growth in Christ, being still "mere infants in Christ" who can only be given "baby milk" - they were not ready for solid food previously, and they are still not ready for it (3:1b-2);

**(c)** They remain "only human" (3:3b-4) or still "simply human", when they should have been transformed into much more than "mere men". Paul cannot level against them a more devastating accusation than this, for it means that in their case something has gone wrong with the outworking of the normal plan of God for Christian growth into maturity. Their divisiveness has stultified and inhibited their growth.

**3:1a** Paul calls the Corinthians "brothers" - an unhesitating acceptance of them as his fellow-Christians; but he then says to them very soberly "I was not able to speak to you as spiritual persons, but as worldly (fleshly), as mere infants in Christ". In the preceding verses (2:14-16) Paul has written of the "natural person" (the unspiritual, unregenerate person) and the "spiritual person", contrasting the two. He now proceeds to deny the designation "spiritual" to the Corinthians.

The way in which Paul speaks here indicates that the Corinthians - or some of them - are applying this description to themselves, regarding themselves as the "spiritual ones". (Paul says of himself [9:26], "I do not run aimlessly; I do not box as one beating the air." What he writes is relevant to the situation at Corinth; when he writes in the way he does in 1 Corinthians about "the spirituals" and gives a judgement on whether or not the term can be applied to the Corinthians, it indicates that this term was being used by some at least at Corinth. It is significant that the word πνευματικος (*pneumatikos*) occurs 26 times in the New Testament, and 15 of those occurrences are in 1 Corinthians.)

51

Paul says that he was not able (that is, while he was with them in Corinth) to accept them as, and treat them as, spiritual people; and in fact they still cannot be described thus (3:2c-4). It would appear that the reason they had thought of themselves as "spiritual" was because of the abundance of the gifts with which the Lord had endowed them (cf.1:4-7, and chapters 12-14); but they are not spiritual in the true sense of being led by and being under the control of the Holy Spirit.

**3:1b** What then is Paul to call them? Are they still to be seen as a "natural person" (NIV, "the man without the Spirit"), as in 2:14? No, Paul cannot use that term of them, for it refers to man as he is apart from God, an unregenerate unbeliever. Paul says they are σαρκινος (*sarkinos*), "people of the flesh", "worldly", a term indicating that though they are Christians (he accepts them as brothers) yet they are under the influence of their old nature, they are still "ordinary men", "mere human beings", "merely human" (3:3-4), whereas they are called to be Spirit-filled men and women of God. Thus the categorizing of people as being "spiritual" or else "without the Spirit" (the categories of 2:14-16E, and evidently the ones being used by the Corinthians themselves) is not enough: there is also the "carnal" or "fleshly" or "worldly" Christian. But this kind of person is described as an infant in Christ - and infancy indicates the existence of different stages of growth. There is nothing wrong in itself with the "infancy" or "nursery" stage of the Christian life; what is wrong at Corinth is that the Corinthians just won't grow up, and after all this time are still behaving childishly. MacArthur 69-71 writes:

> The cause of division in the church was more than an external, worldly influence. It was also internal, fleshly. The Corinthians had succumbed to the pressures of the world, but they were also succumbing to the pressures and enticements of their own flesh.

> Before Paul chastises them for their immature selfishness, he reminds them again that he is speaking to them as *brethren*, as fellow believers. That is a term of recognition and love. It reminded his brothers in Christ that they were still saved, that their sinning, terrible and inexcusable as it was, did not forfeit their salvation. He did not try to diminish the seriousness of their sins, but he did try to diminish or prevent any discouragement that his rebuke might otherwise have caused. He stood with them as a brother, not over them as a judge. ...

> Perhaps somewhat to soften the rebuke, he also compares them to *babes in Christ*. It was far from a compliment, but it did recognize that they truly belonged to Christ.

**3:2** "Milk" indicates the basic doctrines of the Christian faith, and "solid food" refers to progressing beyond this and getting to grips with matters of more substance (see 1 Peter 2:2; Hebrews 5:11-6:3). This is not to imply that foundational matters are unimportant but, rather, that Christian growth requires that we can progress beyond them in terms of our overall grasp of Christian truth. But even now the Corinthians are showing that they are still not ready for this.

**3:3** "Worldly", "of the flesh" (twice) is σαρκικος (*sarkikos*) in this verse, a different word from the σαρκινος (*sarkinos*) of 3:1. Some commentators see a distinction of meaning between these terms - e.g., A. Robertson, who says of σαρκινος (*sarkinos*), "The word is chosen deliberately, and it expresses a shade of meaning different from σαρκικος ..." However, others see them here a synonyms: Newman's Dictionary renders both of them as "belonging to this world, not under the control of God's Spirit".

The Corinthians are behaving as "fleshly" in having the divisions in the church which are Paul's immediate concern in this first section of his Epistle. They are behaving "fleshly" in all manner of other ways as well - for "fleshly" also well describes various other matters which Paul goes on to deal with in the sections which will follow this one.

**3:4** Again Paul quotes what is being said at Corinth, but he does not here refer to Cephas. Perhaps this is because he immediately proceeds (3:5) to discuss the ministries which he and Apollos had fulfilled at Corinth - if Peter had not actually ministered at Corinth, there would be no point in mentioning him in this particular context (see my comment on 1:12).

## 5. Paul's Response To This Situation (3:5-4:21E)

Paul's response is to explain the role of Christian leaders and to describe the concept of Christian growth and how it is to be assessed.

### (a) Christian leaders are the servants of God (3:5)

**3:5** Christian leaders (such as Apollos and Paul) are the servants of God, engaged in doing their assigned work. The reference to both Apollos and himself as "servants through whom you came to believe" indicates that the Corinthian Church included converts from the ministry of both these men. "Servants" is the translation of διακονοι (*diakonoi*). This word is often translated "minister" and sometimes "deacon".

### (b) Each leader does the work God gives him (3:6-9)

**3:6-8** Each does only his part; it is God who supervises the whole and makes their labors fruitful.

I like Augustine's comment on 3:6, in a sermon preached on the anniversary of his ordination to the priesthood, about the nature of ministry. He said (Kovacs 55),

> From outside yourselves receive the one who plants and waters you; but from within receive the one who gives the growth. The fractious have to be corrected, the fainthearted consoled, the weak taken up, the scoffers refuted, the plotters guarded against, the ignorant instructed, the indolent stirred up, the contentious checked, the proud put down, the litigious made peaceable, the poor helped, the oppressed set free, the good approved, the wicked endured, and all loved. In such a great, multiple, and varied responsibility help me, both by praying and by obeying, so that I may have the joy of being not so much your ruler as your benefactor.

Note the mention here (v.8) of a principle frequently referred to in both Old and New Testament: that each person shall be judged and recompensed in accordance with his deeds.

**3:9a** "We are God's fellow workers" can mean "We are fellow workers *for* God" (i.e., we are all workers together in God's service) or, "We are fellow workers *with* God" (i.e., we are all partners with God, sharing in the work which God himself is doing). Both of these ideas can be attested elsewhere in Scripture, though if we must choose between them the former is more likely in this context. However, this choice between the two meanings is a little artificial since the Greek would convey *both* meanings to the reader.

Who is "we" in this sentence? It could be taken to refer to all Christians, and it would be legitimate to construe it in this way. However, the way Paul has used "we" earlier with particular reference to himself and his fellow apostles (see comment on 2:13, and "Reflections" at the end of Chapter Two) and the abrupt change in the middle of this verse from "we" to "you" indicates that again in what he says here Paul is referring to himself and Apollos specifically, rather than to Christians in general (though this is not to mean that what is said would not be true of Christian workers generally). The point that Paul wishes to stress in this entire section of his letter is that he and Apollos are not rivals or opponents but, to the contrary, that they each have their role to play, and in the service of God they are colleagues, co-laborers together.

**3:9b** The change to "you" is significant. "We" are the workers (he is saying), while "you" are our workmanship - a field we have planted, a building we have constructed. Yet, just as we are *God's* workers, so you are *God's* field, *God's* building. *We* are the instruments; *you* are the fruit of our labors; but it is in fact *God* who is doing the work. Thus this verse sums up the thought which Paul has set out in verses 5-8, and introduces the elaboration upon the metaphor of a building which now follows.

## (c) Jesus Christ is the foundation - let each take care how he builds on that foundation (3:10-15)

When the foundation (which is Jesus Christ) has been laid, each Christian individually is then responsible for how they build upon it: their *salvation* is never in question, but their *reward* is involved.

**3:10** Taking up the metaphor of a building, Paul calls himself the expert builder, the skilled master builder, who laid the foundation (i.e., as the founder of the church at Corinth). Paul's description of himself as "an expert builder" is chosen to emphasize that the foundation has been well and truly laid. Others can (and should) build upon that foundation, but the foundation remains secure and unaltered. Others are cautioned to take care how they build upon that foundation, for it is essential that subsequent building shall be appropriate to the foundation upon which it is erected.

**3:11** The foundation which Paul laid and upon which the Corinthian church is built is not its first converts, and certainly not Paul himself: but Jesus Christ. And there can never be any other foundation than this. "Paul does not mean that it would be impossible to construct a community on a different basis, only that such a community will not be the church" (Barrett).

It has been suggested that the Cephas party at Corinth was teaching that Cephas (Peter the rock) is the foundation of the church (based on the words of Christ in Matthew 16:18 and the accepted view in the early church of Cephas as a "pillar" of the church [see Galatians 2:19; and cf. Ephesians 2:20]) - this could in fact be part of the reason for the existence of the Cephas party at Corinth (doubtless without Peter's approval). Whatever may be the case in this regard, Paul is concerned first of all to emphasize the folly and the error - and, in fact, the impossibility - of building a church at Corinth on any foundation other than Jesus Christ himself.

**3:12** Paul proceeds next to warn against the second possible error in building: constructing a shoddy edifice, for such can be erected even upon an ideal foundation. "If anyone builds" does not use the indefinite, hypothetical Greek "if", ἐαν (*ean*), but εἰ (*ei*), the "if" of real circumstances. Thus the meaning is: "When anyone builds upon this foundation (and they shall), let each one (v.13) take care how and what he builds." Re " precious stones": A. Robertson 62 comments, "Either 'costly stones,' such as marble or granite, suitable for building, or 'precious stones,' suitable for ornamentation"; and draws attention to the usefulness of hay, straw and stubble in building (cf. Exodus 5:12) and for thatching. Some of these materials are of little or no value, and very combustible; the others are valuable and enduring. In the church and in the life of each church member, what is being built (even when it is upon the foundation of Jesus Christ) can be worthy, or worthless.

**3:13** The Day (of Judgement) will be a day when the lives and works of Christians come under scrutiny - a truth which Paul also specifically mentions in Romans (14:10-12) and which is referred to frequently in Scripture. What each person has done will be tested by fire, and "the quality of each man's work will be seen when the Day of Christ exposes it" (TEV).

**3:14** The purpose of this judgement is to test each believer's work to determine his reward. Although God's people, when they have done all that they should, can only say (Luke 17:10), "We are unworthy servants; we have only done what was our duty", yet nonetheless God's grace promises a rich reward for faithfulness and obedience (Matthew 5:12; 10:41-42; Mark 9:41; Luke 6:23,35; and earlier in this chapter, 1 Corinthians 3:8). The concluding chapter of the Bible contains the promise, "Behold, I am coming soon! My reward is with me, and I will give to everyone according to what he has done." (Revelation 22:12 - cf. Psalm 62:12.) For all of the builder's work which endures, "he will receive a reward".

**3:15** If any person's work does not survive the test, they will thus suffer loss (in particular, the loss of their reward, and doubtless also the sorrow of seeing that their life has achieved nothing of real value). But their own salvation is never in jeopardy, for salvation is by grace through faith and in no way related to a person's works. They suffer loss, because rewards *are* directly related to a person's works. Such a one is saved as through fire: like a man running from his burning house, with the smell of fire about him, and losing everything behind him.

Some commentators see this passage as referring to leaders in the church, because they are the ones who build the church upon its initial foundation; their "works" are then built through preaching and teaching (for this is to parallel the means by which Paul, the expert builder, laid the foundation). Thus the works referred to would be the doctrines preached and taught concerning which the preachers and teachers carry especial responsibility (cf. James 3:1). This can then be applied to the situation envisaged at Corinth.

Thus Barrett:

> "To abandon the metaphor, and say plainly what Paul appears to have had in mind: if Judaizing Christians, such as the disciples of Peter, attempt to build their old Jewish exclusivism into the structure of the

church (cf. Gal.ii:11-14) they will fail; this rotten superstructure will perish."

Whether or not the meaning can be taken to be this specific, it is clear that Paul intends his metaphor of building to be seen by his readers as relating directly to their situation at Corinth, this section coming as it does between a passage referring specifically to himself and Apollos (3:4-9) and a passage in which he addresses himself to the Corinthians as "you" (3:16-22E). However, this does not justify the conclusion that Paul's words *only* have relevance to the situation at Corinth, or to church leaders. No such limitations are implied by Paul in his teaching here. What he says here to the Corinthians by way of encouragement and warning is applicable to all the people of God throughout all history.

### (d) The Christian Church is the dwelling place of God (3:16-17)

**3:16** Paul draws now a final point from his picture of building construction. Not only are the Corinthians building badly: they are actually engaged in destroying God's building, God's temple, the church. "Don't you know...?" is a favorite Pauline expression and introduces something that his readers certainly ought to know and presumably something that he himself would have taught them. Paul takes up the concept of the Christian body as God's dwelling place, in contradistinction to the temple of stones in Jerusalem. Note the further comments upon this verse in the "Reflections", below.

**3:17** To destroy the temple of God is a serious thing indeed, for if anyone does this then "God will destroy him". But this *IS* what the Corinthians are doing: by fragmenting the church with their divisions and dissensions they are engaged in destroying the temple of God. This is a more serious matter than failing to build well, and losing one's reward. It implies that God's church in Corinth is under attack and its existence as a church is being threatened.

If such a comment appears wildly exaggerated, it is well to remember that Paul is speaking of the community of believers in that place, the local church, and that the churches *did* disappear from many places where they existed in apostolic and post-apostolic times (cf. the early churches in North Africa, and the churches of Revelation 1-3 in Asia Minor).

Who is it who is in the process of destroying the church at Corinth? It could be non-Christian agitators fomenting trouble in the church between brethren: God shall destroy any such. It certainly refers to the behind-the-scenes manipulator of the disputes at Corinth, the devil himself: him indeed God shall destroy.

What is also implied here is that if any Christian is engaged (wittingly or unwittingly) in activity that is destroying the church at Corinth, he is aligning himself with the enemies of God and the enemies of the gospel, and must expect to share their fate. This is not pressed or further explained. What Paul is expecting is that a genuine Christian, made aware of the seriousness of what he is doing, will come to himself and cease to behave in a way that does damage to the church of God. Paul emphasizes the seriousness of the accusation he is making against them by saying "for God's temple is sacred", holy (that is, it belongs to God in a special way, and is set apart exclusively for him) "and that temple are **YOU**". The word "you" (plural) is the last word in the Greek paragraph, and very emphatic. (Paul uses this same concept of believers corporately as the temple of God in another connection in 6:19, and again in 2 Corinthians 6:16.)

## (e) There is no room for
### boasting about wisdom or about men (3:18-23E)

**3:18** He should become a fool, that is, in the estimation of the people of this age, by accepting the wisdom of God which they regard as foolishness (as Paul has explained in the preceding two chapters), in order that he may thus become truly wise, according to God's standards of judgement. The Corinthians (or some of them) are in danger of deceiving themselves in thinking that they are wise, through assessing themselves by the wrong standard, the wisdom of this age.

**3:19** The wisdom of this world is utter foolishness as far as God is concerned - not least because it leaves God out of its thinking. (Paul picks up here what he has mentioned earlier in 1:20ff.) God is the one who wins out over the wise (the quotation is a description of God) - he catches the wise in their own craftiness, he entangles them in their own net, he exposes and shows up the sham, the shallowness, and the perfidy of their wisdom.

The word "craftiness" has the idea of "deceitful cunning", "sneakiness", "trickery". The word picture is of a criminal caught in the act by someone in authority who seizes him firmly by the wrist and prevents him carrying through what he is doing. The quotation, from Job 5:13, is not taken from the Septuagint; Paul here makes a direct, exact translation from the Hebrew (or else he is using a translation into Greek that differs from the Septuagint).

**3:20** The quotation is from Psalm 94:11; in applying it to make his point, Paul changes "men" to "wise". Their "thoughts" are their reasonings, the conclusions which they reach, or possibly their thought-out plans, their crafty schemes. These are all ματαιος (*mataios*), that is, "worthless", "futile", "useless", "unavailing", "ineffectual". A vivid illustration of this is seen in the "trick questions" with which Jesus's enemies so often sought to entrap him, and how he rendered all their efforts ineffective, and exposed their hypocrisy.

**3:21** This is a statement of the consequence of all that has gone before. No one can boast in men - as the Corinthians had been doing in their assertions of factional allegiances (1:12; 3:4). *All* the leaders in the Church belong to all Christians (note the inversion of the thought: the Corinthians were saying that *they* "belonged to" such-and-such a leader; Paul says that all the leaders "belonged to" them). But Paul does not merely say "all the leaders", though this in itself is the decisive answer to the divisive wrangling at Corinth; he says "all things", and encourages them to think more widely still.

**3:22-23E** He explains the "all things" - it includes the leaders concerning whom they are disputing, and beyond this it embraces the world, and the very issues of life and death, and everything that is encompassed in the present and the future as well.

In what sense does the "world" (κοσμος, *kosmos*) belong to Christians? In the same way as is true of life and death, the present and the future: in that all these are in the Lord's hands, and "you are Christ's, and Christ is God's". It is an expression of the absolute lordship of Christ, and of the absolute commitment to Christ of the true Christian, and the total acceptance by the Christian of that lordship.


## SOME PRACTICAL AND PASTORAL REFLECTIONS

### How Many Temples Does God Have?

Frequently we find popular expositions of 3:16 and 6:19 saying to individual Christians, "Your body is a temple of the Holy Spirit." This is totally misexposition, completely wrong. And misleading. And it distorts Paul's point.

Isaiah 28:16 gives the promise: "Therefore thus says the Lord God, 'Behold I am the one who has laid as a foundation in Zion, a stone, a tested stone, a precious cornerstone, of a sure foundation.'" Jesus says (Matthew 16:18), "I will build my church." Jesus takes the words of Psalm 118:22 and applies them to himself - he is himself the cornerstone of the church he is building (Matthew 21:42//Mark 12:10//Luke 20:17;

also Acts 4:11). And in John 2:19 Jesus says to the Jews, "Destroy this temple, and in three days I will raise it up." Not altogether surprisingly, they take him to be referring to the building in front of them. "But he was speaking about the temple of his body. When therefore he was raised from the dead, his disciples remembered that he had said this, and they believed the Scripture and the word that Jesus had spoken." (John 2:21-22.)

Stephen understood that "the Most High does not dwell in houses made with hands" (Acts 7:47-50), and Paul draws all these thoughts together, describing "the church which is his body" (Ephesians 1:22-23) as: "built on the foundation of the apostles and prophets, Christ Jesus himself being the cornerstone, in whom the whole structure, being joined together, grows into a holy temple in the Lord. In him you also are being built together into a dwelling place for God by the Spirit." (Ephesians 2:20-22.)

Note carefully: The people of God (Ephesians 2:22, "you", plural) are being joined together (as each new convert is added) so that "the whole structure grows into a holy temple", because Christians are being "built together into a dwelling place for God by the Spirit".

Peter teaches the same truth (1 Peter 2:4-8), where he says, "you yourselves like living stones are being built up as a spiritual house". A church building is not the house of God: the people of God are *together* the true house of God, each one of them being a living stone.

This then is the strand of biblical teaching which Paul reflects in 1 Corinthians 3:16. "Do you not know this?" Paul asks. "- that you are God's temple, and that God's Spirit dwells in you?" *Not* the individual Christian, but "you" plural. It is a corporate concept: the whole body of Christians together: "all of you together constitute God's temple, and God's Spirit lives in you".

In the next verse Paul goes on to speak of destroying God's temple. He is speaking of destroying the church of God - not of an individual Christian. Then in 6:19 Paul refers once again to the same concept, "Do you not know that your body is the Holy Spirit's temple within you, whom you have from God?" Again, "you" is plural; again, it is referring to the people of God collectively, corporately. And then in 2 Corinthians 6:16 Paul says, "We are the temple of the living God."

So, biblically, you cannot say to an individual Christian, "Your body is a temple of the Holy Spirit." Let me emphasize again: you cannot.

But isn't it all the same thing, singular or plural?

No, it is not.

Oftentimes teachers are saying to someone, "Your body is a temple of the Holy Spirit." And then to another Christian, "And yours." And to another, "And so also is yours." As if God has as many temples as there are individual Christians. At this point frequently the lesson is drawn, "Therefore honor God in your body" - do not treat your body or use your body in a way which is dishonoring to the indwelling Holy Spirit.

Indeed a valid conclusion and application, but an invalid premiss, which misses Paul's point.

For the point which Paul is making in Ephesians 2:20-22, and again twice in 1 Corinthians, is the *interconnectedness* of Christians as the body of Christ, the temple indwelt by the Holy Spirit. If our concept is of an individual as "a temple" of God, then what such a one may do in the body which dishonors the indwelling Spirit is bad enough; but at least it may not directly impact upon other Christians. However, in Paul's application of this biblical truth, it is wider than that. For when (in 6:15-20) Paul writes of a Christian joining himself to a prostitute, and links this with the concept of the body as the Holy Spirit's temple, Paul is saying that in so doing, this person is joining the other parts of the temple of God to that prostitute also. The person concerned may think it is a private and individual thing that he is doing. But "the Holy Spirit's temple" is a corporate concept, so he has involved the whole church in his sin.

This would apply equally to any other sin which a Christian commits in, with, or through his body.

And any exposition of this teaching as of an individual Christian being "a temple" of the Holy Spirit quite misses this dimension of what Paul is saying.

# CHAPTER FOUR

## SECTION 1: DIVISIONS IN THE CHURCH (continued)

### 5. Paul's Response To The Situation (3:5-4:21E)

### (f) The ministry of Christ's servants (4:1-21E)

**4:1** "How then should men regard us?" Paul answers the implied question: "Regard us as servants of Christ and stewards (trustees, custodians, and dispensers) of the secret things of God, the mysteries of God (that is, the things of God which could never be known by human wisdom or through human searching, but which *are* able to be known, because God has been pleased to reveal them).

**4:2** "What is required (ζητεω, *zeteō*)" in stewards, "those who have been given a trust", is that they must prove πιστος (*pistos*), "faithful", "trustworthy" (honest and reliable) in carrying out the responsibilities given to them by their master.

**4:3-4** It seems clear from this and other references (see especially 9:3) that Paul was being subjected to strong criticism by some at Corinth. Paul declines to allow himself to be troubled or diverted from his ministry by this. His own conscience is clear; but what really matters is the judgement of the Lord, and Paul is content to commit himself to this.

**4:5** He warns them against reaching a premature judgement before the appointed time: before all the facts are in, i.e. before the Lord returns, because he will bring to light things which at present are hidden, and expose the inner motives of the heart. This will apply both to Paul and to those who are his accusers. Then each person will receive whatever measure of praise from God is due to him. Paul's words in this passage can well be applied to those today who set up as self-appointed critics of the ministries of God's servants.

**4:6** In what he has said Paul has used himself and his friend Apollos in his comments and illustrations, to make his points. The implication is that other names could have been mentioned specifically also: presumably that of Cephas in particular, and doubtless the names of the troublemakers at Corinth as well. Paul's purpose is "so that you may learn from us the meaning of the saying, 'Do not go beyond what is written [in Scripture]'". (Note that the RSV/ESV translation is less helpful at this point than the NIV.) It would seem that the Corinthians were prepared to "go beyond" what the Scriptures contained, and thus (by following traditions outside Scripture, or by their own "superior" wisdom) they were in consequence becoming conceited and boastful, exalting one person against another. What is said here in the context of one particular situation has application far more widely, in relation to any tendency or temptation to go beyond the warrant of Scripture.

The danger of a person going beyond or ahead of what he has warrant for (in the teaching of Scripture) is also mentioned in 2 John 9. It was a danger into which the Pharisees fell, and for which Jesus severely criticized them (see Matthew 15:1-6). It is also a danger for us to beware of in our church today. I comment further on this in "Reflections" at the end of this chapter.

Paul's corrective in the next verse for the Corinthians' error in "going beyond" indicates a particular fault for which they were in need of correction: they were boasting and exulting and taking pride in the abilities or ministries that some amongst them possessed.

**4:7** The word "for" with which this verse commences shows that what Paul says here is in direct response to the pride the Corinthians are exhibiting. He asks, "Who sees anything different in you?" In themselves, they are not different from each other, so that one person has no right to be given preeminence over another. Insofar as they do differ from each other, the special endowments that any one person possesses have all been received by them (received, that is, from God), so how does that constitute a basis for his boasting?

We have here another reference to the spiritual elitism that was behind much of the dissension at Corinth, the boastfulness in an imagined spiritual superiority, which Paul deals with at length in chapters 12 to 14.

**4:8** Already you have all you want (that is, you are filled with all the gifts with which God could endow you)! Already you have become rich (with every possible enrichment that you could have)! Without any help from us (Paul and Apollos) you have started to reign as kings! Paul pricks their pride with pointed irony. If only it were true, he continues, so that we could have a share in your reigning as kings!

**4:9-13** But as it is, he says, we are humbled and humiliated, rejected and reviled. By contrast with their inflated opinion of their importance, Paul paints a soberingly realistic picture of what it actually means to be a faithful servant of Christ. "Us apostles" (verse 9) can refer to Paul and the twelve apostles, or could be a wider use of "apostles" to include

Apollos (in the light of 4:6) and perhaps others of Paul's companions and associates in ministry such as Barnabas (cf. Acts 14:14). These comments set forth the true nature of ministry for God: it is self-giving and sacrificial.

**4:14** Paul's intention in writing as he has is to bring them to their senses, and to a sober appreciation of the realities of the situation, but not to put them to shame. He assures them that he still regards them very warmly as his "dear children" in Christ, and as such, he has the right and the duty to admonish them. The Jerusalem Bible translates: "I am saying all this not just to make you ashamed but to bring you, as my dearest children, to your senses."

**4:15** He is their spiritual father because "it was I who begot you in Christ Jesus by preaching the Good News" (Jerusalem Bible). They can have ten thousand guardians and guides and tutors in Christ, but they do not have a multiplicity of fathers; no one can ever replace Paul as the one who brought them the gospel and thus brought them to Christ. This verse is no basis for the use of the word "father" for a Christian minister; Paul uses this word as a metaphor for the relationship between an evangelist and his converts.

**4:16** Paul urges them to model themselves on him (become a μιμητης [*mimētēs*], a mimic, of him). This is not pride on Paul's part, nor is it a desire to attract followers for himself in a personal way. But rather, as a father is an example to his children, so Paul must be to the Corinthians an example of what it means to be a Christian and to live a Christian life.

Doubtless included in this is the example he has set them, in the preceding verses (4:9-13), of what it really means to be a servant of Christ. This exhortation is repeated in 11:1, and its justification is given there: "Be imitators of me, as I am of Christ." (Similarly Galatians 4:12; Philippians 3:17; 1 Thessalonians 1:6; 2:14; 2 Thessalonians 3:7-9.)

**4:17** Timothy - also Paul's convert - is sent to them to remind them of Paul's way of life. To remind them, because they would have already been taught by Paul of these things and have seen Paul's ways for themselves. Paul also draws attention to the fact that what he is teaching the Corinthians is identical with what he is teaching everywhere in every other church. This sets the Corinthian situation in perspective: they are being encouraged to see themselves as part of the universal Church of Christ.

Timothy may possibly have been the bearer of this letter himself, but most commentators conclude that Timothy had already left Ephesus before Paul wrote 1 Corinthians, travelling to Corinth via Macedonia (see Acts 19:21-22) - so that this letter, sent more directly by sea, apparently with the returning Corinthian delegation which had travelled to Ephesus to see him (1 Corinthians 16:15-18), would be expected to reach Corinth before Timothy arrived (see 1 Corinthians 16:10-11).

**4:18-20** Paul is not sending Timothy and a letter as a substitute for coming to see the Corinthians personally, as some at Corinth are arrogantly saying. When he comes, he will confront his detractors in person and see their power, not their talk. That is, he will find out whether they are empty talkers, or possess God's power (see 2:4-5). This is the evidence of the kingdom of God.

**4:21E** Paul closes this entire first section (chapters 1 to 4) of his letter with the challenge for the Corinthians to decide for themselves the spirit in which his forthcoming visit will be made. Their decision will be shown by the response they give to what he has written to them.

Implicit in Paul's words is his confidence in his apostolic authority. Robertson & Plummer (xlvii) have commented,

> In our Epistle the Apostle, in asserting and defending his Apostolic status and mission, never for a moment vacates his position of unquestionable authority, nor betrays a doubt as to his readers' acceptance of it.

## SOME PRACTICAL AND PASTORAL REFLECTIONS

### The Danger of Going Beyond

Paul writes (4:6), "I have applied all these things to myself and Apollos for your benefit, brothers, that you may learn by us not to go beyond what is written ..." In the NRSV this reads, "... so that you may learn through us the meaning of the saying, 'Nothing beyond what is written.'"

John writes of this same danger in his Second Epistle, v.9: "Everyone who goes on ahead and does not abide in the teaching of Christ, does not have God. Whoever abides in the teaching has both the Father and the Son." The NRSV: "Everyone who does not abide in the teaching of Christ, but goes beyond it, does not have God; whoever abides in the teaching has both the Father and the Son."

The AV/KJV is most unhelpful in its rendering of Paul's meaning in 4:6: it reads, "... that ye might learn in us not to think *of men* above that which is written" - which misses the point.

The danger that Paul and John are pointing out, in its most basic form, is a dissatisfaction with the silences of Scripture, and an attempt to "add in" the information which Scripture does not give.

In many cases this is completely harmless: as when a Sunday School teacher embroiders one of the stories of Scripture to make it more vivid for her Sunday School class. Harmless, that is, provided the details she adds are validly taken from what we know of the situations in Bible times, and are not misleading.

And there are many "traditional" details which have been added to biblical narratives to the point where most people would believe that they are part of the original account. One example would be that in the Garden of Eden, Adam and Eve ate an apple (Genesis does not name a fruit, calling it "the fruit of the tree of the knowledge of good and evil" [Genesis 2:17; 3:3].). Another would be that the wise men who visited Jesus as a babe were three in number (Matthew 2:1 simply calls them "wise men from the east", their number unspecified).

In the early church many people felt that the information about the life of Jesus given in the Gospels was a little too sketchy, and so various accounts were written which "filled in the details": the different infancy stories. In similar fashion numerous "Acts" were written to tell of other experiences of Paul and the rest of the apostles. Some were merely speculative fictions; some contained heterodox teaching.

Somewhere here we should draw the line as to what is acceptable. Paul says, "Do not go beyond what is written." Certainly we should not be more strict or less strict than Scripture in its moral code. This would certainly be encompassed within the prohibition of Revelation 22:18-19 about adding to or taking away from the words of this book. And however one interprets precisely the binding and loosing of Matthew 18:18, it can be agreed that this verse forbids both the "tightening" and "loosening" of what the laws of God allow or proscribe.

Yet this is precisely what some in the church of God have done down the ages. This is one of the things for which Jesus castigated the Pharisees, who "tie up heavy burdens, hard to bear, and lay them on people's shoulders" (Matthew 23:4). And this is still what some Christian leaders and teachers do today: adding requirements for the Christian life or godly behavior for which the Bible gives no warrant. And forbidding things where no such prohibition is found in Scripture, neither explicit or implicit: in fact, there are quite a few sins which the church has invented - they are nowhere found in the Bible. Some such issues will arise in the course of our consideration of this Epistle, and I will draw attention to them at that time.

Then on the other hand there are matters explicitly disallowed in Scripture which some churches today will permit; or else commanded in Scripture which some churches today will not require of Christians. In some such instances, the apologists for differing from Scripture will say, "It is because the biblical teaching on this matter was culturally conditioned, and culture has changed." Now, there can be a considerable extent to which this is so: but even when a biblical command or prohibition is expressed in a cultural context there is normally an eternal truth in it which we need to understand and apply even in our different culture. But often it is simply a situation where biblical standards differ from the patterns of behavior of our present world, and the temptation is always to conform those biblical standards to what is to be found in the world around us.

Instances of all these situations are to be found in this Epistle, and will call forth careful consideration.

But we have this word of warning from John: "Everyone who does not abide in the teaching of Christ, but goes beyond it, does not have God; whoever abides in the teaching has both the Father and the Son." And this instruction here from Paul: "learn through us the meaning of the saying, 'Nothing beyond what is written.'"

For down that path lies danger.

# CHAPTER FIVE

## SECTION 2: CONCERNING SEX AND MARRIAGE

### INTRODUCTION: The Issues Paul Discusses (5:1-7:40E)

The most pressing issue to be faced by the church at Corinth was the dissension which was fracturing its unity and ultimately threatening its very existence. Having discussed this matter at some length, Paul is ready now to turn his attention to the next of the concerns affecting the church. In the letter they have written to him, the Corinthians have raised a number of questions about sex and marriage, and he is ready to answer them about these questions. But first of all, in relation to this general subject of sex and marriage, there are some questions that he wishes to take up with them, some matters that they did not (it appears) choose to mention in their letter to him (7:1) but which he has heard about. The first of these which he discusses is a blatant case of immorality which is being tolerantly accepted by the Corinthian Church (5:1-13E). This is followed by a consideration of another matter reported to him: Christian is going to law against Christian at Corinth before non-Christian judges (6:1-8). And then he proceeds to a comprehensive and systematic consideration of the whole subject of sex and marriage.

First, he covers the matter of the wrong use of human sexuality - he identifies the different types of immorality that were practised at Corinth, underlining the standards of God in this sphere of life and the seriousness of violating those standards (6:9-20E). Then (and this in reply to one of the points raised in the Corinthians' letter to him) he speaks about the right place for sexual fulfillment, in the marriage relationship (7:1-5).

Thereafter he systematically treats the various other marital situations that can occur (which may or may not have been explicitly referred to in their letter): the sexual pressure faced by a person who cannot live in that relationship that Paul has just described (7:1-5) because that relationship has terminated (7:6-9); from this, a discussion of the question of marriage break-up, in general terms (7:10-11) and then a more detailed examination of a specific situation, where one spouse has been converted and the other is not (7:12-16). There follows from this a more generalized comment on "Living the life that the Lord assigns" (7:17-

24), and the discussion concludes with a fairly lengthy treatment of problems concerning the unmarried (7:25-40E). There is thus a traceable sequence in this section, with a logical progression from one topic to the next:

• A blatant case of immorality that Paul has heard about.
• Another abuse that Paul has heard about: Christians going to law.
• The overall question of the wrong use of human sexuality.
• In contrast: the right use of human sexuality.
• The problem faced by a person whose sexual relationship has termi-
  nated.
• The problem of marriage break-up.
• The specific situation of a Christian with a non-Christian spouse.
• General comment flowing from this: Living the life that the Lord
  assigns.
• The situation of the unmarried.

This clear framework and progression of thought in Paul's treatment of the overall subject suggests a carefully planned and structured approach by Paul to discussing the matter, and also indicates his intention of giving a comprehensive coverage of all aspects of the subject.

## 1. Dealing With A Case of Incest (5:1-13E)

**5:1a** Paul here begins the second section of his Epistle, and begins it very abruptly indeed: "Immorality is widely reported among you". The "among you" can go either with the "immorality" or the "reported": i.e., that among you there is immorality, and this is widely known elsewhere: or, that immorality is widely reported in the church at Corinth (and possibly also amongst the non-Christians of Corinth) - this case of immorality is not a secret, but is out in the open. In either case it means that the Corinthian church is well aware that there is an instance of immorality in their midst.

It is, moreover, of a very serious kind "that is not tolerated even among pagans". This does not mean that such a kind of immorality could never *occur* amongst pagans, but that it breached even pagan standards of acceptable behavior so that pagans (even the pagans of licentious Corinth) condemned it. Yet the church allowed an instance of this kind to continue in its midst!

**5:1b** A man has his father's wife. "Has" indicates a continuing sexual relationship. Commentators speculate whether the father was still alive, and if so, whether he is divorced now from this woman, or whether he has died; and even whether the incestuous man has seduced her away from his father. We have no information about these matters. It can be taken however that "his father's wife" means the man's stepmother and not his own mother (or this would have been mentioned), and that the man is (or professes to be) a Christian and the stepmother is not: for Paul says nothing further about the woman but writes in deep concern about the church's relation to the man (cf. 5:12-13).

There is nothing in the New Testament against a man marrying his stepmother, yet Paul takes it for granted that he can speak in this way to the Corinthians and be understood. He feels no need to cite the relevant passages, but his attitude here presumes the teaching of the Old Testament (Leviticus 18:8; 20:11). That Paul can take the applicability of Old Testament moral teaching for granted in this way indicates an attitude on Paul's part both to the Old Testament itself and also to its relevance for the Christian Church as revealing the mind of God upon such moral issues.

**5:2a** Yet the Corinthians are arrogant (ESV, RSV, NRSV) and proud (NEB, NIV, TEV, Jerusalem, and Phillips), literally, "inflated" with self-importance. At first sight, it might seem that they are proud *in spite of* this case of incest; but the way in which Paul goes on to suggest what their response to this situation *ought to be* (5:2b) appears to indicate a contrast with the pride, which is what their response *actually is*. Similarly 5:6a would appear to mean that they are boastful about the situation that Paul is describing, that is, this toleration of the incestuous man in their midst. They were proud and boastful about their toleration and broadmindedness, as some churches today are proud of having practising homosexuals in their membership, or unmarried church members living in a *de facto* relationship. (See further on 5:6a.)

**5:2b** What should be the response of the Corinthians to this situation? *First of all*, they should mourn about it and about the man concerned. They should be filled with grief. It is a serious thing when a member of the church of God not only falls into a sin but continues to live in his sin. It destroys the life and witness of that person, tarnishes the testimony and ministry of the whole church, grieves the Holy Spirit, and causes God's name to be blasphemed among the unbelievers. What Paul says about the Jews in Romans 2:17-24 is even truer when it has to be said about Christians. We all share in what happens to each part of the body of Christ (1 Corinthians 12:26-27). If therefore a church member is continuing unrepentant in sin, it is a matter for deep grief and for the most serious concern on the part of all of us.

*Secondly*, they must put this offender out of the fellowship of the church. This is a matter of obedience to the instruction of Jesus in Matthew 18:17, where he says that if such a person refuses to listen to the church then that person is to be regarded - and treated - as a pagan or a tax collector. It is to be added that, *thirdly*, if he continues in his sin, then he will now be seen not to be a Christian at all - see 6:9-11.

**5:3-4** As Paul is not in Corinth, he is thus unable to take action in person; but he is with them in spirit and has taken action as if he were present: he has considered the facts of the situation and reached a judgement upon it, in the name of the Lord Jesus. But this judgement must be endorsed by the church when it formally assembles (a legal assembly is implied by the word συναγω, *synagō*) and the church must accept responsibility for carrying out that judgement. Paul will be present in spirit - that is, to put his view before them then, as it were, which he is conveying to them now in this letter. When they act, it will be (Paul is confident) to take a serious but necessary step: and this will be because their assembly, and their action, is with "the power of our Lord Jesus".

**5:5a** The judgement then to be executed by the church is "to deliver this man to Satan". This judgement is also found in 1 Timothy 1:20, where it is stated, "I have handed over [Hymenaeus and Alexander] to Satan that they may learn not to blaspheme". It appears that to hand someone over to Satan means to exclude them from the fellowship and privileges of the church (the thought being that outside the church is the realm of Satan). This idea of exclusion from the church is indicated by 5:2b, "Let him who has done this be removed from among you"; and also by 5:13b, "Purge the evil person from among you."

A person cannot be permitted to continue to receive the benefits derived from belonging in the church while he is actively living in continuing sin.

Moreover, if rebuke and warning have not brought him to repentance and amendment (and the passage implies that the time for rebuke and warning has passed) then the only way that the seriousness of his situation can be brought home to him is by putting him out of the church. We can see that this situation has been continuing for some time by the fact that Paul had already written to the Corinthians about it earlier (see comment on 5:9).

A third reason for the necessity of expelling the offender is the effect that his continued acceptance in the church has upon others - which Paul writes about explicitly in the verses which follow (5:6-8).

Paul does not name the offender in this letter: contrast 1 Timothy 1:20, where the judgement has been executed ("I have handed over") and the people concerned *are* named. Presumably the offender's name is not mentioned here (although the matter is widely known throughout the church in Corinth) because formal judgement by the church has not yet been pronounced against him and there is still the possibility that the man, even at this late stage, may repent.

**5:5b** There are two purposes for handing him over to Satan: in the short term, "for the destruction of the flesh"; and in the end, "so that his spirit may be saved in the day of the Lord". Commentators and translators vary in their understanding of the first purpose.

*Some* take "flesh" in the sense of "the old sinful nature within man", the meaning being that when the man is cut off from the Christian community he will realize the enormity of his sin and its consequences from being cast into the realm of Satan, and this will bring him to his senses and cause him to subdue his sinful desires and terminate his illegitimate relationship with his stepmother and return to the people of God. An illustration of this that is cited is the story of the Prodigal Son (Luke 15:11-32E). This approach is found in the NIV which translates, "so that his sinful nature may be destroyed and his spirit saved on the day of the Lord".

*A second interpretation* is to take "flesh" to be equivalent here to "body", so that the handing-over to Satan is an equivalent to physical death, the death of the body, which (in the view of some commentators) will then follow as God's judgement upon the sin. The execution of Ananias and Sapphira (Acts 5:1-10) is cited as a parallel. Alternatively, this verse is understood to mean that when the man is put outside the protective sphere of the church, Satan will attack him directly and bring about his death. That Satan and his minions have the power to inflict death is shown from Matthew 10:28, Luke 12:4, and Revelation 2:10. Translations along these lines include the following: "hand this man over to Satan for his body to be destroyed" (TEV); "he is to be handed over to Satan so that his sensual body may be destroyed" (Jerusalem Bible); and "this man is to be consigned to Satan for the destruction of the body" (NEB).

*A third interpretation* is that "flesh" here has the common meaning in the Bible of "man in his humanity, especially man in his human state apart from the working of the grace of God". Thus the interpretation would be that the handing over to Satan means putting the man out of the church and "letting Satan have him", as he is persevering in following Satan, with the result that the sin he is pursuing will follow its course and wreak its own ravages upon what he is as a human being. As a person in this world he will become destroyed, but because he still is a Christian his spirit will ultimately be saved. This would then be seen as being the inevitable outworking of the basic principle of Galatians 6:7,

"Do not be deceived: God is not mocked, for whatever one sows, that will he also reap." Thus we may note the Phillips translation: "the man should be left to the mercy of Satan so that while his body will experience the destructive powers of sin his spirit may yet be saved in the day of the Lord."

Whatever the interpretation of the first purpose, the meaning of the second purpose is clear: the ultimate salvation of the man's spirit at the day of judgement. But it is not clear whether this ultimate salvation is thought of as certain (i.e., the man is a Christian, and so will be saved in the end, cf. 3:15); or whether his ultimate salvation is the hoped-for goal, but is uncertain (that is, he bears the name of brother - 5:11 - but his actual state before God is uncertain, because he is continuing in his sin; or, he has been a Christian but may lose his ultimate salvation because of continuing in his sin). This verse does not lend definite support to either viewpoint in the doctrinal difference of opinion amongst Christians as to whether a Christian can lose his salvation.

**5:6a** Paul is concerned about the situation as it affects the immoral offender at Corinth. He is equally concerned (some commentators would say, more concerned) about this situation as it affects the Corinthian church itself, so that this section of his letter is not so much dealing with a case of immorality as dealing with a case of church order. The Corinthian response to the situation is seriously wrong. Not only do they fail to act decisively against the offender, and tolerate the continuation of his involvement in the church, but they are proud and boastful of their spirituality.

This could mean that they were proud and boastful about their spirituality *in spite of* the toleration of this sin in their midst, and is taken this way by Godet: "the apostle declares to them that their ground of self satisfaction is of bad quality ... 'Ye are proud of the state of your church; there is no reason for it.'" So also Barrett: "A church with a rotten spot in its structure was in too perilous a position to boast."

Alternatively, it could mean that they were proud and boastful *because of* their toleration of this man. Morris says of Paul's comment, "It shows that the Corinthians did more than merely acquiesce in the situation. They were proud of their attitude." Clark 81 has a similar interpretation: "The trouble was that the Corinthians boasted about their tolerant views on incest." For a similar issue of interpretation, see 5:2a.

Lenski 219 comments on καυχημα (*kauchēma*), the word Paul uses:

> "The term καυχημα [*kauchēma*] denotes the thing in which one glories and makes his boast, as distinct from καυχησις [*kauchēsis*], the act by which one glories."

Thus Paul is saying here "the thing about which you are boasting is not good", and not "the fact that you are boasting is not good". If Paul is thus saying that the Corinthians are boasting about something which is not good but which (by boasting about it) they are treating as if it is good, this indicates that what they are boasting about must include their attitude of acceptance and toleration towards this man's behavior. "Not good" is understatement, a figure of speech called *litotēs* - Paul means it is "bad"; but his choice of words, denying that it is "good", is additional support for the view that the Corinthians were asserting that it *was* a good thing (not necessarily that the man's incest was a good thing; but that their tolerance of it was a good thing).

**5:6b** This underlines the point of Paul's concern. For a Christian to be living in sin is serious enough; for the church of God to accept this situation is worse still. It shows how the effects of this sin are spreading: at this stage it is being tolerated - how long before it is being emulated? As yeast in a lump of dough spreads to affect the entire lump, so sin permitted within the Christian church in this way will spread in its influence and affect the whole church. How can the church preach against sin and bear witness in the community against sin, while tolerating a notorious example of sin within its own membership?

Thus the yeast (leaven) here certainly must refer to the offender in their midst. But its meaning is wider than this alone. The toleration of the Corinthians for this sin, and their attitude of arrogance, pride and boastfulness, is also yeast at work in the church which is dangerous and damaging. Note once again Paul's use of "Don't you know", "Surely you realize" (cf. 3:16) relating to something he had taught them or (as here) to something that was common knowledge.

**5:7** Therefore the old leaven must be completely cleaned out - both the attitude of toleration by the Corinthians and then, as a result of such a changed attitude and a new resolve, the offender himself must be put out of their midst. Lenski comments,

> Paul traces the Corinthian disinclination to take action against this one vicious case to its real source, the old worldly and fleshly disposition that was carried over in their hearts from their former life.

In this passage Paul is using imagery taken from the Passover ritual in which the Jews cleaned every bit of yeast and leavened bread from their houses before the Passover could be celebrated (Exodus 12:39; 13:6-9; 23:15; Deuteronomy 16:1-4; Matthew 26:17; Mark 14:1,12; Luke 22:1,7; Acts 20:6). Leaven (yeast) is used here (and in most other places in Scripture) as a symbolic representation of evil. They are to do this as they themselves really are unleavened - they really have been cleansed from sin by Christ and are genuine Christians. This is the basis on which they can, and must, act - "Christ, our Passover lamb, has been sacrificed."

**5:8** The "feast" to be kept is the whole Christian life, which is to be lived as "without yeast", "unleavened" - that is, with all that is sinful and evil purged and removed, and replaced by purity (or, sincerity) and truth.

**5:9-10** When Paul says "I wrote to you in my letter ..." he is referring to a letter written to them prior to our 1 Corinthians, as is evidenced by what he mentions here of the contents of that letter, and by the circumstance that he must now correct a misunderstanding by the Corinthians of his meaning. This "previous letter" or "earlier letter" (as it is sometimes called) is what is designated as "Corinthians A" in the Introduction.

As I also mention there, we have references in 2 Corinthians to another "lost" Pauline letter, written between the two that are extant, and usually designated "Corinthians C". Other "lost" Pauline letters are also mentioned (or implied) elsewhere in those that we have: the "Epistle to the Laodiceans" (see Colossians 4:16), and Paul's comment in 2 Thessalonians 3:17, "This is the sign of genuineness in every letter of mine: it is the way I write", which implies several prior letters, when we only have two letters written before 2 Thessalonians (Galatians and 1 Thessalonians). Johnson 91 explains about this:

> [1 Cor. 5:9] is the first clear reference in the New Testament to an apostolic letter that has not survived in our canonical collection. There were apparently others as well (cf. Col. 4:16). This should not be troublesome for us. Not all the apostolic instruction was universal enough in scope to address different congregations' needs, and the Holy Spirit worked providentially to give us those writings in the collection (canon) that would best serve the church in its continuing witness to the gospel of Christ.

"To associate with" is συναναμιγνυμι (*sunanamignumi*), a double-preposition verb meaning "to get mixed up together with". Paul's earlier letter had instructed them not to be (the form here is continuous aspect) mixed up together with the immoral. The Corinthians misinterpreted this (deliberately?) as referring to forbidding any contact at all with immoral people. This injunction was patently impossible to keep, especially in a city like Corinth, and thus it would seem that they felt free to ignore it.

Hurd's opinion is (152),

> The Corinthians had, Paul maintained, attributed to him an impossible idea, not out of innocence, but, as their own actions indicate (5:1,2), out of a deliberate desire to make him appear ridiculous.

It is possible that the incestuous relationship now being dealt with had already existed at the time of Paul's previous letter, and that he had intended it to be included in the scope of what he said then. If so, then the situation has changed between the two letters in that the Corinthians have (inadvertently or deliberately) sidestepped his instruction by misunderstanding what it referred to, and the details of the relationship have become reported more widely (5:1).

If however the present case of immorality had arisen since Paul wrote (or was not known to Paul when he wrote) his earlier letter, then he was speaking more generally in that letter. In such a case the fact that he had to write that earlier letter would show that at that earlier stage there were other cases of immorality in the church at Corinth - even if not of incest - that had to be dealt with. This highlights even more vividly the attitude of the church at Corinth in tolerating sin in their midst, and suggests that their toleration (indicated by the fact that Paul had to raise this matter in his previous letter, and that the Corinthians it seems took no action as a result of that letter) may well have been a factor in encouraging the incestuous offender in entering or continuing his relationship.

Paul mentions that to avoid the immoral of this world, and the greedy and swindlers and idolaters, one would need to go out of the world - a stark comment indeed on the moral situation at the time in Corinth.

**5:11** Paul's initial words here could be translated (with the NASB, RSV, and Jerusalem Bible), "I wrote to you", referring again to that previous letter, and reiterating just what it was that he did say in it. Alternatively, his words could be rendered as meaning, "what I am writing to you now in this present letter", referring to a present explanation of his previously intended meaning (taken thus by AV/KJV, ESV, NEB, NIV, NRSV, and Phillips).

In either case, he is now making his meaning crystal clear: if any person who is called a brother (either by himself or by those in the church) is immoral or greedy, or an idolater, reviler, drunkard or swindler, then Christians are not to associate with him (συναναμιγνυμι [*sunanamignumi*] is used again), and this prohibition extends as far as sharing a meal with him. To associate with such people (especially socially, as in sharing a meal) gives the impression of condoning their behavior, and thus one can become by association a partaker in their sin. (For the expression of this idea elsewhere in the New Testament, see 1 Timothy 5:22; 3 John 10-11; Revelation 18:4.)

In the world of the first century, to eat with a person was a sign of mutual acceptance and fellowship. Moreover, especially for the Jew, a meal was a sacred occasion: it began with the "breaking of bread", the thanksgiving to God for his gracious provision (thus see how Jesus began the meals at the Feeding of the Five Thousand, Mark 6:41, and at Emmaus, Luke 24:30) - it is this that lies behind the Jewish attitude to eating with Gentiles which was an issue in the early church: cf. Galatians 2:11-13.

Note that in the church at this time the accepted word for a Christian was "brother". However, Paul refers to the kind of person of whom he speaks as "one who is called a brother": Paul himself makes no pronouncement as to whether such a one would be a genuine Christian or not. (Probably in some such cases the answer would be "yes" and in others "no".)

Paul here adds to the four examples of reprehensible sin that he gave earlier (5:10) a further two: a reviler, and a drunkard. The list is primarily of matters which are considered sinful by the church but are likely to be more readily condoned by the world, so a crime like murder is not included.

**5:12** In writing, "For what have I to do with judging outsiders?" he further clarifies the fact that his previous letter cannot have been intended to refer to non-Christian sinners: it is not his business to judge them.

While a Christian will need to review constantly the nature of his association with non-Christians, so as not to be compromised in relation to behavior in which such non-Christians may indulge, this association with non-Christians is not forbidden (cf. later, 10:27). Jesus was wellknown for just such a willingness to mix with sinners. Such contact is essential, if the gospel is to have a bridge across which it can be brought to outsiders. But such association is not of necessity going to be interpreted as the Christian condoning the moral behavior of the non-Christian.

The matter is different regarding those *inside* the church. They *are* Paul's concern. Moreover, they must also be the concern of the whole Corinthian church.

Note the change of pronoun: "Is it not those inside the church whom *you* are to judge?" (RSV, ESV.) If the church of God does not exercise discipline but tolerates open sin amongst its members, then the yeast of such a person's sin will work its way through the whole church of God: everyone can become contaminated by the sin, others are led to follow the sinful example, the standards of the whole church are lowered, and its witness is compromised and its holiness is lost. No wonder then that this question of the disciplining of a church member is treated with such seriousness.

**5:13E** Paul makes it clear that making this distinction (in 5:12) does not mean that the non-Christian will go unjudged and unpunished, but that this is a matter to be left directly in the hands of God. However, in regard to the offender in their midst, the responsibility of the Corinthian church (at a formal assembly of its membership, 5:4) is clear and plain: Expel this evildoer from among you. Paul ends his treatment of the issue with an authoritative word, a quotation from the Old Testament Scripture, where it occurs with slightly varied wording in Deuteronomy 17:7; 19:19; 22:21,24; and 24:7.

Jesus taught that a brother who sins and who will not respond to correction by the church is to be regarded and treated as a pagan and a tax collector (Matthew 18:15-17). Paul's instructions are on identical lines. Such a one is to be put outside the fellowship, if he will not accept correction as a member of the fellowship. He is to be expelled "from among you", and left to the judgement of God for "God will judge those outside" (5:13). The hope is that this drastic action will result in his eventual salvation (5:5). If he continues in his unrighteous behavior then the assurance is given that those who do such things will not "inherit the kingdom of God" (6:9-10).


## SOME PRACTICAL AND PASTORAL REFLECTIONS

### What Are We To Make of This Offender?

In the world of today it is not always possible to know who in the assembly of the church are genuine Christians and which ones are those who only have the appearance of being Christians. At times there is a tendency to think that these matters were much more clearcut, black and white, in apostolic days.

This however is not really so, as we can see from this chapter. The offender is clearly a member of the congregation of the church at Corinth: Paul says (5:1) that "there is sexual immorality among you", and in any case Paul disclaims any responsibility for passing judgement on outsiders (5:12a), whereas he has passed judgement on the man who has done this thing (5:3-4). The man is to be delivered to Satan with the intended purpose of his ultimate salvation (5:5) - but is he actually a Christian at this time, or not?

It may be that he is a Christian who has fallen back into sin (perhaps because of the apparent attitude of toleration towards sin, especially sexual sin, which seems to have been prevailing in the church at Corinth).

Every minister of the gospel today is aware of the reality of this possibility; he has had backsliding Christians in his congregations; he has seen keen servants of Christ stumble and fall into sin and he knows the desperate relevance of the warning which Paul gives later in this letter (10:12), "So, if you think you are standing firm, be careful that you don't fall."

Even the minister of the gospel himself is not immune from the possibility of such a fall.

If the offender is a backsliding Christian, the intention is that putting him out of the fellowship of the church and delivering him afresh to Satan - whose kingdom he left at his conversion - will compel him to face the seriousness of his sin. This he will do, of course, only if he first sees that *the church* views it seriously. Without the church's fellowship, acceptance and support, without the ministry of the church and participation in the Lord's Supper (implicit in the prohibition of 5:11, "With such a man do not even eat"), he is made to recall his old life and compelled to see that he cannot have a foot in both worlds, but must choose, *for* Christ or *against* him. In a situation which has some parallels with that of the Corinthian offender, King David was compelled to face his sin (2 Samuel 12:1-14), and was brought to repentance and restoration (Psalm 51).

Alternatively, the offender, though a member of the Corinthian congregation, may not have become a Christian at all, and may be seeking to continue living in accordance with his old standards of morality while attracted to the Christian message and Christian standards in other ways. But if he were merely an interested listener to the gospel it is hard to see that Paul would have acted in this way; for the man (even if unconverted) has obviously become accepted in the church at Corinth as "one of them".

Again, this possibility will surprise no one. The Parable of the Sower, the key to all the parables (Mark 4:13), warns that there will be those who give every indication of a genuine response to the Word which is sown but who fall away and by their falling away make plain and clear what otherwise was not: that they are not those in whose hearts the Word of God has been fruitful (Mark 4:14-20; Matthew 13:18-23; see also 1 John 2:19).

Jesus explained further in his next parable (Matthew 13:24-43) that in the field there will be weeds growing amongst the wheat. The Corinthian offender may be not yet a Christian but may think himself to be a Christian, and consider that his behavior is within the tolerable limits of Christian liberty. When the church takes a firm stand on the question of sin in their midst, this can bring the man to recognize his true situation, and thus to realize that he cannot hesitate between the two alternatives but must commit himself fully to Jesus Christ who said, "Whoever is not with me is against me" (Matthew 12:30; Luke 11:23). Thus the church's severe response to the man's sin can lead to his ultimate salvation (5:5).

Some students of this passage accept a third interpretation of the situation: that the offender was indeed a Christian, but that he has, by his act of turning his back upon the moral standards of God, rejected Christ and lost his salvation. If the church now will act to reject the man from their fellowship, this will force the man to realize that he is no longer a member of Christ's church, for his behavior is incompatible with his profession of faith. Being thus brought to see that he is once again an outsider and a lost sinner, he may come back to faith and receive salvation again.

It is possible that Paul and the Corinthians are more fully aware of the man's spiritual standing than we are able to be, for we lack the fuller knowledge of the situation that they would have had. But it is also quite possible that Paul himself cannot be sure at this stage whether the man is a Christian or not. Certainly when he writes in more general terms of the church's attitude towards those who are open and continuous sinners, he speaks concerning "anyone who bears the name of brother" (5:11) - referring to the situation where a person "calls himself a brother" (NIV) or has been accepted as a Christian by the church, but has then by his unchristian moral behavior called in question the genuineness of his Christian standing.

John's First Epistle gives a very carefully balanced view of the situation: to commit an act of sin does not prove that a person is not a Christian, nor cause him to cease to be a Christian, for "If we say we have no sin, we deceive ourselves, and the truth is not in us. ... If we say we have not sinned, we make him a liar, and his word is not in us." (1 John 1:8-10). Yet, "My little children, I am writing these things to you so that you may not sin. ... Whoever says, 'I know him' but does not keep his commandments [that is to say, who continues in disobedience to his commandments] is a liar, and the truth is not in him." (1 John 2:1-4).

A similar balance is found in what Paul writes. In what follows (6:9-10) he sets before the Corinthians various forms of unrighteousness, from which (6:11) they have been forgiven, cleansed, and delivered. But these comments also make it starkly plain that those who persist in such behavior show by that fact that they are not of the people of God, and, they will not inherit the kingdom of God.

## What Then Should We Do?

The application of the teaching of this chapter to the circumstances of today's church will present many problems in practice. What are we to do in the church as a result of what Paul has said here? What is its relevance for today? This requires some thoughtful reflection. Ask yourself: if our church today finds itself confronted by a parallel situation, what are we to make of what Paul says, and, in particular, how is our church to respond to his teaching?

At its worst extreme of implementation, we can find the dissension in a church exacerbated, with two warring factions each "excommunicating" the other, or the more powerful group or party in a church crushing a minority with whom they differ. At the end of the first century, dissension still divided the Corinthian church - though at that time it was a dispute between the elders and the young radicals in the church - and this was the occasion for the writing of *1 Clement*, the letter of Clement of Rome to the Corinthians. Disputes of modern times can often be due to "personality clashes", or are frequently concerned with doctrinal issues or questions of worship, liturgy, sacraments, church order or practice, or the like. Now, without denying the seriousness of such issues, one should nonetheless recognize that they differ from the question of publicly-known immorality and the church's attitude towards the scandalous behavior of one of its members.

Sometimes modern attempts to implement the Pauline teaching have had unscheduled consequences, where the "excommunicated" have taken the church authorities to court for alleged defamation of character. Moreover there have been occasions when a person has been put out of fellowship for relatively minor infringements of the behavioral code of a particular group when those offences were simply not to be compared with the sin being practised by the Corinthian offender.

And it all too frequently happens that a church will fail to take account of the repentance of an offender but will continue to punish him for a sin for which he has sought and received the forgiveness of God.

At the opposite extreme, one can find Christian groups who, mindful of the real dangers of intolerance and excess of zeal in enforcing a particular code of morals, adopt a policy of total tolerance which does not enforce upon its membership any church discipline for moral lapses. Thus there comes to be no difference between the moral standards and practices of its members and those of the non-Christians outside the church, so that the concept of the church standing for and witnessing to a specific standard of moral life is completely nullified. This in fact was the exact situation at Corinth which called forth Paul's concern.

So then: what are we to do in the church as a result of what Paul has said here? Let us consider these issues.

First, let us recognize that Paul expected action to be taken. It is not possible to read this chapter and conclude that Paul was not serious about the matter. The Christian understanding of the Bible as authoritative and normative for church teaching and practice compels us to recognize that in similarly appropriate circumstances similarly appropriate action is required in the church today.

Second, we must note the seriousness of the offence. It was something that was so reprehensible that even the pagans condemned it; it had been continuing for some time and was still continuing; and it had become public knowledge in the church and (apparently) in the community as well. The seriousness of the sin must be commensurate with the seriousness of the action taken against it, as we seek to implement Paul's teaching in today's church. (Notice the kind of sins listed by Paul in 5:11.) We do not take drastic and extreme action against a culprit guilty of a minor misdemeanor. But nor do we allow serious, continuous, public sin on the part of a church member to go unchecked, unrebuked, and unpunished.

Third, just as this chapter presumes and implies prior attempts to bring the offender to a change of heart and mind, so must we first challenge such a person about his sin and give him time and opportunity for repentance - it is the gracious mercy of God to allow this first (see Revelation 2:21; 2 Peter 3:9). The clear evidence, found throughout Paul's epistles, of his close familiarity with the teaching of Jesus makes it highly probable that he knew and had already followed Jesus's teaching in such a situation (Matthew 18:15-17) in his previous comments about this man's offence, which was, it seems, discussed in Paul's earlier letter to the Corinthians (5:9-11). What necessitates drastic action now at Corinth is that the offender is unrepentant and the offence is still continuing. But if we were to act too precipitately in thrusting an offender out of our fellowship we may do more to prevent than to procure the favorable outcome that we seek.

Fourth, we are to act as a church. No one individual or group of individuals in a church is here being authorized to act on their own authority. Quite the contrary. We may consider that Paul the apostle had the authority to act himself against this offender. But it was necessary, and important, that the whole church be involved and be seen to be involved. They are to meet in formal assembly to consider the matter and decide what is to be done (5:4). There is absolutely no question about what Paul is telling them is to be done in this situation (see 5:3-5 and 11-13), but the point is that *they* are to do it (5:5a). The act of putting a person out of a Christian fellowship is an act of that whole fellowship formally assembled to discuss and decide the issue.

Fifth, we are to be completely clear in our minds about our objective. It is, through this discipline by the church, to censure the offender for his behavior with the purpose of bringing about his repentance and restitution, in hope of his restoration, and with a view to his ultimate salvation (5:5)

Sixth, we are to sever our association with a person who calls himself a brother (or who has been accepted as a brother) and who persists in flagrant sin - not only referring to immorality, but other serious sin (5:11). The circumstances of our doing this, through the act of a formal meeting, must be so clearly laid before the person in question that he understands what is being done, that it is being done by the whole church, that it is because he has failed to respond to the efforts of the church to help him to amend his ways, and that it is the last step open to us in our concern for his spiritual wellbeing and for our witness to the Lord in the world. It is to be made clear also that he will be welcomed back into fellowship when he has repented and made such restitution as the circumstances require. After making this clear, we withdraw our fellowship from the offender.

This is the point where the practical problem is most acute in our present denominational pattern, and with our modern mobility. The person concerned, if he wishes to retain his church links, simply goes to another local church or another denomination, once he is put out of our fellowship. What was meant to be an act of severe church discipline - the most drastic act of which the church is capable - becomes for the offender simply the occasion for a change of membership or denominational affiliation.

And when he links up somewhere else, he is not highly likely to mention the circumstances of his departure from his previous congregation or that he is under discipline from them. He has moreover a fresh opportunity of keeping concealed whatever the sin is that he is committing and which had come to light in his last church.

The apparent hopelessness in these circumstances of effecting any kind of actual church discipline has caused some to abandon the attempt as being about as successful as carrying water in a sieve.

Two comments should be made about this.

First, the fact that to a considerable extent the offender can "slip out from under" the discipline when the church acts as it should is no valid reason for the church failing to act as it should.

Second, the church which imposes this discipline can, through its leaders, seek to retain a contact (perhaps by an occasional visit) with the offender so that he is reminded that the church still loves him and cares for him though it cannot countenance what he is doing - and that in this attitude the church is reflecting the attitude of God.

If his former church learns that the offender has linked up somewhere else, should they inform his new church about their own action against the offender?

There is no easy answer to this question, and it may well depend upon the details of the specific situation. But they most certainly (through their leaders) can and should seek to make the offender aware that if he has not repented and abandoned his sin then his transfer to another local church solves nothing in regard to the serious fracture of his relationship with God; and if he has, then he is welcome to return to his former congregation. But in the latter case, the person concerned may feel a preference for making a new start elsewhere, and his former church may decide to consider this a reasonable outcome.

# CHAPTER SIX

## SECTION 2:
## CONCERNING SEX AND MARRIAGE (Continued)

### 2. Christians And Lawsuits (6:1-8)

Paul has dealt with a particular issue at Corinth - a case of incest - and in the course of doing so he treated the entire situation in more general terms, including the matter of the church's attitude to that situation. His next topic is that of lawsuits between Christians, and his approach is similar. A specific case of one Christian going to law with another (or possibly, more than one such case) had occurred at Corinth (6:6). Learning of this through his contacts with the church (who here, as in 5:1, are unnamed), he takes up this issue with them, but deals with it on a wider base than that of the specific instance or instances which led him to raise it, and again considers the issue of the attitude of the church itself.

**6:1** "Dare any one of you...": "Dare" comes first in the Greek in an abrupt commencement of this topic, and is emphatic. There is the sense of "How dare you!" as in the Jerusalem Bible translation: "How dare one of your members take up a complaint against another in the law courts of the unjust instead of before the saints?" The verb is present tense, indicating that some of the Christians (or at least one of them) were in fact doing this.

"The unrighteous", "the ungodly", ἄδικος (*adikos*), refers to the judges of the pagan Corinthian courts before whom the Christians were placing their disputes for judgement. It does not mean that these judges were especially corrupt or sinful, but that they were "ungodly" or "unjust" in the sense of not knowing or judging according to God's standards of justice and righteousness. The word is the negative of "just" or "justified" and thus also means "unjustified", i.e. "non-Christian", "pagan" or "heathen" (and is translated thus in TEV, NEB and Phillips). Paul is highlighting the incongruity of a Christian seeking for justice before such a one. The question carries with it the connotation, "Shame on you for doing such a thing", made explicit in 6:5.

**6:2-3** "Do you not know...?", a favorite expression of Paul's, is used six times in this chapter (twice here and also 6:9, 6:15, 6:16, and 6:19; see also 3:16 and 5:6). It usually is used to call the attention of his readers to something that he himself would have taught them previously, and that is the meaning here. Re "...that the saints will judge the world" and "...that we are to judge angels": for the idea of the twelve apostles judging Israel, see Matthew 19:28 and Luke 22:30; the one who conquers will be given authority over the nations to rule them, Revelation 2:26-27; cf. also Revelation 20:4. There is no general teaching in Scripture about the saints judging the world, and no other mention of Christians judging angels. Thus if (as Paul indicates) the Corinthians were expected to know this already, it must be because Paul taught it to them personally. Paul may have received this knowledge by revelation directly from God, or by inspired interpretation of the scope of the meaning of Scripture which would not otherwise directly suggest it (e.g. Daniel 7:22 and the teaching of Jesus in my previous references).

We know no more than is said here: we do not know which angels (good or bad, or all angels) we are to judge, and so forth. This is not Paul's point here. Rather he says, If we are to judge this world (in the future judgement), do we now go before the people of this world and get *them* to judge *our* cases? If we are to judge angels one day, are we not now capable of judging the matters relating to our present life?

**6:4** The "if you have" is in the hypothetical form; Paul is not going to assert that they actually do have cases that *need* a court hearing. The second part of the verse can be (as in the ESV, RSV, and NRSV) a question, with "those who have no standing in the church" referring back to the pagan judges mentioned in v.1. A second interpretation is to take the verb as imperative (as in the NIV), so that Paul is saying that if the Corinthians have such cases needing to be dealt with, they can appoint to consider them even the persons of least account in the church (the thought being that even the lowliest person in the church would be a better choice to judge the matter than any person who is not a Christian). These alternative interpretations are reflected in the varied translations to be found.

Fee 235f. carefully examines these two alternative views as to "who is intended by the designation 'those of little account' (lit. 'those who are despised'), believers or the pagan judges". He gives his judgement against the interpretation that Paul could be referring to believers in such harsh terminology, for

> It is difficult to imagine Paul, even in irony, so referring to fellow believers ... Furthermore, the softening to "even men of little account" simply has no lexical basis. ...

> [B]ut that they are those people whose values and judgments (*sic*) the church has rejected by its adoption of totally different standards. To

go to pagan courts is to ask those to make a ruling among Christians who have absolutely "no standing within the church" (GNB, NAB).

**6:5** This verse begins with quite a sharp and abrupt exclamation in the Greek: "For shame! I say to you." It seems rather softened in the usual English translations. As the individual concerned merits censure for taking his dispute with a brother to a pagan court, so the church as a whole should be ashamed also ("to your shame", with plural "you", refers to all of them). Their shame is that they have not found some one of their number who is "wise enough" to handle the dispute and thus prevent it being taken before outsiders. Paul has been using the weapon of ridicule to show the foolishness of Christian going to law against Christian before the pagans, and his point is doubly sharp because of the way (as we have seen in earlier chapters of this letter) that the Corinthians prided themselves on their superior wisdom.

The Greek says literally, "between his brother", i.e. between one church member and his brother, the use of the singular "no one" indicating that what is envisaged is appointing a person to adjudicate in the particular matter that has arisen at Corinth; Paul is not referring to appointing a Christian judge or arbitrator to officiate in a formal Christian court on a permanent basis.

**6:6** "Unbelievers" (ἄπιστοι, *apistoi*) refers to the same people as "ungodly" ("unrighteous") in verse 1, but whereas in that verse the word indicated a person being asked to administer justice who did not follow God's standards of justice, here the choice of word has in mind the thought of a believer going on trial before one who is not a believer.

**6:7** So far Paul's criticism of what is happening at Corinth has been:

**(a)** Christian going to law against Christian before a pagan court is not a good thing;

**(b)** The church itself shares the shame that such a thing is occurring;

**(c)** Disputes between Christians should be adjudicated and settled within the congregation, through the arbitration of one of its members.

Now Paul goes behind the situation to a more fundamental issue. He has been talking about acceptable and unacceptable ways of handling disputes between Christians; he now challenges the very existence of such legal wrangles that have to be judged by some third party. No matter what the outcome, no matter the judgement that is given, or who "wins" the dispute, the person who engages in such litigation at all has already suffered defeat, or loss: defeat in the battle to live and witness as a Christian in a godless age, loss of the gentleness and humility which is to characterize Christ's servant, and loss of something of honor and integrity, and certainly of love within the fellowship. To "win" at litigation against a brother is hardly to be victorious. Again, Paul's questions point the way of Christian response: it is better to allow oneself to be treated unjustly (Paul uses here the verb form of the word he used in verse 1 of the "unjust" judge); it is better to allow oneself to be defrauded.

This is an application of the "turn the other cheek" teaching of Jesus in Matthew 5:39-42; but there Jesus was speaking of the believer's response to the greed and thirst for power and domination of the unbeliever; here, Paul speaks of having the same attitude of submission to injustice when the one responsible is in fact a fellow-believer. No wonder he has declared (v.5), "I say this to your shame"!

John Chrysostom, in speaking of this verse (Kovacs 95f.), comments at some length on the "benefits" of being separated from our possessions. He says,

> If it were an evil thing to suffer injustice, God would not have told us to do it, for God does not enjoin what is evil. Do you not know that he is the God of glory? He does not wish to cover us with shame and ridicule and loss but to give us the opposite of these. For this reason he orders us to suffer injustice, and he does everything he can to separate us from worldly things and to make us see what is glory and what is shame, what is loss and what is gain (Phil 3:7).

> But someone will say, "It is a terrible thing to suffer wrong and be maltreated." No, my friend, it is not terrible at all. How long will you be distressed about present things? God would not have commanded it if it were terrible. Consider this: the one who has committed injustice leaves the court with money but a bad conscience, but the one who has suffered injustice, even if he is deprived of his money, has confidence before God, a possession more precious than countless treasures. ...

> Consider that present things are temporary; take note of the tombs of your ancestors. Observe clearly what has happened, and you will see that the one who wronged you has made you stronger. He has made his own passion fiercer - I mean his love of money - but he has weakened your passion by taking away what nourishes that wild beast.

A sentiment indeed which accords with the word of Jesus, "a person's life does not consist in the abundance of one's possessions" (Luke 12:15), but much at variance with the emphasis we place these days upon our claim to affluence.

**6:8** Lest it be thought that Paul is here condoning this wrongdoing, he now attacks those guilty of acting unjustly and fraudulently (using the active voice of the two verbs which in v.7 he used in the passive). But he is not really now turning to address a different group of people; the emphatic "you" in the Greek shows that his remarks are being strongly made to the same ones. They themselves, he accuses them, are also engaged in the practice of injustice and robbery (the present tense is used) - and this wrongdoing is even directed against their brothers in Christ. This does not imply that somehow such conduct would have been less reprehensible if it were the heathen being wronged and exploited, but expresses Paul's incredulity in the face of the astonishing situation that in the church at Corinth they were willing to act like this towards a fellow-believer and servant of God. This salutary challenge must surely compel them to face the nature of their behavior and bring them to repentance and a willingness to live by Christian standards.

**6:9** There follows here a transitional paragraph that links what Paul has just been saying with the discussion of sexual morality which is to follow. The link is in particular the word ἄδικος (*adikos*), "wicked", "unrighteous", in v.9. This word only occurs three times in Paul's writings in the New Testament: once in Romans in speaking with horror of the accusation that God is unjust (3:5), and the other two occurrences being in this chapter of 1 Corinthians. V.1 uses this word about the "unjust" or "unrighteous" (NIV, "ungodly") judges of the pagan courts; v.9 now uses ἄδικος (*adikos*) of all who behave unrighteously.

The thought follows on from v.8: "You are acting unrighteously" (ἀδικεῖτε, *adikeite*, spoken to the Corinthian Christians). Then, v.9, "Surely you know that those who are unrighteous will not inherit the kingdom of God?" That is to say, unrighteousness should be a thing of the past for those who are the inheritors (through Christ) of God's kingdom. The converse of this, also clearly conveyed here, is that a person who is continuing in his unrighteous behavior is showing thereby that he is **not** an inheritor of the kingdom of God. This would certainly be aimed at making the Corinthians to whom his words apply "examine yourselves, to see whether you are in the faith" (as he specifically writes to them later, in 2 Corinthians 13:5).

Here in the next verses he follows this generalized comment with an explicit cataloguing of ten examples of unrighteousness which show that a person is not an inheritor of God's kingdom. It is not that the committing of these offenses **excludes** from God's kingdom but rather the practising of these things **discloses** or makes clear that a person is not a member of God's kingdom. Amongst them Paul includes "the greedy" and "swindlers", which reflects back again to his description, in the preceding verses, of the behavior of some in the church at Corinth. Moreover, these words echo the list of those who are the wrongdoers of this world which he gave in 5:10, and again in 5:11, immediately prior to embarking upon his discussion of lawsuits.

It thus appears that the sequence of his thought can be traced:

**(a)** He discusses the case of incest at Corinth, and the attitude of the church to it;

**(b)** He mentions such immorality as being a reason for the church to disassociate from such a so-called brother;

**(c)** He adds a reference to other serious sins which are similarly of a kind that should lead the church to disassociate from a so-called brother who practises them;

**(d)** This leads him to deal with a situation at Corinth where members of the church are acting in such blameworthy ways, concluding this passage by accusing some at Corinth of unrighteous behavior and fraud (v.8);

**(e)** He again lists the vices of this kind, in this list going further and pronouncing that those who practice them are outside the kingdom;

**(f)** In his list he now expands his references to types of sexual immorality, preparatory to resuming his discussion of this subject;

**(g)** He emphasizes, "And such were some of you" - for all such behavior is (or most certainly ought to be) a thing of the past.

From this point forward he takes up the question of sexual immorality which his discussion of lawsuits interrupted, and after this transition paragraph (6:9-11), this topic occupies the remainder of the chapter. To this we shall shortly turn our attention.

First, however, there is another view of the function of 6:1-8 which we should note at this point.

In *Novum Testamentum* (January, 1983), Peter Richardson discusses the nature of the dispute or disputes at Corinth that had caused litigation. His thesis can be summed up in this paragraph from his introduction (37):

> 1 Cor. 5 and 6 have been regarded as a *locus classicus* for an understanding of Paul's sexual ethic. Not only do these chapters include a dramatic account of sexual impropriety (5:1-8), they also include three vice-catalogues in which sexual sins are dominant (5:10; 5:11; 6:9b-10) and an impressive discussion of the body and problems of immorality (6:12-20). But 6:1-11 (or 1-8) is almost universally excepted from the discussion of Paul's sexual ethic, being viewed for the most part as an intrusion. The thesis of this article is that all of chapters 5 and 6, including 6:1-11, has to do with sexual questions.

Richardson notes that there is absolutely nothing in the passage itself "describing the nature of the lawsuit" in which the Corinthians were engaging. Therefore the nature of this lawsuit is something that "we are forced to infer from hints that lurk below the surface". He continues (40):

The fact that it is a legal matter narrows the range somewhat. It must be a case which can, but need not, be properly brought before judges, and one of sufficient concern that it ought to be dealt with by the Christian community (6:1-6). To put it differently, it must be an issue which is sufficiently against the law of the land that it can be taken to a court, but not absolutely against the Christian community's basic minimal standard of behavior. ... Six arguments will be developed to support the claim that 6:1-11 presupposes a sexual problem. Though not of equal weight, all contribute something to the case. None is absolutely decisive, but the cumulative force is persuasive. No countervailing argument requires that the issue is the one generally assumed: monetary fraud.

This introduction is followed by the detailed consideration of the six arguments that Richardson advances, which relate to questions of the overall structure of 1 Corinthians and the immediate context of 6:1-11, the connection with the Old Testament, and possible parallels in 1 Thessalonians 4:1-8 and James 2:1-11 and 4:1-12. After this discussion and a short consideration of other background factors, Richardson 53 assesses where he sees the evidence leading him. He says:

I have argued that there is a sexual case (*pragma*) behind the lawsuit discussion of 6:1-11. ... But what kind of case was it? First, it involves two males; second, both are within the church; third, the case involves some kind of sexual defrauding; and fourth, it is a case which properly can be brought before local authorities, whether Roman or Corinthian. The following cases seem possible.

Here Richardson (55) lists eight specific issues which meet these requirements, summing them up thus:

These are proposed only to suggest the range of possibilities and to show that the kinds of problems afflicting the Corinthian church are such that a case involving two brothers could arise. I have suggested several cases, most of which fall into the following categories:

a father and son-in-law over the status of the younger man's wife;

two men involved sexually or even non-sexually with the same woman;

a man charging an influential 'leader' in a congregation with 'tampering' (i.e. with the normal functioning of his marital relationship with his wife, or in relation to a father's responsibilities and prerogatives with regard to arranging the marriage of his daughter).

Indeed, as Richardson says, the section 6:1-8 (or 1-11) can be explained (and usually is explained) as a digression in Paul's discussion of the topic of sexual immorality at Corinth. A digression which arises because Paul, in instructing the Corinthians to put the incestuous offender out of their fellowship, also mentions (5:11) other issues requiring the same response, and then begins to discuss another serious moral issue which has arisen at Corinth before returning again to his main subject.

But Richardson's thesis shows that it is quite possible that the legal case which had arisen at Corinth was also to do with general questions of marriage and sexual morality. He makes, by way of illustration, a number of suggestions as to what this issue could have been and asserts that even if it is not possible for us to know its exact nature for certain, we nonetheless have good reason for concluding that it was a problem of this type.

Richardson's presentation gives us grounds, in interpreting 1 Corinthians, for regarding chapters 5 to 7 as all concerned with the overall subject of sex and marriage in its various ramifications, though it does still remain a possibility that in 6:1-8 Paul is diverting aside from his main topic to deal with a similar - but unrelated - problem at Corinth.

It now remains to enquire what is the practical application of this passage in the life of the church today; and this is discussed in "Reflections", below.

## 3. Sexual Fulfillment - Getting It Wrong (6:9-20E)

**6:9a** For the third time in this chapter (see 6:2 and 6:3) Paul asks "Do you not know...?", as he reminds them of basic facts of which they should need no reminder.

As in 6:1, which is the only other place in 1 Corinthians where "unrighteous", *adikos*, is used, the word is the negative of the word for "righteous". It means a person who practises unrighteousness, a person who has not been made righteous with the righteousness which comes through faith in Jesus Christ (as Paul explains in detail in Romans 3-5). "The unrighteous" (as it is rendered in most translations) does not have the article ("the") in the Greek and means "any person, whoever he is, who is unrighteous", with the stress being upon the unrighteous character of such a person. "Will not inherit" means "will not come to possess", "will not enter into" the kingdom of God - not in this world, and thus not in the next.

"Do not be deceived" is a warning which Paul gives on a number of occasions (1 Corinthians 15:33; Galatians 6:7; similarly 1 Corinthians 3:18; Galatians 6:3; Ephesians 5:6; 2 Thessalonians 2:3; and also found in James 1:16; 1:26; 1 John 3:7). However, the implication here is that the Corinthians **are** in danger of being deceived and must be on guard against this happening: they must not imagine that it is possible for a person to be unrighteous and to practise unrighteousness, and simultaneously to be an inheritor of God's kingdom. That is to say, to acknowledge God as king and to practise unrighteousness are mutually exclusive.

**6:9b** Paul now lists ten categories of unrighteousness. That a person practises these things is evidence that he is not an inheritor of God's kingdom.

The vices which Paul mentions here are those that he sees as most relevant to the Corinthian situation. The list does not include some from the Decalogue (the only Commandments from the Decalogue that are covered are the Seventh and Eighth, and perhaps by implication the First and Second in the reference to idol worshipers, and the Tenth in the mention of "the greedy".

Instead, this list of ten is in two parts, the first five relating to different types of sexual immorality and the second five to other types of wrongdoing. Six of the ten were mentioned earlier (5:11) and this is a list which has been progressively built up during these two chapters.

Each list builds on the one before, adding further vices to the ones in the preceding list. Every list commences with *pornos*, "the immoral", but the order of the other vices varies from one list to another. (The order in the table below is that of 5:11, and the others have been accommodated to this order, to facilitate comparison.) There is one thing you will notice about them as we look through them now: Paul says that they are totally unacceptable behavior for a Christian, but most of them were quite accepted in the non-Christian world of Paul's day, or deplored very lightly indeed. And the attitude found in the non-Christian world today is much the same.

| 5:9 | *pornos* immoral | | | | | |
|-----|------------------|--------------------|------------------|---------------------|------------------|----------------------|
| 5:10 | *pornos;* immoral; | *pleonektēs;* greedy; | *eidōlolatrēs;* idolater; | | | *harpax* swindler |
| 5:11 | *pornos;* immoral; | *pleonektēs;* greedy; | *eidōlolatrēs;* idolater; | *loidoros;* reviler; | *methusos;* drunkard; | *harpax* swindler |
| 6:9 | *pornos;* immoral; | *pleonektēs;* greedy; | *eidōlolatrēs;* idolater; | *loidoros;* reviler; | *methusos;* drunkard; | *harpax* swindler; |
| | *moikos;* adulterer; | *malakos;* catamite; | *arsenokoitēs;* pederast; | *kleptēs* thief | | |

What exactly are these ten vices to which Paul here calls the Corinthians' attention - and ours?

**6:9** The first five vices, which relate to sexual immorality, are:

**(a)** πορνος, *pornos*, "immoral person": originally the word referred to a male prostitute or one who frequented prostitutes, and thence by New Testament times came to be used of a person who engages in sexual intercourse outside of marriage (a fornicator) and, more generally, as a generic term for a sexually immoral person. In its context in 6:9, where particular words are used for other types of sexual vice, *pornos* has its more specific meaning of a person who engages in sexual intercourse outside of marriage.

**(b)** εἰδωλολατρης, *eidōlolatrēs*, "idolater": a sin reprehensible in itself as it involves worship of other gods, but also usually associated with gross sexual immorality. The religion of the Canaanites who dwelt in the land before the Israelite conquest, and of other nations around Israel, included cultic prostitution and fertility rites involving symbolic religious sexual intercourse with "priests" and "priestesses" of those cults. When these religions invaded Israel then cultic sexual practices were adopted too (Numbers 25:1-9 with 1 Corinthians 10:6-8; 1 Kings 14:22-24; 15:11-13; 2 Kings 23:7; Ezekiel 16:15-17; Hosea 4:10-18; Amos 2:7-8).

Similarly, idolatry in Corinth included ritual sexual intercourse with the sacred prostitutes of the temple of Aphrodite on the acrocorinth overlooking the city (as we noted in the Introduction to this Epistle).

Thus "idolaters" refers not just to the worshiping of idols but to the fact that the devotees of idols engage in sexual practices with the cult prostitutes of the pagan religion. Idolaters were thus practising another form of sexual abuse - hence the listing of idolaters with those who practised sexual sin.

**(c)** μοιχος, *moichos*, "adulterer": that is, a person who engages in sexual intercourse when (at least) one of the parties is married to someone else. This form of sexual sin not only involves immorality in itself, as did the previous two that have been mentioned, but in addition it offends against the marriage relationship and in particular is an act of disloyalty against one's marriage partner.

**(d)** μαλακος, *malakos*, "catamite": the Greek word means "soft" and "effeminate", and was used as a technical term for the male who takes the feminine role in a homosexual relationship between men. The English technical term for this person is "catamite". Usually in Greek homosexual practice the catamite was a boy, kept by an older man for sexual purposes. (Details of the use of the word *malakos* in Greek literature are given by Danker-BAG.)

**(e)** ἀρσενοκοιτης, *arsenokoitēs*, "male homosexual": the word can be used as a general term for a male homosexual, or (especially when coupled, as here, with *malakos*) refers to the active partner in a male homosexual relationship, that is, a *sodomite*, or especially a *pederast*, a technical term from Greek word roots meaning "boy-lover", a male who has sexual relations with a boy (a catamite). Garland has a very good treatment of these two words. It can be noted that many translations do not render Paul's words *malakos* and *arsenokoitēs* precisely but resort to imprecise and vague generalizations such as "sexual perverts" (RSV of 1971), "homosexual perverts" (TEV, NEB), "men who practise homosexuality" (ESV), "homosexuals" (RSV of 1946) for both words taken together. The most accurate are the NIV ("male prostitutes and homosexual offenders"), the NRSV ("male prostitutes, sodomites"), and Jerusalem Bible ("catamites, sodomites"). Paul does not explicitly mention female homosexuals (lesbians); it may well be taken that he intends his listing of both types of male homosexual to imply equal condemnation of the role of both participants in female homosexuality. This implication is made explicit when he writes from Corinth to the Romans about these issues (Romans 1:26-27).

**6:10a** continues Paul's vice-list with a further five:

**(f)** κλεπτης, *kleptēs*, "thief": someone who steals; cf. the Eighth Commandment.

**(g)** πλεονεκτης, *pleonektēs*, "greedy": that is, a person who is covetous; cf. the Tenth Commandment. Greed, covetousness, is regarded by Paul as a serious sin - it is included in his vice lists in 5:10 and 5:11, and is frequently mentioned in his writings; it was a sin about which Jesus himself often warned: "Watch out! Be on your guard against all kinds of greed; a person's life does not consist in the abundance of one's possessions" (Luke 12:15).

**(h)** μεθυσος, *methusos*, "drunkard": a person who has become intoxicated. This vice is also included by Paul in his list in 5:11. Paul criticizes the Corinthians in 11:21 because some of them have become drunken. In Ephesians 5:18 (RSV) he commands, "Do not get drunk with wine, for that is debauchery". A person who is under the influence of alcohol is not able to place himself under the control of Christ; thus this vice also is an indicator of a person who will not inherit the kingdom of God.

**(i)** λοιδορος, *loidoros*, "slanderer, reviler": a person who is abusive. This word only occurs twice in the New Testament, here and in 5:11 (in both places in association with *methusos*, "drunkard"), but the verb form, λοιδορεω (*loidoreō*), occurs once in Paul's writings, in 1 Corinthians 4:12, where he speaks of how "we" (apostles) respond when reviled. The inclusion of "revilers" in this list of those who will not inherit God's kingdom may appear extreme; being abusive may be unkind and unloving, but is it in the same class as the other sins listed? From the mention here and in 5:11 of those who are revilers and in 4:12 of the fact that Paul was being reviled (especially as these three are the only occurrences of the noun or verb in all of Paul's writings), it appears that some people at Corinth were pouring out upon Paul and perhaps upon some others (see "we" of 4:12) a flow of vituperative insults and vitriolic invective. This attitude of abuse and hatred is incompatible with the calling as a member of God's kingdom.

(j) ἁρπαξ, *harpax*, "swindler": a person who is grasping and rapacious, who seizes for himself whatever he wants with utter disregard for the rights and entitlements of others. Whereas "thief" [see (f) just referred to] refers to stealing, often by night, or surreptitiously, the *harpax* snatches or appropriates what he takes - the word has the sense of "suddenly", "vehemently", probably "forcibly" and "violently".

**6:10b** Paul repeats now in relation to people who act in these ways what he said in verse 9a of the unrighteous (for these are ten ways in which people can act unrighteously): that those who do these things will not inherit (i.e., participate in) the kingdom of God.

**6:11a** Some of those in the church at Corinth had once lived in this way. But such behavior should now be a thing of the past - "And that is what some of you *were*". However, the kind of questions that Paul has to deal with in his correspondence with the Corinthians indicates that (for some people, at least) the break with their past way of life had not been as complete as it should have been, or that, at the very least, the influence of aspects of their former lifestyle still lingered with them.

**6:11b** Literally, not "you were washed" (most versions), but "you cleansed yourselves" (Phillips) - the verb is aorist middle in Greek, indicating a decisive action carried out by them ("you") in relation to themselves. Concerning this, Lenski 250f. writes:

> "This middle ἀπελούσασθε *apelousasthe* does not mean 'you were washed' (passive) ... but 'you let yourselves be washed' (causative or permissive middle), 'you had yourselves washed', as we translate. ... This causative or permissive middle ... adds what the passive would omit, namely that with their own hearts the Corinthians themselves desired and accepted this washing and cleansing."

The only other occurrence of this verb ἀπολουω (*apolouō*) in the New Testament is in Acts 22:16, where Paul in recounting the story of his conversion puts it into the mouth of Ananias, "Get up, be baptized and wash your sins away."

Numerous commentators take it here to be referring to baptism, as if

Paul had written "But you were baptized". However there is no justification for importing baptism into Paul's comment "you washed yourselves clean": it means literally "washed from", and certainly implies "washed from your sins"; it refers to the initial cleansing of a person from his sins at conversion when he receives God's forgiveness and is made clean and righteous before God through Jesus Christ.

Johnson says,

> *Washed* speaks not primarily of baptism, but of the deep spiritual cleansing from sin's defilement and guilt that the person of faith experiences when she is brought into Christ.

True. Thus Paul is saying, not, "you got yourselves baptized", but, "you washed yourself clean (from all these sins) ... in the name of the Lord Jesus Christ and by the Spirit of our God." That is, it refers here not to baptism but to the **reality** to which the sign and symbol of baptism points: the believer's cleansing by faith in Christ. That is, its meaning is similar to that of Peter's comment in Acts 15:8-9, referring to the conversion of Cornelius and his household, "God ... cleansed [purified] their hearts by faith." I agree with Hodge who says, "The reference which so many assume to baptism, does not seem to be authorized by any thing in the context."

Thus Paul's point here is the extension of what he has just said: such behavior is for the Corinthians a thing of the past because - by the grace of Christ and the power of the Spirit of God - they have cleansed themselves (the aorist indicates, definitely and finally) from all these things in their lives.

**6:11c** "But you were sanctified, but you were justified ..." - Paul twice more uses the emphatic "but" (ἀλλα, *alla*). It has seemed to some commentators that the more logical order would have been "justified" and then "sanctified" (cf. Paul's discussion of these issues in Romans). Paul's thought here, though, is simply "you have been made holy before God" ("sanctified"), and "you have been made righteous before God" ("justified"), in each case the use of the aorist indicating that this is referring to what God did at the point of one's conversion. The use of the passives "you were sanctified, you were justified", indicates that it is God who sanctified and justified them. This is their status and standing before God; they are now called to live this out in practice in lives of righteousness and holiness.

"In the name of the Lord Jesus Christ" means "according to the character of and by the authority of the Lord Jesus Christ". "By the Spirit of our God" points to the Holy Spirit by whom these things - cleansing, sanctification and justification - have been effected, and by whom also these things shall continue to be brought to fulfillment in the lives of Christians.

**6:12-20E** At this point Paul leaves the general discussion of sins, and gives his attention to one sin specifically: *porneia*, sexual immorality, and in particular "fornication", sexual intercourse outside of marriage.

The practice of fornication had virtually universal acceptance in the ancient world. Thus Anderson Scott (*New Testament Ethics*, p.116ff.) quotes W.H.S. Jones's pungent comment (p.118f.) on the situation:

> It is hard to find a passage in pre-Christian Greek literature where loose intercourse is looked upon as in itself a moral offence. Sexual indulgence stood upon exactly the same moral level as eating and drinking.

It is this attitude which is still influencing some of the Corinthians, and which lies behind this passage - they are saying, "Just as food is intended to go into the stomach and the stomach is intended to receive food, so sex is similarly an intended activity of the body and the body is intended to be sexually active." The conclusion to which this argument led is that having sexual intercourse is no more involved with questions of morality than is having a meal - and is equally as necessary; and not to engage in sexual activity is to place curbs and restrictions upon one of the most basic ways in which the body was intended to function. Some things have changed little over the centuries; this line of argument has a very modern ring to it. Behind Paul's discussion in this passage it can be seen that this is the argument that he is combating.

**6:12** "All things are lawful for me" (ESV, RSV, NRSV), "Everything is permissible for me" (NIV). The way in which Paul uses this saying (twice in this verse, and again twice in 10:23) indicates that it was a saying in current use at Corinth, which Paul is quoting. Indeed, there is much to commend Hodge's comment, "Paul was accustomed to say 'All things are lawful for me' [in certain specific situations]", and the Corinthians are now quoting and misapplying Paul's own words. These words are an expression of the scope of Christian liberty. But they are being used by some at Corinth as a justification for decidedly unchristian licence.

The scope of our freedom in Christ is limited, Paul shows, by two things: first, by the test of advantage; second, by the test of enslavement. The first test is positive: not everything that I might do is helpful (that is to say, useful, beneficial, advantageous, profitable); some things could have the reverse result. This test directs my attention to the results of my actions in themselves. The wisdom and validity of an action or course of action is to be evaluated in relation to its consequences. The application of this test will mean that of all the things that I might do, of all the alternatives open to me, I am to choose those that are advantageous (according to Christian standards). The second test is negative: some things that I do can bring me under their power so that my self-control is reduced and my freedom is restricted. Thus my freedom to do as I choose actually leads to my enslavement. This test directs my attention to the results of my actions upon myself. Actions or activities which affect me adversely in this way are thus clearly wrong for me.

The point is that if someone is asking, "Is such and such permissible for me?", they are asking the wrong question.

**6:13-14** Again Paul quotes the Corinthians, the quotation and his comment on it revealing the line of argument being used by some at Corinth to justify their view of sexual freedom. Food and the stomach are indeed correlated, as the Corinthians assert: but only as long as this life lasts, for then both equally are destroyed. The contrast of this with the Christian as a person is implied here, and made more explicit later, for the Christian is one spirit with the Lord (v.17) and thus is eternal.

It is to be noted that Paul in answering the Corinthians about their attitude does not simply say, "This is wrong!" - he rightly recognizes that this approach would leave them unconvinced. Rather, he shows them logically that, for reasons they can see for themselves, their position is untenable for a Christian. There is a time for an emphatic "Thus says the Lord", and there is also a time for patiently explaining why something is right or wrong so that the doubting and unconvinced can be brought to appreciate the force of clearsighted explanation.

Thus, he explains, the body is not meant for immorality (unrestrained sexual activity) - as some of the Corinthians were asserting, on the basis of the analogy of food and the stomach. On the contrary, the body is intended for the Lord, that is, to be handed over to the Lord for his use and service. Paul expounds this idea explicitly in Romans 12:1-2, "... present your bodies as a living sacrifice, holy and acceptable to God". Moreover, the Lord is for the body - as God raised the Lord from the dead (in his body, transformed as a resurrection body), so also he will raise us, our bodies similarly being resurrected and transformed.

That then is why what we do with our body in sexual intercourse is a very different matter from the Corinthians' so-called parallel of eating a meal.

**6:15** Again Paul makes his point through the question "Do you not know...?", "Surely you must realize...?" (see 6:3). Not merely, "Your bodies belong to Christ", but "Your bodies are Christ's limbs", they are connected to him and he to them, they are the means by which he acts, and are to be used by him for his purposes. Shall I then take Christ's limbs and organs and attach them to a prostitute? Thus the Lord himself becomes, through my body, engaged in an act of immorality! Paul aims to show the absolute incongruity of such a thing, and climaxes the imagery with his emphatic μη γενοιτο (*mē genoito*), "never let it be so!"

**6:16** Again he asks, "Do you not know...?" What they surely must realize is that a person who joins himself (in sexual intercourse) with the prostitute is one body with her, is united physically with her. Paul then quotes from Genesis 2:24. His meaning is examined in "Reflections", below.

**6:17** But the Christian who joins himself to the Lord is one spirit with him. Paul uses here the same words as in 6:16a, changing only "to the prostitute" to "to the Lord" and "one body" to "one spirit", the parallelism of wording highlighting these differences. The spiritual union of the believer with the Lord shows up the wrongness of physical union with a prostitute: the believer joining himself to the Lord (which implies and requires the dedication of his body to the Lord - v.15) is in stark contrast to the believer joining himself to the prostitute. When the believer's body is dedicated to Christ and his service, then body and spirit are a unity and operating in harmony; if a believer's body is used in fornication with a prostitute there is a complete clash between this physical relationship with the prostitute and his spiritual relationship with the Lord.

**6:18a** The answer to a situation of temptation to sexual immorality is simple and stark. Flee. Get up and run. Remove yourself immediately from that situation. [A vivid illustration of doing this is found in the account of Joseph, Genesis 39:12: when Potiphar's wife attempted to seduce him he "fled and got out of the house".] The use of the present tense for "flee" in this verse can mean "start fleeing and keep on going" or, more probably, it is a *habitual durative*, "on any occasion when you find yourself in this situation, flee from it".

**6:18b** The comment "Every other sin a person commits is outside his body, but the sexually immoral person sins against his own body" is usually taken to mean, "Sexual sin is unique in that the body is the vehicle for the sin and this is not true in quite the same way of any other sin." There are however three significant difficulties with such an interpretation:

**(a)** This interpretation is based not upon what Paul said but upon something that he did not say. The interpretation derives from the word "other" which is found in this verse in most translations (not in the

AV/KJV, the RV or Wand, but is in the ESV, NAB, NASB, NEB, NIV, TEV, Jerusalem Bible, Beck, Knox, Moffatt, Phillips, Weymouth, Williams, etc.): whereas in fact the word "other" does not occur in the Greek.

**(b)** This interpretation has Paul making a difference between sexual sin and all other sin. This is at odds with what is found in the whole of the rest of the Bible, where sexual sin is not treated as being different from other sin.

**(c)** This interpretation has Paul saying something which is not true: that other sins are external to the body, i.e., do not involve the body. However, there are numbers of other sins that can involve the body and that cannot really be committed apart from the body. A thief can steal with his hands. Pain and injury can be inflicted on others through the body. Pride can be exhibited in the body, both in the body's prowess or beauty, and in the displaying of the body (apparel, jewelry, and so forth). Love of ease, comfort, and apathy, can be closely related to the wants and desires of the body. Gluttony is a sin of the body. So is drunkenness. It simply is not true that immorality is the only sin that involves the body, so that all other sins are external to or outside the body.

There is an alternative way in which this verse can be understood, which takes note of this point. Taken as literally as possible, the Greek reads, "All sin, whatever it is that a man may commit, is outside the body." This should be recognized as the response of the Corinthians to Paul's comment. It is a continuation of their minimizing of the significance of promiscuous sexual behavior, which they do not see as being sinful, and in fact it is an antinomian extension of their attitude: "Sinning is quite a separate matter from any bodily activity".

**6:18c** Paul's response to this is: "But the one who commits immorality is sinning against his own body. Don't you see that your body is the Holy Spirit's temple?"

This is the better way to understand the verse.

In his Commentary on 1 Corinthians, Jerome Murphy-O'Connor 50 writes:

> "We have already had occasion to allude to the Corinthian attitude towards the body which underlay a number of their practical decisions. Here it comes out into the open because Paul actually quotes a number of statements made by the Corinthians. The section, therefore, is really a dialogue, and unless this is recognized it is very difficult to follow the argument. If we structure the text as a dialogue we get the following result:"

Murphy-O'Connor then sets out this section of 1 Corinthians almost identically with the way I set it out (see the following pages). Each of us found that the evidence has led us to the same conclusion. He then carries forward his discussion (51) in these words:

> "Let us look first at the Corinthians' position. Their key argument is in v. 13, which can be restated in this way. The body has no permanent value because it is swept away by death. God concurs in this assessment because he permits the destruction of the body. Hence, anything done in and through the body has no moral value. Reformulated positively this means that 'All things are lawful' (v.12). If no physical action has a moral character, everything on the corporeal level is permissible. We can eat what we like and go to bed with whom we like.

> "This is not to say that the Corinthians denied the possibility of sin. Sin was possible - but only on the level of motive and intention, and they refused to concede that these could be evaluated on the basis of the actions in which they were embodied. Hence, 'every sin which a man may commit is outside the body' (v.18b) - not 'every *other* sin', RSV." [Original author's italics.]

Murphy-O'Connor then traces Paul's response, concluding (52f.),

> "The body, therefore, is morally relevant, and Paul is therefore forced to reject the Corinthian statement in v.18b. 'On the contrary,' he says [in reply], 'the immoral man sins against his own body' (v.18c), because he does not use it for the purpose intended by God."

I find myself in very close accord with Murphy-O'Connor's assessment.

It is interesting to note, in the early church, the different evaluations that we find of the seriousness of sexual sin. On the one hand, Oecumenius says very definitely (Kovacs 101):

> Paul wants to emphasize the seriousness of sexual immorality since that is the subject of his present exhortation. But it is not the case that sexual immorality is the worst of all sins.

But Augustine says firmly (Kovacs 100),

> It seems that the blessed apostle, through whom Christ was speaking, wished to make the evil of fornication greater than other sins.

The viewpoint of Augustine prevailed in the church (in no small measure due to the negative teachings of Augustine himself about sex).

Thus 6:18 maintains the pattern of this entire passage, which continues to be cast in the form of a dialogue between Paul and the Corinthians.

**6:19-20E** Again Paul asks, "Do you not know...?" Your body, he says, is the temple of the Holy Spirit of God whom you have received from God and who dwells in you. The words "your" and "you" are plural; the application is different but the wording is similar to 3:16.

In both places Paul is *not* saying that each individual Christian is *a* temple of the Holy Spirit (as if there are as many such temples as there are Christians), but that Christians corporately comprise the *one* temple of God. Individually, Christians are "living stones" in that one temple. [See the further discussion in "Reflections" at the end of the commentary on chapter 3.]

Paul adds: You do not belong to yourself (to do whatever you choose with your own body) for you were purchased at a price (that is, Christ's sacrifice on the cross).

## SOME PRACTICAL AND PASTORAL REFLECTIONS

### Christians and Secular Courts Today

How does this teaching in 6:1-8 apply in the situations of today's world?

First, it is going well beyond the meaning and intention of this passage to say that a Christian is being told not to have anything at all to do with secular courts or legal systems. By their participation as lawyers and judges, Christians can assist in the administration of justice in the truest sense, and make a contribution towards human laws and their administration, operating upon the basis of the ultimate justice which derives from the nature of God. Certainly Paul does not argue against this; on the contrary, he advocates the Christian recognition and acceptance of civil authority (Romans 13:1-7).

Similarly, Paul is not pressing for the introduction of some system of church courts. The wording of what he says shows he is speaking of appointing an arbiter to adjudicate in a *particular* dispute if such a person is needed when such a dispute arises; he is not speaking of appointing someone to permanent office of this kind in the church.

Moreover, Paul is not forbidding Christians to defend themselves if they face adversaries who take them to court, especially if such adversaries are non-Christians. Such an interpretation *may* be given to Jesus's teaching in Matthew 5:39-40, but is not a *necessary* conclusion from his teaching there. While Paul's 1 Corinthians comments certainly show a similar spirit to Jesus's teaching, and may well reflect a knowledge of what Jesus said in the Sermon on the Mount, they are more concerned with the question of one Christian choosing to take another Christian to court.

There are two main thrusts in Paul's teaching here.

First, a Christian should not take another Christian to court before the civil jurisdiction: if he has a dispute which *must* be handled in this way, let the parties take the matter before a Christian who can arbitrate in the matter.

Second, the Christian brother contemplating this action should ask himself seriously whether he ought not rather to forego his right of action and be willing instead to accept the loss which (it is presumed) is being caused by his brother. Furthermore, there is a rebuke to those who cause such harm or loss to their brother in Christ.

The application of this in the church today would suggest that where possible Christians entering into (for example) business contracts should provide for matters of dispute which may arise to be referred to arbitration by a mutually agreed arbiter or arbiters.

It is not uncommon for contracts between Christians to contain such a clause. However, when a dispute arises, the way of Christian grace is for the parties in dispute to work out the problem between themselves, and the way of Christian love is for each to do this in a spirit of willingness to yield to the other and suffer loss if need be rather than damage Christian fellowship in the body. Furthermore, if a member of the fellowship is acting in a way that is treating a brother unjustly or defrauding him, then this is something that requires rebuke, and the church (through its leaders) should intervene with such a rebuke to whoever merits it, as Paul did for the Corinthians (6:8).

Two issues are not easily resolved.

Firstly, should a Christian take a non-Christian to court where he finds himself wronged? At times the right answer may be not to fight but to suffer the injustice. On the other hand, not to act in a particular case may be to encourage the wrongdoer to continue with his wrongdoing - to fail to act is to indicate to him that, if your victim is a Christian, crime *DOES* pay. For example, if a confidence trickster defrauds a Christian and the Christian declines to prosecute, the result may well be that the conman decides that Christians are easy marks and do not fight back, and therefore henceforth he makes them his chief target.

Each individual case will need to be carefully considered in the light of the circumstances of that case.

Secondly, many court cases these days are held in order to establish by due legal process what is the right thing to do, or the best thing in the circumstances. This could apply to an action for damages after a motor vehicle accident, for property settlement and/or custody of children in connection with a divorce, to determine the due amount of compensation in a worker's compensation case or a civil action, and so on - the list could be extended indefinitely. In some of these situations, Christians should seek for a fair settlement between themselves without going to court, but in numerous instances they may have difficulty in working out on their own what does constitute a fair settlement, and in some situations in the nature of the case one party may be at a negotiating disadvantage and need the impartial protection of the court. Again, there are "test cases" which are held in order to determine what the law is in a particular matter.

In all such cases, wherever it is possible to do so without disadvantage or unfairness to one party, an agreement should be reached without the matter going to law. But it may be that circumstances will arise where two Christians will take an issue to court in order to have the court make an impartial legal ruling as to what is right. If this is done in a mutual effort to seek justice and fairness, and not in a spirit of bitterness and wrangling, it may be that it does not offend against Paul's teaching here. But the spirit of Paul's teaching is quite clear, and is best observed by avoiding involvement in such legal action.

If Richardson is correct in his view that the legal battle at Corinth was concerned with some issue in the area of marriage and sexual morality, this will define for us the particular instance of resorting to law which called forth Paul's comments, but does not greatly affect what has been said in regard to seeking to draw out the principles at stake, and apply them.

## Some Implications Concerning Flesh and Body

A major issue involving different views of interpretation centers upon Paul's intended meaning in v.16, concerning the explanation which Paul is giving for why sexual union with a prostitute is completely wrong for a Christian. The common interpretation of Paul's meaning is as follows:

> He who joins himself to a prostitute becomes one body with her, because this is the consequence of the teaching of Scripture when it states 'The two shall become one flesh'. That is to say, becoming 'one flesh' is brought about by having sexual intercourse with a person, even if that person is a prostitute, because he who joins himself to a person in sexual intercourse becomes one body with her, and 'one body' and 'one flesh' have the same meaning.

E.g. Conzelmann (111) says explicitly, "Paul presumes that σάρξ, 'flesh,' is the equivalent of σῶμα, 'body'." So completely was this identification of "one body" and "one flesh" accepted by the translators of the original (1946) RSV that the Greek word "flesh" was left untranslated, leaving the reader to identify the "two shall become one" with the "one body" of the sentence which precedes it. The revised RSV of 1971 inserted "flesh" to translate σαρξ (*sarx*), so that at least the reader is now aware that two different words are used in the Greek.

The deficiency of this interpretation is that it denudes Paul's argument of any specific point. Paul is made to be saying:

> Shall I therefore take the members of Christ and make them members of a prostitute? Never! Do you not know that the Scripture says that he who joins himself to a prostitute becomes one flesh with her?

Why this should be wrong is not explained - that is left for the Corinthians to work out for themselves. Paul is shown as building his argument up to a point - and then he fails to make the point!

The following verse (6:17) draws the contrast between bodily union with a prostitute and spiritual union with Christ without explaining why the former is wrong. But the fact that I am spiritually united with Christ does not make *all* sexual union wrong for me. If Paul's point is that sexual union is wrong if my partner is a *prostitute*, then verse 17 is not helping to make that point.

We know that sexual union with a prostitute is wrong because of Paul's question about this that he answers with an emphatic "Never!" But we are left without any meaning in his purported explanation of *why* it is wrong. This consequence should make us somewhat suspicious of an interpretation that brings us to such a situation.

Our suspicion of this interpretation must be considerably increased when its wider implications are considered.

If sexual union with a prostitute makes a customer "one flesh" with her, then it will do the same for all her customers - so *either* each customer is in a one-flesh relationship with the prostitute until the advent of the next customer (a very short-term relationship!); *or else* the "one flesh" term refers only to the actual act of intercourse and not to a relationship at all (so that Paul is here quoting Genesis 2:24 with a meaning quite opposed to that of all other biblical occurrences of this passage); *or else* a prostitute can be, and remain, simultaneously one-flesh with *all* her customers, who themselves are *also* one-flesh with any other prostitutes they consort with - a conclusion which evacuates the term of any meaning at all!

However, the fact is that Scripture uses "one flesh" to refer to the marriage relationship (Genesis 2:24; Matthew 19:5; Mark 10:7; Ephesians 5:31). To equate becoming "one flesh" just with physical union itself ("one body") is to make the establishment of a marriage to be solely a matter of physical union.

This could not be restricted to liaisons with prostitutes. On this view, any two people who had sexual intercourse together would have to be held to be, in God's sight, married to each other. The theological and pastoral implications of this are far-reaching! Some Christians, being consistent, have reached this conclusion, and thus they give pastoral counseling based on this interpretation of the passage, telling two people who have had sexual intercourse to become formally married as they have already become married in God's sight!

Moreover, if physical union in itself ("one body") is equated with "one flesh" (6:16) and this is then contrasted with being "united to the Lord" and becoming "one spirit with him" (6:17), then it is hard to resist the conclusion - from this interpretation - that all sexual activity (even the "one flesh" of marriage) is covered by Paul's contrast with a spiritual relationship with Christ, and thus is wrong in itself and apparently condemned by the generalization of 6:18, "Flee from immorality". Now this conclusion is impossible to sustain from the wider context: the instruction "Therefore honor God with your body" (6:20) is followed within a couple of verses by injunctions to both husband and wife to give sexual fulfillment to their marriage partner, and the assertion that each has the control, for sexual purposes, of the partner's body (7:3-4).

If then respect for the whole of what Paul says in this total passage will prevent us from regarding "flee from sexual immorality" and being one spirit with the Lord as a blanket condemnation of all sexual relations, we are thereby compelled to backtrack and think afresh whether we are correct in accepting the identification of "one body" and "one flesh" (6:16) as synonymous.

Consider some of the pastoral and theological implications, in a few real-life pastoral situations, of the interpretation of 6:16 that to be "one body" with a prostitute means the same as to be "one flesh" with her - that is, that an act of sexual intercourse is what makes two people "one flesh":

**1.** George goes away to a Convention with his workmates, and while they are in a distant city together he gives way to peer pressure when the others decide to hire a few call girls for the evening. So he's become "one flesh" with one of these girls, has he? What exactly does that mean? He doesn't even know the girl's name. He will never see her again. What exactly does it mean now to say that George is "one flesh" with her, in terms of Bible teaching? And what is the nature now of his relationship with his wife, theologically speaking? - he was "one flesh" with her before the Convention: is he still? You are his pastor, and - deeply ashamed - George comes to you for clarification. Theologically, what do you tell him? Oh, yes, and of course the call girl had several other customers that night - are *they* all "one flesh" with her also? Simultaneously? How many people can you be "one flesh" with simultaneously - is there a limit?

**2.** Muriel and her husband split up many years ago, but she never bothered with a divorce as she did not contemplate marrying again. Recently she joined a gym club, and felt attracted to one of the instructors. One thing led to another, and one day they had sex together. It was just a passing infatuation - she doesn't love him, and they would not be a good match to get married. But where does she stand with him now, theologically speaking? If she is "one flesh" with him now, does that mean she is actually married to him in God's sight? So is she to put through her divorce now, so that she can legally marry this gym instructor? You are her pastor, and in great distress, remembering your sermon last year on "one flesh" in 1 Corinthians 6:16, Muriel comes to you now for you to explain her situation to her theologically. What will you tell her?

**3.** One wet Saturday afternoon two teenage members of your youth group are fooling around, not really understanding what they are doing. And while playing around together, they end up having intercourse. Now, if having intercourse means becoming "one flesh", they must now be married in God's sight, right? They certainly didn't intend to get married that wet afternoon. Judy's mother finds her in tears, and brings her to you. What can you tell them both about the concepts of *intention* in relation to getting married, and giving *consent* to a marriage, and all the other things that you would normally say to a couple contemplating marriage? Judy and Jim don't want to marry - they just want to complete their schooling. Do you tell them they *are* now actually married in God's sight? And what must they do about this?

Or, seeing all these people this week, will you decide that being "one flesh" is not the same thing as being married before God? What will you do then with all the Bible verses that say that being "one flesh" is in fact the inner meaning of being married?

Or will you perhaps rethink now what started it all - the interpretation of 6:16 that says becoming "one body" with a prostitute means in fact becoming "one flesh" with her, with all that the Bible means by this intimate term?

The fact is, this approach is an extremely unsatisfactory interpretation, both on internal grounds, and on the basis of the other teaching of Paul (e.g., Ephesians 5:22-33) and the teaching of the rest of the New Testament. For it is difficult to deny that such an interpretation sets this verse in conflict with the meaning of Genesis 2:24 ("one flesh") both in its original context and in each other place where it is quoted in Scripture.

There are several commentators who have noted the unsatisfactory nature of this usual approach. For example, in the Anchor Bible Commentary on 1 Corinthians, the authors William F. Orr and James Arthur Walther, write:

> Since human bodies are parts of the body of Christ, Paul declares it unthinkable that they participate in prostitution. Based on his understanding of creation he believed that sex union makes the two participants one body. [Whereas] to become one flesh is the proper destiny of those who incorporate their sex desires into a total relation of love and loyalty, so that they can become one joint personality and in their relationship express faith in God and love for the other. This cannot be done in the isolated, commercial action of prostitution. The mysterious unity of the flesh where there is no concern, loyalty, or love is sharply rejected by Paul.

That is, these authors affirm that Paul sharply rejects the idea that "the mysterious unity of the flesh" can exist "in the isolated, commercial action of prostitution", "where there is no concern, loyalty, or love".

The commentator who seeks to face the problem squarely, and to wrestle with it realistically, is Calvin. In his commentary he begins his discussion of what Paul says in v.16 thus:

> He makes it plainer how seriously Christ is harmed by the man who has intercourse with a harlot. For one body is formed, and so tears a member away from the body of Christ. Paul adds a quotation from Genesis 2:24 but it is not clear what connection he means it to have with his theme. For if he quotes it in order to prove that two people who commit fornication with each other become one flesh, he is distorting the meaning, from the true one to [a different] one quite alien to it. For Moses is not speaking here [Genesis 2:24] of the scandalous and forbidden cohabitation of a man and a woman, but of the marriage union which God blesses. For he teaches that that bond is so close and indissoluble that it surpasses the intimacy which exists between a father and son; and that certainly cannot be said about fornication.

Having thus totally rejected this explanation, Calvin suggests two other ways in which the passage may possibly be understood. My suggested interpretation is akin to, though not completely identical with, the second of Calvin's two alternatives.

The true understanding, I suggest, of Paul's meaning in 1 Corinthians 6:16 proceeds upon the basis that when Paul has chosen to use two different words here, "body" (*soma*) and "flesh" (*sarx*), it is with two different meanings. That is, he uses these words not as synonyms but in order to contrast them.

While "flesh" (*sarx*) **can** be used as a synonym for "body" (*soma*), its normal use is with different meaning. It refers to all that is means to be human. To say, for example, that "the Word became flesh" (John 1:14) means more than that Jesus had a body. A "one-flesh relationship" means that marriage is a union of all that two people are as human beings in this life.

Paul asks, "Do you not know that he who unites himself with a prostitute becomes one body with her?" He is about to use a quotation containing the word "flesh". If he intended his readers to see that this word links directly with what he is saying, with the same meaning, he had only to use the word "flesh" instead of "body" in this lead-up to the quotation. That he used **different** words should at least give us pause, and lead us to consider whether by them he meant different things.

Let us trace Paul's whole argument. His emphatic "Never!" (v. 15) makes it plain that sexual intercourse with a prostitute is wrong. He is now clarifying **why** it is wrong. Sexual intercourse with a prostitute is a union of bodies, a coming together into one body. Moreover, that is **all** that it is.

This thus raises the question, unspoken but implicit in Paul's reasoning, "Why is this wrong?" His answer is, "Because the Scripture says 'The two shall become one flesh'" (6:16). The one-flesh union is a total union of two people. This is God's intended type of union for sexual fulfillment. The one-body union, in contrast, is a mere physical coupling. So then, why is it wrong? Because it is a willful substitute for, and a rejection of, the full one-flesh union, which is God's plan for mankind and the only legitimate sphere for the expression of our sexuality according to the will of the Creator.

Taking "body" and "flesh" as synonyms in this passage deprives Paul's logical argument of any point and forces us to some very bizarre theological and pastoral conclusions. Taking "one-body" and "one-flesh" as being contrasted here (that is, accepting that Paul choose to use different words because he wanted to express different meanings) gives us the interpretation that Paul is showing sexual union with a prostitute to be wrong because this is only a union of bodies whereas God's plan for the expression of human sexuality is that it takes place within, and is limited to, the total union of two human beings which Scripture refers to as the one-flesh relationship of marriage.

We should note now the way in which Paul is refuting the Corinthian position using a dialogue approach - which also he continues in Chapter Seven.

## PAUL'S DIALOGUE APPROACH IN 6:9-20E

It significantly helps our understanding of 6:9-20E to recognize that this passage is cast by Paul in the form of an imagined dialogue with those at Corinth whose views he is opposing: something we may not immediately see because Paul in his day lacked the conventions in writing which we now have for setting these things out. His meaning would however have been quite clear to his readers, because they knew the views which were being propounded at Corinth which Paul is answering. In more modern format, the interchange would appear something like this:

Paul: "Do you not know that the wicked will not inherit the kingdom of God? Do not be deceived: Neither the sexually immoral nor idolaters nor adulterers ... will inherit the kingdom of God. And that is what some of you were. But you were washed, but you were sanctified, but you were justified in the name of the Lord Jesus Christ and by the Spirit of our God."

Corinthians: "But everything is permissible for me!"

P.: "But not everything is beneficial!"

C.: "No, everything is permissible for me!"

P.: "But I will not be mastered by anything!"

C.: "Food for the stomach, and the stomach for food - and it's the same thing with sex."

P.: "But God will destroy both stomach and food! The body is not meant for sexual immorality but for the Lord, and the Lord for the body. By his power God raised the Lord from the dead, and he will raise us also. Do you not know that your bodies are members of Christ himself? Shall I then take the members of Christ and unite them with a prostitute? Never! Do you not know that he who unites himself with a prostitute is one with her in *body*? Whereas what God says is, 'The two will become one *flesh*.' But he who unites himself with the Lord is one with him in spirit. You must flee from sexual immorality."

C.: "All sin, whatever it is that a man may commit, is outside the body."

P.: "But the one who commits immorality is sinning against his own body. Don't you see that your body is the Holy Spirit's temple? You have received him from God and he dwells in you. You are not your own; you were bought at a price. Therefore honor God with your body."

# CHAPTER SEVEN

## SECTION 2:
## CONCERNING SEX AND MARRIAGE (Continued)

### 4. Sexual Fulfillment - Getting It Right (7:1-5)

**7:1** The opening words of this chapter, "Now concerning the matters about which you wrote", show that Paul is turning to a new section of his topic. The systematic way in which he is dealing with each aspect of the subject one by one indicates an intention to be comprehensive. There is only one type of consensual sexual relationship between human beings that he has not already referred to in chapters 5 and 6: which is, between a husband and wife. This then becomes the first of the matters raised by the Corinthians with which he deals; and he has left this topic till now so that it becomes the bridge from his discussion of sexual issues which *he* is raising with the Corinthians (chapters 5 and 6) to his discussion of marriage issues which *the Corinthians* are raising with him (the balance of chapter 7), in a letter they have sent him, apparently carried by Stephanas, Fortunatus, and Achaicus (16:17).

There is a dichotomy about marriage and sex in the early church fathers. Kovacs 104 writes,

> Patristic commentary on this chapter reflects the wide influence of the ascetic ideal in the early centuries of the Church, evident, for example, in the many treatises on virginity composed by fathers such as Athanasius, Ambrose, John Chrysostom, and Gregory of Nyssa .... Most commentators, taking their clue from verse 38 where Paul says that marriage is "good" but remaining single is "better", agree that the celibate life is superior to married life. ...

> Within this widespread consensus, some fathers give a more positive assessment of marriage than others. Clement of Alexandria devotes a whole book of his *Miscellanies* to a discussion of marriage and sex ... Like other fathers, however, Clement sees sexual desire as a threat to the spiritual life. He advocates continence within marriage and, like many other fathers, says that sexual relations are allowable only for the purpose of procreation.

> The Roman monk Jovinian ... aroused Jerome's ire by arguing that married and celibate Christians have equal merit. ...

Jerome writes (Kovacs 110) about Jovinian:

> A few days ago my holy brothers in Rome sent me the treatises of a certain Jovinian, asking me to reply to the foolish ideas they contain and crush this Christian Epicurus with the force of the gospel and the apostles ...

> Jovinian says that virgins, widows, and married women, once they have been cleansed by Christ, have equal merit as long as their other actions are similar ...

Jovinian sets out texts from Old and New Testaments showing the role of marriage in the purposes of God for his people, and then continues,

> From this it is clear that you [who discourage marriage] are following the doctrine of the Manichaeans, who forbid marriage and eating food that God created for use, and who have consciences seared with a hot iron.

Jerome responded (Kovacs 110) to Jovinian with unrestrained vehemence:

> We must fight the enemy [i.e., Jovinian] with all our might and marshall our battle lines to repulse the disorderly forces of the enemy, who fight like brigands, not soldiers. ... Let us return to the chief point of Paul's witness: It is well, he says, for a man not to touch a woman. If it is good not to touch a woman, it is bad to touch one; for nothing is the opposite of good except bad.

We need to consider the question as to the extent to which the fathers have perceived the correct intent of Paul's teaching in many places: a question which is to be asked also of not a few modern writers.

The first issue which Paul is going to discuss in this chapter is the question of a man not touching a woman. Johnson 108 points out that "In Hebrew and Greek it is a euphemism for 'not to have sexual intercourse with a woman' (Gen 20:6; Prov 6:29)." (We use a similar kind of euphemism today when we speak of "to sleep with" someone, and we mean "having sexual intercourse".)

Then the next word in this verse, γυνη (*gunē*), means both "woman" and "wife": which poses a translation problem here.

Some versions (e.g. the NIV) try to get around it by translating it, "It is good for a man not to marry", that is, translating it as if it had said "It is good for a man not to take a woman as his wife". But if that was what was meant we might have expected that to be what the Greek actually said here. Or for the normal word for "to marry", γαμεω (*gameō*), to have been used: it is quite a common word, used 28 times in the New Testament - why not here? What we actually have is a euphemism for sexual intercourse. This indicates pretty plainly that it is not the question of **marriage** as a whole which is being raised, but one particular aspect of it: **sex**.

There are several issues to consider in seeking to understand the meaning of this verse. One helpful approach to the problem of clarifying its meaning is by asking ourselves, In dealing with the matter raised by the Corinthians (whatever it was), what is it that Paul does in fact discuss? When we look at what he says in the verses which follow, we see that his subject is: sexual relations within marriage.

If we were to take it that the issue being raised in v.1 is whether or not to marry (following the NIV), we have to face several anomalies, including: (a) that the issue is phrased in the oddest possible way in the Greek; (b) that Paul contradicts himself - saying in v.1 that it is good not to marry, and then in v.2 that each man should have his own wife, and each woman her own husband; (c) that in these verses (1-5) Paul discusses the question of whether or not to marry exclusively in terms of sexual relations - and even if one believes that that was how Paul viewed marriage (improbable as this seems in the light of what we know of his views from his other writings), verses 2 to 5 still do not flow smoothly from v.1, covering as they do questions of sexual rights and obligations, in what circumstances to abstain from intercourse, and so forth.

So taking v.1 to be raising or answering the question of whether or not it is a good thing to marry is pressing an interpretation upon it which does not arise naturally from the Greek words used, nor from what the context indicates of its meaning.

But if, rather, we take "to touch" to be referring to sexual intercourse - which is what it was used for in the language of the day (and how else can we take it? - no one takes "touch" to be used in an actual literal sense) and if we take γυνη *(gunē)*, as "wife" (which is how it is translated in every other place where it occurs in this whole context), then we see that the issue that is being raised is whether or not a man, now he is a Christian, should continue to have sexual relations with his wife. And that, as we find in the verses which follow, is **exactly** the issue which Paul deals with.

The sequence which we can thus recognize in Paul's thought (from wrong sexual behavior in chapters 5 and 6 to the right sexual behavior in 7:1-5) reinforces the interpretation of γυνη *(gunē)* in this verse as referring to a man's wife, and the meaning of 7:1b as being "It is good for a man not to have sexual relations with his wife".

A factor which can be advanced against this view is the absence of the pronoun "his"; the Greek reads "for a man not to touch a wife". The explanation of this is that the issue is being discussed in general terms, not in relation to a *specific* man and wife, but *any* man and wife, and this can account for the omission of the article "the" with both words. It is not uncommon in Greek for the pronouns "his", "her", "my", "our", "your", etc., to be omitted when referring to parts of the body and to close relationships when the person whose parts or relations they are is mentioned in the context.

Moreover, we need to think carefully about who it is who is saying, "It is good for a man not to touch a γυνη *(gunē)*". The Greek here can be taken in either of two ways:

**(a)** That this is a statement made by Paul in answer to what the Corinthians said; or,

**(b)** That this is what the Corinthians said, which Paul then proceeds to answer, from verse 2 onwards.

Taking Paul as the speaker here leaves us still with the problem of a contradiction between v.1 and what follows. Hodge 108 interprets v.1 as Paul himself speaking. He writes: "Paul says, It is good for a man not to marry" - and then Hodge spends the next page (108f.) seeking to reconcile this (supposed) saying of Paul in v.1 with the rest of the passage, because (to quote him) "in the following verse he [Paul] declares directly the reverse".

And such a teaching would also contradict the rest of Scripture. Indeed, such an interpretation makes Paul to be saying something which comes very close to being an explicit contradiction of Genesis 2:18-24, where God says, "It is not good for man to be alone", creates Eve for him, and then says, "Therefore a man shall leave his father and his mother and be united to his wife, and they shall become one flesh."

But all anomalies vanish if we translate it as, "Now concerning the matters about which you wrote - [then quoting the Corinthians] 'It is good for a man not to have sexual relations with his wife'", recognizing that Paul is quoting from their letter before replying to the point raised. It is taken as a quote from the Corinthian letter by the NRSV and the ESV. As we have noted, Paul quotes what the Corinthians were saying at several points in his letter as he answers them (e.g. 1:12; 3:4; 6:12-13; 6:18b; 8:1, 4; 10:23, 28; 12:3; 15:12, 32, 35 - quite apart from their own letter to him, his sources of knowledge of what was being said at Corinth were Chloe's people, 1:11, and Stephanas, Fortunatus and Achaicus, 16:17).

This not only explains all the anomalies we have noted, but also the use of the euphemism "to touch" - which is odd if it originated with Paul, in view of his plain speaking in the verses which follow, but understandable if he is quoting the views of some in the church at Corinth.

Hurd 163 sums up thus:

> Thus we conclude that, as a number of scholars have suggested, the statement "It is well for a man not to touch a woman," was a quotation from the Corinthians' letter.

But note: this verse is concerned with a man having sexual relations *with his own wife* (the issue of a man having sexual relations with someone *not* his wife Paul has dealt with in chapters 5 and 6).

Some of the Fathers read it this way. Hurd 156 notes:

> Chrysostom in his homily on 1 Cor 7:1,2 said of the Corinthians, "They had written to him, 'Whether it was right (δει) to abstain from one's wife, or not'."

Similarly Tertullian on these verses.

The evidence suggests that the background situation at Corinth was a diverse reaction in the church to the question of sex. Many (most?) of the Corinthians had, prior to their conversion, been living quite immoral lives. Some of them were slow to turn from this behavior - and chapters 5 and 6 of Paul's letter (cf. 6:9-11, "and such were some of you") deal with various abuses of human sexuality: incest, fornication, adultery, homosexuality, male and female prostitution, and sexual promiscuity generally. But others in the church at Corinth, with the zeal of new converts, had swung to the opposite extreme and had condemned all sexual activity as wrong, including sexual relations between a man and wife in marriage. This ascetic faction had now written to Paul expecting his support for their viewpoint - it will be noticed that in what they wrote they were not so much putting a question for him to answer as putting a point of view for him to agree with.

As Hurd 165 puts it,

> Thus on the particular issue under discussion the Corinthians appear to have advocated sexual abstinence for married couples, and to have defended their position with the general principle that "it is well for a man not to touch a woman."

Johnson 109 comments on this further:

> When we see that this negative assessment of all types of sexual intercourse, even within marriage, is not Paul's but one he rejects in the following verses, a great deal of misconception that has plagued the church regarding the apostle's negative attitude towards marriage is dispelled.

Yet this ascetic attitude, as shown by these Corinthians towards sexual relations within marriage, can be found evidenced in the Church over the centuries. Still today there are some who hold that married couples are more spiritual if they engage in sexual intercourse only infrequently.

Origen looks at the excessive zeal of the Corinthian ascetics' advocacy of abstinence in marriage, and writes (Kovacs 107):

> The standard, therefore, which is neither excessive nor deficient but in due measure, is to know how we should live. Are you bound to a wife? If so, then you are acting according to an excessive standard if you do not consider your wife but say, "I can practise continence and live in a purer way." Be aware that your wife will perish if she cannot endure your purity, she for whom Christ died.

> Something like this was happening in Corinth, and there was dissension in the households of the brethren: in some the men and in others the women were seeking to be continent, and they were at odds with each other. And so the Corinthians wrote a letter about this to the apostle, and in response to their letter Paul writes the words recorded here.

But we must note that Paul does **not** agree with the ascetics at Corinth. Rather, just as in chapters 5 and 6 Paul condemns the wrong use of sex, so in chapter 7:2-5 he explains and vindicates the right use of sex. Marriage is the God-given provision for human sexuality (as the expedients mentioned in 6:9-20 are **not**).

So we see that the verses which now follow are intended as guidance for Christian couples concerning the place and role of sex in their married life. It is sad to see that in church history the Church did not follow Paul's teaching here: rather, under the influence of Greek and Persian mystery cults, when their adherents entered the Church without a genuine conversion, the Church adopted an attitude of regarding sex as wrong and sinful, necessary perhaps for procreation and even then barely tolerated. (There were some church leaders who actually said, "Leave procreation to the heathen, and let Christians keep themselves pure".) Even in marriage, abstinence from sex was advocated as the better way, and marriage itself was forbidden for clergy and nuns, etc. For a history of the situation in the Church down the ages, see Appendix C of my book *Marriage and Divorce*. Still today something of this attitude remains. Therefore we ourselves need to pay careful heed to these verses.

**7:2a** If (in the way that has been suggested by some translators and interpreters) Paul is in this section answering a question about whether or not a Christian should marry, then verses 2 to 5 make rather strange reading as being addressed to those who are unmarried and contemplating marriage. On the other hand, they make perfect sense and are most appropriate in their context if addressed to the married who have become Christians and are wondering about the place of sex within the married relationship for a Christian couple. These verses are clearly intended as guidance for Christian married couples.

If Christian couples were to carry out the Corinthians' suggestion of refraining from sexual intercourse in marriage, this would expose both of them to very severe temptations to all kinds of immoralities (the Greek word here, πορνειαι, *porneiai,* is plural). This sexual pressure is referred to again in verses 5 and 9 (and, by implication, in v.7 also). And such a suggestion, besides being dangerous in exposing people to strong temptation, negates the whole plan of God in creating mankind in complementary sexes, as male and female. In making mankind sexual beings, God did not intend that they should (by marrying and then not satisfying each other's sexual needs) be placed in temptations to immoralities. He intends that each person should have their own wife or husband, who would be their sexual partner. "Have" in this verse carries two levels of meaning: to have in the sense of possessing a spouse, of being married; and to "have" your spouse in a sexual sense (as opposed to "having" someone sexually who is not your own spouse, which is immorality).

Paul is not saying that the reason for marrying is to avoid immorality, nor that every person is obliged to marry, but that a person's sexual partner is to be his own spouse, and for the spouse not to fill that role is to expose the partner to temptation to immorality.

**7:2b** Note that this verse leaves no place for polygamy, for each person should have their own spouse. (For a detailed discussion of polygamy, see my *Marriage and Divorce,* Appendix E.) It is very significant that in the second part of this verse Paul does not say simply, "Each man should have his own wife," as if that were the whole of the issue. He adds, "and each woman her own husband". He thus gives the woman a position alongside the man. What applies to the man applies to the woman also. This is one of the very remarkable features of this entire section. Paul, so careful in certain situations to delineate the precise relation between husband and wife and to emphasize the position of husband as the head of the combined "body" of marriage (1 Corinthians 11:3; Ephesians 5:23, 28) is now, in this whole passage on sexual relations, putting the two partners on exactly the same level and saying of each of them exactly what he says of the other (for he writes similarly in verses 3-5).

We must also note another significant factor here: that Paul fully recognizes and accepts the sexual nature and sexual needs of the woman. "Each woman," he says, "should have a husband of her own." Why? ESV: "Because of the temptation to sexual immorality." Similarly the RSV. ["Temptation" does not represent a Greek word but is a legitimate inference here from the context.] But πορνειαι (*porneiai*) is plural, "temptations to **immoralities**". Is this plural just a reference to the different forms that immorality can take, or does it not rather amount here to a recognition that both the man *and the woman* can be subject to sexual temptation?

This recognition by Paul of the sexual needs of the woman is far in advance of the general opinion of his day, which saw in the woman just a convenience for the satisfaction of the man. In fact, Paul's insight in this passage into the woman's sexual nature is quite unique in literature in the ancient world. But it goes to the heart of Paul's total concept of marriage as a partnership, and his specific view of it (as expounded here) as a *sexual* partnership. And his words in v.2 do not stand in isolation.

**7:3** The AV/KJV translation of this verse reads, "Let the husband render unto the wife due benevolence", i.e. let the husband treat his wife kindly, as she deserves. This is the translation of the wording of the *Textus Receptus* version, which has had an extra word (a "gloss) inserted at this point, together with a slight change to another word, the effect of which is to blunt the sexual reference of what Paul actually wrote.

Findlay (in *The Expositor's Greek Testament*) says, "The gloss of the T.R., as old as the Syriac Version, is a piece of mistaken delicacy." Robertson & Plummer 133 suggest the other alternative: that the alterations which have been made to Paul's original wording "may be ascetic periphrases to obscure the plain meaning".

Though most modern versions are based on older and more reliable manuscripts, the wording of some of these translations is rather general so that it may not be immediately obvious to the reader that what is being referred to is the spouses' sexual responsibilities to each other. For example, the Jerusalem Bible wording is: "The husband must give his wife what she has the right to expect, and so too the wife to the husband."

The next verses emphasize the responsibility of each marriage partner to recognize and respond to the sexual needs of the spouse. Notice in each verse the emphasis on mutuality, and the absolutely evenhanded way in which Paul carefully sets out the sexual needs and responsibilities of both husband and wife: they are placed on absolute equality in this matter (as also we saw in v.2). Thus in v.3 the husband is told that he should give to his wife her sexual dues (i.e. the fulfillment of her sexual needs), "and likewise the wife to her husband."

**7:4** Moreover, "For the wife does not have authority over her own body, but the husband does. Likewise the husband does not have authority over his own body, but the wife does." Note this accurate translation from the ESV and NRSV. Contrast the NIV: "The wife's body does not belong to her alone, but also to her husband. In the same way the husband's body does not belong to him alone but also to his wife." The point of what Paul has said is being watered down in the NIV by the unjustifiable insertion of "alone" and "also" in each case.

Note that the wife is explicitly stated to have the right to - the Greek literally says, "the rule over", ἐξουσιαζω (*exousiazō*) - her husband's body, as he hers.

Commenting on this, John Chrysostom says (Kovacs 109):

> In the passage before us, however, there is no superiority or inferiority, but the spouses' authority is the same. ... The husband does not rule over his own body, nor does the wife rule over hers. Their privileges are entire equal; neither one has any advantage at all.

**7:5** "Do not deprive one another" shows that the wife is as entitled to (and as likely to) lead into sexual intercourse as the husband. In Paul's exposition of the sexual relationship within marriage, the wife's needs and rights are as important as those of the husband.

The view was widely held by the early church Fathers that procreation was the reason for sex, and even then you should not enjoy sex or engage in it too often.

Clement of Alexandria (Kovacs 107) writes,

> To state in a general way our teaching about marriage and food and other such things: we should do nothing out of desire, but our will should be directed only toward those things that are necessary. For we are children not of desire but of will. And the man who marries to have children must be continent, feeling no sexual desire for his wife. He ought to love her and beget children with a will that is holy and chaste.

Augustine is very strongly of this view that procreation is the purpose and the justification for engaging in sex; concerning the partnership of marriage he says (Kovacs 111-112):

> The next bond of community between them is children. These are the sole honorable result, not of the marriage of male and female, but of their sexual relations; for even without sexual intercourse there could be between them a true union of friendship, with one of them ruling and the other obeying. ...

> In my opinion [marriage] is not merely for the sake of procreation of children but also because there is a natural affinity between the sexes. If this were not the case, we could not call it a marriage when the spouses are old or have lost their children or never had any at all. But in actuality in a good marriage, no matter how old the partners, even if the youthful ardor between the husband and the wife has withered away, the ordered love between them continues. The better the partners are, the sooner they refrain from intercourse by agreement (v.5), so that their

abstinence be not merely a matter of necessity because of inability in their later years to act on their desire. Instead it is to their credit to decline to do what they are able to do. ... Marriage produces a further good: it uses carnel and youthful incontinence, which is a fault, for the honorable task of begetting children, so that intercourse within marriage creates something good out of the evil of lust. Furthermore, the desire of the flesh is subdued and its blazing passion becomes more moderate since parental love tempers it. A certain seriousness is imposed upon the heat of their pleasure, since in the act of cleaving together they are intending to become father and mother.

We may note, from his teaching, that in marriage "carnal and youthful incontinence ... is a fault", sexual desire is the "evil of lust", but from it can come children, and marriage "creates something good" in "the heat of their pleasure, since in the act of cleaving together they are intending to become father and mother." Further concerning the "sin" of sexual desire, Augustine says (Kovacs 115):

Even if married persons, overcome by lust, consort with one another more than is necessary for begetting children, I see this as one of those things for which we pray every day: Forgive us our debts, as we also have forgiven our debtors.

Yet Augustine has no doubt as to how these matters are regarded by God. He says also (Kovacs 130):

If you consider your blessings separately, the celibate man is better than his father for spurning marriage, and the celibate woman than her mother. For virgin holiness is better than conjugal chastity. ... Conjugal chastity is a good thing, virgin holiness a better one. ... The mother, who is married, will have a lesser place in the kingdom of heaven than the daughter, who is a virgin ... but both will be there. Just as with a bright star and a star of lesser magnitude, both will be in the heavens.

There is something of a difference between on the one hand the beliefs of Jerome and Augustine and those who share their ideas, and on the other the teaching here of the apostle Paul. It is noteworthy that, while such church Fathers see the begetting of children as the only justification for sex, Paul does not even allude to procreation a single time in this entire passage. To the contrary, Paul discusses married sex in terms of the relationship between husband and wife. And so far from implying that the partners are more holy before God if they refrain from sexual relations, Paul teaches clearly that each spouse has a responsibility towards the sexual needs of the partner.

In the sexual side of the marriage relationship there is to be no sign of a supreme right being given to the male, no sign of passive obedient submission being required of the female. Quite the opposite: the emphasis is upon the role and the contribution of each partner, upon the ideas of mutuality, of agreement, of doing things together. It is greatly to be regretted how often this has been overlooked by exegetes of Paul, and how often it has been absent from so many marriages between Christians.

Abstinence from sexual intercourse is perhaps permissible, Paul says, if both partners come to a mutual decision on this - but it must not be prolonged to the point where they give Satan an opening to tempt them. The word ἀποστερεω (*apostereō*) translated "deprive" or "deny" or "refuse" carries the implication that for one partner to act in this way is robbing or cheating the other - abstention is not to be at the choice of one partner but by agreement; is to be only for a time, καιρος (*kairos*); and is to be "so that you [plural - husband and wife] may devote yourselves to prayer".

Robertson & Plummer 134 comment,

> After what has been stated it is evident that refusal amounts to fraud, a withholding what is owed. The present imperative may mean that some of the Corinthians, in mistaken zeal, had been doing this: [so Paul says,] "cease to defraud." Three conditions are required for lawful abstention: it must be by mutual consent, for a good object, and temporary.

For neither spouse is to refuse the other unilaterally but the two partners are to agree on abstention from intercourse, and on coming together again in their sexual relationship.

But even as important an activity as prayer must not be made a ground for continued abstinence, as that is to leave the way open for "Satan to tempt you [again plural, and so referring to both husband and wife] through the strong desires of your sexual nature".

When Paul gives prayer as a possible reason why a married couple may temporarily discontinue sexual intercourse, this is not implying that marital relations and prayer are somehow incompatible. Alford's Commentary shows that the reference is not to "your ordinary prayers", as this would be inconsistent with the direction that it be only for a short time; rather "the aorist expresses this temporary purpose and shows that the prayer meant is not ordinary but extraordinary - seasons of urgent supplication."

But to say that abstention must be by agreement and that each should give the other their sexual dues is not to say that either partner has the right to make demands on the other: this is precluded by what Paul says of each partner having the rule over the other's body. If *that* is the operating principle in a married relationship, then the one partner can restrain as well as encourage the other. There is nothing in the passage about either partner having rights which may be asserted over the other. Rather, the passage is about each partner being aware of, and acting to meet, the sexual needs of the other. The passage is not about a partner's *rights*; it is about a partner's *responsibilities* to the other.

Paul here describes the way a happy sexual adjustment will work out in marriage. But this "working out" is shown to depend upon a spirit of mutuality within the marriage. Without that, sexuality will be a source, not of marital harmony, but of discord.

Thus we are to note that sexual activity within marriage is being set forth in this passage as an end in itself, which of itself is a satisfaction (the right and the only true satisfaction) of human sexual nature, and thus it fulfills an important role within the marriage.

This is Paul's answer to those who asked him whether it were not desirable for a Christian couple to refrain from intercourse.

### Explanatory Translation of 1 Corinthians 7:1-5

This passage could be paraphrased as follows, to bring out these aspects of the Corinthians' proposal and Paul's response to it:

> "Now concerning what you wrote: 'It is good for a man not to have sexual relations with his wife.' But what about the temptations to immoralities? Because of these each man should have his own wife, and each woman should have her own husband. The husband owes it to his wife to give her her sexual dues, and in the same way the wife also owes this to her husband. It is not the wife who has the rights over her own body, but her husband - and in the same way also it is not the husband who has the rights over his own body, but his wife. Do not deny yourselves to one another - except perhaps if you both decide together that you abstain for a while, in order to spend a period of time in prayer. But then come together again: otherwise you leave yourselves open for Satan to tempt you through a lack of self-control."

Reflect a moment upon the point noted earlier, that in this entire discussion of the fulfillment of human sexuality in marriage, Paul makes no mention of sex as being given for or even directed towards procreation. Sexual relations are shown to have a role and value in their own right as a constituent of the total marriage relationship. This is wholly consistent with the rest of biblical teaching. Note the reference to the sexual dimension in marriage in the foundational verse, Genesis 2:24: "Therefore a man shall leave his father and his mother and be united to his wife, and they shall become one flesh." Being united to (cleaving to, being joined to) one's wife and becoming one flesh means more than the sexual relationship, but it certainly refers to and includes this. There is no justification in Paul's teachings or anywhere else in the Bible for the notion that sexual intercourse is solely or even primarily for the purpose of procreation - the only biblical support that can be adduced for this is Genesis 1:28, "Be fruitful and increase in number", but seeking to base such teaching on this verse is a misinterpretation and misapplication of its meaning and role.

This then raises a very important issue here - the question of the legitimacy of contraception, both in biblical times and today. This is discussed in "Reflections", below.

In regard to this and other issues in the total area of marriage and sex, later church traditions are still being read back - totally wrongly - into the writings of Paul. We must not be diverted by this from taking note of what Scripture itself actually says.

## 5. Problems Concerning The Married (7:6-16)

### (a) Problems if a relationship has terminated (7:6-9)

**7:6** "I say this as a concession, not as a command" means that what Paul is saying is not a **requirement** that they **must** follow, but is a **recommendation** which they can follow if they wish - and if they are so gifted by God.

The word "this", οὗτος (*houtos*), can refer back to what he has just said in v.5 (a married couple can choose to agree to discontinue marital relations if they wish for a limited time for some special reason); or it can refer forward to another matter of choice which he is just about to lay before them (verses 7-9) and to which therefore this comment is the introduction. [There are numerous occasions in 1 Corinthians, and elsewhere in Paul's writings, where he uses οὗτος (*houtos*) to refer forward to something he is just about to say: for example, in this Epistle in the Greek of 7:29; 9:3; 11:17; 15:50.] In view of the openness and balance of 7:7, and the way 7:9 is worded as an instruction to do something that Paul himself suggests against, it is more reasonable to take v.6 as referring to what **follows** rather than what **precedes** it. In fact, there is no valid justification for taking this verse to refer back to the overall instructions in what he has just written in verses 2-5: this would be to nullify any force and authority in his teaching and render it pointless. If this concession of v.6 were to be taken as referring back, it would be only to the "exception" of v.5. But I concur with Garland 270 that "Taking the 'this' to refer to what follows makes the best sense."

**7:7a** These next verses have a common theme: the question of remaining unmarried. Paul expresses the wish, "I wish that all were as I myself am." But this "wish" is a concession, not a command, for "Each person has his own gift from God, one of one kind and one of another." It was standard, in the Jewish milieu from which Christianity emerged, for people to marry. What Paul is now in effect doing here is to give explicit recognition to the fact that, in the providence of God, some people are being given the gift of celibacy and living unmarried. And Paul commends this option: he sees it as able to offer certain advantages (7:33-34), and he almost certainly has in mind here also Jesus's words about being unmarried "for the sake of the kingdom of heaven" (Matthew 19:12). But this is not a command, and counterbalancing the fact that one person is now given the gift of celibacy, another is given the gift of being a marriage partner (7:7).

Moreover, his instructions (7:9) for those who are unmarried to marry in certain circumstances may also be taken as a concession.

Note that when Paul here expresses the wish that all people would remain as he himself was, the meaning of his wish is of course totally tied to the question of what his own marital state was. It is obvious that he was not married at the time he wrote this Epistle, but: had he been married before? It is very frequently taken for granted that Paul was a bachelor who had never married, so that what he is here wishing for is that everyone would remain celibate and never marry. But is this assumption really so? Johnson 112 informs us:

> We don't know whether Paul was married earlier in his life, as were most Jewish men, especially rabbis and Sanhedrin members (Acts 26:10), and then was divorced some twenty years before the writing of 1 Corinthians, at the time of his conversion (his wife leaving him). Or perhaps he became a widower, or had never married (unlikely).

Indeed, the evidence is overwhelmingly indicative of Paul having been married. This evidence, and its attestation, is set out in my book *The Ministry of Women in the Church*, pages 27 to 31. I have included its key points in "Reflections", below. We may note that there is no evidence at all for the idea that Paul had never married. Rather, the evidence is all best explained on the basis that he was a widower who did not remarry after the death of his wife: this is much more probable than that Paul had never married. Thus his comment here about being like himself is an introduction to the issue he is dealing with in verses 8 and 9.

**7:7b** Paul now says (to paraphrase him): "But this is not really a matter of personal preference, because each person has his own individual gift from God in this regard: for one person, it is the gift from God of being equipped to live as a partner in a marriage relationship, and for another person, it is the gift from God of being able to live a full and complete life without marrying, that is, as celibate."

Robertson & Plummer 136 tell us, "Origen points out that if celibacy is a χαρισμα [*charisma*, divine gift], so also is marriage, and those who forbid marriage forbid what has been given by God."

In this verse it is likely that Paul is consciously expounding the teaching of Jesus in Matthew 19:10-12: we know Paul was familiar with this teaching of Jesus because in v.10 he quotes what the Lord said in Matthew 19:6.

**7:8** To understand fully the meaning and application of Paul's teaching in these verses, we need to see which people Paul is writing to at this point. V.8 starts off, "To the unmarried and the widows". This seems quite clear, but it is possible to misread the meaning of this passage through not recognizing the significance of the word that Paul is using here. Who are the "unmarried" he is addressing?

Paul uses two different words in this chapter in reference to people who are not married: παρθενος (*parthenos*; plural *parthenoi*), which is the word for a person, male or female, who has never had sexual intercourse, a virgin; and, secondly, ἀγαμος (*agamos*; plural *agamoi*), which means a person, male or female, who is not at the time a member of a marriage relationship, but it does not imply that such a person has never been married.

What is the word Paul uses in v.8? It is ἀγαμος (*agamos*), not παρθενος (*parthenos*), it is "unmarried", not "virgin". But can you see the ambiguity in the translation "unmarried"? It is still so easy for people to take this simply as meaning "never been married". Whereas, as we are about to see, this word ἀγαμος (*agamos*) is the word that Paul uses in v.11 in describing the woman with a broken marriage!

Some of the translations can get us a bit mixed up here. For example, while Paul has used these two very different Greek words in 1 Corinthians 7, in the RSV both are translated as "unmarried" - παρθενος (*parthenos*) is the word translated "unmarried" in the RSV in v.25, where Paul addresses himself to virgins. Then Paul uses ἀγαμος (*agamos*) in verses 32 and 34, where the RSV also translates it "unmarried".

But when Paul uses ἄγαμος (*agamos*) in verse 11, in referring to a wife who is separated from her husband, the RSV translates it "single".

The New RSV, the NIV, and the ESV help unscramble this confusion by uniformly translating ἄγαμος (*agamos*) as "unmarried". But - as we shall see - they translate παρθενος (*parthenos*) in variant ways.

It makes quite a bit of difference in our understanding of Paul's meaning when we see that in verses 6 to 11 he is talking to, and talking about, those who are ἄγαμοι (*agamoi*), not those who are παρθενοι (*parthenoi*).

Then ἄγαμος (*agamos*) occurs again in v.32, in contrasting the concerns of the unmarried man and the married man, and again in v.34 - which has both ἄγαμος (*agamos*) and παρθενος (*parthenos*), in order to cover both categories of women without a husband, those who are virgins and those who have been married before. These four occurrences of ἄγαμος (*agamos*) in 1 Corinthians 7 - verses 8, 11, 32, and 34 - are the only usages of this word in the New Testament.

Who then are those addressed in v.8 who are ἄγαμοι (*agamoi*)? This covers those who are widowers, and also those who have been divorced.

Note the progression of Paul's discussion in this chapter. In 7:1-5 Paul speaks concerning the sexual relationship of marriage. This, he says, is not to be discontinued or interrupted except by agreement for short periods for some special purpose such as prayer, and then the couple is to resume their sexual relationship lest Satan make their continence an occasion of temptation.

Then in v.8 Paul considers the situation of a person who has had a sexual relationship which for some reason has been terminated, so that the person has become ἄγαμος (*agamos*). Such a person would be under some pressure to establish a new sexual relationship - a pressure much greater than would normally be experienced by someone whose sexual nature had not been aroused as yet.

Paul's first guidance to those who are ἄγαμος, *agamos* (that is, not at the moment in a married relationship) and widows, is that it is a good idea for them to remain as he is. (The word "single" in the RSV and ESV of this verse, "unmarried" in the NIV and NRSV, is a translator's interpolation, and represents no word in the Greek text.) This advice would certainly operate as a brake upon a person too precipitately entering a new relationship. Why are widows mentioned specifically in this verse? Lenski suggests:

> "The term 'unmarried' really includes all individuals mentioned in this first group, yet '*kai*' adds 'widows'. This conjunction is often used thus to single out a part from a whole in order to give it special attention. Widows

might, indeed, have had special reasons for thinking their state a sad one and thus for desiring to have it changed."

Lenski's interpretation suggests that Paul is writing, "And to the ἀγαμοι (*agamoi*), especially to the widows, I say ..." etc.

**7:9a** "If they cannot exercise self-control", that is, if after seeking to live now as celibate, they find that God has not given them the gift of living without a marriage partner (as set out in v.7). Verses 7 and 8 make it plain that Paul commends his marital state as an example for the Corinthians to follow - but only if it is given them by God to do so. This verse makes it equally plain that if they do not have the gift of celibacy, then they ought to marry.

Not to remarry when a person has received from God the gift of a nature needing fulfillment in marriage, is **not** recommended by Paul. Inevitably such a person will in those circumstances find himself continually burning with the desire for sexual fulfillment. Paul's word to such people is rendered as "let them marry" (AV/KJV, NASB, Knox, Moffatt, Phillips, Wand, Weymouth), as if it is a permission; or "they should marry" (NAB, NEB, NIV, RSV, NRSV, ESV, Jerusalem, Williams), as if it is a recommendation. But these translations do not unambiguously convey the full force of what Paul wrote. In the Greek it is in fact rather stronger, an aorist imperative which is instructing them what in those circumstances they are to do: thus, Barclay, "they must marry", Beck, "get married", and TEV, "go on and marry".

Paul's concession which is not a command (7:6) would thus be for the ἀγαμοι (*agamoi*) and widows to remain without remarrying, which it is good for them to do, but those who "cannot exercise self-control" (ESV) or who "are not practicing self-control" (NRSV) are instructed (imperative) to marry.

**7:9b** "To be aflame with passion" is present tense, and refers to living in an ongoing state of sexual tension. Paul is not here advocating marriage solely for sexual reasons. He is stating that the sexual relationship of marriage is the **right** answer, in the economy of God, to the pressures of one's God-given sexual nature (in contrast to the **wrong** answers of immorality). Some people, not noticing this distinction, have decided on the basis of what Paul says here that he has a very low view of marriage. Paul's comments must however be understood within the context in which he writes them.

Moreover, there is another possibility concerning this verse: it is possible that when Paul says "It is better to marry than to be aflame with passion", he is being somewhat jocular. There is no *a priori* reason why apostles are not permitted to make jokes, or why we are compelled to think of Paul as a totally serious, humorless man. He is capable of sarcasm, irony, hyperbole and punning (1 Corinthians 9:1-7, 2 Corinthians 11, esp. verses 16-21; and 12:13; Galatians 4:15-16; Philemon 10-12). In this also he is but following the precedent of his Lord (see Elton Trueblood's book, *The Humor of Christ*). This present verse may well be a case of the "many a true word being spoken in jest".

And in speaking thus he could perhaps have in mind the very real problems of some who fall specifically into none of the categories which have been mentioned: they were not divorcees or widowers for they had not been married, but nor were they παρθενοι *(parthenoi)* - they were those who in licentious Corinth had been (before their conversion) fornicators and frequenters of prostitutes (1 Corinthians 6:9-20; note v.11, "And such were some of you"). Being now Christians, and aware that such behavior was wholly outlawed, and yet without the gift of continence, and plagued by unfulfilled sexual feelings, what were they to do? Should they try to live celibate lives now? Perhaps Paul's jocular words could have an especially attentive reception from such men: "It is better to marry than to be aflame with passion."

Thus Paul addresses all such people with his instruction to marry: for otherwise their unfulfilled sexual nature will cause problems for them, and "it is better for them to be married than to be tormentcd by unsatisfied desire" (v.9, Phillips).

We should note specifically that this instruction, "they should marry", clearly applies to divorcees, amongst others. Paul's guidance is exactly applicable to their situation and their needs, irrespective of the grounds of divorce, or whether the person in question was the "innocent" or "guilty" party. Such people can find that they still have sexual needs, which they now cannot legitimately satisfy because of the break-up with their former partner. Are we to take it that, because of the sin and mistakes of that marriage break-up, they are supposed to go through the rest of their lives without ever again experiencing sexual fulfillment? Paul recommends first of all that such people do not remarry: but this, he says (v.6), is advice, not a command: and if they find themselves under strong sexual pressure (v.9), then marriage is the answer.

So it needs to be noted that 7:8-9 is not directed primarily to those who have never been married and are virgins, παρθενοι *(parthenoi)*. While such people may well be aware of their developing sexual potential, their situation is not on a par with that of people who have been part of an ongoing sexual relationship which has (for whatever reason) now terminated, and who are the ones whose situation is discussed in 7:9.

Commenting on this point, Clement of Alexandria says (Kovacs 114),

> But when the apostle says, "If he is aflame with passion (v.9), let him marry," he is speaking of second marriage.

There are some commentators who would expressly seek to restrict the scope of Paul's comments in 7:6-9 so as not to include divorcees. This is the approach found (for example) in Fee 288-296. He notes firstly (288), concerning *agamos*, "that in his [Paul's] regular usage it denotes not the 'unmarried' in general but the 'demarried', those formerly but not now married." I totally concur with him on this. He adds further (289),

> "In this case, then, Paul is not so much offering marriage as the remedy for the sexual desire of 'enflamed youth', which is the most common way of viewing the text, but as the proper alternative for those who are already consumed by that desire and are sinning."

But then from v.11 he draws the conclusion:

> The wife who may happen to divorce her husband may not use her present unmarried condition as an excuse for remarriage to someone else (295). ... What is *not* allowed is remarriage, both because for him that presupposes the teaching of Jesus that such is adultery and because in the Christian community reconciliation is the norm (296).

As Fee thus excludes any remarriage for a divorcee, his interpretation of *agamos* in v.8 is (288): "On balance, 'widower' seems to be the best understanding of the word here."

Everything I have said so far tells against Fee's approach. Fee recognizes the sexual pressure which could engulf the *agamoi* who do not now have the gift of celibacy and continence so that "they are already consumed by that desire and are sinning". He recognizes that Paul's response to that situation is the instruction, "they must marry". And while Paul's word in 7:9 relates to all who are *agamoi*, without restriction or limitation, Fee applies to this situation an interpretation that he draws from Mark 10:11//Matthew 19:9 to conclude that all remarriage after divorce is adultery (Paul does not mention adultery) - an interpretation which is opposed to the natural meaning of this verse, and is in contradiction with the rest of Scripture.

What Jesus actually says is that "whoever divorces his wife and marries another commits adultery" - the package deal, and doing the first in order to enable you to do the second, i.e. changing from one woman to another, and covering the whole transaction with a veneer of legality. Jesus's teaching is very far removed from his categorizing all remarriage as adultery - and neither does Paul, as we shall see more particularly when we consider 7:28. (A detailed discussion of these issues will be found in chapter 14, "Remarriage After Divorce", in my book *Marriage and Divorce - the New Testament Teaching*.)

But thus and thereby Fee allows 7:8 to refer only to those who are *agamoi* because widowed and excludes from it those who are *agamoi* because divorced - although in relation to the "burning passion" of 7:9 the latter would be in exactly the same position as the former.

One must also mention that Fee's discussion does not refer to the grace of God in forgiveness, available upon repentance for those who have sinned, nor the new start granted to those who are cleansed and justified.

Fee 296 writes against those who "turn the text into law and make divorce the worst of all sins in the church", and then virtually does this very thing in regard to remarriage: which Scripture does **not** categorize as a sin at all. No, rather, we must allow 7:9 to refer to all those who are *agamos* - and note now what Paul says about a broken marriage.

### (b) Problems that split a marriage (7:10-11)

**7:10** Next Paul here addresses himself to the married, and says "I give this command (not I, but the Lord): A wife must not separate from her husband. And a husband must not leave (or, send away, or, separate from, or, divorce) his wife." Then in the middle of this basic statement of the position Paul includes a parenthesis which covers the case where a separation has occurred.

Here Paul may be answering a specific question addressed to him on this point, such as, "If a person is already married when they are converted, should they separate from the other partner, if the partner is a Christian?" Alternatively it may well be that the issue is raised here because Paul was being asked for guidance in relation to a specific case which had arisen at Corinth where a wife had separated herself from her husband. If so, this would explain the mention of the wife first, and the parenthesis about what a wife was to do if she had separated.

It has sometimes been taken that this section of Paul's marriage chapter is dealing with marriage between Christians, in contrast with verses 12-16 where the central point is that one of the partners is not a Christian. Thus Fee 291 says concerning 7:10, "In speaking to the 'married', Paul is presupposing in this first instance that both partners are believers." This approach to the passage is also very common among Roman Catholics and those who, like them, take a sacramentalist approach, for they hold that only a marriage between Christians (by which they mean "baptized persons") is sacramental and indissoluble.

However, whatever the form in which the matter was raised with Paul, and whatever the background circumstances, his reply is *not* directed exclusively towards Christians any more than was the word of the Lord on which he bases it. In fact, we may recall that *that* word (in Matthew 19:6) was spoken to the Pharisees engaged in tempting Christ. Thus Paul's word here must be taken as having unrestricted application. *No* wife should separate from her husband; *no* husband should leave (or repudiate) his wife. Those who are not Christians are not just for that reason excused from the operation of this word of the Lord: though as a question of fact it may be that they are less likely to avoid a broken marriage or divorce than a Christian.

It is also to be noted that the passage is not primarily concerned with divorce, although that is frequently the level on which it is discussed: thus the kind of approach which is often followed is, "Paul here re-echoes Christ's prohibition of divorce". The word of the Lord on which Paul's answer is based is recorded in Matthew 19:6//Mark 10:9, "What therefore God has joined together, let not man separate." The pivotal word used by Jesus, "put asunder" (RSV), "separate" (NIV, NRSV, ESV), χορίζω (*chorizō*), is the same word "separate" used by Paul here in v.10. Paul's concern is not divorce, but *any* sundering of the marriage relationship - for that was what Christ was concerned with also.

The first point therefore which Paul is making in this passage is this: "In accordance with the word of the Lord, a wife is not to sunder the marriage relationship with her husband, and the husband is not to sunder the marriage relationship with his wife - by letting her go, sending her away, leaving her, deserting her, or, of course, formally divorcing her." To this absolute prohibition of separation and of sundering by any means at all, Paul allows *no exception*: because Christ allowed none (Christ's teaching does *not* contain any exception that *allows* divorce - Matthew 5:32 is not an exception permitting divorce; and Matthew 19:9 is not an exception at all but a mistranslation of μη [mē], "not" - see my *Marriage and Divorce*). And also because to breach this prohibition is to breach the marriage itself in terms of how marriage was understood by Paul (and by Christ). The mutual self-giving of the marriage (1 Corinthians 7:2-5, and Ephesians 5:21-33) cannot exist if the partners have deliberately separated. The will of God for a marriage *cannot possibly* be fulfilled if one partner deliberately separates from the other: such separation is obviously therefore an act against the will of God. Hence Paul forbids it, as Christ forbad it.

**7:11a** Some Christian expositors and theologians who strongly oppose divorce have permitted separation (without divorce or remarriage) as the solution for an intolerable marriage situation, citing 7:10-11 for this. Thus Fee 294 is representative when he writes,

> 'No divorce' is what is 'commanded' for believers; nonetheless, just as in all the other situations addressed in this chapter, Paul allows an exception: 'but if indeed she is separated.' ... the previous sentence expresses the ideal situation (in this case, no divorce), while the following conditional clause introduced by a *de* ('but') 'describes the alternative possibility which is permissible but not ideal' (in this case, separation, but without remarriage).

Usually these authors base their prohibition of divorce upon the words of Christ to which Paul refers, recorded in Matthew 19:6. The irony of this teaching of theirs is that what Christ forbids in Matthew 19:6 is **exactly** what Paul forbids in 1 Corinthians 7:10 - both use the same word χορίζω (*chorizō*), "separate", "sunder", "split apart", and in this verse Paul expressly cites the teaching of the Lord Jesus Christ as the source of what he says in forbidding separation.

Contrary to the interpretations placed upon it by such commentators, this passage gives neither authorization for nor justification of separation between marriage partners. The view that it does is a most grotesque inversion and thus repudiation of what Paul - and Christ - actually taught. What is happening at this point in Paul's discussion is that he quotes, and affirms, Christ's teaching, and then (v.11) explains what is to be done in a situation where, in disobedience to Christ's word, separation has in fact occurred. To teach - as some do - that this verse gives **permission** for separation is to mangle and distort Paul's words to have a meaning the exact opposite of what Paul is in fact saying.

We have a parallel in 1 John 2:1: "My dear children, I write this to you so that you will not sin. But if anybody does sin, we have one who speaks to the Father in our defence." Applying to this verse the same twisted reasoning that is used on Paul's prohibition of separation would produce the interpretation that John is authorizing sin because he says, "But if anybody does sin ..."

Where (contrary to the Lord's prohibition) separation **has** occurred, a person in such a circumstance should remain unmarried, ἀγαμος (*agamos*): to act otherwise would close off the desired outcome, which is that the couple should become reconciled and resume their marriage relationship. If a person who has thus become ἀγαμος (*agamos*) genuinely seeks to be reconciled and is forced to recognize that this is impossible, and then seeks to ascertain whether God has now given him the gift of living unmarried (v.7) by continuing to live as a single person (v.8) and finds that he does not in fact have this gift but is still in need of being part of a marriage relationship (v.9a), then Paul's word directed to precisely this situation applies expressly to him: he should marry (v.9b).

In 1 Corinthians 6:9-20, Paul gives a list of things which are wrong, and subject to the condemnation of God. The list includes fornicators, adulterers, homosexuals, and frequenters of prostitutes, and Paul adds that those who do such things will not "inherit the Kingdom of God" (verses 9, 10).

But it is significant to note that this list does **not** include divorce and subsequent remarriage. Why not, if these are similarly subject to the condemnation of God? The answer certainly cannot be that divorce and remarriage were unknown in the Mediterranean world of Paul's day - we know from contemporary historical evidence that they were widespread and common. The most logical explanation is that divorce and remarriage were not regarded by Paul as being always and in themselves sinful *in the same way* as the other matters listed. One must be careful about placing too much weight on an argument like this from silence, but we ought to reflect upon the logic and the biblical validity of the policy found in the Church (or at least, in some sections of the Church) which forbids ministers officiating at the marriage of a person who has been divorced, but does not forbid them officiating at the marriage of a person who has been a practising homosexual, a frequenter of prostitutes, or living in a fornicatory relationship - all of which are condemned in this Epistle in the strongest possible terms.

So beware of those exegetes who take this verse as a permission to separate so long as "if she does, she must remain unmarried or else be reconciled to her husband" - with this verse in fact being treated as if Paul here changed his mind and completely reversed what he has just said; as if he were here actually saying, "However, she *may* separate if she then remains unmarried or else is later reconciled to her husband."

Such a reading of the text is to make nonsense of Paul's careful wording, and to nullify completely the word of the Lord which Paul has just cited - for there is no such permission to separate in the teaching of Christ, upon which Paul is basing what he says. Paul makes no exception to his (and Christ's) prohibition of separation.

Rather, he is (being a realist) dealing with the situation, "If this prohibition is broken and separation occurs, then, what next?" He is stating what is then to be done, in order to prevent the further worsening of a situation which is already bad enough.

His answer is very logical and straightforward: she must remain unmarried (in order that the split is not made permanent - the bad situation is held where it is) or she is to be reconciled to her husband (so that

the wrong of the separation is set right, and obedience to the commandment of Christ is restored).

It should be noted that after the separation the γυνη (*gunē*) is ἀγαμος
(*agamos*), "unmarried", so remarriage is possible. It is *forbidden*, but it
is *possible*. As the wife broke the first prohibition (of v.10) in separating,
so it is *possible* that she might break the second one and remarry. Paul
does not say here, "She is still married to her first husband, no matter
what appearances may be. Therefore if she takes another man this is
adultery." He is not upholding the idea of some "marriage bond" which
continues in existence independently of whatever action the parties to
the marriage may take. Quite the reverse. He says that the woman is now
ἀγαμος (*agamos*), "unmarried" (the same word as in v.8, "To the
unmarried and the widows I say ..."). He does not point to some marriage
bond. By his choice of this word, Paul says *there now is no marriage
bond* - by separating from her husband she has broken it.

Christians differ in their interpretation of how the prohibition of
remarriage in 7:11 for an *agamos* relates to the instruction to the *agamoi*
in 7:9, "They should marry".

The first view is that 7:8-9 give a statement about *agamoi* in general,
which instructs them that when they do not have the gift of now living a
celibate life, then "they should marry"; while 7:11 refers to one specific
instance of becoming one of the *agamoi* (viz., through the break-up of a
marriage relationship), and instructs that when *this* is the reason for becoming *agamos* then remarriage is forbidden.

On this first interpretation, Paul's words about "remain unmarried"
mean, "permanently". Thus a person in such a situation has two choices:
be reconciled to her spouse, or remain unmarried always - or at least
until the spouse dies.

The weakness of this interpretation is that it fails to take account of
the fact that the person who is *agamos* through the break-up of a marriage relationship is quite definitely covered by the comments of 7:7 and
7:9 - for that person may now receive from God the gift of living a
celibate life, *or else* may instead have the gift of such a nature as
requires its fulfillment in the marriage relationship. If so, they will for
that reason be in exactly the situation of sexual pressure which Paul
describes in 7:9 and in response to which he says of such people, "They
should marry".

The alternative interpretation, then, is to see 7:7-9 as a general statement of the situation, whereas 7:10-11 is setting out what is to be done
initially in a particular case. First, the wife should not separate from her
husband. Second, if she does, then she should remain unmarried, ἀγαμος

(*agamos*), and this is linked with being reconciled with her husband, which is the hoped-for outcome. To marry another person would rule out the possibility of such a reconciliation, and reconciliation must be sought first. But if such a reconciliation cannot be achieved - if the marriage is now quite dead and reconciliation is impossible - then the person has done what Paul instructed in remaining unmarried, and 7:7-9 applies. So, that person should test their gift to live without remarrying (7:8), but if they do not have this gift from God (7:7), then Paul's instruction "They should marry" (7:9) applies to them in the same way as to any other person who is ἀγαμος (*agamos*). See further, "Reflections", below.

**7:11b** The wording of v.10, and the discussion in v.11a of the situation which exists after separation, are both couched in terms of the wife. Then follows the prohibition that the husband μη ἀφιεναι (*mē aphienai*), must not renounce or repudiate, his wife; and as the whole passage is addressed to those who are married (v.10a) it is clear that the instruction given in v.10 to the wife would apply in the same way to the husband if he were to separate from or otherwise sunder the relationship with his wife.

It is a matter of regret that most English versions have used "divorce" as the translation of the husband's forbidden action in v.11b: though the NASB and Jerusalem Bible render it as "send his wife away", while Phillips has "A husband must not desert his wife."

But if this verse is taken at its face value in the majority of English translations, it means that a husband is precluded from *divorcing* his wife, but *not from anything else*: not, for example, from sending her away without a formal divorce, or separating from her or deserting her himself. But if those options are not excluded by these various English translations, they most certainly *are* excluded by the Greek which Paul wrote.

The word here translated "divorce" is not the usual Greek verb for divorce, ἀπολυω (*apoluō*) (as in Matthew 1:19; 5:31, 32; 19:3, 7, 8, 9; Mark 10:2, 4, 11, 12; Luke 16:18 - *that is, in every other place in the New Testament where divorce is mentioned*). Rather, the verb being translated "divorce" in verses 11, 12 and 13, ἀφιεναι (*aphienai*), is nowhere but in this passage translated "divorce", nor is it used for "divorce" anywhere in the New Testament or in early Christian literature (as is shown in Danker-BAG).

*Aphienai* has a wide area of meaning which does not of course *exclude* the idea of divorce, but which also *includes* "let go", "send away", "leave", "abandon". (Details and examples of these in New Testament usage are set out in Danker-BAG.)

To limit the connotation of this word in 1 Corinthians 7:11-13 just to the meaning "divorce" is thus to restrict materially the scope of what Paul was saying.

If therefore we would not mistake Paul's meaning at this point, we must take care to avoid allowing the issue to become confused through giving to the word just this one English meaning. For words in any language have an area of meaning, and the meaning of this Greek word is much wider than that of the English word "divorce".

So then, why did Paul not use "divorce", ἀπολυω (*apoluō*), in 1 Corinthians 7:11? Because he is not concerned simply to preclude a formal divorce. He is concerned the rather (as was Christ) to outlaw *every possible way in which a husband could sunder the marriage relationship* - and ἀφιεναι (*aphienai*) is ideally fitted to express this meaning. A better English translation here would be "repudiate" or "renounce", which has something of the breadth of scope of ἀφιεναι (*aphienai*).

Similarly in verses 12 and 13 an understanding of the meaning of what Paul is saying will involve a recognition of the full meaning of the verb ἀφιεναι (*aphienai*) which he uses.

## (c) Problems of a divided marriage (7:12-16)

**7:12a** Paul now addresses himself "to the rest", τοις λοιποις, *tois loipois*. "The rest" is usually taken to be "the other people whose case has not been already covered thus far". But Paul has discussed the ἀγαμοι (*agamoi*) and widows (v.8), and the married (v.10): who are left? Only the παρθενοι (*parthenoi*), virgins - but he has a word to them in verses 25ff. when, making a new start, he says, "Now concerning the παρθενοι (*parthenoi*) ..." And in any case he is not in fact in v.12 leaving the group under discussion (the married) to discuss another group; he is proceeding to consider a particular case which can (and presumably did) arise among the married. Thus it may be better to take τοις λοιποις (*tois loipois*) as "concerning the remaining cases or situations affecting the married" - that is, presumably, the remaining cases concerning which the Corinthians had asked him.

He has already discussed two situations (the married who may be contemplating separation, the case where separation has occurred). Now he proceeds to other issues which affect the married.

"I say this (I, not the Lord)" is not some kind of disclaimer by Paul of inspiration or authority (as a few interpreters have mistakenly taken it) but a simple statement of the situation that contrasts with v.10. There, he was able to quote the actual teaching of the Lord in dealing with the issue under consideration; but there is no teaching of the Lord that he can cite in the matter that he is now taking up, for Jesus did not deal with this at any time in his teaching ministry. Therefore Paul gives the answer to the issues raised, upon his own authority.

Contrast here Paul's "I say, not the Lord" with v.10, "not I but the Lord". We see that Paul is very careful to differentiate between what the Lord said and what he himself is teaching upon his own authority. This declaration indicates that Paul lays claim to a very high awareness of the teaching ministry of Jesus: both what the Lord did say, and what he didn't say. We may note here the comments of Fee 292,

> These twin data from vv. 10 and 12 speak in their own way to the basic authenticity of the Synoptic tradition. It has become common in NT scholarship to assume that early Christian prophets created many of the Jesus sayings as need arose in the churches. These two texts suggest otherwise. Paul himself was a prophet, yet he felt no constraint to have Jesus speak to the new situations he faced.

Following upon Fee, Garland 282 says,

> Paul's careful distinction between his own command and that of the Lord also undercuts the assumption in modern scholarship that the early church invented sayings of Jesus as the need arose. ... He did not declare his own commands to be the Lord's words ...

Similarly Paul's disclaimer in 7:25, "I have no command from the Lord, but I give my judgement as one who by the Lord's mercy is trustworthy."

Robertson & Plummer 141 sum up, concerning Paul's comment:

> He means that he is not now repeating the teaching of Christ, who is not likely to have said anything on the subject. He does not mean that he is speaking now, not with Apostolic authority, but as a private individual. All his directions are given with the inspiration and power of an Apostle, and he speaks with confidence and sureness.

We are reminded of his statement in 2:12-13 that he and his fellow-apostles are able, through the Spirit, to understand what God reveals to them, and that they then "impart this in words not taught by human wisdom but taught by the Spirit."

**7:12b-16** The underlying situation in this passage is that of a brother or sister married to an unbeliever. We can see how the specific issues are covered in Paul's treatment of this situation.

**7:12b** Again, in view of the broad area of meaning of ἀφιέναι (*aphienai*), it is best rendered by "renounce" or "repudiate". Is the brother to ἀφιέναι (*aphienai*) an unbelieving wife if she is willing to live with him? (Paul says, No.)

**7:13** Similarly, is a γυνη (*gunē*) to ἀφιεναι (*aphienai*) an unbelieving husband if he is willing to live with her? (Paul says, No.)

**7:14** Paul adds three other comments to his answers. *Firstly*, The believing partner sanctifies the other. (Presumably Paul here gives the sanction for continuing the close and intimate relationship of marriage, which otherwise the believing partner may have felt obliged to break off.) If this were not the case, the children of the union would be unclean, but as it is they are holy. This does not mean "saved" or "Christian", as if this is something which one obtains by inheritance. What Paul is saying is that the children of even one believer, where the other parent is not willing to be converted, are "holy", "set apart for God", in the same way as are the children of two believing parents. That is, through the believing parent the children have access to the gospel and can respond to God's call by personal faith.

**7:15a** If the unbelieving partner separates (χοριζω, *chorizō*), what should the believer do? (Paul says, Let the unbelieving partner separate.) If such cases arise, is the believer still bound? (Paul says, No.) The ESV translates, "In such cases the brother or sister is not enslaved." The usual rendering of the verb is "not bound" (RSV, NIV, NRSV, Beck, Phillips, Williams, etc.; TEV: "free to act"; Jerusalem: "not tied").

There is a difference of interpretation about the meaning of "not bound", as to whether or not it allows remarriage. The general opinion is that no marriage bond (no matter how conceived) can be held to continue existing when Paul says a person is not bound; though some say that Paul means that the believer is "not bound" in the sense of "not required" to try to prevent the separation of the unbelieving partner (NEB: "under no compulsion"). However, although "required", in this sense, is a possible meaning of the English word "bound", it is not the normal meaning of the Greek word used here, δουλοω (*douloō*).

**7:15b** Then *secondly*, God has called us to peace. Or, in peace. NIV: "to live in peace". Presumably this is the reason why the unbeliever is to be allowed to separate without difficulties being placed in the way. If the unbeliever wishes to depart and is in some way prevented from doing so, "peace" is hardly likely to be a feature of the resultant marital situation. If we take "peace" to mean "concord", the spirit of happy contentment in a true marriage, then the fact that this is lost if continued cohabitation is retained by some kind of coercion (e.g., social or economic) constitutes a reason for allowing the unbelieving partner to depart. Alternatively, we could take it, with Garland, that what Paul is saying is that if husband and wife have a harmonious marriage even though one of them is not a believer, then this religious difference is not a valid ground for breaking up that harmonious relationship.

**7:16 *Thirdly*,** You do not know whether you shall save your unbelieving partner. This is quite ambiguous. It could mean, "You cannot be sure that you will save your unbelieving partner, and by keeping him/her from leaving, you may be condemning yourself pointlessly to a life without peace; so let them go." It could equally well mean, "You cannot rule out the possibility that you could save your unbelieving partner if you stayed together, so make every effort to continue the marriage if at all possible."

If we must choose between these two, the second may be more likely in view of Paul's attitude in verses 12-13, and in the light of 1 Peter 3:1. However the uncertainty may be intentional, and the meaning along these lines: "You do not know how things would turn out if the marriage continued, whether your partner would remain an unbeliever or would become a Christian, so do not take the initiative yourself in ending the marriage, but accept it if the unbelieving partner separates."

As is the case in v.11a, Paul is dealing in these verses with a real life situation. In the present case, the ideal solution to the problem is not capable of achievement, as the unbeliever is leaving. The ideal is that the unbelieving spouse continues the marriage and is saved (v.16): but what is a Christian to do in other cases? The answer is: accept the dissolution of the marriage.

This is not an acceptable solution, not a solution of which Paul approves. It is not in fact a solution of the problem at all, and Paul certainly is not happy with the break-up of the marriage. Rather, it is a realistic recognition of the fact that, as Jesus himself said (Luke 14:26; 18:29), there would be occasions when the impact of the gospel would separate husband from wife.

It is unfortunate when this is what happens rather than the other partner becoming a Christian - but it does happen, and when it does, it must be accepted (v.15). The marriage relationship is being sundered by the unbelieving partner in separating: there is no use trying to hold together the outward appearances of a marriage which has been shattered because the inner union of husband and wife has gone.

We may take it from 1 Corinthians 7:39 ("in the Lord") and 2 Corinthians 6:14 that Paul is considering here, in 7:12-16, the case where one marriage partner becomes converted, rather than that of a believer marrying a non-believer: we see in v.12 that the brother *has a wife* who is not a believer, not *marries a woman* who is not a believer. Similarly a wife *has* an unbelieving husband, v.13.

John Chrysostom brings this out clearly (Kovacs 117):

> Paul is not addressing those who had never married, but those already married. He does not say, "If someone wants to marry an unbeliever," but "If anyone has a spouse who is an unbeliever." This means: if someone received the Christian faith after marrying, and the partner remains an unbeliever but is content to continue living together, the Christian should not seek a divorce.

Similarly Tertullian writes (Kovacs 117):

> Perhaps by understanding this admonition concerning married believers in an unrestricted sense they think it is permissible to marry unbelievers. God forbid! Anyone who interprets this way knowingly ensnares himself! It is plain that this scripture names those who were found by the grace of God when already married to a non-believer.

Even so, Paul's comments would also apply if a Christian, contrary to the command of Scripture in this matter, were to marry a non-Christian.


# SOME PRACTICAL AND PASTORAL REFLECTIONS

## Questions of Contraception and Birth Control (7:2-5)

In many parts of the Church today there will be found doubts and hesitations about the Christian use of contraceptives, or certain types of contraceptives. The whole issue of birth control is considered suspect by some Christians. What light is thrown upon this issue from Scripture?

Seeing that in 7:2-5 Paul has clearly shown the relational role of sex in marriage as quite distinct from the function of sex in procreation, then equally clearly it is legitimate for husband and wife to engage in sexual intercourse in fulfillment of its *relational* role while taking appropriate steps (viz, contraception) to exclude fulfillment of its *procreational* role. This is a direct and immediate application of Paul's teaching which would have been as relevant in Paul's own day when contraception, although rather less efficient than today, was widely discussed, accepted, and practised.

So what do we know about the attitude to, and practice of, contraception in the ancient world? An important expert in this field is John T. Noonan. In his major work, *Contraception* 9-18, Noonan sets out what is known of the contraceptive practices of the ancient world, particularly amongst the Egyptians, Jews, Greeks, and Romans. To quote some of his relevant comments: he says,

The existence of contraceptive technique in the pre-Christian Mediterranean world is well established. The oldest surviving documents are from Egypt. Five different papyri, all dating from between 1900 and 1100 BC, provide recipes for contraceptive preparations to be used in the vulva. ... [Descriptions of the contents of the five papyri are given.] ... These prescriptions, aimed at blocking or killing the male semen, were rational ways of attempting contraception. ... The desire to prevent pregnancy by artificial means will be found even more characteristic of the society the Christians knew. ... Probably the effectiveness of these methods varied widely. ... How much was contraception practised? ... One possible limitation on diffusion scarcely existed: most writers do not speak of any moral objection to the dissemination of contraceptive information. The Hippocratic oath rejecting the use of some forms of abortion is famous; no similar pledge was made as to contraception.

So similarly, Peter Fryer, *The Birth Controllers* 17ff.

The post-apostolic church came to condemn contraception, but there is no evidence of this attitude in Paul's teaching, or indeed anywhere in the Bible. Noonan on pages 35f. discusses the Old Testament milieu and teaching, and in particular the story of Onan in Genesis 38:8-10, which is often adduced as a condemnation of contraception. His conclusions on this story and on the more general issue are:

That contraception as such is condemned is unlikely. There is no commandment against contraception in any of the codes of law. A comparison between the provisions on other sexual matters and on contraception points up the omission. ... It is surely strange that ... the illegality of contraception [be] left to inference, if the compliers of the Pentateuch believed contraception to be unlawful. It can scarcely be surmised that there was no occasion to legislate on contraception. The story itself [i.e. about Onan] shows that coitus interruptus was a practice known by at least the first millennium B.C. The Egyptian documents reflect the practice of contraception in a country that had great cultural influence on the Jews. The people of Israel knew no immunity from the sexual customs of their neighbors. There is explicit post-Exilic legislation against homosexuality, against bestiality, and against temple prostitution (Lev. 18:22, 20:13, 20:15-16, Deut. 23:18). If these acts had to be prohibited by law it seems unlikely that, in the absence of clear prohibition, the Jewish people would have believed that coitus interruptus or the use of contraceptives was immoral.

Similarly, the evidence given by Noonan and by Fryer shows the wide extent of the knowledge of and use of contraception in New Testament times. There are many sexual issues dealt with explicitly in the New Testament, and many wrong practices condemned, but contraception is *not* included amongst them.

To sum up: Paul's teaching in 1 Corinthians 7:2-5 about the place of sexual expression in marriage, in which procreation is never once mentioned, thus strongly indicates the legitimacy of fulfilling the **relational** role of sex in marriage while excluding the **procreational**, and thus the legitimacy of the use of contraception to this end.

The post-apostolic church, contrary to Paul's teaching here, came to the opinion that (to quote Clement of Alexandria): "To have coition other than to procreate children is to do injury to nature", so that "husbands use their wives moderately and only for the raising up of children". (Noonan 76 gives these and similar quotations.) Within such a view there was obviously no place for contraception, and therefore it is rejected with varying degrees of condemnation, John Chrysostom going so far as to regard "contraception as worse than homicide, a mutilation of nature" (Noonan 79). These views are totally without biblical warrant.

For further discussion of issues of birth control, including contraplantives (which inhibit implantation) and sterilization and vasectomy, see Chapter 11 and also Appendix B of my book *Marriage and Divorce*.

Furthermore, we need to recognize the huge and fundamental difference between animal sex and human sexuality. Re this, see my same book, Appendix A, for a detailed comparison and contrast of the character of animal sex with human sex, highlighting the totally misguided, unchristian, nature of the use of animal sex, "the birds and the bees", as a basis for teaching children about human sexuality.

### The Significance of the Matter of Paul's Marriage (7:6-9)

It is sometimes assumed (especially on the basis of 7:6-9, and also 9:5) that Paul was a bachelor who never married, and who commended that unmarried celibate state for others to follow also. This assumed example of Paul has often been used as the basis for the pastoral encouragement for a young person not to marry at all. We should therefore examine the evidence concerning Paul's marital state. These are the relevant factors to note (based on my *Ministry of Women in the Church* pages 27 to 31):

**(a)** It was the cultural norm for every Jew to be married by their mid-twenties at the latest. Marriages for Jewish young people were arranged by their parents, and it was a matter of some shame if a marriage could not be arranged. There are no grounds of any kind for thinking that this normal Jewish pattern would not have taken place in Paul's family.

**(b)** Paul expressly states (Acts 22:3, Philippians 3:4-6, and especially Galatians 1:13-14) that he followed the traditions of his people. It is hard to credit that he could have said about himself, "I was advancing in

Judaism beyond many Jews of my own age and was extremely zealous for the traditions of my ancestors" if he had failed to conform to the Jewish tradition about marriage.

(c) There is external evidence that to be a married man was a requirement for membership of the Jewish high Council, the Sanhedrin. And it would appear, from the New Testament evidence, that Paul (Saul) was a member of the Sanhedrin - he was well qualified for this office; his statement in Acts 26:10 that he voted for the death penalty for Christians is most naturally to be taken as referring to his participating in the formal vote in the Sanhedrin; the witnesses against Stephen brought him before the Sanhedrin (Acts 6:12, 15); the wording of Acts 7:57 shows that the members of the Sanhedrin accompanied the witnesses against Stephen who (according to custom) carried out the stoning, and it is more reasonable to read this account as indicating that the witnesses entrusted their clothes to a known member of the Sanhedrin group (i.e. Saul) than to an unknown stranger who happened along at that time (see also Acts 22:20); the ready access of Paul (Saul) to the high priest and the way the latter delegated authority to Paul (Acts 9:1-2; cf. 22:4-5) is also more likely if Paul were a Sanhedrin member.

(d) Paul was a chosen and prepared vessel for the ministry he was given. His perception of the nature of the marriage relationship (especially in 1 Corinthians 7:2-5 and Ephesians 5:21-33E) strongly suggests that the Lord is enabling him to understand the nature of a relationship which he himself knows from experience.

Now, it would be *possible* for the Lord to use, as the vehicle for the Bible's teaching about the nature of the marriage relationship, a person who had never been married: but the Lord's usual way is to work through someone whom he has prepared for that role, and the normal preparation for a person to write about the nature of marriage would be to be married.

(e) It cannot be argued that Paul rejected marriage from Christian conviction or because of the dangerous nature of his future ministry, because his parents would have arranged his marriage at a time prior to his conversion.

(f) Paul accepted that Christian leaders would be married, and that in this regard he and Barnabas were exceptions (see 1 Corinthians 9:5).

(g) Paul does not ever refer to himself as παρθενος (*parthenos*), or suggest in any way that he had never married; on the contrary: in 7:8 Paul writes, "Now to the ἀγαμοι (*agamoi*) and widows I say: it is good for them to stay as I am." That is, he classes himself with those who had previously been married, and had not subsequently remarried, and recommends to his readers that in this regard they follow his example.

There is no evidence on the other side, that is, in support of the view that Paul had never married; and there are no reasonable grounds for holding such a view. The evidence that we do have, as set out here, is best explained on the basis that Paul was a widower.

A second possibility is that his wife, being (as one would expect for the wife of such a man as Saul) a committed Judaist, may have left him after his conversion to Christ: in Philippians 3:4-8 Paul refers to his old life in Judaism before his conversion, and adds, "... Christ Jesus my Lord, for whose sake I have lost all things", which may have included his wife (cf. Luke 14:26; 18:29).

The least likely possibility is that Paul had never married at all.

### Sex, Marriage, Divorce, And Remarriage; And How Long to "Remain"

The background circumstances at Corinth, and a consideration of the linguistic issues in a given passage, are both relevant in assessing the meaning of numbers of passages in the Corinthian correspondence. We have been considering several passages in 1 Corinthians 6 and 7 in the light of the interaction of these two factors.

We have seen in chapter 6 that some of the new converts at Corinth believed that they were free to continue to satisfy their sexual wants through promiscuity, in the manner of everyone else around them. Paul points out that all the members of our bodies belong to Christ, and we cannot take the members of Christ and give them to a prostitute: for union with a prostitute is only a "one-body" union, and this conflicts with the plan of God, that our sexuality is to be fulfilled only in the - different - total "one-flesh" union of marriage.

Others of the converts at Corinth had gone to the opposite extreme. Aware of the abuse of sexuality that was practised at Corinth, they had concluded that *all* sexual activity was wrong, or at least, "not good", even in marriage between husband and wife. They wrote to Paul about this, seeking his support (it would appear) for this view. Paul rejects the idea categorically and shows how sexual fulfillment in marriage for husband and wife is God's intention for us.

Others again at Corinth had marriages (or at least, sexual relationships) which, for whatever reason, had terminated. What now was God's word to them in their situation? Paul counsels against precipitate action. Remain, he advises, as *he* is.

When this situation has arisen from the break-up of a marriage relationship, then a particular aim is mentioned: reconciliation between the spouses - which of course would become impossible if one of them married a third person. But Paul recognizes that God has given to some people the gift of living a single, celibate life, and to others the gift of being a marriage partner. If persons whose previous relationship has terminated (for whatever reason) should find, after seeking now to live the single life, that this is *not* the gift that God has given them but that their sexual nature remains a force within them and they need to live as a marriage partner, then Paul's word to such people is - v.9 - "They must marry".

How is Paul's teaching to be interpreted and applied? In his comments on verses 10 and 11, Hodge 113 presents a widely-held view:

> The wife had no right to leave her husband; nor had the husband the right to repudiate his wife. But although the marriage bond cannot be dissolved by any human authority, because it is, in virtue of the law of God, a covenant for life between one man and one woman; yet it can be annulled, not rightfully indeed, but still effectively. Adultery annuls it, because it is a breach of the specific contract involved in marriage. And so does, for the same reason, willful desertion, as the apostle teaches in a following verse. This is the Protestant doctrine concerning divorce, founded on the nature of marriage and on the explicit instructions of our Lord, Matt 5:32; 19:3-9; Mark 10:2-12; Luke 16:18. According to this doctrine nothing but adultery or willful desertion is a legitimate ground of divorce. ... The plain doctrine of the passage before us, as well as other portions of the word of God, is that marriage is an indissoluble covenant between one man and one woman for life, admitting neither of polygamy or of divorce. If the covenant be annulled, it can only be by the sinful act of one of the parties.

Although I have a very high regard for Hodge's scholarship, on this point I consider that he is completely mistaken, and that this common view is an absolute distortion of what Scripture actually teaches. I have set out my objections more fully in my book *Marriage and Divorce: The New Testament Teaching*, but it is relevant to summarize the major points here:

Scripture knows nothing of "annulling" a marriage on the basis of adultery or desertion. Jesus and Paul both say that husband and wife must *not* χοριζω (*chorizō*, sunder) the marriage relationship that God has joined together. Contrary to Hodge, these things are *not* "legitimate grounds of divorce". There are *no* "legitimate" grounds for divorce. But Paul recognizes in this passage that there are numbers of factors which can destroy a marriage. Not, as Hodge puts it, "breach a contract" or "annul a covenant", but demolish a relationship.

Now, being a realist, Paul addresses himself in verses 6 to 11 to this situation: what to do after a marriage has ended.

I particularly draw attention to the tacit assumption that is often being made concerning the ex-wife in 7:11, when she is instructed to "remain unmarried". The assumption is that this means, "for the term of her natural life" - so that all possibility of her ever having another marriage partner is completely ruled out. Or, at the very least, some would say, until her ex-husband dies.

That is to say, on this view, you get one shot at marriage - even if, perhaps, you married in haste before becoming a Christian - and if for any reason that marriage doesn't work out, it doesn't matter, that was your one and only chance. You don't get another. All that Paul says in this chapter about not having the gift of living celibate, being subject to overwhelming temptation and sexual pressure, and needing a partner, may apply to you, but you still must "remain unmarried". Well, that's how some teachers see it.

How long does Paul say you must "remain unmarried"? Actually, he doesn't say. What Paul does do, however, is give the reason for it: it is to leave open the possibility of reconciliation. Garland 283 points out,

> It may seem that Paul presents the Christian wife with two options: either remain unmarried or be reconciled to her believing husband ... But he directs her to remain unmarried *in order to* be reconciled with her husband. ... In Paul's Jewish tradition, a wife who has been divorced and has married another is forbidden to her former husband (Deut 24:4 ...) If there was to be a reconciliation she must remain unmarried.

Now, some situations may be borderline or uncertain. But in the majority of cases a person will be able to know within a reasonable period of time whether there is, realistically, any possibility of a reconciliation with one's former spouse - whether whatever were the problems between them can be resolved. Paul's teaching clearly envisages giving this possibility a real chance. His instructions weigh against taking any precipitate action which would rule out this possibility prematurely. But when it becomes quite clear that reconciliation is not any longer a genuine possibility (if it ever was), what is the reason then for being bound to "remain unmarried"? The reason which Paul has given for it no longer applies.

All too often one learns in pastoral ministry of cases where a spouse, in obedience to this verse (as they suppose), will pass up all opportunities of a second marriage and condemn themselves to a solitary life and a lonely old age. But in fact when they have sought for a basis for reconciliation, and have seen beyond question that this can never happen, then they have thus done what Paul in v.11 has instructed them to do.

We need to recognize that while a broken marriage and divorce is a sin of disobedience against the clear word of both Paul and Christ himself, yet it is *not* the unforgivable sin, and by grace a divorcee can seek and receive God's forgiveness.

A person should follow Paul's outlined procedure: first, "remain unmarried" to seek for reconciliation; if this proves impossible, what then? Then they are back in the general situation of ἄγαμοι (*agamoi*) as described in verses 7-9. They must consider whether they are now being given by the Lord the gift of celibacy, as shown in v.7 - if so, then they are to continue unmarried, as Paul did, v.8. But if instead they find themselves in the situation Paul describes in v.9, and if the opportunity is available, then they must do what Paul tells the ἄγαμοι (*agamoi*) in that verse: "they must remarry".

### Popular Prejudice Against Paul: and His Actual Teaching

Johnson 105f. sums up the situation re opinions about Paul:

> Throughout church history and to the present, Paul's remarks on sex and marriage in chapter 7 have been viewed quite differently depending on the commentator or reader. Opinions range all the way from seeing Paul as a great supporter of marriage and sexual relations to viewing him as having quite a negative view of sex and marriage and being an enemy of women. Augustine and other early church fathers, for example, took verse 1 as the basis for rejecting, as a venial sin, sexual intercourse for mutual enjoyment, even within marriage (*Confessions* 2.3). ... While not all of the apostle's views in the chapter resonate with modern sympathies, much of the negative attitude towards Paul's views is based on misunderstandings of what he actually said.

Indeed, a careful examination of what Paul actually says in 1 Corinthians 6 and 7 (with attention to the Greek) shows that the commonly-held negative picture of Paul and his teaching about marriage and sex is completely unsupported by the facts and indeed is a serious misconception. It is an interesting study in itself (but beyond the scope of our present purposes) to trace how such views about Paul's teaching arose in the church and have been perpetuated down the years in an interpretational tradition. If however we pay heed to Paul's actual words, assume that he chose them carefully to convey his intended meaning, and give them their full weight, we see that he is not anti-sex, nor anti-woman, nor anti-marriage.

Paul does not affirm that a relationship with a prostitute is on a par with the one-flesh relationship of marriage: rather, he contrasts the two.

He does not affirm that an act of sexual intercourse establishes a marriage between a man and a woman: rather, he shows how the purely physical union ("one body") with a prostitute does violence to God's plan that sex shall be part of a total one-flesh union.

He does not affirm that sex is somehow unspiritual or contrary to God's perfect will: rather, he affirms the positive plan of God for sex in marriage.

He does not affirm that sex is for the purpose of procreation: rather, he describes sex entirely in terms of the relationship between a husband and wife, a vital component of their total relationship that is not to be treated as unimportant nor to be foregone (except perhaps by agreement for a short time for good reason).

He does not denigrate woman as the "unequal" partner in marriage: rather, he gives her an honored equal place alongside her husband in the sexual sphere of marriage and shows a recognition of her sexuality which is quite without parallel in the ancient world, and says about her absolutely the same things as he says about her husband.

He does not affirm that celibacy is a higher calling than marriage: rather, he emphasizes that it is by God's gift that some people are to be single and equally by God's gift that others are to be married - and, unless given by God the gift of being single, each man should have his own wife, and each woman her own husband.

He does not affirm that separation is the solution for a difficult marriage: rather, he quotes and underlines Christ's prohibition on separation, and then gives guidelines for a person caught in such a situation, aimed at facilitating reconciliation.

He does not affirm that marriage is incapable of dissolution: rather, he recognizes that a person is unmarried (single) when a marriage relationship has been discontinued, and asserts that a person is not bound in the empty shell of a marriage when the reality has gone.

He does not affirm that remarriage is either wrong or impossible: rather, while affirming categorically that husband and wife must not separate he confronts realistically the situation that does result when a person becomes ἄγαμος (*agamos*) and he instructs that, if such a person has tested whether he now has the gift of being able to live a celibate life and found that he cannot, then that person should marry.

We must beware of "trendy" interpretations of Scripture which simply adjust the teaching of the Bible so as to make it more congenial to contemporary thinking. We must also beware of elevating traditional interpretations of Scripture to a position of authority co-equal with the text of the Word of God itself.

## 6. Leading The Life That The Lord Assigns (7:17-24)

Paul now interrupts his specific treatment of marriage to set what he
has said on this subject into a wider context, and to give a few comments
and general principles. The underlying theme of this passage may be
stated in these terms: "In all aspects of a person's life, the normal principle to follow is: after a man is converted, he should still continue in the
life he was leading before. So the instruction to continue if at all possible
to live in marriage with an unconverted spouse is one instance of a general rule that is to be followed in other areas of life as well."

Hillyer's Commentary on 1 Corinthians 7 describes this thus:

> The conditional liberty allowed in the matter of mixed marriage is
> exceptional. Normally a Christian is to continue to *lead the life* he was
> living when God's call to become a Christian came to him; i.e. he is
> socially, etc., to stay put. No violent changes should be made simply
> because of conversion; this applies to differences of racial custom and
> social status. Paul twice underlines this principle (verses 20, 24) as he
> discusses the great dividing factors in religion and society in his day,
> circumcision and slavery.

Paul gives two comments concerning this principle; that it is his rule
for all the churches (v.17) - i.e. it is not something which applies exclusively to the Corinthians; and, secondly, that this principle that everyone
should "follow the life that the Lord has assigned to him, the vocation to
which God has called him" applies not only in relation to marriage but
throughout life generally (verses 18-24).

**7:17** Paul's teaching does not mean - and is not to be interpreted to
mean - that whatever a man is in every way when converted, that he
must always remain thereafter; rather, if a slave has the opportunity of
gaining his freedom legally, by all means let him take it (v.21). But
Paul's teaching is directed against violent and sudden changes when one
is converted: such as separating from a spouse who is not a Christian,
perhaps because of the idea that the close intimacy of marriage would be
impossible for a Christian with a non-Christian.

**7:18-19** Another issue of importance which Paul mentions in this section is: "Circumcision is nothing and uncircumcision is nothing. Keeping
God's commands is what counts." (NIV.) This reminds us forcibly of
Paul's viewpoint, the principle underlying his whole theology: it is not
the outward, the fleshly, that counts (circumcision or uncircumcision),
but that which goes to the root of the matter, one's relationship with
God.

And this relationship, which Paul refers to on other occasions in a
multitude of ways - being "in Christ", having adoption as sons, living by

faith, and so on and so on (cf. for example Galatians 5:6) - he here speaks of as "keeping God's commands". Such a wording is, in the context of this chapter, quite significant. Paul only gives one logion as specifically a charge of the Lord (v.10), but he writes here (v.19) of "commandments of God" (plural). Doubtless these words of his have general applicability, but it seems that they also apply in particular to his own instructions in this chapter, and that this verse is to be understood in the light of his confident claim to God's inspiration in verses 25b and 40b.

**7:20-24** Paul here thrice reiterates the principle (verses 17, 20, and 24), "Each one should remain in the condition in which he was called": which applies even if it means having to accept slavery (v.21a) - though this is not intended to prevent a slave from regaining his freedom if he can (v.21b). "You were bought with a price" repeats 6:20, though here with fresh application. MacArthur 169ff. writes, concerning this passage:

> Much has been said and written about the social role and responsibility of the church. Periodically throughout church history, and strongly in our own day, people have claimed that Christianity should be an agent of external social reform, even of revolution if necessary. ...

> First Corinthians 7:17-24 is not a full treatise on that subject, but it plainly teaches the basic principle by which Christians should look at and respond to the civil and social conditions in which they live. The principle is this: Christians should willingly accept the situation into which God has placed them and be content to serve Him there. It is a principle against which human nature rebels, and Paul states it three times in these 8 verses, so that his readers could not miss his point. ...

> When it is faithfully followed, however, biblical Christianity cannot help having radical effects on every person, institution, and practice around it. But the primary purpose of the gospel is to change people, not change society. Its focus is on inward change, not outward. We should be satisfied to be where God has put us, to accept what the Lord has assigned us, and to be faithful in whatever condition God has called us. ...

> Christians can be Christians in a dictatorship, a democracy, or even under anarchy. We can be Christians whether we are man, woman, child, married, single, divorced, Jew, Gentile, slave, or free. ... The gospel can be planted and take root wherever there is a person to hear and accept it, even in countries or in families that are pagan, atheistic, humanistic, and avowedly anti-Christian. As the saying goes, we should bloom where we are planted. Where the Lord has assigned and where God has called is where we should walk. ... God allows us to be where we are and to stay where we are for a purpose. Conversion is not the signal for a person to leave his social condition, his marriage or his singleness, his human master, or his other circumstances. We are to leave sin and anything that encourages sin; but otherwise we are to stay where we are until God moves us.

## 7. Problems About The Unmarried (7:25-40E)

### (a) Preliminary Question:
### To Whom Is Paul Writing In This Passage?

This final section of Paul's discussion of sex and marriage - verses 25 to 40 - is quite ambiguous for us. Doubtless his readers at Corinth knew exactly what he was talking about. But we do not.

At issue, basically, is the question of just who it is that Paul is addressing in this entire section in general, and in verses 36 to 38 in particular. To a large extent these verses are the crux of the matter, so we need to look at them first of all.

Hurd 171 maintains:

> This passage is one of the most difficult and controversial in the New Testament, because a number of serious ambiguities occur in these three verses.

Indeed: this passage is possibly the most completely ambiguous passage in the entire New Testament - so much so that translations sometimes give two completely different versions of it (as in the NIV, and Barclay's translation).

In the Greek text, Paul is discussing the question (quite possibly raised by the Corinthians in their letter to Paul) of what a man should do about his virgin. What are we to take this to mean?

There are three views found in the translations: (a) These verses could be referring to a man and his fiancée to whom he is betrothed (taken thus by the ESV, RSV, NRSV, NIV, TEV, and Phillips). (b) The verses could be referring to a custom that was known from later centuries but is not attested from New Testament times, of "a man and a woman living together under vows of chastity" (Jerusalem Bible margin; also taken this way by the NEB). Or (c) the verses could be discussing the responsibility of a father to arrange for the marriage of his daughter, and who was seeking to know what was the right thing for him to do in the present crisis situation at Corinth in the light of Paul's teaching (7:26) about "holding to the status quo" (NASB, NIV margin, Jerusalem Bible).

Hodge and Garland present the case for the two main, differing, positions, Hodge taking the older, traditional interpretation, and Garland arguing for the major alternative position.

Hodge 132f. presents his viewpoint on v.36 thus:

> This and the following verse are addressed to fathers, for with them, according to the usage both of Jews and Greeks, rested the disposal of the daughters of the family. Though the apostle regarded marriage at

that time as inexpedient, he tells fathers that they were perfectly free to exercise their own judgement in giving their daughters in marriage, or keeping them single.

Hodge then proceeds to exegete the passage from this perspective. Similarly Robertson & Plummer 158f., who say,

> The verse indicates that the Corinthians had asked him about the duty of a father with a daughter of age to marry. The question is what he ought to do, not what she ought to do: his wishes, not hers, are paramount. This is in accordance with the ideas of that age, and the Apostle does not condemn them. ... It is wholly improbable that *tis, autou,* and *hos* (v.37) refer to the suitor, the prospective bridegroom. The Corinthians would not have asked about him. It is the father's or guardian's duty that is the question.

To the contrary, Garland sets out the three views I have mentioned above, and then argues against two of them. The interpretation that the reference is to a non-sexual "spiritual marriage" is effectively refuted by his arguments against it, and I consider we can put this possibility aside. Our choice is thus between the other two views: that Paul is discussing (a) a father and his virgin daughter, or (b) a man and his fiancée.

Which approach to the passage is correct? Both are well supported. Hodge's approach is the traditional one - it was the common interpretation amongst the early Church Fathers. Thus for cxample on these verses Theodoret says (Kovacs 128):

> If a father thinks that his daughter's remaining unmarried is a disgrace and so wishes to unite her with a husband, let him do as he sees fit. For there is no sin in marriage.

On the other hand, Garland argues for the interpretation that this passage refers to a man in relation to a possible marriage to his betrothed fiancée.

This is the usual one taken by commentators today - though not all of them: for example, in his recent (2000) Commentary on 1 Corinthians, Barnett says (on v. 36), "Apparently a father from the congregation has expressed concern that in barring the way for the marriage of a daughter who is somewhat older than the norm ... he may have acted in an unseemly way", and Barnett then interprets this passage accordingly. So also does Naylor 150ff. (1996). But unquestionably most of the recent commentaries - and translations - take Paul to be referring to a man and his fiancée.

Do Garland's arguments against the father/daughter scenario effectively demolish this viewpoint? I do not believe they do. It seems to me that the two possibilities are much more evenly balanced than would appear from Garland's presentation. Numerous commentators have specifically referred to the difficulty of deciding the case. Garland himself cites one of them - Moiser; while Hurd, as we have seen earlier, called this issue "one of the most difficult and controversial in the New Testament". And Orr & Walther 223f. write, "Few passages of Scripture of such length bristle with more difficulties than does this."

Garland's arguments against the "father/daughter" interpretation are effectively rebutted in the literature on the passage. For example, as to Garland's arguments #3 and #5 (pages 337f.), regarding "virgins", and γαμιζω (*gamizō*), Orr & Walther 223 point out:

> There is considerable ambiguity in the phrase *his virgin*. Again, no line of argument offers incontrovertible evidence; the explanation given will usually support the overall interpretation adopted ... There is evidence in Greek literature for the use of *parthenos* as both 'fiancée' and 'daughter'. This passage must finally be understood without a sure decision about this phrase ... By interpreting the person in question as a father, v.38 readily makes sense. The meaning of the New Testament word *gamizō* is clearly 'to give in marriage' in the only other [New Testament] occurrences."

Robertson & Plummer 159 are definite in their judgement:

> The γαμιζων [*gamizōn*, give in marriage] is decisive: the Apostle is speaking of a father or guardian disposing of an unmarried daughter or ward.

How then do we come to a position on this issue? I myself am influenced in my own decision by three factors:

**1.** *What we know of the situation existing in New Testament times, when Paul wrote*: that is, what are the background circumstances prevailing behind this Epistle? The answer is: that in this society, marriages were normally arranged marriages - arranged by the parents between their families (i.e. marriage had wider implications than just the feelings and preferences of the bride and groom). Frequently we do not give this factor due weight: we are in danger of reading-back our twenty-first century attitudes into the first century world. We shrink from the idea of our parents arranging who we are to marry, and so we recoil from the recognition of the fact that this is the way it was in the first century. Actually, this is still the way it is, in a large number of societies in the world today, and if we think our "free romantic choice" approach is so much better, we could perhaps reflect upon (a) how many people today of both sexes do not marry because they "do not find the right person", and so they are "left on the shelf", matrimonially speaking, and (b) the fact that our society's approach is not all that markedly successful in steering people towards lasting and satisfactory marriages, if we note the number of marriages today that end in divorce or separation. So, given the cultural circumstances of the day - that the person who was primarily responsible for whether a young virgin married or not was her father - there is an *a priori* presumption, other things being equal, that this is the implied situation Paul is discussing.

**2. What the early Church Fathers thought.** This is not always decisive - they could be wrong. But they did live so much closer than we do to the apostolic age, and they would in many ways be in a better position than we are to judge how to take ambiguous passages. And in relation to the present passage, their common view was that Paul was speaking of a father and his virgin daughter.

**3. The actual words Paul used.** I take it that Paul chose his words accurately, under the inspiration of the Holy Spirit, so we should take careful note of them. And in v.38 Paul speaks of giving or not giving the virgin in marriage, γαμίζω (*gamizō*). Concerning this word Orr & Walther 223 write,

> The verb *gamizein* regularly means 'give in marriage' and not 'marry' in the New Testament, and it does not occur in Greek literature prior to the New Testament literature.

A fact that Garland omits to mention. So there is no adequate reason here for us to depart from its usual meaning, and I do not consider that we should do so. For these reasons I agree here with Hodge's interpretation, not Garland's.

## (b) The Question of the "Present Crisis" or "Impending Distress"

In introducing this section of his discussion, Paul again disclaims (v.25b) any specific command of the Lord applicable in this particular situation, but again also he gives his own opinion, here adding, "as one who by the Lord's mercy is trustworthy". Together with his authority to make these suggestions we notice his tentativeness, his "I think" (v.26), "I would spare you that" (v.28), "I want you to be free from anxieties" (v.32), "I say this for your own benefit, not to lay any restraint upon you" (v.35). His whole attitude in this section is conditioned by one factor which he mentions three times: "in view of the present distress" (v.26), "the appointed time has grown very short" (v.29), "For the present form of this world is passing away" (v.31).

The word describing the situation to which Paul is referring can be translated as either "impending" or "present": the Greek term refers to something that is just at the point of happening, like a wave overhanging and just about to break. Garland presents a case for taking it here as something that has become present amongst them.

Exactly what Paul is referring to we cannot say with certainty. A common interpretation is that Paul was expecting the promised Second Advent of Christ at any time, so that this teaching in 1 Corinthians 7:25-40 is an "interimsethik", an ethic for a temporary situation, because the end of the age was approaching. Support for this view is drawn from 1 Corinthians 15:51, "We shall not all sleep, but we shall all be changed", which can be taken to indicate that he expected that some of his readers would be alive at the *parousia*, the Appearing of Christ.

Now, it is clear, from the prominence of the theme in his writings and the explicit teaching that he gives concerning it, that the expectation of the Second Advent was very real to Paul. The question is whether it was *this* expectation which he meant when he said, "the appointed time has grown very short". He is certainly giving, in 1 Corinthians 7:25-40, instructions (or should we say, suggestions) which are conditioned by his belief in some "present crisis" or "impending distress" - is this referring to the *parousia*? Is Paul's ethical teaching in 1 Corinthians conditioned by this expectation? How does that affect us today, as we still await the *parousia*?

Against such a view is Paul's attitude in the two Thessalonian epistles, which were written earlier. In the First Epistle he expounds the theme of the Second Advent with explicit detail, and great enthusiasm (4:13-5:11). But there are no exhortations there in 1 Thessalonians in the ethical area such as we find in 1 Corinthians 7. However, the Thessalonians took him to mean that the Second Advent *was* imminent, and, in fact, just about to burst upon them. Paul therefore sends a short and hasty second letter in which he explicitly states that that day is not yet upon them nor indeed will come until some other events have first taken place (2 Thessalonians 2:1-12). Therefore those who have ceased their work to live in idleness (apparently influenced by the nearness of the end of all things) are to do their work normally and live their lives normally, and not to be supported by the charity of others (2 Thessalonians 2:15; 3:6-14).

If Paul writes thus in the Thessalonian epistles, how can we reconcile this with his completely different approach in 1 Corinthians 7? The answer may be, "Because when he wrote 1 Corinthians the *parousia* was that much the closer; hence more extreme measures were called for." If this be so, then it would be reasonable to see Paul's eschatological conviction showing itself again in 2 Corinthians, and also in Romans, both epistles written shortly after the time of 1 Corinthians, when the *parousia* must have been even nearer still. But although ethical issues **are** raised in these epistles (particularly in Romans) there are no short-term, hold-fast-to-the-status-quo instructions like those in 1 Corinthians 7. We do indeed find in Romans 13:11-12a,

> Besides this you know the time, that the hour has come for you to wake from sleep. For salvation is nearer to us now than when we first believed. The night is far gone; the day is at hand.

But Paul draws from this exactly the same kind of ethical injunction to purity as does the apostle John some years later: and neither is in any way parallel to 1 Corinthians 7:

Romans 13:12b-14:

> So then let us cast off the works of darkness and put on the armor of light. Let us walk properly, as in the daytime, not in orgies and drunkenness, not in sexual immorality and sensuality, not in quarreling and jealousy. But put on the Lord Jesus Christ, and make no provision for the flesh, to gratify its desires.

1 John 2:28; 3:2, 3:

> And now, little children, abide in him, so that when he appears we may have confidence, and not shrink from him in shame at his coming. ... We know that when he appears, we will be like him, because we shall see him as he is. And everyone who thus hopes in him purifies himself, as he is pure.

Romans is more explicit in regard to what constitutes "pure behavior", and 1 John is more general; but the theme is the same. And there is nothing in either that could be said to be an "interimsethik" in the sense of an ethic which had application to the special circumstances before the *eschatos*, the end, and not otherwise.

I find this interpretation of Paul's comments to be totally unconvincing. It involves believing that Paul got things wrong, and had to change his mind on the subject when the *parousia* didn't arrive as expected. Some interpreters believe this: for example Stanley 127 holds

> 'the impending calamities ... to be the precursors of the end of the world, ... and this brings us to a point on which we are forewarned by Christ Himself, that even Apostles might be in error, for "of that day and that hour knoweth no man, no not the angels in heaven, neither the Son, but the Father."

This entire line of interpretation runs contrary to what we actually find in Paul's writings. And if 1 Corinthians 15:51 suggests that some will still be alive at the time of the *parousia*, it also equally suggests that some will **not**. It seems to be symbolic of this whole argument. The evidence can be made to point in whatever way one wants.

The evidence for this crisis or distress is limited to the period of 1 Corinthians, and it is not mentioned by Paul in such terms in any other letter. (The "sudden destruction" of 1 Thessalonians 5:3 and the vengeance and punishment of 2 Thessalonians 1:8-9 are specifically shown to be for the non-Christians and not the Christians.)

Instead, the "present crisis" or "impending distress" may well have been a situation of persecution or affliction. Or quite possibly (see Rosner 162f., Garland) it was a time of famine.

Therefore we see that Paul is here speaking in relation to a particular situation - probably such a period of trouble and persecution or other problems which was at that time hanging over their heads.

Whatever it was, it had apparently passed even by the time of 2 Corinthians - there he is busy organizing the collection for the saints (2 Corinthian 9:1ff.; this collection was already in hand in 1 Corinthians 16:1-4; but why plan such an extensive program, and - verses 3-9 - itinerary, if the end of all things was momentarily about to come?).

Moreover, in 2 Corinthians 6:14 he is prepared to exclude the marriage of unbelievers with believers, and by his selectiveness apparently to approve the marriage of believers together. Thus 1 Corinthians 7:27 seems no longer to apply.

So we cannot take the "present crisis" or "impending distress" of 1 Corinthians 7:26 to be the *parousia*. (For why would Paul call the *parousia* a "present crisis" or "distress"? The expectation of the *parousia* is a source of comfort - 1 Thessalonians 4:18.)

All this evidence shows that "the present distress" (whatever it was) does **not** refer to the *parousia*.

## Exegesis:
### (c) A Temporary Holding To The Status Quo (7:25-31)

**7:25-31** In the particular, limited, short-duration, local situation to which Paul addresses himself in 1 Corinthians 7:25-40, he recommends (it is no stronger than that) a temporary holding to the status quo. It is **not** an advocacy of celibacy - if a man is married (v.27), he is not to seek to be free. Grant's comment on 1 Corinthians 7 describes Paul's position:

> It was not a fundamental solution of the problems of marriage, but a temporary one. A parallel might be a group of shipwrecked passengers and crew on a lonely island, awaiting rescue. The best rule would certainly be, no change of status, marital or other!

The reason given by Paul for his suggestion is that the pattern of things was in a state of flux (v.31b) and to take upon oneself in those circumstances the added commitment of marriage, with its particular problems and troubles and responsibilities (v.28b), could prove burdensome.

Garland 370 says, "Throughout 7:25-38 this one issue - What should the betrothed do about marriage? - is in view." In looking at verses 36-38 Garland has put on a pair of theological spectacles, and now he sees everything through them. So Garland 320, agreeing with Fee 323, says that "It is more logical for the word ['virgin'] to retain the same meaning throughout, unless compelling evidence leads one to decide otherwise", and therefore he concludes that "The most plausible option is that 'virgins' comprise betrothed women" - which is consistent with his view of the interpretation of verses 36 to 38.

The ESV, following this line on interpretation, actually renders v.25a as "Now concerning the betrothed", putting an *interpretation* into the text instead of a *translation* (something which is quite reprehensible). Irrespective of how one sees the meaning of verses 36 to 38, there is no valid reason for departing in v.25 from the general sense "virgins".

Having thus far discussed the immoral (chapter 6), then those now married, the previously married, and those with an unbelieving spouse, Paul comes naturally to the remaining group: virgins. This would include the betrothed, but irrespective of how many of the virgins may have been betrothed, there is no valid justification for limiting the meaning of παρθενος (*parthenos*) to this sub-group.

**7:25** With the words "Now about virgins", Paul returns to his main theme and (presumably) to the next issue raised by the Corinthians in their letter to him. Paul's comments up to this point have been addressed to the married and those who had previously been married. He now addresses a word to virgins, those who have not been married - though (as we shall see) he also has a word for the married together with those who have previously been married.

"About virgins" is περι των παρθενων (*peri tōn parthenōn*), which may be either masculine or feminine, i.e. either female virgins or male virgins or probably, in this instance, both. It seems to be taken thus by the TEV and RSV translators, in their rendering "the unmarried"; similarly the AV, NASB, NIV, and NRSV translate literally as "Now concerning virgins ...". On the other hand Phillips restricts παρθενος (*parthenos*) to its more usual meaning and translates, "Now as far as young unmarried women are concerned"; while the NEB and the Jerusalem Bible take a different line altogether and render it, "On the question of celibacy".

The section deals with both unmarried men as well as unmarried woman (cf. vv. 27b, 32b), which seems to indicate against Phillips's version, and it discusses the question of whether the unmarried should marry or not, as distinct from the question of celibacy, so that the Jerusalem Bible and NEB rendering is unjustified by the context as well as unjustified as an accurate rendering of the Greek.

Some sceptical scholars regard numbers of the sayings attributed to Jesus in the Gospels to the creative flair of the apostolic church, which could just invent them as the occasion required. Garland, agreeing with Orr & Walther, notes (282 and 321) how this does not happen but, to the contrary, that Paul carefully distinguishes when he has a teaching of Jesus to refer to (as in 1 Corinthians 7:10; 9:14) from situations where Jesus has said nothing on a subject and so Paul himself gives his own authoritative teaching on the issue (1 Corinthians 7:12; 7:25). This is a point well taken, and worthy of note.

Paul's comment that the Lord did not teach upon a given subject is also an indication that Paul had a very confident view of what was (and what was not) covered by the Lord in his teaching ministry. This is hardly compatible with the opinion of some scholars that Paul was not really at all well acquainted with the life and teaching of the human Jesus.

**7:26** To virgins, Paul says that he considers that it would be a good idea for them to remain as they are. These words have often been lifted out of their context and used as justification for exalting virginity and advocating celibacy, or considering celibacy a better state than marriage.

This is not legitimate exegesis. *First of all*, Paul's reason for saying this at all is clearly stated to be "Because of the present distress", and cannot be pressed as an all-time principle for situations not parallel to the one which existed when Paul wrote. *Secondly*, this is not a commendation of virginity or celibacy as such, nor a statement that this is to be preferred for spiritual reasons, but a recommendation based on pragmatic considerations related to the particular troubles which were impending or present at that time. *Thirdly*, Paul makes exactly the same recommendation against a change of status (in the following verses) to those who are married and those who are divorced, and his advice must be taken as a whole. As we have seen, it is advice to hold fast to the status quo, whether that means to continue unmarried or to stay married.

**7:27a** Paul now addresses those who are married: he says, literally (see ESV, NASB, NEB, RSV, NRSV), "Are you bound to a wife?" The verb used is present perfect in form: "Have you entered, and are you still in, a binding relationship with a wife?" Thus NIV, "Are you married?"

Then he wants to make clear that nothing he is saying should be taken to mean that you would be better off not to have a wife, for he says plainly to the married: "Do not seek a divorce." The marriage relationship is to be maintained even in the face of the difficult circumstances which they were facing. That is to say, "Maintain things as they are."

Garland (318 and 325), viewing everything as he does as relating to the betrothed, sees the "being bound" as being bound to a vow to a betrothed, not to a wife: "Are you bound to a woman (by engagement)?"

Yet this same verb (the perfect of δεω, *deō*) is used in v.40, where it clearly refers to being bound in marriage. There is no reason (apart from a theological disposition) for seeing it differently in v.27.

Garland 325 rules out the possibility that "Do not seek to be free" (ESV, NRSV) could mean "Do not seek a divorce" (NIV) from your wife, on the grounds that Paul has already dealt with this in v.10, where he said he has a word of the Lord to cite, whereas here he says he does not (v.25). But Paul might well make a further specific comment on this same issue because his readers could be wondering whether, in this context, the "present distress" made any difference to the general rule. Paul says "No it doesn't: don't seek a divorce."

**7:27b** Paul again uses a present perfect form, this time of the verb λυω (*luō*), "to release" or "set free", indicating the situation resulting from a prior action: "Have you been freed from a wife?" The translation of the NIV here, "Are you unmarried?", is inadequate and ambiguous, because it can be read as if Paul is simply repeating here his recommendation of v.26 to virgins that they should remain unmarried. In fact, as the use of the perfect tense indicates, the circumstance which Paul is now discussing is when a husband has been freed from the relationship of being bound to a wife; that is, Paul is discussing the situation of a person whose marriage has terminated. This could be as the result of death or divorce. However, some translators consider that divorce is primarily in view here: "Are you bound in marriage? Do not seek a dissolution. Has your marriage been dissolved? Do not seek a wife." (NEB; - Barclay has almost identical wording for v.27b.) Numbers of commentators also interpret Paul's meaning here in this way: thus Jay Adams 84 says, "Paul is speaking here to the previously married who have been divorced."

**7:28** The "you" in v.28 is the same person who in v.27 is said to be "having been freed from a wife", and who is being advised in the present circumstances not to seek a wife. Underlining the point that he is making a recommendation (v.25) in the light of "the present crisis" at Corinth, Paul now continues to address this person, i.e., a divorcee, and states quite clearly, "But if you do marry, you have not sinned." Having made this comment to those who remarry after "having been bound in marriage" previously and then "having become freed from a wife", he now says the same thing concerning a virgin who marries: "And if a virgin marries, she has not sinned." [The other recommendation that Paul gave in this passage was (v.27a) that the person who was married should not seek a divorce: it is noteworthy that he does not add that the married person can feel free to disregard *that* comment.]

Paul's word to divorcees here, recommending that they do not remarry, but stating that they are not sinning if they do, is completely in harmony with his previous guidance (7:7-9) for the person who was *agamos*. However, a person who does remarry in these circumstances can expect to have troubles in this life (NIV, NRSV), which Paul wants to spare them. Note that this is stated explicitly as being the motivation for Paul's recommendation that they do not remarry.

**7:29-31** This is not, as some have taken it, a reference to a supposed nearness of the Second Coming, the *parousia* - see my introduction to this section. Rather, it is on the one hand a serious reflection of the crisis they were then facing - probably a sharp period of persecution. And on the other hand, more generally, it is a comparison of the matters of this life when weighed in the scales of eternity. The best of earthly relationships, all the sadnesses and the joys of life, and all matters of commerce and business, are secondary; for the span of our time (ὁ καιρος, *ho kairos*) in this world is short and the "present form (το σχημα, *to schēma*) of this world" is in the process of passing away (present continuous tense). Hodge 129-130 comments succinctly,

> It is the design of God in allowing us but a brief period in this world, or in this state, that we should set lightly by all earthly things. ... We should set our affections on things above, and not on the things on the earth. ... The fact that the present condition of the world is not to last long, and that our participation in its joys and sorrows is to be so short-lived, is the reason which the apostle urges why we should not be wedded to earthly things.

Of the various matters which Paul has just mentioned, he now turns to consider one of them - the marriage relationship - more particularly.

### (d) The Danger of Being Distracted from the Lord By a Spouse (7:32-35)

**7:32-34a** Paul states first of all his purpose in writing this present section of his letter: he would like his readers to be "free from concern" or "from anxieties". What follows makes his meaning clear: he wants a married man to be free from a concern (anxieties) about the affairs of this world, and in particular how to please his wife, which competes with his concern about the Lord's affairs and how to please the Lord, so that his interests are divided.

**7:34b** Paul now refers to the same problem facing a woman. He here writes of the woman (γυνη, *gunē*) who is ἀγαμος, *agamos* (unmarried), and the παρθενος, *parthenos* (virgin). His comment refers to two groups (this is shown by the second use of the article in front of παρθενος, *parthenos*, indicating that it refers to different people from those women just mentioned before, who are ἀγαμος, *agamos*). So the ἀγαμος, *agamos* woman is differentiated from the παρθενος, *parthenos*, that is, those that are **not at the moment** married from those that are virgins, thus covering both groups of women who are unmarried. And thus, his comments cover those who have been married before and those who have never married. So now in these verses he refers to a particular temptation which confronts those who are married: to be more concerned about matters involving their spouse than for the things of God, so that their interests are divided. By contrast, those who are unmarried find themselves freer to devote themselves to the Lord.

**7:35** This verse explains more fully Paul's purpose for writing as he has. Paul has spoken of the danger faced by a married person: this person's concern for his wife can distract him from giving his undivided attention to Christian growth and holiness and to serving the Lord, and similarly for the wife in relation to her husband; by contrast, the unmarried man or woman is not subject to this same distraction. What then is Paul's purpose in making this point? Is it to assert that the unmarried state is higher or more spiritual than marriage? Is it to encourage his readers not to marry?

The reason which Paul himself gives is neither of these. He is warning them of the potential danger inherent within the commitment of marriage, by its very nature: that one spouse can distract the other from giving undivided loyalty to the Lord, so that they get their priorities wrong.

Paul's solution to this problem is **not** a recommendation that they do not marry (he says explicitly that he has no intention of laying any restraint upon them in any such way). Rather, it is to seek to promote their good by drawing this danger to their attention so that, aware of it, they can avoid it and give their "undivided devotion to the Lord".

It is interesting to note the comments of the early church fathers on this passage. Some of them found being married and serving the Lord without distraction to be quite incompatible.

Thus Basil of Caesarea writes (Kovacs 125):

Thus we achieve the discipline that is pleasing to God, and in accordance with the gospel of Christ, by withdrawing from the anxieties of the world and becoming completely estranged from its distractions.

For this reason the apostle, even though he allows marriage and gives it his blessing, contrasts the busyness marriage requires with anxiety for God, the two being mutually exclusive. ... Therefore one who truly follows God must dissolve the bonds that bind him to this life. ... Otherwise we cannot achieve the goal of pleasing God ...

Similarly Gregory of Nyssa says (Kovacs 127-128):

In ordinary life there are so many distractions, as the apostle says. So we are compelled to propose the life of virginity as a door to the holier life. ... For no one who has turned towards this world, taken on its cares, and devoted himself to pleasing men ... can fulfill the first and great commandment of the Lord, which is to love God with your whole heart and all your might. For how will someone love God with his whole heart when his heart is divided between God and the world, and when he steals the love he owes God alone and uses it up in human affections?

However, this view is not unanimous, but, as Kovacs 105 notes, "Clement of Alexandria argues that the married can be just as holy and undistracted in their love for the Lord as the unmarried."

We should note carefully that Paul is *not* saying here, "Do not marry"; he *is* saying, "Do not allow marriage to distract you from your total loyalty to the Lord."

At the same time however it must be recognized, in the application of this teaching in living the Christian life, that situations can arise (possibly only temporarily) where celibacy is of advantage in a particular sphere of service (e.g., in pioneering missionary work); and God does give to some people the gift of living without marriage (cf. 7:7) because of the nature of the particular ministry to which he is calling them, for the sake of the Kingdom of heaven (Matthew 19:12).

## (e) The Question of What To Do With One's Virgin (7:36-38)

**7:36-38** We have already considered these verses at the beginning of this section of the Epistle (at 7:25), in discussing how to understand Paul's meaning in the entire section, and I have given already my reasons for taking Paul to be discussing what a father should do about marriage plans for his daughter. This seems the best way to understand the passage, seeing that the person responsible for a virgin's marriage was her father, and the passage speaks of giving her in marriage (v.38). Paul repeats his advice to refrain, in the present troubled circumstances, from marrying, but he specifically allows freedom of choice, and acknowledges that to proceed with the marriage would be in order.

It should be noted that Paul nowhere says or implies that the advice he gives to refrain from marriage is permanent, but on the contrary is only due to the "impending distress" or "present crisis" and the particular circumstances of the time. What he says here in this way in this special case cannot be pressed to contradict his more general teaching elsewhere.

### (f) The Question of a Widow (7:39-40E)

**7:39** In similar fashion Paul deals with the next issue - the remarriage of widows. A widow may remarry, so long as it is "in the Lord" (ESV, RSV, NRSV), that is, "he must belong to the Lord" (NIV). Note that Paul speaks here of a wife being "bound to" or "tied to" her husband, as in 7:27 he spoke of a husband being "bound to" or "tied to" his wife.

This verse clearly teaches the intention of God that marriage is to be for life. The verse does not mention divorce, as this has no place in God's perfect will; the absence of reference to divorce does not mean that divorce is *impossible* but that in view of the binding nature of marriage in God's purposes, divorce is *wrong*.

Moreover, we must note that Paul is speaking about the woman's situation. *She* is bound to her husband whilever he lives: under Jewish law, *she* was not able to divorce *him* - for a wife, the bond of marriage could be broken by nothing but death. If her husband dies, then indeed she is free to remarry. (Note the close parallel between this verse and Romans 7:2.)

But what Paul says of the *wife* would not be true in respect of a *husband*, because the option of divorcing her (though against Christ's teaching) was available to him.

**7:40a** However, Paul's judgement is that a widow would be happier if she remained unmarried. It is interesting to see that the reason he gives for her not remarrying is not some (supposed) idea of this being more pleasing to God, but rests upon Paul's estimate of her welfare - compare v.26, "in view of the present distress, it is good for a person to remain as he is"; v.28, "those who marry will have worldly troubles, and I would spare you that"; v.35, "I say this for your own benefit". His specific comment here on this issue is fully in line with what he has already said more generally (7:6-11).

**7:40b** Paul's closing remark is not to be taken as a tentative-but-uncertain claim to God's guidance - he does not mean, "I suppose that I have the Spirit of God, but I could be mistaken." Such an idea would be completely out of character with Paul's consistent attitude to his own apostolic authority!

He had a high view of the apostleship, and was most emphatic in asserting his own call to be one of the apostles. We have his claim in this same letter (2:12-13) that he and the other apostles speak in very words taught by the Spirit when they teach spiritual truth; in this same chapter he teaches authoritatively upon his own judgement, and claims explicitly to be trustworthy in doing so (7:12; 7:25). He does not now end the chapter by effectively repudiating this.

Rather, in this verse he is stating that it is his considered judgement that he has the Spirit of God in what he says. His claim here is low-key and understated, but nonetheless definite for all that. His "I too" directs his teachings against the self-designated "spiritual ones" at Corinth who are claiming to teach by God's Spirit, and who are repudiating Paul's teaching and challenging his status (see 4:3-5; 9:3). Thus with gentle irony and considerable understatement he makes his own claim to be led and taught by the Spirit in what he says.

**In sum:** Paul counsels the unmarried - both virgins and those previously married (those divorced or widowed) - not to marry, on the grounds that in his judgement they will be better off in the circumstances of the time.

I myself consider that many commentators overstate Paul's personal commitment to the "ideal" of celibacy: rather, Paul's preference for celibacy is pragmatic and based on expediency - and on the specific gift of God (v.7). But if any of these unmarried ones choose to marry (to the contrary of his recommendations), then to do this (and Paul states this explicitly, 7:28) is not a sin.

# CHAPTER EIGHT

## SECTION 3(a)
## CONCERNING FOOD SACRIFICED TO IDOLS

### 1. The Issue Stated (8:1-13E)

**8:1a** Paul now turns to a fresh subject, which he introduces with περι δε (*peri de*), "now concerning ..." [NIV translates: "Now about ..."] (as in 7:1 and 7:25).

What is meant by the term the ESV renders as "food offered to idols"? Thiselton 620 says:

> Since the social, socioeconomic, cultic, and religious dimensions of τις εἰδωλόθυτα [*tis eidōlothuta*] are so multidimensional and complex, we propose the translation *meat associated with offerings to pagan deities*.... The translation is cumbersome, but it hardly overtranslates a Greek term which is almost impossible to translate into English otherwise without further explanation.

The issue which occupies Paul's attention for the next three chapters is, "What should be the Christian attitude towards eating food which has first been sacrificed to idols - and towards one's fellow-Christians who do?"

Corinth was a city steeped in idolatry, and it permeated the whole of life. For many people the idols were absolutely real, and their worship was a very serious business indeed. It is very difficult for those of us with a background of generations of Christian tradition to understand fully what this would have been like for the majority of people when they first became converted and were learning to break from this past, in order that we can put ourselves into the scene that Paul is describing here. John Chrysostom sought to explain it (Kovacs 139) to the people of his day:

> They still tremble before idols, Paul says. Don't think of the present situation, where several generations of your forebears were Christians. Carry your mind back to those earlier times. Imagine a time when the Christian gospel was just beginning to be proclaimed, when pagan impiety still held sway, fires burned on the altars, sacrifices and libations were being performed, and the pagans were in the majority. Imagine people who had inherited paganism from their ancestors and were descendants of pagan fathers, grandfathers, and great-grandfathers, people on whom these demons had inflected much suffer-

ing. Consider what their situation would be when all at once they were converted, how they would tremble in fear at the demons' designs.

The problem at Corinth results from the fact that it was somewhat difficult in the social circumstances of the ancient Mediterranean world to avoid meat which had been part of an animal sacrificed in an idol's temple. Morris explains it thus:

> First, it was an accepted social practice to have meals in a temple, or in some place associated with an idol. ... The kind of occasion, public or private, when people were likely to come together socially was the kind of occasion when a sacrifice was appropriate. To have nothing to do with such gatherings was to cut oneself off from most social intercourse with one's fellows. ...
>
> Secondly, most of the meat sold in the shops had first been offered in sacrifice. Part of the victim was always offered on the altar to the god, part went to the priests, and usually part to the worshipers. The priests customarily sold what they could not use. It would often be very difficult to know for sure whether meat in a given shop had been part of a sacrifice or not. Notice that there are two separate questions: the taking part in idol feasts, and the eating of meat bought in the shops, but previously part of a sacrifice.

**8:1b** Edwards 209f. comments:

> "for all have knowledge touching this matter": I take it to be an allusion to the other Apostles and their decree at the Council of Jerusalem. Even when they forbade the Gentile converts to eat things offered unto idols, they did so because they saw that partaking of idol-feasts was one of the sorest temptations to fornication that would beset Christians in the heathen cities of that age.

Edwards has also said (208): "Besides, as Paul assented to the decree, it would be nothing less than a breach of faith on his part afterwards to ignore it." Like Edwards, I believe that Paul would have passed on the Apostolic Decrees (Acts 15:29) to the Corinthians, as part of his basic foundational Christian teaching. We know that this was his practice in his teaching to his churches: Acts 16:4, "As they went on their way through the cities, they delivered to them for observance the decisions that had been reached by the apostles and elders who were in Jerusalem". We have no reason to think Paul would have done anything differently in Corinth.

Most modern commentators and translations take the words "we know that all of us possess knowledge" (or the words after "that") as what was being said at Corinth, and put them in inverted commas (ESV, NEB, NIV margin, RSV, NRSV, TEV, Jerusalem Bible, etc.). So there is very general agreement amongst scholars that v.1 contains a quotation from the Corinthians, but its extent is disputed. Willis 70 says:

> The extent of the quotation is not a decisive issue. But, it seems bet-
> ter to say it begins with οἴδαμεν [*oidamen*, we know] both on grammati-
> cal and theological considerations.

Numbers of scholars seem to consider that the background of this is
that the Corinthians apparently asked Paul in their letter to him (7:1) for
his advice about eating idol meat. I don't get this impression at all. The
Corinthians are not requesting advice from Paul: they are arguing with
Paul. I agree with Hurd 126: "In effect the Corinthians' question is not
'may we?' or 'should we?' but 'why can't we?'"

I take it that chapters 8-10 are Paul's answer to their response to his
teaching to them (including the Apostolic decree forbidding idol meat).
From Paul's reply it would seem:

**(a)** they are defending their practice of eating idol food on the
grounds that they know that an idol has no real existence (so whether the
food has been offered to an idol makes no difference to it), and

**(b)** they are saying something like, "Anyway, how do we know
whether a given bit of meat has been part of an idol sacrifice or not? Are
we expected to enquire about the source of each piece of meat we buy?
Are we to refuse to eat meat we are offered on the grounds that it might
have been sacrificed? This would just about totally rule out ever accepting an invitation to have a meal with our friends!"

**8:1c** What Paul says next in this verse is then seen as being his comment upon what the Corinthians are saying, as they are virtually elevating "knowledge" (γνωσις, *gnosis*) to the preeminent place in the situation. Paul says: "Knowledge puffs up, but love builds up." Paul is not
denigrating knowledge itself; he is pointing out its dangers when it is *by*
itself. It must be accompanied by love - then it builds up (i.e., the individual Christian, and the whole church of God). "The rest of the chapter
is an expansion of the statement that love buildeth up." (Edwards 210)

**8:2-3** Paul's contrasting of knowledge and love is expanded and
developed fully later in this letter (chapter 13, and the wider context of
chapters 12-14). In this present chapter, Paul responds to the issue of
idol meat by considering how the exercise of love will influence how
one acts upon the "knowledge" that one has. Edwards 211 says that in
v.2, "here τι [*ti*] must express the knowing man's assumed modesty: 'if
any one pretends to have *some* knowledge'."

"If anyone considers that he knows something" [with the implication,
"and that this knowledge is what matters"], then [that very fact indicates
that] "he does not yet know as he ought to know" [i.e., he has not yet got
this "knowing things" business straight]. But "if anyone *loves God*" [ah,
that is the main thing!] then "he is known by God" [- that's the kind of

knowledge that *really* matters.] Edwards 213: "According to St Paul, therefore, two distinct elements combine to form an enlightened conscience - knowledge and love."

**8:4** Now Paul picks up again from the beginning of v.1, saying in effect, "So now then, let's look at this issue of idol meat". "So now then" or "Therefore", he says resumptively, repeating his heading quoted from the Corinthians. But he adds in a word now which changes the focus somewhat. Compare his initial statement of the issue (v.1) with his restatement of it here (v.4):

1 Now concerning (περι)                 the food offered to idols
4 Now concerning (περι) the eating of the food offered to idols

There is a subtle change of emphasis here, from the issue of the food itself to the question of the *eating of it*. Paul will go on to show that it is not the *nature* of the meat which is at stake but the question of eating it: when, where, and in what circumstances. It's as if he is saying, "Now follow me carefully in this: it's not what you do but the way that you do it."

Again, as in v.1: "We know that ..." (οἰδαμεν ὁτι, *oidamen hoti*): the Corinthians are being quoted here, stating their viewpoint, and giving the (theological) basis for the behavior that they were engaging in (v.10), and why they feel free to be eating meat in an idol's temple - and why they consider themselves fully entitled to continue their practice. It is because eating idol meat (they are saying) is a nothing-issue, seeing that "an idol has no real existence" (with the implication "You yourself taught us that, Paul") - seeing that "there is no God but one" (an allusion to Deuteronomy 4:35, 39 and particularly 6:4, quoted by Jesus in Mark 12:29) - ("and we believe in him [they imply], and that's what counts").

Numbers of translations place these statements in inverted commas to indicate that Paul is quoting what the Corinthians were saying (as in the ESV, RSV, NRSV - though the NIV sets this out as being Paul's own comment).

Paul is in a bit of a bind here: how is he going to handle this? John Chrysostom explains the problem (Kovacs 135):

> See what a tight spot Paul has fallen into. He wants to argue two different points: that it is necessary to refrain from such a meal, but also that it cannot harm those who partake of it. These things do not fit together easily. For if the Corinthians learned that the meal was harmless, they would be prone to treat it lightly, as if it were a matter of indifference. On the other hand, if they were prohibited from touching

such food, they would suspect that they were being forbidden something that could do them harm.

**8:5** In this verse it may be the Corinthians who are speaking, as in
v.4. Or it may be Paul who is making the assertions - scholars differ in
their views here about this. But it looks to me that in verses 5 and 6 Paul
is responding to what the Corinthians are saying.

There are indeed many gods and lords. These do exist in the sense
that they are given worship and are dominant in the life of the worshiper,
and moreover, the worship and sacrifice given to pagan gods is actually
being paid to demons (see 10:20).

Paul is far from asserting that these gods and lords exist objectively,
but, rather, they are very real in the understanding and beliefs of the
pagans (and they still are also, for the recently converted Corinthians).

John Chrysostom says (Kovacs 135) that "By 'things on earth', Paul
means the demons and all those men who were made into gods."
Edwards 216 gives this assessment:

> The Greek conception of the independence of every unit in nature
> and society was embodied in the mythology. Every city had its tutelary
> deity; every spring of water was haunted; every crop of corn was under
> the protection of a goddess; every movement of the elements and every
> human action might assume a sacred character and become, the one a
> prayer, the other its answer. There were gods on the earth.

In the next verse Paul contrasts the objective reality of the situation
(and here he agrees with the ones who "know these things" at Corinth
[v.4] - there is only one God) with the subjective perception of the situation as it impacts upon those at Corinth who have a "weak" conscience
(v.7) in this matter: there are many "so-called" gods in heaven and on
earth. In saying "so-called", Paul is acknowledging that this is how it is
in the understanding of many at Corinth.

"In heaven and on earth": this encompasses their great variety in the
Greek heavenly pantheon and in earthly idols, plus, people were at that
time being encouraged to regard the Roman emperor as a god.

There were "gods many and lords many": as they could plainly see,
as the shrines of these deities are all around them in Corinth: who could
deny that they were many? Yes indeed there are gods many and lords
many: this is the perception of the people in Corinth, some of whom
have just become Christians and are now trying to break free from this
mindset.

**8:6** But (whatever others may believe), for us it is different.

"But for us": strong adversive ἀλλα + ἡμιν (*alla* + *hēmin*) - that is,
for Christians, in contrast to how it is for pagans, which Paul has just set

out in v.5. This one God whom we worship is the supreme source of the entire physical universe and everything else one can conceive of. And this includes in particular ourselves - *we* exist "for him" (i.e., for his purposes). Moreover, all God's creation came into existence through this Lord Jesus Christ: and that includes us too.

"There is only one God (in contrast to this false belief in 'many gods') and he is the Father; and only one Lord (in contrast to this false belief in 'many lords'), and he is Jesus Christ (and, by implication, the Son)."

From the Father all things exist. Edwards 218 notes that "the purpose of the passage ... is to prove that eating meat offered to an idol is not sinful [i.e., in itself], inasmuch as *all* things were made through Christ". That is, "all things" - even food - have their source and origin from God through Christ.

The problem is, some Christians, knowing that there is only one God, one Lord, and that an idol has no real existence, draw the conclusion that they can therefore eat this idol meat.

Oftentimes commentators, in expounding Paul's teaching from this chapter, call these people "the strong", in contrast with those Paul calls "weak". Not so. Paul does indeed write of the weak (8:9; 8:11; 9:22), or to be more specific, of those whose conscience is weak (8:7; 8:10; 8:12), but he *never* refers here to others as "strong". Rather, he contrasts the weak with the "know-it-alls" or the "knowers" (to use Garland's term for them). Or we could call them respectively the "scrupulous" and the "liberal".

This verse contains a very compact theological package. Paul is not setting forth duotheism, two Gods, the Father and the Lord Jesus Christ. This teaching is totally monotheistic: there is only one God - but this God is Father and Son. This summarizes (without explaining) what "we" Christians (including new converts at Corinth) already know. It is in fact the first part of a trinitarian formula (but Paul does not go on to include the Spirit, as this teaching is not his purpose here).

Note Paul's high Christology here, referring to Jesus Christ as "the one Lord, through whom are all things and through whom we exist" - an anticipation of what he later says more fully in Colossians 1:16-18. Lord, κυριος [*kurios*] not only answers to the "lords many" of v.5 - there is only one Lord, and that is Jesus Christ - but also is applying to Jesus Christ the word which in the Old Testament referred to the Lord God, Yahweh. There is an implication here that Christ is Yahweh. It is a tightly-packed verse, that a Christian will be able to unpack.

Fee 375 says,

In the same breath that he can assert that there is only one God, he equally asserts that the designation "Lord," which in the OT belongs to the one God, is the proper designation of the divine Son. One should note especially that Paul feels no tension between the affirmation of monotheism and the clear distinction between the two persons of Father and Jesus Christ.

Edwards 217 points out:

ὁ πατηρ: not to be joined with θεος, "God the Father; but in apposition to it, "God who is the Father"; as, in the corresponding clause Ἰη σους Χριστος is in apposition to Κυριος, "one Lord, who is Jesus Christ." Again, πατηρ [patēr] must not be restricted to God's being the Father of Jesus Christ ... the subject of the whole passage is, not what God is to Christ, but what he is to us.

**8:7a** Now the point that is relevant to the present issue is that *we* know this, but not everyone possesses this knowledge. As can be seen from the context, Paul here is contrasting the "know-it-alls" at Corinth, who fully understand and accept (and live in the light of) this truth, with those in the church who are just one short step out of paganism - those who "through former association with idols, eat food as really offered to an idol, and their conscience, being weak, is defiled".

Gordon Clark 133 says,

Paul's problem here was double. Obviously he had to instruct these ignorant Christians so that they could eat this meat without sinning, but he also had to protect them from their immature condition and prevent them from worshiping idols by an action that, properly understood, was no sin at all.

**8:7b** Paul explains the issue now as it affects the brothers with a "weak" conscience. Their conscience tells them that it is idolatry to eat such meat, whereas now as Christians they have turned from idols to the living God.

Re "conscience", Edwards 221 says, "In our passage it means the sense of guilt which a Christian has when he thinks he has contracted moral defilement by contact with an idol"; and Willis 90f. tells us: "There is a general agreement that the normal use of συνειδησις [suneidēsis], both in and outside the New Testament, is to refer to the universal capacity to evaluate one's own actions."

Conscience enables us to recognize the existence of right and wrong, and that there is a difference between them. But conscience does not automatically tell us what is right and what is wrong. Unless it is specifically taught differently, an uninstructed conscience will only reflect the standards we have picked up from our family or our peer group (or society in general) - mostly an outlook on right and wrong that is very far from Christian.

Thus our conscience will often tell us that we should do (or not do) such-and-such, and will make us feel guilty when we do something different: and all it is actually telling us is what the world around us thinks. How hugely important it is, then, to give specifically Christian moral teaching to the members of our family, and in our churches. And that we model Christian ethical standards to the world at large, and that by our godly behavior we show there is a difference between Christians and non-Christians!

It appears that the "weakness" of some Corinthian Christians was that their "consciousness" or awareness of the non-existence of idols is what is weak.

Garland 384 describes the "weak" as those with a "faulty moral compass" who are in danger of reverting to their previous idolatry, to their eternal spiritual doom (8:11).

Note the contradiction between v.1 and v.7: The Corinthians (or some of them) assert that "we all have knowledge" (γνωσις, *gnōsis*) and on this basis - because we all know that an idol has no real existence - we can eat idol meat in the temple. Paul's response is specifically (v.7), "But not everyone has this knowledge" (again γνωσις, *gnōsis*) - and the "know-it-alls" at Corinth are not taking this factor into account.

Paul does not identify himself with the "knowers", as we may have expected - he may have agreed with them that "we all have such knowledge", but he proceeds to address such people as "you" (8:9-11), and thus dissociates himself from them. He identifies himself with the weak (9:22a). He does not address himself to the weak, so that they will become better informed for the future. Rather, he directs his teaching to the "knowers", and states the issue strongly to bring them to an awareness of the seriousness of the consequences of what they do. The Bible is very emphatic in stressing that we are responsible for, and accountable for, the consequences of what we do, even when those consequences were neither deliberately caused nor intended.

**8:8** Some take this verse as Paul's own affirmation, while some see it as (once again) a Corinthian statement which Paul is quoting. In fact, the difference is moot, seeing that, if the latter, it is nevertheless a statement that Paul agrees with - as far as it goes.

What is the reality of the situation? The reality is that eating idol meat will not make a skerrick of difference to us one way or the other: there is nothing in the *meat* that will affect us. As Stanley 139 puts it succinctly, "The whole question of food is in itself absolutely indifferent." Eating or not eating is morally neutral: it has the same spiritual impact upon you as whether you choose to wear brown shoes or black, a red dress or a blue one. We are morally no worse off and no better off one way or the other.

So from that point of view you can eat or not eat, just as you choose. Lenski 343 stresses,

> Food has no power to determine our relation to God in one way or in another. The emphasis rests on "food" and on "with God": the former is too small and the latter too great to produce such an effect. The verb is neutral: "will not affect our standing," literally "will not place us beside God." i.e. beside him in a favorable position or in an unfavorable position.

And Gordon Clark 134f. avers:

> Neither doing nor abstaining commends us to God. That is to say, these choices are morally neutral. In God's sight, it makes no difference how we decide. ...

> In view of the fact that Paul so clearly indicates that some choices are not moral choices, that one with good conscience can do either this or that, is it wise for popular Christian leaders to tell young people that "God has a plan for your life" and that one should take care to find it? Then, the teenager worries whether God would have him become a stockbroker or an automotive engineer, or whether he should marry the blonde or the brunette? Paul says that it makes no difference - do what you like; only in the second example, the blonde and the brunette must both be Christians. Otherwise, it makes no spiritual difference; neither choice pleases God more than the other.

Very true, in relation to the morality of such decisions. But still: deciding one way rather than the other may well turn out much better in the future. In view of the way the future is known to God, our choice (although both alternatives are morally legitimate) still needs to be made with prayer and care. [See further, "Operating in the Gray Areas of Life", in "Reflections", below.]

**8:9** Now Paul warns, "take care". Because there is more. What really counts is not just the facts of the situation, but the impact upon others. For your right to eat idol food if you want to, can have a serious effect upon a fellow-Christian with a weak (that is, inadequately taught) conscience in this area: it can cause him to stumble. How can that be? Surely what you choose to do is just between you and the Lord? Not so!

**8:10** Because you know that "an idol has no real existence" (v.4), you "know-it-alls" have no qualms about eating in an idol's temple.

In many cases this eating in an idol's temple would be in full view of the world. Edwards 223 considers it "A banquet in a public place". And so a "weak" brother sees you, and will he not be encouraged to do the same thing? That is, to accept invitations to functions at the temple, where quite clearly the meat eaten will first have been part of a sacrifice to that idol. Or, to eat meat in other circumstances where it is known to be "food offered to idols".

And when he does this, it has for him all the connotations of the idol worship from which he has so recently emerged (v.7), and he cannot but see himself as participating still in idol worship. But you do it, and therefore he cannot see any Christian reason why he is not to do it also.

Christians will see you there - but unbelievers will also. Augustine (Kovacs 141) looks at the impact on unbelievers when they see Christians apparently participating in idolatry:

> Can you not imagine how people are led astray by images if they think the images are being honored by Christians? "God knows my mind," someone demurs. But your brother doesn't know your heart. ... Those who see you do these things are encouraged to do other things: they want not only to eat in the temple but also to sacrifice. Look at the result: "the one who is weak is destroyed by your knowledge." ... We want the rest of the pagans to be converted, but you are rocks in their path; though they want to come they stumble over these rocks and turn back. They say in their hearts, "Why should we abandon the gods when Christians themselves worship them as much as we do?"

Now, the significant question is, Why on earth would you want to do so? Why would the Corinthians (or many of them) have wanted to participate in the idolatrous temple meals and related activities?

Actually, there are several reasons we can identify.

First of all, it provided an opportunity for those who attended to enjoy eating meat - an opportunity not often available to most of them in ordinary circumstances, as meat was expensive and infrequently on the dinner table (unless you were quite rich).

Thiselton 619 points out,

> "As Theissen and Yeo observe, this would be all the more difficult and seductive for the socioeconomic "weak" or poor, who could not otherwise afford the luxury of eating meat, but were consigned to an endless diet of wheat bread or barley-based cereals."

Again, social activities in the temple were an "ordinary" and "normal" part of everyday life. Some immature new believers may have considered that for unbelievers to know that becoming a Christian would mean having to give up such a significant part of life would be a disincentive to becoming a Christian.

Then Willis 63 tells us:

> Third, it has been seen that sacrifices and common meals were normative features of Hellenistic cults and associations. Since these meals were characteristic expressions of Greek public life, it is

altogether understandable that the Corinthian Christians should desire to be involved in them, at least to the degree they considered permissible. Since they probably did not see such meals as religiously significant, their enlightened Christian monotheism would have been sufficient to overcome any qualms about eating - except among some members "weak in conscience". The social character of cult meals would also have emboldened the Corinthians to ask defensively of their founder-apostle reasons why they must abstain from such normal functions of life.

The assessment of the cult meals as occasions of good company, good food, and good fun makes it obvious why the Corinthian Christians would not have wanted to miss out. It probably was not regarded as pagan worship to participate in the various "socials" held in the temple precincts.

**8:11-12** For a young Christian, the result of eating in an idol's temple is going to be severe damage to this Christian's relationship with the Lord. John Chrysostom has some serious comments to make on these verses (Kovacs 139-140) which are worth citing at length:

> So the brother who is weak will be destroyed by your eating - the brother for whom Christ died. When you commit such an injury, there are two things that make it difficult to pardon: first, that the injured one is weak, and, second, that he is a brother. In addition, there is a third, even weightier than the others. What is this? That while Christ was willing to die for him, you don't have the patience even to make allowance to his condition. By these words Paul reminds the mature Christian what he himself used to be and that Christ died for him. ... But after your weak brother has been saved in this way, will you allow him to perish, and - what is even worse - for the sake of food? ... In the end, there are four accusations, and very weighty ones at that: that the man is a brother, and a brother who is weak, and one whom Christ valued so highly that he died for him, and, on top of all this, that he is destroyed for the sake of food. ...
>
> In fact, it is the height of folly for us, if we regard those who were so precious to Christ that he chose to die for them as so insignificant that we cannot even abstain from food for their sake. And this accusation could be addressed not only to the Corinthians but also to us, who care nothing about the salvation of our neighbors and utter words worthy of Satan. For to say, "What does it matter if this man falls or that one is destroyed?" is to partake of the cruelty and inhumanity of the devil.

When Paul says, "You are destroying a brother for whom Christ died", he uses a strong word here, ἀπολλυμι, *apollumi*, "destroyed", and treats the situation with great seriousness. What does he mean?

Some scholars see "this weak person is destroyed" as meaning he has fallen back into idolatry and has lost his salvation. For example, Fee 387,

In saying that the brother "is destroyed" Paul most likely is referring to eternal loss, not simply some internal "falling apart". ... What is in view is a former idolater falling back into the grip of idolatry.

Others would differ: e.g. Blomberg 163:

Verse 11 thus spells out the second reason for voluntary abstinence. Flaunting one's freedom was actually damaging the spiritual lives of the weak. "Is destroyed" is probably better rendered "is in the process of being ruined." It is doubtful if Paul could imagine that these inherently amoral issues could actually jeopardize a Christian's salvation. Rather he saw the strong believers' behavior as "an obstacle to Christian sanctification."

**8:13E** To eat meat in such circumstances is unthinkable. It violates the foundation of our Christian life and behavior: love (v.1). What you (a "knower") may know about the "nothingness" of idols is irrelevant. What counts is acting in love. Perhaps the only meat I can get is idol meat. Then if that is the case (or if that is how my brother sees it), I will never eat meat again "lest I make my brother stumble". Barnett 145 assesses the situation:

Meat was a luxury beyond the reach of most people, and doubtless a special treat for rare occasions of celebration. But not even for this will Paul break his commitment if such eating caused the spiritual downfall of a brother or sister for whom Christ died.

In writing of himself, Paul is obviously regarding his example as being for them to follow: he will surrender and renounce his right to eat meat if through such eating he would cause his brother to stumble (ESV), to fall into sin (NIV).

His consideration of these issues can lead to only one outcome: I will cease to do what is harming my brother. If my eating meat is going to cause my brother to fall (because it had been part of an idol sacrifice), then "I will never eat meat again". This is the decision to which love will lead.

But it is not the end of the matter. Paul has some further implications that need to be considered, and thus this verse is the lead-in to what he has to say (chapter 9) about surrendering one's rights for the sake of others.

In fact, 8:13 is the principle and the theme which is then taken up and developed throughout chapter 9. His climax in chapter 9 is to say in effect (9:22b): "All that I do is subordinated to this one goal: that by all means I might save some." Thus chapter 9 is an illustration and explication of the thought of 8:13.

# IN SUM

In this short chapter Paul has dealt with the first of the ramifications of this issue: where a Christian is actually openly eating in an idol's temple (v.10).

The situation here is absolutely clear-cut: in the restaurant attached to an idol's temple, the meat served would undoubtedly first have been offered in idol sacrifice, and everybody would know it - no one would be in any doubt about the situation. So for the "weak" Christian brother to see a fellow-Christian thus openly participating in idol worship by partaking of the sacrificial meat with other idol worshipers would offend their Christian conscience.

For a Christian, falling back into idolatry remained a real danger in a community in which it was so rife. Garland 384 writes,

> Paul fears that the person with a weak conscience might follow the example of those presumed to have knowledge, and eat idol food as truly offered to an idol, that is, as a sacrificial act. This person will be led astray in his or her moral judgement to think that such polytheistic practice is permissible for a Christian ... This person's conscience is then defiled through idolatry (cf. Rev. 3:4).

Paul is not just concerned with the "weak". He is concerned with the "knowers" also - concerned about the danger that, in sharing thus in idol worship they become partners with demons (1 Corinthians 10.20).

Thus the very spiritual life of a Christian was being endangered - indeed, both that of the "weak" and of the "knower". Garland 391 calls idol meat "spiritually toxic". Paul's response leaves no room for any alternative: "Can I do this? No, never!!"

# SOME PRACTICAL AND PASTORAL REFLECTIONS

In his own 1 Corinthians commentary, Blomberg 167 has said:

> Yet for most readers of this commentary, idol meat and its analogues in other world religions will not rank among their top one hundred moral dilemmas in life! Still, when one realizes the overarching principles involved, applications clamor for attention at every turn.

For Christians of today, two very significance questions emerge from Paul's teaching in this chapter. The first is, how the actual issue of idol meat and its consumption (or not) affects us today.

The second is the lessons we are to learn, from the principle involved, of how we should handle issues which fall into the "gray" areas of life.

## Some Present-day Alternatives

We may well tend to think that this chapter has no real relevance for us today, in our society. We need to think again.

*Firstly*, in many missionary situations in today's world, new Christians are in real danger of being pulled back into the idolatry of their society. Sad to say, in numbers of places this has resulted in a so-called Christianity which is a syncretistic amalgam of aspects of the gospel with elements from idolatrous paganism.

*Secondly*, many societies around the world have experienced an influx of immigrants from cultures in which idolatrous practices are followed. In some places restaurants have been opened by devotees of such other religions, offering good food at cheap prices - restaurants to be avoided by Christians for precisely the reasons Paul sets out in this chapter.

*Thirdly*, our own culture has its own twenty-first century equivalents of idol worship: we may not immediately see these for what they are, but we need to be alert to recognize them when they confront us. Sometimes Christians will participate in these "just for a bit of fun - it's not serious, and there's no harm in it." An example might be: a church fete where someone will read your palm or your tea leaves, or "tell your fortune". Or a person looking up a magazine's astrology columns "just out of interest - I don't take it seriously, of course." Or joining in Halloween observances - "the children love the dressing up, and we go along with them to ensure they're quite safe." Or more overtly occult activities, such as sharing in an experience using a ouija board, or participating in a seance, and so forth. Or our observing various superstitions ("It's good luck to do this, or bad luck to do the other", and the like) will fall into the same category.

Even when all these are done (supposedly) lightheartedly, they are of the same genre as the eating in an idol's temple in the first century by the "knowledgeable" Christian who acknowledges only one God and one Lord (8:6). For this behavior is capable of opening a door of opportunity for Satan to deceive the unwary: "I know there's nothing in astrology, but nevertheless it's uncanny the way in which ..."

And the example set for "weak" Christians in this way can be devastating. Moreover, this "dabbling" can swing wide the door of a person's heart or experience to the occult, so that real demonic bondage results. Never risk this destructive result!

Then there are semi-religious or quasi-religious organizations (such as the Masons) which can entice a person with their rites and ceremonies and observances, and can grow to become the focus of interest.

Ultimately anything which involves a recognition of some power in the universe other than the true God worshipped in the way Scripture teaches, becomes a snare by which Satan can entrap us and entangle us: and he has a variety of offerings to suit every taste. Although as Christians we would not intend it, we end up with an acknowledgement of Satan and his demons that he accepts as worship (10:20) - for behind Halloween and astrology and tarot cards and fortune telling and their ilk lies an acknowledgement of another supernatural being that is in competition with our Lord God. It is the twenty-first century face of idolatry.

Paul gives us fair warning (10:14): Keep well clear of any form of idolatry! For some have walked this route and have had their faith destroyed.

## Operating in The "Gray Areas" of Life

Blomberg 164 has commented:

> Possible applications range far beyond the specific issue of idol meat, but they do not include that which is inherently good or bad. Rather, 1 Corinthians 8 speaks to the gray areas of Christian living. Sometimes Scripture makes plain whether an issue is fundamentally immoral or amoral [no moral issue involved]. ... Christians must then ask if the practice in question has any inherently pagan (or anti-Christian) elements or if it is necessarily destructive and hurtful to the individuals involved. More positively, if [it is the case that] the practice in question seems acceptable in light of both these tests, might our participation enhance our outreach to the non-Christian world by cultivating friendships and social activities that unbelievers enjoy (cf. 9:19-23)? Two dangers remain ever-present: a separatism that prevents Christians from being the salt of the earth and the light of the world (Matt. 5:13-16), and a syncretism (a mixture of religions) that adopts pagan practices with damaging consequences."

Then Friesen says in his significant book *Decision Making and the Will of God*, 377f.:

> One of the major premises of this book is that in those areas where the Bible gives no command or principle (in nonmoral decisions), the believer is free and responsible to choose his own course of action. Any decision made within the moral will of God, we have argued, is acceptable to God.
>
> Ironically, there are some decisions in which it is easier to please God than to please our fellow Christians. Given the nature of humanity and the reality of freedom of choice, it is inevitable that believers are going to come to differing conclusions concerning what is permissible and what is not. ... God does not view differences of opinion in the area

of freedom as a bad thing. ... And so, instead of trying to eliminate divergence of opinion, the Holy Spirit has given specific instructions to guide our response to it. Most of that revelation is concentrated in Romans 14 and 15 and 1 Corinthians 8-10.

Friesen then discusses how these chapters deal with this matter, and how they are to be applied to the issues Christian face in the very different circumstances of today's world.

This is a book which has a great deal to say in regard to how to identify matters of this kind and how to put Paul's principles into effect - and it covers many more things besides, about the will of God in life, and how to make godly decisions. I recommend it warmly.

# CHAPTER NINE

## SECTION 3(a)
## CONCERNING FOOD SACRIFICED TO IDOLS (Cont.)

### 2. The Nature Of Freedom (9:1-27E)

In this chapter Paul is arguing a case: that as an apostle he has a number of rights. And he argues very cogently and at length for one right in particular: the right to receive support from the Corinthians. Then having validated this beyond question he claims the right not to exercise this right of being supported, on account of the gospel; and he concludes by explaining the overriding principle that guides his behavior: that by all means he should save as many as possible for Christ.

These things he sets out so as to show that it is necessary for us to yield up our rights when they are in conflict with our primary goal of making the gospel freely available to everyone. In all this, his behavior is their example. This bears directly upon the issue that he has confronted in chapter 8: for the sake of their witness, their example, and their ministry, they must not eat in an idol's temple.

There are some in the church at Corinth who have adopted a stance of opposition to Paul: they are challenging his teaching, and, it would appear, his status as an apostle. One of the arguments being raised against Paul seems to be, "Apostles and Christian leaders are supported by those to whom they minister. Paul cannot be much of an apostle - he did not take support from us but he has worked for his own living himself." The corollary of this would be: "He has thus put his own valuation upon his ministry: he does not charge anything for his teaching, because it is worthless."

Paul forcefully argues in support of the main premiss of this argument: that a Christian worker is indeed to be supported by those to whom he ministers (verses 4 to 14). But (Paul asserts) he also has the right not to take advantage, if he so chooses, of this right to be supported (verses 15 to 18).

Further, these Corinthians appear to be saying something like: "Paul keeps changing his mind - and his behavior. No one knows where he stands on anything. He is completely unpredictable - we don't know from one occasion to the next just what he is going to do." So in verses

19 to 22 he is helping them to see that indeed there is one consistent principle behind what he does.

This explains the defensive note that can be detected in chapter 9; in this chapter Paul explains, justifies, vindicates, his own conduct.

In chapter 8 we have had "Part 1: The Issue Stated". Chapter 9 may strike us as an abrupt change of subject. For in chapter 8 Paul is discussing eating idol food, and he returns to this in chapter 10. Why the sudden change of topic in chapter 9? The basic integrating factor is that the conclusion reached in 8:13 is about the surrendering of rights that one may have: and in chapter 9 Paul uses himself to exemplify this.

Paul ends chapter 8 by pointing to a restriction upon his (and thus upon anybody's) freedom as to what they may do. He commences chapter 9 by proclaiming his freedom. Then he will proceed to explain how this works out in practice and what his freedom actually means.

Some scholars have found the change of subject in chapter 9 so substantial and so unexpected that they have postulated another explanation: that a later scribe has divided a continuing discussion of idol meat (chapter 8 and 10) by inserting here another Pauline document in the middle. There are three reasons why this "explanation" does not hold up:

**(a)** No First Corinthians manuscripts exist which lack chapter 9 - so such a modification would have had to have been made at the very beginning, before this letter was sent and commenced being circulated: a highly improbable idea.

**(b)** Some scribe who had an extra bit of Pauline material he intended to insert would hardly have chosen to intersperse it in the middle of a discussion of something else - there are so many better places for an insertion (e.g., in front of this whole section on idol meat, between our present chapters 7 and 8).

**(c)** This theory presupposes that chapter 9 has in fact no real connection with its context, and requires some such explanation to account for it: but if we can recognize the nature of that connection, the need for "explaining" how chapter 9 came to be included there by Paul disappears and thus this theory has no point or purpose.

To those who hold this "change of subject" view (it is an ancient one) Origen gives this comment (Kovacs 148):

> Now if someone is not paying close attention to Scripture, it may seem that in this section the apostle is forgetting the subject under discussion. But this is not true; Paul is sticking closely to his argument. His concern is to teach about food offered to idols (1 Cor 8:1), so that if someone claiming to have knowledge says he is not hurt by consuming food offered to idols but becomes the cause for harm to others, he will be obliged to care about his neighbor and not become the reason other

people come to ruin. So he offers examples, saying, "Because we have a right to do something, we should not in all cases make full use of the right (1 Cor 9:18). For if someone is a soldier, he does not serve as a soldier so as to have nothing left over from his wages for himself. Or if he is a farmer, he is not content with his wages, but he also eats from the grapes. If he is a shepherd, in addition to his wages he gets a share of the milk. So too I ought to receive in this world, in addition to the promises made to me if I serve well as a soldier or farmer or shepherd, a share in the things I need from the soldiers who serve under me or from the fields I farm or the flocks I tend.

But nonetheless, even if I (Paul) have a right to the things I need, in consideration of what builds up (1 Cor 8:1), I do not make full use of this right (1 Cor 9:18). I am careful not to put an obstacle in the way of the gospel of Christ (1 Cor 9:12) ... Therefore, just as I do not make use of the right my teaching gives me, so also you who claim to be wise should not make use of your right but should take thought for the building up of your neighbors. And if some of you should think this teaching has no support and is merely human reasoning, let them hear the law which says: You shall not muzzle an ox when it is treading out the grain (Deut 25:4; 1 Cor 9:8).

**9:1** As so often in this letter, Paul makes his points through a series of sharp questions. *First of all*, he vindicates his apostleship on the grounds (a) that he has seen the Lord (a basic requirement of apostleship, Acts 1:22; he elaborates this point further later in this Epistle, in 15:8-11); (b) that the Corinthians are his workmanship, i.e., converted through his ministry; and (c) that their conversion is the seal of his apostleship (not implying that only an apostle could have converted the Corinthians, but that in thus working through Paul's ministry the Lord had authenticated that ministry, and thus also Paul's claim to apostleship, for the Lord would not have thus blessed the ministry of a liar and fraud).

**9:2** Garland 405 says,

More likely the "others" refers to churches that he did not found. ... He may not be the apostle of other churches, but he is without question the Corinthians' apostle. Their very existence as a church is the seal of his apostleship.

Stanley 147 paraphrases Paul: "You are the last men who ought to have questioned the authority, of the genuineness of which you are yourselves the most striking proof."

**9:3** The words "defence" (ἀπολογια, *apologia*) and "examine" or "investigate" or "sit in judgement" (ἀνακρινω, *anakrinō*) are terms from the lawcourts, and Paul's use of these words indicates that he is being subject to scrutiny and criticism by some at Corinth, and that in what he writes he is making a response to this criticism.

Scholars differ in their views as to whether Paul's "this" refers back to what Paul has just said, or forward to what he is about to say. Stanley 148 asserts concerning αὐτη (*hautē*), that it means "namely, what he has just said; *'This* contains all my defence.'" I concur: Paul's defence of his behavior is primarily that he is an apostle, from which a number of consequences will flow. Thus, "this" refers back to what is already said - for this is Paul's answer to those who are in effect putting him on trial. All else in this chapter is examining the significance and the consequence of this.

**9:4-5a** Paul discusses now the "rights" he has as an apostle. First of all, he claims the right to receive support not merely for himself and other Christian workers (v.4) but also for his wife. He and others "have the right to take a believing wife along with us" (NIV; cf. also ESV, NASB, NRSV, and most other translations, but the RSV is not adequate at this point). The Greek says "a sister, a wife", so that the wife is a sister in Christ, a fellow Christian, and therefore a suitable companion in the work of God.

Let us note that what Paul defends is not merely the right to *have* a wife (i.e. to be married), but - more than this - the right to *be accompanied* by a wife. A wife left at home is not a companion, and the idea of the companionship of marriage loomed large in Paul's teaching, as in Christ's.

Why is a man to have the right to be accompanied by a wife, instead of being under the necessity to forsake her for the sake of the gospel (Luke 14:26; 18:29)? Because the wife of whom Paul speaks here is also a Christian sister. Those words of Christ apply when the gospel divides, but here the gospel unites the couple in Christ's service.

But more than only the right to have your wife as a companion: she is a wife who is a sister, Paul says. She is a companion and *partner in Christian ministry*. In many situations this would be significant and important. Clement of Alexandria (Garland 407)

> believed the apostles' wives worked as fellow ministers who spoke to the women of the household, so that the gospel could penetrate the women's quarters without causing scandal.

Similarly Stanley 148:

> The fact of these women accompanying their husbands on their journeys may be explained by the necessity of females to gain access to and baptize the female converts in Greece and other oriental countries.

**9:5b** "as do the other apostles": Paul points to this as a basic right not only for himself, but for the other apostles also.

Some commentators maintain that Paul's point is to claim for all of them the *right* to do this, not to say that they necessarily are exercising that right. But Paul's wording in making this claim shows that he is aligning himself with recognized practice, what the other apostles do: which is rather a pointless thing to say unless in fact this is exactly what the others are doing! Therefore I must agree with Gordon Clark 143, who says, "All of them, or at least most of them, were married, as the present verse makes clear."

It was normal Jewish practice for men and women to marry quite young, and these matters were arranged for each family by a professional matchmaker: it was a matter of shame for the family if in any particular instance this could not done. It is almost certain that these men each would have been married before they met Jesus - as was certainly the case for Peter (Matthew 8:14//Mark 1:30//Luke 4:38).

**9:5c**: "and the brothers of the Lord": These brothers are named in Matthew 13:55//Mark 6:3 as James, Joses (or Joseph), Simon and Jude, and Matthew 13:56 refers to "all his sisters", indicating at least two, and thus that Jesus had at least six siblings. With Joseph and Mary, this would indicate that Jesus was a member of a family of at least nine.

Three main views have been held as to the identity of these brothers.

The first: that they were children of Mary and Joseph by natural birth, taking the word "brothers" with its normal meaning in Greek. The implication is accepted from Matthew 1:25, that after the visitation from the angel of the Lord in a dream, Joseph "took Mary home as his wife, but he had no union with her until she gave birth to a son ... Jesus" (NIV). Thus Mary gave birth to "her firstborn son" (Luke 2:7), to be followed by others, so that Jesus was the eldest child in the family.

The second view arose in the church when virginity came to be a prized virtue and, in tandem, sex was deprecated and regarded (as we have seen in chapter 7) as tainted with sin if not actually sinful in itself. Thus it grew to be held that Mary the Lord's mother must always have remained "pure" and could not have engaged in marital relations with Joseph. The development of this dogma of "the perpetual virginity of Mary" meant that (on this view) she could not have given birth to other children after Jesus, so another explanation was required for the New Testament references to such siblings.

The *Protevangelium* ("Gospel of James"), an apocryphal Gospel written more than a century after the crucifixion, describes Joseph as being an older man who already had children when Mary was espoused to him. On this view, then, Jesus would be the youngest child in the family.

Objections to this view: There is no contemporary historical evidence at all for this theory: the view is special pleading to provide an explanation of the New Testament references to the "brothers of Jesus". In the narratives of the nativity of Jesus there is no mention of other, older, siblings in the family. When Joseph was warned in a dream to flee to Egypt, "he rose and took the child and his mother by night and departed to Egypt" (Matthew 2:14) - no mention of other, older, children.

And similarly no mention of other children in the account (Luke 2:41-51) of the visit to the temple in Jerusalem when Jesus was twelve. Children younger than Jesus could have been left behind with other family members, but children older than Jesus (or at least some of them) would be expected to accompany the parents on this journey.

Matthew 13:55 identifies Joseph as a carpenter, and Mark 6:3 names Jesus as "the carpenter" of Nazareth. This is by no means unexpected if Jesus is the eldest son in the family, but it is considerably less likely to be the case that Jesus would take Joseph's role and profession if there were four older brothers in the family.

The John 7:1-5 account implies that Jesus's brothers were still living at home in the family - a highly improbable situation if these brothers were children of Joseph, and thus older than Jesus, but logical if they were somewhat younger.

An alternative view upholding the perpetual virginity of Mary was proposed by Jerome in AD 382: that in Scripture the word "brothers" is not only used to mean "children" of the same parent, but is also used more widely, as "kinsman" or in particular, "cousin". It is held that "brother" simply denotes relationship - in fact (depending on context) it may just mean "friend", and in relation to the "brothers of the Lord" it is to be understood as referring to "cousins", children of Mary's sister. But Paul used the normal word for "cousin" (ἀνεψιος, *anepsios*), elsewhere, when he needed it (Colossians 4:10) - why not here if that was what he meant?

The Gospels several times refer to Jesus's brothers being in the company of Mary (John 2:12; Matthew 12:46-47//Mark 3:31-32//Luke 8:19-20). Why would this be the case if they were not her children but Jesus's cousins?

Advocates of this theory are pushed into further unfounded speculation, such as that their own parents had died and that Mary adopted them. Which contradicts another "leg" of the "cousins" theory as usually held: that these "cousins" were the children of Mary's sister Mary the wife of Cl(e)opas. So we have (in this version) two sisters, both named Mary! But both Mary's sister and Cl(e)opas were alive at the time of the crucifixion, and are mentioned in the Gospels. And speculation is added to speculation to get around each contrary fact as it is encountered.

Support for the idea that Jesus's brothers could not be natural children of Mary has been drawn from the fact that (John 19:26-27) on the cross Jesus committed Mary to the care of his disciple John, and she went to live in his home. It is argued that if Mary had had other children, Jesus would have committed her to *their* care. It can be responded that Mary was *there*, at the cross, and other brothers (or sisters) of Jesus were *not*; that Jesus had plainly said that his disciples were his family and that his mother and his brothers were *not*, if they did not believe in him and accept his teaching and his ministry (Mark 3:20-21, 31-35); and that John was "the beloved disciple" who would provide Mary with a warm and loving home, whereas at that time his brothers were unbelieving mockers and scoffers (John 7:1-5). It is understandable that Jesus did not commit her to the care of someone who was "against him" (Matthew 12:30//Luke 11:23).

After the resurrection his brothers became believers - but that lay in the future.

The rationale for the belief in "the perpetual virginity of Mary", so that she bore no other children but Jesus, is the idea which developed in the early church of the "purity" of virginity, and the wrongness (in varying degrees) of marital sex, with the consequent deduction that Mary and Joseph could not ever have had sex together. Once we reject this idea as a total misreading of Scripture about sex, there remains no reason for disallowing the normal meaning of "brothers of the Lord" as a reference to other natural children of Mary, born after Jesus.

These brothers were unbelieving during Jesus's time on earth (John 7:5). Accompanied by Mary they went out from (presumably) Nazareth to where Jesus was living in Capernaum (Matthew 4:13), "to seize him, for they were saying, He is out of his mind" (Mark 3:20-21), and when they arrived they were rejected by Jesus as "family" unless they would "do the will of God" (Mark 3:31-35) - which presumably, in that context, included recognizing and receiving his ministry and his teaching.

This entire issue of the identity of the brothers of Jesus, and the question generally of the perpetual virginity of Mary, is examined in full detail by Eric Svendsen in his valuable monograph *Who Is My Mother?*

His brothers were not present at the cross. But after the Resurrection, Jesus appeared to his brother James (1 Corinthians 15:7), and this clearly was the turning point. In consequence, after the ascension "Mary the mother of Jesus and his brothers" joined the apostles and the women disciples in their gathering in "the upper room where they were staying"

(Acts 1:12-14) . James grew to hold a position of leadership in the Jerusalem church (Acts 12:17; Galatians 1:19 and 2:9, 12) and presided at the Council of Jerusalem (Acts 15:13 - see also 21:18). His leadership in the Jerusalem church is well attested from church history, and he was martyred by the Jews in AD 62.

This same James is generally recognized as the author of the Epistle of James; and another brother, Jude, as the author of the Epistle of Jude.

From our present verse 9:5 we learn that the brothers of the Lord were now engaged in Christian ministry, and in this ministry were accompanied by their Christian wives.

**9:5d** We note that Paul mentions Cephas (Peter) by name, even though he would have been included within the term "the other apostles". Why should Paul thus single out this man for special mention?

This would seem to indicate that the ***married status of Peter*** was a matter of significance within the Corinthian church, and that this was one of the points of difference between the "Cephas faction" and the "Paul" and "Christ" factions there (1:12) - Peter being the most prominent married apostle. If so, we can see the relevance of Paul's argument here. He cuts the ground from under the feet of those who make a difference between Peter and himself on this issue when he says, "I have every right to be accompanied by a Christian wife, just as Peter is, if I choose to be." This would link further with the words of v.3, "This is my defence to those who sit in judgement on me" (NIV) - suggesting that the dispute at Corinth which involved Paul's name also touched on the question of his (and Peter's) married status. (We do not know the matrimonial status of Apollos.) Otherwise it is very difficult to see why Peter is singled out for special mention.

This verse is also important for showing that marriage was the norm for the apostles and other church leaders. Paul was aware that (with Barnabas) he was the "odd man out" in the apostolic company by being unmarried, but far from suggesting that the others should be like him, he defends his right to be like them - even if it is a right that he chooses not to use. This verse, coming as it does from the apostle of the ἀγαμοι, *agamoi* (7:8), is the strongest possible testimony against the teaching that celibacy is a better state than marriage, and the idea that those engaged in Christian ministry should be unmarried. Even now, says Paul, I have the right to marry and to take my wife with me on my journeys.

**9:6** Why would Paul link Barnabas's name with his own here? Barnabas was not one of Paul's companions when he ministered in Corinth, nor was Barnabas in Ephesus at the time when Paul was writing. The simplest explanation is most likely also the correct one: that

Barnabas, like Paul (and unlike the other leaders of the early church), was unmarried. This may well have been a factor in Barnabas's availability to be partner with Paul on the First Missionary Journey, and he would be the "we" with Paul in v.5 ("we have the right to take a believing wife along with us") as well as in v.6 (working to earn one's own living while preaching the gospel - something that would be rather more difficult if one had a wife to support as well as oneself). Thus Paul has moved on from his "right" to be accompanied by a wife to the question of his "right" to receive financial support for his ministry.

**9:7** These three illustrations from everyday life support the principle that the Christian worker is entitled to be provided for in return for his ministry.

"Whoever (τις ... ποτε, *tis ... pote*) goes to fight a war at his own expense?" A soldier will have his needs supplied. The owner of a vineyard receives the benefit of its produce. The text says next, "Whoever tends a flock and does not *eat* (ἐσθιω, *esthiō*) some of its milk?": referring not just to *drinking* some of the milk but getting to eat the dairy produce in general (cheese from the milk), and other things purchased from the proceeds of the milk. Stanley 149: ἐκ του γαλακτος [*ek tou galaktos*], i.e. "from the proceeds of the sale of the milk," or "from the food made out of the milk."

Garland 409 sums up the implication:

> "The analogies of army, vine and flock have a rich heritage as imagery for God's people in the OT ... Those who are soldiers in the army of Christ, working in God's vineyard, and shepherding God's sheep also can expect to receive upkeep from their service."

**9:8-9** These illustrations are followed by a quotation from the Law (Deuteronomy 25:4; also quoted in 1 Timothy 5:18). As it stands, the question "Is it for oxen that God is concerned?" would have to be answered "Yes", seeing that the Old Testament shows clearly that a merciful and compassionate God *is* concerned about the welfare and treatment of his animal creation. At times, sentences of this kind need the insertion of "only" in English to bring out their meaning correctly: "Is it only for oxen that God is concerned?"

Similarly παντως, *pantōs* (v.10), translated "entirely" in the RSV, NRSV, ESV, does not limit the application of this quotation to people and exclude God's concern for animals; this word is better rendered here "surely" (NIV, Phillips), "really" (TEV), "clearly" (NEB) or "an obvious reference to ourselves" (Jerusalem Bible).

**9:10** "It was written [i.e. this Scripture in Deuteronomy 25:4] for our sake": Robertson & Plummer 185 declare that "we must understand the ploughing and threshing as metaphors for different stages of missionary work. Such work, and indeed teaching of any kind, is often compared to agriculture."

**9:11** "τα πνευματικα [*ta pneumatika*], that is, the things of God" (Edwards 231); "... normally denotes the things of the (Holy) Spirit in Paul" (Thiselton 689). This is the same expression which occurs in 12:1 (in the genitive) and 14:1, where it is so frequently rendered in the translations as "spiritual gifts". We may note that it is never in *this* verse thus rendered by them: which allows us to recognize that the addition of the word "gifts" in these later verses is not part of the meaning of the expression, but is an idea *added in*. When we reach these chapters we shall consider the significance of this further.

**9:12** This section reaches its climax with Paul's reference to the "others" who are claiming support for their ministry from the Corinthians, and Paul's assertion that he has an even more legitimate claim. This is immediately followed by his reminder that he had not used this right.

"Endure anything" indicates that his policy has its difficulties for him: which is part of the reason for the implied unhappiness of the Corinthians about it.

Garland 413 remarks that what he has said

"indicates that he was in need. His poverty caused the Corinthians some consternation ... they interpreted his penury as demeaning to himself and an embarrassment to them. Paul apparently considers the Corinthians' disapproval of his choice of low social status as only a minor impediment in their relationship compared to the possible negative repercussions that accepting support would have had on possible converts. His strategy of supporting himself freed him to serve all, not just his patrons."

For there could be hindrances to the gospel if he took support from the Corinthians for his ministry - he gives no hint at this point as to what these might be, but says merely that he will under no circumstances permit anything to put an obstacle in the way (ESV) or hinder (NIV) the gospel of Christ.

These down-to-earth everyday illustrations are given almost certainly with his Gentile readership in view. After he makes his point for the first time in this verse about not using his rights, he builds again to the same point a second time in v.15 - but this second time he uses illustrations from Scripture to appeal to his Jewish readership.

**9:13-14** A further example is taken from the Old Testament sacrifices (see Leviticus 6:16; 7:6, 31-36; Numbers 5:9-10; 18:8-24; Deuteronomy 18:1), the practice still at that time being observed in Israel.

Then the parallel is drawn and the principle is stated: "In the same way, the Lord commanded that those who proclaim the gospel should get their living by the gospel." This passage (and similar teaching elsewhere, e.g. 2 Corinthians 8-9; Galatians 6:6) lays it down clearly that the Lord's people are responsible for supporting the Lord's work by providing generously for the Lord's servants whom he calls to minister in the gospel.

Again we have here (as in 7:10) a citing of what the Lord has commanded: referring to commandments the Lord Jesus had given during his earthly ministry. This command is found in the teaching of Christ in Matthew 10:10//Luke 10:7 - the latter verse is also quoted exactly by Paul in 1 Timothy 5:18, where he again uses the same saying from Deuteronomy 25:4 that he quotes here (9:9). Paul's references to the commandments of the Lord indicate a high degree of familiarity on his part with what the Lord taught during his earthly ministry (cf. also 7:10 - and 7:12 and 7:25 for Paul's awareness that Christ had *not* given any teaching on certain matters).

Drawing upon these Old Testament passages and the teaching of the Lord, Paul states the principle: "In the same way, the Lord commanded that those who proclaim the gospel should get their living by the gospel." This is a principle of basic importance in the administration and structure and ministry of the church: see further in "Reflections", below.

**9:15** After insisting emphatically upon the responsibility of the church to provide the livelihood of those who minister, Paul now states that those who minister are also able, if they choose, to forego these rights, in part or in whole. Garland 415 points out,

> Paul did not understand himself to be disobeying a decree from the Lord, but interpreted it as a right that he was free to accept or refuse. ... He regards "these things" in 9:15, including the Lord's command, as a "right" (cf. NRSV, NIV), not an obligation. We might imagine that preaching in pioneer areas in a pagan environment would also have required greater flexibility. Paul could hardly go to a new community and say, "The Lord commanded me to be supported by you."

Why would Paul have adopted this attitude towards receiving support from the Corinthians? Paul himself tells us here that it is so that no one can deprive him of his grounds for boasting. This indicates his concern lest the purity of his preaching of the gospel be compromised in some way. We can identify several specific factors which he is likely to have had in mind.

One probable reason lies in the circumstances of his visit there. It was while in Corinth that Paul received news about the progress of the Thessalonian church, through the arrival of Timothy (1 Thessalonians 3:6),

and this news included details of the continuing opposition from the
Jews in Thessalonica. Morris (*The Epistles to the Thessalonians* 21f.)
comments:

> One part of their campaign was a personal attack on Paul himself.
> They urged that he had no real love for his converts (else why did he
> not come back to them?), and that he had never been motivated by any
> genuine concern for them, but only by the desire for personal profit. ...
> Paul devoted a considerable amount of space [in 1 Thessalonians] to the
> refutation of such slanderers. ... He pointed to the way he and his com-
> panions had steadfastly refused to take anything from the Thes-
> salonians, but had worked hard night and day to support themselves.

In these circumstances, then, Paul had thought it wise similarly to
take no support from the Corinthians. For Paul has decided it is pre-
ferable for him to give no grounds for anyone at Corinth to say that he
was only engaged in his ministry for the material benefits it brought him.
Robertson & Plummer 186: "Obviously, if he took maintenance, he
might be suspected of preaching merely for the sake of what he got by
it."

There is another reason which we can see to be very relevant in rela-
tion to the Corinthians and what he is saying to them in this Epistle.
Basically, by declining to accept financial support from the Corinthians
Paul was retaining the right to rebuke and criticize them. As Robertson
& Plummer 187 describe, "He must be free to rebuke, and his praise
must be above the suspicion of being bought."

Furthermore, as Garland 413 points out,

> Potential converts may have shied away from converting to the gos-
> pel if they suspected that it came with strings attached: acceptance
> would cause them to incur financial obligations to support the one who
> brought them the gospel.

Blomberg 173 contends that a significant factor was:

> The powerful patrons in the Corinthian church doubtless would
> have preferred to have Paul accept their money but give them deference
> and political support in return. When he refused and continued to rely
> on tent-making instead (cf. Act 18:1-4), they charged that his unwilling-
> ness to go along with their patronage demonstrated that he did not have
> the same authority as other itinerant apostles or preachers

Thiselton 662f. notes

> the extent of the social obligations to which Paul would be
> understood to have committed himself if he had made use of his
> "rights" in the Corinthian situation. ... no doubt the rich "patron" would
> expect some *quid pro quo* in terms of status, influence, or leadership
> role within the church.

Paul was willing - and indeed grateful - to accept support from another church: that is, from a church he was not currently ministering in (see his response to the gifts from Philippi, Philippians 4:10-20; cf. 2 Corinthians 11:9). But to accept support from the Corinthians would involve too many issues, some of which could compromise his ministry and "put an obstacle in the way of the gospel" (9:12). Fee 414ff. says:

> His overall concern seems clear enough: to explain, in terms of his own unique relationship to the gospel, why he has deliberately not accepted their patronage. ... He has the right to such patronage, he has argued, as even the Lord has commanded. His restraint with regard to that right is not to be understood as not having it, but as related to his own calling. That calling is so interwoven with the gospel itself that he can do nothing that might hinder it, including accepting patronage.

**9:16-18** Paul preaches the gospel, he explains, not for reward, but to fulfill his commission, which lays upon him his compulsion to preach. This commission he received on the Damascus Road (Acts 9:6, 15; 13:2; 22:21; Galatians 1:15-16).

His reward is being able to make the gospel freely available to all: preaching the gospel is its own reward. Paul's exclamations should find an echo in the hearts of each believer, as God provides opportunity: "Woe to me if I do not preach the gospel! I am still entrusted with a stewardship!"

**9:19** Paul asked, "Am I not free?" (v.1), and now tells them what freedom in Christ means. Paul is free - to be everybody's slave. That is how Paul explains the nature of Christian freedom. The paradox of the Christian life: we do not have freedom to do what we like, but freedom to do what we should.

**9:20-23** Fee 423:

> After the extended defense of his rights, and his right to lay them aside, he now sets out to explain his apparently chameleonlike stance in matters of social relationships.

Paul outlines the principles of his policy: he adapts himself and his message to those to whom he ministers. This is not compromise, much less hypocrisy or insincerity. Rather, it is a high degree of sensitivity to the views and situation of those he seeks to persuade, and a willingness to learn to act and speak in ways that will be understood and which will commend his message. He wishes to avoid artificial and unnecessary barriers of culture or practice getting in the way between himself and his hearers. He seeks to show the total relevance of the gospel message to the needs and aspirations of each group of listeners to whom he speaks.

As the "law" in this verse is indubitably the Mosaic law, most commentators appear a titch puzzled (cf. Fee 428) as to what Paul had in mind when he differentiated between "the Jews" and "those under the law".

Suggestions include: (a) they are synonyms, but in "those under the law" Paul refers to this aspect of Judaism in particular (Fee 429); (b) Paul is showing an awareness that there are some Jews not much concerned about keeping the law, and some non-Jews who do keep it: "The one refers to nationality, the other to religion; and there were some who were under the Mosaic Law who were not Jews by race": (Robertson & Plummer 191); (c) Samaritans (put forward by Origen, Kovacs 154); (d) proselytes to Judaism; Stanley 157: "To those that were under the law," i.e. (as distinguished from Ἰουδαιοις), Jewish proselytes, or Jewish converts to Christianity." (e) godfearers; (f) Gentiles with a respect for Jewish standards of behavior; (g) Jewish Christians, with "win" meaning not simply to bring to salvation but to build up in the faith.

We can see the outworking of this policy if we look at the approach he follows in each of the speeches recorded in Acts: a very Jewish approach, thoroughly grounded in the Old Testament, when he speaks to Jews, and an approach to Gentiles that commences at the point where they are (cf. his speech at Lystra, Acts 14:8-18; and at Athens, Acts 17:16-31).

Thus today missionaries in a foreign culture will adapt themselves to the features of that culture as far as they can, and change from aspects of their own culture, lest these incidental trappings of culture be confused by their hearers with aspects of the gospel message itself.

**9:20** This certainly means that Paul could and would behave as a Jew when the circumstances so required. This would include when he attended the Jewish synagogues as the first step in his evangelism in a new town (Acts 13:5; 13:10; 14:1; 17:1-2; 17:10; 17:17; 18:4; 18:19). Other examples of his Jewish conformity to gain and retain as smooth a path as possible for the gospel would include having Timothy circumcized (Acts 16:3), taking a vow (Acts 18:18), and joining with others in their purificatory rites (Acts 21:21-26). After the Romans took him into custody, Paul said to the Jewish crowd, "I am a Jew" (Acts 22:3). Paul submitted to the discipline of the Jewish community to retain his membership and his acceptance in it, for the sake of the gospel (9:23) - even though he now regarded himself, in Christ, as "not being myself under the law" (9:20c - cf. Galatians 5:18). His goal is to win Jews - those under the law (9:20c).

**9:21** Similarly he became as one outside the law (i.e. the Jewish law: he is thus referring to the Gentiles) - not, he hastens to add, that he is outside God's law, but he is subservient to the Law of Christ. The concept of the Law of Christ, the "Royal Law", is paralleled in the Epistle of James, where this is a significant theme: see "Reflections", below.

**9:22a** Commentators acknowledge some uncertainty about the identity of the "weak", and thus what Paul means when he says "I became weak" (there is no "as", ὡς, *hōs*, here). Garland 433 informs us that

> Many contend that the "weak" refers to Christians who are "weak in faith" (Rom 14:1), whom Paul tries to win to a fuller knowledge of the faith or to prevent from falling away from Christ (1 Cor 8:10-11). ... In 10:31-33, Paul states his aim to seek the benefit of the many in order that they might be saved, and he lists three groups: Jews, Greeks, and the church of God (10:32). If the "weak" refers to Christians, the order in 9:20-22 would match that in 10:33: Jews, those without the law, and the weak.

Garland himself argues against this interpretation, but (mainly because of how it links with the context of chapter 8 and then chapter 10) I myself prefer it.

**9:22b-23** Blomberg 160 states that in this section we find the Epistle "enunciating Paul's underlying principle for all of his behavior in these gray areas of life: what is most likely to bring more people to Christ."

In this policy, Paul is not pretending to be something he is not. Rather, he is flexible, conforming to those he is seeking to win. He became (as each different situation required) all things to all people, in order to save them. He was responsive and perceptive, and in tune with his listeners. He was not insisting upon his rights: he was willing to yield in all non-essentials in order that what was essential to the gospel could be clearly seen. Stanley 157 mentions: "πάντως, [*pantōs*] "by all means," the double meaning, as in English."

**9:24-25** Two analogies from the Greek Games illustrate his motivation and his aim. He runs with all his might and skill, in order to succeed in winning the prize (and he exhorts the Corinthians to run in the same way).

"Only one wins": Paul is not speaking of competing against fellow-Christians for a limited number of prizes. Fee 435: "His point does not lie with the fact that only one receives the prize, as if the Christian life were a competition of some sort." We are each running our own race, the race of life - and an obstacle race at that! Each of us is to run *our* race with a determination and one-eyed commitment equal to that of a winning athlete, so as to be successful.

**9:26** He boxes effectively, not "as one beating the air", or shadow-boxing. He fights, in other words, in such a way as to counter the attacks of his opponents, and to get in effective blows that will defeat them. Robertson & Plummer 196 describe this: "he uses his fists as one in deadly earnest, and does not miss: he plants his blow."

This gives us an insight into the purpose of what he says in his various epistles: he does not write lightly and thoughtlessly, but with definite objectives in view in each thing that he says, and with the intention of answering and silencing his opponents and detractors. We should recognize the application of this purpose throughout his entire corpus, not just here.

**9:27E** To this end, he makes his body his servant in Christ's service, so that he can accomplish this purpose and not be "disqualified". The body is not an enemy to be defeated or punished, but a servant to be held in check, a vehicle of his ministry, to be properly serviced and maintained.

"Disqualified": Thiselton 717 stresses, "However, Paul does not specify that he would be not approved ... as if to imply eschatological rejection or loss of salvation." Paul is not speaking here of "losing his salvation" in any sense, but rather of being put on one side by the Lord for service and ministry, if he does not keep himself trained and available. He intends to guard against this possibility by ensuring that he is always in control of himself, and thus always able to "run" and "fight" in Christ's service.

In writing in this way about *himself* being "disqualified", Paul is implying a similar and much more real danger of this happening to the self-satisfied, complacent Corinthians.


## SOME PRACTICAL AND PASTORAL REFLECTIONS

### Providing and Accepting Financial Support

Paul affirms (9:14), "In the same way, the Lord commanded that those who proclaim the gospel should get their living by the gospel."

Is Paul disobeying the Lord's command by not accepting Corinthian support? No: the primary thrust of this command is directed to those who receive the ministry or (in missionary and similar situations) those who send out the workers (Romans 10:15).

On the one hand, Jesus is telling those whom he calls to ministry that it is fully right and proper for them to be supported by that ministry. On the other, it is a clear word from Jesus which lays down the responsibility of those who receive such ministry to support those who provide it.

Fee 413 says, "The command is not given *to* the missionaries, but *for* their benefit."

Paying the one who ministers is not like paying a tradesman who is doing work for you - "payment for services rendered" - or a salesman providing you with goods. It is establishing a reciprocity of a different order: I am doing this (supporting you) while you are doing that (preaching the gospel and teaching the faith). I am not paying you *for* doing that so much as paying you *to enable* you to do that.

It is the shame of the modern church in many places that it commits itself to explaining why the tithe as the minimum level of giving for a Christian does not apply to us today (in spite of the fact that it was the one thing for which Jesus commended the Pharisees: Matthew 23:23), and thus the work of outreach and world evangelism is proceeding much more slowly than it could.

We need to move out of our comfort zone and surrender our rights to our little luxuries (which so often, totally unjustifiably, we deem necessities) and ensure that those whom the Lord calls to his service are provided for.

God be praised for those who go forth anyway, paying their own way in ministry, like Paul. For Paul's life is bivocational: he spends his time both in working, earning his livelihood, and in engaging in Christian ministry. We have no idea how much time he spent in each. Obviously a similar flexibility is open to us in seeking to follow in his footsteps in this.

Blomberg 176f. notes that:

> Bivocational ministry has numerous advantages: freedom from human "strings", not imposing a financial burden on any group of believers, and exemption from charges of mismanaging funds or ministering primarily for financial gain. Although ... verse 14 allows us to generalize Paul's principles to any one in full-time gospel ministry verses 9-11, with their metaphors of sowing and reaping, suggest that such ministry need not even be full time."

Paul was not adverse to accepting support, when it was sent freely, no strings attached, and no complications involved (as we see from 2 Corinthians 11:9 and Philippians 4:10-20). But he did not depend upon it, for his commitment to the proclamation of the gospel impelled him forward notwithstanding. For this was his priority. As the Lord had called and empowered the prophets (cf. Jeremiah 1:4-10; Amos 3:8), so Paul felt himself swept along under this internal compulsion. This is the "fire in the belly" which constrains the dedicated herald of the Lord. Blomberg 179 notes:

> A good test for would-be full-time Christian workers is to ask them-
> selves the question if they could imagine being truly happier doing any-
> thing else. If the answer is yes, they probably have not been called.

So Paul will minister in Corinth finances notwithstanding. And in the circumstances at Corinth, Paul has decided that he declines to use his apostolic right to be supported by them in his ministry (though he is will-ing to have them finance his journey when he leaves them and moves on elsewhere - see the notes on 16:6, where Paul asks the Corinthians to send him on his way wherever he goes).

But he has established clearly the right and the need for the ministers of the gospel to be fully supported by the people of God. To finance the worldwide ministry of the gospel: this is to be our priority. The gospel ministers may support or partially support themselves. But they can do a much more effective and focussed job if Christians support them adequately so that they are not cumbered with the necessity of financing their ministry.

As we shall see, Paul gives us some further guidelines in relation to supporting others in chapter 16, below.


## Christians and The Law of Christ

There are those who live under the law and to them Paul became, he tells us, as one under the law ("though not being myself under the law"), that he might win them. And to those who do not have the law he became as one "without law" (ἄνομος, *anomos*) that he might win them also. He cautiously qualifies this by saying also, "not being outside the law of God but under the law of Christ". He is careful to show us that he is not without law, or outside the law, i.e. "lawless", but he is subject to the law of Christ. So there are those who are under law, and those without law, and those who are subject to the law of Christ.

And what exactly does this "law of Christ" mean?

The New Testament regards the teaching of the Lord Jesus Christ as authoritative and definitive. We have seen that Paul has already cited teachings from Jesus as the decisive word of the Lord on a point (7:10 and 9:14). Jesus himself referred on a number of occasions to his "com-mandments", and in the Missionary Mandate of Matthew 28:20, when commissioning his followers to go throughout the world and make dis-ciples from all nations, he instructed them to teach these converts "to obey all that I have commanded you".

Paul refers specifically to the "law of Christ" in 9:21 and also in

Galatians 6:2. John refers several times to his commandments in his First Epistle. James writes of the "Royal Law" in James 2:18 and of the "perfect law, the law of liberty" in 1:25 and again of the law of liberty in 2:12. And there is, throughout the New Testament, an attitude that in Jesus God has spoken and is to be obeyed at all costs (e.g. Acts 5:32).

Jesus placed his imprimatur upon the two greatest commandments as "love God" and "love your neighbor" (Matthew 22:37-40//Mark 12:29-31), and Paul summarized all the commandments of the Mosaic law as "love your neighbor as yourself" (Romans 13:9-10). John emphasized that we are to "keep his commandments and do what pleases him", and identified in particular that "this is his commandment, that we believe in the name of his Son Jesus Christ and love one another, just as he has commanded us" (1 John 3:23; cf. 2:8).

Jesus made his commandments definitive of the relation of the disciple to him. "If you love me, you will keep my commandments" (John 14:15). "If anyone loves me, he will keep my word" (John 14:23). And supremely, this is because it is to be recognized that "The word that you hear is not mine, but the Father's who sent me" (John 14:24). Again Jesus said, "You are my friends, if you do what I command you" (John 15:14). John echoes this: "By this we know that we love the children of God, when we love God and obey his commandments. For this is the love of God, that we keep his commandments. And his commandments are not burdensome." (1 John 5:2-3.)

The Lord's primary commandment is love (John 13:34-35). There is a sense in which all the rest of the teaching of Jesus is explicatory of how this commandment is fulfilled in practice, as Paul has said (Romans 13:10). But those "explanatory details" are important for clarifying how we are to behave in day-to-day living.

This does not mean that the commandments of the Old Testament have been abrogated or discontinued in some way, but rather, that they are now internalized and reapplied: and this, initially and primarily through the life and teaching of Jesus Christ himself. Indeed, a major distinction in the New Testament era in which we live is that all the commandments of God are now internalized: for the Christian, they are written by the Spirit of the living God, not on tablets of stone (like the Ten Commandments at Mount Sinai), but on the tablets of human hearts (2 Corinthians 3:3).

This happens as the Christian responds to the exhortation to "grow in grace and the knowledge of our Lord and Savior Jesus Christ" (2 Peter 3:18). The Lord himself instructed, "Take my yoke upon you, and learn from me." (Matthew 11:29).

Paul reminds us that we "are not under law but under grace", which means that Christians, "who were once slaves of sin, have become obedient from the heart to the standard of teaching to which you were committed" (Romans 6:14-17).

Then, thus knowing the commandments of the Law of Christ, each of us will keep them because of the motivation of love for Christ. "If you love me, you *will* keep my commandments." Paul is not "lawless": he lives in submission to the "Law of Christ". So also must all Christ's followers do.

# CHAPTER TEN

## SECTION 3(a)
## CONCERNING FOOD SACRIFICED TO IDOLS (Cont.)

### 3. Examples, Issues, Principles (10:1-30)

### (a) The Example Of The Fathers (10:1-13)

**10:1** In discussing the matter of food offered to idols, Paul has first stated the issue under consideration (chapter 8), and followed this with a consideration of "The Nature Of Freedom" (chapter 9). He has been simultaneously defending himself against the calumnies of his detractors and using himself as an example for the Corinthians. He has recognized the need for self-control in his life, in order that his whole being (including his body) can be under Christ's control - and he has exhorted the Corinthians to do this also. "Run in such a way to get the prize" (9:24b, NIV). "They do it to receive a perishable wreath, but we an imperishable" (9:25b). Now Paul moves from an implied warning to the Corinthians to a very explicit one, which he draws from Israel's history: what happened to the Israelites in the wilderness. There is a close connection in the Greek (γαρ, *gar*, "for") between this passage and what has gone before in chapter 9, a connection which many translations (including the ESV) overlook (it is found though in the NASB, NIV and Phillips).

Paul's thought is that the danger of being disqualified, which he has just set before them, is not vague and hypothetical, but a very real possibility, for that is exactly what happened to "our forefathers" (NIV). Paul addresses himself to the "brothers" at Corinth - that is, to the whole church - and then writes of the Jews as "our forefathers", showing that he regarded the Church, the people of God in the new dispensation, as the heirs and successors of ancient Israel, and in full continuity with the people of God under the old covenant. Thus the Church is Israel (Galatians 6:16) and Abraham is the father of all "those who believe", for "If you are Christ's, then you are Abraham's offspring, heirs according to promise" (Galatians 3:6-29). Thus Paul draws out lessons for the Corinthians, for "these things took place as examples for us, that we might not desire evil as they did" (v.6) and "they were written down for our instruction" (v.11).

Paul commences this passage, "I want you to know, brothers", not implying that they did not know the *facts* of the Exodus from Egypt, but that they had not paid sufficient attention to the *significance* for themselves of the lessons to be learnt from these facts.

"The cloud" refers to Exodus 13:21, "The Lord went before them by day in a pillar of cloud to guide them along the way".

**10:2** The Israelites were baptized in the cloud and in the sea: they themselves were not in the water, but they had the cloud above them and they "walked on dry ground through the sea, the waters being a wall to them on their right hand and on their left", and the Egyptians in attempting to follow them were engulfed and overwhelmed in the waters (Exodus 14:28-29).

Why is this called being "baptized into Moses"? Gordon Clark 152 says,

> The similarity between Moses' baptism and Christian baptism must be sought in their significance, or in a part of it. In both cases, the baptism is a visible sign that the baptized persons are the disciples of him into whose name they are baptized.

Godet's comment is,

> The Israelites, placed under the cloud and crossing the sea, possessed the visible pledge of Divine blessing and salvation. This miraculous crossing separated them thenceforth from Egypt, the place of bondage and idolatry, exactly as the believer's baptism separates him from his former life of condemnation and sin.

Morris writes,

> Probably we are to think of Moses as a type of Christ. Just as baptism has as one effect, the bringing of a man under the leadership of Christ, so did the participation in the great events of the Exodus bring the Israelites under the leadership of Moses.

**10:3** They ate manna, "spiritual food" (ESV, NASB, NIV, NRSV, TEV, Jerusalem Bible, Phillips, etc.) - Paul's term does not imply that it was not physical food, but indicates that its source and supplier was God.

**10:4** In the wilderness they obtained water from a rock by divine providence. Calling it "spiritual drink" indicates (as also in "spiritual food" in v.3) that its source and supplier was God. The account mentions that the Israelites received water from the rock twice. On the first occasion, Moses was told to strike the rock, and did so, and life-giving water flowed out of it (Exodus 17:6). On the second occasion Moses was instructed to speak to the rock only, but Moses - in anger with the contentiousness and grumbling of the Israelites - disobeyed God and struck the rock twice (Numbers 20:7-11), and in consequence of this act of disobedience neither he nor Aaron was permitted to enter the Promised Land (see Numbers 20:12, 24; 27:12-14; Deuteronomy 3:23-27).

Paul explains that the Rock which supplied their needs was Christ. That is, Christ is shown as pre-existent, and the One who followed them - Christ was with them in their wilderness wanderings, and it was Christ who provided water for them. Moses was to strike the rock once, and thereafter to speak to it but not to strike it: for the Rock "was" Christ, and Christ was smitten once for us to bring us life, but only once. When Moses struck the Rock twice more he damaged the symbolic imagery of the Rock as Christ.

"The Rock 'was' Christ" indicates that Christ miraculously sustained them in the wilderness, and this saying can best be understood in the same sense in which Christ said "This is my body ... this is my blood" - see my comment on 11:25.

Commentators vary considerably in their explanations of "the spiritual Rock that followed them, and the Rock was Christ". Garland 456 poses the problem when he speaks of:

> "ancient readers wondering what the Israelites did for water between the two accounts of the miraculous rock, when water gushed out (Exod. 17:1-7; Num 20:2-13). Surely, in forty years God gave them water more than twice."

I consider we may say with F. F. Bruce 91, "Paul ... affirms that Christ accompanied his people as a spiritual source of refreshment throughout this period." As God miraculously provided his people with spiritual bread during this period - the manna from heaven - so he also miraculously supplied their ongoing need for water, from a "spiritual Rock" always with them, and "the Rock was Christ". Details of this miraculous water supply are not given in the Old Testament (hence the way this problem is posed in Garland), and no more are such details given by Paul, other than to say, "the Rock was Christ". This was enough for Paul's purpose, which is to proclaim: these people received God's provision of spiritual food and spiritual drink, but nonetheless because of their idolatry and their rebelliousness most of them perished in the wilderness. And Paul's point is plain.

**10:5** In the first four verses of this passage Paul has five times emphasized that God's guidance and God's providential care, in Christ, were made available to them ***all***. Now comes the telling punchline: "nevertheless" (the strong adversive conjunction "but", ἀλλα, *alla*)

***almost all*** of them failed to profit from these tremendous advantages and, instead, incurred God's wrath. This forcefully illustrates Paul's point that receiving God's blessing and being a participant in all the privileges of the people of God gives no basis for believing that one can safely presume upon his mercy and ignore his standards.

**10:6-10** The application is made explicit. These things are warnings to us, because God's standards do not change, and therefore we can expect to encounter his judgement if we act as did the Israelites in the wilderness. These events are "warning us not to crave after evil things as they did" (Phillips). In particular, the Corinthians are warned, "Do not be idolaters" (relevant to the issue that is before Paul, of taking a meal in an idol's temple or eating meat offered to idols); we must not indulge in sexual immorality (very frequently associated with idolatry - see my comment on 6:9; Paul's command here underlines what he has said in chapters 5 and 6 about immorality); we must not put God to the test (by seeing how far into sin and disobedience one can go); nor grumble (because in its essence, as with the Israelites, this springs out of unbelief). Each of these commands is followed by a specific reference from the account of the Exodus, showing when the Israelites did such a thing, and what happened to them in consequence.

**10:11a** This section ends as it began, with the strong assertion that these events which occurred in Old Testament times contain warnings by which we are to be instructed: God's dealings with his people were warnings to them at the time; moreover, these events have been recorded so that we of subsequent generations can learn from them. This comment is significant in showing that in the providence of God the events of history which are written in the Bible are not recorded merely as history, but in order that we should draw from them examples to follow and warnings to heed: this thus authenticates the theological use of biblical history.

**10:11b** "On whom the end of the ages has come": this is not asserting that (in Paul's view) the end of all things was immediately at hand. Rather, he saw that the age in which he was living was the age of fulfillment to which the whole of the Old Testament pointed, and it is the final age in that when it ends it will be with the Return of Christ and the Consummation of all things. Thus in this sense the New Testament can (and does) refer to writer and readers as living in the "last days". We today are still living in the "last days" or "the last age" because, however long it lasts, this age will culminate in the sovereign reign of Christ, as Paul further elucidates later in this letter (15:24ff.).

**10:12** These solemn warnings must shatter all complacency. The one who is confident of his standing would be well advised to "take heed", "watch out" (from βλεπω, *blepō*, "I see"), for he is at risk of falling. "Fall" may mean "fall from grace", "fall from salvation", but in the light of the preceding verses about sin, and the next verse about temptation to sin, it is more appropriately taken as "fall into sin", especially sin of the kinds just mentioned. This verse makes it plain that it is always possible for us to fall: no matter how long we have been a Christian, and no matter how committed we are to Christ, sin is never impossible.

**10:13** This verse is one of the greatest assurances provided for the Christian in all of Paul's writings. The connection of Paul's thought thus far in this chapter is: "From the Old Testament record we see how the people of God fell into sin and how disastrous for them was the outcome. We are to take warning from this, lest we similarly fall into sin and condemnation. The person who is complacent and self-confident about his standing must watch out - he may be in grave danger of falling." Now there comes a tremendous word of encouragement: "But you do not have to fall into sin - it is *never* inevitable for a Christian to sin, but there is always a way of escape open for him."

The individual parts of this verse will repay our careful attention, as we too can learn much from them. See "Reflections", below.

## (b) The Significance of Sharing In Worship (10:14-22)

**10:14** Paul began in 8:1 to deal with the matters of idol worship and food offered to idols. After an initial consideration of these questions (chapter 8), he entered upon a much wider discussion which has led him to a general warning about the seriousness of sin and the certainty that by God's grace it *is* possible to resist temptation - for there will always be available a God-given way of escape.

Now he states this conclusion in relation to idolatry: "Therefore, my beloved, flee from idolatry". The word "therefore", διοπερ (*dioper*), is emphatic. What he says now is the conclusion which must follow from what has gone before - on the one hand, the seriousness of sin and its consequences, and on the other hand the certainty that we *can* resist temptation. The way of escape from idolatry, Paul says, is simple: flee from it. Keep well away from it. The present imperative (durative aspect) indicates that this is to be one's habitual response to any possible situation of involvement with idolatry. Garland 474 pictures this vividly: "Idolatry is like radioactive waste: it requires them to bolt from this area immediately to avoid contamination and certain death."

What is said in this section (10:14-24) has particular reference to the first of the two questions with which Paul has to deal, that of taking a meal in an idol's temple.

**10:15** The Corinthians had been priding themselves on their wisdom, and Paul appeals to them on that level. Sheer common sense will show them the logic of what he says.

**10:16** "The cup of thanksgiving" or "blessing" refers to the thanksgiving, or grace, said at meals. It is referring here to the cup used in the observance of Holy Communion. The breaking of bread was the act with which the Jews commenced a meal, and was accompanied by a prayer of thanksgiving to God for his goodness in graciously providing for the needs of his people. In the New Testament there are a number of occasions when the breaking of bread is alluded to where clearly it is not referring to Holy Communion (e.g., at the feeding of the five thousand, Mark 6:41; the feeding of the four thousand, Mark 8:6; the beginning of the meal at Emmaus, Luke 24:30). That is, the breaking of bread is the beginning of a hunger-satisfying meal, and was used as a term for the whole meal (e.g. Acts 2:42).

In Paul's use here, it refers to the meal in which Christ's death is commemorated, where the breaking of the bread is a reminder to them of Christ's words at the Last Supper about his death (Mark 14:22).

The word twice translated "participation" (ESV, NIV and RSV), "sharing" (NRSV), is κοινωνια (*koinonia*), "fellowship", which is sometimes (e.g., AV/KJV and Jerusalem Bible) translated "communion" and it is from *this* verse that is taken the name of "Holy Communion" for the eating the bread and drinking the cup in remembrance of Christ's death for us. To drink from the cup and eat the bread is to participate in Christ's blood and body.

**10:17** The bread which they used is all one, and is broken and distributed among them to be eaten; and this oneness of the bread is seen as a reminder and a symbol of the unity of the body, the Church.

**10:18** Similarly, those who eat the sacrifices in Israel "participate in the altar", i.e. are participants in the worship of the God of Israel at that altar.

**10:19-20** On the basis of these truths, the significance of eating a meal in an idol's temple is now shown. The worship of Christ in Holy Communion is real. The worship of the Lord at Israel's altar is real. Paul is wanting to avoid any suggestion that by what now follows he is saying heathen gods are real - but when a person participates in a meal in a heathen temple, he is participating in the worship of that heathen deity. And behind that heathen god stand Satan and his demons, so that pagan sacrifice is actually the worshipping of demons; eating a meal in an idol's temple is thus to be seen to be being "participants with demons" (ESV, NIV) or "partners with demons" (RSV, NRSV). Note, as Hurd

135 points out, "It is not the meat of and by itself, but the idolatrous eating of it which effectively produced fellowship with demons."

**10:21-22** To do this creates an impossible conflict for a Christian. He cannot share in worshipping Christ (in Holy Communion) *and* eat in an idol's temple, thus sharing the cup and the table of demons. God is jealous of his worship (this reflects the wording of the Second Commandment, against idolatry, Exodus 20:4-6) - dare we (by participating in idol worship) provoke his jealousy?

Note that the Lord's Supper the Holy Communion is observed upon a table, not an altar. (There is never in Scripture a mention of an altar in connection with Holy Communion: this would convey a totally incorrect and inappropriate connotation in connection with the meaning of the observance.)

### (c) When You Can Eat Meat, And When Not (10:23-30)

**10:23-24** Paul twice repeats here a common saying at Corinth that he also quoted in 6:12. (See also my comment on that verse.) The justification which the Corinthians gave for their behavior was that all things are permissible or lawful for the Christian. But, Paul repeats, not everything is beneficial. Not everything is constructive - not everything builds up the church, or the individual Christian. And *these* are the tests to be applied to whatever we do. Our aim - and the yardstick by which we assess our behavior - is to be what is of benefit (not just for myself, but) for my neighbor. Thus Paul has clearly answered the issue of a Christian eating in an idol's temple: both on the grounds that it is participating (albeit unintentionally) in demon worship, and that it is leading other Christians astray, it is behavior that no Christian can join in.

**10:25-30** Paul now turns to the second issue: eating meat which has been offered to idols. His principle here is a simple one. If you obtain the meat from the meat market, or if it is served up to you in an unbeliever's home where you are a guest, and the question of whether it has been offered first to an idol does not come up, then you are to eat it with a clear conscience, as this issue is not at stake. But if the question *is* raised, then the situation is different.

**10:25** Paul gives instructions not to raise the issue, when buying meat in the meat market, as to whether it has first been offered to idols. This shows clearly that the fact that it has been part of an idol sacrifice makes no difference to the meat itself. This may be self-evident to the modern reader, but it was a question under consideration in the early church. (Compare also views held today in some parts of the Christian church that the bread and wine of the Holy Communion is actually changed in its nature by consecration during the service.)

Thiselton 618 quotes Murphy O'Connor (from *St Paul's Corinth* 161), "About the only time that meat came on the market was after pagan festivals, and it had been part of the victims sacrificed to the gods", and then he adds:

> This meat could be purchased for use in private homes, where the "strong" in socioeconomic status could afford it and the "strong" in "knowledge" about the nonexistence of pagan deities could enjoy it without scruple.

**10:26** The reason why one can eat anything, even food that may have been offered in pagan sacrifice, is that it and all else in the earth ultimately belongs to God and comes from him - and this fact cannot be altered because something has been part of an idol sacrifice. (Paul's quotation is from Psalm 24:1.)

**10:27** The same principle applies when a Christian accepts the hospitality of an unbeliever's home: eat whatever is set before you without raising the issue about idol sacrifice. Paul's words "eat whatever is set before you" are almost identical with Jesus's words in Luke 10:8 - the identity of the thought and the closeness of the wording strongly indicate that Paul was familiar with this part of Jesus's teaching and was consciously basing what he said upon what Jesus taught. (Paul similarly uses this same teaching of Jesus in 1 Timothy 5:18, where he quotes the exact words of the preceding verse, Luke 10:7, and refers to this as what "the Scripture says".)

Also noteworthy is Paul's presumption that unbelievers would invite believers to dinner, and that believers are free to accept such an invitation if they wish: contrast 5:11, where believers are instructed not to eat with one who claims the name of brother and is living in a way that belies his Christian profession.

There is no objection however to a Christian eating with an unbeliever; often such dining together can be the foundation upon which bridges of friendship are built, across which the gospel can be taken. Paul's attitude here reflects that of Christ, who often ate with "outsiders", ranging from Pharisees (e.g. Luke 11:37) to tax collectors (e.g. Mark 2:13-15; Luke 19:1-10) - something for which Christ was criticized (Mark 2:16) and which he justified on the grounds that such people were the ones who needed his ministry (Mark 2:17).

Paul here allows the eating at a neighbor's of food which *may* have been sacrificed to an idol, if no issue about it possibly being idol meat is raised. Hurd 145 comments:

Moreover, if idol meat were completely forbidden, table fellowship of the Corinthian Christians with their non-Christian neighbors would be almost impossible. Thus the Christians would have become a socially segregated group like the Jews.

**10:28-29a** The RSV puts this sentence in brackets as if it is a parenthesis in Paul's thinking. The brackets are misleading, and again the ESV, NIV and NRSV are more correct here. This is not an aside - it is the other part of Paul's answer to the problem he is considering. If someone says (and this can be *anyone*, not just the host) that the food has been offered in sacrifice, then the Christian must not eat it. The issue of idol worship has been raised, and to eat the food in those circumstances would be to give the impression (at the least) of condoning idol worship and possibly even of participating in it by eating something that had been sacrificed to the idol.

What Paul says here is in clear concord with the judgement issued by the Council of Jerusalem (Acts 15:19-20, 29). It is sometimes said that Paul's teaching in 10:25-27 is in conflict with the Council of Jerusalem's edict, but a more thoughtful consideration of his complete teaching here will make it clear that this is not the case. Rather, Paul is *interpreting* that edict in relation to how it is to be applied in practice. Where it is *known* that the meat has been part of an idol sacrifice, then clearly to eat it would be in breach of the instruction "You are to abstain from food offered to idols" (Acts 15:29).

The question at issue is, How does the edict that you abstain from idol meat apply when you do not know whether or not some particular food *is* idol meat? Paul interprets the edict: one must not eat it where the fact that the meat has been sacrificed to idols is known or is said to be the case (and thus is a factor in the situation); but he regards it as no issue if it is not known whether the meat was part of a sacrifice (because no one is making it an issue). Paul's view is thus not inconsistent with the Council of Jerusalem's decree.

Nor is it inconsistent with Revelation 2:20, which condemns the teaching that encourages a Christian to practice immorality and to eat food which has been sacrificed to idols. The context in Revelation is clearly speaking of the deliberate and knowing eating of idol meat, which is a participation in idolatry. And Paul has strongly condemned such a thing in his teaching to the Corinthians.

Why does Paul not invoke the Council of Jerusalem's edict in answering the Corinthians' queries?

First of all, it is an open question whether Paul writes as he does *because* this is what the Council of Jerusalem decided (that is, in order simply to interpret and apply their edict) or - which is a great deal more likely - because he himself happens to be in accord with the Council in condemning any involvement in idolatry. It is to be expected that in this matter his views would agree with the Council's. He himself was at the Council; and in any case the Old Testament condemnation of idolatry is absolutely clear, and Paul would share this condemnation and teach it.

Secondly, it is questionable whether in faction-ridden Corinth the quoting of such a decree would carry weight in itself with more than a small number. Paul's chosen way was to appeal to their own commonsense (10:15) to see the obvious for themselves: a Christian must not eat idol meat for conscience' sake - not the conscience of the person himself who knows an idol is nothing, but for the sake of the conscience of the person who raised the issue and thus who is sensitive about it.

The most likely situation, however, is that Paul had previously delivered to them the decree of the Council in his initial ministry after founding the Corinthian church: we know from Acts 16:4 that it was his practice to give it to his churches. It would appear that the Corinthians were querying this decree and its application in their circumstances (probably in their letter to him), and that in chapters 8 to 10 Paul was responding to issues they had raised, following on from what had been said in the Council's decree.

**10:29b-30** The person who is not troubled by the thought of eating idol meat, because he is strong in the Lord, is thus not in danger of having his own faith affected; he can eat any meat he buys in the market without troubling to enquire if it is idol meat, as his conscience is not sensitive on this point (v.25). But such a person is, it appears, under attack from other Christians because *their* scruples do not permit this.

Paul puts himself hypothetically into the position of such a person and asks, "Why should my freedom (the fact that I am free from the control of idols and from belief in their power) be subject to the judgement of another man's conscience? If I eat this food with thankfulness to God, thus recognizing him as the giver (as in v.26), why am I denounced for eating what I have thus thankfully accepted as from God?" This can thus be another of Paul's rhetorical questions, here showing that a person who has a strong conscience concerning idol meat is not to be condemned - for not checking the source of his food (v.25) - by those who *are* troubled in conscience at the thought of eating idol meat (even if inadvertently).

Alternatively, 10:29b-30 can be seen as another instance of Paul quoting the Corinthians in order to answer them, and these two questions are taken that way by the TEV and NEB. These translations thus see

Paul as quoting those Corinthians who object to Paul's pronouncement (verses 28-29a) that a Christian must not eat, with 10:31-11:1 being Paul's reply to them.

*Had* Paul eaten idol meat at Corinth? Hurd 130f. thinks it probable: he says,

> Thus the clear implication of these three chapters is that Paul believed that he had been "denounced" for having eaten meat offered to idols. If, as seems probable, Paul's conduct was inconsistent to the extent that at certain times he had eaten idol meat, then ... The defensive tone of 1 Cor 9 is entirely understandable. ... We conclude, therefore, that Paul's own inconsistencies in this matter produced some sort of criticism from the Corinthians.

In view of what Paul says overall, I would think not, unless it had been in the kind of situation he describes, eating it inadvertently at a friend's place where the issue is not raised.

## 4. Paul's Summary: Principles of Action (10:31-11:1)

**10:31-33E** Paul now gives his concluding summation of where the entire discussion leads, and enunciates three guiding principles for conduct (in relation to the question of food offered to idols in particular, and Christian behavior in general). These are:

**(a)** Everything that a Christian does is to be done for God's glory. This applies to eating and drinking, and also to whatever else is done. When this principle is used to test the present problem, the conclusion is plain. We honor God when we thankfully receive what God supplies for our good (verses 26, 30). But if we eat a meal in such circumstances as to imply that we countenance idolatry, then this is not to God's glory (verses 20-22). And similarly it does not glorify God if we offend another man's conscience (verses 28-29a).

**(b)** In what we do, we must seek to avoid giving offence to others - to Jews or to Greeks (Gentiles), i.e. to non-Christians of different backgrounds and viewpoints, as well as to the Church of God. (Paul's wording here implies a three-fold division of mankind: into Christians and non-Christians, but with Jews distinguished from Gentiles amongst the non-Christians; then when they become Christians this division is lost and together they now are "the Church of God".)

**(c)** This negative requirement (v.32) is, however, not sufficient. We must act positively, to "try to please everyone in every thing I do". This is done, Paul adds, by my "not seeking my own advantage but that of many". The purpose of this - indeed of everything that Paul has said in this entire Part of his Epistle - is "that they may be saved".

**10:33E** There is a superficial contradiction here with Galatians 1:10, where Paul says "Am I now seeking the approval of man, or of God? Or am I trying to please man? If I were still trying to please man, I would not be a servant of Christ." But in Galatians Paul is speaking of modifying the gospel message in order to make it more palatable to the rebellious hearts of men (1:6-9) - this he steadfastly refuses to do, for turning the gospel into another gospel is perverting the gospel. In contrast, Paul is speaking now to the Corinthians in a completely different context. No question of modifying the gospel is involved. Rather, it is a question of commending the gospel to everyone in every possible way by caring about the impact which our behavior has upon others, and placing their advantage and benefit above our own, so that this can help them to be saved.

**11:1a** In what he has just said, Paul has used himself as an example - this, he says, is how he himself acts; this is the basis upon which he directs his own behavior. He now concludes his discussion of the entire question by exhorting his readers to imitate him: specifically, in relation to seeking the good of others, not oneself; more generally, in his whole attitude to the problem.

Why does he use this approach, setting down what he himself does and instructing them to follow his example, rather than simply telling them (as previously) what they are to do? I would say the explanation is because of how much easier it is to copy an example than to carry out an instruction for which you have no example. Firstly, the Corinthians are being required to reflect afresh upon Paul's own life and ministry in their midst, and to pattern their behavior upon what they have seen of him. Secondly, it is always more effective when a person can say, "Do what I do", rather than merely, "Do what I tell you".

The significance of Paul's teaching here shows the value and importance for new or weak Christians of having mature, established Christians as models upon whom they can pattern their own lives. Each Christian should become such a pattern which displays to the outsider what life is like as a servant of the Lord, and which shows the next generation of Christians what they by God's grace are to be.

**11:1b** This is an awesome responsibility, and we would be likely to hesitate about saying to immature, uncertain Christians, as Paul did, "Imitate me", "Follow my example". But the basis upon which this can be said is quite clear: "as I follow the example of Christ". Ultimately the model for Christian living is not another Christian, but Christ himself, for he is the example to all (1 Peter 2:21). Christ's example then is to be seen in the lives of his people, and this is what is to be followed. The confidence with which Paul (and we) can say "be imitators of me" is grounded upon his (and our) firm commitment to live as an obedient follower of the Lord Jesus Christ.


# IN CONCLUSION

It is interesting to note the assessment given by different scholars to Paul's situation vis-a-vis the Corinthians, and how he has responded to it. Hurd 146 gives his reconstruction of the Corinthians' question about idol meat thus:

> We are now in a position to summarize the preceding discussions by suggesting the content of the Corinthians' question concerning idol meat:

> "We find nothing wrong with eating idol meat. After all, we all have knowledge. We know that an idol has no real existence. We know that there is no God but one. For those in Christ all things are lawful, and as far as food is concerned everyone knows that 'food is meant for the stomach and the stomach for food'. We fail to see what is being gained by the avoidance of idol meat. You know yourself that when you were with us you never questioned what you ate and drank. Moreover, what of the markets? Are we to be required to enquire as to the history of each piece of meat we buy? And what of our friends? Are we to decline their invitations to banquets because of possible contamination by idol meat?"

> For reasons which we have discussed above we hold that: ... The Corinthians were primarily voicing an objection to the subject to Paul, and were not asking for guidance from him.

Hurd has based this reconstruction of the Corinthians' question on a detailed examination of what Paul has actually said in response to the Corinthians. We cannot of course be sure that the Corinthians raised with Paul all the points which Hurd has set out in his reconstruction - but we *can* see that these are exactly the points that Paul deals with in his letter back to them.

And what happened next? In the years which followed, what were the subsequent attitudes in the Church towards eating idol meat? Edwards 208 reports:

> Justin [and others] abstained ... We cannot suppose that these Fathers were conscious of being in opposition to the Apostle. The explanation is that in times of persecution tasting the wine of the libations or eating meat offered to idols was understood to signify recantation of Christianity.

## SUMMARY OF PAUL'S ANSWER
## RE FOOD OFFERED TO IDOLS

It is sometimes said that this section of the Epistle is dealing with a "doubtful issue", and that this teaching is to be applied in that way by us today. Paul's teaching is taken to be that we must decide such doubtful questions as best we can, on the basis of love.

Certainly we would have to agree that we are to operate on the basis of love, but this approach could imply that Paul's approach is a great deal more open than in fact it is. His instructions are quite definite and specific, and the Christian response is not left to the "discretion" of his hearers.

### ISSUE: EATING FOOD OFFERED TO IDOLS

| | | | | |
|---|---|---|---|---|
| **Situation:** | In idol's temple | Bought at markets | At friend's home | At friend's home |
| **References:** | 8:10 | 10:25 | 10:27 | 10:28 |
| **Background:** | Always idolmeat | May be idolmeat | May be idolmeat | Said to be idolmeat |
| **What to do:** | Do not eat it | Eat without questioning | Eat without questioning | Do not eat it |
| **Why:** | (a) Stumbling block to others (8:9-13) (b) Eating is participating in idolatry - a Christian cannot eat of the table of demons (10:14-24) | The earth is the Lord's (10:26) | The earth is the Lord's (10:26) | Someone has raised the issue - another man's conscience is involved (10:29) |

## SOME PRACTICAL AND PASTORAL REFLECTIONS

### The Truth About Temptation To Sin

I want to draw attention to the great assurances which Paul brings us in 10:13.

The first section states, "No temptation has overtaken you that is not common to man." At times when we find ourselves severely tempted, we are likely to feel that this is a quite unique or particularly strong temptation - and we may be in danger therefore of thinking that in these circumstances we cannot resist it, or even that we are justified in giving in to it. Hence the relevance of this first encouragement: the temptations that we face are the same kind that everyone else has to face. Our temptation is not unique and we are not alone in having to face it.

Next, Paul says, "God is faithful", πιστος (*pistos*), that is, "reliable", "dependable", "trustworthy". We are not facing this temptation on our own; God is with us - we can rely upon that absolutely.

Then, "he will not let you be tempted beyond your ability". There are some temptations which would be so strong that they would totally overwhelm us; but God does not permit temptations like that to come to us. He allows us to be tempted; but he filters the temptations that could come to us, and only permits those that we can bear.

At times when some particularly strong temptation is attacking us and we feel almost overcome by it, we may marvel at the level of confidence that this indicates God has in us!

But we have this word of absolute assurance that whatever that temptation is, we can endure it. This is the clearest possible statement of a great biblical truth: that it is *never* necessary for us to sin; succumbing to temptation is *never* inevitable, because "God can be trusted not to allow you to suffer any temptation beyond your powers of endurance" (Phillips translation).

Finally, we are told how this can be so. It is not because of the inner strength and determination of the individual person. This strength and determination *is* required - the Hebrew Christians were rebuked because (Hebrews 12:4, NASB), "You have not yet resisted to the point of shedding blood, in your striving against sin."

We need to strive against sin. The encouragement of Paul's word to the Corinthians is that we can know that we can strive *successfully*. Thus we will not give up the struggle. We are assured that with the temptation God will also provide the way of escape, so that we are able to endure it.

What *is* the way of escape?

Paul does not give the answer here as fully as we might have wished - but the way of escape will vary according to the nature of the particular temptation.

It will involve prayerfully appropriating the grace of God and the power of the indwelling Spirit, putting on the armor of God, and taking hold of the teaching of Scripture; it will also involve something appropriate to each type of temptation to sin. To the rich man who was beset by covetousness Jesus said "Sell all that you have and give to the poor" (Mark 10:21); to the person being tempted to immorality Paul says, "Flee" (6:18). He has a similar word of instruction now in relation to idolatry.

Notice the careful balance in these two verses. In verse 12 we are reminded: sin is *never* impossible. And in verse 13 we are assured: sin is *never* inevitable. We find a similar balance between these two truths in 1 John 1:8 and 2:1: "If we say we have no sin, we deceive ourselves, and the truth is not in us ... My little children, I am writing these things to you so that you may not sin."

# CHAPTER ELEVEN

## SECTION 3(b): CONCERNING
## BEHAVIOR IN THE CHURCH OF GOD

### 1. Women And A Covering (11:2-16)

We need in this section to be more than usually careful to attend to the exact wording of Paul's comments. As Garland 505 warns in relation to this passage, "The danger lurks that interpreters will try to make it say what they would like it to say."

**11:2** In turning next to other questions affecting behavior in the Church of God, Paul begins by commending the Corinthians for maintaining the teachings or, more literally, the traditions that he had delivered to them. "Tradition" means something formally handed down, whether orally or in writing; Paul's use of this word indicates that he regards himself as a link in a chain, as he passes on to successive generations of Christians the facts about the life and teaching of Jesus Christ which he himself had received - a process of receiving and handing on the message to which he refers even more specifically in 15:1-3.

These authoritative traditions have now become written down in the Bible, which has become for us the deposit of Christian truth that one generation of Christians hands on to the next. There is no support here for any idea of a line of tradition originating from Jesus and still being handed down orally independently of the Bible (cf. Roman Catholic teaching about authoritative traditions handed down orally in the church).

**11:3** However, there are some matters relating to their conduct (within presumably the general area for which he had just commended them) that are in need of correction. Paul's "I want you to understand" could indicate that this is new teaching. He gives a word of introduction to the issue, on the subject of headship. In this passage Paul utilizes the full range of meaning possessed by this word (κεφαλη, *kephalē*).

Numbers of scholars see this word as indicating "source" (e.g., see Philip Payne). I am persuaded, rather, by those holding an alternative view.

In Greek as in English, "head" refers both to that part of the anatomy and also to the concept of the one who, in a given organizational hierarchy, has authority in relation to another or others; e.g., head of a school, head of a government department, head gardener, and so on. The meaning of the word initially, in Paul's use of it, is "the one who has headship". Thus Christ has headship over every man, and the man has headship over a woman, and God has headship over Christ.

Be aware: The passage is not saying that *every* man has headship over *every* woman, but that the **husband** has headship over **his wife**: again we note that the Greek word ἀνήρ (*anēr*) means both "man" and "husband", and similarly γυνή (*gunē*) means both "woman" and "wife".

Thus some versions translate these words in this verse as "woman" and "man", which can be misunderstood as if the words were in the plural and applied more generally (e.g. AV/KJV, NIV, NASB, NEB, Jerusalem, Phillips). But these words are more helpfully translated as "wife" and "husband" in other versions (e.g. ESV, NRSV, TEV, Beck, Williams, Lattimore) - thus making it clear that Paul is speaking here (as is shown by both the immediate context and other passages in Paul's writings) about the "headship" relation of marriage.

The *fact* of this headship is taught specifically here, but the *nature* of the headship is not fully explained. Paul sets out his teaching about this in more detail in Ephesians 5:21-33E, where it can be clearly seen that the man to whom the woman submits is the one who loves her as he loves himself, as a part of his own body: that is, her husband - there are close affinities between the thought of Paul's teaching here and in Ephesians 5:21-33E.

It is to be noted that Paul (and the Bible generally) teaches the headship of the husband, and that a wife is to be in submission to her husband. What we are able to see from these two passages is what is meant by that headship and submission. It is not an oppressive, coercive headship, but it is in its nature to be of the same kind as the headship of God over Christ, and the headship of Christ over man (1 Corinthians 11:3) and over the church (Ephesians 5:23) - that is, a self-giving headship exercised in love.

This is why the church responds to Christ, and this is why the wife submits to her husband. Frequently the nature of the biblical headship of a husband in relation to his wife is misunderstood and generally either becomes repressive or else, at the other extreme, is abdicated, whenever people lose sight of the pattern for this headship which is given here, viz, the parallel with the relation of Christ to the man and with God to Christ.

The wording here is not to be taken to mean that Christ is not the head of the woman, being related to her only through man - Paul is not dealing with relationship to Christ as such, but is showing the hierarchical authority or headship structure as an introduction to what he needs to deal with next. The question of the relationship of man and woman to Christ is covered in what Paul wrote in Galatians 3:28, where he shows that in Christ Jesus male and female are equal. In regard to "the head of Christ is God", Paul presumably has in mind such things as were taught by Jesus in Matthew 24:36; Mark 13:32; John 14:28.

**11:4** The two meanings of "head" are invoked in Paul's next comment: every man who prays or prophesies with his head *covered* dishonors his head (that is, Christ), but every woman who prays or prophesies with her head *uncovered* dishonors her head (that is, her husband). The reference apparently is to the wearing of a veil over or hanging down from the head. What is the point of this head covering? Garland 517-518 explains this as a pious practice when engaging in pagan sacrifice. But in his *Commentary on the New Testament from the Talmud and Hebraica*, John Lightfoot's explanation is:

> It was the custom of the Jews that they prayed not, unless first their head were veiled, and that for this reason: that by this rite they might show themselves reverent, and ashamed before God, and unworthy with an open heart to behold him.

There may perhaps be a connection between this and the veil which Moses wore (2 Corinthians 3:13). In the context of Moses's veil, Paul continues (2 Corinthians 3:14-18),

> But their minds [i.e. the minds of Israelites] were hardened. For to this day, when they read the old covenant, that same veil remains unlifted, because only through Christ is it taken away. Yes, to this day whenever Moses is read, a veil lies over their hearts. But when one turns to the Lord, the veil is removed. Now the Lord is the Spirit, and where the Spirit of the Lord is, there is freedom. And we all, with unveiled face, beholding the glory of the Lord, are being transformed into the same image from one degree of glory to another.

Paul's teaching to the church at Corinth which he explains in this passage of is diametrically opposed to Jewish practice - they would pray and preach while wearing a covering on their head, and Paul states emphatically that if any man were to do this he dishonors his head (that is, Christ). Quite possibly this discussion of veils in 2 Corinthians 3:12-18 is by way of Paul explaining to the Corinthians the reason for the attitude he takes in 1 Corinthians 11 to men being thus veiled.

In any case it seems clear that for a Christian man to wear a veil and signify, as we have seen, that he is "ashamed before God and unworthy with an open heart to behold him" is dishonoring to the Christ who saved him, because the veil is a symbolic denial of that salvation and of the Christian's freedom in Christ, for "when one turns to the Lord, the veil is removed" (2 Corinthians 3:16). As the veil over the heart and mind is removed when a man is converted, so also must be the physical veil, because "we all, with unveiled face, are being transformed" - we approach the Lord with all boldness and should not wear a symbol of being ashamed and unworthy before God, because we are now his children and are taught to cry to him "Abba", "Father".

**11:5a** Why then should the very opposite be stated for a woman - that she dishonors her head if she is uncovered when she prays or prophesies? Surely a Christian woman is also a child of God, and cleansed and forgiven, and able to approach God with boldness in the same way as a man?

So, why the difference? It lies in the meaning of the veil for each, and in the circumstances of the activities in which they are engaging.

Concerning "praying and prophesying", Adam Clarke explains that this refers to

> Any person who engages in public acts in the worship of God, whether prayer, singing, or exhortation: for we learn, from the apostle himself, that *propheteuein*, 'to prophesy', signifies to 'speak unto men to edification, exhortation, and comfort', chapter 14:3. And this comprehends all that we understand by 'exhortation' or even 'preaching'.

It needs to be noted that Paul takes it for granted that there will be women as well as men who do this in the assembly. Adam Clarke's Commentary continues,

> Whatever may be the meaning of 'praying' and 'prophesying' in respect to the *man*, they have precisely the same meaning in respect to the *woman*. So that some women at least, as well as some men, might speak to others to *edification*, and *exhortation*, and *comfort*. And this kind of prophesying or teaching was predicted by Joel 2:28, and referred to by Peter, Acts 2:17. And had there not been such gifts bestowed on *women*, the prophesy could not have had its fulfilment. The only difference marked by the apostle was, the man had his head *uncovered*, because he was the representative of Christ; the woman had hers *covered*, because she was placed by the order of God in a state of subjection to the man, and because it was a *custom*, both among the Greeks and Romans, and among the Jews an express *law*, that no woman should be seen abroad without a *veil*. This was, and is, a common custom throughout all the east, and none but public prostitutes go without veils. And if a woman should appear in public without a veil, she would 'dishonor her head' - her 'husband'.

Similarly Barrett's Commentary is worth noting:

> The verse is meaningless unless women were from time to time moved, in the Christian assembly in Corinth, to pray and prophesy aloud and in public (not simply in family prayers and other small groups - Bachmann). If moreover Paul had thought it wrong for them to

do this he would certainly not have wasted time in discussing what, in these circumstances, they should do with their heads; he would simply have forbidden the practice. ... Paul assumes that women will offer public prayer, and utter the kind of public speech known as prophecy, and simply regulates the way in which they shall do this.

Similarly Garland 516, 518.

Thus in summary: women can pray and prophesy in the Church in the same way as men. The symbolism of the veil for a man is utterly inappropriate to his standing in Christ, and it must not be worn. The symbolism of the veil for women in the ancient world was quite different, and it was right that the veil for Christian women should continue to be worn to continue to convey that particular symbolism in that society. The man is the head of the woman, and when the woman prayed and prophesied using the covering of the veil she acknowledged that she was not engaged in an act of exercising authority but was acting under authority (i.e., the authority of the council of elders of the congregation).

Moreover, only immodest women in that society went abroad without a veil, and thus for a Christian woman to abandon the veil was to convey symbolically a comment about her morals that was absolutely in contradiction of her profession of the moral standards of a Christian. To be without the veil would thus on both counts be to dishonor her husband.

Re the application of this teaching today, see "Reflections", below.

**11:5b** When a wife goes about uncovered, "it is the same as if her head were shaven". An adulteress (and sometimes a woman guilty of other faults) could have her head shaven - a woman who did not have her head covered placed herself in the same class as a woman who had been shaven: immodest, and immoral.

**11:6** If a woman is going to throw off the veil (apparently in a surge of emancipation resulting from the appreciation of woman's enhanced standing in Christ), she may as well go as far as having her head shaven, for that is how her action will be interpreted in society (i.e. as "liberated" in the sense of morally and sexually "free and easy"). If this is disgraceful (and the definite "if", εἰ [ei], indicates that clearly it is), then "let her be covered". In the Greek, what she should cover is not specifically mentioned, but is clearly her head. Garland 522 comments,

In this particular context, it refers to her head. In other cultures, other parts of the body may need to be covered to prevent conveying inappropriate sexual messages. Interpreters must be mindful that fashions vary and that ideas of proper decorum vary from culture to culture and among differing classes. ... one does need to bridge the contexts to discern what is eternally valid. Paul's concern that Christian honor sexual decorum in worship and avoid what a culture deems to be suggestive attire is a broadly applicable, though elastic, concept. He is not trying to repress women and restrain their expression of spiritual gifts but to impress on them the need to project modesty and virtue in their dress.

**11:7** A man *does not* cover his head, as he is both the image and glory of God ("glory" here apparently expressing the same concept of hierarchical authority as earlier); a woman *does* wear a veil as she is the "glory of man" (i.e. acknowledging the headship of man). Paul here is indicating a difference between man and woman. This is a difficult verse to understand, but we can note that woman is *not* said to be "the image and glory" but only "the glory" of man, for she also and not man alone is made in the image of God (Genesis 1:27).

**11:8-9** Paul makes further comments upon the creation story. Man was not made from woman but woman from man, i.e., Eve from Adam's rib; man was not created by God for woman but woman for man, i.e. as companion and helper (Genesis 2:18-23).

Notice that Paul anchors the differentiation of husband and wife in the nature of God's creation. This would include the husband's headship role, and the submission asked of the wife (Ephesians 5:22, 24). Those teachers and commentators who have assigned this headship/submission as the outcome of the Fall have failed to take adequate account of the actual wording of Genesis 2:15-25, which lies behind Paul's teaching here. For there are in fact several significant points of difference in this passage between what applies to Adam and what applies to Eve.

These commentators (those who view man's headship as resulting from the Fall) are not really coming to grips with the fact that in biblical teaching this headship role for the husband is that of *leadership*, not *rulership*. The result of the Fall was that this benign, helpful, caring headship/leadership has become twisted and distorted in so many instances into a "ruling" over the woman, such a ruling over her being the fruit and the outcome of sin. Then the effect of Christ's redemption is not to remove man's leadership role, but to redeem and renew it, and transform it afresh into what it ought to be. And in this passage and Ephesians 5:22-33E this is what Paul is explaining.

A common misunderstanding should be clarified at this point: neither in these passages nor anywhere else in the New Testament will there be found an instruction that wives are to obey their husbands. Though in 1 Peter 3:6 Peter commends Sarah for the way she obeyed Abraham, he still uses the word "submit" (see 1 Peter 3:1) for the attitude which women are to have towards their husbands. This distinguishing between "obey" and "submit" is no empty quibble over words, and its significance should not be overlooked.

I have discussed all these issues in considerable further detail in my *The Ministry of Women in the Church*, pages 86 to 96.

**11:10** Adam Clarke's dry comment on this verse is,

> There are few portions of the sacred writings that have given rise to such a variety of conjectures and explanations, and are less understood, than this verse, and v.29 of chapter 15.

Literally the verse says, "That is why a woman ought to have authority upon her head, because of the angels." The woman having authority upon her head can be taken (as in the NIV) to mean "a sign of authority" or (ESV, NRSV) "a symbol of authority" upon her head, that is, that she is acknowledging the authority of man. If this comment still has the specific situation in view of the woman preaching and prophesying in the congregation, this sign can be an acknowledgement of the authority of the council of elders, under whose jurisdiction she is thus ministering. A great variety of ideas has been put forward about the reference to angels, the two most widely accepted being that Paul is making passing reference to a Jewish belief that angels are present in our worship to assist us (cf. the hymn line in "Praise, My Soul", "Angels, help us to adore him"); and, that angels are custodians and administrators of God's order in the universe, and by wearing the sign of authority women are acknowledging to the angels their role under the authority of the man.

**11:11** Paul has been explaining the difference between the roles assigned by God to men and women in relation to authority. He now makes quite clear that this is not in some way an indication of any inferiority being ascribed to woman. On the contrary he emphasizes (again grounding this upon the creation account) the interdependence of man and woman.

"In the Lord": that is, "in the Lord's plan", "in the way the Lord has created men and women"; this does not restrict what Paul says only to those people who are "in the Lord" as if he meant to speak only to Christians. Beck's translation of this verse is particularly clear and helpful: "In the Lord a man needs a woman and a woman needs a man." God has so made man and woman that neither is independent and autonomous, but each has a need for the other.

**11:12** "As woman was made from man" - again, a reference to the account of the creation of Eve in Genesis (2:21-22). Paul balances this with the fact that each man is now born of woman, and the whole plan, in every detail, is God's design.

**11:13** Paul invites the Corinthians to recognize that it would not be fitting for a woman to pray with head uncovered, expecting them to see for themselves how inappropriate this would be i.e. in terms of the symbolic meaning of the covering in the culture of their day.

**11:14-15a** Our own feeling for what is natural for men and women in regard to long hair, he continues, will help us in recognizing what is fitting and what is degrading or disgraceful. This endorses the need to be aware of what is regarded as acceptable and unacceptable in one's particular culture.

**11:15b** "For her hair is given to her for a covering": We may note that some commentators regard this as the key to the entire passage, so that they take the "covering" for the woman that is referred to throughout the passage as being properly-tended hair, not a veil. The NIV gives this approach as an alternative translation in its margin, and this approach is developed and explained fully by J Keir Howard in the January 1983 issue of *The Evangelical Quarterly*. He challenges the belief that wearing a veil was customary in the ancient world and says that it was almost exclusively a Jewish custom, and Paul would not foist this on the church, especially a church like that at Corinth, which was largely Gentile. Howard 35 says,

> The clear implication of the argument there [i.e. in v.15] is that a woman's hair is the equivalent of a covering. ... The apparent requirement of a veil in the earlier verses is thus odd to say the least. The ... translation ... 'to be veiled' and 'unveiled' respectively ... must be called into question.

He concludes (36):

> "It is argued therefore that Paul is not advocating the use of a veil or shawl to cover the head and face, as was common in the east, because he saw long hair as being an adequate covering in itself. He does insist, however, that women wear their hair in a way that is conducive to good order and modesty. The woman's dressed hair is thus her mark of 'authority'. ... In this context it can only mean the authority to act and speak in the open assembly of the local congregation. ... The main thrust of Paul's argument is thus to insist that the proper distinctions between the sexes should be maintained.

Similarly, Payne. Thus there are differing approaches to understanding this passage.

**11:16** Paul anticipates that some at Corinth may continue to be contentious about this issue, and closes the discussion by reminding them, in effect, that they are not, as a congregation or even a group within a congregation, entitled to concoct their own set of rules and regulations about all such matters, and that what Paul has set out for them is the only practice which he and his associates ("we") recognize, and indeed is the agreed practice of all the churches.

# SOME PRACTICAL AND PASTORAL REFLECTIONS

## Wearing A Head Covering Today?

A major question which arises from any consideration of this passage is, What is its relevance for today? Some practices have been drawn from it, in particular that women should wear their hair long, or that women should wear hats in church.

It should be noted that if *that* is the conclusion to be drawn from the passage, then hats should be worn whenever engaging in praying or prophesying (teaching or preaching God's truth) and on all public occasions, not just in church.

However, what is at stake in the passage is the question of how a person's behavior will be interpreted. If a particular society requires women to wear a covering, and it has the same symbolic significance if she does or does not as it had in Paul's day, then his words will apply directly. If a head covering does not have any such significance in a given culture, it is hard to see any point in requiring a head covering for women today, as this would be meaningless.

But one thing is reasonably certain: the point of the passage is that a person should not give offence and risk misunderstanding through acting against his/her culture. The principle to be followed would be that a Christian today should act in such a way that their behavior will be correctly interpreted by the culture as accurately representing Christian truth. But if a culture does not attach an adverse meaning to a particular practice (e.g. a woman who does not wear a head covering), then observance of such a particular practice, being meaningless in that culture, is not required of a Christian belonging to that culture.

## 2. The Lord's Supper (11:17-34E)

In this passage in 1 Corinthians we have the only explanation that the Bible contains of the observance of this sacrament. It is appropriate, therefore, that we begin with some words of introduction to the whole concept of the Lord's Supper.

Some scholars find multiple references to the Lord's Supper in the New Testament. Let us first consider these as we approach this passage. This list gives all the references in the New Testament to the Lord's Supper, possible and certain. The actual text of the "possible references" is set out here for ease of consideration.

They fall into five groups:

**GROUP 1: Christ's Discourse On The Bread Of Life (John 6:32-35, 41, 43, 47-58)**

**GROUP 2: Possible New Testament References To The Holy Communion (NIV):**

**(a) Hebrews 6:4** It is impossible for those who have once been enlightened, who have tasted the heavenly gift, who have shared in the Holy Spirit ...

**(b) Hebrews 13:10** We have an altar from which those who minister at the tabernacle have no right to eat.

**(c) 1 Peter 2:3** Now that you have tasted that the Lord is good.

**(d) 2 Peter 2:13** They will be paid back with harm for the harm they have done. Their idea of pleasure is to carouse in broad daylight. They are blots and blemishes, revelling in their pleasures while they feast with you.

**(e) Jude 12** These men are blemishes at your love feasts, eating with you without the slightest qualm - shepherds who feed only themselves. They are clouds without rain, blown along by the wind; autumn trees, without fruit and uprooted - twice dead.

**GROUP 3: References to The Breaking Of Bread**

**GROUP 4: Gospel Narratives of the Last Supper**

**GROUP 5: References in 1 Corinthians 10 and 11**

Some exegetes regard John 6:32-58 (Group One) as providing an explanation of the meaning and significance of this sacrament: but this passage does not discuss or imply the observance of a sacramental ceremony in the churches.

The passages of the New Testament in Group Two, which some scholars cite, *may* be references to the observance of the Lord's Supper: but at best it can be said they are ambiguous in this regard, and in any case they do not add to our knowledge of the practice of the early church in this matter.

It is possible - as some believe - that the expression "the breaking of bread" that occurs five times in Acts (2:42, 46; 20:7,11; 27:35) may refer to the rite of the Lord's Supper - but if so, it gives us no information at all about it. However, we shall further examine this possibility below, in Excursus One, "The Breaking of Bread".

The three Gospel narratives of the Last Supper (Group Four: Matthew 26:26-29; Mark 14:22-25; Luke 22:14-20) give us the record of the historical occasion which lies behind the observance of the Lord's Supper, but are presented in those Gospels purely as a record of what happened on that occasion and not explicitly set out as, nor stated to be, a model for the church to imitate.

The majority of ancient manuscripts contain the Lord's instruction "Do this" in Luke 22:19, but some other early manuscripts omit any instruction to Jesus's followers to re-enact this celebration, and the authenticity of these words in the original text of Luke is uncertain.

In his comment on 1 Corinthians 11:24 Morris says:

> 'This do' is present continuous, 'Keep on doing this.' This is important, for there is some textual doubt about Luke 22:19. If it be judged that the latter part of the verse [in Luke] is no part of the true text, this [i.e., 1 Corinthians 11] is the sole record of the command to continue the Communion.

And our sole New Testament source for information about the *observance* of this ceremony in the church comes from 1 Corinthians - from what is said in chapter 10:16-21, plus our present passage. Thus we may note that if there had not been problems in the church at Corinth which caused Paul to discuss the Holy Communion in detail as he does, we would have no knowledge at all from Scripture about the observance in the church of this sacrament. I will comment further about this when we reach these verses.

In the providence of God this account *has* been provided in 1 Corinthians, so that we can be informed about his instructions to his people regarding this sacrament, and its meaning.

These five groups exhaust the New Testament references to the Lord's Supper, certain and possible. And when these five groups are examined, it will be found that only Paul's comments in 1 Corinthians give us any information about *how the Lord's Supper is to be observed in the church*.

Before we examine Paul's teaching in this chapter, we shall consider further the relevance, for our understanding, of the passages about the breaking of bread.

## EXCURSUS ONE: THE BREAKING OF BREAD

All the New Testament references to the breaking of bread (including Gospel parallels) are (NIV):

(a) **Mark 6:41 (cf. Matthew 14:9 and Luke 9:16)** Taking the five loaves and the two fish and looking up to heaven, he gave thanks and broke the loaves.

(b) **Mark 8:6 (cf. Matthew 15:36)** He told the crowd to sit down on the ground. When he had taken the seven loaves and given thanks, he broke them and gave them to his disciples to set before the people, and they did so.

(c) **Luke 24:30,35** When he was at the table with them, he took bread, gave thanks, broke it and began to give it to them. ... Then the two told what had happened on the way, and how Jesus was recognized by them when he broke the bread.

(d) **Acts 2:42,46** They devoted themselves to the apostles' teaching and to the fellowship, to the breaking of bread and to prayer. ... Every day they continued to meet together in the temple courts. They broke bread in their homes and ate together with glad and sincere hearts.

(e) **Acts 20:7,11** On the first day of the week we came together to break bread. Paul spoke to the people and, because he intended to leave the next day, kept on talking until midnight. ... Then he went upstairs again and broke bread and ate. After talking until daylight, he left.

(f) **Acts 27:35** After he said this, he took some bread and gave thanks to God in front of them all. Then he broke it and began to eat.

Is the expression "the breaking of bread" being used in the New Testament with reference to the Lord's Supper? This is very widely assumed to be the case. Let us examine this assumption.

The "breaking of bread" is in fact a standard Jewish expression from pre-Christian times which refers specifically to the action of "breaking bread" at the commencement of a meal, and then, by extension, to the meal itself. The act of breaking the bread was performed by the head of a household or by the host presiding at the meal.

The form of blessing used by the Jews for the bread was: "Blessed art Thou, O Lord our God, King of the universe, who bringest forth bread from the earth."

The breaking of bread was thus associated with the prayer of thanksgiving, and had a religious significance of joint fellowship in sharing and enjoying the blessings of God. A.B. MacDonald, in his *Christian Worship in the Primitive Church* (125), points out:

> The taking of food was accompanied, or rather, preceded, by a certain formal and conspicuous action, namely, the pronouncing of a blessing over the bread that was to be eaten, followed by the breaking of the loaf in two, preparatory to its distribution around the table. This was an old Jewish custom, corresponding to our grace before meals, but conveying far deeper suggestions of religious fellowship, and carried through with greater solemnity and ceremony, and *reserved for certain meals of a pronouncedly religious character*.

The blessing pronounced over the bread applied to the other food eaten in conjunction with the bread; A. Edersheim, in his *The Life and Times of Jesus the Messiah*, Vol. II, 206, writes:

> Bread was regarded as the mainstay of life, without which no enter-
> tainment was considered as a meal. For the blessing was spoken over
> the bread, and this was supposed to cover all the rest of the food which
> followed, such as the meat, fish or vegetables - in short, all that made
> up the dinner, but not the desert."

Similarly we read, in the IVF Bible Dictionary, 750: "'To break bread' was a common Jewish expression for the sharing of a meal."

All of the New Testament usages of this expression are set out above. The three Gospel references to the breaking of bread, in accord with normal use, are clearly to the commencement of a hunger-satisfying meal (the feeding of the five thousand, the feeding of the four thousand, the two disciples at Emmaus).

The first two of these are particularly so, for the hunger of the crowd was the motivation behind the feeding taking place, and it is equally clear that the two disciples were inviting the unrecognized Christ to an ordinary meal at Emmaus, for they expected him to stay the night with them.

Occasionally we encounter some fanciful interpretation of these accounts (e.g. Schweitzer in *Quest for the Historical Jesus*, 374, held that at the feeding of the five thousand Jesus administered an "eschatological sacrament", giving a minute portion to everyone, much as we would today in a celebration of the Lord's Supper); but the accounts in each case make it clear that the "breaking of bread" marked the commencement of a meal intended to feed the recipients.

In each of these three incidents the breaking of bread is coupled with giving thanks to God for the bread. It is interesting to note that in John's account of the feeding of the five thousand he mentions our Lord giving thanks (John 6.11) but not his breaking of the bread, though this is implied.

It is readily recognized that Paul's breaking of bread and giving thanks during the storm at sea (Acts 27:35) falls into the same category with the other three passages that I have mentioned. Thus these passages all illustrate the current Jewish custom of commencing a fellowship meal with the giving of thanks and the breaking of bread, thereby investing the meal with a religious significance of conscious joint participation in enjoying the blessings of God.

The circumstances of Jesus's life with his disciples made it inevitable that they often ate together, sometimes on their own and sometimes as a guest in the house of others (e.g. at the home of Mary and Martha at Bethany). On many of these occasions Jesus would preside, and thus would be the one who broke bread and gave thanks. It would seem that he had a unique and distinctive way of doing so; certainly it was through his breaking of the bread that the two at Emmaus recognized him (Luke 24:30, 35).

It is clear that after the resurrection of Jesus the disciples began to meet together in fellowship assemblies and that they shared meals together. The risen Christ on occasions joined in eating common meals with them (Luke 24:29-31; 24:41-43; John 21:9-15; [Mark 16:14]). After the Lord's ascension and the events of the day of Pentecost, the disciples continued their fellowship together. Their common meals would now also be a conscious remembrance of the meals they had shared with the Lord during his physical presence among them, and as they broke bread and gave thanks they would be reminded of the times he did this in their midst and they would be conscious of his continued presence with them through the Holy Spirit.

There is absolutely no reason at all for doubting that they would continue the pattern of their years of association with Jesus (and in fact the pattern of all pious Jews) by beginning their ordinary hunger-satisfying meals with the breaking of bread and thanksgiving. The question is, is this all that is meant when Luke speaks (Acts 2:42,46) of the breaking of bread? Certainly it is *possible* that this exhausts the meaning of the expression "breaking of bread" in these verses.

However, it is claimed by some that after the crucifixion and resurrection the disciples would have in their minds one particular occasion when Jesus broke bread: the Last Supper. Moreover, as the remembrance of that occasion would fill their minds whenever they broke bread together, so the significance which Jesus placed upon the broken bread ("This is my body which is [given] for you") would be primary in their thoughts. Thus they would be consciously remembering the death of Christ and its significance when they broke bread together, and thus the expression "breaking of bread" must refer to a celebration of the Lord's Supper.

But is it to be maintained that *every* main meal which the disciples had (on which occasions bread would be broken at the commencement) is to be regarded not only as a meal *per se*, but as a celebration of the Lord's Supper? It could be answered that only at one meal a day, the main meal, would bread be ceremoniously broken, and that this meal was also a celebration of the Lord's Supper, this meal being seen as the meaning of Acts 2:46, "And *day by day*, attending the temple together, and *breaking bread in their homes* ..."

But if the custom of a daily observance of the Lord's Supper was *ever* followed, it clearly was not long continued. After it became weekly (which in the view of many commentators is what shortly happened), was the term "breaking of bread" to be then used for the observance of the Lord's Supper *alone* and no longer to be used for the breaking of bread which Christian Jews would still observe at the beginning of their regular daily meals? Or are we to assume that Christian Jews discontinued the practice of breaking of bread at the beginning of their main daily meals?

It is much more likely that in Acts 2 and also in Acts 20 (Paul at Troas), Luke uses the expression "breaking of bread" or "to break bread" in exactly the same way he has used it in his Gospel, and in accordance with the regular usage of the day, to denote the preliminary act at the commencement of a fellowship meal in which God's gracious gift of food is gratefully accepted.

If so, then the meals referred to in Acts would indeed have a definite religious significance and would doubtless be regarded as a remembrance of Jesus and a conscious participation in fellowship with the risen Lord, and may well therefore have been invested with a special significance for Christians - *but* they would not be comprised of the six characteristics which (as we shall see) were features of an observance of the Lord's Supper as Paul sets it forth in 1 Corinthians. So what the disciples did when "breaking bread together" could not be called an observance of the Lord's Supper.

To summarize:

The expression "the breaking of bread" found in Acts 2 was commonly used amongst the Jews to refer to the sharing of a meal in conscious religious fellowship, and this usage is found in the New Testament, not least in the Gospel by the same author as Acts and even elsewhere in the Acts.

The significance of the religious aspect of the breaking of bread would be greatly heightened for the disciples in the light of the Last Supper, but *this is not the same* as saying that they held a ritual meal deliberately re-enacting the Last Supper in conscious obedience to the command of Christ, commemorating his death through eating bread and drinking a cup; and these features would be necessary if we are to regard the "breaking of bread" as equating with the Lord's Supper.

Rather, the evidence indicates that in the New Testament the expression "the breaking of bread" or "broke bread" refers to the usual Jewish practice of prayer with which a hunger-satisfying meal commenced. When we recognize that references to the breaking of bread are *not* references to the Lord's Supper, we see the significance of what we learn from Paul's teaching in 1 Corinthians.

## Exegesis

**11:17a** In v.2 Paul had commenced his discussion of "Women and a Covering" by praising the Corinthians for the way in which they were carefully observing the traditions which he had brought them. He now comes to deal with a tradition which he had also delivered to them (v.23), but which they were not following as they should. "In regard to this instruction that I gave you," he says, "I cannot praise you."

The Greek is τουτο δε (*touto de*), "now in relation to this matter". This expression *can* refer back to what has just been said, but is much better taken as the introduction to a new point, the "this" pointing forward to what is to follow. This is the way it is usually taken here (i.e., as "In the following instructions ..."), and it makes clear sense to take it this way (though Gordon Clark's Commentary is an exception, in seeing it as referring back to what has gone before).

The sense of the chapter is thus: "I praise you for how you are keeping the traditions, but there is one further thing I want you to know (he instructs them concerning women and head coverings, 11:2-16). Now in this next matter I cannot praise you because, although I delivered this tradition to you also, you are not faithfully observing it."

It is worthy of note that 7:6 begins in the same way, τουτο δε (*touto de*), "Now as a concession, not a command, I say this", so that this other verse in similar fashion and for similar reasons should be seen as referring to what follows it rather than to what precedes it (see my comments on 7:6).

**11:17b** When the church of God assembles it is intended to be for the benefit of its members, through being built up in the faith. Paul notes with concern that when the church of God at Corinth assembles to eat the Lord's Supper (v.20), their assembly does not in fact turn out for their betterment. It is not even simply that they gain no benefit from meeting together - what happens in their assembly is actually being detrimental to them (both to their fellowship together, and to their growth in Christ). How this is so will be seen in the account which follows.

**11:18** "For", γαρ (*gar*), indicates that Paul is now about to explain his meaning, and show why this is so.

"In the first place" would normally suggest that he intends to follow this later with a "secondly" and perhaps a "thirdly", but he does not do so. The planned continuation may have been intended to deal with other related matters which he has in mind and which in the event he decides can be deferred until he actually sees them face to face (as he in fact says in v.34b). Alternatively, Paul's "firstly" may be qualitative, i.e., that this is a serious issue, a matter of first importance (see for a similar question of interpretation, 15:3).

"When you come together as a church" or "as the church": "the church" in the New Testament refers primarily to Christians assembled in the name of Christ, though the word is also used of the concept of "all who are believers".

"I hear": Paul's comment shows once again that he has been kept closely informed about what is happening at Corinth. This comment also indicates that it is upon his own initiative that he raises the question of disorders in the observance of the Lord's Supper at Corinth - this clearly is not a matter about which the Corinthians have asked him. (This point should be noted in relation to the division of 1 Corinthians that is sometimes made, whereby chapters 1 to 6 are said to deal with issues that Paul raises, and chapters 7 to 16 are considered to consist of answers to questions asked in the letter the Corinthians wrote to him, to which he refers in 7:1.)

"Divisions", σχισματα (*schismata*), is the same word as in 1:10 - what is said in 1:10-11 concerning Paul hearing of divisions amongst them is very similar to what is said here. However, the context of the present comment indicates that Paul is now speaking of divisions occurring in a particular situation: when the church assembles for the Lord's Supper.

"To some extent I believe it", or, "I believe it in part", or, "I believe it to be partly true": the report that Paul has received may have been somewhat exaggerated, but Paul has become convinced that there is some truth in it; or else perhaps, Paul believes that the disgraceful behavior of which he has been informed is indeed occurring but it is only affecting part of the congregation.

Alternatively, to quote Garland 537, "Hayes avers that he sounds a note of incredulity, 'I can't believe it,' to heighten the outrageousness of what they are doing."

**11:19** "Differences", "factions", is αιρεσις (*hairesis*), our word "heresy". There must be factions (heresies) either because, as Gordon Clark says, "The reason that heresies occur by necessity and not by chance is that God decreed them"; or, as Findlay affirms, because in the nature of the case "these divisions were inevitable ... 'it is necessary', δει, *dei*, affirms a necessity lying in the moral conditions of the case ... they serve to sift the loyal from the disloyal".

ESV: "in order that those who are genuine among you may be recognized"; NIV: "to show which of you have God's approval": δοκιμοι (*dokimoi*), means "those who are approved after having been put to the test". "Approved", that is, by God. They would be tested by being faced with the factions, which compelled them to sift out and choose what is right; the existence of such factions is necessary if people are to be tested.

However, Garland 538 calls v.19 "surprising". After considering different explanations for it he concludes (539),

> It is far more likely that [Paul] expresses bitter irony about these factions rather than affirming their eschatological necessity. If that is the case he does not use the οἱ δοκιμοι (*hoi dokimoi*) in a favorable sense to mean those who will show themselves to be the "outstanding Christians". Rather, οἱ δοκιμοι (*hoi dokimoi*) denotes the dignitaries. ... [and thus] Paul refers to the requirement foisted on the Corinthian church by its well-to-do members.

**11:20** Paul's wording here indicates that he is speaking of the occasion when the church assembles together with the ostensible purpose of eating the Lord's Supper, and he informs them that because of the abuses that are occurring it is not the Lord's Supper that they eat; i.e. these abuses prevent their meal having this spiritual significance because it has ceased to be honoring to the Lord. The way they are acting towards each other is unloving and divisive, the very opposite in fact of the unity of the body which the Lord's Supper is meant to express (as we saw in 10:17); and of the attitude of the Lord at the Last Supper.

It is from this verse that the term "the Lord's Supper" is derived.

**11:21** The connective "for", γαρ (*gar*), indicates that Paul is now explaining why they are not eating the Lord's Supper. It is because each person proceeds with his own meal, so that one has nothing to eat and another has too much to drink. The verb προλαμβανω (*prolambanō*) may mean "to take before" and thus may indicate that some people were eating their meal beforehand, that is, before the arrival of others (presumably, the arrival of slaves and the poorer members, who were delayed by their duties). The consequence was that there was nothing remaining for the latecomers, and while the earlier starters had more than enough the latecomers were left hungry.

However, B W Winter presents a carefully argued case (in *The Reformed Theological Review* of September-December, 1978) for a different assessment of the circumstances. He argues (77) that

> The use of the verb is meant to convey the idea of the selfish eating of their own food. 'Devour' then would be the most fitting word to convey his response to their actions.

If each person ate what he himself had brought, then in the nature of the case some people would not be in a position to bring anything, or only very little, and thus while the others ate in front of them they were being allowed to remain hungry. The situation which is presupposed in this passage is that the remembrance of Christ in the Lord's Supper took place in the context of a regular, hunger-satisfying meal for which the church assembled, a communal meal in which all were to share.

Winter's interpretation of what was happening is supported by the facts -

**(a)** that the abuse which Paul is rebuking occurred when not just some members but *all* the church was assembled (the verb "to assemble together", συνερχομαι, *sunerchomai*, is used in vv. 17, 18, and 20);

**(b)** that the verb's prefix προ-, *pro-* (in προλαμβανω, *prolambanō*) can mean "in front of" as well as "prior to"; (c) and that each person ate his own meal (v.21), be it much or virtually nothing - the word "each", έκαστος, *hekastos*, implies that the comment refers to everyone, and it would thus not fit as well an interpretation that each person went ahead with his own meal *before* others arrived, as in such a case it obviously could only be true of *some* people, not of all, that they went ahead of others, because the "ones going ahead without waiting" could not be referring to the ones who were late in arriving.

Garland 540 agrees with Winter, concluding,

> The problem is not that some jump the gun by dining before everyone arrives, and that Paul must respond by insisting that they restrain themselves and politely wait for the others to arrive. The problem is that they devour their own ample amounts of food in the presence of their fellow Christians who have little or nothing to eat. His complaint is this: During the common meal, each consumes his or her individual food. The disparity in the amounts that each one brings to consume results in one group being drunk and sated, and another pinched with hunger.

"Drunk" (μεθυει, *methuei*) could mean "has had an ample sufficiency to drink". Or it could imply being "intoxicated" - if so, this is an additional ground for Paul's rebuke, as he has already had occasion to include those who get drunk in his list of serious sins (see 5:11 and 6:10).

**11:22** Once again Paul pinpoints what is wrong in their behavior with a series of sharp questions. The communal meal was an important opportunity of table fellowship in the early church, when social and racial distinctions which outside the church divided society were swept aside in Christian fellowship and sharing and mutual concern each for the other. This characterized the church from Pentecost onwards (Acts 2:42, 46; 20:7, 11). A breach of this sharing of table fellowship together was the occasion of a major dispute of Paul with Peter (Galatians 2:11-12).

These occasions for table fellowship, which were referred to as "love feasts", were also sometimes abused by others (Jude 12; and also 2 Peter 2:13 in some texts of the New Testament).

In the situation at Corinth, Paul demands, "Don't you have homes to eat and drink in?" This is not implying (as some have incorrectly taken it) a criticism of the practice of the communal meal, as if they ought not to eat together when they meet together as the church. Worshipers of idols met together to eat in an idol's temple (8:10), and these events were significant social occasions in the life of Corinth. How much more appropriate for Christians to eat together! What is at issue here (as the context makes plain) is the question of *purpose*. If all you are thinking about (he is saying to the offenders at Corinth) is consuming food and drink, you have homes of your own where you can do that. This highlights the offence that they were committing - they were transgressing against the *purpose* of the church meal, which was: the purpose of Christian fellowship and sharing.

Perhaps also Paul's comment was intended to be something of a poignant contrast with the circumstances of "those who have nothing". This may mean merely "have no food to eat on this occasion" but it is a starkly absolute statement, in Greek "the have-nots", and may well therefore be referring to poorer church members who did *not* have homes to eat and drink in. The church's communal meal was thus the one opportunity for these people to enjoy a good meal, through a sharing together.

By their selfish actions the culprits are despising the Church of God, whereas the Lord's Supper was to be specifically an occasion for demonstrating the unity of the Church of God (as we have noted from 10:16-17); and instead of caring for and sharing with the poorer members of their fellowship they are humiliating them. Again Paul repeats (as in 11:17) that he cannot commend them for their behavior.

**11:23-26** The meal which had thus been abused by some at Corinth should have been the occasion for remembering what Christ had done to accomplish their salvation.

Paul goes on next to describe what happened at the Last Supper, and its significance.

The Last Supper is recorded in Matthew, Mark, and Luke, and here in 1 Corinthians. As an introduction to our consideration of what Paul says about this, it is relevant to compare now the four accounts from the Last Supper, set in parallel for comparison, noting carefully their similarities and differences.

**11:23a** An examination of these four accounts of the Last Supper shows that Matthew and Mark are very similar, and Luke and 1 Corinthians are very similar, and that these pairs differ from each other in a number of points of detail.

Also noteworthy is that the second half of the Lukan account (22:19b-20, placed in brackets and printed in italics in the Table) is absent from some early manuscripts, a fact which has led some scholars to conclude that it was not part of the original text of Luke's Gospel but was a later insertion based upon our present passage in 1 Corinthians.

The four passages are set out for comparison on the following page.

It is noticeable that Paul's narrative contains several details that are not in Matthew or Mark or the textually certain part of Luke. This leads us to enquire as to Paul's source for his account. Paul himself says of this, "I received from the Lord what I also delivered to you."

Paul's words "I received" (παραλαμβανω, *paralambanō*) and "I delivered" (παραδιδωμι, *paradidōmi*) are virtually technical terms used of the passing on of the Christian tradition. What do they tell us of the source of Paul's information? Does he mean that he received this teaching in a special revelation?

In a single sentence Garland 545 offhandedly dismisses this possibility, when he says: "It does not imply some communication from the risen Lord, but does affirm the authoritative nature of this tradition." Garland is thus representative of those who hold that Paul's comment is to be taken to mean, "For I received from *others*, who received it from the Lord ..."

Hodge 221ff., on the other hand, emphasizes at length that this is *exactly* what Paul is saying: that he received directly from the Lord the revelation about celebrating the Lord's Supper. Similarly Alford 572 takes Paul to mean he received a "special revelation", and he argues in refutation of the view that would "deny that this revelation was made to Paul himself". That this should be the case is entirely consistent with the numerous references in the New Testament to other such direct revelations and messages from the Lord to Paul.

Thus two main views are possible here:

**(a)** that Paul obtained his account *in toto* from what has often been called the common heritage of the church, by the ordinary means of human communication (though the form in which that common heritage reached him contained material not in Matthew's and Mark's accounts);

**(b)** alternatively, that Paul received his account (in some respects at least) by direct revelation from Christ.

A comparison of the four passages:

| Matt 26:26-28 | Mark 14:22-24 | Luke 22:19-20 | 1 Corinthians 11:23-26` |
|---|---|---|---|
| And while they were eating, | And while they were eating, | And | |
| Jesus | he | he | The Lord Jesus, on the night he was betrayed, |
| took bread and | took bread and | took bread and | took bread and |
| when he had | when he had | when he had | when he had |
| blessed it | blessed it | given thanks | given thanks |
| he broke it and | he broke it and | he broke it and | he broke it and |
| giving it to his disciples | gave it to them | gave it to them | |
| he said, | and said, | saying, | said, |
| "Take, eat; | "Take it; | | |
| this is my body." | this is my body." | "This is my body *[given for you; do this in remembrance of me."* | "This is my body, which is for you; do this in remembrance of me." |
| And taking | And taking | *And in the same way, the cup after the supper,* | In the same way also, the cup after the supper, |
| a cup and | a cup and | | |
| giving thanks, he gave it to them | giving thanks, he gave it to them, and they all drank from it. | | |
| saying, | And he said to them, | *saying,* | saying, |
| "Drink from it, all of you; for this is my blood | "This is my blood | *"This cup is* | "This cup is |
| of the covenant, | of the covenant, | *the new covenant in my blood, which is poured out for you."]* | the new covenant in my blood; |
| which is poured out for many for the forgiveness of sins." | which is poured out for many." | | |
| | | | do this, whenever you drink it, in remembrance of me." For whenever you eat this bread and drink the cup, you proclaim the Lord's death until he comes. |

If indeed Paul drew his facts from the "common heritage" of the church, why did Matthew and Mark not get a similar account of the Last Supper from the same common heritage? (For, as we can see, they lack any reference to Christ's command to "Do this in remembrance of me".)

Concerning Paul's source we may note, firstly, that Paul on a number of occasions claimed to receive direct revelations from the Lord: caught up into the third heaven (2 Corinthians 12:2); speaking by revelation (1 Thessalonians 4:15); learning the fate of those with him in the ship (Acts 27:24); and the circumstances of his conversion and learning the gospel (Acts 9:3-6; 26:19; 1 Corinthians 15:8; Galatians 1:11,12). Here therefore we could expect that we are to understand Paul as claiming to have received his account of the Last Supper by direct revelation when he says, "For *I received from the Lord* what I also delivered to you, that the Lord Jesus on the night when he was betrayed took bread ..."

But this could not reasonably be taken to mean that Paul received the full set of *facts* about the Lord's Supper by revelation. Although this actually is Hodge's view, it would be a needless miracle. Rather, what would be meant then is that what Paul received from the Lord was that it was the Lord's will for Christians to commemorate the Last Supper by the regular holding of a ceremony with a particular focus centered in the death of Christ. That is to say, the essence of what Paul received was what is stated in the words "Do this in remembrance of me" (vv. 24, 25).

Secondly, if this "common heritage" were where Paul received all that he hands on to the Corinthians, why did he say he received it "from the Lord"? Such language is rather pointless, and a little confusing, to say the least.

On the basis of the grounds I have outlined, including in particular the parallels with other direct revelations which Paul received (e.g. Acts 9:3-6; 18:9-10; 22:18-21; 23:11; 26:14-19; 27:23-25; 1 Corinthians 14:6; 15:8; 2 Corinthians 12:2, 7; Galatians 1:11-12; 2:2; 1 Thessalonians 4:15), it is reasonable to accept his words here at face value: the Lord revealed to Paul the form and the significance of observing of the Lord's Supper, and this revelation was taught by Paul to the church at Corinth.

**11:23b** Note the frequency with which Paul uses the term "Lord" - either (as here) with "Jesus", or alone (as in "the Lord's table", 10:21; "the Lord's Supper", 11:20; "received from the Lord", 11:23; "the Lord's death", 11:26; "cup of the Lord", 11:27a; "body and blood of the Lord", 11:27b; "judged by the Lord", 11:32).

Paul identifies the time of the Last Supper by the description "on the night he was betrayed". The verb is imperfect tense (durative aspect), "on the night when he was being betrayed": while Jesus was delivering to the eleven apostles the bread and the cup, the symbols of his death, Judas was engaged in betraying him - perhaps still sitting at the table with Jesus and at that moment deciding finally to go ahead with the betrayal (see Luke 22:21-23 in context). Or, as many think more probable, having already left the room (see John 13:21-30) Judas was at that moment engaged in arranging the details of the arrest of Jesus (see John 18:2-3) in accordance with his agreement with the chief priests (Luke 22:3-6).

**11:23c** It is uncertain whether the term "the Lord's Supper" (in v.20) was applied to the entire communal meal or only the specific remembrance of Christ's death which was observed within it: probably the whole meal, as the term is used in that part of the passage which is discussing the meal rather than the remembrance alone, and as this whole occasion is explicitly derived from the occasion of the Last Supper, which was a hunger-satisfying meal.

But in any case, Paul now describes that part of the meal in which there is a specific observance of a rite of remembrance.

We should recognize that the Pauline observance of the Lord's Supper had these six characteristics:

**(a)** It was based on an historic event - the Last Supper - and was a deliberate re-enactment of portion of that event.

**(b)** It was held as an act of conscious obedience to the command of Christ, who had said, "Do this in remembrance of me".

**(c)** It was a ritual meal as distinct from a regular meal; that is, the eating of the bread and the drinking of the cup was done because of its ritualistic and symbolic significance as distinct from the purpose of satisfying hunger and nourishing the body, which is the intention of what may be called a "regular meal". Now, this ritual meal could be held in conjunction with a regular meal, and clearly, as we can see, the Corinthians ate a regular meal on the occasion when they met together to "eat the Lord's Supper". Moreover, taking note of what took place at the Last Supper we may conclude that the participants in the meal could actually be engaged in consuming significant quantities of bread and drink, as distinct from purely token quantities, at the point where they would "Do this in remembrance of me". But Paul's comments here are expressly intended to emphasize the ritual aspect of the meal and its spiritual significance.

**(d)** It involved eating bread and drinking from a cup.

**(e)** Its significance was to commemorate Christ's death and the new covenant in his blood.

**(f)** It looked forward to the Return of Christ ("until he comes").

**11:24** Jesus did four things with the bread: he took it, gave thanks to the Father for it, broke it, and gave it to the disciples. This was the normal procedure at a meal: Barrett says,

> What Jesus is here related to have done would have been done at any meal (but with special solemnity at a Passover meal) by the head of any Jewish household. The blessing (cf. 10:16), or thanksgiving, over bread was, 'Blessed art thou, O Lord our God, King eternal, who bringest forth bread from the earth.'"

Jesus may have varied this prayer or used different words: the explanation in Luke 24:35 that Jesus was recognized by his two companions from the road to Emmaus when he *broke the bread* indicates that there was something distinctive about Jesus's practice. At this "last supper" his prayer of blessing (see Matthew and Mark) and thanksgiving (see Luke and Paul) would possibly also relate specifically to this particular occasion and thus prepare the apostles to recognize its special and unique significance.

When Jesus gave the pieces of broken bread to the apostles he spoke to them words of explanation of this significance: "This is my body." It can be seen from the four-account comparison (above) that Matthew, Mark, and the shorter text of Luke contain only these words, while the longer text of Luke and 1 Corinthians continue, "... which is (given) for you. Do this in remembrance of me." [Luke contains the word "given"; while the AV/KJV text of 1 Corinthians 11:24 has the word "broken", the manuscript evidence indicates that this was not part of the original text.]

But a comparison of the four accounts raises the further question of whether Christ actually said the words "Do this in remembrance of me" at the Last Supper. At first sight it may appear not to be a question at all, if we take seriously what the Bible says. For both Luke and 1 Corinthians agree in recording that he did.

However, there is more than one way of viewing the Scriptural evidence. And this in turn raises the entire, wider, issue: When did the observance of the celebration of the Lord's Supper commence in the early church? This is discussed below, at the end of this chapter, in Excursus Two: "When Did The Lord's Supper Begin?"

**11:25** Note from the comparison of the four accounts (set out above) the differences between Matthew-Mark and Luke-Paul in the exact wording about the cup. Matthew-Mark say that Jesus "took a cup", and mention that again Jesus gave thanks and gave the cup to them saying "This is my blood of the covenant"; Luke-Paul mention that this occurred "after supper", and quote Jesus's words as, "This cup is the new covenant in my blood [Luke: which is poured out for you]." The meaning is the same in all four, but each pair of witnesses thus clarifies and expands the testimony of the other pair.

Paul's account continues with a repetition of the command to "Do this ... in remembrance of me" and with the addition of the words "... whenever you drink it. For whenever you eat this bread and drink the cup you proclaim the Lord's death until he comes." All of this wording is without parallel in the historical accounts of the Last Supper in the three Synoptic Gospels and thus can, it would seem, be attributed to the revelation about the Lord's Supper which Paul tells us that he received from the Lord.

A great deal of discussion amongst Christians has centered on the meaning of the word "is" in this context. The Roman Catholic teaching is that, after consecration, the bread literally and genuinely has become the actual body of Christ, while similarly the cup now contains the actual blood of Christ (the doctrine of transubstantiation).

We will hardly come to this view if we note carefully what Jesus says: "This cup is the new covenant in my blood" - this is not saying that the *content* of the cup *is* blood, but that the *cup* is the *covenant*, so the meaning of "is" must be "portrays", "represents", or "stands for". One view is that the representation whilst real is symbolic, as if one person in a restaurant explaining a traffic situation says to another, "The saltpot is my car, the pepperpot is the other fellow's car, the cup is the bus and the box of toothpicks is all the pedestrians at the traffic lights" - there is no close link between the symbols selected and what they stand for.

A closer link is seen in another analogy where a man passes you a photo and says, "This is my wife." Assuming he is speaking truthfully, he cannot hand over a photograph of some other person and say of it, "This is my wife." There is an identity between the photograph and the wife, and the former communicates truth about the latter; but there is a limitation of the identity between the two, for no matter how well the photograph can portray the wife it still falls short of the reality.

Other theologians yet again consider that Christ is present in the bread and drink, though in a spiritual as distinct from a physical sense; however, it is difficult to derive this from the biblical narratives, as none of the four accounts mentions what was in the cup (for consideration of this, see below, at the end of this chapter, Excursus Three: "The Content of the Cup"). Matthew states that Jesus gave a cup to them and instructed them all to drink out of it (πίετε ἐξ αὐτοῦ, *piete ex autou*), and Mark states that "they all drank out of it" (the referent of "it" being "cup"). Similarly when Jesus says "This is my blood of the covenant" (Matthew and Mark), the "this", τουτο (*touto*), is neuter gender, referring to "cup", ποτηριον (*potērion*). As we have noted, Luke and Paul make this explicit, "This cup". Now if it is the *content* rather than the *cup* which "is" Christ's blood, we must derive this by inference, as it is not stated as such. In these circumstances we must note that we have an *inference* not a Scriptural statement that the content of the cup is Christ's blood. This supports a view that in some sense the content *represents* Christ's blood rather than in some sense the content *is identical with* Christ's blood.

This consideration will assist us also in our understanding of "This is my body", concerning the bread.

Fee 549ff. writes:

> The ordinary Jewish meal began with the head of the house giving the traditional blessing over the bread, breaking it, and giving it to those at table with him. Jesus as the "Teacher", undoubtedly played that role in meals with the disciples. ... Hence Jesus' action in blessing and breaking the bread at the Last Supper would have been in the natural course of things. If in fact this was a Passover meal, then the remarkable thing that he did was to reinterpret the meaning of the bread, as he was distributing it, in terms of his own death: "This is my body, which is for you." Several things about this bread saying need to be noted:
>
> (1) The identification of the bread with the body is semitic imagery in its heightened form. As in all such identifications, he means "this signifies/represents my body". It lies quite beyond both Jesus' intent and the framework within which he and the disciples lived to imagine that some actual change took place, or was intended to take place, in the bread itself. Such a view could only have arisen in the church at a much later stage when Greek modes of thinking had rather thoroughly replaced semitic ones.
>
> (2) The use of the term "body" has elicited considerable discussion: does it mean "himself" or "his flesh"? Most likely it means neither, but refers to his actual body, which was about to be given over in death. ...
>
> (3) The phrase "which is for you" is unique to the Pauline-Lukan version at this point. ... By giving them a share in "his body" in this way, he invited his disciples to participate in the meaning and benefits of that death. ...
>
> (4) Almost certainly Paul also understood the phrase "which is *for* you" in this way. Whenever he uses this preposition in reference to Christ, it expresses either atonement, his death in "our behalf" ... or substitution, his death in "our place".

It is nowhere directly stated in the Bible what the content of the cup was. There is an implication from Matthew 26:29//Mark 14:25//Luke 22:18 that it was "the fruit of the vine", grape juice, as Jesus refers to this in the context: see Excursus Three below, "The Content of the Cup".

**11:26** We should note, as I have mentioned, that there is no parallel to this verse in the Synoptic accounts of the Last Supper. Paul indicates that the Christians are to "eat this bread and drink the cup" in remembrance of him, and "whenever" they do this they proclaim his death. No hint is given concerning the frequency of this commemoration.

Church practice has varied, some denominations holding the Lord's Supper at least once a week and others observing it quarterly, preceded by a period of special preparation. The correlation which Paul makes of the Lord's Supper with the Passover (5:7-8) could have suggested to the Church an annual observance, but the once-a-year frequency of the Passover has not been adopted for the Lord's Supper by Christian groups.

The Lord's Supper points back to the Lord's first coming so that when Christians participate in it they proclaim his death (καταγγελλω, *katangellō*, means to make it known publicly, to draw attention to it); and the Lord's Supper also points toward the Lord's second coming, when believers will enter in the fullest sense into what the Lord's death has obtained for them.

**11:27-32** The closing section of Paul's discussion of the Lord's Supper centers upon the importance of worthy participation. The passage opens with "therefore" or "it follows that" (TEV, NEB), showing that what Paul now says is the consequence of the truths which he has been setting out. In fact, he has been explaining about the meaning of the observance of the Lord's Supper in order to lay the basis upon which he can now make these points to the Corinthians. But his comments here are made as a consequence of all that he has had to say about the Lord's Supper, in chapter 10 as well as chapter 11.

Paul recognizes three classes of people (10:32): the Jews, the Greeks (the word is used in a wide sense, referring to Gentiles generally), and the church of God. In the practice of Israel, those who eat the sacrifices are partners in the altar (10:18); those who participate in pagan sacrifices make their offerings to idols and to the demons who stand behind the idols (10:19-21). Those who participate in the cup and the bread are united in one body in Christ (10:16) and in sharing together in feeding upon Christ spiritually and in remembering his death for them (11:24, 25).

The comments upon the three classes are parallel. Though the detail is different in each case the central concept is the same: each group, in its own way, is worshipping (and is visibly demonstrating its allegiance to) its God or gods. If therefore a person participates in the bread and the cup without recognizing (discerning) the body (11:29) - without recognizing that Christ's body was given for him on the cross, and without giving Christ his allegiance in response - then in taking the bread and cup he is acting a lie, for he is accepting the representation of Christ's love for him while in his own life denying its reality. Thus by his unworthy participation he profanes (desecrates, despises) the body and the blood of Christ (11:27).

Paul does not give any detail concerning how a person may eat and drink unworthily, beyond saying that such a person fails to recognize the body (11:29); rather he stresses (verses 28-32) the importance of the participant carefully examining himself before participating, for the consequences of unworthy participation are serious. For the Christian, this will not involve rejection by God and condemnation with the world, but it will involve chastisement (11:32). So we see that Paul warns in strong terms against light-hearted or careless eating and drinking of the Lord's Supper.

The answer to this problem is not absenting oneself, but examining oneself (11:28) and judging oneself (11:31). There is no ***automatic*** benefit or efficacy from the bread or the cup, or from the act of participating: the value of the ordinance is shown clearly to be completely linked with the participant's spiritual perception (11:29) and self-examination (11:28), and therefore, it may be presumed, repentance.

We have noted earlier (on 11:26) that no frequency is ever mentioned for the observance of the Lord's Supper. In view of the very solemn words of Paul in this section (11:27-32), it may be questioned whether the observance would have been weekly, or even rather less frequently such as fortnightly or monthly; it may more likely have been at irregular intervals by special decision, rather than of a predetermined frequency. This seems to accord also with the indefiniteness of "whenever you eat and drink ...".

**11:33** The members of the fellowship must act in fellowship, and with regard for one another. Winter's study (note my previous comment on 11:21) gives grounds for translating ἐκδεχομαι, *ekdechomai* (11:33), not as "wait for one another" but as "receive one another", that is, a mutual acceptance of each other. Winter says (page 82),

> The issues revolve around *ekdechomai*, "to receive one another". The Corinthians could only declare their love for God by demonstrating their love for their needy brother. To refuse to ***receive*** at the Lord's Dinner (*deipnon*) in the fullest sense of the word, those whom Christ has unreservedly received, both denies the reality of the Gospel to break down all barriers, and brings to light in the banquet of the new age those socio-economic divisions that belong to the age that is passing away ... It makes sense to argue that Paul's solution in v.33 involved the sharing of the haves' dinner with those who were hungry.

**11:34E** This verse re-echoes the thought of 11:22a. The intention is not to **prohibit** the idea of communal church meals but to underline that they are an act of fellowship as well as being for the purpose of satisfying hunger. If satisfying one's hunger is a person's whole purpose, then let him do that at home! Otherwise, by eating in the church fellowship and not sharing with those who have nothing, you repudiate by your actions the whole concept of coming together in fellowship, and you humiliate your brother (11:22). And for this you stand condemned.

Finally Paul refers to other matters (presumably, concerned with aspects of the observance of the Lord's Supper) - possibly a "secondly" and a "thirdly" to follow on from the "in the first place" of 11:18 - but these do not seem to be of pressing concern and Paul prefers to leave them until he arrives in person.

## EXCURSUS TWO:
## WHEN DID THE LORD'S SUPPER BEGIN?

Hodge has no doubt at all about the answer to this. He takes it as common ground and accepted by everyone that (222) "the Lord's supper had been celebrated without interruption from the time of its institution". And this viewpoint is very widely held and is usually taken as self-evident.

Books about worship in the early church routinely assume that the observance of the Lord's Supper dates from the earliest times. For example, the continuity of the observance of the Holy Communion is assumed by Garratt 35 to be completely obvious and requiring no proof at all. He says:

> There was no need for the writers of the books of the New Testament to explain to their original readers what the Eucharist was and how it should be celebrated. They presume that they already know, and [they] presuppose the rite as an already established and oft repeated act of the Church's worship. This creates difficulties for us who would like to know more about the way they performed it; but it also assures us that its centrality in the Church's worship goes right back to the beginning. It was not a later development, for it underlies every stratum of the New Testament tradition.

What Garratt is really saying is that we have little New Testament information concerning the way the Eucharist was celebrated (or "performed", to use his word), and he attributes this relative silence to the fact that the observance of the Eucharist was so well known that it required no specific comment.

C. F. C. Moule 21 establishes the continuity from earliest times of the Lord's Supper by seeing almost every meal eaten by the early Christians as being a reminder of the Last Supper. He says,

> Christians could hardly have participated in meals together without often recalling at them the close link thus established not only with Christ, but, more explicitly, with his death. To break bread and share a cup together would be to recall not only the unseen presence of the Lord and many meals formerly shared with him, but also the New Covenant which he had inaugurated at that particular meal in the upper room, in the context of his sacrificial self-surrender at Passover-time in which they found themselves bonded into God's people ... It was because Jesus was recognized by Christians as God's chosen King, because his death and the solemn meal anticipating it were seen to be the inauguration of the New Covenant sealed by his blood, that every meal together was at least capable of meaning for the Christians a renewal of their commitment as true Israel, as the real People of God. There is no need to believe that every meal explicitly carried this significance ... but if the Pauline tradition is a true one, it is difficult to believe that there was not, from the very first, a vivid awareness of this aspect of the Christian breaking of bread also. And to concede this is to recognize something *sacramental* as an original element in distinctively Christian worship.

But even if what Moule says were to be accepted as true, there is a difference between the bread and the cup at a fellowship meal reminding Christians of the Last Supper on the one hand, and on the other hand a specific and deliberately ritualistic celebration of a re-enactment of the Last Supper held as direct Christian worship in conscious obedience to a commandment of the Lord to "do this" in his remembrance.

After reviewing the references in the New Testament, and giving heavy weight to the implications of the "do this" in Luke 22:19 and 1 Corinthians 11:24,25, Moule feels able to say,

> ... It is impossible, at an early period, to draw hard and fast lines between 'mere' eating and 'sacramental' participation, between mere grace before meals and Eucharist. What does seem to be justified is the recognition of the early existence of a sacramental 'Eucharist'. [27], ... To sum up thus far, there appears to be sufficient evidence for believing that, from the earliest days, a sacrament such as came to be called the Holy Communion or Eucharist was celebrated, probably weekly, and usually in the context of a communal meal. [29]

But we need also to consider the question of the cup.

Is it to be accepted that the disciples drank a cup when they "broke bread" together, the cup having the significance explained by Jesus at the Last Supper? This also is usually taken for granted, but should be questioned. It is often considered that the disciples would have had a cup of wine regularly at their meals in any case, and that as the bread was invested with sacramental significance, so would be the wine. But even if we are to accept for the moment that wine was in the cup at the Last Supper (and this is far from being beyond dispute - see below, at the end of this chapter: Excursus Three: "The Content of the Cup"), it is not likely that the disciples had wine with their meals, and in the absence of evidence that they did, such an assumption cannot be made. This point is explained by Joachim Jeremias 50-52:

> Wine was drunk only on festive occasions ... Otherwise wine was generally used in everyday life only for medicinal purposes; it was regarded as an excellent medicine. In everyday life water was drunk. The daily breakfast consisted of 'bread with salt and a tankard of water', and even at the main meal bread and water were the chief ingredients ... It is ... quite out of the question that Jesus and his disciples should have drunk wine with their daily meals.

It seems therefore that (in the absence of particular reasons for believing otherwise) either no cup was drunk with the meal covered by the term "breaking of bread", or, if a cup was drunk, it contained water.

But Maxwell 4-5 and Martin 121-122 take it for granted that the pattern of the Lord's Supper described in 1 Corinthians 11 had been followed from earliest days, on the grounds that the manner of Paul's presentation in this chapter implies that he is not teaching anything new but that "he is recalling the Church to what is traditional teaching".

This is also the view of Garland 545, who says of Paul,

> He does not intend to teach the Corinthians something new about the Lord's Supper or to correct their theology of the Lord's Supper. He cites it only to contrast what Jesus did at the Last Supper with what they are doing at their supper.

However, the position regarding New Testament evidence is well summed up by Martin 120-121 in these words:

> It is true to say that the doctrine of the Lord's Supper in the New Testament is distinctively Pauline doctrine ... All in all, we are dependent on St. Paul's teaching for our knowledge of the doctrine, and that teaching is contained for the most part within one letter - the first Corinthian epistle.

Martin is understating the position when he says, "is contained for the most part within one letter" - the fact is, Paul's teaching about the Lord's Supper is *totally* contained within this one letter: Paul doesn't mention it in any of his other writings.

This evidence is usually interpreted thus:

**1.** The Gospel of Luke (22:19) and 1 Corinthians 11:24 record Christ's command to "Do this in remembrance of me" and it is unlikely in the extreme that such a commandment could have been forgotten, ignored or misunderstood, i.e. it may be taken that such a command would be followed from the beginning. The thinking runs thus: When our Lord commands something, and when his Church is later found to be observing a rite in obedience to that command, then the strong presumption is that the Church has observed that rite from the time of the command, and the onus is on the disputer to show that there is evidence that the rite was **not** observed from the first. Thus in the absence of any such evidence it is to be accepted that the Lord's Supper was observed from the first, i.e. Pentecost. [In effect this argument claims that the Scripture's silence about the Lord's Supper prior to 1 Corinthians supports the early origin of this observance.]

**2.** The breaking of bread (at least in Acts 2 and Acts 20) refers clearly to some special meal of religious significance, and can refer to nothing else but the celebration (albeit in primitive fashion) of the Lord's Supper.

**3.** Paul in 1 Corinthians 10 and 11 is certainly referring to a celebration of the Lord's Supper in bread and cup as a remembrance of Christ's death and passion, and he refers to it in terms which suggest it is long established, i.e. that it dates from Pentecost.

**4.** It is certain that such regular celebrations of the Lord's Supper were later a regular part of church life (cf. Justin Martyr, A.D. 150) and the comparative silence on this point in the New Testament records is most readily explained if we recognize that such celebrations were held from the beginning and therefore were too well known to require special reference, apart from the question of correcting some abuse, such as that at Corinth. If the Lord's Supper were introduced at any time later than the very beginning, there would at that time have been quite a great deal said about the innovation, and evidence of this would have come down to us.

This is the majority view among commentators - though they tend to take it for granted rather than argue their case.

However, Lietzmann 204ff. in *Mass and Lord's Supper*, and also MacDonald in *Christian Worship in the Primitive Church*, interpret this same evidence differently: they strongly disagree with all these assumptions, affirming rather that the observance of the Lord's Supper dates from the Lord's revelation about it to Paul which he reports in 1 Corinthians 11:23.

Let us consider this alternative view of the evidence:

**1.** In spite of 1 Corinthians 11:24 and the present text of Luke 22:19, the Christians of the first two decades did not in fact celebrate the Lord's

Supper. The fact that Christ gave his disciples a particular commandment is not in itself, and without other evidence, final proof that they
obeyed what he asked.

We must ask the question: If the Lord's command was given at the
Last Supper, did the disciples adequately understand this command from
the first? That is, did they recognize that they were intended (if indeed
they were from the first intended) to hold a regular ceremony based on
the Last Supper? There is every evidence that they were repeatedly slow
to grasp the meaning of the Lord's words (for example: they did not
understand his advance teaching about his death and resurrection in spite
of his many repetitions about it).

And the disciples did not interpret Christ's instruction to wash each
other's feet (John 13:14) to mean that they should regularly hold a rite of
this kind; and it would appear, from the evidence, that they did not
understand Christ's words "Do this in remembrance of me" to mean that
they should institute a ceremony based on the Last Supper.

**2.** As we have seen, the expression "breaking of bread" is used before
Christ's death in a context excluding the possibility of reference to a
celebration of the Lord's Supper (i.e. in the narratives of the feeding of
the five thousand and the four thousand), it is used on the resurrection
day of a simple meal at Emmaus that was certainly not the ceremonial
observance of the Holy Communion, and it is used of an ordinary meal
eaten by Paul on shipboard during the storm (Acts 27:35) to encourage
others to take food also. Therefore, without other supporting evidence, to
take such an expression in Acts 2 and Acts 20 to refer to a ritualistic
ceremony of particular significance in which bread *and a cup* are used,
is quite gratuitous and without foundation, and is reading back the practice of a later age into something quite different which was done at an
earlier time. The establishing of the early observance of the Lord's Supper from references to the "breaking of bread" is in fact a circular argument in which you prove your point by means of evidence which
assumes the point you have to prove.

**3.** Paul is certainly in 1 Corinthians 10 and 11 referring to a ceremonial meal in which bread and the cup are used to remember the death of
Christ, in a conscious re-enactment of the Last Supper; and he does
indeed say that this teaching is something which he had previously
delivered to them (1 Corinthians 11:23). However, this does not establish that this practice was any older than Paul's first visit to Corinth,
which was *twenty years* after Pentecost. It cannot be used as proof that
the practice was followed during those two decades.

**4.** The argument from silence is always precarious, and a very fallible guide, for it points equally well in two directions. Clearly, if the Lord's Supper had **not** been observed during the first two decades after Pentecost, silence on the point in the record of those decades is **exactly** what we would expect. And the expected record of the introduction later on of such a practice need be no greater than what in fact we actually have in the writings of Paul. And some aspects of the early silence can be significant. If, for instance, Matthew and Mark were in their regular church worship accustomed to holding the Lord's Supper in fulfillment of the Lord's command given to them at the Last Supper, how could they possibly come to leave out that command from their Gospels? And if the view is held that either or both the first two Gospels were the production of a later period, then this omission is even more inexplicable.

Thus the evidence routinely put forward for the Lord's Supper having been held from the beginning can be equally well interpreted to show the very opposite.

This brings us back again to the four narratives of the Last Supper: to the strange absence of the command "Do this ..." in the accounts in Matthew and Mark, and the fact that this command *is* in Luke and Paul.

We have noted earlier that as some early manuscripts do not contain Luke 22:19b-20, the words in italics in the Table of the four accounts (above), numbers of scholars therefore regard these words as later interpolations.

These scholars tend to ask, "Which is more likely: that Luke 22 originally contained 'Do this in remembrance of me' - the only such command in the Gospel accounts (as Matthew and Mark do not have it) - and that some copyists a century or two after New Testament times left it out, or else that some copyists, familiar with 1 Corinthians 11, incorporated these additional words into Luke, consciously or unconsciously, thus bringing Luke and 1 Corinthians into much closer parallel?"

If Luke 22:19b-20 is not original in Luke's Gospel, there is still much similarity between Luke 22:17-19a and 1 Corinthians, and a simple explanation of the manuscript evidence is that this similarity led some scribe or copyist to insert additional information into the Gospel from his recollection of 1 Corinthians 11. Once these words were added into Luke, no subsequent copyist would remove them, for they were authenticated by the text of 1 Corinthians.

Or if we may take it, on the other hand, that verses 19b and 20 in Luke 22 *are* original with Luke, then they represent an independent line of information for Luke and we may well enquire, Where did Luke receive this information, and in particular the command "Do this ..."? It can hardly be said to be from the "common heritage" of gospel tradition in the early church, because, as evidenced by Matthew and Mark, this "common heritage" did not contain such a command. But there is a very obvious explanation. The close verbal similarities with 1 Corinthians are too significant to be waived aside; the most reasonable answer could well be that Luke obtained this information from Paul. Alford 572 says,

> I may remark that the similarity between this account of the Institu-
> tion and that in Luke's Gospel is only what might be expected on the
> supposition of a special revelation made to Paul, of which that
> Evangelist, being Paul's companion, in certain parts of his history
> availed himself.

Paul wrote 1 Corinthians in about AD 55, and I am persuaded that Luke published his Gospel about five years later, in about AD 60 (some scholars would say, even later still). During this period Luke was accompanying Paul on his travels, so that for some years Luke saw Paul teaching about the Lord's Supper and instituting this rite in his churches, and thus he learned what the Lord had revealed to Paul about this sacra-ment. And this information was reflected in what he wrote in his Gospel.

But what are we to say about the fact that these words are in Paul? Indeed, what are we to make of the significance of the four accounts of the Last Supper? In sum, we can come to any one of three basic posi-tions to account for the evidence:

**1.** That the command "Do this ..." was given by the Lord at the Last Supper, and it was understood and obeyed by the apostles, so that this rite was observed in the church from the beginning - and it was so "nor-mal" and taken for granted that no one had occasion to refer to it until Paul did in AD 55 in 1 Corinthians; and Matthew and Mark simply did not think to mention it when writing their accounts of the Last Supper.

**2.** Or else: That this command was given by the Lord at the Last Sup-per, and that it was misunderstood or overlooked by the apostles until the Lord brought it again to the attention of the Church through a special revelation given to Paul, who taught this to his churches.

**3.** Or else: That the command "Do this ..." was not in fact spoken by the Lord at the Last Supper, but, rather, this command was given by the Lord to Paul in a revelation, and thence the observance of the Lord's Supper was taught by Paul to the Church in obedience to the command of the Lord. That is, the words "Do this ..." are to be understood as instructions given to Paul in the Lord's revelation, which Paul is to pass on to the churches, and these words are additional rather than part of what the Lord said at the Last Supper, in the same way that 1 Corin-thians 11:26 is additional.

We must note that whichever of these scenarios we come to accept -

whether these words were spoken by Christ at the Last Supper, or by Christ to Paul in the course of the revelation which Paul received of the meaning of the rite of the Lord's Supper - they *are* the Lord's command, and they represent his will for the Church. One of the factors which the thoughtful reader may ponder in seeking to weigh the evidence for the different possibilities is, "What are we to make of the absence of the command in Matthew and Mark (and thus, it seems, in the common gospel tradition in early times, apart from Paul)?"

Indeed, how *do* we account for the fact that the accounts of Matthew and Mark omit these words, though every other significant element of the institution narrative is mentioned? It is rather extraordinary that of the four authors who give accounts of the Last Supper, the two who were *not* present, Luke and Paul, include these words, while the two who give eyewitness accounts, Matthew and Mark (if we see Peter as standing behind Mark's narrative, as the early Fathers tell us) omit them.

The omission of these words by Matthew and Mark is *absolutely unaccountable* if we believe that from the time of the resurrection Matthew and Peter and Mark had been participating in weekly celebrations of the Lord's Supper which had their rise in the events of the Last Supper and which had their motivation in the fact that Christ himself commanded them at the Last Supper. How could an author who recognized that at the Last Supper Christ had given a command to be obeyed by his disciples, and who was weekly involved in an act of obedience to that command, possibly write an account of that Last Supper and *omit that command*?

To deny (as some do) that the traditional authors Matthew and/or Mark wrote the Gospels bearing their names does nothing to solve this problem; for if the actual authors of these Gospels were in fact neither an eyewitness nor writing from the preaching of an eyewitness, then they would be that much the more liable to be influenced by church practice, and if church practice included a celebration of the Lord's Supper based on the command of Christ given at the Last Supper, then that command would inevitably be included in their Last Supper narrative.

Two other matters I find significant:

Firstly, (apart from Paul's teaching in 1 Corinthians 10 and 11) there is not a single indisputable reference in the New Testament to the holding of a rite having the six characteristics we have identified in the Lord's Supper of Paul's writings. To say that this was because it was too well known and widely observed to merit comment by New Testament writers is really too facile and gratuitous - it should have appeared *some-*

*where* in their teaching, for what other Christian doctrine is so notable by its absence from the pages of the New Testament?

Secondly, the sermons of Acts (Paul's excluded, perhaps) do not reflect the teaching of Christ's death as being to ransom mankind from sin - a theme which would inevitably have been included if it was proclaimed weekly by the observance of a Lord's Supper of which this was the primary significance. This understanding of the meaning of Christ's death came later, with reflection upon the meaning of Christ's teaching - it was not there from the first. Rather, the emphasis in the early church was upon the resurrection (Acts 4:33; 17:18; 23:6) and the testimony that this gave to the fact that Jesus was indeed the promised Christ of God (Acts 2:36). The call was to repentance and faith in Christ (e.g. Acts 5:31; 20:21); but **nowhere in the speeches of Acts is Christ's death set forth as the basis upon which God can forgive sins**: instead his death is seen as a tragedy and a disaster which was turned to joy by the resurrection; it is seen as the results of the evil work of men and the devil, which God in his plan and foreknowledge transformed by the resurrection (Acts 2:23,24; 3:13-15; 4:10; 4:26-28; 5:30-32; 7:52; 10:39-43).

It may not be too much to suggest that the understanding that Paul was given of the meaning of the Lord's Supper was linked with his proclamation of Christ's death (notably in this same epistle, 1 Corinthians) as the foundation of salvation from sin.

These evidences therefore point strongly towards only two alternatives: either the Lord did not say at the Last Supper, "Do this ...", *or* he indeed spoke these words but the disciples did not fully appreciate their significance and thus **did not obey them in the early years of the Christian era**.

Of these two alternatives, it seems to me more reasonable to suppose that the words "This do ..." *were* spoken by the Lord at the Last Supper but that their significance was not wholly appreciated from the beginning, so that this instruction was not acted upon by the apostles for the first twenty years or so after the crucifixion. Paul was thus charged with the task of bringing the Church to the observance of this rite.

It may well be that the observance of this rite, with its remembrance of the death of Christ, was not necessary for the Church during the first Christian generation, but would be valuable for subsequent generations who had not known Christ or his apostles personally.

A parallel may be seen perhaps in the observance of the Sabbath, which was based in its significance on the day of rest at Creation (Genesis 2:2; Exodus 20:11) but was not instituted and observed in Israel until Exodus 16.

I would summarize then by saying that the evidence appears to point to the conclusion that the Lord's Supper as characterized by the six features described by Paul in 1 Corinthians 11 was not observed for the first twenty or so years of the Christian era, but that it was Christ's will and purpose that it *should* be observed according to a pattern which included these six characteristics, and that therefore the Lord used Paul to draw the attention of the Church to this aspect of the narrative of the Lord's Supper, an aspect which they had not hitherto noted fully nor obeyed.

From the foregoing I would draw this further conclusion: that the Lord's Supper is to be regarded as a most desirable feature in the life of the Church, for our Lord did indeed command it, but when considering its significance we need to take into account (especially in relation to those who regard it as indispensable to the spiritual well-being of the Church) that during her formative years, years which in many ways saw her at the height of her vigor, the Church did not observe the Lord's Supper at all.

## EXCURSUS THREE: THE CONTENT OF THE CUP

What should be in the cup that is drunk by the members of the congregation when they participate in the Holy Communion?

This is clearly to be linked to the answer to a prior question: What was in the cup which Jesus gave his disciples to drink at the Last Supper?

Nowhere in the New Testament is it *expressly* stated what was in the cup at the Last Supper. There is however a very strong implication that it contained "the fruit of the vine": note that Luke 22:17-18 records Jesus taking the cup, giving thanks, and saying, "Take this and divide it among you. For I tell you that I will not drink again from the fruit of the vine until the kingdom of God comes." (Similarly, Matthew 26:29//Mark 14:25.)

Note that the word "wine" is never used in the New Testament of the contents of the cup.

It is however commonly *assumed* by commentators that the cup at the Last Supper actually contained alcoholic wine. In consequence it is then unquestioningly accepted by many that alcoholic wine is to be drunk in the Lord's Supper.

How has this interpretation come to be so widely accepted - and followed?

There appear to be seven lines of argument which have led to this assumption. These seven, with a response to each one, are:

**1.** Many commentators, accepting the implication in the Gospels that there was the "fruit of the vine" in the cup, then take it as self-evident that "the fruit of the vine" would mean alcoholic wine.

*But* if Jesus meant wine, it would have been quite possible for him to say so. It is almost as if Jesus himself in what he is saying - and the Gospel writers in recording it - are all deliberately avoiding use of the word "wine", which itself (as we shall see below) is quite ambiguous in its meaning. If indeed there *was* wine in the cup - especially if it were fermented, alcoholic wine - why does no New Testament writer say so? Instead, Jesus spoke of "the fruit of the vine", an expression which was used in reference to grape juice, not of alcoholic wine. For example, in *Antiquities of the Jews* 2, 5, 2, in relation to the story of Joseph in Egypt, Josephus uses this expression in reference to unfermented grape juice. In this story, we find (Genesis 40:11) the cupbearer of the king describing to Joseph how in his dream "Pharaoh's cup was in my hand, and I took the grapes and pressed them into Pharaoh's cup and placed the cup in Pharaoh's hand." The implication of the story is that providing fresh grape juice was his normal duty which he did regularly in serving Pharaoh (verses 13 and 21).

In his careful and thorough study *Wine in the Bible*, Samuele Bacchiocchi presents solid grounds (163-168) for holding that there was unfermented grape juice in the cup at the Last Supper, and then cites a great many writers from the early Christian centuries who refer to, or describe the use at Communion of, juice straight from the grape or freshly squeezed. After presenting his evidence he concludes (169) that this testimony "has shown that all of these indicate that our Lord used, and commanded the use of, unfermented, nutritious grape juice to perpetuate the memory of his blood shed for the remission of our sins".

**2.** It is not infrequently objected - ofttimes as a throw-away comment - that the possibility of there being grape juice in the cup was ruled out because Passover fell a long time after the grape harvest, and grape juice would not have kept that long without fermenting: fresh grape juice would only ever be available for a short time at the appropriate season.

*But* this uninformed comment can distort our understanding of the situation in the ancient world. Those commentators who say this should make themselves aware of the four different methods in use in the ancient Mediterranean world for the preservation of grape juice. Bacchiocchi describes these methods in detail (106-127), quoting the descriptions from the ancient writers who give them. He shows clearly (128) "that the means of preserving grape juice without fermentation were known and used in the ancient world".

One common method was to boil the grape juice to evaporate most of the water and produce *must*, a thick paste, which was kept in sealed, airtight wineskins and was reconstituted for drinking with the addition of water.

Those of us well familiar with ready access to supermarket shelves groaning under the weight of a multiplicity of modern beverages should pause and ask ourselves: In biblical times, what alternatives were available for ordinary people to drink in the ordinary course of their lives, to quench their thirst?

The fact is, grape juice was a common drink of the time: it was drunk fresh when it was available, or reconstituted when grapes were out of season. There are numerous mentions in the Old Testament to how beneficial and enjoyable a cup of cold grape juice is. Trouble is, we frequently do not recognize these references for what they are because the usual translations use here the word "wine" and we interpret these as references to alcoholic wine.

A measure of this confusion is generated initially by the fact that in its everyday use the English word "wine" is almost invariably referring to alcoholic wine, whereas "wine" is the word regularly used to translate the Hebrew words *tirosh* and *yayin* and the Greek oivoç (*oinos*). The first of these, *tirosh*, refers to grape juice, must, unfermented wine; the latter two are used in the Bible to refer to the liquid product of the grape at all stages, from when it is still in the grape on the vine to when it has become intoxicating wine. Examples of the use of these words:

*(a) Wine as the juice within the grape in the cluster on the vine:*

Isaiah 65:8: "As the new wine is found in the cluster ...";

Jeremiah 40:12 " ... then all the Judeans returned from all the places to which they had been driven and came back to the land of Judah, to Gadaliah at Mizpah. And they gathered wine and summer fruits in abundance." [As is clear in context, what they gathered were grapes and fruit, from the vines and trees of the deserted land; alcoholic wine is not "gathered" from the fields.]

Isaiah 62:8-9: " ... foreigners shall not drink your wine ... but ... those who gather it shall drink it." [What are gathered are grapes, and "wine" here refers to the juice while still within the gathered grapes.]

So also Deuteronomy 11:14.

*(b) When the juice is extracted from the grape in the winepress:*

Jeremiah 48:33: "I have made the wine cease from the winepresses; no one treads them with shouts of joy ..."

Isaiah 16:10: "no treader treads out wine in the presses ..."

Nehemiah 13:15: the Judeans were treading winepresses on the Sabbath, and when this produce is loaded onto donkeys for transport it is referred to as "wine".

Proverbs 3:10: "... your vats will be bursting with wine." Also Joel 2:24: "... the vats shall overflow with wine and oil." Similarly Hosea 9:2. [The vats are where the wine (i.e. grape juice) is collected from treading the grapes.]

*(c) Where wine is fresh grape juice, at times referred to as "new wine"*:

Judges 9:27: the men went out into the field and gathered grapes from their vineyards, which they trod, and then held a festival where they ate and drank: in context, they were consuming what they had just produced: which was grape juice.

Lamentations 2:12: in the terrible time of famine "infants and babies faint in the streets of the city. They cry to their mothers, 'Where is bread and wine?'" They are not crying for alcoholic wine! They are crying for the grape juice which would have been a part of their normal diet.

Zechariah 9:17: "New wine" (*tirosh*) makes young women flourish.

*(d) Wine as causing intoxication:*

Numerous examples of intoxicating wine will be found, in the Old Testament all of them being the use of Hebrew *yayin*. The earliest are in Genesis (Noah: 9:20-21; Lot: 19:32-35). Proverbs warns against wine that makes one drunk (*yayin*, when fermented): 20:1; 21:17; 23:20-21; 23:29-35; 31:4-5); also Isaiah 5:11; Habakkuk 2:5. In Isaiah's time both prophet and priest succumbed to wine, with vividly described consequences (28:7-8). Woe to those inflamed by wine! (Isaiah 5:11-12).

There is no such condemnation of *tirosh*, which is "must, fresh or new wine" (*Westminster Dictionary of the Bible*, 641; and also *Theological Wordbook of the Old Testament*, 969): *tirosh* is never associated with drunkenness. The translation of *tirosh* into English varies - sometimes "juice", sometimes "new wine", often just "wine".

***Tirosh is a blessing provided by God***: Genesis 27:28; Deuteronomy 7:13; 11:13-14; 33:28; Proverbs 3:9-10; Jeremiah 31:12; it is the wine which "cheers God and men" (Judges 9:13; similarly Psalm 4:7); it is the "best of the wine" (Numbers 18:12). These are some of the references to *tirosh* as the provision of God.

The Hebrew *yayin*, which can be used in reference to either fermented wine or unfermented wine (grape juice), is invariably rendered into English simply as "wine". Concerning this, Bacchiocchi 65 notes, with reference to the Ph.D. dissertation of Robert Teachout,

According to Robert Teachout's tabulation of the 141 references to *yayin* in the Old Testament, 71 times the word refers to unfermented grape juice and 70 times to fermented wine. This tabulation may not necessarily be accurate, since in certain instances the context is unclear. ... [But] it is important simply to establish that *yayin* is sometimes used in the Old Testament to refer to the unfermented juice of the grape.

Similarly in the Greek New Testament, the word "wine", οἶνος, *oinos*, is a generic term for the produce of the grape, whether fermented or unfermented (grape juice). We can recognize this, first of all, from the way in which *oinos* is used regularly to translate *yayin*, with its parallel range of meaning. On 33 occasions the LXX translates *tirosh* simply as οἶνος, *oinos*: unfermented juice is included in the range of meaning of this Greek word.

Secondly, in Matthew 9:17//Mark 2:22//Luke 5:37-38 Jesus speaks of putting new wine into new wineskins. This is not referring to putting wine into new wineskins while it ferments there, for no matter how good these new skins they would not be able to resist the expansive force of the gas generated by fermentation, and they would most certainly explode. Bacchiocchi 72 explains that it seems clear Christ is

> "referring to wine fresh from the press which was strained and possibly boiled, and then placed immediately into new wineskins made airtight, possibly by a film of oil on the opening of the wineskin. ... Christ's words suggest that 'new wine' was placed into fresh wineskins to insure the absence of any fermentation-causing substance."

Such problems could be expected in old wineskins. Christ's illustration indicates the intention to retain the wine in its unfermented state.

Further, Bacchiocchi 168-169 provides references from early Christian writers which illustrate the way in which *oinos* was used in reference to unfermented wine, must, grape juice.

Those who fail to take account of this range of meaning of "wine" in the Bible and in early Christian writings are virtually certain to misread the meaning of numbers of passages which refer to wine.

Although there is no mention of "wine" in any New Testament passage referring to either the Last Supper or to Holy Communion, the use of *oinos* in early Christian writers in reference to what is drunk at ***their*** observances of the Holy Communion is then being "read back" historically into the Gospels and the conclusion is being drawn that it indicates that, in the opinion of the early Fathers, ***alcoholic*** wine was used at the Last Supper. Thus this caution applies very much to how the comments of the Fathers are to be understood, for such a deduction cannot be validly drawn from the evidence.

Noting the practice sometimes mentioned, in connection with the

Holy Communion in the early centuries, of mixing wine and water, Leon C. Field (*Oinos: A Discussion of the Bible Wine Question*, 91; cited in Bacchiocchi 169) points out that this water was "not necessarily in the weakening of alcoholic wine, but in the thinning of boiled wines and the thick juices of crushed grapes." Thus for instance Thomas Aquinas (*Summa Theologica*, vol. 2, part III, question 74, article 5) specifically says, in relation to the wine in the communion cup, "this sacrament can be made from must".

Awareness of this is relevant, for example, for understanding his meaning when Justin Martyr refers (*First Apology* 65, 67) to the church practice of using wine mixed with water. What kind of wine is he referring to here? Is this to **fermented** wine mixed with water to break down its alcoholic strength (as many scholars take for granted) - or to the diluting of thick, unfermented must into a more suitable consistency for congregational use?

Thus, first of all, we can recognize that it was perfectly possible to preserve unfermented grape juice as must, and to reconstitute it for drinking when required at any time of the year; and that this was practised in the ancient world. There is therefore no validity in the assertion that there could not have been unfermented wine available on the occasion of the Last Supper - or for that matter for early church observances of the Holy Communion.

And we need to recognize, furthermore, that the meaning of "wine" in its use in the Bible, and by the early church writers, needs to be interpreted in terms of its context in order to identify whether it refers to grape juice (unfermented wine) or alcoholic wine. Although the word "wine" is nowhere used in the New Testament in reference to the Holy Communion, it is relevant to draw attention here to this fact.

**3.** A third line of argument used in support of the contention that alcoholic wine was drunk at the Last Supper is that this meal was being held on the occasion of the Passover, when (fermented) wine would be drunk.

**But** there is a strong body of opinion that the meal was held the evening before the Passover, and was not itself the Passover (see for instance John 13:29). If however the occasion was indeed the Passover, then we should note that at the Last Supper Jesus certainly departed in a number of ways from what we know of the traditional Jewish Passover practice. (It is interesting to note, for instance, that there is no mention of a lamb in the account of the Last Supper.)

In any case, there is strong evidence from Jewish sources (Bacchiocchi sets it out, 159-162) that either fermented or unfermented wine (i.e., grape juice) could be used at Passover: there were differing traditions followed by the Jews in this regard. There is no cogency to an argument from Jewish Passover practice to support the "alcoholic wine" position.

**4.** Fourthly, it is argued that Paul specifically referred to those who got drunk at the gatherings at Corinth, and the conclusion is drawn: this indicates the use of alcoholic wine at Holy Communion in the apostolic church.

***But*** note: If some at Corinth had brought in wine, and drank it during the meal, this certainly does not establish that ***this*** is what was used in the cup for the ritual drink at the Last Supper (nor, for that matter, in the observance at Corinth), any more than we are to suppose that because bread was eaten in the ritual this would therefore be the only type of food consumed in the common meal that is being referred to.

If the word which is used in this context (μεθύω, *methuō*) means to be intoxicated, then it does certainly indicate the presence at the meal of an alcoholic drink such as wine. And such behavior is being mentioned by Paul in order to be condemned - such evidence of the presence of alcohol could not be used in support of what ***should*** be drunk in any observance of the Lord's Supper.

But does the verb μεθύω, *methuō*, really mean here that there was drunkenness on these occasions at Corinth? The verb also means simply to have drunk one's fill, and the context in this passage points to this as the meaning here: "while one was left hungry, another was filled to the full", i.e. until fully satisfied. Insisting that in this passage this verb means "to be drunk" is to overlook the scope of the verb's meaning, the thrust of the passage - and the nature of Paul's criticism. Bacchiocchi (182-187) develops this point fully, together with biblical examples of this meaning of μεθύω, *methuō*.

**5.** Fifthly, wine was used (it is said) for the cup at the Last Supper because, being red, it would carry well the symbolism of blood.

***But*** this is really no argument at all against the use of grape juice, which would equally have been of an appropriate color.

**6.** Sixthly, it is said by some that wine was the common drink of the day, so it would be the normal and natural beverage to use, not only on the initial occasion at the Last Supper itself but on the subsequent occasions when a congregation came together to observe the Lord's Supper.

***But*** this view is very definitely open to question. I have quoted earlier (in Excursus Two) the conclusion of Joachim Jeremias 50-52, who ends up by saying on this issue: "It is ... quite out of the question that Jesus and his disciples should have drunk wine with their daily meals." A similar comment is made in other reference volumes: such as Bromily,

ISBE 4. 1070, "wine": "Wine is not attested as the normal table beverage of OT times. It seems to have been reserved for special occasions."

This fact does not *disprove* the possibility that there was (alcoholic) wine on the table at the Last Supper, but it does counter the glib assumption that there must have been, on the basis that it would have been a normal part of meals in general at that time.

7. Seventh, it has been said that as wine was definitely used in the Holy Communion at a later time, we may take it that this usage commenced very early; i.e. from the beginning.

I have already answered in part (in my comments, above) this argument of the "reading-back" of later details into the practice of early days: to say the least, this is not always very accurate in the conclusions to which it leads.

However, in any case, the fact of the matter is that later writings do not point so clearly as is sometimes supposed to the widespread use of wine (whether fermented or unfermented). In the first centuries there are many references to celebrations of the Lord's Supper which were held with water in the cup, not wine (Acts of Thomas 120; Acts of Peter 2; Epistle of Cyprian 63, which states that this practice was widespread in Africa in the third century; Acts of Pionius 3; the practice was also found among the Marcionites, the Encratites and the Ebionites). Much could be said in favor of the symbolic value of water for use in the Lord's Supper, for as Scripture calls Christ the Bread of Life so it calls him also the Water of Life (John 4:14; 7:37, 38; 1 Corinthians 10:4).

In Justin's description of the Lord's Supper (*First Apology* 65 and 67) both wine and water are used - which may (as I have mentioned earlier) be an instance of must being diluted with water to produce a suitable non-alcoholic drink for Communion use. On the other hand, this could be a transition stage in a use of water giving way to wine, or a fusion of two separate traditions.

Concerning the use of water in the cup, McGowan says (143):

> Yet the most widespead practice other than the use of bread and wine is a case of less rather than more; many church groups seem to have used water rather than wine for the cup of the eucharistic meal ...This and the next two chapters will have the nature of a catalogue of the cases where bread and water (or bread alone) are the elements of the eucharistic meal.

Other early writings refer to other contents for the cup such as milk, honey, and a mixture of the two. (These two became officially prohibited by the Council of Trullo in AD 692: Canon 57; cf also the Third Council of Braga in AD 675: Canon 1.)

Andrew McGowan's book *Ascetic Eucharists* (Oxford University Press, 1999) gives a comprehensive coverage of all these variants, particularly relevant comments being in Chapter 3, "Food and Drink in Early Christian Meals"; "Milk and Honey"; and Chapter 4 on bread and water.

It is not so much a case, in these various early references, of wine being considered and then rejected in preference for one of these other alternatives: these references (above) to the use of other liquids are rarely the result of some early Christian group having a divergent viewpoint to press. In their context the references tend to show, rather, that their authors consider the use of these other liquids quite normal.

The foregoing seven are the arguments I find advanced for the belief that there was alcoholic wine in the cup at the Last Supper. If these arguments are as forceful as some of their advocates feel, it is worth asking how it was that in the first several centuries of the church there could be such a diversity of practice as to what was used in the cup, including the incontrovertible use, on many occasions and in different areas, of non-alcoholic wine or grape juice, as history reveals.

Thus we are able to say: The arguments in support of the contention that there was (alcoholic) wine in the cup used at the Last Supper do not have much substance. Or perhaps rather we should say, The evidence of the Gospels indicates what kind of wine was in the cup at the Last Supper: "the fruit of the vine", which is grape juice.


## THE SIGNIFICANCE OF THIS MATTER

Several interpretational consequences flow from the information we have been considering - logically, these four conclusions can be drawn from our study of this issue:

The simple fact is, there is nowhere in Scripture which lays down what should be used in the cup at the Lord's Supper, as there is for the way the use of bread is very definitely set out. The Gospel references to "fruit of the vine" strongly indicate the use of grape juice, but there is nowhere in Scripture which even enables us to be certain *beyond all doubt* as to what was in the cup at the Last Supper, or at any observance of the Lord's Supper. Our passages in 1 Corinthians, which are in all other matters definitive regarding the different aspects of the ritual, are totally silent on this point (lacking even the hints about "fruit of the vine" found in the Gospels). In fact, in 1 Corinthians the emphasis upon "the cup" - and not what was in the cup - is very striking, and appears deliberate. Our interpretation of 1 Corinthians must take account of the fact that in the Lord's Supper we are not said to drink wine (or any other liquid) but we *drink a cup* or *out of a cup.*

That is to say, though we are to drink out of the cup (i.e. what was in the cup) - for Jesus said "Drink from it, all of you" (Matthew 26:27; cf. Luke 22:17), and Paul said, "he eats of the bread and drinks of the cup" (1 Corinthians 11:28) - yet the entire emphasis is upon *the act of drinking* and never upon *what is drunk.* This fact must guide our understanding of the Lord's Supper. We notice for example that it is *the cup* which is the new covenant in Christ's blood (1 Corinthians 11:25; cf. Matthew 26:27-28//Mark 14:23-24//Luke 22:20) and before we put this down simply as metonymy we should note the link which it gives with Matthew 20:22-23//Mark 10:38-39; Matthew 26:39//Mark 14:36//Luke 22:42; and John 18:11: a link which would be lost if the emphasis were placed upon the liquid to be drunk rather than the cup itself.

Secondly, we are not given any basis in Scripture, either by instruction or example, for the use of alcoholic wine for the Lord's Supper.

Thirdly, the nature or form or composition of the liquid in the cup does not in itself carry or convey any meaning: but rather, merely the fact that it is in *the cup* and that we share it and drink it. Jesus said (Matthew 26:27-28), "Drink of it, all of you, for this is my blood of the covenant ..." Therefore this liquid could be any beverage (such as, for example - and very appropriately - water, which [as we noted earlier] would have much Christian symbolic value - cf. John 4:14; 7:37,38; 1 Corinthians 10:4), for *any beverage* would be equally suitable for a completely valid celebration of the Lord's Supper. Indeed, in the church's early centuries either there were some churches which did not believe that originally wine was used in the cup for the Lord's Supper; or they accepted that this was so, but they did not consider that this was necessarily a guide to be followed.

Fourthly, we should recognize a distinction between the commonly accepted understanding of the meaning of the English word "wine" (which is regularly taken to be a fermented, alcoholic drink) and the use of this word in translations of the Bible and in extra-biblical literature, where it is used in translation of *tirosh, yayin,* and *oinos.* For these words can be and are used both of the fermented and unfermented product of the grape. Sometimes they refer to this entire range of meaning, and more frequently to one or the other, as the context indicates.

It is an error of understanding to take "wine" in the Bible and early Christian writers to refer always to an alcoholic drink - the breadth of the range of meaning in these contexts always needs to be borne in mind.

To summarize the matter:

The use of bread is specifically stipulated, but not the nature of the beverage in the cup. What is the significance of the fact that the Scripture does not mention what was in the cup? Whilst the Lord's Supper consists of the bread and the cup, what is drunk from the cup is never made to bear any meaning in itself. It *represents* the blood of Christ, but no liquid is ever specified to carry that representation and therefore *any liquid could do so*. The drinking is an act of remembrance of Christ's blood poured out for our salvation. The benefit is conveyed by the drinking, and not by the nature or composition of what is drunk.

Whilst any beverage may function for this purpose, the most appropriate would be grape juice, because of the implication of what Jesus says (Luke 22:17-18), i.e., that this is what was used in the cup at the Last Supper.

# CHAPTER TWELVE

## SECTION 4:
## GIFTS AND MINISTRIES IN THE CHURCH

### 1. The Nature Of Gifts And Ministries (12:1-11)

### (a) Jesus Is Cursed, or Jesus Is Lord (12:1-3)

**12:1a** In his introduction to this section of the Epistle, Thiselton exclaims (902), "Hardly any statement about chs 12 and 14 remains uncontroversial". How true this is! It seems that every commentary you read has a different explanation to offer for these chapters - indeed, for just about every verse of these chapters. On some matters it is possible to be reasonably certain of the meaning of what Paul is saying; on some other matters there will be a clear difference between two (or more) opposing viewpoints or interpretations, and the reader will seek to make a choice between these competing alternatives; and on yet other matters it will be found difficult to decide at all upon just what may be meant.

Why is this so? Why isn't the meaning always simple and straight-forward? Because in the providence of God the Epistle reflects real people struggling with real-life issues - and real life isn't always simple and straight-forward. And, as John Chrysostom declares (Kovacs 196),

> This whole passage is hard to understand because we do not know the situation in those times and how this differs from our own experience.

Garland 561 says of one particular issue,

> The ambiguity reflects the fact that Paul picks up an issue raised by the Corinthians, which they would understand even if we do not.

The way forward is for readers to weigh the evidence for themselves, particularly taking note of issues arising in the Greek, for usually the issue will be decided by factors affecting that language. For the benefit of readers without a knowledge of Greek, I explain the nature of what is at issue.

The initial question, upon which there is general agreement, is that when Paul commences in v.1 with Περι δε *(Peri de)*, "now concerning", "now about" (as also in 7:1, 7:25; 8:1), he is indicating that he is taking up a new topic, and he is commencing to deal with an issue which has been raised by the Corinthians, presumably in their letter to him.

But while it is probable that this would be the next issue about which the Corinthians asked him, this does not mean that the Corinthians would have raised every aspect of the subject with which Paul deals. His detailed attention in this section of his letter to some of the abuses at Corinth is more likely to result from his own sources of information about the church than from all these matters being mentioned in their letter to him.

The subject to which he now turns, των πνευματικων (*tōn pneumatikōn*), which will occupy him to the end of chapter 14, is almost invariably rendered in English translations as "spiritual gifts". Some versions go even further: thus, TEV, "Now, the matter about the gifts from the Holy Spirit"; Living Bible, "And now, brothers, I want to write about the special abilities the Holy Spirit gives to each of you." And in fact many versions actually insert a heading for chapter 12, "spiritual gifts" or similar. But in the Greek text that Paul wrote, there is no word here for "abilities" or "gifts". The translations which italicize words that have been inserted by the translators do at least put "gifts" into italics to indicate that it is not in the original Greek.

The literal translation of Paul's wording would be, "Now concerning the spirituals ..." The words των πνευματικων (*tōn pneumatikōn*), could be neuter, "spiritual things". Or they could be masculine, which would mean "the spiritual ones", and thus pick up from chapters 2 and 3 the discussion of those at Corinth who were (or, rather, who described themselves as) "the spiritual ones". This is a description which Paul refused to allow them (see 3:1, where the word is unambiguously masculine, but is otherwise identical with the word here).

It seems clear that these people regarded themselves as the spiritually elite in the church, and this section of Paul's letter allows us to learn why: they possessed particular endowments which gave them prominence, and also, it seems, prestige and status. This (together with the way "the spiritual ones" were behaving) was making all the others in the church at Corinth feel that they were only "Class B" Christians, and led them to envy their (as they saw it) more fortunate brethren. So, as Paul is now tackling the issue of these people in the church, the translation here could be, "Now concerning the spiritual ones ..." Several older commentators take it this way, including Adam Clarke, who says,

> The words ... may [just] as well be translated 'concerning spiritual persons' as 'spiritual gifts': and indeed the former agrees much better with the context.

Several translations give "spiritual persons" in the margin as an alternative translation (e.g. ESV, NRSV). Barrett's judgement is, "it seems impossible to find objective ground for a decision between the two possibilities."

Garland examines the ambiguity at some length (561ff.). He says initially,

> If the genitive plural των πνευματικων (*tōn pneumatikōn*) is read as masculine, then the issue revolves around 'the spiritual persons' and their characteristics. If it is read as neuter, then the issue concerns the nature of 'the spiritual things' or 'the spiritual gifts'.

But thereafter he effectively drops the alternative "spiritual things" and regards the choice as between "spiritual persons" and "spiritual gifts". In the outcome, he himself decides upon the translation of 12:1a as "Now concerning the spiritual ones", taking this to be the Corinthians' meaning - he comments (563),

> Paul cites the Corinthians' question about the 'spiritual ones' in the announcement of the topic, and then seeks to correct their misconceptions. In my opinion, they constricted its meaning to denote only those who gave evidence of the spiritual gifts prized by them - in particular, speaking in tongues. ... It is important to recognize, however, that Paul quotes from the Corinthian letter in announcing the topic. As in 7:1, he uses their language without necessarily giving it the same meaning or value that they do. In this particular case, the genitive plural is obligingly ambiguous, 'the spirituals', and Paul can cite their terminology but develop his own interpretation so that it refers to gifts given by the Spirit to all Christians.

Then Garland explains further (564),

> I have opted to translate it 'spiritual ones' for two reasons. First, to capture the rhetorical setting and the argument's flow, it is best not to impose the understanding of the term that Paul unfolds in what follows onto this announcement of the topic, which is taken from the Corinthians' letter. When he uses this term here, he quotes from the Corinthians' letter, but will reinterpret what it truly means. Second, the translation 'spiritual ones' matches its usage at the conclusion of the discourse in 14:37, where he refers to a Corinthian outlook - those who regard themselves as spiritual.

However, I cannot agree with Garland that our choice is between "spiritual gifts" and "spiritual people". I do not see Paul's thinking as being quite as narrowly confined as Garland does.

One reason why των πνευματικων (*tōn pneumatikōn*) is so often treated as meaning "spiritual gifts" in 1 Corinthians 12-14 is that it is taken by many interpreters virtually to be synonymous in meaning with χαρισματα (*charismata*), "gifts", a word which Paul often uses in this context (e.g., Fee 576: "at points the two words are nearly interchange-able"; Conzelmann 207: "χαρίσματα is an equivalent for πνευματικα")

But χάρισμα (*charisma*), which is an expression of χάρις (*charis*), "grace", refers to a "gift" with a very wide range of meaning, and (as we shall see in the following commentary), is by no means limited to what are usually thought of as "spiritual gifts".

And on the other hand, the adjective πνευματικος (*pneumatikos*) refers to "spiritual" without in any way necessarily implying "gift". In fact, Garland 561f. gives an analysis of the use of πνευματικος (*pneumatikos*) in the New Testament, which shows that it **never** on its own means "spiritual gift" - on the sole occasion where it is used with this meaning (Romans 1:11), the Greek word for "gift" has to be added.

The one thing about which a firm comment can be made concerns the customary insertion of the word "gifts" into the verse. This is completely without any justification in the Greek. I want to emphasize that "gift" is not part of the inherent meaning of this Greek word πνευματικος (*pneumatikos*), which is used in this Epistle on numbers of occasions where no one would think of adding "gift". E.g. 9:11 ["If we have sown spiritual things among you, is it too much if we reap material things from you?" - see my comments on this verse]; and 15:46 ["But it is not the spiritual that is first but the natural, and then the spiritual"]. Not only is "gift" not required with "spiritual" by the context of 12:1, but this addition in English translations is quite misleading and distorts the context. It causes reader to expect (of course!) to read about "spiritual gifts" and (not surprisingly) they are then inclined to read and interpret what follows in the light of that expectation.

Thus this is an interpretative translation which biases the readers in their understanding of what Paul is about to say. In particular, it predisposes these readers to overlook manifestations of the Spirit other than those explicitly called "gifts"; to see the gifts mentioned as all being "spiritual gifts" (often interpreted in a way which excludes from consideration the role of "natural gifts" in Christian work); and to view the gifts as being "given by the Spirit", instead of noting carefully what the text actually says.

But nor can we limit Paul's opening topic to "spiritual people". Paul does not commence this topic by saying "spiritual people" (contrary to what Garland affirms), but he uses a term with a deliberately wide connotation. Quite a few scholars have taken this wider view.

Thiselton 910 raises the question of whether Paul would have been unaware of the ambiguity in πνευματικος (*pneumatikos*), commenting,

> It refers to *either*. But if both the writer and the readers well knew

that the Greek ending included *both* genders (i.e. excluded neither), why should the meaning be construed in either-or terms at all?

Thus he translates, "Now about things that come from the Spirit". Similarly Findlay's Commentary translates it as "spiritual things"; while amongst translators, Phillips renders the expression as "spiritual matters", and Lattimore says, "But concerning matters of the Spirit".

To sum up: Assigning this term (as many do) to the Corinthians, used in their letter to him, obscures the issue. That may or may not be the case: we may guess but we are not here in a position to know. But what we do know is that *this* is the word Paul has chosen to use in announcing his topic. Paul's discussion is going to range over the question of the so-called "spiritual ones" at Corinth, the role of the Holy Spirit in the ministry of a believer, and endowment of spiritual power for spiritual living. His very general term covers all these. Lacking in English a word of comparable scope, we can only approximate with "now concerning spiritual issues" or "questions about the Spirit". But the rendering "spiritual gifts" is a dangerous interpretation, for it sets the readers up from the first verse to interpret everything which Paul now says as being related to "spiritual gifts", instead of allowing it to be seen as much wider, in accord with Paul's actual choice of words, "spiritual matters". The rendering "spiritual gifts" is unnecessarily restrictive, and inaccurate, and *wrong*.

**12:1b** Paul's concern that they should not be uninformed (present tense, meaning to continue in ignorance), wording which is identical with 10:1, indicates that it is his judgement that in this matter they *are* uninformed. In the context of chapters 12 to 14, it may well be that the Corinthians see "being spiritual" as a question of certain spiritual manifestations. But this is not at all what being spiritual means - concerning this they are quite mistaken.

Other matters can await his arrival in Corinth for his attention to them (see 11:34E, the preceding verse): but this matter cannot be left, and must be dealt with promptly.

**12:2** Previously, Paul says (RSV), "You know that when you were heathen, you were led astray to dumb idols"; that is, they were brought to idolatry. To quote Gromacki:

"Somehow or other" [RSV, "however you may have been moved"] contains the idea of being "controlled by outside forces. ... Unconsciously, they were deceived by the world of evil spirits."

But Paul's emphasis is not upon *what* or *who* (e.g. peer pressure) may have been responsible for the leading astray - his point is that, in their former way of life, however they were led, it ended with leading them to dumb idols. As Hodge 239 sums up the contrast:

> Here, as in Ephesians 2:11, the apostle contrasts the former with the present condition of his readers. Formerly, they were Gentiles; now they are Christians. Formerly, they were the worshipers and consulters of dumb idols, now they worshipped the living and true God.

**12:3** When they were under the control of idolatry they may well have said "Jesus be cursed"; but now as Christians their perspective is completely reversed. With the Spirit of God activating them, no longer would they ever say such a thing. Rather, they now acknowledge "Jesus is Lord", and the acceptance of Jesus's authority as Lord is only possible through the work of God's Spirit within. Paul's comment does not mean that a person cannot utter the words "Jesus is Lord" meaninglessly. The word Paul uses, εἰπεῖν (*eipein*), means "to say" with the meaning "to declare, to state a particular content", i.e. to say it and mean it. Thus, that a person genuinely acknowledges the lordship of Jesus is the result of, and the evidence of, the work of the Holy Spirit. In the early church, the recognition that "Jesus is Lord" was the touchstone of what it meant to be a Christian (Acts 10:35; 11:20; Romans 10:9; 2 Corinthians 4:5; Philippians 2:11; 1 Peter 3:15).

But Paul's reference to someone saying "Jesus be cursed" is puzzling. Some commentators consider the reason is that there was ecstatic speaking within the Corinthian church, in the course of which a person could utter the cry "Jesus be cursed" (so Barrett and Grosheide). However, it is difficult to believe that Paul needed to inform the Corinthian Christians, as though of something of which they were ignorant (12:1), that if one of their number said "Jesus be cursed", it was not the Holy Spirit who was speaking through him!

A more likely explanation is the background of Jewish/ Roman persecution, where Christians were being pressured to renounce their faith with the declaration of a curse upon Jesus - Paul himself tells us (Acts 26:11) that before his conversion his mission was thus to compel the Christians to blaspheme.

Garland 571f. comments:

> Since the evidence reveals that this cursing of Jesus actually occurred in the synagogues, it is the most likely background ... This [is] ... the contrast in 1 Cor 12:3: Jews call Jesus *anathema*; Christians, through the Spirit, call him Lord.

So Paul's first response to this question of "spiritual matters" at Corinth is a negative and a positive: the Spirit leads no one ever to say

"Jesus be cursed" - but he does empower a person to declare "Jesus is Lord".

Thus every person who is really a Christian - recognizing Jesus as Lord - is a person who has the Spirit. For Paul's point at the outset is to remind all the Corinthians that every Christian has the Holy Spirit. *That*, as it were, is the starting point in considering this entire issue of spiritual matters.

We shall see this more clearly in the next verses, where Paul says in fact that the whole Trinity is involved, though in different ways.

For Paul now proceeds to consider all these spiritual matters in detail, and on a broad canvas, and in doing so, to set the particular concerns of the Corinthians into their correct context, and place them into proper perspective.

Upon two things there is general agreement amongst expositors: first, that the Corinthians had a preoccupation with two particular gifts, that of speaking in tongues and prophecy, and second, that in coming to write to them about these issues Paul saw that it was necessary to tread gently and to lay a careful foundation rather than deal immediately with them - that is why he provides the explanations of chapters 12 and 13 before getting to grips with these particular matters in chapter 14.

### (b) The Varied Manifestation of the Spirit (12:4-7)

In v.3 Paul has shown how through the enabling of the Holy Spirit the believer is able to declare, "Jesus is Lord". What follows now in 1 Corinthians 12 to 14 has reference to all those who acknowledge Jesus as Lord.

In this section of his letter Paul is in effect expounding the teaching of Jesus about the gift of the Spirit (John 14-16). The key to understanding this passage is recognizing that Scripture nowhere refers to "gifts [plural] of the Holy Spirit", as of something given *by* the Holy Spirit. In the two places where this may appear to be the case in an English version, it is an incorrect translation for *distributions* made by the Holy Spirit (μερισμοις; *merismois* in Hebrew 2:4; and the verb, διαιρουν, *diairoun* in 1 Corinthians 12:11).

So to speak of "gifts of the Holy Spirit" is a misnomer. In the terminology of the Bible, there is only one *gift* of the Spirit, which *is* the Spirit. That is, "the gift of the Spirit" means the *giving* of the Spirit. The Spirit is the *gift*, not the giver. Always. Every time. God is the giver, as Jesus taught (John 14:16; 14:26) and as the Apostles also taught (Acts 2:38; 5:32: 10:45). The Holy Spirit, given by the Father (Acts 1:5;

Romans 5:5; 2 Corinthians 5:5), sent by Christ (John 15:26; 16:7), indwells all believers and empowers them for service and witness (Acts 1:8; 4:31; etc.).

That is, the Holy Spirit is God's supreme gift to his people. Indeed, Paul says in Romans 8:9 that if a person does not have the Spirit, he does not belong to Christ. The Lord explained to his disciples in John 14 to 16 that it was the Father's plan to give his people the Spirit; and in fulfillment of this promise the Spirit came at Pentecost. Scripture frequently refers to this giving of the Holy Spirit, e.g. Luke 11:13; John 14:16; Acts 5:32; Acts 15:8; Romans 5:5; 1 Thessalonians 4:8; 1 John 3:24; 4:13. And whenever Scripture mentions the "gift of the Holy Spirit" (as for example Acts 2:38; 10:45; 11:17; 2 Corinthians 1:22), the gift *is* the Holy Spirit, who is the one given.

The Holy Spirit distributes and activates God's gifts, but the Spirit is not the *source* of gifts: Ephesians 4:7-13 explains that Christ is the one who gives the gifts of ministry, and James 1:16-17 says "Do not err: every good and perfect gift comes down from the Father in heaven."

Paul now shows how the indwelling Holy Spirit manifests himself, expresses himself, reveals himself in a variety of different ways in the life of believers.

**12:4** Paul sets God's gifts in their proper perspective in his opening explanations. There are more than half a dozen words in Greek for "gift", but this one, χαρισμα, plural χαρισματα (*charisma*, plural *charismata*), is distinctive. *Charisma* is an allocation of God's *charis*, God's grace, apportioned to a person. This word is only used in Scripture of a gift which comes from God: never of a gift which one person gives to another, or to God. It is a "grace-gift", a part of God's own being, God's own nature, mediated through the Spirit. It is the outworking, the expression, in a person's life of something of the nature and character of God. This expression is thus and therefore an activity of God.

Paul affirms in verses 4 to 6 that God is a God of difference and diversity, and never more so than in how he is at work in the lives of his people. Moreover, this working of God involves the whole Godhead, the Trinity. In fact, Orr & Walther 281 describe these verses as providing "raw theological material out of which the church developed trinitarian doctrine" - speaking as these verses do of the Spirit, the Lord Jesus Christ, and God, being at work in and through the lives of believers.

There are, Paul points out, differences of χαρισματα (*charismata*), but the same Spirit. The same Spirit in two senses:

*First*, the Spirit who is at work in and through the χαρισματα (*charismata*) is the same Spirit to whom Paul has just referred in v.3, who enables the believer to affirm, "Jesus is Lord!" The Spirit who does the one also does the other. The Spirit who unites Christians in their common recognition of the Lordship of Jesus also expresses himself through their diversity of χαρισματα (*charismata*).

**Second**, it is the one and the same Spirit who is thus seen in each of these χαρισματα (*charismata*), so that each of the diverse χαρισματα (*charismata*) is to be recognized as an activity of that same Spirit. This lays the basis upon which Paul will shortly make the point that each of these gifts is as important as any other in the economy of God.

Moreover, there are διαιρεσεις (*diaireseis*) of χαρισματα (*charismata*). This word means both "diversities" and "distributions". In this verse it refers both to the differences between one *charisma* and another (so that Paul will go on to underline the great variety to be seen in the gifts of God's grace), and also to the way in which these gifts are distributed by this same Spirit. Paul states this explicitly in v.11, where he sums up by saying that one and the same Spirit is at work in each of the manifestations he has been mentioning, distributing them (same word, in verb form) to each person as he chooses.

No matter how distinctive and diverse these different gifts, it is the same Spirit who is seen in them all.

The NIV muddied the water and confused the issue considerably concerning Paul's meaning in this chapter by translating πνευματικων (*pneumatikōn*) in v.1 and χαρισματα (*charismata*) in v.4 in exactly the same way: both as "spiritual gifts"! This made the second reference identical with the first in the mind of the reader. Clearly the NIV translators took Paul to be meaning exactly the same thing when he used these two different words. They thus inserted their ***interpretation*** right into the text of what Paul said. There are numbers of commentators who are of a similar opinion (e.g., Conzelmann 207, "χαρίσματα is an equivalent for πνευματικα"). But they are confusing things that differ.

Earlier (when introducing v.1) I discussed in detail the meaning of πνευματικων (*pneumatikōn*). I have just explained χαρισματα (*charismata*) as an expression and outworking of the χαρις (*charis*), the grace, of God. Paul has more, much more, to say about χαρισματα (*charismata*) as this section of this Epistle develops. We must allow him to be able to use his own words, and to expand and to explain their meaning, and not make him out to be saying one thing when he says another.

And χαρισμα (*charisma*) does ***not*** mean "***spiritual*** gift". It means "grace-gift" without any designation or restriction added, such as "spiritual": something which in the thinking of many people would limit its meaning and would exclude numbers of gifts and endowment and attributes (such as natural gifts), when no such exclusions exist in what Paul is saying.

If you have an NIV, you can test the age of your edition by seeing how it translates 12:4. Because eventually the translators responded to the protests, and removed the word "spiritual" in this verse, so that the more recent NIV editions read, "There are different kinds of gifts" - without "spiritual"!

So beware: χαρισμα (*charisma*) is sometimes interpreted so as to place an unjustified restriction upon the meaning of this word, which actually covers every kind of gift that a person has, including salvation itself. See for example how this same word is used in Romans 5:15-16; 6:23; 11:29; 1 Corinthians 7:7; 2 Corinthians 1:11. The word should certainly be translated simply as "gifts", as indeed it is in most translations.

**12:5** But the χαρισματα (*charismata*) are not the only way in which God works in his people. This is a major point which Paul wishes to make, and which (we may conclude, if we judge aright their emphases) the Corinthians did not see. Paul now points out that there are also differing kinds of διακονια (*diakonia*) - of ministries, of service: but it is the same Lord who is being served. "The Lord" is Paul's normal way of referring to the Lord Jesus Christ, which is certainly his meaning here.

Paul is saying, God's people serve the Lord in a great variety of different ways. Some of them will indeed serve through the exercise of χαρισματα (*charismata*): but some through διακονια (*diakonia*). The original meaning of this word was "domestic service, serving at tables". The servants at the wedding feast in John 2 are διακονοι (*diakonoi*). In Luke 10:40 Martha was busy with διακονια (*diakonia*). This was the ministry - serving tables - to which the Seven were appointed in Acts 6:1-4, where this word διακονια (*diakonia*) is also used (v.4) of the **ministry** of the Word. From this we see that the members of a congregation who look after the domestic arrangements or provide the cups of coffee after the church service, and the ministry team who are leading that service, are equally engaged in διακονια (*diakonia*), and it is the same Lord Jesus Christ whom they are engaged in serving.

I warmly endorse the words of that great hymn (#652 in *The Book of Common Praise*):

"They who tread the path of labour follow where my feet have trod;
They who work without complaining do the holy will of God;
Nevermore thou needest seek me - I am with thee everywhere;
Raise the stone, and thou shalt find me; cleave the wood, and I am there.

Where the many toil together, there am I among my own;
Where the tired workman sleepeth, there am I with him alone."

And:

"Every task, however simple, sets the soul that does it free;
Every deed of love and mercy done to man is done to me."

In what he is saying here in v.5, Paul is of course reflecting the teaching of the Lord himself, who said (Matthew 25:40): "Truly I say to you, as you did it to one of the least of these my brothers, you did it to me."

Then this word διακονια (*diakonia*), and its related words διακονος (*diakonos*) and the verb διακονεω (*diakoneō*), come to be used throughout the New Testament of specific Christian ministry of every kind. Whatever form our ministry might take, whether in up-front leadership or humble, mundane, behind-the-scenes domestic drudgery, as we serve each other it is serving the Lord. As I read Paul's comments about the Corinthians, I do not think that they all properly understood this. It is to be hoped most fervently that we do.

**12:6** There is more. There are also different kinds of ενεργηματα (*energēmata*). This word is variously translated as "workings", "operations" (or energizing, empowering, enabling, activating) and the like. It means "to be at work in", and thus "getting something done". You will recognize that it comes straight into English in our word "energy".

Those with the ενεργηματα (*energēmata*) are those who make things happen. The entrepreneurs. The organizers. The facilitators, the enablers, the planners, the co-ordinators. The ones who bring together the various components of a ministry, an activity, an organization, a structure, an event, and see that - whatever it is - it gets done as it should. But in this diversity of activity it is the one God who is at work.

This is a special skill, and very important to the total working of the Church of God. The gifted speaker who will minister the word of God effectively is not necessarily skilled at organizing the arrangements for the meetings or services at which he will minister. Whereas the one who plans and provides for the meetings or services is not necessarily equipped to speak at them. These are skills of a different order.

So often the gifts which God has given his people are not being utilized as effectively as they might in the work of the Kingdom for lack of persons with the ability of ενεργηματα (*energēmata*) to come forward and play their part and make it all come together and ***happen***. Again, this is a skill which is usually very much behind-the-scenes, and which may not be fully recognized and acknowledged for how important, how crucial, it is. But Paul draws attention to it here.

And then he uses the same word again, in the form of the participle
ἐνεργῶν (*energōn*), which now refers to God. For God is shown to be
actually the one who is at work in whatever it is which we are doing.
This can be translated "who works everything *in everyone*" or "who
works everything *in every way*" - depending whether πασιν (*pasin*) is
taken as being masculine or neuter. But I do not think we are to choose. I
take it that Paul, in using a word form which is both masculine and
neuter, is here deliberately embracing both meanings.

In all this, God is to be seen as working together with and in and
through his people. I am very much reminded of what Paul also said in
Colossians 1:29, in respect of his total ministry: "To this end I labor,
struggling with all the energy he so powerfully energizes in me." I need
hardly mention that the words "energy" and "energizes" here are this
same word ἐνεργηματα (*energēmata*), though here its two occurrences
are in the noun form ἐνεργειαν (*energeian*) and the participle
ἐνεργουμενην (*energoumenēn*).

When something is happening in a church, it is actually God at work
making it happen. But so often when it appears that God is not at work,
the problem is that the people with the various kinds of ἐνεργηματα
(*energēmata*) are asleep on the job. A good summary of these points is
expressed by Carson in *Showing the Spirit* 33f. He says with discernment and insight:

> (1) verses 4-6 do not so much suggest that the Spirit *gives* gifts, the
> Lord *gives* forms of service, and God *gives* 'workings', as that diversity
> of distributions of these 'gifts,' for want of a more generic term, goes
> hand in glove with one Spirit, one Lord, one God; and (2) in the ensu-
> ing verses in this chapter, everything is ascribed to the Spirit (though
> still not so much as the giver of the gifts as the one who distributes them
> and 'energizes' them [12:11]). ... More important, nowhere do these
> chapters explicitly make the Spirit the giver of spiritual gifts.

**12:7** Paul describes each of these διαιρεσεις (*diaireseis*) as being a
manifestation (φανερωσις, *phanerōsis*) of the Holy Spirit. They are, each
of them, ways in which the Holy Spirit works in the church. More than
that, they are, each of them, ways in which the Holy Spirit is *seen* to be
working in the church, for that is the implication of φανερωσις
(*phanerōsis*). The Holy Spirit is not to be seen only in the impressive,
noticeable, gifts which apparently have caught - and held - the Corinthians' attention. The Spirit's ministry, and his working, is much wider
than that - and it needs to be identified and recognized as such.

Some commentators regard these "manifestations" - the *charismata*,
the *diakonia* and the *energēmata* - as referring to the same thing. Thus
Hodge 243, in writing of this passage, says, "They are all and equally

gifts of the Spirit, modes of serving the Son, and effects due to the efficiency of the Father." And similarly Fee 587 considers that "they are simply three different ways of looking at what in v.7 Paul calls 'manifestations' of the Spirit."

I disagree. Paul uses "manifestations" to embrace all three ways in which the Spirit expresses himself in the life of the believers in the church, but they can be quite different and distinct. Fee goes on to say (589) - and I agree with him here:

> First, "each one", standing in the emphatic first position as it does, is his way of stressing diversity. ... He does not intend by this to stress that every last person in the community has his or her own gift. That may or may not be true, depending on how broadly or narrowly one defines the word *charisma*. ... Second, what "each one" is given in this case is not a "gift" but a "manifestation of the Spirit" ... His urgency, as verses 8-10 make clear, is not that each person is "gifted", but that the Spirit is manifested in a great variety of ways. His way of saying that is, "to each one is given the manifestation of the Spirit".

Thus in one believer, the Spirit manifests himself in a gift for more obvious Christian service, whether by activating a natural endowment (such as a musical ability) dedicated to the Lord's service, or through a special gift (such as the calling of being an evangelist); in another believer the same Spirit is manifested through that believer giving conscientious, reliable, dedicated service in the Lord's work, often behind the scenes and unnoticed; in yet another believer the same Spirit is manifested in "activating": that is, in motivating, planning and directing the work of others - the work of management and administration. But in every case, this gift, or ministry of service, or administration, is the outworking, the manifestation, of the indwelling Holy Spirit.

Moreover, Paul emphasizes that the manifestation of the Holy Spirit is given to **each** person. To each person, that is, who acknowledges Jesus as Lord, by the Holy Spirit, v.3. This manifestation is not something for a select few, that is, for an "elite" group within the church, as appears to be implied as being the thinking of some of the Corinthians. No: the manifestation of the Spirit is given to **each believer**, whether male or female, old or young, new believer or mature Christian. There is no Christian in whom the Spirit does not manifest himself. As Paul will go on to show, this has far-reaching implications for the activities and functioning of the church.

Next, Paul gives us the test by which we assess a particular "endowment", the yardstick by which we measure it, as to whether it really is an endowment from God. For Paul tells us that each endowment is given by

God "for the common good": that is to say, for the benefit of others rather than for the recipient of the gift themself.

Recognizing this truth allows us to double-check our interpretation of the nature of a *charisma*, and to verify that its use is in accord with the intention of God. If in our understanding of a gift, it is benefiting only the recipient, then we have not understood correctly the nature and purpose of that gift, or else it is not being used correctly. All the gifts, all the forms of service, and all the energizings, are ways of ministering *to each other*. They are given for "the common good", the total advantage of the whole Church of God (TEV, "for the good of all"). This is what the Corinthians need to see. And this is what *we* need to see, from Paul's letter.

Notice that in this verse there is no mention of who the giver is. "The manifestation of the Holy Spirit" is what is given to each believer. This is passive: someone unstated is the giver. In a passive of this kind, the implication is that God is the one who is acting. (The "divine passive" is a recognized grammatical feature of the New Testament.) Then later in this chapter (12:28) it is stated explicitly that it is God who does these things. Thus, the Holy Spirit is given to each believer from God (as Jesus promised, and as Peter proclaimed at Pentecost), and then, indwelling each believer, the Spirit manifests himself in each one in different ways, as Paul now proceeds to explain in what he says next.

All the gifts in 1 Corinthians 12:8-10 are encompassed in this explanation in 12:7. In that sense I suppose they *can* all be called "spiritual gifts" - not gifts *given by* the Spirit (this way of describing them is totally alien to the New Testament), but gifts from God the Father through Jesus Christ which are encompassed within "*the* gift of the Holy Spirit", and are the ways in which the indwelling Holy Spirit acts in expressing himself through the believer for the benefit of the church.

### (c) Ways In Which The Spirit Manifests Himself (12:8-11)

Paul now lists nine χαρισματα (*charismata*) in verses 8 to 10: which we will go on to consider in careful detail. But before we do, as an introduction to this, we need to set Paul's comments in a wider context.

These nine χαρισματα (*charismata*) are, as we have seen, the imparting in some way of something of the nature of God to the church. But they do not exhaust God's grace. That is to say, they are not an exhaustive list of God's *charismata*. There are other places in Scripture where other χαρισματα (*charismata*) of God are mentioned, and when we put these all together even then God is greater by far than their sum.

Other similar lists are also given in 1 Corinthians 12:28-30; 13:1-3; 14:6; 14:26; Ephesians 4:11; Romans 12:6-8; and 1 Peter 4:9-11. The last reference does not add anything which is not found in Paul, while each one of the Pauline passages contains at least two items which are not found in any of the others. The various passages contain different numbers of items or gifts or ministries, these numbers being respectively, 9, 8, 7, 5, 4, 7 and 3 - a total of 43. (Ephesians contains either 4 or 5, depending on whether "pastors and teachers" is taken to refer to two functions or one; it is better taken as being a reference to those who are both pastors and teachers, so I count Ephesians as mentioning four *charismata*.)

There is overlapping between the lists of course, but it is not always possible to be certain whether an item in one list corresponds with one in another. For example, is the "ability to speak with knowledge" (ESV, etc.: "utterance of knowledge") in 1 Corinthians 12:8 the same thing as "to understand all knowledge" (1 Corinthians 13:2) and as "speaking the very words of God" (1 Peter 4:11) or "to teach" (various references)?

Making the best assessment I can for correlations of this kind, I end up with a list of twenty-four items:

The ability to communicate wisdom; the ability to communicate knowledge; faith; gifts of healings; performances of works of power; prophecy; discernings of spirits; kinds of tongues; interpretations of tongues; apostles; teachers; helpers; administrators; generosity or liberality; giving the body (martyrdom); having a hymn or psalm (i.e., music); having a revelation; marriage/celibacy; evangelists; pastors (or, better, pastor-teachers); ministry (service); exhortation; giving aid; performing acts of mercy.

The meaning of some of these is quite clear; the meaning of others is obscure or open to question. Let us note five overall characteristics.

*Firstly*, the fact that Paul can give so many different kinds of references spread out over six different passages in three of his epistles suggests very strongly that not any one list nor all of them together can be (nor was intended to be) taken as exhaustive but rather as illustrative. These are *ways* in which the Spirit manifests himself (to use Paul's language in 1 Corinthians 12:7), but he may also manifest himself in Christians in other ways which are not listed here.

*Secondly*, the Spirit manifests himself in these ways in Christians for the benefit of the whole church, the body of Christ. This is explicitly emphasized in 1 Corinthians 12:7 and 12:14-27; Romans 12:4-6; Ephesians 4:12-13; it is implicit in the contexts of all the passages. When individual Christians meet within the congregation and make their contribution as the Spirit enables them (1 Corinthians 12:11), other Christians are then and thus equipped for the work of ministry, and the whole body of Christ is build up (Ephesians 4:12).

*Thirdly*, it is not anywhere said that these are gifts, ministries, or enablings which are given to people *as Christians* or *because* they are Christians or *after* they become Christians. This may well be true in some cases: a person could for example hardly exercise a ministry as apostle or evangelist before being a Christian. On the other hand, there are able administrators and teachers who are not Christians, so that in such cases the meaning is seen to be that the Spirit energizes or activates their natural ability (which they had apart from and probably prior to their becoming a Christian), and enables it to be used in God's service.

In such cases their natural ability is God's gift in the sense in which every gift of nature, which every person has, is something that they have as the result of the gracious generosity of God (cf. James 1:16-17). Thus we may recognize the distinctions (mentioned earlier) to which Paul refers in 12:4-7: "Now there are varieties of gifts, but the same Spirit; and there are varieties of service (διακονια, *diakonia*), but the same Lord; and there are varieties of activities, but it is the same God who empowers them all in every one. To each is given the manifestation of the Spirit for the common good."

The word which we may use to cover all the items in the lists that Paul gives is "manifestations" of the Spirit. Some of these are specific gifts; some may be, on the other hand, different ways of serving the Lord, and some may be carrying out different activities which God "energizes". What is common in each case is that they are all ways in which the Spirit manifests himself for the *common good* of the body of Christ.

*The fourth factor* to note, which follows on from what has just been said, is that the Spirit manifests himself in different ways through different individuals: "All these are empowered by one and the same Spirit, who apportions to each one individually as he wills" (12:11). Thus the fact that any person has any one or more of these gifts or abilities is the result of the sovereign choice of God.

Here then is the basic, fundamental aspect of these various gifts and ministries which we are considering: their source is God, and not the church. It is God whose gift it is for a person to be an apostle, prophet, evangelist, pastor or teacher (see Ephesians 4:11) and this gift is there stated to be not primarily a gift *to* the individual, but the gift *of* the individual, thus equipped, *to the church*. The role of the church is that of discernment, of recognizing when God has given a gift to a person, and accepting his or her ministry.

*Fifthly*, these "manifestations of the Spirit" are both natural and supernatural. It is extremely important, in order for us to have an accurate understanding and interpretation of what Paul is saying here, that we note this. Paul's point is that the activities of the Spirit in the lives of believers (i.e. what are sometimes being called "spiritual gifts") encompass, as well as "supernatural gifts", what we would regard as "natural gifts". Indeed, often the supernatural "spiritual gifts" are the enhancement of innate talents and abilities which the Spirit uses and through which he works, as well as special endowments and miraculous enablings. This is clear from the varied kinds of manifestations of the Spirit mentioned in our present passage, and similarly in all the other passages that mention gifts, and particularly in the introductory description in 1 Corinthians 12:4-6 of "gifts", "service", and "working" or "activities".

If we choose to use the term "spiritual gifts", we must be careful not to restrict it to supernatural or miraculous endowments, for this violates the point of this chapter, which is that God is at work in *every kind* of gift or service or activity.

Pastorally, it can be very frustrating for those Christians to whom the Lord has given some kind of natural ability as their manifestation of the Spirit (a talent for administration or organization, perhaps, or for quiet service, or rendering behind-the-scenes assistance). They are told by some writers and teachers that things of this kind are not "spiritual gifts" because they are not "supernatural" but are just normal human skills and aptitudes which they may in fact have had before they were converted. But these skills and aptitudes are needed in the work of the church, and the Lord indeed gives people equipped in this way to the church for its benefit.

Yet these people can be made, by such comments, to feel sub-standard Christians, and thus induced to be dissatisfied with the ministry that God in fact is giving them. In this way they are being caused to have the very attitude of comparison of themselves with others, and a longing to be what others are and they are not, which Paul so trenchantly and effectively condemns in the next section of this chapter (12:14-26).

It is because it can be very misleading, and used wrongly, that I myself am not very comfortable with using the term "spiritual gift", which, as we have seen, is imposed on the text of this letter and is not used by Paul in what he actually wrote.

We can see at the core of a gift something of the natural endowment which God gives to each person as part of who they are as human beings, and then there is the level of divine, supernatural enhancement of this in each person who is a child of God. As an illustration: there is a natural ability to teach, which one person as an individual will have more than another, being able to enjoy it more and do it better - having a greater capacity for it - than others. Then there is the special divine enhancement of that natural gift which enables one person rather than another to exercise a special and effective ministry of teaching in God's church.

We shall see how this is the case as we consider the gifts and ministries to which Paul refers in these chapters of 1 Corinthians. It will assist us in evaluating a major area of controversy between Christians: whether there are gifts which have ceased in the church after the apostolic age, or whether they are all to be found today amongst the Lord's people.

So in 1 Corinthians 12:8-10 we have a representative and relevant listing of God's graces, given to mankind.

The ones he mentions make Paul's points in this chapter: there is great diversity in the varied manifestations of the Spirit; every person has some measure of God's gifting; it is God who is at work in them; and they are given for each of us to use to exercise a ministry towards each other in the church which is Christ's body.

Are these gifts, once bestowed by God, to be considered permanent in and for the recipient? Garland 578 says no: he quotes with approval Baker who says,

> the gifts listed should not be reckoned as 'permanent abilities but possible ways in which the Spirit may choose to work at a particular time in a particular individual'.

He does not explain his view, and I do not see that he could be correct on this point.

*Firstly*, there is the ordinary natural meaning of the word "gift". Would the term "gift" be used of something which you gave to someone, but he/she only had the use of it temporarily, and then you snatched it back?

*Secondly*, there is the nature of these endowments. They are all, basically, the gift of the Holy Spirit himself to a child of God, and then they are expressions, noted for their diversity, of the ways in which the Spirit expresses himself in that individual. What would we say, theologically, about the situation in which the Spirit, who had activated in a particular person such and such an endowment and mode of working, then ceased to act in and through that individual in that way?

And *thirdly*, if it is a totally *ad hoc* matter, as Garland is suggesting, why should not the Spirit just use whoever is at hand for whatever purpose when the exercise of a gift is required? This would be distinct from what is clearly set out in Scripture as being the pattern, that the Spirit continues to be active in a particular way (i.e. in the exercise of a particular gifting) through a particular individual.

Therefore I take it that once a person has received such-and-such an endowment, that person will continue to possess it and to be able to use it - though of course they will need (and will receive) divine guidance as to when, how, and in what circumstances it is to be exercised. E.g. presumably Peter and John had passed the crippled beggar at the Beautiful Gate (Acts 3:1) numerous times before the occasion on which they healed him. But recognition of divine guidance in using a gift is very different from concluding that the gift "comes and goes" or is available only spasmodically. Can we think for example that a person with the gift of teaching is only in possession of it or able to use it on certain days of the week? I find this idea ludicrous.

To sum up thus far: Seeing that each person is given a manifestation of the Spirit (v.7), and as Paul now goes on to list nine gifts (verses 8-10), it would be possible to link these ideas so as to arrive at the conclusion that each member of the church must have one or more of these nine gifts. This would be a totally mistaken conclusion.

**Firstly**, these nine are representative and illustrative - as we have seen, Paul gives several "gift" lists, which mention different gifts, and although this list is the longest, there are quite a few gifts mentioned elsewhere but not included here: this list is not, and is not intended to be, exhaustive in any sense.

**Secondly**, what each person has is a "manifestation" of the Spirit (v.7), and this covers χαρισματα, *charismata* (v.4) διακονια, *diakonia* (ministries, v.5) and ἐνεργηματα, *energēmata* (activatings, v.6). Some commentators have expressed the view that these are all aspects of the same gifts, but in my understanding it is a much more natural reading of the text to see them as additional. That is, the Spirit may be manifested in some persons through χαρισματα (*charismata*) given to them; in other persons, through ways of service to the Lord opened up for them; and in yet others, through opportunities for activating others or for organization or administration (or, in the case of numbers of people, more than one such manifestation of the Spirit). In every instance, it is God at work through the Spirit, expressing his will and his choice, to the glory of God, and for the benefit of the church.

We shall review now the individual gifts and callings which Paul goes on to list in this passage. This brings us to a consideration of a major issue where Christians are divided in their understanding of gifts: the "cessationists" and the "continuationists" - those who hold that the "sign" gifts (or some of them) ceased at the end of the apostolic age, and those who believe in the continuation of these gifts in today's church.

What is my position on this? My understanding is that in the gifts as they were exercised in the apostolic age there were two components: the underlying, basic, gift itself, and - to varying extents - a supernatural, miraculous element that was an important part of a gift's "sign" value at that time (e.g. in the gift of healing or performing a miracle). What I have described as the "supernatural, miraculous element" and the "underlying, basic gift", Jonathan Edwards [*Charity and Its Fruits* 29-30; cited by Wilson 174-175] calls the "extraordinary" and "ordinary" gifts. He says:

> The extraordinary gifts of the Spirit, such as the gift of tongues, of miracles, of prophecy, etc. are called extraordinary, because they are such as are not given in the ordinary course of God's providence. They are not bestowed in the way of God's ordinary providential dealing with his children, but only on extraordinary occasions, as when they were bestowed on the prophets and apostles to enable them to reveal the mind and will of God before the canon of Scripture was complete, and so on the primitive church, in order to the founding and establishing of it in the world. But since the canon of Scripture has been completed, and the Christian church fully founded and established, these extraordinary gifts have ceased. But the ordinary gifts of the Spirit are such as are continued to the church of God throughout all ages; such gifts as are granted in conviction and conversion, and such as appertain to the building up of the saints in holiness and comfort.

Similarly I have concluded that the "miraculous" component did only apply to, and exist in, the apostolic age, and thus is not operative today, but what I call the "gift" element still is: and is still activated by the Spirit today and is still used by - and needed in - the church. My understanding of how this is so will emerge in the discussion of the various gifts.

So for each of these gifts we will consider what is the basic core nature of the gift and what it does, how it was supernaturally and miraculously used in New Testament times, and in what way it functions in the church and for Christians today.

**12:8a** The first gift Paul mentions here is λογος σοφιας (*logos sophias*). This has been translated in many different ways: by the NIV as "To one there is given through the Spirit the ability to speak with wisdom"; by the NEB as "One man, through the Spirit, has the gift of wise speech", also by Williams, "wise speech"; by the RSV, NRSV and ESV as "the utterance of wisdom"; by Phillips as "to speak with wisdom"; by the TEV as "a message of wisdom"; by the Jerusalem Bible as "the gift of preaching with wisdom".

These various translations do not all mean exactly the same thing. Just what it is that Paul means here? The meaning of *logos* is described by Souter's Lexicon (147) as "speech in progress", and then more specifically as "a word, an utterance, speech, discourse, saying".

But what exactly does Paul mean by *wisdom*? We shall examine this carefully. But initially, let us ask: Why is this gift first? Two reasons in particular have been suggested:

**(a)** Because Paul is saying to us that it is the most important. The early church writer Origen first put forward this view in *Against Celsus* 3:46 (cited by Thiselton 940). Origen says,

> in the catalogue of charismata bestowed by God, Paul placed first λογος σοφιας ... because he regarded proclamation (λογος) as higher than miraculous powers.

Concerning this gift Hodge 245 states, "That gift stands first as the most important", and Lenski 500 says, "The ability to state this wisdom to others is the best and highest spiritual gift." Others similarly.

**(b)** Because Paul is picking up on a Corinthian keyword: wisdom is something upon which they prided themselves.

Fee's comment (591f.) is:

> With a considerable stroke of inspiration Paul now does two things: (a) He uses one of their own terms to begin his list of manifestations in the assembly that demonstrate the great diversity inherent in the one Spirit's activities; and (b) he reshapes that term in light of the work of the Spirit so as to give it a significantly different content from their own.

These two ideas need not be mutually exclusive possibilities: it seems there were numbers of "gifts" which some Corinthians valued and exalted, and Paul has totally agreed with them about this one, wisdom - so long as they get it right. So he wants them above all to have the gift of wisdom: but to recognize afresh, as he pointed out at the very beginning of his letter, that true wisdom - godly wisdom, the wisdom from the Spirit - centers in Christ and him crucified. The supreme gift is to see this, and more than that: to be able to communicate this glorious truth to others.

As Hodge 245 puts it, "The *word* of wisdom is the gift of speaking or communicating wisdom". Thiselton 939 describes it as "the *articulate utterance* of this *wisdom*. Hence it relates to God's plan of salvation and its articulation or communication."

And in the words of MacArthur 298:

The use of *logos* (word) indicates this is a speaking ability. ... *Wisdom*, then, refers basically to applying truths discovered, to the ability to make skillful and practical application of the truth to life situations - communicating wisdom.

We can see that there are two elements involved in this gift: first that of **wisdom**, and then the *logos* of wisdom: i.e. to **possess** wisdom, and to **communicate** this wisdom.

A great deal has been written about wisdom, in commentaries, monographs, and journal articles, and many are the views put forward as to what it is. Some of these regard it as a divine endowment bestowed on a given occasion in response to a particular need of that time, a version of "divine revelation" appropriate to the occasion. Others regard it as a natural innate awareness of the right response to a situation.

In their *Spiritual Gifts and the Church* (IVP, 1973), Donald Bridges and David Phypers 48 alert us to a serious misunderstanding about "an utterance of wisdom", which has had dangerous consequences.

They say,

some writers have concluded that this gift is one of uttering an inspired wise saying in some sort of church meeting which solves a problem or points the way forward in a hitherto intractable situation. Being inspired by the Spirit the word of wisdom is immediately so recognized by the rest of the congregation who then act on the advice supernaturally given.

Bridges & Phypers 49 then point out the problems with this idea:

Once it is accepted that *any* individual Christian may give infallible, detailed guidance to a church or other Christian group, the door is opened to all sorts of problems and difficulties. No-one (and this includes Christians) finds it easy to understand the mind of God (see Rom. 11:33,34). ...

But in Crawford *Baptised with the Holy Spirit and Spiritual Gifts* 47 this gift of "the utterance of wisdom" is interpreted as "A supernatural revelation of wisdom, given in that moment to meet a particular situation".

Authenticating Scriptures which are given for this are Matthew 21:24-25 (an example of Jesus's wisdom in dealing with the Jewish leaders - though wisdom is not mentioned); Acts 6:1-4, 10 (a passage chosen presumably on the grounds that the apostles acted with wisdom in appointing the Seven; wisdom was a qualification required of the Seven, and Stephen is said to have such wisdom that the disputants could not withstand it); Acts 15:19-21 (another example given: James's judgement at the close of the Council of Jerusalem - but wisdom is not mentioned in the passage).

There is no basis in Scripture for the definition given by Crawford for an utterance of wisdom. The examples indicate wise behavior on the one hand and recognition of the value of wisdom on the other, but they do not establish or support the definition given.

This approach is summed up thus by Fee (592f.):

> In Pentecostal and charismatic circles this "gift" is often understood to be that special word of insight given by the Spirit when the community is going through a time of difficulty or decision. See e.g., Bittlinger 28, who thus defines this gift: "In a difficult or dangerous situation a word of wisdom may be given which resolves the difficulty or silences the opponent." One need not doubt that the Holy Spirit speaks so in today's church, but it is unlikely that Paul had this in mind by this "gift". If he were to "label" such a phenomenon, it would probably be ἀποκαλυψις [apokalupsis] ("revelation"); cf. 14:6. The same is true of the so-called word of knowledge that has become such a frequent occurrence in these communities.

The λογος σοφιας (logos sophias) is not a divinely ordained substitute for careful planning and thinking ahead. It does not relieve us of the necessity of thought, still less of studying the Scriptures. It is not an alternative for effort on our part, a way in which God takes the hard work out of serving him. It is not just an "easy way" to get "good results". We need the warning from Bridges & Phypers 49-50, that:

> there is no short cut to knowing God's guidance. God guides through day-to-day obedience to His Word in the circumstances in which Christians find themselves, and humility is a constantly-needed grace in this area of Christian living. If individual Christians get the idea that through some supernatural gift they can give infallible, detailed guidance to their church or Christian Union, then deep trouble will almost inevitably ensue.

They then describe situations where "carefully thought-out policies" have been reversed on the basis of some member giving a "word of wisdom", existing leadership has been denounced as "unspiritual" for not immediately following this "word", churches and other Christian fellowships have been split apart or divided into opposing camps. They add:

> That this has often happened with consequent heartache and disappointment to many involved cannot be denied. Had Christians understood more accurately from Scripture the nature of the gift of wisdom such difficulties could well have been avoided.

But it's so attractive an idea - that somebody has a "word of wisdom" which will substitute for careful analysis and application of what the Bible says. So simple - it saves us all that trouble of wrestling with biblical teaching. But what happens ultimately is that this "word of wisdom" becomes a substitute for the Bible.

You can't sever these two words λογος σοφιας (*logos sophias*) from the rest of Scripture and endeavor to explain their meaning apart from the rest of Scripture. Paul has already had a great deal to say about wisdom in chapters 1 and 2 of 1 Corinthians, in which he distinguishes the wisdom of this world, natural wisdom, from the wisdom that comes from above (cf James 1:16-17), godly wisdom. Seeing that Paul himself has explained the nature of wisdom in these opening chapters of this letter, we go far astray if we ignore what he has himself said so far about this concept. Therefore, to understand what Paul means here by wisdom, we must look back at his own explanations of it - he does not spend the first two chapters of his letter explaining wisdom, and then refer to wisdom again in 12:8, and *mean something else*.

In what Paul says, the whole focus of wisdom is upon what God has done in accomplishing the salvation of the world. This is a demonstration and a display of the plan of God, whereas the whole of this is foolishness according to human wisdom.

But what we are often seeing today is that some teachers are conducting their consideration of 1 Corinthians 12:8 divorced from all Paul has already said in the letter, as if this part of the letter is quite separate and independent of everything that has one before. This is to strip this passage of all connection with its context, and to do great and grave damage to Paul's total teaching.

What was the nature of the basic *charisma* λογος σοφιας (*logos sophias*) in New Testament times? It was an effective insight into the wisdom of the plan of God revealed in Christ - a plan which could never have been guessed at by human insight, and which the rather, as Paul has set out, appeared total foolishness to human minds, even to the wisest of people.

What was the supernatural, miraculous enhancement of this in New Testament times for those with a special gift of λογος σοφιας (*logos sophias*)? It was, first of all, the initial gift to see all of this and reveal it to the church, as Paul did in this Epistle. And it was the insight and discernment, the perception, to see the relevance and application of the Old Testament Scriptures to the coming of Jesus as the Messiah. For example, in the way Matthew, in 2:15, applies Hosea's reference about the Exodus of Israel from Egypt to Jesus returning with his family from their flight to Egypt, "Out of Egypt I called my son" (Hosea 11:1). This is based on a recognition that Jesus is the true Israelite, and a greater than Moses in fulfilling the role of Savior.

And, further, this λογος σοφιας (*logos sophias*) can be seen in the way the New Testament apostles and prophets and writers had come to have the mind of Christ, as Paul puts it (1 Corinthians 2:16) - and how they thus had explained the hidden wisdom of God's plan to the church.

As the revelation of God through his apostles and prophets and writers has been completed, and embodied in Scripture and the canon is closed, there is - and can be - no further supernatural and miraculous component now in a λογος σοφιας (*logos sophias*). So then, is there a gift of λογος σοφιας (*logos sophias*) for today's church? Yes, indeed there is.

It begins similarly with a recognition of the wisdom of God in his plan as revealed in Scripture. First there is the promise in James 1:5 of a general wisdom which God grants in response to our prayer: "If any of you lacks wisdom, let him ask God, who gives generously to all without reproach, and it will be given him." All true wisdom comes from God, and God our Father will give wisdom to all who ask.

Then there is a special enhancement of this which God through the Spirit grants to particular individuals. John MacArthur 298 puts it this way:

> Communicating wisdom is the function of the expositor, who draws not only from his own study of Scripture but from the many insights and interpretations of commentators and other Bible scholars. It is also the ability a counselor must have in order to apply God's truth to the questions and problems brought to him. It is a feature in the gift of the pastor, who must know, understand, and be able to apply God's word in order to lead his people as he should.

There is a sense in which all Christians are called upon to seek, and develop, and exercise, this godly wisdom, for there is a general possession of wisdom as a Christian grace. There is also a specific wisdom gift or enabling, for to some people God grants a special endowment, a "heaped measure" of wisdom. Thus God granted especial wisdom to Solomon (1 Kings 3:5-28; 4:29-34E).

"To one person there is given through the Spirit ..." (12:8) - note that this is **through** (*dia*) the Spirit, not **by** or **from** the Spirit. Lenski says this word is used "to denote the mediation of the Spirit with regard to the first gift". The second gift in this verse is *kata* the Spirit, that is, according to the Spirit's choice, as the Spirit determines.

The λογος σοφιας (*logos sophias*) is not a "flash of divine inspiration" which everybody else must then obey. It is an insight into the gospel and the mind of Christ, based upon Scripture, which we can see illuminates a situation. As this wisdom is communicated to the people of God, it gives God's answer to a situation. And above all it will honor Christ crucified.

For there is no suggestion here or elsewhere in this Epistle (or any-where else in Scripture) of a special revelation of God which is given to one person as a message of God. That is not the meaning here of *logos*. Rather, this word means the **communication** of wisdom: the gift and the ability to give wise counsel, in accord with the gospel of Christ. The gift of being able to look at a situation with a gospel world view, and explain this. For most Christians, the world is too much with us, and it clouds our vision and our perception. Note that this gift is the *logos* of wisdom - there is no point having the wisdom of God if you cannot communicate this to people: that would be of no benefit to the people of God.

Wesley 622f. sums up "the word of wisdom" thus:

> A power of understanding and explaining the manifold wisdom of
> God in the grand scheme of gospel salvation.

If we have been given this gift λογος σοφιας (*logos sophias*) this does not mean that we can use it without any training. Paul refers to God's gift to Timothy - but Timothy was told to train and learn to develop his gift (1 Timothy 4:13-16).

Some people seem to think that receiving God's gift is intended to relieve us of any effort of our own, any hard work. This is wishful think-ing rather than biblical teaching. We can see this more readily in relation to gifts like teaching or music or administration. Though we may have such a gift, we are to develop it through training so that we may use it for the fullest benefit of the church of God.

Thus also with the communication of wisdom. We are to train in the things of God and God's ways. This enables us to perceive, to recognize, whether God has given us this gift of λογος σοφιας (*logos sophias*) which the Spirit is activating in us. A good second step (after the first, which is our prayer for wisdom) is to get out our Bible concordance and read all that God has to say about wisdom in the Scripture. Then to see the world and the church from a gospel-oriented perspective. Happy indeed the church to which God gives a person gifted like this!

So then, this gift implies and requires that we train and develop the skill of communication, in order that the church will benefit and be built up. For example, when God grants this gift of wisdom to a person and the church gives heed to it, they will know how to avoid seeking to do the work of God in ungodly ways, by just following the wisdom of this world; they will see rather that the weapons of our warfare are spiritual.

So: how do you recognize if God is giving you this gift of λογος σοφιας (*logos sophias*)? Often this (as for many gifts) is a question of its recognition in us by others, heightening a sense of our own Spirit-led awareness. Paul tells us (see 1:26), Not many wise are called - God grant that there will be some in your congregation!

**12:8b** Paul writes next of the second gift, λογος γνωσεως (*logos gnōseōs*): the communication of knowledge.

Thiselton 941 says: "'Knowledge' (γνωσις, *gnōsis*) is no less a Corinthian catchphrase than 'wisdom'." And Garland 581: "Wisdom and knowledge are apparently of particular interest to the Corinthians."

As "the ability to speak with wisdom" means an utterance (*logos*) the content of which is the communication of (God's) wisdom, in line with Paul's earlier teaching in this Epistle about wisdom; so now "the ability to speak with knowledge" means an utterance (again, *logos*) the content of which is the communication of knowledge which the speaker has gained.

We will recall Fee's comment (592f.) which I quoted earlier concerning both a so-called "word of wisdom" and "word of knowledge" - which in some Christian circles is understood to refer to a special word of revelation granted to an individual for the church. Fee rejected this interpretation, pointing out concerning λογος σοφιας (*logos sophias*) how unlikely it is

> that Paul had this in mind by this "gift". If he were to "label" such a phenomenon, it would probably be ἀποκαλυψις [*apokalupsis*] ("revelation"); cf. 14:6. The same is true of the so-called word of knowledge that has become such a frequent occurrence in these communities.

And MacArthur 299 says further concerning this λογος γνωσεως (*logos gnōseōs*):

> The human writers of Scripture had the gift of knowledge in a unique way. God gave them truths directly, which they recorded as part of his written Word. Since the closing of the canon of Scripture, however, that gift has not involved the receiving of new truth, but only understanding of truth previously revealed. Anyone today who claims to have a divine revelation is a deceiver, and contradicts God's own Word, which expressly warns that if anyone adds to it or takes away from it he will suffer God's judgement (Rev. 22:18). Any word of divine knowledge or wisdom must be based on the Word of God, "once for all delivered" (Jude 3).

The first part of the gift of λογος γνωσεως (*logos gnōseōs*) is the *acquiring* of knowledge.

Now, each Christian is to "grow in the grace and knowledge of our Lord and Savior Jesus Christ" (2 Peter 3:18).

Paul commends the Romans as those who are "full of goodness, filled with all knowledge, and able to instruct one another" (Romans 15:14). Paul reminds the Jews that they are those "having in the law the embodiment of knowledge and truth" (Romans 2:20). He describes himself as "an apostle of Jesus Christ, for the sake of the faith of God's elect and their knowledge of the truth" (Titus 1:1). The end result of Christ giving apostles, prophets, evangelists, pastors and teachers to the church was so that "we all attain to the unity of the faith and of the knowledge of the Son of God ..." (Ephesians 4:11-13).

The knowledge in all these cases is obtained by being taught, and also by other ordinary means of finding out, not by miraculous revelation which bypasses the process of learning. Scripture contains a number of exhortations to learn (including the instruction of Jesus, "Learn from me ...", Matthew 11:29). It is precisely by applying ourselves to the process of learning that knowledge is gained. Timothy was commended for what he had learned (particularly in Scripture), and exhorted to continue in it (2 Timothy 3:14-15); he was instructed to devote himself to the public reading of Scripture (1 Timothy 4:13); the early converts devoted themselves to the apostles' teaching and to the fellowship (Acts 2:42); everything that was written in the past was written to teach us (Romans 15:4); we are to judge and act on the basis of the teaching we have learned (Romans 16:17).

This is the ordinary acquiring of knowledge of the things of God. On the other hand, beyond this, we read of a miraculous knowledge exhibited by apostles and prophets.

Thus "through the Spirit" Agabus spoke of the coming famine (Acts 11:28), and warned Paul about what lay ahead of him (Acts 21:11). Peter's awareness of the deceit of Ananias and Sapphira (Acts 5:1-11) was an instance of supernatural knowledge, parallel to the special revelation given to him about the person of Jesus (Matthew 16:16-17). Paul knew what was to happen to the ship and its company, through the appearance of an angel to him (Acts 27:21-25). Paul frequently refers to the knowledge that he received by direct revelation from the Lord (see Acts 9:3-6; Acts 18:9-10; Acts 22:6-10; Acts 22:17-21; Acts 23:11; Acts 26:14-19; Acts 27:21-25; 1 Corinthians 4:1; 1 Corinthians 11:23; 1 Corinthians 14:6; 1 Corinthians 15:8; 2 Corinthians 12:2-7; Galatians 1:11,12; Galatians 2:2; Ephesians 3:2-11; 1 Thessalonians 4:15).

Knowledge of the mysteries of God was granted by God to his apostles and prophets (Ephesians 2:13-3:12). In comparing himself with the "super-apostles" at Corinth, Paul says (2 Corinthians 11:5-6), "I consider that I am not in the least inferior to these 'super-apostles'. Even if I am unskilled in speaking, I am not so in knowledge; indeed, in every way we have made this plain to you in all things." The "knowledge" to which he is referring is something that demonstrates he is "not inferior" to the "super-apostles" at Corinth, and this is thus a reference to the special gift of knowledge which he has as an apostle.

Thus we may note that in the New Testament we find a miraculous acquiring of knowledge, on the one hand, which came by specific divine revelation; and on the other, a natural acquiring of knowledge, which came by the ordinary process of being taught and by application to learning.

Now, like the λογος σοφιας (*logos sophias*) which we have just considered, this second *charisma* also has two aspects: the gaining and then the communicating. As Lenski 501 writes:

> The "expression" or *logos* of knowledge is the ability to impart this personal knowledge to others.

I am persuaded God still gives people this gift, and the church needs them. What will having the gift of λογος γνωσεως (*logos gnōseōs*) mean for a Christian in the church today?

A person today possessing the gift λογος γνωσεως (*logos gnōseōs*) will be a person with a love of study and thus of acquiring knowledge. Such persons will probably excel at academic courses, and will want nothing more than to be able to bury themselves in a library (their own, or someone else's) and wrestle with some academic problem. Research will be a major interest of their life. Then they will want to share in some way - to ***communicate*** - the things they have learnt, by writing books or giving lectures or holding classes, or finding some other opportunities for passing on the γνωσις (*gnōsis*) they has gained. These people have an important contribution to make to the life of the church.

**12:9a** "Faith", the third gift on Paul's list of χαρισματα (*charismata*), is something which every Christian has to some extent - without it, that person would not ***be*** a Christian. But (as Paul says), in (the sphere of) the same Spirit it is granted to some people to have faith in more abundant measure. In chapter 13:2 Paul refers to it again, more fully, and I shall make a further comment on this special gift of faith at that point.

**12:9b** "Healings", fourth on Paul's list, is plural, and is the only one in this list explicitly called a "gift", χαρισμα (*charisma*). The gift may be the ability to heal others (and is most frequently so interpreted); but there is little evidence in Scripture to support the idea that a person is given the ability to heal others at his own choice and decision. (This ability ***may*** have been given by Jesus to his apostles for their missionary tour, Matthew 10:8; there is no evidence for such a gift ever having been given to other than apostles or the deacons they directly appointed to assist them [Acts 6:8; 8:6-7].) Rather, when God in his sovereignty so chooses, *he* heals whom he will, through whom he will, and leaves others without a miraculous healing. Garland 582 notes,

> χαρισματα ιαματων [*charismata iamatōn*] ... does not refer to the power to heal all diseases but to instances of actual healing.

There are numbers of instances in the New Testament of people being ill and *not* being healed: Paul himself, 2 Corinthians 12:7-10; Epaphroditus, Philippians 2:25-30; Timothy, 1 Timothy 5:23; Trophimus, 2 Timothy 4:20.

An interesting feature of the picture of healing which we find in Acts is the timing of miraculous healings. Peter and John would undoubtedly have many times passed by the crippled beggar at the Beautiful Gate (Acts 3:2) before the particular occasion when they stopped and healed him. We are told that the Philippian slave girl had followed Paul and his companions "for many days" (Acts 16:18) before he healed her of her demon-possession. Undoubtedly God's power was "present to heal" at a particular and appropriate point in time, and the apostles then responded to the prompting of the Spirit within, to perform the healing.

It is also interesting to note that Paul was the instrument of God's healing on many occasions until he reached Malta on his voyage to Rome. There he performed several healings, but there is no record of him ever healing anyone after this time.

In the expression "gifts of healings", χαρισματα ιαματων (*charismata iamatōn*), it is almost invariably taken that the ιαματων (*iamatōn*) has an active sense, the gift of *performing healings*. But it is equally possible for it to be taken as passive in meaning - the gift of *receiving healing*, "the gift of being healed", as God intervenes directly to raise up one person or another from illness to be able to continue his/her ministry in the church: e.g. Acts 14: 19-20, Paul at Lystra after he was stoned almost to death. As we consider the significance of Paul's use of two plural words, *gifts* of *healings*, I rather wonder whether we should not see this word as encompassing here both meanings, active and passive - performing healings, and being healed - as God's gifts.

There can be no question about the way in which God still performs miraculous healings today: but they occur from time to time in his sovereign choice, rather than "on demand", as it were. God may grant an instant miraculous cure. Or he may work slowly through the body's natural healing properties and the medical profession's knowledge of healing. Or in God's sovereign choice, for the purposes of his own will, he may not grant healing at all. I guess all of us will be aware of occasions when each of these outcomes has occurred.

Three further specific comments need to be made:

1. There is **no** place in Scripture which promises that healing will happen today for **everyone** - any more than that this happened in New Testament times. Death and illness is a part of the human condition in this world, and the planet would be overwhelmingly overcrowded if it were not so.

2. The healing ministry which has developed in some churches has been a great blessing to many people, and can be a modern vehicle for the exercise of *gifts of healings* - so long as it is based, not on the (supposed) "healing ability" of some minister, but on prayer to the sovereign God who can grant healing by any means he chooses, or withhold it if he chooses.

3. It is clear in Scripture, as it is also to be seen in the world today, that healings are the direct act of the sovereign God who heals whom he wills, and he has not given this power into human hands. We can pray for healings, and then we must leave the outcome in the Lord's hands: "if the Lord wills it". And we must never expect that we can force God's hand. The way in which some people have attributed a lack of healing to a lack of faith is a great cruelty to many committed Christians who were not healed. Similarly we must not make it appear sinful for a Christian to be ill.

**12:10a** The nature of the miraculous powers (ἐνεργηματα δυναμεων, *energēmata dynameōn*) is not explained, but there are numbers of occasions where such miracles are apparently referred to. Thus Acts 8:13, 14:3, etc. And Paul writes (Romans 15:18-19) of "what Christ has accomplished through me to bring the Gentiles to obedience - by word and deed, by the power of signs and wonders, by the power of the Spirit of God." And again in 2 Corinthians 12:12 he says, "The signs of a true apostle were performed among you with utmost patience, with signs and wonders and mighty works."

What are these mighty works, these miracles? Some would see, as examples of such miracles, the fate of Ananias and Sapphira (Acts 5:1-11, which is followed in the next verse by the statement "Now many signs and wonders were regularly done among the people by the hands of the apostles"); the fate of Elymas the sorcerer (Acts 13:6-12); the raising from the dead of Dorcas (Acts 9:36-41) and Eutychus (Acts 20:7-12). Garland 582 says that this gift of performing miracles "refers to the actualization of God's power in mighty deeds" but then adds that "Paul also warns that the 'lawless one' will come according to the working (ἐνεργεια, *energeia*) of Satan and will work miracles (δυναμις, *dynamis*) (2 Thessalonians 2:9)."

Some Christians claim that similar miracles are performed in the name of Christ today: others regard these claims as unauthenticated, and say (e.g. MacArthur 301f.) that the effecting of miracles was a temporary sign gift and

> Those signs accompanied God's Word only so long as he was revealing the Word - when revelation stopped, the sign gifts stopped.

Thus there is considerable difference of opinion in the church today about these things. In John 14:12 Jesus refers to the miracles he has been performing and promises that, through faith, his followers will perform "greater works than these". As I reflect upon these words, I see them fulfilled today when, through the proclamation of the gospel, one person and then another accepts Christ's salvation and - as Paul puts it in Colossians 1:13 - is delivered from the power of darkness and translated into the kingdom of God's beloved Son. In the scale of eternity this is a far greater and more wonderful miracle than if someone could accomplish some supernatural feat touching our natural life in this world; and there is far more rejoicing over this than if someone were to counteract the normal laws of physics for a few minutes.

**12:10b** I discuss the nature of prophecy, tongues, and interpretation in the Commentary on chapters 13 and 14.

The other manifestation of the Spirit mentioned here is "the ability to distinguish between spirits" (διακρισεις πνευματων, *diakriseis pneumatōn*). This is most frequently taken to mean the ability to discern whether something is a manifestation of good spirits/the Holy Spirit, or on the other hand of evil spirits, and perhaps may be linked back with the fact that it would not be the Holy Spirit leading a person to say (12:3), "Jesus is accursed". I would question this. There are two difficulties with this view.

***Firstly***, this link with 12:3 is rather tenuous and hardly is making the point, as it would not really take a special *charisma* of God to recognize that a person saying this is not being led by the Holy Spirit of God. And there is nothing else in the entire context referring to evil spirits, or the need to discern them, nor a *charisma* from God to enable some Christians to do so. And a consequence of this view, and of having people claiming as a result of it to possess this gift, is a tendency to see evil spirits everywhere and to attribute too much to them.

***Secondly***, as Johnson 226 points out,

> Paul nowhere else uses the term *spirit* for evil spirits, with only one exception (1 Tim 4:1, 'deceiving spirits and things taught by demons'). He uses 'spirits' for human spirits (1 Cor 14:32; Gal 6:18), not for evil spirits.

So this previous view would be to attribute to Paul on this occasion an uncharacteristic use of such an expression. Johnson continues:

> Therefore, the more probable sense is distinguishing between manifestations of the divine Spirit and of merely human spirits. One who exercises this ministry discerns how the Spirit is working, whether certain manifestations promote the lived-out lordship of Christ as self-effacing, loving service, rather than self-serving status seeking or deceptive uses of Scripture ... James's crucial discernment at the Jerusalem Council seems to exemplify such Spirit-directed discernment between the Judaizers' mistaken understanding and that of Barnabas and Paul (Acts 15:13-21).

Such a ministry of discernment would recognize whether someone was being led by the Holy Spirit or was speaking or acting (possibly sincerely, but) from within the promptings and motivation of their own human spirit. This discerning ability would be very advantageous in the churches in assessing ideas and proposals and activities. Johnson climaxes his comments, "How the churches today need this Spirit-given ministry!"

**12:11** Different manifestations of the Spirit are given to one believer and another: but it is the **same** Spirit who is at work in each one. And it is the sovereign decision of the indwelling Spirit how he manifests himself through each person. Note: Paul does not say that the Spirit **gives** them; he says the Spirit **distributes** or **apportions** them to each person individually just as he chooses (as in ESV, NASB, NEB, RSV, NRSV, Jerusalem, Phillips; contra NIV).

The three crucial points which Paul makes in this summary, in the wording of the ESV, are:

1. "All these are empowered (ἐνεργεῖ, *energei*, cognate with ἐνεργήματα, *energēmata*) by one and the same Spirit
2. who apportions to each one individually
3. as he wills."

Thiselton 988 comments on v.11 that

> Virtually every Greek word and phrase takes up the vocabulary of 12:4-7 to recapitulate the principles articulated in verses 4-7.

## 2. The Reason For Gifts And Ministries (12:12-26)

**12:12** Just as our body is made up of many parts and yet is a single unit or entity, so it is with the church, the body of Christ. Paul now proceeds to spell out in detail, with some vivid illustrations, the points he has just been making. We should reflect upon the way that he does this. Note Lenski's comment at this point:

The idea contained in the verb διαιρειν [*diairein*] is that the Spirit separates and portions out the gifts. ... In his distribution the Spirit never ignores the make-up, characteristics, age, position, and other particular features of a person. The gift fits the man. ... 'Even as he wills' should remove all complaint on our part and thus all envy, on the one hand, and all boasting, on the other. What a blessing it is for all of us that the distribution lies in the Spirit's hands, and he allots the gifts as he does!

Therefore we must recognize that the Spirit's allocations and activation of gifts and ministries are for the benefit of the body as a whole, not for the benefit or exaltation of any one part. This is the central point which Paul is making in this section. For, as Paul puts it here, "All the parts of the body, though many, form *one* body."

As we move forward, we should take careful note of a consequence of what Paul is saying now: It would be a mistake to think that all gifts will be represented in equal numbers in a church. The body does not need as many tongues as it does fingers: the congregation does not need the same number of each of pastors, teachers, helpers, and leaders.

It would also be a mistake to think that all gifts will be represented in each congregation. One congregation will be in need of one set of gifts amongst its members; another congregation will have need of slightly different (or even *very* different) gifts. And the same congregation will have need of different gifts at different periods of its life and growth. Related to this: most congregations will need most gifts most of the time, but the proportion - the number of people who are needed with each of the various gifts - will vary from one congregation to another, and from one period to another in the life of a given congregation.

Thus: there will be more need at one time (or place) than another for those with the gift of generosity, or faith, or wisdom, or certain kinds of leadership (e.g., with young people).

But in any given congregation at any given time, all the parts make up the one body.

**12:13a** In our conversion we all become baptized by the Spirit into that one body - we become united, that is, with the people of God, the church which was baptized with the Spirit at Pentecost (Matthew 3:11; Mark 1:8; Luke 3:16; John 1:33; Acts 1:5; Acts 11:16). This is the *only* verse outside the Gospels and Acts which refers to being baptized by the Spirit. All these other verses refer to Pentecost, when the Spirit baptized the Christians into one body: Christ's body, the church. Often Pentecost is referred to as "the birthday of the church" - and so it is. There is total continuity in the New Testament of the church with the faithful people of God in the Old Testament, and yet Christ said "I will build my church" (Matthew 16:18).

The benefits of the once-for-all event of Calvary apply to us at our conversion, when we receive Christ as our Lord. Christ's death happened in history centuries ago - yet it was for us who are alive today. And so today, when we become one of Christ's people, we become part of the church and we inherit all the blessings that Christ won for us at Calvary.

Similarly, the benefits of the once-for-all event of Pentecost, when the church was baptized in the Holy Spirit, become ours at our conversion, when Christ comes to live within us through the Holy Spirit whom Christ promised. "If anyone does not have the Spirit of Christ, he does not belong to Christ" (Romans 8:9).

In his book *Baptism and Fullness* 20-21, John Stott comments on this verse:

> [Pentecost was] the long-promised outpouring of the Spirit consequent upon [Jesus's] death, resurrection, and ascension. As such it completed the inauguration of the new or Messianic age, the age of the Spirit. In itself, it is unrepeatable, as unrepeatable as the Saviour's death, resurrection, and ascension which preceded it. But its blessings are for all who belong to Christ. All Christians since that day, without any exception, have become participants in this new age and have received the gifts of forgiveness and the Spirit which Christ made available by his death, resurrection, ascension, and outpouring of the Spirit. In this sense those converted on the Day of Pentecost as a result of Peter's sermon were typical of all subsequent believers.

Thus when each new convert receives Christ, that person is incorporated by the Spirit into the church, the Lord's body. That person has become part of, incorporated into, a Spirit-baptized community. That is to say, at their conversion each person is baptized by Christ with the Spirit into the church. This verse makes that clear, for as Paul says, "we were all baptized with one Spirit into one body ..."

Numbers of commentaries and many translations, in rendering this expression as "by the Spirit", take it as an instrumental use of ἐν (*en*), making the Spirit the one who baptizes. But Fee 605f. argues otherwise:

> The prepositional phrase "in the Spirit" is most likely locative, expressing the "element" in which they have all been immersed, just as the Spirit is that which they have all been given to drink. Such usage is also in keeping with the rest of the NT. Nowhere else does this dative imply agency (i.e. that the Spirit does the baptizing), but it always refers to the element "in which" one is baptized.

MacArthur's similar comment [312] is:

> It should also be noted that the phrase "baptism *of* the Holy Spirit" is not a correct translation of any passage in the New Testament, including this one. *En heni pneumati* [ἐν ἑνὶ πνεύματι] [can be rendered] "by

or with one Spirit". Because believers are baptized by Christ, it is therefore best to translate this phrase as "with one Spirit". It is not the Holy
Spirit's baptism but Christ's baptism *with* the Holy Spirit that gives us
new life and places us into the Body when we trust in Christ.

John Stott 38 reaches the same conclusion. In examining what is
meant by "baptism by, in, or with the Spirit" he discusses the six other
occurrences in Scripture of this expression, all of which refer to the
events of Pentecost. Stott then goes on:

> The seventh - and only other - occurrence of the expression is to be
> found in 1 Corinthians 12:13. ... This cannot be a simple reference to
> the Day of Pentecost, for neither Paul nor the Corinthians were there to
> share in the event itself. Yet both he and they had come to share in the
> blessing which that event made possible. They had received the Holy
> Spirit, or rather, to use his own terminology, they had been "baptized"
> with the Holy Spirit and had been "made to drink" of the Holy Spirit. ...
> So the baptism of the Spirit in this verse, far from being a dividing fac-
> tor (some have it, others have not), is the great uniting factor (an experi-
> ence we have all had). It is, in fact, the means of entry into the body of
> Christ. ... It is difficult, then, to resist the conclusion that the baptism of
> the Spirit is *not* a second and subsequent experience enjoyed by some
> Christians, but the initial experience enjoyed by all. ... I think we must
> even dissent from the RSV translation of 1 Corinthians 12:13, "*by* one
> Spirit we were all baptized ...*" The Greek preposition in this verse is ἐν
> [*en*], just as in the other six verses, where it is translated "with"; why
> should it be rendered differently here? ... If we put the seven references
> to this baptism together, we learn that Jesus Christ is the baptizer, as
> John the Baptist clearly foretold. According to 1 Corinthians 12:13 the
> baptized are "we all". The Holy Spirit is himself the "element" with, or
> in (ἐν) which the baptism takes place. ...

We must note that plainly Paul's teaching was that baptism with the
Spirit took place at conversion. If the baptism with the Spirit was an
experience subsequent to conversion, then it would not be true that *all*
Christians had been baptized with the Spirit into one body, for at any
given time there would always be some Christians who were in the
period between their conversion and their Spirit baptism.

John Stott 43 comments further:

> Having [seen] that 1 Corinthians 12:13 refers to Christ baptizing
> with the Spirit and causing us to drink of the Spirit, we must note next
> that "we all" have shared in this baptism and this drinking.

MacArthur 312 stresses:

> It is not possible to be a Christian and not be baptized by Christ with
> the Holy Spirit. Nor is it possible to have more than one baptism with
> the Spirit. There is only one Spirit baptism, the baptism *of* Christ *with*
> the Spirit that all believers receive when they are born again. ... Paul's
> central point in 1 Corinthians 12:13 is that baptism with the one Spirit

makes the church one body. ... He is using the doctrine of baptism with the Spirit to show the unity of all believers in the Body. Many erring teachers today have used a wrong interpretation of the baptism with the Spirit to divide off from the Body an imagined spiritual elite who have what the rest do not. That idea violates the whole teaching here. ...

And Thiselton 997f. comments:

Any theology that might imply that this one baptism in 13a in which believers were baptized by [or in] one Spirit might mark off some postconversion experience or status enjoyed only by some Christians attacks and undermines Paul's entire argument and emphasis.

Concerning the idea of a "second work of grace" subsequent to our conversion, MacArthur 313f. adds:

Well-meaning and otherwise sound Christian leaders have caused great confusion, frustration, and disappointment in the lives of many believers by holding out the prospect of a second work of grace - which is called by many names. Time and energy that could be used in simply obeying the Lord and relying on what He has already given is spent striving for what is already possessed completely and in abundance. ... The being "filled up to all the fulness of God" of which Paul speaks in Ephesians 3:19 has to do with living out fully that which we already possess fully, just as does the working out of our salvation (Philippians 2:12). When we trust in Christ we are completely immersed into the Spirit and completely indwelt by Him. God has nothing more to put into us. He has put His very self into us, and that cannot be exceeded. What is lacking is our full obedience, our full trust, our full submission, not His full salvation, indwelling, or blessing.

John Stott makes one further point here which it is relevant and important to note. He assesses the teaching, exhortations, and commands which the apostles gave to the church, and then he says (45):

But never, not once, do they exhort and instruct us to "be baptized with the Spirit". There can be only one explanation of this, namely that they are writing to Christians, and Christians have already been baptized with the Holy Spirit.

**12:13b** Paul here is again reflecting - and reflecting upon - the teaching of Christ.

Paul says, "all were made to drink of one Spirit." In John 7:37-39 we read: "Jesus stood up and cried out, 'If anyone thirsts, let him come to me and drink. Whoever believes in me, as the Scripture has said, out of his heart will flow rivers of living water.' Now this he said about the Spirit, whom those who believed in him were to receive, for as yet the Spirit had not been given, because Jesus was not yet glorified."

When we come to Jesus now - after Pentecost - he gives us the "living water" to drink: and when Jesus said this, then "by this he meant the Spirit". John Stott 53f. points out,

Now the verbs (thirsting, coming, drinking, believing) are all in the present tense. So we are not only to come to Jesus once, in penitence and faith, but also thereafter to keep coming and to keep drinking, because we keep thirsting. We do this physically - whenever we are thirsty, we get a drink. We must learn to do it spiritually also. The Christian is a spiritual dipsomaniac, always thirsty, always drinking. And drinking is not asking for water, but actually taking it. ... Then "drinking water" becomes "flowing water". We cannot contain the Spirit we receive. As William Temple wrote: "No one can possess (or rather, be indwelt by) the Spirit of God and keep that Spirit to himself. Where the Spirit is, he flows forth; if there is no flowing forth, he is not there." We must beware of any claim to the fullness of the Spirit which does not lead to an evangelistic concern and outreach. Moreover, notice the disparity between the water we drink in and the water that flows out. We can drink only small gulps, but as we keep coming, drinking, believing, so by the mighty operation of the Holy Spirit within us, our little sips are multiplied into a mighty confluence of flowing streams: 'rivers of living water' will flow out from within us. This is the spontaneous outflow from Spirit-filled Christians to the blessing of others.

Now, these subsequent *fillings* of or with or by the Holy Spirit, of which Scripture speaks, are to be differentiated from baptism with the Spirit, which is an unrepeatable event for a Christian. For there is and can be only one "baptism with the Spirit", and that was at Pentecost: which we appropriate and enter when by faith and through the Spirit we are incorporated into the Spirit-baptized church, the body of Christ.

John Stott 47 refers to this thus:

When we speak of the baptism of the Spirit we are referring to a once-for-all gift; when we speak of the fullness of the Spirit we are acknowledging that this gift needs to be *continuously and increasingly appropriated.* [Stott's italics.]

Stott then goes on in some detail to clarify and differentiate the two concepts in the New Testament. He pithily sums up this understanding of the Bible's teaching in the statement (68), "One baptism, many fillings."

In the life of many Christians there may be a major experience of the grace of God subsequent to their conversion, possibly a significant encounter with the Spirit in their lives. This could certainly be a filling with the Spirit, but it would be an error - and misleading, and contrary to biblical language - to describe this as being "baptized by the Spirit". All that we are offered in and through the Spirit is available for us at conversion: there is no need for an interval or a period of waiting before further blessing from God is available to us. Though in practice it can often happen that our appreciation of all that is ours through Calvary and

Pentecost may take a while for us to grasp, so that we may not immediately understand and appropriate all that is ours in Christ.

But the fullness of the baptism with the Spirit, with all that this means, is available to us at our conversion.

Indeed, *every* blessing of God is fully available to us in Christ from the time of our conversion, for in the indwelling Spirit he gives us himself. But not all Christians reflect this glorious truth in their daily lives.

John Stott 65-66 puts this problem clearly when he says,

> Our disobedience and our unbelief have robbed many of us of our full inheritance. It is still ours by right, because we are Christ's, but we have failed to enter into it. We are like the Israelites when they had been given the promised land but had not yet taken possession of it. We need to repent and to return to God. We have indeed been baptized with the Spirit, but we continue to live on a level lower than our Spirit-baptism has made possible, because we do not remain filled with the Spirit.

As, therefore, we read and reflect upon the significance of Paul's teaching in this verse, let us by faith appropriate and enter into all that is ours through Christ's gift of the Spirit at our conversion.

**12:14-17** The body is made up of many parts, each of which contributes uniquely to - and is essential for - the best functioning of the entire body.

The foot and the ear may complain as much as they like, but it changes nothing: they are, and they remain, part of the body, no matter what they say. This - in the members of the church - is a false humility, and an attitude (almost self-pitying) of "I don't matter, I don't count."

In these verses Paul now sums up the import of what he has said, and makes a point of great significance in his whole argument. For the right functioning of the whole body, God has designed it for diversity in unity. In stressing that this is God's will, God's design, Paul lays an incontrovertible foundation for the parallel he will go on to draw, that we do not choose our gifts or our roles in the Body of Christ.

In this section Paul makes two points: (1) That no part of the body should disparage its role because it is not something else which may be thought to be more important, and (2) that each part of the body has its role and function as the result of the will and purpose - and the choice - of God himself. The knowledge of this spiritual truth will transform our attitude to the humblest task we may be called upon to perform.

**12:18-19** "But as it is (νῦν δε, *nun de*), God arranged the members in the body, each one of them, as he chose." So that what the Corinthians believe about gifts is an absurd idea: it implies we think we can improve upon what God has done.

The fact is, their diversity is *God's* choice, and actually this diversity is essential for the smooth functioning of the body - for indeed "If all were a single member, where would the body be?" Thus Paul answers the Corinthians who wanted to chose for themselves the gifts they would prefer to have: and they all wanted the more obvious and spectacular "up-front" gifts. God has planned it, Paul says, so that the human body has every kind of part and organ that it needs, and their functions have been allocated by God (v.18). That also is how it is in the church (verses 12, 13, 27). Thiselton 1004 comments thus:

> To try to rank some gifts as "more essential" than others, let alone as necessary marks of advanced status to which all should aspire, is to offer a blasphemous challenge to God's freedom to choose whatever is his good will for his people both collectively and individually. The unexpected ἐν ἕκαστον αὐτων [*hen hekaston autōn*], which in a different context might seem redundant, here intensifies the emphasis *each single one of them* (thus inviting *single* as a comparably redundant intensifying device in English). How dare anyone either boast or exult in his or her own gifts as if these were a status symbol, or devalue other people's gifts, as if God had not chosen them for the other?

**12:20** Once again, νῦν δε (*nun de*), "But as it is".

Note the μεν/δε contrasting: "πολλα μεν μελη, ἐν δε σωμα" (*polla men melē, hen de sōma*): many parts - one body.

The consequence of this, which Paul now draws, is that each part of the body has need for each other part.

**12:21** After directing his teaching to those who were **undervaluing** their gifts and ministry ("if only I were something else"), Paul now addresses those who were **overestimating** the importance of their own gifts and ministry to the point of seeing no need for those with other, "lesser", gifts.

"... cannot say 'I have no need of you'." But this, it appears, is precisely what some members of the body *were* saying to the other members of the body at Corinth! This was individualism and self-sufficiency taken to a ridiculous extreme.

Some commentators see the "eye" and the "head" as an obvious reference to the self-styled "spiritual ones" at Corinth, the "elite", the favored and privileged ones; whereas the "hands" and the "feet" are the "ordinary" church members, just the - unnecessary - rank and file members. In particular, as Orr & Walther 285 say,

> The foot might be regarded as servile and lowly since it carries the rest of the body and gets soiled in the dust of the ground.

But they themselves reject this approach, adding,

> Their anatomical significance is probably not to be pushed, for they first of all are illustrative of the writer's main point. ... Paul, of course, intends his readers to understand that such attitudes are ridiculous.

Paul's comments do not constitute an allegory, where each thing represents something else, but an analogy, a parallelism, an extended illustration - and we must be careful not to push the comparisons beyond the points that they serve to illustrate.

**12:22-24** The more "gifted" at Corinth - with the more "showy" gifts - perceived themselves as the "core" of the church, essential to its functioning, its very being. Just the opposite, says Paul.

The ESV and NIV (and numerous other versions) translate Paul as speaking of treating some parts of the body with more honor because we think of them as less honorable, and of treating the parts that are unpresentable with greater modesty. In line with this approach, Paul's comment is sometimes thought to refer to covering some parts of the body (i.e., the sexually significant parts) for the sake of modesty.

Thus Gordon Clark 198 says:

> The less honorable parts have been identified, by imaginative commentators, as the feet and the intestines. The only certain identification of what Paul meant is that the indecent parts are the organs of sex and excrement. When the text says that the indecent members have more abundant decency, it probably means that we take especial care to clothe them. They are decently covered. The decent members, the face or arms for example, do not have to be clothed.

Johnson 233 is even more precise and explicit:

> These verses can be obscure unless we realize Paul is referring to the bodily parts that have to do with procreation (male organ and female vagina) and nurture (female breasts).

Johnson does not argue for this interpretation or explain it further, but takes it as self-evidently obvious once he has stated it. The approach of Clark and Johnson is, in general, well supported among commentators: there is a high degree of agreement that Paul is referring to the genitalia. As Paul does not in fact elaborate further, or identify any particular parts of the human anatomy in these verses, we cannot say for certain: and so this interpretation may be correct. But two significant problems with this view lead me to reject it.

*First of all*, this approach seems to derive from a mistaken interpretational attitude that views Paul as being opposed to (or at least uncomfortable about) sex. But we should understand his views differently from this after considering his teaching in chapter 7. Here, as elsewhere, there is a danger of reading into Paul's teaching things which he did not say.

And **secondly**, this common interpretational approach runs into some difficulties when we look carefully at what Paul actually says. For in v.23 the point is that some parts of our body are regarded as unpresentable or unsightly in some way, and therefore we pay them particular attention to make them look good - attention that the body parts which are already presentable do not require. Commentators suggest that what this means is, we cover them up with clothing! That might serve modesty, but it hardly serves to make them **look good** in themselves - this interpretation is actually looking in quite the wrong direction.

The Orr & Walther (283f.) translation of verses 23b, 24a is: "and our unpresentable parts have greater presentability which our presentable parts do not need" - i.e., greater presentability, as a result of the greater attention which we pay them precisely because we consider them "unpresentable".

The significant part of Paul's comment, for interpretation, is 12:24a, "while our presentable parts need no special treatment". Thus some parts *do* merit special treatment, in order to make them more presentable. This is quite inconsistent with the idea of a reference to the sexual areas of the body. Paul is not saying that we give these special treatment with the result that they are then and thereby made to look more presentable!

Rather, Paul is drawing an example from life, and speaking of the way in which people recognize that, in physical appearance, some features of their bodies are more attractive than others, and we pay attention to our less attractive physical features in our endeavors to improve on them. Thus, TEV: "Those parts that we think aren't worth very much are the ones which we treat with greater care; while the parts of the body which don't look very nice receive special attention, which the more beautiful parts of our body do not need."

Similarly, Phillips.

However the ESV translates verse 12:23b thus: "and our unpresentable parts are treated with greater modesty". [Similarly the NIV and others.] But this quite misses the point of Paul's contrasting of words here. He speaks of parts which are τα ἀσχήμονα *(ta aschēmona)*, which he then says have (ἔχει) εὐσχημοσύνην, *(echei) euschēmosunēn*. Notice: same word root. What is **unpresentable**, or not very attractive, about our body is made to be more abundantly **presentable**, attractive - which is not the same as "being modestly covered up".

This verse does not make sense if taken as a reference to genitalia etc., for our genitalia do not "become decent" by being covered up - rather, they stay the same and are simply hidden. But the meaning is that something *less* attractive in our body is made *quite* attractive by the honor (i.e. the attention to what it looks like) that we give it.

John Chrysostom (Kovacs 207f.) says on this passage,

> What part of the body could be less important than hair? But remove this small thing from the eyebrows and the eyelids, and you destroy the beauty of the entire face, and the eyes no longer appear lovely. Though the loss affects only a little thing, nevertheless it destroys all the beauty.

We give especial care and attention to a part of our body which is not looking its best or not functioning as it should. So, we exercise, or we wear special clothing, or we use cosmetics, to change or cover up deficiencies or blemishes in our physical appearance and thus to enhance the attractiveness of our bodies. That is, we take steps to compensate for any physical shortcomings we may perceive that we have.

Paul's point, of course, is that this is the appropriate kind of treatment we are to have for the apparently "lesser" members of the church. (He is not talking of hiding these people!)

**12:25-26** But it is God who has arranged all the parts of the body, and made it an undivided unity. It is God who has appointed all the roles, offices, ministries, and gifts in the body and for the body. It is God's concern that the body as a whole functions properly, and that each part within it has an appropriate (and satisfying) role.

John Stott 110 sums up this section of Paul's teaching in this incisive comment:

> The voice of self-depreciation says, "I'm no good; you don't need me", while the voice of self-importance says, "You're no good; I don't need you". But the voice of God says, "You need each other".

I have referred several times to, and quoted from, John Stott's book *Baptism and Fullness*. This book is a short (119-page) discussion of the nature of baptism with the Spirit, as set out in the New Testament, which compares this Spirit baptism with Scriptural teaching about receiving the fullness of the Spirit. It is a very helpful treatment of the issues.

## 3. Allocating Gifts And Ministries (12:27-31E)

**12:27** Having completed his comments on the nature of the human body, Paul now punches home the point of his analogy: "Now you are the body of Christ." So that all that he has been saying about the relationships of the different parts, limbs, and organs of the human body he is actually saying about the body of Christ, the church.

"... and each one of you ...": every single Christian has a role to play and a function to fulfill as a member of the body of Christ.

**12:28** Paul next says, "God has appointed in the church ..." Note the parallelism of this verse with v.18:

**18:** God has set (ἔθετο, *etheto*) the parts, each one of them,
　　　　　　　　　　　　　in the body　as he chose.
**28:** God has set (ἔθετο, *etheto*) in the church firstly apostles ... [etc.]

We should notice carefully that it is **God** who appoints, that God in his supreme sovereign wisdom allocates the different roles to each person. Individual Christians are not invited to choose **their** preferences, as from a kind of theological smorgasbord.

And Paul then gives us another list, but with a difference.

The difference is that whereas in verses 8 to 10 he lists **gifts**, here he lists first three categories of **persons**, and thus of roles and offices - ministries -, which he identifies as "first", "second", "third". Thereafter the rest of his list is of what we are able to call, as in v.7, "manifestations of the Spirit". Following the lead of the first three, many translations turn these into roles for persons also. Thus Paul lists miracles, gifts of healings, helps, guidings, and kinds of tongues, and the ESV translates the text carefully, as it stands, but the NIV (for example) makes it refer to people, and renders it as "workers of miracles", "those having gifts of healing", "those able to help others", "those with gifts of administration", and "those speaking in different kinds of tongues".

But I would see some significant difference between the two parts of Paul's list:

1. For the first three - apostles, prophets, teachers - Paul gives them a ranking, as if this has some significance. (I will discuss this further, below.) The remaining five are not ranked: from which I deduce that either ranking is inappropriate or irrelevant for them, or they are not differentiated in such a way in Paul's thinking. Thus after the first three, order or ranking does not matter. (Though several commentators see significance in the fact that "kinds of tongues" is mentioned last.)

2. The first three - the only ones which are numbered - are of **persons**, of what we should recognize as roles or offices or positions. The others listed are of **functions**, of activities - of gifts or manifestations or of concepts, distributed in the church without being attached to or utilized in specific offices. I see this difference as significant: that there were permanent positions of apostle, prophet, and teacher in the early church from the beginning, to which people were appointed in some way, and that they occupied those roles "for life", as it were. Thus there was an office of "apostle" in the early church, and in this strict sense it was known who was appointed to that office.

So also, it seems to me, it was likely that prophets and teachers, when called of God, were recognized by the church and appointed to that office in the church. But the evidence about this is meager and inconclusive: though we may for example note passages like Acts 13:1, "In the church at Antioch there were prophets and teachers [these men were then named]." This looks to me like a recognition of men who had been appointed to those offices. Similarly I take it that 2 Timothy 2:2 refers to Timothy formally appointing people with appropriate gifts of teaching to the role and office of "teacher". In addition, others would have gifts of prophecy and teaching - and exercise them - without holding formal office.

And similarly others with other gifts and abilities would use them without their functioning being formalized into the office of "healer" or "tongues-speaker", etc.

3. So I see there as being formal appointment to the three listed offices; whereas other people had gifts and ministries which they exercised more informally as opportunity offered and as the Spirit led them. The emphasis here, after the first three - in Paul listing the endowment, not the person - is thus upon the existence of this manifestation in the church community, not upon the person exhibiting that endowment.

Thus we differentiate office and role on the one hand from *charisma*, "gift" or endowment on the other. Everyone who has the office needs the gift, but not everyone who has the gift needs to hold an office nor needs an office to use the gift. But tragedy comes when people are appointed to an office (e.g. presently: pastor, evangelist, teacher) who lack the appropriate gifts.

**12:28a** Paul's list commences with "firstly, apostles ..."

Those who were at first the twelve disciples (Matthew 10:1, etc.) then become the twelve apostles. Why is this? Because of the purpose of Christ, as the Scriptures reveal. *Disciple* means "learner", and *apostle* means "one who is sent out on a mission". *Disciple* is what they were called first of all, because that's what they were: learners; this word focuses specially on the teaching and training Jesus gave them. But they were chosen and called in order that they would be sent out. Thus Mark 3:14 tells us, "He appointed twelve - designating them apostles - that they might be with him, and that he might send them out to preach." After calling them the twelve disciples in Matthew 10:1, in the very next verse Matthew refers to them as the twelve apostles. This is a recognition of what they were - and what they were in training to become. After the resurrection came their commission: "Go therefore and make disciples of all nations ..."; "you will be my witnesses in Jerusalem, and in all Judea and Samaria, and to the end of the earth." (Matthew 28:20; Acts 1:8.)

When Matthias was appointed to replace Judas, and Paul was chosen and commissioned as one of their number, the roll-call was complete. After James the brother of John was martyred (Acts 12:2), no one was appointed to fill his shoes. There was a very real sense in which this was a closed list.

"Firstly, apostles ..." The word πρωτον (*prōton*) can mean "first in rank", "as of first importance", as it clearly does when Paul uses it a few chapters later, in 15:3. Then of next importance, "secondly," would be the New Testament prophets, then thirdly the teachers. And this undoubtedly may be the meaning.

Some years later Paul writes in more detail about these roles, in Ephesians. The church, he tells us there in 2:20, is built upon the foundation of the apostles and prophets, for to them has been revealed (3:5) God's plan in the gospel. And (4:11) Christ has given to the church some who are apostles, some who are prophets, some who are evangelists, and some who are pastor-teachers.

But in view of the way in which Paul points out here that the church is founded upon the apostles and prophets, we should take it also (I conclude) as **chronological**. First came the apostles and the prophets, who laid, under Christ, the foundations of the church. Then came evangelists and pastor-teachers, who built upon their work. Paul has already himself told us of this in 1 Corinthians 3:10-11: "According to the grace of God given to me, like a skilled master builder I laid a foundation, and someone else is building upon it. Let each one take care how he builds upon it. For no one can lay a foundation other than that which is laid, which is Jesus Christ."

As the foundation of the church, the apostles and prophets are unique. And irreplaceable. As MacArthur 324 says,

> Once the foundation was laid, the work of apostles and prophets was finished. The work of interpreting and proclaiming the now-written Word was taken over by evangelists, pastor-teachers, and teachers.

John Stott 100f. elaborates the thought:

> [The apostles] were unique in being eyewitnesses of the historic Jesus, especially of the risen Lord ..., in being personally appointed and authorized by Christ (Mark 3:14) and in being specially inspired by the Holy Spirit for their teaching ministry (e.g. John 14:25-26; 16:12-15). In this primary sense, therefore, in which they appear in the lists, they have no successors, in the very nature of the case, although there are no doubt "apostles" today in the secondary sense of "missionaries".

As the role and office of apostle and prophet has ceased in the church, so also, it will follow, have the authenticating marks of their ministry to which Paul refers in 2 Corinthians 12:12, where he writes, "The signs of a true apostle were performed among you with utmost patience, with signs and wonders and mighty works."

So have there been apostles and prophets after the apostolic age? And: do we have them today? In the nature of the case, no. They laid the foundations. After the foundations are down, as Paul says (1 Corinthians 3:12ff.), the task and responsibility goes to others, with other gifts, to build upon them. So, the miraculous aspect of this gift has ceased. The apostles and prophets, through whom God revealed the full nature of the gospel (as Paul said in Ephesians 3) were replaced in this sense by the written revelation of the New Testament; and their task was completed when the recording of God's revelation in Scripture was completed. So in that sense there have been no apostles and prophets since then.

John Stott 100-101 explains incisively:

> What about prophets? ... In ... the essential biblical meaning, I think that we must say that there are no more prophets, for God's self-revelation was completed in Christ, and in the apostolic witness to Christ, and the canon of Scripture has long since been closed. Moreover, "prophets" come second to apostles in the Ephesian and Corinthian lists mentioned above, and "apostles and prophets" are bracketed in several texts, and said to be the foundation (because of their teaching) on which the church is built (Ephesians 2:20; 3:5). Now the simplest knowledge of architectural construction is enough to tell us that once the foundation of a building is laid and the superstructure is being built, the foundation cannot be laid again. So in the primary sense of "prophets", as vehicles of direct and fresh revelation, it seems we must say that this *charisma* is no longer given. There is no longer anyone in the church who may dare to say "The word of the Lord came to me, saying ..." or "Thus says the Lord". ...

> It seems to be ... that Paul brackets "apostles and prophets" as the most important of *charismata* ... and in that sense (whatever may be said about subsidiary meanings and ministries) we must say they no longer exist in the church. God's way of teaching in today's church is not by fresh revelation but by exposition of his revelation completed in Christ and in Scripture.

But there is a secondary sense for these words, for in the New Testament there are some others who are referred to as apostles: Barnabas (Acts 14:14); Silas and Timothy (1 Thessalonians 2:6); Epaphroditus (Philippians 2:25 - ἀποστολος [*apostolos*] here is rendered "messenger" in the ESV, NIV, and NRSV); brothers who are apostles of the churches (2 Corinthians 8:23 - rendered "representatives" in the NIV and NRSV, "messengers" in the ESV).

The word *apostle* (ἀποστολος, *apostolos*) is the noun from the Greek verb ἀποστελλω, (*apostellō*), "I send out on a mission", and this verb is used in Romans 10:15, 1 Corinthians 1:17 and 2 Corinthians 12:17. Several writers have drawn attention to the fact that in this sense *apostle* is equivalent to *missionary*. Michael Griffiths 24 points out that in this secondary sense of the term, we do have *apostles* today: pioneer missionary evangelists engaged in founding churches. Griffiths says,

> This meaning is supported by the interesting expression in 1 Corinthians 9:2, "If to others I am not an apostle, at least I am to you", i.e. as the missionary founder of the Corinthian congregation. This can be paralleled by the expressions "I planted" (3:6), "as a wise master-builder I laid a foundation" (3:10), and "I became your father through the gospel" (4:15). When a pioneer missionary goes to a new tribe, they have no Bible of their own. The missionary is initially their only source of apostolic doctrine so that, even in this special sense, he carries apostolic authority. It does not seem biblically necessary to deny the continuing existence of apostles in this secondary sense of pioneer church-planting missionaries. In missionary societies today, we need this charisma more than any other. It is the "first" of the gifts, and the planting of new congregations still needs to be done cross-culturally in many parts of the world.

Michael Griffiths also goes on to warn against a wrong understanding of modern-day *apostles* in the church. He adds,

> On the other hand, I think there is a great danger in a recent book which says, "Let us watch and pray for apostles to be raised up ... let us recognize and submit to them as they appear." This doctrine is currently taught in some of the more extreme and separatist parts of the house-church movement, and seems quite different from that of the New Testament, where an apostle brings a congregation into existence. Surely only missionary founders of new congregations could claim this kind of secondary apostolic status. We should beware of self-styled apostles who wish to put themselves in authority over us and of status-seekers who divide congregations in order to grasp a prominence denied them both by society and responsible church discipline.

Following Griffiths, we can recognize a modern-day type of apostle, requiring special gifts appropriate for missionary evangelism and church planting, though without the first-century miraculous aspects. This includes two gifts with a miraculous dimension which Paul mentions in this verse: the "working of miracles", and "gifts of healing" as in the apostolic age, though the "miraculous dimension" of these gifts is no longer found. We have already discussed these specifically in considering verses 9 and 10, and their sense and application today.

And we shall see something similar in relation to prophets: we shall review this ministry when we discuss Paul's teaching in chapters 13 and 14.

One other thing we should note at this point: Those who were called to the office of apostle were given by God the gifts required for apostleship. But not all those who had such gifts were appointed to the office of apostle. Those who held the office of prophet were those who had the gift of prophecy; but not all who had the gift of prophecy were appointed to the office of prophet, nor designated *prophet*. And this will be true of every office in the church.

Similarly our appointments to offices in the church today should involve the requirement that the candidate has the appropriate gifts. As MacArthur 316 notes,

> Churches often fall back on organization because the organism is not functioning right. Because a hand is not doing its job, a foot is called on to do that work, and so on.

Too true. Part of the responsibility of the church is that of recognition of who has been given which gifts. Only those whom God in his sovereignty has gifted for an office should be appointed to that office.

What is the difference between a "secondly", a prophet, and a "thirdly", a teacher?

Their roles overlap, and each contains elements of the other. Indeed, as Garland 580 points out - as do many other commentators - there is much overlapping between all the various gifts and ministries mentioned.

But we may note the explanation given by Thiselton 1017-1018:

> It is the work of teachers to expound and explain what is the case about God's dealings with the world through Christ by the Spirit, on the basis of which the pastoral and situational speech-acts of prophets can have their effect. ... The two primary sources of teaching are the OT scriptures and the primitive creeds of the early church. ... By the time of Irenaeus teaching of this kind begins to be recognized as what amounts to the beginnings of a Christian NT canon of scripture. Thus Irenaeus stresses the integral role of the four canonical Gospels as a cardinal and authentic source of teaching, while the earliest commentators begin to reiterate their common body of what is to be taught through creed and catechesis. [What now] has shifted is a switch from prophets to pastorally gifted preachers who announce God's dealings with his people and with individuals among them.

As in Paul's day, so also today: in our understanding of Paul's teaching about what a prophet does, between prophet and teacher there is a difference of emphasis. The role of the prophets is applying spiritual truth to a situation, to people; they are actively exhorting, encouraging, promising, asking, etc. The role of the teachers is making people aware of the nature and content of spiritual truth; it is ensuring that people know what Scripture says; it is informing, instructing. These roles may well be expressed in differing ways: prophecy in a sermon, teaching in a lecture; prophecy by oral means, teaching by a wide variety of means, including in writing.

But they are by no means mutually exclusive. Ephesians 4:11 speaks of pastor-teachers, which I take to mean that a minister of the gospel should have both gifts, and exercise them both: though not necessarily at the same time or in the same manner.

**12:28b** Most of the endowments or gifts which Paul now goes on to mention here in v.28 have been included in his previous list, but there are two new items here: "helps" (ἀντιλήμψεις, *antilēmpseis*) and "guidings" (κυβερνησεις, *kubernēseis*). These are not common words, and there is much discussion in the commentaries about their precise meanings.

The first word means the helpfulness of a person stepping in to lend a hand when assistance is needed. It has been likened, for example, to the assistance given to Paul by the various members of his staff of associates who are so often mentioned in passing in Acts and the Epistles, sometimes by name and sometimes not named. Thus Thiselton 1020 includes within the meaning of ἀντιλήμψις (*antilēmpsis*),

> support in the sense in which in modern cultures we speak of support staff, i.e. in the plural, kinds of administrative support. ... In our judgement this gift is coupled with κυβερνησεις exactly because both concern practical administrative tasks essential in any concept of the body as both a sociopolitical and a theological entity.

I see the word ἀντιλήμψεις (*antilēmpseis*) as corresponding exactly with those manifestations of the Spirit that Paul refers to in 12:5 as service to the Lord.

The second word (κυβερνησεις, *kubernēseis*) originally referred to a ship's steersman or pilot, and thence came to mean the person who guides a project through to a successful conclusion, or administers an activity or manages an enterprise. John Stott 95 writes of this gift,

> κυβερνησις [*kubernēsis*] would seem, then, to be the gift of guiding or governing others, including perhaps organizing ability to take responsibility for some part of the church's programme, or the leadership to take the chair at a meeting and "steer" the committee's proceedings with wisdom.

And concerning this *charisma* Johnson 238 writes:

> This work of the Spirit through individuals who can steer the ship of the church through troubled waters is sorely needed in today's church.

I see this word κυβερνησις (*kubernēsis*) as referring to the endowment of those with ἐνεργηματα (*energēmata*) that Paul mentions in 12:6, who make sure that something gets done.

**12:29-30** So now, having given his teaching, Paul asks a series of related questions to see whether his readers have grasped the point of that teaching: "Are all apostles? Are all prophets?" etc. Here we have Paul's quick quiz questions upon what he has just being saying. In this way Paul confronts his readers with the requirement to think through and assess the significance - and the consequence - of his teaching. This is Paul's way with his teaching: for another similar example, see Paul's series of questions in Romans 10:14-15, commencing "How are they to call on him in whom they have not believed?"

The form of each of these questions in Greek - they all commence with μη (*mē*) - indicates in every case that the expected answer is "no". There is no gift or ministry that all Christians will have, and there is no Christian who will be given all these gifts or ministries. Through his questions Paul makes it plain that these are not roles or ministries given to all Christians but only to some. He has also made it plain that it is God who allocates the role to each Christian (verses 7, 11, 18, 28). It is not for a Christian to want something else, but rather to accept from God and use what they have been given.

Thiselton 1023 writes thus about the authentic exercise of a gift,

> it is first of all whether it coheres with the proclamation of Christ through apostles, next, whether it builds up like the pastoral preaching of prophets, and, third, whether it coheres with what teachers expound from the OT and from apostolic tradition. But even if all are not apostles, prophets, teachers, the other gifts are no less authentic gifts from God, which all have an honored and respected place within the body of Christ.

In a very thought-provoking treatment, Berding (2006) propounds the view that the emphasis here is not upon *gifts* as such, but rather upon *ministries* to which God calls, and which he then enables. Thus Berding 102 says that this passage:

> begins as a list of persons ("members") in their ministries whom God has placed or appointed in the church, then shifts to a list of ministries themselves.

He argues (137) that Paul's lists here, and in Ephesians 4:11-12 and Romans 12:6-8,

> should be categorized as lists of ministry assignments that God has given to believers, and to the church through those believers.

**12:31a** The chapter concludes with a much controverted challenge. Fee 623 introduces his discussion of this verse with these comments:

> After the argument of verses 4-30 and especially after the rhetoric of verses 29-30, the imperative with which this verse begins, "But eagerly desire the greater gifts", is a puzzle.

Indeed so. At the outset of our consideration we need to recognize that the Greek word ζηλουτε (*zēloute*) in this verse can either be translated as in, "But *eagerly desire* the greater gifts" (NIV text), taking this verb form as an imperative, or, "But *you are eagerly desiring* the greater gifts" (NIV margin), taking the alternative possible meaning of ζηλουτε (*zēloute*) as an indicative, a statement of fact.

How do the commentators treat v.31 and Paul's words about "higher gifts", "greater gifts", "more important gifts"?

The interpretation of the verb as *imperative* (i.e., an instruction) would be that the Corinthians (and Christians generally) must eagerly desire the greater gifts - and these gifts would then be seen as certain ones selected from the catalogue in verses 8 to 10 and/or 27 to 30. Perhaps the interpreter of this passage may then go on to say that Paul is now placing before them, as a further goal for their seeking, the "most excellent way" (12:31b), which is to seek love, the best gift of them all.

Other expositors, emphasizing that love is the fruit of the Spirit and not a gift, see Paul's meaning, rather, as being to improve their focus on gifts. For we all recognize that the whole point of this section of the Epistle is Paul's intention to correct their focus, because they already have their own agenda and they have already made up their minds which are the "greatest" gifts: which is why Paul is dealing with this issue in the first place. There is general agreement amongst commentators that the Corinthians' major focus is on tongues-speaking, and (many would also add), upon wisdom and knowledge and prophecy, as the Corinthians perceived them: so Paul has given them a wider list of gifts, ranking some as better, and inviting them to choose from the greater gifts.

Thus Gordon Clark 201 says,

> He urges the Corinthians, who made so much of languages, to seek the better gifts. Although God distributes His gifts as He pleases, yet it is right for us to desire one or another and to express our desires.

But Thiselton 1005 expresses his concern:

> It is hardly mere speculation to imagine that those who perceived themselves as possessing the "high-status" gifts of knowledge and wisdom, or of the power to heal or to speak in tongues, could be tempted to think of themselves as *the* inner circle on whom the identity and function of the church really depended. In modern times, the tendency to

select either one or more of the "gifts" in 12:8-10, or to interpret the baptism by or in the Spirit in 12:13 as the sign of "advanced" status, comes perilously near to the Corinthian heresy which Paul explicitly attacks.

Yet to varying degrees this type of approach that Thiselton deplores is being widely followed. And Thiselton himself takes ζηλοῦτε (*zēloute*) as imperative. What is the alternative?

If the verb is taken as *indicative*, the interpretation is:

"Here Paul is stating that what they *are* doing is eagerly desiring the greater gifts, whereas what they *should* be doing - which he is now setting before them - is something different: instead of regarding the possession of certain gifts as important and pursuing them, the Corinthians should be seeking love."

Thus this is actually a statement to rebuke them for what they are doing - not an instruction that they do it all the more.

The idea that ζηλοῦτε (*zēloute*) is to be taken as an indicative rather than an imperative is the conclusion reached by significant numbers of scholars, including the German Bittlinger, *Gifts and Graces (1 Corinthians 12-14)* and G. Iber, 'Zum Verständnis von 1 Corinthians 12:31', ZNW, 54 (1963), 48; together with Professor John Ruef in the Pelican NT Commentary, *Paul's First Letter to Corinth* (1971), 140; George Gardiner, *The Corinthian Catastrophe* (1974), 28; David Prior, *The Message of 1 Corinthians*, 223; John MacArthur, *I Corinthians*, 325; Michael Griffiths, *Cinderella's Betrothal Gifts* 10.

Thus for example MacArthur 325 writes,

Because the Greek indicative and imperative forms are identical, the first half of the verse could be translated, "but you earnestly desire the greater gifts." That rendering seems much more appropriate to the context, both of what precedes and what follows. It certainly is consistent with the tone of the letter and the sin of the Corinthians. Because they clearly prized the showier gifts, the seemingly greater gifts, it would seem foolish of Paul to command them to do what they already were eagerly doing. The Corinthians were to stop seeking gifts, because to do so is both presumptuous and purposeless. Every believer already is perfectly gifted in the way that God planned and which best suits their ministry for Him.

And Michael Griffiths 10 says:

The teaching of 1 Corinthians 12 as a whole appears to be that we should accept the gifts sovereignly distributed by the Holy Spirit, and the place in the body which the Father has sovereignly assigned to each of us. Accordingly, it seems probable that 1 Corinthians 12:31 is not a command to "seek" or "covet" gifts (an imperative), but rather a rebuke against being "jealous" of the gifts exercised by others (an indicative).

In other words, the verse should read, not "Earnestly desire ..." but "You earnestly desire the greater gifts. But I show you a still more excellent way." The traditional interpretation depends upon the English translation as "seek" or "covet", but, as we shall see, this may not be the best understanding of the original words in the original context.

If this is so, then we ought not to urge people to seek any gift. Thus we may allow that all the gifts mentioned in the New Testament (and others not mentioned) may be sovereignly given today if God so chooses. Whether they are or not depends *not* upon our seeking, but upon God Himself who sovereignly chooses to bestow or to withhold gifts from congregations or individuals, just as *He* pleases. Such an approach removes a great deal of heat and anxiety from the whole issue. To state it even more simply, gifts are given (as the basic meaning of the word would suggest) and not sought.

Which meaning is Paul likely to be intending? Imperative or indicative? Instruction or rebuke?

Let us apply the context test to these two interpretations.

*First of all* it should be noted that in 1 Corinthians 12 Paul describes these various gifts as something that one Christian has and another does not. The essential nature of each one of these gifts is that that gift is given to one Christian or another for them to exercise for the benefit of others; *none* of these gifts is given to *every* Christian (see the whole of chapter 12, especially verses 4 to 11 and 27 to 30). But love is not such a gift. On the contrary: Paul's whole point in our context (i.e., 1 Corinthians 13) is that the full measure of Christian love (which he here describes) is something that *every* Christian should have and should display, without which we are nothing. Love is the fruit of the Spirit (Galatians 5:22). The difference between a gift and a fruit is significant.

A fruit is something that is produced by a tree from within its own nature and which thus reveals of what nature it is. It is the nature of an apple tree to produce apples: if it produced oranges it would not *be* an apple tree. The Holy Spirit, indwelling every Christian, is engaged in producing from within his own divine nature the fruit of the Spirit within that Christian. We are to understand the role of the Spirit in this, and to desire him to produce this fruit in us, and to co-operate with his ministry in us in the ways that Scripture teaches. By contrast, to repeat, a gift is something given specifically and directly by God to particular Christians, *some* Christians as distinct from *all* Christians, for mutual ministry and in which the Spirit manifests himself.

*Secondly*, it should be noted that the whole thrust of Paul's teaching in 1 Corinthians 12 is that while all Christians have *some* gifts, no Christians have *all* gifts and there is no gift in Paul's list which *all* Christians have (verses 4 to 10, 29 and 30). And it is God the Holy Spirit in his sovereignty who determines which gifts will be distributed to which Christians (verses 11, 18, 24, 27 and 28). Therefore to seek for particular gifts for ourselves is to intrude into the sphere which Scripture *specifically* says that God has reserved for himself.

The fact that Paul wrote 1 Corinthians 12 indicates that the Corinthians were in need of teaching on these matters.

Which then is more likely as Paul's intention in v.31: that Paul should explicitly state that the Corinthians were engaged in seeking after the greater gifts (greater, that is, in the estimation of the Corinthians), thus mentioning the factor that led him to deal with the issue in his letter; or instead that Paul should instruct the Corinthians to seek for any particular gifts when he has just taught that the distribution of gifts is God's prerogative? And that Paul should imply that some gifts are greater than others, when he has just been at pains to stress the importance of the exercising of every gift for the right functioning of the whole body of Christ?

A consideration of the whole of this chapter can lead us to this conclusion:

This verse can hardly be a command to desire particular gifts. This would be a contradiction of everything that has gone before, where Paul has been emphasizing God's sovereignty in apportioning gifts (as distinct from our choosing them!), and that it is God's plan for those in the church all to have different gifts, for the benefit of the body of Christ.

Rather, this verse (as in the NIV margin) is a statement that the Corinthians were seeking after the "greater" gifts (greater, that is, in their own estimation), and their attitude is being *contrasted* with the plan of God, as Paul has set it out. Instead of longing for what God has *not* chosen to give you, Paul says, "I will show you the most excellent way - what you should be seeking for" (v.31b). And then he writes to them about love, which is not a gift, but the fruit of the Spirit.

Numbers of commentators have drawn attention to the way in which Paul begins v.28 with και ούς μεν (*kai hous men*), to which there is no corresponding ούς δε (*hous de*), as strictly should be expected. True. But I see a corresponding δε (*de*), though it is a few verses away, which sets up a significant contrast - if one views ζηλουτε (*zēloute*) as an indicative:

And **God** has placed some in the church with various roles and gifts
But **you** are eagerly desiring [particular] gifts [which you regard as] greater.

The weakness of this is that the μεν (*men*) is contrasting, not "God", but the οὓς (*hous*) in the first leg with the ζηλοῦτε δε (*zēloute de*) in the second leg, so that we would have to take it that Paul had changed his grammatical construction when he interrupted the μεν ... δε (*men ... de*) to ask his questions in the middle. But then, he did that anyway, seeing that (apart from this approach which I am suggesting) there is no answering δε (*de*) to his μεν (*men*). And this suggestion certainly brings out the contrast between what **God** has done in appointing people and gifts, and what **the Corinthians** are taking it upon themselves to do, or seek to do, in wanting to choose gifts for themselves.

Why is the verb form ζηλοῦτε (*zēloute*) taken by so many as imperative, not indicative? Fee, in considering the "indicative" option, states (624) a widely-held view,

> What basically stands against this option is the appearance of the same verb form in 14:1 and 39, where it can only be an imperative and not an indicative. Despite some attractive features to this second option, the more likely alternative is that the verb is an imperative, as in 14:1.

The whole question of the validity of this using of 14:1 to decide 12:31 is linked with the significance of πνευματικα (*pneumatika*) in 14:1. But a major problem with this view is that we are being asked to accept that when the Corinthians reached 12:31 in reading the Epistle, they were expected to hold judgement on how to take ζηλοῦτε (*zēloute*) (i.e., whether as imperative or indicative) until they reached this same verb again a couple of chapters later.

I don't find this believable, or that Paul expected it of them. No! They were expected to understand its meaning on the basis of what they had just read in chapter 12. And that meant they would see it as an indicative, which was **contrasting** what they were wrongly doing regarding gifts, with the pattern of God's plan with gifts and ministries, as Paul has just set it out.

An assumption behind this equating of Paul's use of ζηλοῦτε (*zēloute*) in 12:31 and 14:1 is that when in 12:31 Paul says ζηλοῦτε χαρισματα (*zēloute charismata*) he means the same as when he says ζηλοῦτε πνευματικα (*zēloute pneumatika*) in 14:1. But, as I say more fully when discussing 14:1, far from **equating** χαρισματα (*charismata*) and πνευματικα (*pneumatika*) in these two verses, he is **contrasting** them. "You are earnestly seeking χαρισματα, 'gifts'," he is saying (12:31), "when what you should be doing (14:1) is earnestly seeking πνευματικα, 'spiritual things', 'to be spiritual'" - a very different thing! Just as some commentators suggest, the Corinthians **may** have equated being spiritual with possessing certain χαρισματα (*charismata*), but Paul most certainly did not! But to make the unjustified assumption that he did - contrary to all the evidence - and then upon this assumption to base an interpretation of the form ζηλουτε (*zēloute*) in 12:31, is most certainly not valid exegesis.

It is absolutely incredible the way in which when Paul on occasions is using *different* words - deliberately chosen, I would believe - many commentators take it that he means the *same* thing by them. We should give Paul more credit than that for choosing his words with care - not to mention the inspiration of the Holy Spirit behind those words. You may recall that we saw a similar situation with Paul's use of σαρξ (*sarx*) and σωμα (*soma*) in chapter 6:16.

In this section I have referred several times to, and quoted from, Michael Griffiths's small (78-page) book *Cinderella's Betrothal Gifts*. This discusses God's gifts in relation to the life and witness of the church today. It is a thoughtful and stimulating consideration of the original meaning and current application of Paul's teaching about God's gifts and ministries.

## SOME PRACTICAL AND PASTORAL REFLECTIONS

### Tourist or Team Player?

How are we to view all that Paul has been saying?

The church is not a tour bus, with one driver plus a tour guide, who comments on the scenery and the sights as the tour members travel along.

Rather, the church is a symphony orchestra, with a conductor and a manager and possibly a soloist singer or performer - but every member has an instrument to play and a job to do. You don't have members of the orchestra who sit and do nothing, and just watch and listen while the others play their instruments. Some instruments in an orchestra are numerous, with many players - like the wind section and the strings; for others there are only one or two - like the percussion or the harp. Some instruments are playing continuously or almost all the time; while other instruments are only involved occasionally in playing. But every orchestra member has a task - there is some skill or another which they have - and when the music requires it, they are there to perform.

That's the analogy that appeals to me. But those of you who are into football might relate more to the picture of a team of football players in a match, where every player on the field is there because he has a role to fulfill and a skill to use.

Certainly we can all relate to Paul's picture of the members of the church, the body of Christ, being like parts of the human body: each part has an indispensable role to play in the optimum functioning of the entire body. And not only an indispensable role but a unique role - one part does not attempt to take over the proper role of another part. And all the parts are needed.

In some areas of the church today we have certainly got this mixed up. In numerous places some "parts of the body" - with certain God-given endowments, functions, and roles - are seeking to (or at least wanting to) take over other roles, which need different skills and gifts.

Or, alternatively, like tourists on the tour bus, they are content to be just going along for the ride, enjoying the sights.

Johnson 220, comparing the pattern of the involvement of all Christians in the life and worship of the church as Paul sets it out here with what is often found today, says,

> greater emphasis on the multiplicity and diversity of the Spirit's ministry is needed in many churches, where the congregation's role has been severely reduced to being spectators to the "dance of the clergy".

What are to be our responses to all these truths? We are to have a threefold response:

*Firstly*, we need to identify, and train and develop, and use, our own gifts for the benefit of all, as God intended.

*Secondly*, we have a responsibility, as a church, to help others do the same. So we need to mentor people to find their gifts, and then ensure that, as a church, we provide them with training and practice, and opportunities to use their gifts.

And then, *thirdly*, we need to recognize the "more excellent way". The Corinthians were vainly chasing after what they considered to be "higher" or "better" or "greater" gifts. "No," says Paul. "I will show you something far better and far more important than that!" And he writes for them - and us! - about a way of living, a way of life: chapter 13, "The Way of Love". It is as if he is saying here, "Pause and ponder: Fruit is more important than gifts - any gift. And fruit is something for all Christians to cultivate."

Paul now interrupts his discussion of "gifts and the Corinthians" to explain the Way of Love. But really it is not an interruption of his theme: it is a clarification of it. For Paul is not disparaging gifts in these chapters - to the contrary, he has been emphasizing how vital, how indispensable they are. And he is not setting up here some kind of conflict between gifts and love and saying, "Choose love."

He *is* saying that love is for every Christian to have and show, whereas gifts are each only for particular individuals. But far more than this: he is showing that love is the sphere within which a gift - any gift, every gift - is to be exercised.

Whichever view we adopt concerning 12:31a - whether we accept it as an imperative, "But seek for the greater gifts" or take it as an indicative, "But you are seeking for the greater gifts" - it is concerned with the seeking of gifts. And so Paul's response now to this situation is, "And I will show you a still better way - a way more surpassing, more outstanding, more superior than any gift in itself can ever be, a way which far surpasses all others." He then speaks to them of the way of love, and in the first stanza (13:1-3) of what some have called a poem to love he emphasizes that any gift and every gift without love is pointless and useless and valueless. This is followed, in his second stanza (13:4-7), by the setting forth of the intrinsic excellence of love, and then by a final stanza demonstrating the eternal value of love (13:8-13E).

The chapter personifies love, giving it a life and dimension of its own. In fact we can see how what Paul writes is fulfilled in Christ, so that it can be said of him: "Christ is patient and kind; Christ is not jealous or boastful", and so on throughout. Or perhaps, even better, we can see how it is really Christ's love which fulfills all that Paul says here.

But more than this: chapter 13 is an unconscious self-portrait. When in his introduction in 12:31 Paul says that he is going to show the Corinthians the most excellent way, his choice of verb is interesting. Significant. He uses δεικνυμι (*deiknumi*). Present tense, "I show"; or alternatively, "I exhibit or demonstrate". This is usually taken to mean that he "will tell" them of the "more excellent way", and then he does so in the chapter which now follows.

And I do not doubt that this is so. But he does not use here the future "will tell" - he uses δεικνυμι (*deiknumi*). He is saying, "*I am showing* you the way.*"* And I would say that whether he had this point consciously in mind or not, he did indeed show them, and present to them, and exhibit, this love in his own life and dealings with the Corinthians: for he exemplified this love.

That is, I take it that in describing how love behaves he is speaking out of his own understanding and experience. Because in this, as he says in 11:1, "I follow Christ."

So that when we are (as Paul says in 14:1 that we are) to pursue after love, it is to love like Christ himself that we are to seek. This love, God's own love, is poured out into our hearts through the Holy Spirit whom he has given to us (Romans 5:5).

# CHAPTER THIRTEEN

## SECTION 4:
## GIFTS AND MINISTRIES IN THE CHURCH (Cont.)

### 4. The Far Superior Way - The Way Of Love (13:1-13E)

### (a) The Need For the Way of Love (13:1-3)

**13:1** In the first stanza (13:1-3) Paul speaks again of some of the gifts to which he has referred in chapter 12. We are at the point of transition between Paul's general teaching about gifts, and his specific consideration of those two - tongues and prophecy - which he is about to discuss in detail in what he says next, in chapter 14.

He has laid a comprehensive foundation concerning the nature of gifts, to provide the background and context for his specific teaching about these two.

Paul's treatment of the concept of gifts and ministries that we have seen in chapter 12 is in a sense a detailed exposition, elaboration, and application of Jesus's parable about the talents in Matthew 25:14-30. In the story that Jesus told, a master (κυριος, *kurios*) gave different talents to different servants, more to one, fewer to another; the talents were given to be utilized; and the servants were held accountable to their κυριος (*kurios*) concerning how they used them. There are numerous points of difference, of course, between Paul's teaching and Christ's story, but there are enough points of overall similarity to lead me to conclude that Paul knew this story from Jesus, and had it in the back of his mind during his own exposition of the will and plan of God with respect to gifts.

At any rate, Paul has just been explaining how the Lord has given gifts and ministries to all his servants, for them to use, and before he goes on to give detailed consideration to tongues and prophecy, he explains first the overriding consideration in their use, all of them: the all-embracing importance of love. He has ended chapter 12 by saying, in effect, "You are chasing after spiritual gifts that you like. I will show you something so much better than that."

He begins here: "If I were to speak in the tongues of men and of angels" - Paul is undoubtedly reflecting the question of speaking in tongues which he has mentioned three times in chapter 12 (verses 10, 28, 30) and which he will discuss in some detail in chapter 14. But what exactly does he mean by what he says here?

"If" is ἐαν (*ean*), the Greek hypothetical "if" which, as Alford's commentary explains, "supposes a case which never has been exemplified". "The tongues of men" (ἀνθρωπων, *anthrōpōn*) mean the actual languages spoken by human beings; and similarly "and of angels" would indicate speaking the language of angels. And note that certainly this is *not* something which Paul is claiming he can do.

The concept of the "tongues of angels" has been the subject of much scholarly discussion. Some commentators look for Paul's meaning in Jewish speculations about what languages angels might speak. But Carson 58f. prefers to think that

> Paul may be writing hyperbolically to draw as sharp a contrast as possible with love. ... But I shall leave the question as to what language or languages we shall speak in the new heaven and new earth to those more gifted in speculation than I.

There is no need to suppose, as some do, that Paul's comment indicates the existence of a supernatural language which is then identified as the language which can be spoken by tongues-speakers. What we know for certain from Scripture about angelic language is that when angels speak they are perfectly understood by mankind and they perfectly communicate God's message to those they address. There is no reference anywhere in the Bible, not even a suggestion, that they themselves speak some other kind of language - any idea of angels having another language of their own is totally speculative, and in any case whether they do or not is irrelevant here.

For clearly the idea in Paul's mind is that of having the language facility, the command of language, which an angel has for doing his work: that is, communicating God's message, God's truth.

The common context in the whole first stanza is that of serving God to the fullest, as he deserves. The meaning in v.1 then must be, "If I could communicate the message of God entrusted to me as effectively and accurately as do God's messengers the angels ..."

Thus Calvin says here, "Paul begins with eloquence". So also John Wesley 625 on this verse: "with the eloquence of an angel." And in this vein Phillips translates, "If I speak with the eloquence of men and of angels". Similarly the Jerusalem Bible.

Commenting adversely on this approach to this verse Fee 630 says,

> This opening sentence is the reason for the entire argument: "If I speak in the tongues of men and of angels". One may be quite sure that

the Corinthians believed they did; indeed this best accounts for the sudden shift to the first person singular (cf. 14:14-15). On its own this could mean nothing more than "speak eloquently," as some have argued and as it is popularly understood. But since it is not on its own, but follows directly from 12:28-30 and anticipates 14:1-25, most likely this is either Paul's or their understanding (or both) of "speaking in tongues." "Tongues of men" would then refer to human speech, inspired by the Spirit but unknown to the speaker; "tongues of angels" would reflect an understanding that the tongues-speaker was communicating in the dialect(s) of heaven.

But Fee's rejection of what he calls the way "it is popularly understood" is based - as he says - upon his belief that either the Corinthians or Paul (or both) thought that the tongues-speaking at Corinth was in the language of angels, the language of heaven. In this belief Fee is representative of numerous other commentators. Thus similarly Barrett says, on "tongues" [comment on 12:10 and then on 13:1]:

> Here unintelligible speech is in mind, and not only discrimination but also interpretation is needed. ... apparently Paul thought that the unintelligible speech (unintelligible except to inspired interpretation) used by inspired participants in Christian worship was that in use among angels; this was not normally understood by human beings.

One question which comes to mind is: if the reference is to the language of heaven, why (in 13:1 and elsewhere) does Paul say "tongues", plural? Are the angels supposed to speak a variety of different languages in heaven?

If we do not agree with Fee in his belief (and I emphatically do not, as I explain next chapter), then there is no reason at all for rejecting the more traditional understanding. Therefore, much to be preferred is MacArthur's analysis (331):

> First, Paul imagines himself able to speak with the greatest possible eloquence, with the tongues of men and of angels. ... Paul's basic point in 13:1, however, is to convey the idea of being able to speak in all sorts of languages with great fluency and eloquence, far above the greatest linguist or orator. That the apostle is speaking in general and hypothetical terms is clear from the expression "tongues ... of angels". There is no biblical teaching of a unique or special angelic language or dialect. In the countless records of their speaking to men in Scripture, they always speak in the language of the person being addressed. There is no indication that they have a heavenly language of their own.

But Paul is not thinking merely of eloquence in itself, but rather of ***effectiveness in speaking, effectiveness in proclaiming the message of God***. He did not claim eloquence as such, and would have considered it a small virtue for God's service (see 1:17; 2:1-5). However, to be as effective in speaking not merely as the best of men but as an angel of God:

that would be something worthwhile! And to make his point pointedly here, he needs to postulate a possibility that on its face would be seen to be important or significant for God's service.

That is what gives weight to his contrast, "but have not love ..." The highest speaking ability not merely to which we could attain (tongues of men) but to which we could imagine attaining (tongues of angels), is only empty noise apart from love. It is likely that Paul is intending to indicate here something of the real situation of tongues-speaking at Corinth, where all that this "gift" was producing was a discordant cacophony.

**13:2** Next, Paul takes another three manifestations of the Spirit from his list in chapter 12. "If I were to have prophecy [as in 12:10b - the word used, προφητεια (*prophēteia*), is identical] so that I knew all mysteries; and to have all knowledge [as in 12:8b - the word used, γνωσις (*gnōsis*), is identical]; and if I were to have such total faith that I could move mountains [πιστις (*pistis*) as in 12:9a], and do not have love, I am nothing."

Hodge 267-268 gives a helpful comment here. He writes:

> The understanding or apprehension of mysteries, and not the posses-sion of knowledge, in its distinctive sense, was the result of the gift of prophecy. *Mysteries* are secrets, things undiscoverable by human rea-son, which divine revelation alone can make known. And the gift of prophecy was the gift of revelation by which such mysteries were com-municated (see 14:30). ... "And all knowledge": i.e., "and though I have all knowledge." By knowledge is meant the intellectual apprehension of revealed truth. It was the prerogative of the prophet to reveal, of the teacher to know and instruct.

Paul recognized, we can see, that there were more "mysteries of God" than had thus far been revealed to him.

He speaks here of the ultimate limit: to know - to understand, to com-prehend - *all* mysteries. But even if he were to know the whole lot, he is nothing without love. But, as we have just seen, knowing mysteries is an aspect of being a prophet, and so in this verse it goes with having prophecy. Whereas all knowledge looks back to "if I have". So the verse is to be understood like this:

"And if I have:
        (a) prophecy, and know all the mysteries, and
        (b) all knowledge,
and if I have (c) all faith so as to move mountains,
but do not have love,
I am nothing."

At first glance "know" (εἰδῶ, *eidō*) appears to govern both mysteries and knowledge, but taking it this way will end up with Paul saying "if I know all knowledge".

The key to 13:2 is to recall that Paul was not only an apostle but also a prophet and teacher (as we are told in Acts 13:1), and that to the apostles and prophets were revealed the mysteries of God (as Paul explains to us in Ephesians 3:2-9). Paul also refers to this in 1 Corinthians 4:1, where he tells us that they are stewards of the mysteries of God. And Jesus said to his disciples in Matthew 13:11 and parallels, "The knowledge of the mysteries of the kingdom of heaven has been given to you, but not to them."

Paul several times alludes to one mystery or another which God has revealed to him - and through him, to the church. Thus: Romans 11:25; 16:25; 1 Corinthians 2:7; 15:51; Ephesians 5:32; Colossians 2:2; 2 Thessalonians 2:7; 1 Timothy 3:9; 3:16. All these verses have the Greek word μυστεριον (*musterion*) - almost always translated "mystery" in the ECV, though the NIV and some other translations sometimes render this as "secret" or "secret things", etc. A μυστεριον (*musterion*), as is shown from a consideration of these references, is an eternal truth of God which has been kept secret until it is revealed to the apostles and prophets.

Paul's reference to "faith" here throws light on what is meant in 12:9 by that faith, πιστις (*pistis*), which is a specific manifestation of the Spirit and which is given to some believers only. For Paul's comment about moving mountains is a clear reminiscence of Jesus's teaching about faith moving a mountain (Matthew 17:20; 21:21; Mark 11:23), and this shows once again Paul's familiarity with a great deal of Jesus's teaching.

Thus "faith" here (and in 12:9a) is seen to mean, not "saving faith", which every believer must have in order to *be* a believer, but "miracle-working faith", which is vouchsafed to those to whom the Spirit wills (12:11).

Further, Lenski 550 writes:

> The faith referred to is mentioned by Jesus in Matt.7:22: "Lord, Lord, have we not ... in thy name cast out devils? and in thy name done many wonderful works?" Yet the Lord rejects these people.

Paul is not denigrating these gifts. Rather, he is setting them in perspective. To have all these, and yet to lack love, is to be nothing.

Again in this verse, as in v.1, the ἐαν (*ean*) form of "if" is used, with the subjunctive; Paul is not to be understood to be claiming such things for himself or postulating them for any of the Corinthians, but is making

out an extreme hypothetical case - "even if these things were to be possible" - to emphasize his point about love.

Carson 59 says:

> Certainly verse 2 finds Paul playing with hypothetical superlatives.
> He himself does not think that any prophet "can fathom all mysteries
> and all knowledge," since he goes on to say that at present "we know in
> part and we prophesy in part" (13:9).

**13:3** "If I were to give all I possess to the poor and if I were to deliver
up my body to be burned, but have not love, I gain nothing." Paul is not
continuing to draw other examples from his list of manifestations of the
Spirit (12:8-10); possibly he has used those that best suited his purpose.
Instead he now uses two illustrations of acts that on the face of them
would be worthy and helpful. The first, generosity, giving away one's
possessions for the benefit of others, is drawn once again from the teaching of Jesus (Matthew 19:21; Mark 10:21; Luke 18:22; 19:8).

The text of the second is uncertain. The commonly accepted reading,
of giving one's body to be burnt, is usually (and rightly) taken to refer,
in context, to some act of self-sacrifice on behalf of others. This *could*
refer to being martyred by being burnt, and it was understood in this way
by the early church Fathers (Kovacs 216f.). The commentaries point out
that there were no incidents of this kind recorded at the time Paul wrote,
but later there were many such, commencing with the burnings of Christians by Nero after the Fire of Rome. But Paul may have in mind the
three men in Daniel 3 who were consigned to the flames, and also the
Maccabean martyrs who were burnt (2 Maccabees 7 - 7:37 reads that the
last of the seven martyred brothers says, "I, like my brothers, give up
body and life for the laws of our ancestors, appealing to God" [NRSV].)

The alternate reading in v.3 is, "that I might give my body in order
that I may boast", that is to say, "in order that I would have something to
boast about". The thought would be that in some way the yielding up of
his body would be in circumstances to be considered praiseworthy, and
valid grounds for boasting.

With either reading, the point is that Paul is speaking of yielding up
his body in some way which would ordinarily be considered worthwhile
and meritorious. His argument in this verse proceeds thus: (a) If I were
to give up all my possessions to help the needy, so that I were left with
nothing but myself, and then (b) if I were to give up all I had left - that
is, my body itself.

If Paul were to act thus, but without love, he would not achieve anything by it or be benefited or advantaged in any way. Paul here, in a very
vivid and emphatic way, takes the emphasis off *what* a person actually

does in God's service and in the church, and puts it on *how* he does it and *why* he does it. Lenski 552 comments on this verse:

> Since Paul speaks hypothetically in both instances, and since we know about no actual cases of either kind, it seems best to abide by the hypotheses and to go no further. Both are suppositions of an extreme action and no more. These acts are apparently prompted by love yet in reality are not the result of love.

## (b) The Explanation of the Way of Love (13:4-7)

**13:4** After emphasizing the absolute necessity of love in whatever we do, Paul now explains in the second stanza the way in which love acts. Love is patient - it is slow to show resentment but bears with provocation. Love is kind, that is, acts in a kind-hearted, gracious way - this is possibly a verb which Paul himself has coined and "denotes the disposition to put oneself at the service of others" (Godet). Love is not envious; love is not boastful nor full of conceit ("nor does it cherish inflated ideas of its own importance" - Phillips).

Garland's analysis of this section of the Epistle (607-608) is worthy of note:

> Since virtually every behavioral problem at Corinth is mentioned in verses 4-7, Paul seems to say that the real problem is their lack of love, for love does not behave in the way they do. The section becomes quite ironic, because while Paul is praising love he is at the same time blaming the Corinthians.

**13:5** Love does not display bad manners - it is not forgetful of politeness and respectfulness; it does not seek to gain its own advantage; it is not irritable or touchy - it does not take offence; it does not keep a record of wrongdoing.

**13:6** Love takes no delight in evil or injustice; but it is full of joy when truth prevails.

**13:7** Love is always ready to excuse, and anxious to offer protection; it is full of trust in every way - it does not lose faith in people; it continues to have hope; it endures everything, bearing up under any burden.

Numerous people have declared that they consider this presentation of the nature of love to be the greatest thing Paul has ever written. We need to note carefully, and take much to heart, what Paul says here concerning love: what it is, what it is not.

But we must not fail to take account at the same time of how this chapter relates to the issues of the wider context of gifts and ministries at Corinth. Paul now proceeds to tell us important truths concerning these.

## (c) The Permanence of the Way of Love (13:8-13E)

**13:8-10** Love never ends. In this it differs from prophecy, tongues, and knowledge, for they (says Paul) *will* come to an end. Paul commenced this chapter by showing that it is love that gives meaning to these three (see verses 1 and 2); now he shows that love is permanent while they are but temporary. But just what is Paul speaking about here? What exactly is he telling us?

Consider: now, in our present day, we have available for ourselves the revelation of God's will and plan recorded in Scripture. But in the nature of the case there was an Interval, a term for the gap between the ending of the Old Testament era and the availability of the revelation for the new age which is now found in the New Testament Scriptures.

The Old Testament was God's revelation in the old era, the former dispensation, leading up to the coming of the Messiah. But in the new era inaugurated by Christ's coming, there would be new insights, new revelations of God's eternal plan for mankind.

Paul many times refers to this.

For example, in Romans 16:25-26, "... the revelation of the mystery that was kept secret for long ages but has now been disclosed and through the prophetic writings has been made known to all nations according to the command of the eternal God." And also earlier in our present Epistle when he says (1 Corinthians 2:7) "we impart a secret (μυστεριον, *musterion*) and hidden wisdom of God, which God decreed before the ages for our glory." And in Ephesians 1:8-10: "in all wisdom and insight making known to us the mystery of his will, according to his purpose, which he set forth in Christ as a plan for the fullness of time, to unite all things in him, things in heaven and things on earth."

And Paul tells us that during this Interval the Holy Spirit was giving direct guidance to the church by revealing God's truth to the apostles and prophets. For in addition to the apostles, God now raised up prophets to teach and instruct the church. This was a gift and a calling parallel to apostleship and second only to it ("And God has appointed in the church first apostles, second prophets ...": 12:28; cf. also Ephesians 4:11, "And he gave the apostles, the prophets ... to equip the saints").

Paul explains something of this in Ephesians 3:2-5: "... the stewardship of God's grace ... was given to me for you, how the mystery was made known to me by revelation, as I have written briefly. When you read this, you can perceive my insight into the mystery of Christ, which was not made known to the sons of men in other generations as it has now been revealed to his holy apostles and prophets by the Spirit."

So here we have it, in these verses: Paul is telling us how God effected the change-over from the old era to the new era, and what God's "transitional arrangements" were. It was by the Spirit's direct miraculous revelation to "his holy apostles and prophets" of the new truths for the new era, things up to this point hidden in the secret counsels of God.

Thus the ministry of the apostles and prophets was unique in the establishment and spread of the church - Paul goes so far as to state that the church is "built on the foundation of the apostles and prophets, with Christ Jesus himself as the chief cornerstone" (Ephesians 2:20) - because this special gift of prophecy, and the revelations of knowledge which were granted in the early church, were a part of the process of its foundation and establishment.

So, as we can see from the records of the speeches and writings of the apostles during the period of the Interval, this prophecy, this "communication of wisdom" and "communication of knowledge" (to use Paul's terms, 12:8), consisted of three things:

The teaching and explanation of,

*firstly*, the life and ministry of Christ on the one hand, and,

*secondly*, on the other hand, of the Old Testament, the Bible of the early church: the message of which had to be taken and interpreted and applied, and expanded and supplemented as required, in order to give the Christians the knowledge that they needed for what to believe, and how to live.

Then, *thirdly*, as required, this was supplemented further by inspired prophetic insights and direct supernatural revelations of knowledge, as we have seen Paul explaining in Ephesians 3.

To all of this Paul refers in these verses 1 Corinthians 13:8-9, when he speaks of prophecies and knowledge. In v.8 he mentions also that tongues will cease, παυσονται (*pausontai*) - I shall talk further about tongues in considering the next chapter. But in reference to both prophecies and knowledge Paul uses a different word, καταργεω (*katargeō*), in the future passive. Both of these, he says, will be brought to an end.

Their disadvantage, their shortcoming, their limitation, was (as Paul tells us in v.9), that they were partial and incomplete.

What in fact next happened was twofold:

On the one hand, the prophetic teachings and the revelations of knowledge became superseded by and incorporated into the New Testament.

Think here for example of Paul's own teachings in his Epistles; but this is true of all the New Testament writings.

And on the other hand, with the writing and dissemination of the New Testament books, these special gifts exhibited by apostles and prophets (to which Paul has so many times referred) ceased in the church (as Paul had said that they would). Concerning these gifts, Jonathan Edwards [*Charity and Its Fruits* 29-30; cited by Wilson 174-175] sums up thus:

> They ... were bestowed on the prophets and apostles to enable them to reveal the mind and will of God before the canon of Scripture was complete, and so on the primitive church, in order to the founding and establishing of it in the world. But since the canon of Scripture has been completed, and the Christian church fully founded and established, these extraordinary gifts have ceased.

And thus these special revelations through apostles and prophets, partial and incomplete as they were, became replaced by the complete form of God's revelation for this present age, which we refer to as the New Testament - which of course is also the completion of the canon of the Bible.

So I take it that ***this*** is what Paul is referring to in v.10: that "the complete", the το τελειον (*to teleion*) - which has replaced the partial and incomplete, the ἐκ μερους (*ek merous*) - is the fullness of God's revelation which we have in Scripture. For the completeness of v.10 is the completeness of which the prophecies and knowledge of the Interval were only partial.

So as I read this passage, this το τελειον (*to teleion*) can only refer to the totality and completeness of the New Testament as the revelation of God for this age. If we take seriously the New Testament as being the completion and the completeness of God's divine revelation to us, this fits perfectly (it seems to me) with what Paul is saying here.

But this is not the only way that το τελειον can be taken. Carson 68f. identifies three approaches to the interpretation of το τελειον: that it refers to:

**(a)** the maturity of the church, or
**(b)** the completion of the canon of Scripture (i.e. the view that I myself accept), or
**(c)** the *parousia*, the *eschatos* (which Carson terms the majority view).

Garland holds this third view, which he summarizes (622) thus: "'the perfect' refers to the state of affairs brought about by the parousia"; and he interprets the passage from this perspective.

Carson 70 shows the significance of this difference of interpretational approach when he says,

> the gifts of prophecy, knowledge and tongues ... will pass away at some point future to Paul's writing, designated by him 'perfection'. If this point can be located in the first or second century, then no putative gift of prophecy, knowledge or tongues is valid today. Conversely, if this point is located at the parousia, then there is nothing in this passage to preclude a valid gift of tongues or prophecy today.

On balance, Carson himself opts (70) for the same view as Garland, but he qualifies it (72) with a reference to "historical objections that argue the gifts of prophecy and tongues actually did cease."

To the contrary of Garland, Gordon Clark 211 states,

> The usual Protestant doctrine is that prophecy, miracles, and the gift of speaking in foreign tongues ceased at the end of the apostolic age. Second century Christian literature seems to be devoid of accounts of these gifts.

Clark's summary (215) of Paul's meaning is, "Hence, the time of cessation that Paul implies is not the return of Christ, but the completion of the canon."

**13:8-12** It will assist an understanding of what Paul's meaning is here to notice several Greek key words and expressions. Oftentimes the standard versions give misleading or unhelpful renderings of the Greek where more literal translation would help us to understand how Paul is using his words, and expressing his meaning.

First, to take an overview of this section of chapter 13, and look at the structure and some key words. Let us consider these verses set out in a table, so as to compare their wording with each other, in order to note the meaning Paul is bringing out from the clear pattern he gives us. And then we look at the ways in which they are translated, especially in the NIV.

8. "But as for    prophecies, they will be  καταργηθησονται
                                                (*katargēthēsontai*);
   or   as for   tongues,     they will    παυσονται (*pausontai*);
   or   as for   knowledge,  it    will be   καταργηθησεται
                                                (*katargēthēsetai*).

9. For we know    in part (ἐκ μερους, *ek merous*),
   and we prophesy in part (ἐκ μερους, *ek merous*).

10. But whenever (ὅταν, *hotan*) the complete (το τελειον,
                                          *to teleion*) should come,
    that which is    in part (ἐκ μερους, *ek merous*)
                          will be καταργηθησεται (*katargēthēsetai*).

11. When (ὅτε, *hote*) I was                an infant (νήπιος, *nēpios*),
              I used to talk    like      an infant,
              I used to think   like     an infant,
              I used to reason like    an infant.
    Since (ὅτε, *hote*) I   have reached         adulthood
    I have κατήργηκα (*katērgēka*) the things of an infant.

12. For at the present time (ἀρτι, *arti*) we see through a mirror
                                      indistinctly/indirectly,
    but at that       time (τοτε, *tote*)          face to face;
      at the present time (ἀρτι, *arti*) I know in part (*ek merous*)
    but at that       time (τοτε, *tote*) I shall know       fully,
            just as also     I have been known  fully."

It is important to note Paul's distinct pattern in these verses - the parallels and contrasts. The NIV is an unreliable guide here (it obscures it). The ESV/NRSV is much more accurate.

Gromacki's Commentary on v. 8 gives this explanation:

> Both verbs used for prophecy and knowledge are identical [καταργεω, *katargeō*] and indicate that their purpose will be rendered useless by the influence of something outside of themselves. However, the verb for "tongues" reveals that its purpose will cease on its own even before the coming of that which will render the other two unnecessary.

The verb which refers to tongues, παυω (*pauō*), means "stop" or "cease", and it is in the middle voice, and thus the meaning can be taken (as by Gromacki here), "tongues will cease of themselves", or "tongues will come to an end by themselves".

Lattimore translates v.10: "For we understand in part and we prophecy in part, but when completeness comes, what is in part will vanish away." And Phillips translates this as: "For our knowledge is always incomplete, and our prophecy is always incomplete, and when the complete comes, that is the end of the incomplete."

In fact, Phillips's New Testament itself is a prime example of this very thing. First, J B Phillips translated and published the Epistles under the title *Letters to Young Churches*. Then the Gospels, and *The Young Church in Action*, i.e. the Acts; then finally Revelation. Each of these was, of course, just a part of the New Testament, but these portions, these "partials", existed separately. But then after Revelation was completed, the entire Phillips New Testament was published. And today *Letters to Young Churches* or *The Young Church in Action* are not in print. Why? Because when that which was complete had come, that which was partial was absorbed and superseded.

And this is exactly what is true also of the ***content*** of the revelations of prophecy and knowledge: they were absorbed into the New Testament as a whole when the canon was completed.

Gordon Clark 212f. comments thus on this passage:

> Miracles and tongues were for the purpose of guaranteeing the divine origin of apostolic doctrine. They ceased when the revelation was completed. Even the word *knowledge* is better understood this way. Instead of comparing present-day extensive study of the New Testament with Justin's painfully inadequate understanding of the Atonement, it would be better to take *knowledge* as the apostolic process of revealing new knowledge. This was completed, and revelation ceased.

The NIV translates v.10 as: "But when perfection comes the imperfect disappears." As can be seen from where I have set this passage out above, the expression that the NIV has translated as "imperfect", which is being contrasted with το τελειον, *to teleion* (and which it has translated as "perfection") is actually ἐκ μερους (*ek merous*), the ***same words*** that in the preceding verse it twice translated as "in part".

To translate το τελειον *to teleion* as "perfection" here is pushing the reader to take it as a reference to the end time, for where but then shall we find perfection? And thus the NIV's term "imperfect" will then be given a moral sense by the reader.

Instead, rather, the NRSV translates: "But when the complete comes, the partial will come to an end." This is much better: for ***that*** is what is under discussion - partial prophecy and partial knowledge in v.9, contrasted with what is complete (v.10), at which time what is partial will be καταργηθησεται (*katargēthēsetai*). And, in context, the "completion", το τελειον (*to teleion*), is clearly the completion, the completeness in God's intention, of prophecy and knowledge.

This is clearly shown in the translations of this verse (set out above) of Lattimore and Phillips. Similarly others.

It seems to me a rather forced interpretation to take "the perfect", το τελειον (*to teleion*), to refer to the Second Coming or the "Age of Perfection" to come. The word is never used with this meaning elsewhere, which reduces the likelihood that it would have such a meaning here. And it would break the normal rules of grammar for it to refer to the coming of Christ, "the Perfect One", because it is neuter gender (it would need to be masculine if it referred to Christ). The meaning of το τελειον (*to teleion*) is "completed", "whole", "entire", "mature", and it is being used here in contrast with that which is ἐκ μερους (*ek merous*), "in part", "partial" or "incomplete".

As this expression with which it contrasts, "in part", refers to the communication of God's truth to the church, which is "incomplete" through prophecy and gifts of knowledge, the natural meaning of Paul's words is that a complete and final communication of God's truth will come, and when it does then the need for the incomplete means (that is, the special direct revelation of prophecy and revelation of knowledge through apostles and prophets) will have passed away.

Some have objected to this interpretation on the ground that Paul was expecting Christ's Return at any time and he knew nothing of the idea of a New Testament canon. The answer is **(a)** that this objection is speculative not factual (there is evidence that Paul was aware of an interval before the Second Coming even if he did not know how long it was to be - see 2 Thessalonians; I have discussed this earlier at 7:25), **(b)** that Paul could know anything God chose to reveal to him, and **(c)** that in any case it was not necessary for Paul to "know" about the New Testament canon as such for him to be led by the Spirit to understand that the existing special revelations of prophecy and knowledge were about to be superseded by a more complete form of inspired revelation. This at any rate is what Paul says. And I hold that the most reasonable understanding of his words is that these words were fulfilled by the writing of the New Testament.

It is difficult to give a particular time as the actual date by which any of these things came to an end, but it is worthy of note that Hebrews 2:3b-4 says, "such a great salvation ... was declared at first by the Lord, and it was attested to us by those who heard, while God also bore witness by signs and wonders and various miracles and by gifts ('distributions', μερισμοις, *merismois*) of the Holy Spirit distributed according to his will." This comment is written referring to the past (the aorist tense has been used) and appears to indicate that the miraculous attesting manifestations of the Holy Spirit (and this would include the miraculous gifts of prophecies, tongues, and knowledge) had ceased before Hebrews was written.

**13:11** Paul gives two illustrations of the coming change. In this first one, Paul contrasts the speaking, thinking, and reasoning ability of a man with himself when he was an infant (νηπιος, *nēpios*). As an adult, Paul says he has κατηργηκα (*katērgēka*) the things (the speaking, thinking, reasoning) of an infant. The word Paul uses - again, καταργεω (*katargeō*) - is a key word here. As can be seen from the Greek of these verses (set out above, on v.8), Paul uses this same word four times in these four verses (though you would not know this fact from the NIV, which translates it differently for each of these four occasions). Its meaning is (in the passive): "to be nullified, canceled, superseded, to be rendered ineffective or inoperative". The ESV and the NRSV render it consistently all four times: the ESV, in the first three occurrences, where it is a future passive, as "will pass away" and in v.11, where it is perfect active, as "I gave up"; the NRSV, "will come to an end" (when future passive), and then in v.11 as "I put an end to".

But in Paul's illustration, has the man, as an adult, really "put an end to" the speaking, thinking, reasoning he did as an infant? No: rather, the infant's processes of speaking, thinking, and reasoning, have grown and developed, and they have reached a maturity, a stage of fruition, of completion, in adulthood. There has been an expansion, a development, but it can hardly be said that somewhere along the road there was a discontinuity, a point where one's speaking, thinking, reasoning, was brought to an end - and replaced with something else.

Paul uses imperfect verbs here: "I used to speak, used to think, used to reason", allowing for the process of growth. There has been total continuity, but *what used to be* has been superseded by the more complete reality of adulthood.

When you become a man you do not abandon everything you were before. Especially your knowledge that you have been gaining. Your "partial", as you were growing up, becomes absorbed into the whole, which you now are as a man.

**13:12** The second illustration is the difference between looking at something in a mirror of polished metal, and seeing that same thing face to face. The metal reflection is partial and not as clear and as accurate as full face-to-face vision. From a mirror you get a pretty good general impression; but seeing something directly allows you to have a much better focus, to get things into perspective, to appreciate the details. So the revelation of God will similarly be clear when "the complete, the perfect" has come. The present partial knowledge will become complete knowledge of all that God wants us to know on earth.

But this does not mean that everything you saw before is totally wrong, so that you have to abandon it completely. No - when you can see something directly rather than indirectly, you refine your understanding of it, especially the details.

Paul's comment in this verse is taken by some as referring to the contrast between the present state of our knowledge compared with what we shall know in eternity. This is indeed a valid understanding of truth; but it is not the meaning of what Paul is saying here. In its present context the passage is contrasting the knowledge that the people of God had (Paul uses himself as a typical example) under the Old Dispensation plus what they received through prophecies and gifts of knowledge, in comparison with the completeness (το τελειον, *to teleion*, v.10) of the New Testament revelation, which tells us everything that God is revealing to us. "But at that time (i.e. when το τελειον, *to teleion*, comes), I shall know the things of God as fully as God - or anyone - has come to know me."

Some expositors say that we do not know and cannot know fully now, in this life, and they therefore draw the conclusion that "to know fully" must refer to after Christ returns, because only then shall we know fully. But this is missing the point here, where the comment is referring to the completeness of God's revelation to us: in this sense, to say that we do not now know fully all that God wishes us to know in his revelation would be equivalent to saying that the Bible is incomplete or inadequate in revealing to us all that God wants us to know. Something I do not think we would really want to say.

**13:13E** Paul sums up: faith, hope and love "remain", or, "continue": that is, during this present time, after prophecies, tongues, and knowledge have come to an end. Of these, love is the greatest. Thus Paul gives us a sense of perspective about the relative values of all the things he has been discussing.

When we look at what Paul explains here we can see that love is about ***behavior*** (what we do), not about ***sentiment*** (what we feel). It is a matter of conduct, not emotion. Love is not a warm fuzzy feeling, but a question of what we do (and don't do).

If we fully allow the truth of what this chapter says to seize our souls, it will above all affect our attitudes. We will be looking for opportunities of behaving in a way that shows, that demonstrates, that puts into practice, loving behavior. It is a very powerful and pervasive challenge.

# CHAPTER FOURTEEN

## SECTION 4:
## GIFTS AND MINISTRIES IN THE CHURCH (Continued)

### 5. The Role of Tongues And Prophecy (14:1-40E)

### INTRODUCTION

In this section of his Epistle Paul has several times so far referred to speaking in tongues. He has said it is a grace gift from God, one of the many grace gifts which God has given his people. He has said that without love it is but empty, chaotic noise. And he has said it is going to cease. But while these were all just passing references, so to speak, they were part of his preparing the ground for a full and careful discussion of this issue: because clearly it was a *major* issue at Corinth, and the Corinthians - or some of them - were getting it wrong, and misusing and abusing it.

Paul's approach now is extraordinarily considerate and conciliatory. He seeks to persuade them gently, but their abuse of this grace gift must be corrected, because it is causing harm to the body and damage to the church's witness to outsiders, who are liable to say that the Christians have gone mad. So Paul's purpose is clear: in discussing this issue in careful detail he intends to help them to set this gift in perspective, and to use it as God intended.

Speaking in tongues is only mentioned four times in the entire New Testament. It is discussed in some detail in this section (chapters 12 to 14), and the other three occurrences are in Acts (2:4-13; 10:46; and 19:6). There is a fifth reference in the textually dubious and highly suspect longer ending of Mark's Gospel (16:17).

When on the Day of Pentecost the pilgrims in Jerusalem heard the hundred and twenty excited disciples speaking in tongues, they exclaimed in amazement and perplexity, "What does this mean?" (Acts 2:12.) Christians since have also been amazed and perplexed, and are similarly asking, "What does this mean?"

And similarly as we read Paul's teaching in 1 Corinthians today we face this serious conundrum: whatever is Paul talking about? For one of the most crucial issues here is whether "speaking in tongues" has the same meaning with Luke in Acts as with Paul in 1 Corinthians. There are several different viewpoints about this that are held in the church - differences which result in completely differing interpretations of what Paul says and, in consequence, differences of putting his teaching into practice.

A vast number of dedicated Christians have written at length and in detail about this issue, and have come to very different conclusions. Some of these books I will mention.

Johnson 226-229 assesses the issue and concludes, "There are at least five plausible interpretations of this kind of speech." He lists these as:

"1. Foreign languages unknown to the speaker."

"2. Audible sounds, languagelike but not structured language."

"3. Liturgical, archaic or rhythmic phrases." (Concerning this view, he comments that "it doesn't seem to fit 14:8-13, 21-25.")

"4. Ecstatic speech."

"5. Language of the unconscious released in 'groans that words cannot express'."

To these we could add a sixth interpretation, as I have mentioned (when discussing 13:1), that it is "tongues of angels".

So: what then does Paul mean in his Epistle by "speaking in tongues"? As we move forward, we should note the wise words of Packer in *Keep in Step With the Spirit* 207:

On the nature, worth, provenance, and cessation of New Testament tongues, much is obscure and must remain so. Various interpretations on key points are viable, and perhaps the worst error in handling the relevant passages is to claim or insinuate that perfect clarity or certainty marks one's own view. The texts ... are too problematical for that.

This is a word of caution for us to keep in mind in all that follows.

But of course, even if there might just possibly be some doubt in our minds at the present moment as to exactly what was going on at Corinth, at least we can be certain of one thing: obviously Paul and the Corinthians knew what was happening, didn't they? Didn't they?

I'm not so totally sure. I wonder whether - in spite of all the information he was receiving about the situation at Corinth - there was possibly a tiny niggly doubt in Paul's mind as to just exactly what was going on. I shall discuss this question in due course.

## i) Foreign Languages Previously Unknown to the Speaker

The first interpretation Johnson lists is the traditional one, which was the standard one - indeed, almost the invariable one - held in the church until about 1900. This older or "traditional" interpretation is stated thus by Gromacki [*The Modern Tongues Movement* 1972: 63, 67-68, and 1977:153]:

> Rather than dividing languages into known and unknown, Paul is affirming that all tongues phenomena were in the form of definite languages, not ecstatic utterances. ... The use of *glōssa* and the description of the phenomenon in the New Testament reveal that only speaking in known languages was involved. ... The gift of tongues was the Spirit-given ability to speak in known foreign languages (unknown and unlearned by the speaker).

What happened at Pentecost can be summed up in the words of Burdick 15-16:

> The term "tongue" (*glōssa*) was commonly used in Greek to refer both to the physical organ of speech (Luke 1:64) and to the speech or language which the physical organ produces. Here the word "other" (*heterais*) [Acts 2:4] suggests that the believers spoke in different languages from that which was native to them, a fact which is borne out by the surprise described in verses 7-8. This is further confirmed by v.6, where it is said that "every man heard them speak in his own language." The word translated as "language" is *dialektō* from which our word *dialect* comes. The two terms *tongue* (*glōssa*) and *language* (*dialektos*) are obviously used interchangeably here, making it clear that the disciples were speaking in other languages. What those languages were is indicated in verses 8-11, namely, the native languages of such areas as Parthia, Media, Elam, Mesopotamia, Judea, Cappadocia, Pontus, Asia and Phrygia.
>
> There can therefore be no doubt that the tongues described in Acts 2 were foreign languages. The phenomenon was a miracle enabling the disciples to speak in languages which were not native to them and which they had not learned by normal educative processes.

Concerning the word "tongue", we see that in Revelation 7:9 John writes of a great multitude "from all tribes and peoples and languages" before the throne - and "languages" is γλωσσα (*glōssa*); similarly 5:9; 10:11; and numerous other references.

The view that "tongues" in Acts and 1 Corinthians (and Mark 16:17) always refers to human languages was the common view of the early church Fathers. Kovacs 229 summarizes the way the situation was understood by early commentators:

> Patristic authors, like many later interpreters, tend to understand 1 Corinthians 12-14 and Acts 2 to refer to the same phenomenon.

John Chrysostom writes of it thus (Kovacs 196):

> One would suddenly speak in Persian, another in Latin, another in the language of the Indians or of some other people. ... Once the

apostles had received this first sign, other believers received the spiritual gift of tongues, and not only this gift but several others as well.

And Augustine says (Kovacs 124):

> There in Jerusalem, when the Lord had ascended into heaven and after ten days kept his promise by sending the Holy Spirit, the disciples, filled with the Holy Spirit, spoke in the languages of all the nations.

John Chrysostom said further, on tongues and interpretation, which he understood to mean "translation" (Kovacs 203):

> The one [speaking] knew what he himself was saying, but he could not interpret for another. The interpreter had both these abilities, or at least the second. Now the former was thought to be a great gift since it was the first that the apostles received, and the majority of the Corinthians possessed it.

Theodoret (Kovacs 230) explains the purpose of the gift of tongues as being to facilitate the evangelism of those of other language groups: many of the Corinthians had received this gift of thus speaking in a foreign language, but under the usual circumstances in Corinth the gift was not helpful to the Corinthian congregation:

> Because of the diversity of human languages, preachers received the ability to speak in tongues so that when they came to the inhabitants of India, they could use their own language to bring them God's message. Again, by using the language of each people, they could proclaim the gospel to Persians or Scythians or Romans or Egyptians. But for anyone speaking in Corinth it was pointless to use the languages of the Scythians or Persians or Egyptians, since the Corinthians could not understand them. That is why the apostle says that "one who speaks in tongues speaks not to men but to God". For he adds this: "for no one understands him."

Thus Pack [71-72] says in summary,

> Irenaeus believed that Paul was able to speak in many languages, and that these languages were human languages he had not learned but was inspired to speak. ... Chrysostom understood the gift of speaking in tongues as the gift of speaking unlearned human languages. While he recognized that by his time these things had ceased ... he describes the gift of speaking in tongues in these words ...

Pack then quotes Chrysostom (as above), and continues:

> Through this entire period there is no other understanding of the New Testament speaking in tongues, *glōssa*, than speaking in human languages that one has not learned but which are somewhere spoken among men.

This also is the meaning of tongues held by Cyril of Alexandria, Aquinas, Luther, Calvin, Wesley, Clarke, Alford, Barnes, Matthew

Henry, Hodge, Ironside, Lange, Lenski, Rice, and numerous current writers.

John Wesley says, in his *Explanatory Notes Upon the New Testament* [625, 629, 631]:

> "Though I speak with all the tongues" - which are upon earth ... "Unless ye utter by the tongue" - which is miraculously given you. "Words easy to be understood" - by the hearers. ... It seems "the gift of tongues" was an instantaneous knowledge of a tongue till then unknown, which he that received it could afterwards speak when he thought fit, without any new miracle.

So also Adam Clarke defines "tongues" in his comment on 12:10 as being

> *Different languages*, which they had never learned, and which God gave them for the immediate instruction of people of different countries who attended their ministry.

However, there are some commentators who, while agreeing that the gift was the understanding of human languages, have said the miracle lay in the *hearing*, not in the *speaking*. Thus Johnson 227 says, "Acts 2 can easily be understood as a miracle of hearing rather than of speaking."

But the wording of the accounts in Acts rules this out. What is decisively against this view is that this miracle is **always** described as "speaking in tongues", and **never** as "hearing in tongues". In Acts 2:4 we are informed that the disciples "began to speak in other tongues, as the Spirit gave them utterance" - i.e. the Spirit gave them this speaking ability. This is stated before there is any mention of anyone *hearing* what was being said. Moreover, in Acts 19:6 it is stated quite explicitly that they **spoke** in tongues, without any mention of "hearing".

Thus we must conclude that in Acts the miracle was in the speaking, and the speaking was in foreign languages that were spoken at that time by the peoples living around the Mediterranean basin and elsewhere. And that, as the listeners described it, the disciples were "telling in our own tongues the mighty works of God" (Acts 2:11) - which we may presume were the deeds of Jesus and then his resurrection from the dead: that is, the gospel message.

Thus we have good reason to take it that the miracle which we see in Acts 2 was the gift of speaking unlearned foreign languages. But was this "speaking in tongues" in Acts the same gift which was being exercised in the church at Corinth?

Numbers of commentators say a confident "No!" to this: the tongues at Corinth must have been different from the tongues in Acts, because the point of the passage in Acts is that everyone understood them whereas the point in 1 Corinthians 14 is that nobody understood them. So Leon Morris 191 says that 14:2 "makes it plain that the gift spoken of here is different from that in Acts ii, where all men understood."

This also is Garland's viewpoint: he examines this issue, and then says quite firmly (584), "This rules out the view that tongues refer to the miraculous ability to speak in unlearned languages."

But that is Paul's whole point: he is criticizing the Corinthians engaging in speaking in tongues when there is no one present speaking that language (or else it would have been a situation parallel to Pentecost) but simply as a show-off, as a "status sign".

We should let our understanding of "speaking in tongues" in Acts guide our understanding of the meaning of exactly the same term when it is used in 1 Corinthians. This is to apply what I take to be the starting point with any biblical exegesis. It is a basic principle of biblical interpretation that one passage of Scripture in which the meaning of something is clear should be used to clarify another passage of Scripture in which the meaning of that issue is more obscure. This has sometimes been expressed as, "The best commentary upon a difficult passage of Scripture is another passage of Scripture."

As we have seen, the meaning of the gift of tongues in Acts 2 is very clear: As the Spirit gave them utterance, the believers spoke in other human languages, for these were recognized by their hearers, who understood what was being said to them in those languages. Therefore our initial expectation will naturally be that "to speak in tongues" (λαλειν γλωσσαις, *lalein glōssais*) in 1 Corinthians 14 will have the same meaning that the same words had in Acts 2:4. This initial expectation must then be tested by the examination of the place where these words occur in 1 Corinthians 14.

Alford [vol II pages 14-16] writes quite strongly on Acts 2:

> There can be no question in any unprejudiced mind that the fact which this narrative sets before us is that the disciples began to *speak in various languages, viz, the languages of the various nations below enumerated, and perhaps others*. All attempts to evade this are connected with some forcing of the text, or some far-fetched and indefensible exegesis. ... How is this ἑτεραις γλωσσαις λαλειν related to the γλωσση λαλειν afterwards spoken of by St Paul? I answer that they are *one and the same thing*. ... I believe this narrative to furnish *the key* to the right understanding of 1 Cor. xiv. [Alford's italics]

On this question Lenski 504-505 clinches the matter:

> Luke's description as given in the Acts is decisive for what Paul writes in Corinthians. This is reversed by some. They seek to determine what happened at Corinth, and then either square Luke's account with

what they think occurred at Corinth or posit two different gifts of tongues. ... This method of approach is unsatisfactory. For Luke is the one who fully describes what the tongues are, while Paul takes for granted that his readers know what they are and therefore offers no description. Luke writes for a reader (Theophilus) who may never have heard of this gift, at least may never have seen this gift in operation. Paul writes for readers who have often heard members of their own congregation speak in tongues. This is decisive as to the Scriptural starting point.

## ii), iii) Audible Sounds or Liturgical Phrases

The other possible interpretations which have been proposed - that the "tongues" is the language of heaven or of angels, or a supernatural language taught by the Spirit, or an ecstatic utterance, and in any case not a human language - have in common that they either consider the "speaking in tongues" of 1 Corinthians to be different from that of Acts, or else they reinterpret Acts 2 against the natural sense of the words (which we have seen), so as to make this passage also refer to non-human speech.

Johnson's second and third interpretations were:

2. Audible sounds, languagelike but not structured language.

3. Liturgical, archaic or rhythmic phrases.

Concerning the third of these, Johnson commented that "it doesn't seem to fit 14:8-13, 21-25" - a comment which is equally relevant to the second one also.

## iv) Ecstatic Speech

Johnson's fourth listed interpretation notes that some writers consider the tongues of 1 Corinthians were not human languages but ecstatic speech. The position of these exegetes is summed up thus by Hillis 102: "While Pentecost featured known languages, 1 Corinthians 13:1 and 14:2 point to ecstatic speech."

But Watson Mills (*Understanding Speaking in Tongues* 34-38) denies the Pentecost experience was known languages:

Even the Pentecost narrative itself does not consistently maintain that a miracle of foreign languages occurred. Some of those present said, "They are filled with new wine." This is not the impression that foreign languages would have made. Further, when Peter begins to preach, he takes his start from the accusation of drunkenness, and he never mentions foreign languages. His introduction presupposes that everyone has *not* understood what he said. ... What then is glossolalia in the context of Acts 2? It is an attempt to express the inexpressible: the indwelling of the Spirit of God in the lives of men. When the *kerygma* sank home to a responsive heart, ordinary human language could not express the emotions that were aroused; therefore, the believer broke forth in ecstatic speech.

This interpretation of Paul's words is that he is here referring to, and encouraging the use of, speaking in an "ecstatic" or "spiritual" language, an "unknown tongue". This interpretation has in some measure derived from the Authorized Version's translation of γλωσσα (*glōssa*) in this chapter: for the AV/KJV renders it as "unknown tongue". Concerning this rendering Burdick [19] says,

> It should be noted first of all that the term "unknown", which occurs in verses 2, 4, 13, 14, 19 and 27, does not occur in any Greek manuscripts. Paul does not say that the tongue is unknown; consequently it is possible that the languages referred to were foreign languages known and used by the various nations of earth. In that case the languages were merely unknown to the people of Corinth just as the Arabic, Urdu, Danish and Russian languages are not familiar to the average church member in America today. There is nothing in this chapter which requires that ecstatic heavenly languages be found here. The statement that the uninterpreted tongue speaks only to God (v.2) demands nothing more than a foreign language which the hearer does not understand. The statement that he who speaks in an uninterpreted tongue only edifies himself (v.4) does not demand an ecstatic heavenly language. Such a speaker edifies no one else because the language used is as foreign to the hearers as Urdu is to the average American.

Ecstatic speaking or speaking in special "divine" languages, was a feature of the pagan religions of Corinth and the Greek world generally. Thus Dillow points out [18-19, 117-118],

> It is sometimes argued that the fact that a gift of interpretation was required in Corinthians and not at Pentecost (Acts 2) suggests that the tongues in Acts 2 were languages but the tongues in 1 Corinthians were ecstatic utterances. ... The effectiveness of glossolalia as an authenticating sign depended on its *difference* from the ecstatic gobbledegook in Hellenistic religion. ... To pray in tongues involves only the human spirit. This tendency probably was brought over [by the Corinthians] from their heathen background of ecstatic speech in connection with Diana worship. They were using the legitimate gift of tongues in the way they used to use ecstatic speech in their pagan worship before becoming Christians. When they prayed in ecstatic speech to Diana, their mind was not engaged. It was this kind of prayer that Jesus had forbidden in Matthew 6:7. They were now praying in the New Testament gift of foreign languages and their mind wasn't engaged either. To pray in ecstatic speech or even in New Testament tongues without engaging the mind is a heathen practice.

If therefore Paul's speaking in tongues (which - v.18 - he did more than any of them) was a speaking of a non-human language or ecstatic speech or gibberish, this would be to do what the pagans did: how would it honor the Lord? If speaking in tongues was not in a human language, how was the behavior of the Corinthian Christians who spoke in tongues any different from that of the devotees of pagan religions in Corinth? For they did the same thing.

Speaking in tongues was to speak as the Spirit gave the word (Acts 2:4), and this was one of the gifts in which the Spirit manifested himself (12:10-11). How was it a manifestation of the **Holy Spirit** if it was the same as the manifestation of heathen spirits? How was it (14:22) a sign from the Lord to unbelievers? How could behaving like heathen religious practitioners ever be in any sense a gift from God?

All these things require that the gift of tongues had to be clearly and obviously a different thing from the speaking in a "divine" language by the pagans.

The NEB has translated "tongues" throughout 1 Corinthians 14 as "ecstatic speech", "ecstatic utterance", "the language of ecstasy", "the tongues of ecstasy" or "the language of inspiration". Thus readers of this version have the matter decided for them by the translators. This translation was criticized by Robert H Gundry in a thorough and scholarly article, "Ecstatic Utterance (NEB)?", pp. 299-307, in which he shows that the "tongues speech" of both Acts and 1 Corinthians can refer only to known languages spoken somewhere upon earth.

### v) Deep Groanings

Johnson's fifth listed interpretation is that the tongues are to be understood as in effect the "groanings too deep for words" of Romans 8:26.

Again, such an approach to understanding Paul's meaning lacks a valid foundation. For a start, Romans 8:26 is referring to the intercession of the Spirit on our behalf, not to any human prayer, and it is referring in any case to something quite distinct from the tongues-speech in the assembly which is the topic at issue in chapter 14 (e.g. see v.27). This approach fails to make sense out of most of the tongues references in this chapter.

### vi) The Tongues of Angels: A Heavenly Language

Sixthly, there is also Fee's affirmation (630) that Paul or the Corinthians (or both) consider the tongues-speech to be the language spoken by angels; concerning which Fee says, most likely this is either Paul's or their understanding (or both) of "speaking in tongues." "Tongues of men" would then refer to human speech, inspired by the Spirit but unknown to the speaker; "tongues of angels" would reflect an understanding that the tongues-speaker was communicating in the dialect(s) of heaven.

Similarly Garland 611 says about Paul's reference to "tongues of angels", "It is more likely that he poses a realistic possibility - that some may indeed believe that they speak in a celestial language."

I have discussed this idea, and drawn attention to its inadequacies as an explanation, when commenting on 13:1.

## Assessment

For myself, after I examine what Paul says in this chapter, I come firmly to the view that by "speaking in tongues" Paul is clearly referring to the miraculous ability to speak in unlearned human languages - the traditional view.

Charles Hodge's Commentary on 12:10 sets forth numerous arguments for this view, which he calls both "the old interpretation of this passage" and "the common interpretation":

> That is, the ability to speak in languages previously unknown to the speakers. ... What was spoken with tongues was intelligible to those who understood foreign languages, as appears from Acts 2:11. ... Though intelligible in themselves and to the speaker, they were unintelligible to others (at Corinth), that is, to those not acquainted with the language used; and consequently unsuited for an ordinary Christian assembly. The folly which Paul rebuked was, speaking in Arabic to men who understood only Greek. The speaker might understand what he said, but others were not profited. ... Though there are difficulties attending any view of the gift in question, arising from our ignorance, those connected with the common interpretation are incomparably less than those which beset any of the modern conjectures.

As Hodge says, "there are difficulties attending any view"; but I maintain that everything in this chapter can be explained quite readily on the basis of this view; it is the natural way of understanding several key verses; it involves far fewer assumptions without adequate evidence; and it gives us a more logical basis for a cohesive overall understanding of the situation at Corinth which was causing Paul so much concern. Above all, it makes the best sense of the idea of tongues-speech as a gift from God which was given to be of use in the church - even if (as Paul is carefully pointing out) its possession is not a matter of major importance.

How this is so I will point out as we now go through what Paul actually says.

## (a) The Contrast of Tongues and Prophecy (14:1-19)

### i) Prophecy Is of More Value Than Tongues (14:1-5)

**14:1a** "Follow the way of love" (NIV), "Make love your aim" (RSV), "Pursue love" (ESV, NRSV): these translations are rather weak. The Greek verb is strong, and means "pursue after love with fervour and determination"; the Jerusalem Bible translates it well: "You must want love more than anything else."

Alongside this and parallel with it Paul adds, "and eagerly desire the things of the Spirit", or, "spiritual things". "Eagerly desire", ζηλουτε (*zēloute* - the same word as in 12:31a), means "be full of zeal for". As in 12:1, Paul writes here about "the spirituals", and most translations uniformly add-in the word "gifts". In my discussion of 12:1, I give the evidence to show that the word Paul uses, πνευματικος (*pneumatikos*), does not mean or imply "gifts", and that when the word "gift" is intended it has to be supplied. The meaning that is being thus introduced here by these translators is that Paul is instructing the Corinthians to seek for "spiritual gifts", i.e. the manifestations of the Spirit as set out in chapter 12. But the word used here, πνευματικος (*pneumatikos*) is **not** the same as "manifestations" (12:11) or "gifts" (χαρισματα, *charismata*, 12:4; 12:31a). And those commentaries - and there are quite a few of them - which equate these two words are quite unjustified in doing so.

To make these words of Paul here into an instruction to "eagerly desire" these gifts and manifestations is to put into Paul's mouth a command *that he did not give* and (as also with the usual translations of 12:1 and 12:31a) to cause him to contradict himself in a way that is completely and absolutely without justification from the context or from *his actual choice of words*. When he used *one* choice of wording he is translated as if he had used *a completely different* choice of wording.

Are we to take it that Paul has obscured his own meaning? That he has said one thing when he meant another? But there are commentators who take this to be the case, and therefore who seek to draw out of his words a meaning other than what the words naturally mean. This is how one reads one's own ideas and doctrines into Paul's writings; it is not how one ascertains Paul's meaning. I propose we do not do this, but that we take it that he is actually saying here just what he means.

Paul has given no grounds for thinking that he regards a person as "spiritual" on the basis that that person possesses a particular *charisma* or even all of them (if that were possible). He regards someone as a truly spiritual person, a person in whose life the Spirit is achieving his goals, if that person's life is lived in love. That is the point which chapter 13 was written to show. Now the climax of that chapter is given when Paul says, "Pursue love and eagerly desire spiritual things (the things of the Spirit)."

These two are parallel. To do the first is to do the second. He is writing this whole section about the nature of spiritual things (12:1), with the additional implication of discussing what it really means to be spiritual men and women. Now he reaches a vital point of his explanation. To be a spiritual person is **not** to pursue *charismata* (chapter 12); it **is** to follow the way of love (chapter 13). His meaning here is, "Pursue love, and thus you will be expressing a genuine desire for the things of the Spirit". His choice of word here (πνευματικος, *pneumatikos*) may well reflect the vocabulary of the Christians of Corinth, as commentators uniformly affirm, but his meaning is the same as in Colossians 3:2 where he says, "Set your mind on things that are above, not on things that are on earth."

**14:1b** "Especially that you may prophesy": this has been the source of the insertion of "gifts" after "spiritual".

The reasoning is: Prophecy is one of the gifts of chapter 12; the Corinthians are in particular to desire this gift; therefore it is one example of the larger category of gifts which they are being told to desire in τα πνευματικα (*ta pneumatika*), "the spirituals". But the logic of this reasoning has not taken account of the two-fold way in which Paul uses these terms "prophecy" and "prophesying".

"Prophet" and "prophecy" are used in the New Testament both in a formal and official sense, i.e. of a role and office, and also in a descriptive and functional sense, i.e. of an activity.

Thus in 12:28 Paul speaks of apostles, prophets, and teachers, and immediately asks "Are all prophets?" with the answer indicated, "No, most definitely not!" But in 14:31 in a somewhat different context he says all can prophesy if they do it one at a time, so that everyone may learn and be encouraged. Then in 14:1 and again in 14:39 he exhorts all to desire to prophesy.

We see that though not all are prophets, nonetheless all believers can, in appropriate circumstances, engage in prophesying. We have already noted the miraculous revelatory role of prophets (in the commentary on 13:8), in which they are coupled with apostles. Here in 14:3-4 Paul is speaking of the **ministry** role of prophecy: to prophesy is to speak to people [men and women] "for their upbuilding and encouragement and consolation ... the one who prophesies builds up the church." In Acts 15:32 we see this in the ministry of Judas and Silas.

On the one hand there is the person who is chosen by God for the office of prophet, an office which (as we have seen previously) func-tioned in the early church alongside that of apostle. To the prophet, as to the apostle, God at that time revealed directly the meaning of new truth for the new era.

On the other hand, there was a much more general ministry of prophesying, as the Holy Spirit was poured out in these last days upon all flesh (Acts 2:17a) so that "your sons and daughters will prophesy ... Even on my servants, both men and women, I will pour out my Spirit in those days, and they will prophesy" (Acts 2:17b-18). This is now being fulfilled in the events of Pentecost, Peter says (Acts 2:16). This ministry of prophecy is thus shown to be for widespread exercise within the church, and not restricted to those who were appointed by God to the *office* of a prophet.

Lenski 503 writes of this thus:

> "Prophecy" is used to designate the gift or the office of a prophet. ... This term is used in a double sense; broadly to indicate any and all ability to communicate the saving will of God to others so that every true teacher and preacher may be called a prophet; and more narrowly to designate the receiving and communicating of direct and specific messages from God.

This parallels the way God works in other things: There were those whom the Lord specifically appointed as his witnesses (Luke 24:45-48), but we are all able to witness to him; there are particular Christians who are called as evangelists (Acts 21:8; Ephesians 4:11), but Christians in general are to evangelize; certain people are given the special ministry of being teachers (1 Corinthians 12:28; Ephesians 4:11), but it is said of Christians in general "by this time you ought to be teachers" (Hebrews 5:12) and those who as reliable men and women have received the gos-pel are to teach others also (2 Timothy 2:2). Similarly, while only a select few were called to the *office* of prophet, the Spirit was poured out upon God's people generally so that they could prophesy.

In order that there may be no doubt in our understanding as to whether Paul is here speaking specifically of the role of a prophet or more generally, he immediately goes on to explain (v.3) what he means by prophesying.

All Christians are potentially able to prophesy: no one is excluded from this possibility. But in the nature of the case some will be found to be more gifted in this than others.

Are prophets to be considered prophets all the time, or only when (and because) they are prophesying? If I read Paul aright, both would be true - but of different people, at different times. Thus there were those called and equipped with the special miraculous gift of discerning and revealing the mysteries of God, as Paul has explained in Ephesians 3:5 (as we noted before), on whom the church was founded, alongside the apostles (Ephesians 2:20), and to whom Paul has referred in 12:28-30. With the completion of the New Testament the office of prophet in this sense has come to an end.

Then there are those members of the congregation whom God is gifting to be able to speak to men and women to instruct, strengthen, exhort, encourage and comfort them. Many members of a church may be granted this gift by the Lord, to use either in gatherings of the whole congregation, or in small groups, or on a one-to-one basis. This gift and calling continues in the church and is greatly needed in every age, including of course our own. It is the gift needed by a counselor, by one who gives consolation and help to those in need of it (for example, in sickness or after bereavement), by Bible study and youth leaders, and by those undertaking a pastoral ministry. With discernment and insight Calvin 271 said,

> From this verse let us therefore learn that prophets are (1) outstanding interpreters of Scripture; and (2) men endowed with extraordinary wisdom and aptitude for grasping what the immediate need of the Church is, and speaking the right word to meet it. That is why they are, so to speak, messengers who bring news of what God wants. ... In a word my view is that the prophets referred to are those who are skilful and experienced in making known the will of God, by applying prophecies, threats, promises, and all the teaching of Scripture to the current needs of the Church.

Different people will possess such a gift to varied extents: due to different levels of endowment from the Lord in the first place, to diverse extents to which they have trained and developed the gift they have, to varying degrees to which they will take the initiative and actually use their gift, and to differences in the extent to which they are given the opportunity to exercise their gift (e.g., preaching opportunities made available for them in their congregations). Just as some are better teachers or administrators than others, so also with the gift of prophecy, or pastoring and preaching. We must each aim to use to the full the measure of the gift we have been given (Romans 12:6). So we will expect that we have this gift to some extent, and use it to the extent we have.

Packer [214-217] explains why prophecy today does not mean receiving special revelatory messages from God, but rather illumination of the Scriptures. He says (I am indicating the essential thrust of what he says in these pages):

First, Joel's prediction, quoted by Peter at Pentecost, was of universal prophecy as one mark of the age of the Spirit (Acts 2:17-21).
Prophesying was thus an activity in which all believers were able and
perhaps expected to share (see Acts 19:6; 1 Corinthians 14:1, 23-25):
though it appears that not all believers could properly be called
prophets (1 Corinthians 12:29) ... In the second place ... the essence of
the prophetic ministry was forthtelling God's present word to his
people, and this regularly meant application of revealed truth rather
than augmentation of it. ... New Testament prophets preached the gospel and the life of faith for conversion, edification and encouragement
... Paul wishes all the Corinthian church without exception to share in
this ministry (1 Corinthians 14:1, 5). So ... a prophetic "revelation" (1
Corinthians 14:26, 30) was a God-prompted application of truth that in
general terms had been revealed already, rather than a disclosure of
divine thoughts and intentions not previously known and not otherwise
knowable. By parity of reasoning, therefore, any verbal enforcement of
biblical teaching as it applies to one's present hearers may properly be
called prophecy today, for that in truth is what it is. ... We should realize that it has actually been exhibited in every sermon or informal 'message' that has had a heart-searching, 'home-coming' application to its
hearers, ever since the church began. Prophecy has been and remains a
reality whenever and wherever Bible truth is genuinely *preached* - that
is, spelled out and applied, whether from a pulpit or more informally.
Preaching is teaching God's revealed truth with application; such teaching with application is prophecy, always was, and always will be.

**14:2-4** In these verses the one who speaks in a tongue and the one
who prophesies are compared and contrasted. The one who speaks in a
tongue speaks not to people but to God, no one understands him, and he
edifies only himself. The one who prophesies speaks to people and
edifies the church.

"No one understands him" - what does "no one" mean? Nobody anywhere in the world? Or, no one who was present at the time the speaker
was using this particular language?

Gordon Clark's commentary states [219ff.],

The account of Pentecost in Acts clearly describes what the apostles
spoke; Paul here presupposes that everyone knows what he is talking
about; therefore the description in Acts should govern the exegesis of 1
Corinthians, and the latter should not alter the former. ...

The present verse is a reason for the preceding verse. The
Corinthians are commanded to prefer prophecy to languages *because*
the latter are of little or no use in the church. Such had not always been
the case. At Pentecost, the Apostles spoke in foreign tongues and the
crowds understood. However, in Corinth, everybody spoke Greek and
no one understood the languages of the Elamites and the dwellers in
Mesopotamia. Thus, in Corinth, the languages were intelligible only to
God, and no one in the congregation heard, in other words, understood.
...

> As has been made clear several times in the previous chapters, mysteries are divinely revealed propositions. Hence they cannot be nonsense; they must be intelligible; and if anyone speaks them, he must use intelligible language. ... Paul gives the reason why those present were not edified: they were not edified because they did not understand what the man was saying. They did not grasp the intelligible meaning. However, if the man, himself, was edified, as Paul says he was, then *he* must have understood; for if he could be edified without understanding, so could the others. This point becomes clearer still as we proceed. It applies even more to the modern Pentecostalists ... for if gibberish could edify the speaker, it could also edify the church, and no translation would be needed.

It is important to our overall understanding of this chapter to grasp clearly the point to which Clark is here drawing our attention. The church is edified, built up, by prophecy because it is intelligible. The church is not edified by (uninterpreted) tongues because this is not intelligible. Thus when Paul says that the speaker in tongues *is* edified when he speaks, this clearly indicates that *he understands the meaning of what he is saying*, "for if he could be edified without understanding, so could the others." As Chrysostom (Kovacs 203) explained, "The one [speaking] knew what he himself was saying."

Thus the tongue spoken must have been a human language, and it was not the glossolalia of modern-day tongues speakers, who do not understand the meaning of what they are saying.

Note also that these verses are *not* talking about praying. The tongues-speaker is speaking in the public congregation, but he is said to be speaking only to God not for the reason that he is praying but because he is speaking in a language which only he and God understand. It may be recalled that, as cited earlier, Theodoret commented (Kovacs 230):

> But for anyone speaking in Corinth it was pointless to use the languages of the Scythians or Persians or Egyptians, since the Corinthians could not understand them. That is why the apostle says that "one who speaks in tongues speaks not to men but to God". For he adds this: "for no one understands him".

But those who support modern "tongues speaking" see this verse as referring to prayer, and thus interpret Paul's meaning as an encouragement to pray in an "unknown tongue", that is, in non-human "tongues". Writing about the nature of "tongues" in 1 Corinthians, Christenson 26-28 says:

> The Bible says that speaking in tongues is addressed to *God* (1 Corinthians 14:2). Therefore the question of whether *people* understand it is actually irrelevant. The question is: Does it express meaning for the speaker, and does God understand it? ... Although one does not know

what he is saying as he speaks in tongues, he does have a clear sense that he is praying to God.

But this question - whether the gift of tongues is of ability in speaking a human language, or of speaking in something that is not human speech - is not "irrelevant", as Christenson has asserted here: this is in fact the issue upon which the whole interpretation of chapter 14 turns.

Those who advocate "tongues-speaking" encourage frequent use of "tongues" as prayer. Thus Christenson writes further [28, 72-73]:

> One speaks in tongues for the most part in his private devotions. *This is by far its most important use and value.* It offers the believer a glorious new dimension in prayer. ... Often a burden of intercession simply overwhelms or baffles us. Then and there a person may pray in tongues, knowing that "the Spirit intercedes ... according to the will of God" (Rom 8:27). ... Speaking in tongues brings to one's private devotions the special blessing of "praying in the spirit" as distinct from praying with the understanding. ... It would seem that prayer in which the mind is unfruitful would have little value. What blessing can it be to pray when you have no idea what you are praying about? Actually, this is one of its greatest blessings - the fact that it is not subject to the limitations of the human intellect. ... Speaking in tongues is a God-appointed manner of praying which can bypass the limitations of the intellect.

Following through a similar line of thought, Campbell says [98]: "It is important for us to worship in tongues every day." But is this really what Paul is instructing the Corinthians (and us) to do? Is it reasonable to interpret Paul's comments here to have this meaning?

Packer 208-209 further clarifies this situation:

> But one thing is clear: Paul is discussing *public* use of tongues throughout 1 Corinthians 13, 14; and it is neither necessary nor natural to refer any of his statements to glossolalia as a private exercise. Charismatics often explain 14:4 ("he who speaks in a tongue edifies himself ...") and 18 ("... I speak in tongues more than you all") in terms of private glossolalic prayer, but exegetically this is a guess that is not only unprovable but [also] not in fact very plausible. It involves a gratuitous modeling of first-century experience on the charismatics' own ("Paul and the Corinthians must have been like us"); furthermore, it is hard to believe that in verse 4 Paul can mean that glossolalists *who do not know what they are saying* will yet edify themselves, when in verse 5 he denies that the listening church can be edified unless it knows what they are saying. But if in verse 4 Paul has in view tongues speakers who understand their tongues, today's charismatics cannot regard his words as giving them any encouragement, for they confessedly do not understand their own glossolalia. And the supposition that these verses relate to private glossolalia cannot in any case be supported from Paul's flow of thought, to which private glossolalia is irrelevant. This supposition can be read into the text, as so much else can in these chapters, but not read out of it.

In epistle after epistle Paul tells his readers of the things that he prays for, and exhorts them concerning what they in turn should pray for. To pray for such things is thus to pray in accordance with the whole sweep of Paul's teaching. Jesus taught his disciples to pray using meaningful words. The same thing is found in the remainder of the New Testament and in the Old Testament. Some writers (as we have seen) have asserted that the "groanings which cannot be uttered" (Romans 8:26, AV/KJV) refers to speaking in tongues; but this expression, "groans that words cannot express" (TEV, NIV), refers to what cannot be uttered in words and is not a description of tongues-speaking, and in any case it is said in reference to the Spirit's intercession directly with God, in which we are not involved at all - it does not refer to human prayer of any kind.

When therefore we pray in human words, framing petitions with our minds and bringing them before God knowing what we are asking, we are doing what Jesus taught and what is taught throughout the *whole* Bible. But if we open our mouths and let utterance flow out which is not intelligible to us (or others, if present) and bring this to God as our prayers to him, we are doing something which is only taught according to *one* interpretation of *three* verses of *one* epistle of the New Testament, where the passage may very well *not* have this meaning in any case.

The one who speaks in a tongue is not understood by people (v.2) not for the reason that he is using "angelic" or ecstatic speech but because he is speaking in a human language that they do not know. This is using the gift of being able to speak in tongues simply to display the fact that one has it, and not in any way to serve the purpose for which it was given. God of course understands the speaker, but he is the only one who does: and that is not the purpose or intention of the gift. The speaker utters mysteries, but instead of them being made clear to the hearers - which *is* the intention when God's mysteries are proclaimed - they remain unintelligible and therefore unknown to the hearers. Paul is not *commending* this situation: he is *contrasting* it with what happens when a person prophesies.

As Lenski 577 points out, numerous commentators make an erroneous assumption at this point: taking it that Paul is stating the speaker's *intention*, "as though he *intends* to address only God. [But] Paul states only the *fact* [not the intention]: he speaks only to God, as indicated."

Paul now makes plain what a person will do when he prophesies. This verse throws light on the scope of Paul's use of this term.

We can see, moreover, that the activity referred to by Paul in v.3, while it will be part of the ministry of a person who is called to the special office of prophet, is also a ministry open to Christians in general, as the Spirit enables them (as I discussed on 14:1b).

**14:4** When Paul says, "The one who speaks in a tongue builds up himself", is he commending this as a practice to be followed? That is, is he saying, "Tongues-speaking is for edifying oneself, as prophesying is for edifying the church"? If this were his meaning he would be completely contradicting his foundational teaching in 12:7 where he has laid it down that "To each is given the manifestation of the Spirit for the common good". If this is the principle concerning the use of the manifestations of the Spirit, then clearly when a person uses a gift to edify only himself he is not using it in accord with God's intention in giving it: he is abusing its use.

Paul's comment that, in the situation that existed at Corinth, a person was edifying only himself when he spoke in a tongue (for no one else present understood him) is a *criticism* of such a practice. A person should *not* be speaking in a tongue in the assembly *unless* others are present who do understand that language or if that is not the case, *unless* what he says is translated for the edification of the church as a whole. Paul is not referring to a person "speaking in tongues" when alone by himself, and it is distorting the meaning of Paul's words in their context to read such an idea into what he is saying in this passage.

**14:5** It is a mistake to take it that Paul is here urging that all should, or even implying that all could, speak in tongues. This verse is often read as if to speak in tongues and to prophesy were being presented as parallel options, of which Paul prefers the second.

Thus the ESV: "Now I want you all to speak in tongues, but even more to prophesy", which clearly sets out that there are two things that Paul wants them to do: to speak with tongues and also to prophesy; and he wants the second one for them more than he does the first. This is the standard approach in translations. Interpretationally, this *could* possibly be the correct way in which to understand Paul's point. But we ought to note that this in *not* how the two matters are stated in the Greek, where the construction of the two clauses is quite different.

The first clause is, "I wish (or, I want) you all to speak in tongues", with the verb of speaking in the infinitive. If the second alternative were merely Paul's preferred option which he wished they would do, it too could be simply the infinitive, "to prophesy". But it is not. It is ἵνα (*hina*) plus the subjunctive. Now ἵνα (*hina*) can be used as no more than "that", thus meaning in this verse, "I wish that you would prophesy". But its normal, usual function is in a purpose construction, "in order that you would prophesy". As Paul is deliberately using this ἵνα (*hina*) construction rather than again the infinitive, as in "to speak", it is highly probable that his reason is because he is doing more than simply laying out two alternative options - that in fact he is giving ἵνα (*hina*) its usual force.

The other word here, μᾶλλον (*mallon*) can possibly be rendered "rather", but means in particular "more, all the more, more than ever, more than that" (Newman's Dictionary 111). Thus its force here is not to present **an alternative** to speaking in tongues but to refer to doing something **more than** just speaking in tongues.

So we can see that Paul is saying, "I want you all to speak in tongues but more than this (more to the point, more especially) I want you to speak in tongues in order that you may prophesy." That is, the speaking in tongues which Paul commends here is not a speaking in tongues which ends there, which is for its own sake alone, but a speaking in tongues which is done for a purpose and that purpose is that it shall become prophesying.

How can speaking in tongues be carried out so as to become prophesying? Paul's very next words in this same verse answer this question. He explains: when someone speaks in tongues and this tongues-speaking is then interpreted so that the church is edified, then that speaking in tongues has thereby been placed on a par with prophesying.

"The one who prophesies is greater ...": not greater in importance or status, so much as in effectiveness in ministry, and thus in value to the church.

The last clause in this sentence is again a "ἵνα (*hina*)-plus-the-subjunctive" construction, and it is customarily rendered by translators (e.g., ESV, NIV, NRSV) as "so that the church may be edified/built up" (or similarly). This ἵνα (*hina*) construction parallels the one that Paul has just used concerning speaking in tongues and prophesying. Speaking in tongues is to be engaged in "in order that the church may be built up", i.e. in such a way that it becomes prophesying; Paul says here that the tongues-speaker becomes equivalent to the one who prophesies when what he says is interpreted so as to edify the church.

The ESV, RSV and NRSV translate, "unless someone interprets..." (and similarly the TEV): this translation can be quite misleading - Paul's wording does not necessarily mean, "someone else", but actually says, "unless he interprets", and the "he" can quite well be the same person who has first spoken in another language. Phillips, Jerusalem Bible and NEB translate so as to refer to the speaker in tongues as the one who also interprets; the NASB and NIV translate literally, "unless he interprets", leaving the question a little more open: it can be the tongues-speaker himself or someone else who interprets.

The word ἑρμηνεια (*hermēneia*), rendered "interpretation" (12:10; 14:26), has the meaning "translation, interpretation" [Danker-BAG], and the compounded forms διερμηνευω (*diermēneuō*) (12:30; 14:5; 14:13; 14:27) and διερμηνευτης (*diermēneutēs*) (14:28) similarly mean "to translate/interpret" and "a translator/interpreter" respectively. Thus in Acts 9:36 this word occurs in the sentence "a disciple named Tabitha (which, when translated, is Dorcas, or Gazelle)", where this word is rendered "translated". We see then that these words can refer to interpreting or translating from one human language into another. Concerning this, Gundry 1966:300 comments,

> Although the verb *might* refer to the explaining of mysterious utterances, its usage in biblical Greek militates against this understanding. Out of 21 uses of ἑρμηνευω (*ermēneuō*) (apart from the uses in 1 Cor 12-14) in the LXX and in the New Testament, 18 refer to translation, 2 to explanation, and 1 to satire or a figurative saying.

In sum, it can be seen from this verse that prophecy is equivalent to tongues-plus-interpretation (viz., translation) i.e., this is what edifies the church. Paul is not commending all tongues-speaking as such, but only that which equates with prophesying, i.e. that which is interpreted (translated), so as to edify the church.

That this is Paul's meaning here is made clear in his practical summary of what is to be done (14:28), which states expressly that there is to be no speaking in tongues in church without an interpretation. This instruction of v.28 is in conflict with Paul's commendation of speaking in tongues in v.5, unless (as I have urged) we take seriously Paul's ἱνα (*hina*) construction in v.5 and recognize that the only speaking in tongues which he commends is that which is done in such a way as to be prophesying, i.e. by being translated, and thus edifying the church.

### ii) Tongues are Valueless Unless Understood (14:6-19)

**14:6-9** Speaking in tongues can only benefit the hearer if it brings some revelation or knowledge or prophecy or teaching; and it cannot bring any of these things to the hearer unless it is understood. Paul uses several analogies as illustrations to make this point. If speech is uttered which (because it is in a tongue which is not understood) is unintelligible, then it is "speaking into the air". There is no way in which you are helped by what you do not understand.

In v.9, δια της γλωσσης (*dia tēs glōssēs*), Paul is making use of the full range of meaning of γλωσσα (*glōssa*). At the first level of meaning he is saying, "unless with your tongue (the physical organ of speech, in your mouth) you utter intelligible speech ...", speaking as a generalization about all speech as communication, and summing up the point of what he has just been saying. But he also is saying, "unless by means of this other language that you are using (i.e. your glossolalia) you are making yourself understood, you are just speaking pointlessly and purposelessly into thin air."

**14:10-11** "There are without doubt a great number of languages in the world": here Paul clearly identifies tongues-speech with the "various languages of the world", none of which "is without meaning". This pretty clearly rules out any interpretation of glossalalia other than that of meaningful human language; this passage strongly points to the understanding of "speaking in tongues" as speaking in foreign human languages that were not known to the congregation as a whole. The inclusion of this comment between the twice-repeated "so with yourselves" (verses 9 and 12) indicates that while Paul is using *himself* as an illustration of the point ("but if I do not know the meaning of the language") he is actually referring to what *they* are doing in their church practice at Corinth.

**14:12** Since they are eager for "the things of the Spirit", they should direct their seeking, then, towards what will build up the church, for that is what it means to be spiritual. Again in this verse the translations uniformly add the word "manifestations" (ESV) or "gifts" (NIV, NRSV) to what Paul actually says. The word he uses is πνευματων (*pneumatōn*), literally, "of spirits". This may legitimately be taken as "the things of the Spirit", "spiritual things", meaning, in the context of 1 Corinthians, to be spiritually-minded people (as in 14:37, and 3:1, and cf. Romans 8:6). There is no textual or contextual justification for adding in here the word "manifestations" or "gifts" - it is inserted because of a doctrinal presupposition on the part of the inserter.

**14:13-14** The one who speaks in a tongue should pray that he may interpret. "If I pray in a tongue my spirit prays" - because "I" understand what "I" am saying; but my mind is unfruitful - that is, produces no fruit from what it is doing, because others do not understand the message. My spirit and my mind must be united in what they do. This verse *does not* say and *does not* mean, "I will pray with the spirit (i.e., on some occasions, when using a 'tongue') and I will also pray with the mind (i.e., on other occasions, when using language that is understood by people)", as if these are two separate activities in which I can engage at different times.

Moreover, "praying with the spirit" does *not* mean praying *without* the person himself knowing the meaning of what he is saying in his prayer. The person who prays in a tongue builds himself up (14:4a) - which cannot happen if he does not understand the meaning of what he says. (As noted above, if one can be edified without understanding, then the church could be equally edified by hearing prayer in a tongue they did not understand, and 14:4b indicates that this is not the case.) The spirit is inseparable from the person: 2:11 says quite explicitly that a man's spirit knows (understands) his thoughts. Further, for Paul to say "my mind is unfruitful" does *not* mean that his mind does not understand something that his spirit does. "To be fruitful" means "to produce fruit". Paul is saying that his mind cannot succeed in its purpose of producing fruit *in the church* - 14:12 - if the members of the church do not understand his meaning.

**14:15-17** These comments make it clear that praying or giving thanks in a language which is not understood is not acceptable *at all*. Both the spirit and the mind (the intention of engaging in fruitful ministry) must operate together. Speaking in a language unknown to the congregation is thus excluded, because it is unedifying (verses 5 and 17), "speaking into the air" (v.9), "unfruitful" (v.14), and does not allow the others (who are "outsiders" as far as this language is concerned) to join in and participate (v.16).

**14:18-19** Paul has more knowledge of foreign languages than anyone at Corinth: but in the congregation of the church he would much rather say five words with his mind (that is, communicating his meaning effectively to others and thus being fruitful) than ten thousand words in another language which is meaningless to them. Hurd 188 says concerning this,

> Since "ten thousand" is the largest number for which the Greek system of numeration had a symbol, we may better translate: "... rather five words with my mind ... than an infinite number in a tongue."

## (b) The Role of Tongues and Prophecy (14:20-33a)

### i) The Significance of Tongues and Prophecy (14:20-22)

**14:20** Paul says, "Stop thinking like children" - he uses the present tense (the durative mode) which refers to a state or an ongoing activity, and says not to do this. Negating a durative command means to stop doing something which you are already doing. In their attitudes and practices regarding tongues, the Corinthians were being like children. Some commentators have pointed out that this comment picks up and builds upon what Paul said in 13:11 about growing up and giving up "childish ways". The Corinthians are being told to become "adults", "grown-up", "mature", in their thinking.

**14:21** "In the Law": that is, in Deuteronomy 28:47ff., and in particular in Isaiah 28:11-12. The "foreigners" are the Assyrian invaders, who come speaking their own language - they are thus speaking "strange tongues" from the point of view of the Israelites, who do not know what is being said. This quotation which Paul cites gives us a clear understanding of what he means by tongues in 1 Corinthians 12-14, for there is no question but that tongues in 14:21 means "foreign languages" (specifically, the speech of the Assyrian invaders), and in 14:22 Paul goes on to apply this comment, saying, "Tongues, then ..." and continues his discussion of tongues in the church at Corinth. The connective used by Paul is ὥστε (*hōste*), which means "so that, consequently, and so, therefore" (Newman's Dictionary), stating the result or consequence of what has gone before. Phillips shows the connection: "That means that tongues are a sign ...". And the Jerusalem Bible translates "You see, then, that the strange languages are meant to be a sign ...", "strange languages" referring on the one hand to the speech of the Assyrians and on the other hand to the tongues-speech of the Corinthians.

Paul's wording shows that the meaning of the word "tongues" is identical in verses 21 and 22 (and in the rest of the whole chapter), and thus this passage indicates that the meaning of "tongues" is "human language foreign to, and thus not understood by, the hearer".

**14:22a** Tongues, Paul says, are a sign to unbelievers. He points out that in the Old Testament the use of foreign languages to the Jews was a sign of God's rejection of them if they did not repent and walk in his ways. Now, in the New Testament era, tongues are also a sign to unbelievers, and we can see how this was so in five ways:

**(a)** When the apostles spoke in foreign languages on the day of Pentecost this was the sign given to the Jews, and it was made quite explicit in the speeches throughout Acts. Peter explains that prophecy has been fulfilled and the last days have begun (Acts 2:17ff.) and God has made Jesus both Lord and Christ (Acts 2:36). The people were told, "Save yourselves from this crooked generation" (Acts 2:40). Judgement and destruction was promised if the people did not heed the message of Jesus (Acts 3:23-26). The apostolic testimony continued for forty years and then in AD 70 the judgement predicted by Jesus (Matthew 24:1ff.//Mark 13:1ff.//Luke 21:5ff.) fell upon Jerusalem, and the city was destroyed and its inhabitants slaughtered or scattered.

**(b)** Signs and wonders were an authenticating testimony from God upon the ministry of the apostles at Pentecost (Acts 4:30), as they had been for Jesus (Acts 2:22). This included, at Pentecost, the miracle of their speaking foreign languages, a miracle which was widely known (Acts 2:6, 14) and could no more be denied or explained away than could the "notable sign" of the healing of the man at the temple gate (Acts 4:16 - the same word "sign", σημειον (*sēmeion*), is used in this verse as in 1 Corinthians 14:22). Peter appealed explicitly to the miracle of tongues to substantiate his message (Acts 2:33).

(c) A band of Galileans (Acts 2:7) speaking languages from all over the world around Israel captured the attention of all those who were in Jerusalem for the Feast of Pentecost, and thus gained an attentive audience for the preaching of the gospel. There would appear to have been two distinct groups in the Pentecost crowd. There were the Jews and proselytes of the Jewish Dispersion, who recognized the native tongue of the country where they lived when they heard it, and who responded accordingly with wonder and amazement (Acts 2:5-12). And then there were the Aramaic-speaking Jews of Jerusalem itself, who saw no miracle and decided that the babble about them was because the believers were speaking gibberish, as a result of getting drunk (Acts 2:13).

(d) Fourthly, tongues were a sign that Babel (Genesis 11:1-9) was being reversed. Until Babel, there was only one tongue spoken by all mankind. Only after Babel were there "languages" (plural). After Babel, moreover, God's attention focussed down upon one nation, through which he planned to work, so that even Jesus would say (Matthew 15:24), "I was sent only to the lost sheep of Israel". But after Pentecost the gospel was for "every tribe and *tongue* and people and nation (Revelation 5:9; 7:9; 14:6; cf. 10:11; 11:9; 13:7:17:15 - the word "tongue" in all these verses, with the meaning "human language", is the same word γλωσσα (*glōssa*) used in Acts 2:4, 11; 10:46; 19:6; and 1 Corinthians 12-14).

(e) Fifthly, the sign of tongues at Pentecost was a foretaste of the program of God which was laid down by Jesus in Acts 1:8. In its fullest sense and its total scope this program will occupy the people of God to the end of this age, for there still remain unreached peoples in "the ends of the earth" to whom the gospel is to be brought; and a realization of how the Gentiles were to be accepted into the church of God was still some years in the future for the apostles: but at Pentecost representatives from the different countries of the then-known world had the gospel of the risen Lord Jesus Christ preached to them. This may well have led to the beginnings of the church in some of those various places, when those amongst the 5,000 converts (Acts 4:4) who were visiting Jerusalem, went home - e.g. the church in Rome may well have begun with the converts amongst those who had come to Jerusalem from Rome (Acts 2:10).

In these five ways tongues at Pentecost were a sign to unbelievers (those, that is, who were not believers when they heard them): for some, a sign for judgement, because they did not accept the message that accompanied and was preached through the miracle; for others, a sign for hope, as they learned what God had done in their day, and in their thousands they thereupon accepted the message of the gospel.

When Cornelius and those with him spoke with tongues, extolling God, this was a sign both to Jews and to Gentiles that Gentiles were now welcomed into the kingdom (Acts 10:44-48) - and as Peter and those with him, reassured by the sign of tongues that God was doing with Gentiles as he did with them at Pentecost, reported this, it soon became widely known (Acts 11:1, 18).

So, similarly, for the small group at Ephesus (Acts 19:1-7). They knew only John's baptism - he had taught them that there was One who would come and baptize them with the Holy Spirit (Matthew 3:11//Mark 1:8//Luke 3:16). Thus they could not be ignorant of the *existence* of the Holy Spirit (as most translations appear to imply), for John taught concerning him; they were ignorant of the fact that "he is here", that is, that John's prophecy had now been fulfilled. (Thus Knowling, *The Expositor's Greek Testament*; cf. RV.) Now the sign of tongues authenticated their incorporation into the church of Christ.

And so also Paul now reminds the Corinthians of this basic intention of God: that the supernatural gift of foreign languages is a sign for unbelievers - of mercy and acceptance for those who accept the gospel, and of condemnation and judgement for those who do not. Whatever was happening at Corinth in the matter of tongues-speaking, it seems it was not being thus used.

Some authors (e.g., D Basham, *A Handbook on Holy Spirit Baptism*, 67) treat tongues as a sign only in Acts, and then as being a sign of what they term "the baptism in the Holy Spirit"; then they say that in 1 Corinthians "we find Paul discussing speaking in tongues as a *gift* among other gifts". This teaching ignores, *firstly*, to whom tongues is a sign (14:22) and what tongues is a sign of (14:21), and *secondly*, that it is in 1 Corinthians (not Acts) that this explanation of the purpose and meaning of tongues is given. Thus the purpose of tongues is the same for both Acts and 1 Corinthians: it is a sign to unbelievers. Paul's words are intended to show the Corinthians how they are mistaking the purpose of tongues and thus misusing the gift.

**14:22b** For tongues to be a *sign* to unbelievers, as Paul says, indicates that the use of tongues must still involve the exercise of a miraculous gift of speaking languages not learnt in the normal way. But what is said in tongues (a foreign language - intended to communicate to the "outsiders" who spoke that language) could still be edifying to the believers if translated for their benefit (see 14:5), for just as prophecy edifies believers so can tongues if what is said is really intelligible. It appears clear from Paul's total comments that the miraculous type of tongues-speaking (i.e. the ability to speak in foreign languages that one has not learnt) was not the only type of foreign-language-speaking that was occurring at Corinth, for some sections of this chapter (e.g. so far, verses 2, 4, 5, 6, 10, 11, 13, 18, 19) could also well include people speaking foreign languages which they knew from ordinary human knowledge. I shall return to this question later (see below, "Reflections: What Was Going On At Corinth?")

Paul is not attempting at all points to identify and differentiate various kinds of tongues-speaking (if there were more than one), but in his comments he aims to cover all and any speaking in a foreign language in the congregation when this is unedifying in the way that he describes. The fact that prophecy is for believers, not unbelievers, indicates that it has no "sign" value for "outsiders", but rather it ministers to the upbuilding of the members of the church, as we have seen earlier (e.g. 14:3-4).

The ESV inserts "sign" into 14:22b (as do some other versions), so that it reads "prophecy is a sign not for unbelievers but for believers"; then a footnote warns that the "Greek lacks *a sign*." The NIV is correct here: "prophecy however is for believers." Tongues is "for a sign" - it has "sign value" in itself, but it is not said of prophecy that this is a sign, but simply that it is "for believers", for the purposes set out in v.3.

## ii) The Effect of Tongues and Prophecy (14:23-25)

**14:23-25** These verses in no way contradict what Paul has just said. Paul pictures an assembly of the church in which (v.23a) everyone is engaged in speaking in tongues - without their succeeding in conveying, or even intending to convey, meaningful communication but just "exercising a gift" for its own sake - into which an outsider, an unbeliever, happens to enter. [The churches often met in private homes which had adequate space, to which strangers, "outsiders", had free access. This may appear bizarre to us, but it was not uncommon at the time, and indeed is the assumption behind several of the stories Jesus told and events which happened (e.g. Luke 7:36-38).]

Such an "outsider" may well (and justifiably) conclude that everyone has gone mad. This is certainly not the use of a gift of tongues as a sign to and a means of reaching outsiders, but an abuse of that gift, either by using it wrongly if one genuinely had it, or by the *pretence* of having it if one did not. (If "*all*" are "speaking in tongues", then clearly something is wrong, for Paul's earlier argument climaxing in his questions of 12:30 clearly indicates that in the plan of God *not* all will "speak with tongues".)

The picture Paul paints here of the chaotic babel in the assembly of the Corinthian congregation may well be a little overdrawn, but it shows that something of the sort must have been happening or the description given here is meaningless and irrelevant, and that is something Paul would not be (cf. 9:26).

Then the contrast is drawn: if the members were all to prophesy, then the unbeliever from outside will **understand** the message that each person gives and thus by all of them he will be convicted of his sin and called to account before God, and will be constrained to fall down and worship God, acknowledging that God is really amongst them. (He would not however be led to acknowledge the presence of God by hearing their much tongues-speaking.)

### iii) The Exercise of Tongues and Prophecy (14:26-33a)

**14:26-28** Now Paul sets out a pattern for the assembly of the church in which everything can have its proper place. This is a list of "gifts of participation". Each member of the congregation shall participate, according to what he/she has. One has a hymn (perhaps to sing or to lead in congregational singing, perhaps a new hymn which he has himself written - the original root meaning of the word is to play a musical instrument). The reference here is to someone exercising the gift of music in some way. Another has a "word of instruction", a "lesson" (Greek διδαχη [*didachē*], "teaching"); another has a revelation (I shall comment further on this in a moment); another has a message in a foreign tongue and this will then be interpreted (translated).

The overall standard by which every contribution is to be judged is, "All of these must be done for the building up of the church." Thus there would be a normal limit of *two* and an absolute limit of *three* upon people speaking in a tongue, and it is possible that there may be none at all ("*If* anyone speaks in a tongue ...").

All such tongues-speaking is to be interpreted (i.e., translated), and no public tongues-speaking is to take place unless there is someone present to interpret. This may well indicate that before the meeting the foreign-language speaker checks around and verifies that someone is present who can translate from this language before that person speaks in it publicly. Otherwise he/she can only speak or pray in this language silently ("the speaker should keep quiet in the church and speak to himself and God").

**14:29-32** Similarly two or three prophets may speak, and the others (i.e. the other members of the congregation) are to weigh carefully what is said. Some commentators take this to mean a very formal "sitting in judgement" upon something offered as a prophecy, and a few go to the extent of saying that this is to be done formally in relation to *every* prophecy. I consider this is over-translating and over-interpreting. If the nature of the prophecy we are talking about here is simply the preaching, expounding, and applying of Old Testament Scripture or of the traditions about Jesus being preserved and passed on in the church at this time (and I follow Calvin and others in taking this to be Paul's meaning here - as in verses 3-5), then this "weighing" of prophecy is just the same as the "weighing" of what is said in a sermon which every congregation does today after that sermon. And it would be totally informal, and usually also totally private and personal. Regarding "weighing" a message: see my further comments on this in "Reflections: Weighing A Message", below.

**14:30** "A revelation" (so also v.26) could be reflecting the situation before the New Testament was available, when God would at times speak by direct revelation to an apostle or prophet (Ephesians 3:3-5). Or rather (and I take this to be his meaning here) it may simply refer to a Spirit-given insight into an issue - maybe a part of their Scripture under consideration, or possibly something raised by another speaker.

**14:31-32** "You all can prophesy in turn" (or "one by one") - not by any means "all" at the one meeting of the church: we should not "read in" this idea - but in orderly sequence over a period of time. Again we note the function of prophecy: it is "so that everyone may be instructed and encouraged." Prophets *can* wait their proper turn in this way because "the spirits of prophets are subject to the control of prophets": the fact that they have the prophetic gift does not mean that they have to, or are entitled to, speak out in ways that would breach good order in the congregation.

Is the description we have here (verses 26-33) a picture of what we could call "normal Christian worship" in the churches of the mid-first century? Johnson 266 says "yes". I discuss this idea below in "Reflections: Worship Then And Now".

**14:33a** The reason why this procedure is to be followed is that "God is not a God of confusion but of peace" - this pattern will promote peace and avoid confusion and disorder, and this is the will of God for his church whenever and wherever it meets together.

## SOME PRACTICAL AND PASTORAL REFLECTIONS

### Worship Then and Now (14:26-33)

Johnson takes 14:26-33 as a total picture of worship in the congregation at Corinth. He says,

> These verses (vv.26-33) give a rare picture of a Christian church service in these early years (c.54-55). We find no leaders, no reading of the Law, no set order, and no single sermon (different from Jewish synagogue worship). Instead we find a democratically functioning group, with one offering a Christian song (*psalmos*, "psalm," "hymn," "Christian song"), then another giving a *word of instruction*, another bringing a *revelation* (cf. v.6), still another speaking in *a tongue* and then giving *an interpretation* (or another giving an interpretation, v.26).

The presumption behind this understanding of these verses 26-33 is that whatever isn't expressly mentioned didn't happen. That is one way of interpreting the evidence, I suppose. There is another. This is to view this passage as addressing issues in need of correction or attention or clarification, and not mentioning those things that were "standard" or "normal" or "correct". For example, there is no mention at this point of celebrating the Lord's Supper - there is lengthy discussion of this a few chapters earlier, of course (11:17-34E). And there is no specific mention in 14:26-33 of prayer or Scripture reading being included in the worship. Yet we would expect its inclusion - and justifiably so. A picture of a time of worship in Corinth (and other churches) needs to be built up on the basis of *all* the evidence available to us.

Firstly, Christian worship was initially patterned on the Jewish synagogue worship. And why not? Christians held the same faith in the same God - but with the conviction that the promised Messiah had come. James the president or bishop of the early church in Jerusalem even refers to the church assembly by the term "synagogue" (James 2:2) - a reference that reveals the concept of the same worship pattern. We may legitimately take it, then, that there would indeed be prayer and the reading of the Scriptures in Christian as in Jewish worship (2 Corinthians 3:15), doubtless plus other features that were an accepted part of the Jewish scene.

For example, that the men and the women sat separately. One reason why such a feature as this is not mentioned specifically in the New Testament is that, if it were, this could well then have been taken as a Holy Spirit-given example for us to follow and so could have become normative for Christian worship, though such a thing was not at all the divine intention.

The conduct of Jewish worship was in the hands of "rulers of the synagogue", elders. There is no suggestion in the New Testament that Christian worship would be different or that Paul would choose to diverge from the synagogue in such matters. To the contrary: Paul and Barnabas appointed elders in the churches they founded (Acts 14:23), and Paul addressed the elders of the churches in his ministry (Acts 20:17; Philippians 1:1), and wrote of the qualifications for elders (1 Timothy 3:1; Titus 1:5). He spoke of the elders who ruled and who taught in the congregation (1 Timothy 5:17). Peter similarly addresses elders (e.g. 1 Peter 5:1). Paul's concern very much included that there be orderliness and decorum in the congregation, so that the people of God could be edified in their gathering without hindrance or distraction: let all things be done decently and in order (14:33a, 40).

It is against this background then that we are to interpret 14:26-33. The singing and the speaking (plus everything else not specifically mentioned here) must all be conducive to edification.

Johnson 268 assumes that opportunity will be given at each Lord's Day gathering for all the prophets to speak (v.31):

> A series of two or three prophets spoke, then there was discussion, followed by another series of two or three prophets and then discussion, until all the prophets had spoken.

The "discussion" he envisages as being when "the congregation as a whole sifts the content of the speech" (268).

There is absolutely no reason from the text for taking "you can all prophesy one by one" to mean, "at the one gathering of the congregation, on the one occasion". Much better to take it sequentially over whatever may be an appropriate period of time, so that the prophets could all share whatever had been revealed to them by the Lord (v.30).

I doubt that a prophet was a prophet for all occasions. On all topics. It is more likely that the Spirit specially leads one person to understand in depth one particular issue or area of truth, and others similarly in different areas. Then from the variety and multiplicity of their respective contributions the whole counsel of God will emerge. Just as now each different book of Scripture makes its contribution to our total understanding. I take it that when Paul says "you can all prophesy" he is not meaning "so that everybody is able to have their say, lest somebody gets offended by being left out"; but in order that all prophets who have received something from the Lord can share it.

The lesson and example of this for our worship services today is that we should also give time and opportunity for prayer and praise, for singing and Scripture-reading, and for proclamation of the message of the teaching of the Lord from the Word of God. Seeing that God's channel of communication prior to the availability of the New Testament canon in the churches was by revelation to (apostles and) prophets, there is a sense in which the prophets at that time sharing a message revealed by the Lord was equivalent to our reading from the New Testament epistles today.

Perhaps, though, the idea of several speakers (tongues speakers - plus interpreters - plus two or three prophets) all contributing on the one occasion to the teaching and edification of the congregation is something which may give us pause for reflection and thought in the light of our usual present-day practice of having one speaker bringing one sermon during a worship service. Alternatively, we may feel that this aspect of a Corinthian gathering for worship was primarily intended for the particular circumstances of those times, and is not intended to be a pattern for today.

One thing is absolutely clear, though, and should also be our goal and purpose in our worship today: that there was an important place in the gathering of the congregation given to the teaching and instruction of the people in the truths of God (i.e. what to believe and how to behave). And in this the practice in the church at Corinth (and as Paul would say, in all the churches - 7:17; 11:16; 14:33) was consistent with what was done in the early church from its beginning (Acts 2:42) when they were all so excited to see that God has broken through into history in a new and special way.

## Weighing A Message (14:29)

The "weighing" of prophecy in this verse means just the same as our "weighing" of what is said in a sermon: which every congregation does today after that sermon. You have - or should have - an opinion about the sermon, a response. And it would be totally informal, and usually also totally private and personal. So this instruction is as important a challenge to the church of today as it was to the church in Corinth when Paul first wrote it. Paul is saying to us today: Don't automatically believe everything you hear, not even everything you hear in a sermon! Assess it! Evaluate it!

It is actually easier and clearer to us today to do this, because we have the complete Scripture available and accessible. They would have had their knowledge of true teaching, pure doctrine, from what they had heard from Paul and others like him. But just as they - and we - are to resist evil, so also it is important to resist error. Jesus himself warned (Matthew 7:15) that false teachers would come like wolves in sheep's clothing, false followers who would be capable of wreaking havoc amongst the flock of God.

In 1 Thessalonians 5:20-21 Paul said again the same kind of thing: Put everything you hear (even from prophets) to the test, and hold fast to what is good. Later, to the Ephesian elders (Acts 20:29-30) he was to exhort them to guard themselves and all the flock of which the Holy Spirit of God had made them overseers, for savage wolves are coming to ravage the flock. (What a clear reminiscence of Jesus's teaching!)

In the same way Peter (in 2 Peter 2:1-3) warns that, as there were false prophets of old, so there will be false teachers invading the church in his day, promoting destructive heresies.

In recent centuries down to present times - as indeed before, throughout church history - there have come false prophets into the church, enemies of the gospel masquerading as children of light (2 Corinthians 11:13-15). And also quite often there are earnest and genuine followers of the Lord who, in their teaching, simply are sincerely astray, sincerely wrong.

Too often the church of God has been too slow to weigh the teaching of the teachers against Scripture, and to denounce error for what it is. The combined result is to be seen in parts of the church today: places where believers were previously true to the Scriptures but who now have accepted wrong teaching about the things of God, and wrong moral and ethical standards which are contrary to the Word of God.

And if we ourselves are called to a ministry of prophecy, of preaching - instructing, exhorting, and encouraging the people of God - this underlines the responsibility we are undertaking. James 3:1 reminds us that teachers will be judged with greater strictness. Paul says to Timothy (1 Timothy 1:3), "instruct certain people not to teach any different doctrine." And Paul says here, "Weigh carefully what is said."

Let us do this conscientiously, testing what is being taught against the whole teaching of the Word of God. Isaiah said (8:20) "To the teaching and to the testimony! If they will not speak according to this word, it is because they have no light." To do this requires that we are diligent and teachable students of the Bible, so that we put ourselves genuinely in a position today to evaluate preaching accurately by biblical standards, and we do not reject something just on the grounds that it is at variance with something else we learnt before. Like the Bereans of Acts 17:11, we must be active in searching the Scriptures for ourselves, as to whether these things are so.

The general teaching of the Scripture is that we are to accept the leadership of our leaders, and give them our loyal obedience (1 Thessalonians 5:12; 1 Corinthians 16:16; Hebrews 13:17). But this is to be balanced by a healthy scepticism which weighs up what is being said by the preacher: for Paul here puts this into balance. The fact that something is said by a prophet, a preacher, a leader in the church, does not automatically **guarantee** that it is right and true, and a word from God. Perhaps if those in earlier generations had been more alert to assess, identify, and counter wrong teaching, we may not have to the same extent the doctrinal and moral confusion which exists in many parts of today's church. Perhaps if we heed **now** these words of warning from Paul, we may do a better job of guarding the deposit of God's truth and handing it on faithfully - and accurately - to the next generation, as Paul in 2 Timothy 2:2 challenged Timothy to do, and as Jude 3 also exhorts us.

### (c) The Question of Women In The Church (14:33b-36)

**14:33b-36** Chapter 3 in my book *The Ministry of Women in the Church* (SPCK Australia) is devoted to the detailed discussion of this short passage, and as this book is readily available I will content myself here with a brief summary of the issues and of my interpretation.

In 11:5 Paul discusses what is required when a woman prays or prophesies; in this passage he instructs that "the women should keep silent in the churches. For they are not permitted to speak." What are we to make of these apparently contradictory statements in the same epistle? There have been various attempts made at reconciling the two passages - sometimes by rejecting one or the other of them.

Thus some scholars hold that the restriction upon a woman in 11:5 shows Paul's tacit disapproval of her engaging in such a ministry at all, a disapproval which he makes completely plain and clear in 14:33-36. Thus Edwards 381 gives his view,

> In 11:5 the Apostle permits the women to pray and prophesy in the assembly under certain restrictions. The discussion of the gifts of tongues seems to have led him to withdraw even that limited permission.

At the other end of the spectrum Anderson Scott 126 solves the problem by regarding the words as a non-Pauline interpolation: "That the verses 1 Corinthians 14:34, 35, which close with the words, 'It is disgraceful for women to speak in church', were written by St. Paul I do not believe." Barrett 332-333 is also inclined to reject these verses, and similarly Fee 699ff. considers them "inauthentic" and a later addition.

Another approach is the suggestion that the embedding of these verses within a passage dealing with speaking in tongues is significant for interpretation, as is the use of λαλειν (*lalein*) for "speak" (verses 34b, 35b), as this is the word uniformly used in the expression "to speak in tongues". Thus the interpretation is deduced that "to speak" here means "to speak in tongues" and that the meaning of the passage is that women are being forbidden to speak in tongues, for this is never permitted for them.

Now, it is sound to take it that this section must relate in *some* way to its context. But the problems with *this* particular interpretation are:

**(a)** It notes only one feature of the surrounding context ("speaking in tongues") and assigns to it the overriding role in deciding the meaning of this passage (the other major element in the context is that of edification, avoiding confusion and promoting peace, and doing all things decently and in order: it is much more reasonable to see that *this*, rather, is the context factor to which Paul's comments about women are related).

**(b)** It does not take adequate account of the words introducing this section, "as in all the churches of the saints" (v.33b), for what would be the point of saying that a comment about women speaking in tongues is identical with what is taught to all the churches of the saints if the question of the abuse of speaking in tongues was (as seems the case) only an issue at Corinth?

**(c)** If speaking in tongues is put on to a par with prophecy when there is interpretation/translation provided (as Paul says in 14:5), and under Paul's rule interpretation/ translation *must* be provided (14:28), so that the result would parallel prophecy, why would this be forbidden to women when a woman can prophesy (Acts 2:17; 21:9; 1 Corinthians 11:5)?

**(d)** The interpretation that Paul's intention is to forbid women to speak in tongues leaves 14:35a as meaningless, for on such an interpretation what is the point of Paul saying, in between the two references to women speaking [in tongues] (verses 34b and 35b), that they should ask their husbands at home about anything they wanted to know?

**(e)** The closest previous reference to speaking in tongues - verses 27 and 28 - is rather a long distance away for it to be clear for any reader to see that the use of the ordinary word "to speak" several verses further on is to be taken to mean "to speak in tongues". This would not be a natural understanding of it. Does it not look very much like a case of special pleading?

I find this approach totally unconvincing.

Hurley has put forward the interpretation that what women are not allowed to do is take part in the public evaluation of prophecies, an interpretation of "let the others weigh what is said" (v.29). This idea was taken up by Grudem 2000, 188ff. and has also been espoused by various other writers. Some scholars (e.g. Bilezikian 245f.) have argued strongly against it.

I consider Hurley's position self-contradictory. He holds that women are not to exercise authority in the church, or to teach, but that they may prophesy; yet that here they are being forbidden to evaluate the prophecies of others. So a man or woman may prophesy, and this prophecy is then evaluated in the congregation: but only by men. This view regards the evaluation of a prophecy as an exercise of authority (and therefore forbidden to women), but not the prophecy itself!

It is absurd to adopt an interpretation of the passage which allows women to *give* prophecies but then not to participate with others in *discussing* prophecies.

But the text itself rules out the Hurley view. The command to silence is directed to women in relation to their wanting to learn: that was the point and purpose of their asking questions. But the assessment of prophecies is an *examining* question - a very different matter! And there would be no point in instructing a woman who might otherwise have engaged in such a discussion and evaluation that the correct alternative for her to follow is instead to ask her husband questions at home so that she might learn something. As Bilezikian 245 points out:

> Questions raised at home would have been irrelevant to the congregation's evaluation of prophecies that had been uttered during its meetings.

Finally, Paul appeals to the Law in support of what he is saying: but there is nothing in the Law to which appeal can be made to stop women evaluating prophecies.

Therefore this view cannot be the meaning of the text.

There is a much more reasonable and valid interpretation. Its starting point is giving attention to the words Paul used in these verses.

The Greek language contains a wide range of words meaning to communicate meaningful content to someone. There are specific words for "to preach" (κηρύσσω, *kērussō*), "to teach" (διδάσκω, *didaskō*), "to proclaim the gospel" (εὐαγγελίζομαι, *euangelizomai*), "to prophesy" (προφητεύω, *prophēteuō*), "to assert" (φάσκω, *phaskō*), "to make an announcement" (ἀγγέλλω, *angellō*), and three common words for "to speak/say" in the sense of "to convey information", "to tell someone something" (λέγω, *legō*, φημί, *phēmi*, and εἰπεῖν, *eipein*). And there are all the various compounds of these words: well over a dozen words in all. These verbs all have primary reference to the **content** of what is being said.

Another Greek verb, λαλέω, *laleō*, refers to saying something with one's mouth, the act and fact of speaking — *laleō* involves **verbal utterance**: it is something that "the mouth speaks" (Matthew 12:34), the act of uttering words. Thus whenever the New Testament refers to a person who had been dumb as now being able to speak, the word used is always *laleō* (Matthew 9:33; 12:22; 15:31; Mark 7:37; Luke 11:14).

Similarly, λαλέω, *laleō*, is the normal word used for when people engage in informal conversation; it refers simply to talking, especially in the sense of conversing, or chatting, or even chattering or babbling.

This verb *laleō* is not the word for preaching, teaching, or giving an address. To say this does not mean that *laleō* was never used where meaning was being conveyed by what was said: it was. The word **could** have the meaning of the informal presentation of a Christian message, as in conversational preaching or teaching. For example, on a number of occasions *laleō* is used of Jesus teaching the people (e.g., Matthew 13:3). But the central idea is that of engaging in oral communication, of being **heard**, and usually the idea of informal utterance is also present.

This differentiation can be noted when λαλεω [*laleō*] and λεγω [*legō*] are used together, as in 1 Corinthians 12:3: "no one **speaking** in the Spirit of God ever **says** ..." (consecutive words in the Greek). The former focusses on the **act**, the latter on the **content**.

When Paul says in 1 Corinthians 14:34-35 that women are not permitted to speak in church, he does not use any of the words that mean to preach or teach or communicate a message. He does not even use one of the ordinary Greek words for "speak" which refer to the conveying of meaningful content (*legō, phēmi, eipein*). What Paul uses (twice, once each in 14:34 and 35) is this word *laleō* — which is a **very** ambiguous and inconclusive word to use if "preach/teach/communicate information to the congregation" is the meaning Paul is seeking to convey.

Let us note, moreover, the significance of the context in 1 Corinthians 14 in which Paul gives his comments about women speaking.

Paul has been discussing the question of good order in the congregation. He has just been talking about this in relation to the issues of tongues and prophecy (14:22-32). The transition verse, 33, which links that topic with his next topic of women being silent, says, "For God is not a God of confusion but of peace". Paul concludes this entire section of his letter, "But all things should be done decently and in order" (v.40). What comes in between these two statements of verses 33 and 40, thus in a sense "framed" by them, can be expected therefore to relate to his overall subject at this point in his letter, the issue to which he is referring both immediately before and immediately after what he says about women not speaking. And this is: the issue of avoiding confusion and of promoting peace, and thus of conducting worship in a fitting and orderly way.

The interpretation to the effect that Paul here discusses whether women can preach or teach or otherwise contribute in spiritual ministry does not fit this context. Rather, the context favours the alternative view: that Paul here discusses a problem of disorder and lack of peace in the worship, which is resulting from the behavior of women talking.

Furthermore, let us recall the circumstances of the day. At that time in the synagogue, and then in the early church, men and women sat separately in the meetings. There would doubtless be occasions during the course of the meetings of the assembly when something was said that some of the women found strange or perplexing.

What happened then? One of the possible ways in which some of the women could respond to such a situation would be to discuss the point amongst themselves, or there and then to ask their husbands about it, where they sat.

If we think it unlikely that the women would do such a thing in church, we need to remind ourselves that (contrary to the Jewish milieu, where the women were not being taught) in the Christian church the teaching was being addressed to the women as much as to the men. And the ground-rules for the handling of new situations which would arise because of changes of this kind from Judaistic practice were still in the process of being developed.

If the practice that ultimately developed was of people not conversing or calling out to one another during the conduct of worship, then it seems possible that some Christian leader at some stage guided the church towards such orderly conduct in the public meetings. My contention is simply: here in 1 Corinthians 14:34-35 we have the record of Paul doing precisely that. That is the point and meaning of these verses.

The exegesis of 1 Corinthians 14:34-35 which I propose is not a new suggestion. It has been advocated by many scholars through the years (alongside the view of others, that Paul is here prohibiting women from preaching and teaching in the church).

For example, Hillyer (*New Bible Commentary* 1070),

> Women had to be wise in using their newly-given liberty in Christ. Paul is here protesting against the disturbance of services by feminine chatter - the meaning of *speak* in verses 34-35. Some women (they sat apart from men) were perhaps calling out questions, and commenting knowingly on things said in the service.

Similarly Nicole 45f.; to the contrary, Grudem 2000, 185ff.

Thus this interpretation is simply to take λαλειν (*lalein*) in its primary sense of "to chatter, prattle, babble" [cf. Danker-BAG; and also Kittel, "[this word is used] of speech when there is a reference to sound rather than to meaning." If then we are correct in giving weight to the particular word Paul has chosen to use, and to the context in which this passage is set, then we can see that Paul is not forbidding women to preach or teach, but is forbidding them to disrupt the meetings of the church with conversation, chatter, or possibly even calling out.

If, alternatively, a person would wish to interpret this passage as forbidding preaching and teaching, then there are three issues with which he will have to come to terms.

***Firstly***, why does Paul choose to use the verb λαλεω *laleō* rather than a word which would have conveyed such a meaning quite clearly and unambiguously to his readers?

***Secondly***, if "women speaking" means women teaching and preaching, then what is the point Paul is making in 14:35 where he says to ***those women*** who (on this view) are speaking by ***teaching and preaching*** that ***they*** should ask their husbands at home if there is anything they want to know? On this interpretation, they are engaging in speaking because they believe they have something worthwhile to communicate to others present: they are not speaking for the reason that they want to find out something! Such a comment as this would be absolutely irrelevant in reference to women "speaking" in the sense of preaching and teaching in the church. Rather, it indicates clearly that the speaking to which Paul is referring is related to their wanting to know something. Grenz and Kjesbo 123 comment succinctly,

> Paul's explanatory command "Let them ask their husbands at home" indicates that he is primarily concerned with women interrupting teaching, not women engaged in teaching.

***Thirdly***, if speaking means preaching and teaching, how can women be permitted, in the light of this passage, to engage in ***any*** kind of preaching or teaching? This passage acts as a ***total prohibition*** of whatever it is that it is prohibiting, for it allows no scope for exceptions — women are not permitted to do it at all (whatever "***it***" is) but are to be silent; thus if it means ministering by speaking, there is no room for the ideas of women preaching to women, women teaching Sunday School, women as missionaries, and so on. It is indeed arguable that for women to engage in public prayer and sing hymns would also be forbidden by this passage. Once λαλεω *laleō* in this passage is taken as referring to the exercise of a spiritual ministry of some sort by women, there is no way in which some exceptions can be fitted in by which any kind of spiritual speaking-ministry within the church can be retained for women.

To sum up: If Paul had wanted to refer to women preaching, teaching, or otherwise engaging in ministry in the congregation, he had a range of a dozen or so such words available to him, general or specific, which referred to the **content** of an utterance. If he had wanted to refer to women conversing in church assemblies, λαλεω *laleō* would be the verb to use. And λαλεω *laleō* is the verb he did use.

Attention to the meaning of the words Paul uses, consideration of the context and background circumstances, and consistency with the overall teaching of Scripture, all point to the same interpretation of this passage: that Paul is rebuking disorder in the assembly caused by the women conversing and asking questions. Let them, he says, be silent while in the church assembly, and at home ask their husbands whatever else they want to know. And once it is recognized that what Paul is forbidding is the opposite of asking their husbands something at home, we can see that he is writing in reference to women conversing in church in a way that disturbs the proper dignity and order of public worship.

The passage 1 Corinthians 14:34-35 has nothing to contribute to the question of whether women ought or ought not to preach (κηρύσσω, *kērussō*) or to teach (διδάσκω, *didaskō*) in the congregation, because it simply does not touch on this issue at all. Certainly this passage does not forbid such ministry to women.

Thus this instruction is no more an absolute and total ban in all circumstances on women speaking in church than is the call to men to be silent (verses 28 and 30). Each takes its meaning from its context and from the circumstances of the time.

It was to be expected in the society of that day (and still may be the case even today in some parts of the world) that some women could need help in understanding the meaning of new teaching: perhaps reduced educational opportunities may sometimes play a part in this. By all means shall the husband be encouraged to help his wife to understand what she hears. But let this be at home, not in the middle of a church service!

**14:36** This is directed against any individual church (in this case, Corinth) thinking it was "a law to itself" and could make individual rules and arrangements for itself, out of kilter with all other churches. It highlights the danger of individualistic and idiosyncratic behavior, usually the result of a strong personality with ideas of his - or her - own dominating the congregation. It seems that Paul sometimes had occasion to be concerned about holding his churches together in a unity of faith and practice.

### (d) The Assessment of Tongues and Prophecy (14:37-40E)

**14:37** "If anybody thinks he is ...": that is, "if anyone considers himself to be ..." Clearly a person who was chosen by God and appointed as a prophet (12:28), and was receiving supernatural revelations of the mysteries of God (Ephesians 3:5), would not be unaware of this. So, this is the secondary type of reference to prophets and prophecy. This person is making a judgement about himself that he has the gift and ministry of prophecy in the non-miraculous sense, and is seeking to exercise it.

Such a person who regards himself as being a prophet or one of the "spiritual ones" (2:13-3:3; 12:1) will recognize and acknowledge that what Paul is writing is a commandment of the Lord. Paul clearly has a high sense of the inspiration and thus of the authority of what he has written.

Christians may come to differing conclusions about the meaning and interpretation of what Paul is saying, but the one option which is not being left open to us regarding any part of this Epistle is to dismiss what Paul writes as irrelevant or outmoded, or purely a matter of Paul's own personal opinions which we are free to ignore as we choose. On the contrary. When we are laboring to understand correctly the meaning of what Paul is teaching, the effort is worthwhile because behind what Paul says stands the full authority of the Lord himself.

**14:38** Acceptance of Paul's teaching and authority is made a requirement for a person to be accepted himself by Paul and the Christian congregation (and possibly - it may be implied - by the Lord himself).

**14:39-40E** In conclusion: the brothers should be eager and zealous to prophesy, for in the sense in which Paul has been using the term in this chapter this, as we have seen, is open to all (14:1, 5, 31) and it is more to be desired than anything else because it provides people with upbuilding and encouragement and consolation (14:3) and it results in the church being edified (14:4). But the existence of the gift of speaking in tongues is to be acknowledged and this is therefore not to be excluded - but everything (speaking in tongues and all else) is to be carried out in a decent and orderly way.

# SOME PRACTICAL AND PASTORAL REFLECTIONS

## What Was Going On At Corinth?

When this chapter is examined, it will be found that there are two places (verses 2, and 14-16) which could be understood to refer to the speaker in tongues using a non-human language, but neither of these places demands such an interpretation to explain them (both places could refer to the speaker speaking in a human language that he himself did not happen to understand, and indeed in both places Paul could be referring to the speaker using a human language which he himself *did* in fact understand - see my comments on these verses).

Some exegetes consider that verses 4 and 28 also indicate the use of non-human language (or at least a language not understood by the speaker), but this idea is being read into the text, not taken from it - there is absolutely nothing in the wording of those verses to suggest that a human language is not meant.

On the other hand, there is strong evidence in the passage for taking "tongues" to mean, as in Acts, human languages.

Verses 10-11 speak of the "all sorts of languages in the world", and add that "none of them is without meaning" - which in context means "meaning to human beings"; and "if I do not know what that meaning is, then I and the speaker are foreigners to each other" (the Greek word "foreigner" here, βαρβαρος *barbaros*, specifically means a person speaking a foreign language). Paul's next words, "So with yourselves" indicate that his comment is *describing what is happening at Corinth*, and thus is a comment about the nature of tongues.

V.21 quotes from "the Law" (Deuteronomy 28:47-51 and, in particular, Isaiah 28:11-12) which refers to "men of strange tongues", and this prophecy from the Old Testament is immediately used (v.22) to explain the purpose of tongues in the church of Paul's day. As the strange tongues then were a sign to the unbelieving Israelites of God's judgement, so also now (i.e., in Paul's day) tongues are a sign for unbelievers. But "tongues" in v.21 refers to the foreign language spoken by the Assyrian invaders! There is no basis upon which "tongues" in Paul's consequence clause, "Tongues, then" (v.22), can be given a different meaning: it similarly is referring to human languages - foreign, but human.

Now that we have looked at all that Paul is saying about speaking in tongues (he doesn't mention it again in any of his other Epistles), what are we to make of it? In particular, exactly what was going on at Corinth?

The core of the situation at Corinth is that there are some there who have the gift of being able to speak a foreign language that they never learnt. This is a perpetual miracle - and it can be called forth on demand. Probably these people were some of the initial one hundred and twenty (Acts 1:15) who were given this gift on the day of Pentecost (Acts 2:1) - and like other grace-gifts, when once given they still have it.

Perhaps others also have subsequently been given this same gift: I do not see any evidence about this one way or the other.

We can imagine that these people are being encouraged by others in the church to use this gift - not for any useful purpose, but just to demonstrate that they have it. It brings them prestige. It is a miracle on tap, they are happy to oblige. This is an example of what we might call the "wow!" factor at work.

But I believe the evidence indicates that there is another group at Corinth also: people who can speak a foreign language anyway (either because they learnt it in the ordinary way or because it is their mother tongue). They are also using this "ability" - as far as others are concerned, it all sounds the same! And they are thus able to gain the same prestige and recognition in the Corinthian church as the first group.

Griffiths 57ff. says about this:

> How are we to understand this word γλωσσα [glōssa]? Does it mean that when we speak in 'tongues', we speak to God in prayer? That is certainly a possible understanding of it. Or could it mean [rather] that if you speak in your "mother-tongue", which may be incomprehensible to the rest of the congregation, that you are certainly understood by God, who understands all languages, but you only edify yourself because nobody else understands what you are saying? ... After all, if on the day of Pentecost Jerusalem was full of people speaking many languages, then it is not too far-fetched to expect that in a large cosmopolitan seaport like Corinth, you would not infrequently have overseas visitors: Parthians, Medes, Elamites, dwellers in Mesopotamia, Judea and Cappadocia, Pontus and Asia, Phrygia and Pamphilia, Egypt, districts of Libya around Cyrene, Cretans and Arabians and visitors from Rome. In such a multi-lingual port, there must have been many occasions when someone wanted to speak in their own language, which would be incomprehensible to the predominantly Greek-speaking congregation. ... Should people be allowed to contribute in unfamiliar languages? Everything Paul says is explicable in terms of regulating this problem.

So, it is highly probable that there were these first two groups in the congregation. But Paul seems surprised by the number of tongues-speakers at Corinth, and I think he suspects there is a third group: those who are just faking it, to receive the same elite status held by these others. At any rate, there are parts of Paul's teaching that seem to me to be deliberately wide enough to cover all three such groups, as if Paul

himself is not totally sure what is going on at Corinth, and he is making
certain he covers all possibilities.

If my suspicions are correct, there is a basic core at Corinth of what
we could call "genuine" tongues-speakers, with a miraculous gift of
speaking an unlearned foreign language, plus some others who have
managed to join this elite group. But whatever the situation at Corinth,
Paul can clearly see its bad effects, and his teaching is directed at bringing it under control without overtly denying the existence and genuineness of miraculous tongues-speaking as a grace gift from God.

Does this gift of tongues exist today?

The miraculous element - the ability to speak, unlearned, a foreign
language? No: that is said by Paul (14:22) to be a sign gift, and it did not
continue beyond the apostolic era.

But enhanced language ability? Most definitely "yes".

This was Calvin's understanding. In his Commentary on 1 Corinthians [286] he describes "the gift of tongues" as "somebody speaking in
a foreign language", for "tongue" "means a foreign language". Similarly
he says [263],

> Interpreters translated the foreign languages into the native speech.
> They did not at that time acquire these gifts by hard work or studying;
> but they were theirs by a wonderful revelation of the Spirit.

Calvin holds that the miraculous ability of speaking and interpreting a
foreign language is not ours today, but God gives to the Church those
people who will study languages using natural ability: "knowledge of
languages" continues in the Church to "serve the needs of this life"
[280], but is now acquired through study. Then he adds [287],

> God has bestowed no gift on His Church without there being some
> purpose for it; and tongues were of some use at that time. ... In our own
> day when there is a crying need for the knowledge of tongues, and
> when, at our stage in history, God in His wonderful kindness has
> rescued them from darkness and brought them to light, there are great
> theologians who, faced with that situation, are loud and violent in their
> protests against them. Since there can be no doubt that the Holy Spirit
> has bestowed undying honor on tongues in this verse [14:5], it is easy to
> deduce what sort of spirit moves those critics who make strong attacks
> against the study of languages with as much insulting language as they
> can muster.

To sum up then: I find that a consideration of the text leads to these
conclusions:

**(a)** That "speaking in tongues" always has in the New Testament the
meaning that it has in Acts 2, that is, speaking in a human language;

**(b)** that the "speaking in tongues" at Pentecost was the miraculous granting of ability to speak in a human language which one had not learnt;

**(c)** that this miraculous ability was used in the preaching of the gospel in those first years of the early church, and that this was a sign to unbelievers;

**(d)** that foreign-language-speaking at Corinth had become a distortion of the Pentecost gift, both in purpose and execution. The speaker may have been given the ability to speak the foreign language by miraculous divine gift, or by heightened natural ability - or in fact he may have been speaking a language he had learned in the ordinary way: or he may have been pretending to have this miraculous language-speaking ability.

Quite possibly all three of these things were happening in the "speaking in tongues" at Corinth; and three similar equivalents apply in relation to "interpretation".

**(e)** that this miraculous granting of the gift ceased in the early church by the time the writing of the New Testament was complete;

**(f)** that such miraculous ability to speak in a language which one has not learnt is not being granted to Christians today, but that the gift of tongues (without the miraculous element) is to have a facility in learning to communicate the gospel in a foreign language, and the gift of interpretation/translation is the ability to translate the message of the gospel from one language into another. Both of these are skills in which by God's choice some people are better equipped than others; and both of them God gives to his church today.

We may well say that so-and-so has a gift for languages, and we speak more truly than we realize. For we refer to a natural flair for learning another language, and this is a God-given ability, just as another person will have a flair for music, or mathematics, or teaching, or administration.

Such a gift is of immense value to a person called to be a foreign missionary. Michael Griffiths 58f., a world missionary leader, explains:

> Nowadays, before accepting somebody as a missionary, we give them a Modern Language Aptitude Test to get a rough idea of whether they have any natural aptitude for languages. ... No missionary discussion today can overlook the fact that an essential component in a missionary's usefulness is going to be his ability to speak one or more languages. For the first term of missionary service, the time involved in learning a language and the restrictions of inadequate language will be a major factor. In several countries people really need to learn two new languages! Any missionary society constantly wrestles with this problem of communication. ... People who do not speak a language are always impressed by another's apparent fluency, and readily call it a 'gift for language'. Anybody who regularly has to preach in a recently-

acquired language recognises how much he needs the grace gift from the Holy Spirit to speak effectively. It is an essential gift for taking the gospel to all nations!

Indeed, if one has such a gift, one may recognize it as equipping you for missionary service. Oh that such people should test out and recognize their calling and equipping of God to take up the challenge of missionary service, whether fulltime or, like Paul for much of his ministry, as "tent-makers"! The need for workers in the fields white for harvest is immense, and a facility for languages is a great asset in preparing for this ministry, and responding to this call.

Similarly, the gift of interpretation for today means the ability to turn what is said in one language into its meaningful and accurate equivalent in another. This is more than just being able to speak both languages - it involves being able to recognize the equivalent of the one in the other. Michael Griffiths's comment (65) about this is:

> Let us remember again that the understanding of the word as "trans-lation" still involves a spiritual gift. Those of us who listen frequently to translated messages, or who have to be interpreted ourselves, are very clear that a gifted interpreter manifests the unction of the Spirit just as much or even more than the speaker whom he interprets. There can be no doubt that the plain meaning "interpreter" (of one known language into another) requires the grace of God to do it effectively to the bless-ing of the congregation.

Thus in today's world the gifts of "tongues" and "interpretation" can be seen as natural abilities which God gives to one person or another. Michael Griffiths 68 describes them as "natural aptitudes which would subsequently become enriched by spiritual gifts".

Griffiths goes on:

> While we must agree that we cannot succeed in spiritual work merely by relying upon natural aptitudes, the sovereign God may well give to his servants from their mother's womb natural abilities which, when surrendered, sanctified and transfigured by spiritual blessings, can be effectively used to God's glory.

This assessment of "tongues" and "interpretation" covers all the issues which arise in the understanding of 1 Corinthians 12 to 14, but it leaves unresolved one remaining major issue: what then is one to make of modern-day "speaking in tongues"? I discuss this below, in Excursus Four, "Tongues Speaking Today: A Comment".

For those of you who would like to look into this further, I recom-mend the very warm and helpful approach to answering this significant question found in J I Packer's book *Keep in Step With the Spirit*.

# EXCURSUS FOUR:
# TONGUES SPEAKING TODAY: A COMMENT

## OUTLINE

INTRODUCTION

WHAT IT IS NOT
1. Glossolalia Is Not Speaking In Natural Human Languages
2. Glossolalia Is Not Speaking In Language At All
3. Glossolalia Is Not In Any Way a Sign of the Holy Spirit

WHAT IT IS
1. Glossolalia Is Religious Enthusiasm
2. Glossolalia Is a Symbol of Peer Group Membership
3. Glossolalia May Be Due to Autohypnosis & Psychologically Induced
4. Glossolalia Is a Learned Response
5. Glossolalia May Be Used By The Devil

WHAT CAUSES THE WISH TO SPEAK IN TONGUES?
1. Consequences of Mistranslation in the New Testament
2. Desire For a Deeper Christian Experience
3. Desire For a Miracle
4. Psychological Pressure

WHAT LEADS PEOPLE TO SPEAK IN TONGUES?
5. Expectancy
6. Acceptance and Conformity to the Expectation
7. Pleasure and Enjoyment
8. Effectiveness in Prayer
9. Belief In the Value and Importance of Baptism in the Spirit
10. A Desire For Power, Control, and/or Recognition
11. A Sense of Spiritual Obligation

A RESPONSE TO MODERN GLOSSOLALIA
1. Recognize the Mistranslation
2. The Correct Path To a Deeper Christian Experience
3. Anyone Can Speak in Tongues - It's Not a Christian Miracle
4. Resist Psychological Pressure
5. What Should We Be Expecting?
6. Acceptance/Conformity Can Confirm Us In Wrong Views
7. Pleasure Can Be Based upon Human Factors/Mistaken Views
8. What Is the True Measure Of Effectiveness In Prayer?
9. Respect For the Interpretation Accepted By Others

10. Wrongness of Using "Spiritual Gifts" in a Power Struggle

11. Being Freed from Feeling Obligated to Engage in Glossolalia

CONCLUSION


## INTRODUCTION

The Commentary on chapter 14 has set out the traditional understanding of "speaking in tongues": that in both Acts and 1 Corinthians, this refers to the miraculous speaking of a human foreign language that the speaker does not know by ordinary means of knowing. This is shown to be the natural meaning of what Paul is explaining in chapters 12 to 14. But this leaves one crucial question unresolved: in that case, what is the nature of modern tongues-speaking? For today's tongues-speakers believe that they are exercising exactly the gift that Paul is talking about.

The issue is broader than tongues alone: it raises numerous other matters relating to the Charismatic movement. Indeed, here is a dilemma so great that it challenges our understanding.

On the one hand, there are those in the Charismatic movement (and they are many) who have been brought to Christ by it, or who had been apathetic or dead Christians and who have been brought to new life by it. Their experience of "being baptized in the Spirit" has refreshed and invigorated them. So how can there be other Christians (and there are!) who deny that there is any such experience as this for the Christian, who say that the baptism in the Spirit is part of conversion.

These Charismatic Christians *know* that it was not part of *their* conversion! For them, it was an experience that came later. They have a new joy and enthusiasm for the Lord. They find that praying in tongues brings them a release and liberty in prayer that was not there before. They see healings and mighty works performed in their midst, they hear prophecies and utterances of wisdom and knowledge, and interpretations of tongues, that bring them a real sense of God directly addressing their situation and their concerns today. For them there is no room for doubt at all - this is genuine; it is God at work in their midst in a mighty way.

So how can there be other Christians (and there are!) who reject all this, and insist on clinging to their old ways? No wonder many of these Charismatic Christians are tempted to say (and they do!) that the traditional Christians are holding back out of fear or are simply unwilling to surrender fully to God and allow him to have his way in their lives, that such people in fact are quenching the Spirit.

On the other hand, there are those Christians (and they are many) who have sincerely searched the Scriptures concerning all these things, and cannot find any warrant or justification in the Bible for such doctrines or such experiences. They believe that this is a mistaken interpretation of Scripture, and that these Charismatic experiences do not line up with God's Word or God's intentions for us. So how can there be other Christians (and there are!) who say that in these various new ways God is exactly meeting their needs today, and speaking directly to them in their problems?

The traditional Christians are amazed to hear that there are well-known and respected Christian leaders in their local community and on the world scene (and there are!) who have accepted the Charismatic view and have spoken in tongues. But nonetheless it is possible to see in the Charismatic movement a frequent concentration upon tongues and healings that throws everything else in the Christian life out of balance, a growing tendency to depend for guidance and instruction upon prophecies and other utterances instead of upon the Bible, so that these Christians are in practice giving these things a greater place of authority in their lives than Scripture.

Traditional Christians can see how many people come for healing and do not receive it, and are left disillusioned and bereft, having been assured that if they had faith they would be healed. Traditional Christians can see how often some Charismatics have abandoned (even at times, actually condemned) the serious study of Scripture because they receive their word direct from today's prophets when they need it. Traditional Christians have noticed how often Scripture is made to fit an experience and authenticate it, whereas Scripture should be our foundation and the standard by which we judge all else, to which our experience is to conform. Otherwise, no matter how we dress it up, we have in reality abandoned Scripture as our final authority. No wonder many of these traditional Christians are tempted to say (and they do!) that the Charismatic Christians are exalting an experience to a place above Scripture.

It is puzzling. Indeed, it is confusing. How can earnest, eager, committed Christians, seeking to live in obedience to the Lord, and to find and follow his truth, come to such opposite, and in point of fact contradictory, conclusions about issues that are so important in the practical expression of our Christian living?

Unquestionably, there is need for greater understanding by each side of the other - and by each side of the ramifications of its own position!

This is certainly true in relation to the whole question of the nature of modern speaking in tongues. If this is identical with the tongues-speaking of the Bible, then God is engaged in performing fresh miracles in our day in this way, and we all of us have to recognize this and adjust our thinking to take proper account of it.

How else may modern tongues-speaking be viewed? Is there any other explanation of what is happening?

There *is* another explanation: an explanation that is based upon thorough careful investigation of tongues-speaking today by those who are both Christian and also expert in this whole area.

The purpose of this Excursus is to outline this explanation and thus to contribute to everyone's understanding of the nature of speaking in tongues today, and to draw some conclusions concerning it.

Our examination in the Commentary of the wording of 1 Corinthians 12-14 has considered and presented the evidence for the interpretation that in the Bible the expression "speaking in tongues" always refers to speaking natural languages, and never to unintelligible sayings or supernatural, non-human languages. Now if this is so, what is to be said about the "speaking in tongues" (technically called *glossolalia*) which is practised by some Christians today?

The definitive study of modern tongues-speaking has been carried out by Professor William J Samarin, and is written up in his book *Tongues of Men and Angels* (1972) and his article "Glossolalia As A Vocal Phenomenon" (1973). Samarin is a Christian, and has written as Professor of Anthropology and Linguistics at the University of Toronto, and a specialist in African languages and sociolinguistics. In this Excursus, I have regarded Samarin's first-hand research as of considerable significance.

His study is quite sympathetic towards the whole tongues-speaking movement - the full title of his book is *Tongues of Men and Angels - A Controversial And Sympathetic Analysis Of Speaking In Tongues*.

He himself accepts glossolalia as a valid religious experience. His endorsement of the movement is based ultimately not on any linguistic factors or indeed anything directly connected with the glossolalia but upon his perception of the overall spiritual enthusiasm and vitality, and quality of life, of those in the movement.

Our present concern is somewhat different. It is not to give an assessment of tongues-speaking on the basis of concomitant features in the lives of tongues-speakers but it is to ask, "Is the modern glossolalia the speaking in tongues of the New Testament?" And having found good grounds for seeing the two as fundamentally different (as set out in the Commentary on 1 Corinthians 12-14), then to ask, "What then is the nature and purpose of modern glossolalia, and what is the reason for its practice?"

## WHAT IT IS NOT

### 1. Glossolalia Is Not Speaking in Natural Human Languages

Charismatics generally consider that modern tongues-speaking is speaking sometimes in an actual human language, and sometimes in a non-human language ("the language of heaven", "tongues of angels"). This is based on 1 Corinthians 12:10, where the spiritual gift is described as (NIV) "the ability to speak in different kinds of tongues", and this is then further identified in 1 Corinthians 13:1 as to "speak in the tongues of men and of angels".

To clarify the technical terms that are used:

We need to note the distinction between *glossolalia* and *xenoglossia*: Samarin defines *glossolalia* [1973:131] as "a vocal act believed by the speaker to be language and showing rudimentary language-like structure but no consistent word-meaning correspondence recognizable by either speaker or hearer." A *glossolalist* speaks a *glossa*, which is [1973:141] "(a) an alleged language, represented by a particular glossolalic discourse; (b) a specimen, either written down or mechanically recorded, of this 'language'." By contrast, *xenoglossia* is [1973:130] "the demonstration of knowledge of a language not learned in the normal ways."

Charismatics commonly believe that, whilst rare, speaking in an unlearned human language (the technical term for which is *xenoglossia*) **does** occur, and most Charismatics will have heard or read reports of this happening.

For example, Morton Kelsey 152-163 recounts several stories of xenoglossia. Johnson 227 relates a remarkable such story. And Basham 1976:37-39 writes:

> But the truth is that today's speaking in tongues *is* miraculous and that many times the languages which are spoken *are* recognized - by other persons present - as foreign languages not naturally known by the one speaking. I could easily double the size of this book simply by setting out to record several dozen such incidents. But three brief illustrations should be sufficient. [Three accounts of xenoglossia are then given.]

The same writer gives further examples of xenoglossia in his other books [1969:77-78; 1971:49 and 61-65]. And in fact these reports of xenoglossia could be multiplied many times over in books by Charismatic authors - there are numerous anecdotes in the literature recounting instances of people today speaking fluently in a language which they have not learnt.

However, as tongues-speakers regard both "tongues of men" and "tongues of angels" as equally the "gift of tongues", and from God, they usually down-play the significance of the question as to whether what is spoken is a natural language or not. Thus Basham [1976:39] says:

> Yet, in spite of the obviously miraculous demonstration such incidents provide, we need to remember that, according to Scripture, *the validity of the experience of tongues is not dependent on the languages being understood.*

Basham makes similar comments in his other books [1969:75, 76, and 79; and 1971:48-49].

But it is **not** a minor question whether modern tongues-speaking is ever in natural languages or not. It goes to the very heart of the matter. If people can, and do, speak in an unlearnt human language, then without doubt this is a miracle, and there is no way that this can be denied. We are then all compelled to say, with the members of the Sanhedrin in relation to the deeds of the apostles Peter and John, "It is evident to everyone ... that an extraordinary miracle has taken place through them, and that is something we cannot deny" (Acts 4:16, Phillips).

Objective observers enquiring into the phenomenon of tongues-speaking have been very actively seeking to locate and investigate any instances of xenoglossia they can learn about. Samarin describes thus [1972:xii] his own investigation of glossolalia:

> The linguistic description is based on a large sample of glossolalia. This was not difficult to obtain. Many people consented to have their glossolalic prayers recorded in one context or another, privately or in group meetings. Large public meetings were also recorded. The clearest recordings were then phonetically transcribed and analyzed. ...

> Over a period of five years I have taken part in meetings in Italy, Holland, Jamaica, Canada, and the United States. I have observed old-fashioned Pentecostals, and neo-Pentecostals; I have been in small meetings in private homes as well as in mammoth public meetings; I have seen such different cultural settings as are found among the Puerto Ricans of the Bronx, the snake handlers of the Appalachians, Russian Molakans in Los Angeles, and *pocomania* sectarians in Jamaica. This "participant observation" was supplemented by interviews and the use of a questionnaire.

As Samarin 1972:112 comments, "Authentic cases of xenoglossia would be miraculous indeed ..., since language is by definition learned behavior." Numerous attempts have been made by investigators to authenticate reports of the occurrence of xenoglossia. Samarin 1972:132 gives an instance:

> For example, the London Society for Physical Research tested in the following way two Englishmen who claimed to speak Temne, a tongue

spoken in Sierra Leone which they claimed never to have learned. They were sent to the School for Oriental and African Languages to speak in the presence of a native Temne. The native categorically rejected that the Englishmen spoke in his language.

Samarin investigated information about reported instances of xenoglossia. Some few of these instances have been found which do contain genuine words in a foreign language. In his 1973 article, Samarin 132 comments that

> many scholars ... accept *cryptomnesia*, or "hidden memory," as a valid explanation. In this phenomenon, conscious thoughts considered to be original are in reality only memories. In a clear case of cryptomnesia it can be demonstrated that a person did know or could very well have known what he now claims not to have known previously.

That is to say, the explanation of apparent xenoglossia is frequently "hidden memory" of foreign words once heard and then forgotten in the conscious memory. However, the great majority of reported instances of xenoglossia have a different explanation. Samarin goes on to say [1973:132f.]:

> Most cases of xenoglossia are reported by uncritical people who are predisposed to believe them. Generally only hearsay evidence is given; bona fide firsthand witnesses are rare. References to xenoglossia in the writings of Christian charismatics cannot be taken as scientifically valid evidence of the instance of this phenomenon. They are valuable only as illustrations of the beliefs of glossolalists.

> An interesting feature of these reports is that they are often set in a frame consisting of the following elements: Person A utters a glossolalic discourse which is identified by person B as being his own language, whereupon some witness to the event (including either A or B) takes it as a God-given sign for some kind of decision. This stereotypic oral transmission of purported history must be considered folkloristic.

> It is particularly noteworthy that when an utterance is identified as being in a known language its content is referred to only indirectly; there is, as far as I know, no example of the translation that would be expected if the witness really knew the language. Only with glossolalia is there 'interpretation'.

> Further, the person who claims to have heard another speak in an unlearned language must be judged competent or incompetent to identify languages. An incompetent witness is not necessarily a fraud. It is possible in good conscience to mistake a glossa for a natural language. This often happens when the whole event is interpreted in terms of some small part of it. For example, if a person thought he heard some Swahili words in a discourse, he would tend to 'hear' many more words as Swahili.

> An ambiguous situation arises when glossolalic discourse is com-

posed of various linguistic materials. Sometimes they include snatches or even whole sections in a language unknown at the level of consciousness but recalled cryptomnesically.

Samarin gives more details and examples of claimed cases of xenoglossia in his 1972 book. His report includes [109-118] the following:

> Since most glossolalists believe that their glossas are real languages, it is not surprising that they find confirmations for this belief. Thus, there are supposed to be numerous cases, if never their own, where utterances have been identified as Hebrew, Chinese, German, etc. What makes this belief religiously significant is that these were languages unknown to the speakers; they were participants in a miracle. If glossolalia is a sign, then xenoglossia is God adding to the impressiveness of the sign. ...

> Early in the century, when glossolalia was almost entirely restricted to groups of poorly educated people, the belief that tongues were real, earthly languages seems to have been stronger than it is today. It is reported that some people even went abroad as missionaries in the firm conviction that they were speaking Chinese, for example, or some African language. ...

> It is extremely doubtful that the alleged cases of xenoglossia among charismatics are real. Any time one attempts to verify them he finds that the stories have been greatly distorted or that the "witnesses" turn out to be incompetent or unreliable from a linguistic point of view. ... That is, one cannot prove that a stream of speech is from a real language just because several syllables remind one of a real language. ...

> Another case is the following, reported to me in person by someone who had grown up in a traditional Pentecostal church but had never been a tongue speaker herself. When a man arose to give a message in tongues, she immediately recognized it as the language she had learned in Africa as a missionary many years before. And as he spoke, she understood the sense of what he was saying. Immediately the meeting was over, she met with her husband and son, who also spoke this language. All of them had been amazed to hear it from the lips of someone who could not possibly have had the opportunity to learn it as they had.

> Probing as politely as I could, I found that she apparently had some knowledge of this language, but she spoke it with quite an accent, in addition to the fact that she ignored the tones that are a part of this language's structure. I could not, of course, determine for myself whether the tongue speaker had in fact made a discourse in this language (the length of which she was uncertain, maybe a minute or less), but I did ask her if the man spoke as an African, or with a "missionary's accent." She said it was the latter, but she had obviously never thought of this point before. In my opinion, this man's glossa, based on English sounds, resembled the version that she and her family spoke, also based on English sounds.

> Moreover, although she claimed to understand what was said, all

that she could report was that the man was praising Jesus, the same kind of message that was given in the interpretation. In other words, cross-examination destroys the credibility of this sincere person who claimed to hear a language she personally knew. ...

Illusions in this way always disappear on close examination, and it is not surprising that one of my respondents should report that he had heard of cases where xenoglossia disappeared (or as he put it, the speaker "lost the ability to speak [for example, German] via tongues") after the person began to study it "in the usual hard-work manner." What apparently happened was that what the person thought was German proved to be something entirely different when compared with real German. ...

Many people do not seem to realize that the occurrence of words from languages known to them is evidence against the supernatural nature of their tongues.

During his thorough investigation Samarin was not able to locate and verify a single authentic instance of xenoglossia. He says [1973:133],

In summary, although Christian charismatists claim that xenoglossia is a part of the tongue-speaking experience, they would be unable to provide a case that would stand up to rigorous scientific investigation. At the most it would prove to be cryptomnesic.

Concerning this and his other findings, he adds, "This is the conclusion I have come to after seven years of intensive study of glossolalia in the charismatic movement" [1973:140]. The final chapter of his book *Tongues of Men and Angels* states his conclusions in detail, and commences thus [1972:227]:

There is no mystery about glossolalia. Tape-recorded samples are easy to obtain and to analyze. They always turn out to be the same thing. *strings of syllables, made up of sounds taken from among all those that the speaker knows, put together more or less haphazardly but which nevertheless emerge as word-like and sentence-like units because of realistic, language-like rhythm and melody.* ... This would also mean that contrary to common belief, it has never been scientifically demonstrated that xenoglossia occurs among Pentecostals: people just do not talk languages they are unfamiliar with.

This conclusion has been reiterated by all others who have engaged in scientific investigation of reported instances of xenoglossia. For example, William E Welmers, Professor of African Languages at University of California at Los Angeles, wrote in *Christianity Today* [VII, November 8, 1963, 127]:

We do know something about representative languages of every known language family in the world. I am by no means unique among descriptive linguists in having had direct, personal contact with well over a hundred languages representing a majority of the world's language families, and in having studied descriptions of languages of virtually every reported type. If a glossolaliac were speaking in any of the thousand languages of Africa, there is about a 90% chance that I would recognize it in a minute.

Thus Vines 218 reports,

No known language is spoken in the tongues movement today. The Toronto Institute of Linguistics has studied tongues extensively. After listening to thousands of tapes of modern charismatic tongues, they have been unable to discover evidence of any foreign tongue. They have, however, discovered that every phonetic sound which the person speaking in tongues uses is a phonetic sound obtained from his own language. In many instances, tongues is even self-induced.

A Charismatic response to this kind of report is that, as investigators only ever examine a minuscule proportion of all tongues-speaking that occurs, it is totally invalid for them to generalize from a quite statistically-inadequate sample to a declaration that xenoglossia never occurs. Thus Hummel 202 quotes the last section of the citation from Samarin which I have just given above, and then comments:

This scientific statement does not take into account a possible miraculous work of the Holy Spirit. By its very nature a miracle is a unique historical event and cannot be reproduced in the laboratory. It is verified by credible witnesses rather than by scientific demonstration under controlled conditions. The Holy Spirit is not known for command performances so that his work can be made scientifically acceptable. The scientist has the right to study religious phenomena, but if he recognizes the limitations of his method he will refrain from pronouncing what people can or cannot do by the power of the Spirit. Speaking in tongues as a recognizable foreign language, while infrequent, has been verified by a number of reliable witnesses.

In support of this statement, Hummel cites no further information but gives an end-note reference to another author.

Thus Hummel and others with similar views hold that there could in fact be any number of glossolalists who speak in a real human language but whose utterances never come to the attention of a linguistics investigator. This comment can sound plausible initially. But these points must be made:

(a) This view is a statement of faith, held by those who believe it without any demonstrable basis but only upon the basis of reports which they wish to accept. They believe in xenoglossia because they believe that this is what is meant by passages in 1 Corinthians. But such a view is speculation, and they are in fact adopting a viewpoint based upon hearsay reports about people understanding glossolalia: but this speculation is unsupported by any actual evidence, and it flies in the face of such investigatory evidence as does exist.

**(b)** On the evidence it would appear that it must be said that those who speak (or consider themselves, or are considered, to speak) in a natural language without learning it cannot do so or at any rate do not do so when the language can be verified by both the presence of objective observers and a competent speaker of the language in question, or when the speaking in this tongue can be tape recorded for subsequent verification. (All attempts by investigators to tape record instances of xenoglossia have so far been unsuccessful.) If a person is given by the Lord a human language previously unknown to him/her, and can speak it at will, why could Samarin (and others) not find *one single such person* during their years of investigation? And why does not at least one person with this gift come forward to investigators and speak in his language in circumstances where it can be confirmed as genuine xenoglossia?

**(c)** A significant part of the meaning of tongues is its sign value in demonstrating the genuineness of the presence of God in the individual and in the Christian fellowship in which this tongues-speaking occurs. It then seems surprising (to speak no more strongly) that the Holy Spirit, who is held to be the source and author of the tongues utterance, has never granted that such an utterance shall be spoken in "the tongues of men" (i.e., an actual unlearnt human language) *on any single occasion* when it can be verified by an objective observer using incontrovertible linguistic means, through which the occurrence of a miracle would be confirmed to the believer in tongues and to sceptic alike. If the Holy Spirit gives such a language only on occasions when in the nature of the case its occurrence cannot be verified and validated, and not when it can, it would seem that he does not want sceptics or the open-minded to know the truth of the matter.

But it is very difficult to believe that the Holy Spirit would indeed act in such a way. Certainly, this is in sharp contrast to the occurrence of xenoglossia in Acts 2:1-11, because then the whole point of the giving of foreign languages was so that they *would* be heard and understood by those who were native speakers of those languages; and it is in contrast also with Paul's point in 1 Corinthians 14:22 when he reminds his readers that tongues are for the benefit of unbelievers.

## 2. Glossolalia Is Not Speaking In Language At All

A very high percentage of practising tongues-speakers affirm that even if what they utter is not a human language, it is nonetheless a language. Some would refer to it as "tongues of angels" or "the language of heaven".

Samarin reports [1972:107-108] the result of asking about this in his Questionnaire: "Although the majority of my respondents are convinced that their glossas are languages, they are uncertain about what languages they might be compared to. Only nineteen out of sixty-nine (or 27%) were not convinced that their glossas were languages. ... In response to another question, 50% of the respondents said that if someone could show that tongues were not like human languages, they would have to be considered heavenly, spiritual, or angelic languages."

We have noted that Professor Samarin carefully differentiates [1973:131] xenoglossia and glossolalia, noting: "Xenoglossia and glossolalia are not identical, A *glossa* is never a natural language, and it resembles a natural language only in very limited ways."

First [1973:133], he considers the possibility that tongues-speaking can be speaking in a natural language not yet discovered or widely known:

> Could [glossic utterances] possibly be specimens of the four to seven thousand languages spoken on earth which have not yet been studied? ... Even though we are discovering new languages every year, glossas cannot be classed with them. First, to "discover" languages is to speak metaphorically; we simply learn that language A and language B are two different languages instead of one. We learn that speakers cannot understand each other even though the languages are obviously related (such as some forms of Spanish and Portuguese). Because of the increasing precision with which languages can now be differentiated, the number of known languages in the world has grown. Of course, many parts of the world have not yet been fully explored, and we must suppose that their inhabitants are using hitherto unknown languages.
>
> Second, it is almost certain that whatever languages are "discovered" will resemble those already known. Thus, the "new" languages of the Indians living in the jungles of South America are not startlingly different from those [that] linguists have already studied; and their discovery does not change our fundamental understanding of the structure and use of human language.
>
> There is, therefore, no justification whatsoever for hoping that future language discoveries will enable us to identify glossas. The science of languages has developed sufficiently so that we can safely assert that glossas are not normal human languages even though they may reveal some of their characteristics. ...

Next, Samarin proceeds [1973:135-136] to explain why "glossas" - the utterances of modern speaking in tongues - are not and cannot be understood as being languages; he says:

> *Meaningless.* A glossa is always meaningless in the linguistic sense. That is, there are no consistent correlations between units of speech, and experience. Glossolalists do not deny this but insist, nevertheless,

that a glossa has meaning because it *is* a language and because it can be interpreted into familiar languages. These interpretations are often strikingly longer or shorter than the glossic utterance; they are never translations in the strict sense of the term. The glossolalist believes, however, that the interpretation is as much a charism or "gift" from God as his own glossic utterance.

Samarin then demonstrates with detailed examination of several examples why this is not and cannot be so. He continues:

> *Repetitious.* Glossas differ from natural languages because they are simple and repetitious. Linguistically speaking, they contain a smaller number of linguistic units and a much higher incidence of some of them. ... Glossic speech is repetitious at all levels. Whole macrosegments recur as do selected syllables and their constituent sounds. As might be expected, a preference for certain sounds gives to a glossa its exotic flavour. ... [Examples are given.]

> *Asymmetrical sound grids.* Asymmetry is revealed by the frequent absence of sounds where one might expect them in an articulatory chart. [This is explained fully.]

> *Simple syllable structure.* Although there is no reason why some glossas could not have phonologically complex syllables, glossas generally have a simple syllable structure. [More information is given.]

Samarin's study contains [1972:121-127] a section headed "Dissimilarities to Language", which gives a detailed analysis of the features of a language. He notes by way of introduction [120-121],

> If we operate with the linguist's canon of language, we can judge whether a glossa is like any human language extant or extinct. And we find that all of the glossas we have examined (recorded by ourselves or others) do have some, albeit incomplete, resemblance to natural language. ... Indeed, there is no doubt that a practised glossolalist, in contrast with a beginner, really sounds as if he is talking a language.

> It is this superficial resemblance to language, surely, that reinforces the glossolalist and helps him maintain the fiction that he is really talking.

Samarin identifies, and explains, a basic semantic difference between natural language and glossolalia, and then comments [122],

> A glossolalist might argue that this is no argument, because the semantics of glossolalia is different from that of human language. In the absence of any evidence, this is, of course, no counter-argument, but just a statement of faith.

This comment by Samarin is directed to the assertion that even if glossolalia does not conform to the criteria of natural, human language this does not mean that it is not a language: it can be regarded as a heavenly language which has its own criteria. Samarin examines the whole concept of what is meant by "language", and shows [124] why glossolalia is not a language:

> In construction as well as in function glossas are fundamentally different from languages.

This difference is then spelt out in detail in his report. He concludes the chapter thus [1972:127f.]:

> This chapter has demonstrated that glossolalia is a derivative phenomenon. Its basic features depend on the linguistic competence and knowledge of each speaker. This will surprise no one who came to this study already convinced that glossolalia was some kind of gibberish. However, now he knows that it is not *simply* that. We have also seen that because glossolalia is not just gibberish millions of tongue speakers are led to believe that they engage in authentic speech. Now they can understand what led them to this conviction. They must realize, moreover, that when the full apparatus of linguistic science comes to bear on glossolalia, this turns out to be only a façade of language - although at times a very good one indeed. For when we comprehend what language is, we must conclude that no glossa, no matter how well constructed, is a specimen of human language, because it is neither internally organized nor systematically related to the world man perceives.

Each person's glossa reflects the phonemes of his own speech knowledge: primarily his mother tongue, and possibly at times phonemes from any other languages to which he may have been exposed. Samarin 1973:138 says:

> When a glossa is compared with the native language of its speaker, it is seen to be both derivative and innovative. Both its inventory of sounds and its sentence melodies are derived from the speaker's first language. In other words, a glossolalist's "accent" gives clues to his native tongue. We find, for example, that if the voiceless stops are aspirated (that is, are followed by a slight puff of air), as with the first sound of "Paul", his everyday speech is probably English. We would expect this sound to be unaspirated in the glossa of a French-speaking glossolalist because voiceless stops in that language are always unaspirated. ...

> Innovating features are the simplification of syllable structure, the increase in the frequency of some sounds, and borrowing from languages other than English. I have already mentioned the first two features in viewing glossas as if they were independent languages. These traits make them look strikingly different from English. Borrowing from other languages occurs when the speaker has had contact with a language other than the one he normally speaks. This has been proven by investigating the biography of the tongue-speaker. ...

> We have seen that glossas are not natural languages and that they are unlike natural languages in significant ways even though they share certain features.

So then, a glossa is individual to each person who speaks in tongues: each has his or her own unique way of speaking, and furthermore their glossa reflects their existing language knowledge and competence. If what is used in speaking in tongues is "the language of heaven" or "the language of angels", then there must be as many different variations of it as there are human language groups on earth. Furthermore, we must also accept that some angels speak with a German accent, others with French phonemes, others again in the sounds of the languages of the Pacific islands, or of African languages, and so on, while not in fact speaking any of those actual human, natural languages.

Thus significant differences exist between the glossas of different individuals: indeed, one person may have more than one distinctive glossa. And there are differences between the glossas of people of different linguistic backgrounds which correspond with the differences between their mother tongues, allowing for the influence of other languages which they may know to some extent.

There are some superficial resemblances between glossas and languages, especially in the case of glossas of glossolalists who are practised at speaking them and who come to speak them in patterns and with characteristics borrowed from their normal way of speaking their mother tongue. It is these features which lead people to conclude that an actual language is being spoken even though not understood.

But upon objective linguistic investigation it can be seen that glossas do not have the essential characteristics of language, in particular that of conveying meaning by means of sounds. In a genuine language there is a direct relationship between a particular set of sounds and a specific meaning. Allowing for homophones (different words with the same pronunciation), there is a consistency between sound-sets and meaning - that is, in a language a group of sounds does not have a different meaning each time it occurs.

And a language is an ordered and organized structure for the use of sets of sounds. That is, there are "rules of grammar" for the use of words and the construction of sentences. It is because these things are so that humans can learn each other's mother tongues. These features of language are lacking in glossas.

That is why one person would not be able to learn to understand the meaning of another person's glossa by studying it. That is to say, a trained linguist, who can enter into a geographical area where a particular language is spoken which he does not know and can learn to understand and speak it by analyzing its sounds and structure, could never learn to speak or even understand a Charismatic speaker's glossa by means of linguistic techniques. If it were a genuine language, a glossa could be "broken into" and understood by a linguistic specialist, like any other language. But it can't be done. Because glossolalia is not a language.

Samarin 1972:227 sums up the data thus:

> Glossolalia is indeed like language in some ways, but this is only because the speaker (unconsciously) wants it to be like language. Yet in spite of similarities, glossolalia is fundamentally *not* language. All specimens of glossolalia that have ever been studied have produced no features that would even suggest that they reflect some kind of communicative system.

This is why "interpretations" of glossolalia do not provide any clue to unlocking the meaning of a glossa. There is no consistent correspondence between the words of the "interpretation" and the sounds of the glossolalic utterance, as there would be in a translation of a genuine language.

Glossolalists respond to this by saying that an interpretation of a glossa is not a translation, but rather just gives the general sense.

Actually, this whole issue of interpretation is related to the question of whether glossolalia is a language.

Samarin 1972:159-162 reports,

> Glossolalia is also used in addressing a group with the intent of passing to them a message from God. Since this discourse is unintelligible by definition, it must be "interpreted". ...

> The interpretation of a glossolalic message - occasionally of a prayer - is a supplementary discourse in natural language that purports to reveal the meaning of the otherwise unintelligible one.

> Mistakes do occur. One charismatic Lutheran minister in Germany informed me that a Czechoslovakian, speaking in his native language, had been "interpreted" in the belief that he was speaking in tongues!

Kildahl 1972:62-63 provides similar information from his researches:

> We attended many meetings where glossolalia both occurred and was interpreted ... In order to investigate the accuracy of these interpretations, we undertook to play a taped example of tongue-speech privately for several different interpreters of tongues. In no instance was there any similarity in the several interpretations. The following typifies our results: one interpreter said that the tongue-speaker was praying for the health of his children; another that the same tongue-speech was an expression of gratitude to God for a recently successful church fundraising effort.

> When confronted with the disparity between their interpretations, the interpreters offered the explanation that God gave to one person one

interpretation of the speech and to another person another interpretation. They showed no defensiveness about being cross-examined and generously upheld alternative interpretations as equally valid. The interpreters offered their remarks with sincerity and good faith; there was no evidence of conscious scheming or manipulation.

We know of a man who was raised in Africa, the son of missionary parents, who decided - rather cynically, perhaps - to test the interpretation of tongues. He attended a tongue-speaking meeting where he was a complete stranger. At the appropriate moment, he rose and spoke the Lord's Prayer in the African dialect he had learnt in his youth. When he sat down, an interpreter of tongues at once offered the meaning of what he had said. He interpreted it as a message about the imminent second coming of Christ.

I myself could add that when I was in Nigeria I personally learnt of a similar incident. The brother of my informant, who had gone to America to study, recited a psalm in his African mother-tongue during a Charismatic meeting. His speaking was interpreted to the effect that this man had been having problems in his relations with his wife and these were now settled, and he was giving praise to God for this. (The man who had spoken the psalm was not in fact married.)

So when we consider the question of interpretation, we see again that a glossa simply does not have the essential features of a language.

## 3. Glossolalia Is Not In Any Way A Sign Of The Holy Spirit

Christian tongues-speakers associate their glossolalia in some way with the Holy Spirit. All would contend that it is given by the Holy Spirit, and most would hold that it is the essential sign (or at least, the usual sign) of the "baptism of the Holy Spirit".

Thus Campbell 49-50 says:

> I know there are some who insist that the supernatural manifestation of tongues was simply a sign of the *birth* of the church. But such people forget that when the second and third instances took place, the church was already well established.

> The fact is that Jesus wants His church to have a continual assurance of His resurrection power. And it is the baptism in the Holy Spirit, evidenced by speaking in tongues, which makes this possible.

Similarly, Basham 1971:33:

> There is overwhelming evidence in the Book of Acts confirming the fact that speaking in tongues is the normal, expected sign or proof that one has received the baptism in the Holy Spirit.

However, how can we agree that modern glossolalic tongues-speaking points to the work of the Holy Spirit in view of the fact that instances of phenomena the same as modern tongues-speaking have been found amongst the enthusiastic devotees of almost all the religions on earth, past and present?

In "Glossolalia in Historical Perspective", Bunn surveys the data for the occurrence of the phenomenon of glossolalia, and sets out the evidence for the practice of unintelligible speaking in the religions of Mesopotamia, Egypt, the Canaanites, the Hittites, ancient Israel, the Arabs, and the Greeks [43-44].

The last-named is particularly significant for our present study, as the Greek religions were the background for many of the Gentiles at Corinth who had entered the church (see 1 Corinthians 6:11: Paul's "and that is what some of you were" included those who had been idolaters (6:9); and also 12:2, "You know that when you were pagans, you were led astray to mute idols, however you were led ").

Glossolalia was, in particular, characteristic of pagan worship at Corinth, especially of the cult of the goddess Diana: Dillow 14 comments,

> In 1 Corinthians 14 Paul is dealing with an error that the Corinthians had fallen into regarding the speaking in tongues: they had begun to use it in the same manner as the heathen did. They were bringing over their old use of ecstatic speech from Diana worship and using the legitimate gift of tongues in a similar way. ... The gifts of the Spirit were all given for speaking and otherwise ministering to men. That one could communicate better with the gods through a language of the gods was the heathen belief. The believer in Christ knows that he has just to lift his heart to God and God understands him better than he understands himself.

Furthermore, the "shaman", found in many religions "in a band stretching from the Arctic through Russia, North Asia, and North America" is identified by Bunn 45 as a "religious figure of formidable power", and "It is the contention of the shaman that while he is in the trance state spirits have spoken through him, and he claims to be unconscious of what he had said or done."

Bunn goes on to discuss "Three other widely scattered manifestations of similar nature": the Polynesians of the Pacific, and "examples ... from ancient India and Persia. ..."

These comments may be cited from Bunn's conclusions [46]:

> Glossolalia is actually a common religious phenomenon. ... Throughout the world and history, there is to be seen in this ... type of religion the ecstatic personality. And among such ecstatics, whether Mesopotamian, Egyptian, Israelite, Canaanite, Greek, or Muslim, there are those who, when possessed by the spirit of deity, delivered messages in strange tongues. No religion, ancient or modern, may claim exclusive rights to such a religious act. ...

Similar comments about the widespread nature of the phenomenon of leaders or members of non-Christian religions and cults speaking in ecstatic speech or unknown "language" are made by numbers of other authors.

L. Carlyle May gives a record of tongues-speaking, especially as used by the "medicine man" or "shaman", in his article "A Survey of Glossolalia and Related Phenomena in Non-Christian Religions" [*American Anthropologist* LVIII, 79]. He gives examples from Hudson Bay Eskimos, North Borneo, and the Mortlock Islands of Micronesia. Burdick 66-67 cites May and several other reports of non-Christian glossolalia. Kildahl 1974:76 reports that "Glossolalia is a common practice for Hindus."

Michael Green 140 says,

> It is salutary to remember that Muslim devotees in the Sudan speak in tongues no less than Christians in Guildford or Cleveland!

Kelsey 58f. draws our attention to the fact that tongues-speaking is part of the platform of Mormonism. And John MacArthur 175,178 writes:

> False religions are known for tongues - ecstatic babblings - euphoric experiences. Mormons and Jehovah's Witnesses claim to be able to speak in tongues.

The possibility of non-Christian glossolalia is recognized by some Charismatic writers. Samarin 1972:141 comments,

> Glossolalists have recognized the existence, or the possibility, of non-Christian non-Spirit-inspired speaking in tongues. This kind of glossolalia they called a "Satanic counterfeit".

But, as Bunn's account has shown us, the "counterfeit" was in existence a very long time before the "genuine glossolalia" appeared: examples of similar non-intelligible speaking in a context of religious enthusiasm have been attested from the records of many ancient religions, and it was a widely recognized occurrence in the Greek religions of the first century into which Christianity came. To an unbiased outside observer it would appear that Christianity was adopting the practices - or at least imitating the behavior - of the pagan religions of its day (if, that is, the speaking in tongues at Corinth was to be understood as uttering unintelligible speech).

Let us reflect upon the significance of this information.

**1.** Jesus expressly instructed his disciples (Matthew 6:7, NIV), "And when you pray, do not keep on babbling like pagans, for they think they will be heard because of their many words." Note the TEV translation of this verse (similarly NASB, Beck): "In your prayers do not use a lot of meaningless words, as the pagans do, who think God will hear them because of their long prayers." This is a completely clear instruction which Jesus gives to his followers: he tells them that they are never to pray in meaningless words like the pagans, who are trusting in the *quantity* of their utterances, completely without regard to any considerations of *thought* and *meaning* in what they are saying.

This, Jesus says, is an example not to be followed but rather to be condemned: Jesus goes on to say, "Do not be like them", and adds, "This is how you should pray". He then teaches his followers to pray for *specific* matters, by means of *known* requests, which are worded in *understandable* language. That is, he teaches them, as a pattern prayer, what we now call "the Lord's Prayer".

We need to ask ourselves: Which type of prayer is modern "praying in tongues" like: what Jesus condemned, or what Jesus commended and commanded?

When a person "prays in tongues", that person is turning away from the type of prayer that Jesus taught, and is adopting a type of "prayer" which in its most significant features is similar to that of pagans, and was condemned by Jesus. Indeed, to "pray in a tongue", not knowing what you are praying, means that you cannot actually be sure that it is really prayer at all.

**2.** The sign value of speaking in tongues depended upon its *difference* from the behavior of the pagans. It would be no sign to anyone about God's unique presence, through the Spirit, in the life of a believer if the believer's "speaking in tongues" was of the same kind (i.e., speaking language without meaning) as was characteristic of the pagan religions in Corinth at the time. Paul commences his discussion of the Corinthian situation (12:1-3) with a reminder that it is important for them not to continue in ignorance of this point (the verb is present tense, with durative force): when they were pagans they were led astray to dumb idols, but Paul is making it known to them that no one speaking by the Spirit of God would say "Jesus be cursed", and it is only by the Holy Spirit that a person can acknowledge, "Jesus is Lord". Paul is stressing the *difference* made by the Holy Spirit of God. The implication of Paul's opening statement is quite incompatible with the apostle then proceeding to endorse a type of tongue-speaking which was *of the same kind* as that practised by the pagans.

**3.** At present many people from vastly different doctrinal backgrounds are united in the Charismatic movement on the basis of having had the same tongues experience. They are willing to acknowledge the validity of each other's doctrine if their experience of "the baptism of the Spirit" is the same. Thus Roman Catholics, Anglicans, Methodists, Presbyterians, Baptists, sacramentarians, liberals, evangelicals, all are willing to see their unity through this experience as more important than any doctrinal differences. Protestant Charismatics are extending recognition to these Roman Catholics as brothers in Christ on the basis of the shared Charismatic experience, which is seen as more important that anything else - while those same Charismatic Roman Catholics still see themselves as having been regenerated in their baptism as infants, and as having their spiritual life sustained by participation in the Mass, in which they receive the actual body and blood of Christ. They testify to the way in which their experience of the "baptism in the Spirit" and glossolalia has enhanced their appreciation of the Mass, their devotions to Mary, the use of the Rosary, and all the other teachings and practices of their church (see Gromacki 155-160; Butler 102-106).

But Campbell 14 extends this "unity" even further:

> Laymen and ministers from most Protestant denominations, from the Roman Catholic Church, and from the Jewish faith ... are receiving the Holy Spirit in the same way the apostles did on the day of Pentecost."

Now, if this experience is the one crucial factor for mutual recognition and unity, logic and consistency would indicate that the hand of fellowship should also be extended to any members of sects (Mormons, Jehovah's Witnesses) who might have similarly spoken in tongues, and then to Muslims, Hindus, animists, and any others.

So we can clearly see that the "glossolalia" kind of "speaking in tongues" - speaking, that is, in what Samarin 1973:140 calls a "pseudo-language" cannot be the sign of or evidence for the indwelling of the Holy Spirit, seeing that *the adherents of Christian fringe sects and outright pagan religions could do exactly the same thing!* We have noted [Bunn, 46] that

> Glossolalia is actually a common religious phenomenon. ... No religion, ancient or modern, may claim exclusive rights to such a religious act.

If to speak in a pseudolanguage indicates the "baptism of the Holy Spirit", then the adherents of just about every major religion on earth, past or present, must have experienced this "baptism". We would all of course vehemently reject such a conclusion. Therefore we must reject the premiss from which it derives: that glossolalia is the biblical gift of tongues, or a sign of the "baptism of the Holy Spirit".

The fact is, any adherents of any religion, or indeed, no religion at all, can speak in glossolalia. Kildahl 1974:76 reports two such circumstances:

> A linguist has reported that he has been able to teach a classroom of students to speak in tongues - without reference to any religious beliefs about it.
>
> An actress once explained to me that verbal expression without using a known language was an important part of the training of her acting class. She proceeded to speak a "language" for me which sounded exactly like glossolalia. She spoke somewhat different "languages" when she was asked to express joy, or warmth, or intensity, or sadness.

To reflect upon these facts will show that there can therefore be no basis for saying that the experience of glossolalia is the evidence of the baptism of the Holy Spirit, or indeed evidence of any other specifically Christian experience.


## WHAT IT IS

### 1. Glossolalia Is Religious Enthusiasm

Christenson 27f. comments thus on "the value of speaking in tongues":

> Those who have experienced this manifestation of the Spirit find that it has great blessing and value. It is no "frill" or "extra" in their Christian life - something which they could now take or leave depending upon their mood. It has had a deep, often a transforming effect on their spiritual life. One man expressed it this way: "Speaking in tongues was a spiritual break-through for me." There is an awareness of having entered a vast new spiritual realm. And this leads to deeper study of the Scriptures, for one wants to know more about this realm which has suddenly taken on new reality. One suddenly finds himself able to understand the Bible far better. One young worker who received this experience said, "For years I have tried to force myself to read the Bible, but I never got anything out of it - I couldn't seem to understand it. Now I read the Bible every day, and I always get some new thought or insight."

A transforming effect on one's spiritual life - a spiritual break-through - a vast new spiritual realm - "one suddenly finds himself able to understand the Bible far better". Is this not what all the Lord's people long for? If the promise of all this blessing is held out to a Christian, to be obtained through speaking in tongues, will this not entice and encourage vast numbers to want, and to seek for, the experience of glossolalia?

It will be noted, from what we have seen above, that glossolalia can express enthusiasm for *any* religion. If one's background or the particular context of a tongues experience is Christian, then it will express enthusiasm for Christianity and Christ.

It is frequently reported that speaking in tongues brings a feeling of release and liberty, a kind of freeing-up from inhibitions, accompanied by a sense of pleasure and joy.

People, having learnt of this, therefore speak in tongues because they have (or desire to have) these feelings.

These feelings are related to the fact that the people believe:

1. That what they are doing is the "speaking in tongues" of Scripture (they would not feel the same way about what they were doing if they believed that it was *not* the biblical speaking in tongues).

2. That what they are doing is communing directly with God in prayer or speaking a message directly given by him (they would not feel the same way about what they were doing if they believed that they were not communicating with God or from God).

3. That what they are doing is in accord with (indeed, is fulfilling) the expectations and perhaps the prayers of other Christians whom they respect - this gives them a sense of spiritual satisfaction (they would not feel quite the same way about what they were doing if all those whom they respected the most as Christians were expecting them to reject this behavior, and did not believe that it was of God).

Evidence for this comes from those who used to speak in tongues and who - although they can still do so - no longer practice it.

They report that, when they ceased to see it as being the same as biblical tongues, or to believe that it came from God, or to hold the same respect for a key person who espoused tongues speaking, then their glossolalia no longer brought any special feelings of liberty or joy.

## 2. Glossolalia Is A Symbol of Peer Group Membership

A significant factor in the practice of glossolalia is the role that it has in linking a person with a group of others who have similar values and experiences and interpretations of Scripture. Samarin 1972:212-214 makes these comments:

> What is a validating experience for the individual .. is a demarcating one for the group: it symbolizes the group's difference from others. In this respect glossolalia serves the same function that any form of speech may have, like the in-group languages of students (slang) or secret societies. ... In these groups, then, it is not enough for a newcomer to identify himself as a Christian. The members will want to know if he

has had "the experience." One of the best answers is simply "Yes, I have spoken in tongues." This marks solidarity with the group. Indeed, reliable reports indicate that some groups will not integrate a person unless he gives evidence of being a tongue speaker. The expression is not theirs, but this is their "requirement for membership." ...

This unifying function of glossolalia is, of course, seen from the point of view of the group itself. Seen from outside, the rise of a charismatic group within a traditional church very often leads to divisions, and the reasons are very often what they were when Paul dealt with them at Corinth ...: a feeling of superiority on the part of the tongue speakers and the disorder that the practice of glossolalia introduces into corporate worship.

If glossolalia is symbolic externally, it is also symbolic internally. That is, it helps the members to reaffirm their difference as often as they will.

## 3. Glossolalia May Be Due To Autohypnosis, And Psychologically Induced

We are all readily able to respond to suggestion and, indeed, to cause ourselves to respond to our own wishes and desires. This is true quite widely in our lives. In particular, it can explain something of the nature of glossolalia. Dillow 174-175 makes these thoughtful comments:

Another possible cause is *autohypnosis*. Several things combine to produce this. In almost every case there is a sense of frustration and inner conflict. This is particularly acute in Christians, in that their lives often do not stack up with what the Scriptures say is possible. This inner tension sets off a search for the 'secret' to the abundant Christian life. Tongues promises to be an end to the tension, and people subconsciously begin to seek it. The autohypnosis is further augmented by the fact that the gift is presented as the acme of Christian experience. To receive it is to gain the hallmark of spiritual prestige, resulting in the feeling of group acceptance and divine approval. Furthermore, everyone around them is assuring them that this gift is the solution to their problems. This has a powerful effect and will psychologically induce the phenomenon in some people. ...

Whatever the circumstances that motivate one person to begin to speak in tongues today, one thing we now know with certainty is that anyone can do it. ... While it is true that tongues speaking today is psychological and that it has been under study for years and observed in the lives of nonreligious people, there are no completely satisfactory explanations of what really causes it. It happens to some people who were not seeking it, didn't even know what it was, and who had no inner tensions at all. One day "it" just happens.

Kildahl 1972:78 reports this finding from his research into glossolalia:

Our finding was that a personal crisis of some kind preceded the initial experience of speaking in tongues in 87% of the cases examined. We noted that where there was not crisis experience, there was less susceptibility toward learning to speak in tongues. Further, one glossolalist reported that as she became more settled in her life, her need to find solace and support from glossolalia was less urgent. It would seem that the use of glossolalia, with its special meaning of acceptance by God and by the group of fellow tongue-speakers, would diminish as a person solved his critical problems and became more independent.

It could not be said that all glossolalia can be explained as autohypnosis or psychologically induced, but it does appear that this is a factor in the overall situation for numbers of people.

## 4. Glossolalia Is A Learned Response

In the course of his first-hand research into glossolalia, published [1972] as *The Psychology of Speaking in Tongues*, Kildahl reached the conclusion that this was a technique which could be taught. He comments [74],

> It is our definite opinion that those who have the necessary psychological characteristics can *learn* to speak in tongues.

He then speaks of "many experiences of watching people teach other people how to speak in tongues". He comments later [1972:86], "We have shown that speaking in tongues can be learned, almost as other abilities are learned."

Samarin 1972:227f. explains,

> Glossolalia is not a supernatural phenomenon. It is, in fact, a very natural phenomenon. It is similar to many other kinds of speech humans produce in more or less normal circumstances, in more or less normal psychological states. In fact, anybody can produce glossolalia if he is uninhibited and if he discovers what the "trick" is. Both the commonplace nature of glossolalia and experiments have proven this fact.
> ...
>
> Therefore there is no need to explain what *causes* a person to produce this form of speech. Nothing "comes over his vocal chords." Speech as people imagine does not originate there anyway. It starts in the brain. That is where the instructions to the vocal organs come from. And when someone speaks in tongues, he is only using instructions that have lain dormant since childhood. "Finding" them and then being willing to follow them are the difficult things. So the only *causes* that need to be found are those that explain why a person should *want* to use these rules again and how he becomes *willing* to do so. The rest is easy.

In babyhood, we each discovered the ability to make noises with our voices, and we enjoyed experimenting with the noises we could make. Our mind led us to do this, because of the enjoyment we derived from this playing with sounds. (It is possible to observe this happening in any young child.) As we matured, we learnt to use our minds to place restrictions upon the range of noises we could make, abandoning those which were meaningless and developing our recognition of, and our ability to produce and use, those that had meaning. This was the process of learning to talk in our mother-tongue. Glossolalia is accomplished by bypassing the controls which we placed upon our speech mechanism as we grew older, to get back to the freedom of unrestricted and unplanned utterance which characterizes a small child.

This has also been noted by Charismatic leaders. Thus in his "Instruction For Receiving" the baptism in the Holy Spirit [1976:59-61], Basham teaches how to begin speaking in tongues by starting with making noises like a baby or child.

In this regard it is of interest to notice that in the course of writing about tongues in 1 Corinthians 13 and 14, Paul says,

> "When I was a child, *I talked like a child, I thought like a child, I reasoned like a child.* When I became a man, *I put childish ways behind me.*" [13:11]

> "Brothers, *stop thinking like children.* In regard to evil be infants, but *in your thinking be adults.*" [14:20]

If in 1 Corinthians Paul was commending a speaking in tongues of the same kind as modern glossolalia, which involves returning to the making of unformed and unrestricted utterances just as a child does, is it really believable that the apostle could have written in the way he has about completely turning from talking and thinking as a child does?

In reaching the end of his book, Samarin 1972:233-236 asks, concerning all that he has written,

> what is the consequence for the glossolalist and for his non- or anti-glossolalist brethren in the Christian tradition? ...

> For some glossolalists there will be no consequence, just incredulity. They will not believe that a linguistic scientist can demonstrate the nonlinguistic, noncommunicative nature of tongues. ...

> The glossolalist's incredulity challenges the linguist's competence, because this competence probes where he [the glossolalist] is most sensitive. But the encounter is an uneven match. We know more about language than the glossolalist does. We know enough to declare what is and what is not language. We know as much as a mathematician, who can tell the difference between a real formula and a pseudo-formula - one that *looks* like mathematical language but does not *say* anything. ...

> Others will wonder if this verbal phenomenon is "of God." If they mean by that "miraculous," then the answer is categorically no. Glos-

solalia is a perfectly human, perfectly normal (albeit anomalous) phenomenon. However, if it is charismatic religion that they question, then the answer will depend on what kinds of things they believe God does today. ...

If they believe that tongues are real human languages, this is not the worst of human errors. The similarity between tongues and natural languages is what misleads them. They are not victims of self-deception.

That accounts for the past. What of the future? If tongue speakers believe what I have written, they can no longer trust appearances. They will have to admit that in one instance at least Pentecostal doctrine is wrong.

## 5. Glossolalia May Be Used By The Devil

Glossolalia may on occasions be demonic. This would certainly be the case in the speaking in tongues which occurs in some religions. For example, the prophecies of the Delphi sibyl have been attributed to demonic activity.

Samarin 1973:141 comments,

Glossolalists have recognized the existence, or the possibility, of non-Christian non-Spirit-inspired speaking in tongues. This kind of glossolalia they called a "Satanic counterfeit."

Samarin's comment refers only to non-Christian speaking in tongues; it does not extend to any speaking in tongues by Christians. However, if non-Christian glossolalia is to be accounted for on the basis that Satan is counterfeiting genuine Spirit-inspired glossolalia, it needs also to be borne in mind that (as we have seen earlier) numerous examples of such speaking in tongues in non-Christian religions are documented *before* the time of Jesus Christ. Are we to explain all this as Satan counterfeiting the gift of the Spirit in various other religions *before* the Spirit was given? To ascribe this to the work of Satan seems reasonable, and in line with the significance of the comment Paul gives in 1 Corinthians 12:1-3; but to call this a *counterfeit* of what did not at the time exist seems to be a questionable use of words.

However, is it justified to believe that the devil would never be able to so influence a Christian tongues-speaker as to produce a counterfeit glossic utterance? Most Charismatics who have considered this question do consider that it is possible (e.g., see Michael Green 139f., 207, 235).

Indeed, glossolalia by Christians has also sometimes been adjudged to be demonic.

Nonetheless, in discussing speaking in tongues by Christians, of whatever kind, and taking note of the occurrence at times of obvious abuses, we ought to bear in mind that when Paul was dealing with the abuses which were occurring at Corinth he did not (after 12:1-3) discuss the possibility that this was demonic. Thus, Samarin 1972:16 notes,

> It is interesting to observe that although nonbelievers may have thought that tongue speakers were drunk or insane (Acts 2:13; 1 Corinthians 14:23), there is no record that people associated this phenomenon with "demons". In the Gospels, demons that possess an individual always seem to talk that person's native language.

Now, it must be acknowledged that demonic influence *may* be a possibility which needs to be borne in mind in any given instance, but those Christians who explain the entire phenomenon as the work of the devil are going beyond the warrant of Scripture.

We need to recognize, though, that even if glossolalia does not necessarily *originate* with the devil, he is able to make use of it to cause distortion of our understanding of prayer, edification, and ministry, to distract us from seeking holiness and Christlikeness, and to cause dissension and division in the body of Christ.

Furthermore, through our equating of modern glossolalia with the biblical speaking in tongues, the devil can mislead us about the need for and benefit of having and using the true gift of tongues - language ability - that the church needs today.

## WHAT CAUSES THE WISH TO SPEAK IN TONGUES?

What purpose, then, is served by glossolalia, and why is it sought and used? Samarin 1972:18 poses this crucial question thus: "Why, in the case of glossolalia, should people in all seriousness indulge in meaningless verbalizations?"

### 1. Consequences of Mistranslation in the New Testament

The Authorized Version/KJV of 1 Corinthians 14:2, 4, 13, 14, 19, and 27 refers to speaking in an "unknown" tongue. The word *unknown* is in italics, indicating that it is not part of the original text and has been added by the translators: but this added word has been very influential this past century in affecting the beliefs of people, three hundred years and more after the AV/KJV translation was made.

It is difficult now to be sure what was in the minds of the translators in adding this word.

Did they intend in this way to make it a little more explicit to the reader that those who heard this language did not know its meaning?

Or did they wish to indicate that the "tongue" was not a human language at all but some other kind of speech? Certainly this is the meaning that many Christians today have taken from 1 Corinthians 14. That is to say, many people have been interpreting the meaning of the passage to be that Paul is discussing speaking in a language not known on earth. Several authors, in writing about the modern "tongues" situation, refer to how influential this added word "unknown" has been in leading people to believe that the speaking in tongues at Corinth was speaking in a non-human language (see Burdick 19, Dillow 17, Glover 143f., Gromacki 1967:63, Meier 79).

But this is a mistranslation: Paul did **not** say, "speaking in an unknown tongue", and there is no justifiable reason for translating *glossa* in this way. Yet it is upon this mistranslation - or rather, upon the interpretation that this mistranslation helped to foster - that the initial "speaking in tongues" teaching was based.

Some modern versions of the Bible have followed a similar line. Thus the Good News Bible (TEV) uses the expression "strange tongues" for *glossa* throughout 1 Corinthians 12-14, irrespective of whether the original Greek has the singular or the plural. The New English Bible renders *glossa* by expressions such as "language of ecstasy" or "ecstatic utterance".

And the Living Bible uses "unknown tongues" several times, and indeed "writes in" the Charismatic interpretation of this passage right into the text. Thus this paraphrase renders 1 Corinthians 14:14-15 as: "For if I pray in a language I don't understand, my spirit is praying but I don't know what I am saying. Well, then, what shall I do? I will do both. I will pray in unknown tongues and also in ordinary language that everyone understands. I will sing in unknown tongues and also in ordinary language, so that I can understand the praise I am giving."

Further, this paraphrase adds the word "privately" into 14:18, to make it read, "I thank God that I 'speak in tongues' privately more than any of the rest of you." This is not **translating**; this is actually **altering the wording of the Scripture** in order to make it conform to the interpretation which the "translator" has decided upon.

More exact translations avoid these interpretative renderings, and indeed to its great credit the NIV gives in the margin the alternative translations "another language" and "other languages" for Paul's use of *glossa* in the singular and the plural.

But the impetus that was imparted by this AV/KJV rendering to the interpretation of *glossa* as "non-human languages" still continues. Thus the biblical "gift of tongues" comes to be identified with modern glossolalia, and when they believe this, some Christians will naturally want to have this "gift" of glossolalia.

## 2. Desire For A Deeper Christian Experience

The major factor that causes most people, most of the time, to want to speak in tongues is their love for the Lord. They very strongly desire a closer relationship with the Lord and a richer fellowship with him. They are longing for, and seeking for, how to come into a deeper Christian experience.

They have been taught or have heard (perhaps from a friend) that speaking in tongues is a gift of the Spirit and a sign of the baptism of the Spirit, which brings them into this deeper experience with the Lord, and they are therefore very responsive to this teaching. They accept this as being correct biblical teaching and they want to experience the baptism of the Spirit as it is explained to them, and to speak in tongues, both as evidence of the experience and also for the sake of the blessing which (they have been assured) such an experience will bring.

These seeking Christians believe that this glossolalic ability is a direct gift from the Lord through the Spirit, and as such it is to be received with thanksgiving and - like every gift that the Lord gives us - it is to be used.

So, not to speak in tongues would be not to accept and use the gift that God gives, and a failure to act in love to the Lord.

But there are frequently other motives involved of which a person may be largely unaware (though they may be recognizable to others).

## 3. Desire For A Miracle

People are being taught that "spiritual gifts" are "miraculous gifts". Many Christians do not perceive in themselves any miraculous gifts, but they have been told on the basis of Scripture, and they believe, that each person is given at least one spiritual gift. They are taught that modern glossolalia is the same as the biblical tongues-speaking, and that this is a gift of the Spirit, a miraculous gift, and they are being given encouragement to seek for it.

All of this leads them to the point of wanting to "speak in tongues", and of believing that they should, and can, do so. That is, they want to have a spiritual gift, and glossolalia is presented to them as one that they can have, so that, if they do speak in tongues they consider that now indeed they do have a miraculous gift.

## 4. Psychological Pressure

A very considerable psychological pressure is brought to bear by Charismatics upon others to engage in glossolalia. The Charismatic movement is being referred to as "Charismatic Renewal" or "Revival", and described by its advocates as the way in which the Holy Spirit is moving in the church today. Thus Thomas Smail speaks [13] of "the charismatic renewal in which I have been a participant for the last fifteen years, for the last seven as a leader". Similarly, Michael Cassidy refers [e.g. 163, 261] to the movement as Charismatic Renewal. Those who do not share in the Charismatic movement are thus seen as (and certainly are subtly pressured to see themselves as) out of step with what the Holy Spirit is now engaged in doing.

This perception exerts strong pressure upon people to abandon their deeply-felt reservations, their traditional interpretations of the Scriptures, and go along with the Charismatic view, with all that that entails - including "tongues".

Unworthy motives are attributed to those who resist this pressure to speak in tongues. Thus Basham 1976:26-28 writes,

> The question is asked everywhere I go, "Why is there so much controversy over speaking in tongues?" Consistent experience in ministering the baptism has convinced me that there are two major reasons for the controversy. One is fear, the other is ignorance. The fear comes from years of dire warnings that speaking in tongues is "fanaticism, emotionalism, or of the devil." And when these complaints have repeatedly bombarded the ears of earnest Christians who have never examined the Scriptures carefully for themselves or heard clear scriptural teaching about the baptism in the Holy Spirit, the result is a deeply embedded emotional prejudice against what God is doing in the church today. ...
>
> Satan's favorite tactic is to throw up an emotional smokescreen, to create controversy and anger when the gift of speaking in tongues is mentioned. ...
>
> Fear and ignorance, combined with false teaching, have proved to be powerful weapons in Satan's hands.

Even the terminology which is used brings this pressure to bear. Thus those who are pro-tongues-speaking refer to Christians as being "Charismatic" or "non-Charismatic", and this terminology is repeatedly used. They thus break up Christians, effectively, into those who accept the *charismata* (spiritual gifts) and those who (by implication) reject them.

But who wants to be classified as a Christian who rejects the "gifts of the Spirit"? So again there is subtle pressure to move out of the unflattering "non-Charismatic" category into that of "Charismatic".

Speaking personally, I find it condescending and presumptuous for self-designated Charismatics to apply to me the term "non-Charismatic". I *do not* reject the *charismata* - how *could* one reject the *charismata* without rejecting the Scriptures?

Rather, I reject the innovative and recent interpretation placed upon them by certain Christians, and I adhere to the traditional understanding of their nature and meaning. Therefore, if you want to label me, you may call me a "Traditional Charismatic". But not a "non-Charismatic", please!

Where in the writings of Charismatics can one see an open acknowledgement that there are numbers of thoughtful, concerned, Bible-believing, Spirit-filled Christians who do not concede that Charismatics have a monopoly on the Holy Spirit, and who oppose the Charismatic teaching about miraculous gifts in general and glossolalia in particular not because they are afraid but because they believe this teaching is wrong?

Charismatics tend to be very dismissive of those who teach an opposing interpretation. Thus Michael Harper 47 dismisses both dispensationalism and the theological work of B B Warfield with these words:

> With the evangelical world thoroughly penetrated now by the charismatic experience, there are fewer and fewer who still subscribe to a dispensationalism that relegates spiritual gifts and miracles to the first century, or to the express views of B B Warfield, whose influence on evangelicalism in the first half of the twentieth century was profound, that the "supernatural" gifts were so wholly associated with the apostles that when they had all died the gifts were buried with them. What we see now is a faith in the "supernatural" breaking out from the narrow confines of Biblical fundamentalism, mechanical sacramentalism and traditional dispensationalism. The ghosts of Scofield and Warfield are being well and truly laid.

It is very difficult to find Charismatic authors who acknowledge the strong doctrinal and interpretational opposition to their position. Very difficult.

The end effect of this attitude is to convey unmistakably to the ordinary Christian who encounters Charismatic teaching that he/she is out of line with the way the Spirit is working - indeed, that one is quenching the Spirit or resisting the Spirit or rejecting the Spirit - if one does not accept the Charismatic viewpoint and open themself to (or actively seek for) speaking in tongues.

## WHAT LEADS PEOPLE TO SPEAK IN TONGUES?

When a Christian has been brought by these factors to accept the Charismatic interpretation of gifts and tongues, what happens next? This will vary from one person to another. Some people may deliberately set out now to learn to speak in tongues, and practise until they can do it - possibly with tuition from a person who is helping and guiding them. Some may be in a warm and stimulating and enthusiastic service or meeting with those who do speak in tongues, and respond when invited to seek the baptism of the Spirit and the tongues gift - they will be conscious of the tongues experience and the expectations and prayers of these others, and so they will want and expect to speak in tongues also. Others may be seeking this gift privately in earnest prayer to the Lord for the experience.

### 5. Expectancy

What actually is the trigger which leads a person to commence glossolalia? Samarin 1972:55-57 says,

> The most common state of mind is expectancy. This is natural, of course, in people who earnestly want something to happen and believe that it will happen. But it is important to note how this expectancy is nurtured (as in the teaching of 'faith healer' Oral Roberts, pp.5-7) and how it becomes as much a part of the situation as the physical environment. This is why one of my respondents described the setting for his first experience as having an 'expectant atmosphere,' as if it were palpable, a force that would descend on him. ...

### 6. Acceptance/Conformity To The Expectations of Others

When they have spoken in tongues, this tongues-speaking (or their testimony to their tongues-speaking) is acknowledged by the group with whom they are fellowshipping as the sign of the baptism of the Spirit, and thus their own full membership of and acceptance by that group is affirmed.

They may never speak in tongues again - in which case their initial speaking is seen as a sign of the baptism of the Spirit but they are said not to have the gift of tongues; or they may continue to do so occasionally or regularly, in church or in private prayer - in which case they are regarded (and they regard themselves) as having the gift of tongues.

One Charismatic pastor was asked how he would feel if no one spoke in tongues in his church for six months. "Devastated", he replied. When we are encouraged by the group of fellow-Christians to speak in tongues, prophesy, etc., it is easy to do so because it is expected of us. This conformity brings a sense of oneness with others in the group (whether it is large, or a small minority in a church), and of identification and belonging and acceptance.

Many people join Charismatic groups because they did not receive this in their previous churches. Now, by conforming, they become part of a warm fellowship.

## 7. Pleasure and Enjoyment

Some people report that to be able to use the tongue without needing to engage the mind brings a great feeling of release, and freedom from constraints and limitations.

This brings a feeling of happiness and well-being. When this is a person's experience, it is understandable that they would repeat the tongues-speaking to have this feeling again.

On the basis of his first-hand investigations, Samarin 1972:202 comments about this:

> *Pleasureful.* Glossolalia is also indulged in, because speakers appear to derive pleasure from the experience. They enjoy doing something they once considered impossible; they like the way their discourses sound; and they enjoy both the fantasy and "ecstasy" that are associated with the use of this pseudolanguage.

> *Mastery.* ... the pleasure is partly derived from becoming proficient in a newly acquired skill.

With practice, the facility of speaking in tongues continues to improve [Samarin, 1972:68, 70]:

> For most people facility in speaking in tongues comes gradually and with much practice. ... When fluency does come, it is easier to speak in tongues than it is in one's natural language.

## 8. Effectiveness In Prayer

Praying in tongues brings a sense of particular effectiveness, of spiritual achievement. Samarin 1972:152-156 explains this thus:

> Praying in tongues is ... much more common than giving messages in tongues, and private prayer is more common than public praying. ... Glossolalists consider praise and petition (including intercession) to be the most important uses of glossolalic prayers, in which they claim to have greater freedom and efficacy by comparison with prayers in natural language. Glossolalia makes it possible for a person to express great joy or profound concern which one is otherwise unable to put into

words. A person may find himself, for example, deeply troubled without knowing the reason. Taking this unease as evidence of God's prodding, he engages in glossolalic praying without knowing for whom or why he is praying. Many times, however, it turns out that someone known to the person or connected with his immediate religious group was in dire need at that very moment. Reporting such "miraculous" events takes a prominent part in Pentecostalist testimony meetings and in Pentecostalist literature ...

Praying in tongues is also better, because a person is able to focus on the object of adoration, God, rather than on the means of adoration, language; one person says that rather than concentrating on the mode of communication, one concentrates on the communication itself. The result of this is experienced psychologically: one feels more relaxed and rested even though one may have prayed "all night".

The freedom that supposedly characterizes glossolalic praying is significant by comparison with the strain that is said to accompany earnest prayer outside this experience. ...

Moreover, since the prayer is uttered by the Spirit himself one has the assurance that he is praying for the right things. It follows from this that there can be no doubt about the prayer's being answered: what the Spirit prays for will be granted by God. This means that when a person is praying in tongues, God is going to do something wonderful, whether one hears of it later or not. Reduced to a formula it reads: "Prayer produces miracles." Since rational prayers are not this efficacious, it is no wonder that glossolalists who hold these views can be sanguine about life.

Because of this peculiar power, glossolalia is supposed to be especially effective in healing and exorcising, even though there is no Biblical precedent for such a belief. Praying for someone with physical problems takes place in very much the same way it would in normal language: one can be in the presence of the needy person or far removed from him; one starts with the conscious desire that the person be healed, delivered from pain, etc. and then engages in glossolalic discourse.

Now, this is more than we experience through praying in our own natural language. It can readily be seen, then, why praying in tongues brings a sense of spiritual achievement. It is also possible to identify speaking in tongues with attaining to some extent - and in a very easy way - the goal of becoming a spiritual person, and this also brings a sense of achievement.

## 9. Belief in the Value and Importance of Baptism in the Spirit

Glossolalists will regard their baptism in the Spirit and their tongues-speaking as being of God, and a very desirable thing, which adds a further and important spiritual dimension to their lives. They will seek to keep up their own tongues-speaking by regular practice, and they will therefore value it for themselves and wish to encourage others who have not had this experience to enter into it.

They will tend to see Christians as falling into two groups: those who are Spirit-baptized, and those who are not (and who therefore are lacking an experience and a level of Christian living which God has provided through the Spirit, and which he intends all his people to have).

## 10. A Desire for Power, Control, and/or Recognition

Tongues-speaking and prophecy marks people out in a group as spiritually gifted. Thus they are looked up to by many as being spiritual leaders - even if they have had no special biblical training, may be recent converts rather than mature Christians, and may not possess the skills of good leadership. Instead, tongues and prophecy is accepted as evidence that the Holy Spirit is choosing these people.

Many instances are reported of those who "spoke in tongues" or prophesied being able to take over the control of groups like university Christian Unions from the former leaders.

Sometimes this take-over has been assisted by prophecies that a course of action should be followed which is different from that mapped out by the leaders, and some of the members have then accepted this as being a direct word from the Lord.

If the existing leadership declines to follow this "word of prophecy", these leaders are "unspiritual" and are rejected by many of the group members; whereas if they do follow the "word of prophecy", then these leaders themselves have taken a significant step in conceding leadership of the group to the ones who are practising the tongues-speaking and prophecy.

Those who thus succeed in gaining control of the Christian Union or other group do not see this as religious manipulation, but as "the Spirit opening up the way for them for a wider ministry". Thus the Charismatic influence spreads.

Other people through their glossolalia and/or prophecy are content with lesser goals: by the exercise of these gifts in their Christian circle they can often achieve a recognition as spiritual Christians - or even just as *people* - which was not previously accorded them. (Especially this may be the case if they were women in churches which provide a limited role for women's ministry, or perhaps members of a congregation where almost all the ministry is kept in the hands of a few clergy or recognized church officers.)

## 11. A Sense of Spiritual Obligation

The experience of glossolalia and other Charismatic involvement is not always so "liberating" as some people have reported it. There are those who find it an obligation which they need to keep up because that (so they believe) is the will of God. They feel under a spiritual obligation: "If this is what God wants, then I have to do it."

Samarin 1973:139f. has commented,

> People speak in tongues - that is, produce pseudolanguage - because they feel they have to. But whether they do or don't, it does not influence the quality of their Christian experience.

## A RESPONSE TO MODERN GLOSSOLALIA

What are we to say to all this? The following comments respond point by point to the preceding eleven sections covering why people speak in tongues.

### 1. Recognizing the Mistranslation

Once we reject "unknown tongue" (and similar renderings of γλωσσα *glōssa*) because they are mistranslations, and thus become set free of the influence of interpretative versions, we can examine the text itself for the meaning that Paul was conveying.

This examination has been set out in the Commentary, where the reasons have been given for preferring the Traditional Charismatic interpretation: that in the New Testament, "tongues" means "natural languages". Modern glossolalia is not the biblical "speaking in tongues".

### 2. The Correct Path To A Deeper Christian Experience

All God's people should indeed be filled with a great desire to know God more fully and to walk in a closer relationship with him. Paul cries out with such a longing (Philippians 3:10, NIV), "I want to know Christ and the power of his resurrection and the fellowship of sharing in his sufferings". Jesus says (Matthew 5:6), "Blessed are those who hunger and thirst for righteousness, for they shall be satisfied". But we must be guided by Scripture: our desire must be for what God says is his intention. We must desire and long for his will and the outworking of his purpose in our lives.

Does this mean we will necessarily know his will correctly and ask correctly?

In Luke 11:9-13 Jesus encouraged his disciples to ask, and promised them that "it will be given to you"; if they would not give a serpent or a scorpion to a son who asked for food, "how much more will the heavenly Father give the Holy Spirit to those who ask him."

Charismatics frequently cite this passage in support of their teaching that God will give us the baptism in the Holy Spirit when we ask him. Campbell commences his book *Baptism In The Holy Spirit* [5] with this quotation; similarly Christenson 126 refers to it, especially in relation to receiving the gift of speaking in tongues. Basham 1969:97, basing his comment upon the use of this passage, says,

> You need have no fear of a counterfeit from Satan. If you ask God for the baptism in the Holy Spirit, then that's what you receive. We have Jesus' own word for it.

And with this "baptism", Basham continues, you "receive and speak the language the Holy Spirit gives" [104].

That is, if we ask God to give us the gift of tongues, and we then begin speaking glossolalia, this promise from Christ is our guarantee that our tongues-speaking is God's gift and has not come from Satan nor simply from within ourselves, from auto-suggestion or psychological causes.

But this simply does not follow. As Christians we are still able to mistake the Lord's will in what we ask: we are still capable of self-deception. It is all too easily possible to ask God for something, and then go out and do it or get it - and attribute the outcome to God and thank him for it, when from beginning to end it was all our own doing, and God may not have wanted us to do it or have it at all. It can be the case that we are simply engaged in persuading ourselves that what we are asking for is what God wants: and therefore when we get it we convince ourselves - wrongly - that it has come from God and is God's will.

Consider: A man infatuated with a non-Christian girl prays to the Lord that he may marry her, and does marry her, and then thanks the Lord for this when it was the *girl* who said "yes", and *not* the Lord. Or a Christian prays to get a new, expensive car that has taken his fancy, and persuades himself when he sees one advertised in the newspaper at a discount that this is the Lord's "provision" and an answer to his prayer. Or again, someone is praying about responding to a call to the mission field and then is offered a safe, secure, and lucrative post in the homeland, and prays about accepting this job, and then does so.

The will of God is that we are to be holy (1 Thessalonians 4:3).

God's purpose for us is that we should be holy and blameless before him (Ephesians 1:4, Philippians 1:10, 2:15, 1 Thessalonians 3:13; Colossians 1:22, 1 Peter 1:15, 2 Peter 3:11-14). We are to grow in the grace and knowledge of our Lord and Savior Jesus Christ (2 Peter 3:18). These are the goals that Scripture sets before us, for which we should seek. This is the teaching to which we should respond.

There is *nothing said in Scripture* about seeking the baptism of the Spirit (because in fact all Christians are baptized with the Spirit into one body - the body of Christ - in their conversion [1 Corinthians 12:13], as they receive and enter into the benefits both of Calvary and of Pentecost).

There is *nothing said in Scripture* about seeking the gift of tongues (because all gifts are manifestations of the Spirit [1 Corinthians 12:7] and are distributed to each Christian entirely as the Spirit chooses [1 Corinthians 12:11]).

### 3. Anyone Can Speak In Tongues
### - It Is Not A Christian Miracle

As we have seen, modern tongues-speaking is not the "gift of tongues" described and referred to in Scripture, which was an ability to communicate in a known human language for the purpose of passing on God's truth and edifying the hearers. On the day of Pentecost, this gift was conferred upon the disciples by a miracle, but such miraculous conferring of gifts was only for a particular purpose in the economy of God (attesting to the credentials of the speakers, making known God's truth to people in their own language, and a sign of judgement upon unbelieving Israel).

Today's glossolalia is not a miraculous gift from God. As this Excursus has shown, it is a natural ability which we had from childhood, innate in all of us, and able to be exercised by any adherent of any religion or of no religion at all. It is a completely faulty view that when this is done by devotees of other religions or by atheists, glossolalia is not miraculous, but when it is done by Christians *this same kind of glossolalia* is a miracle from God.

Sincere Christians are turning to speaking in tongues because they are told that "spiritual gifts" are miraculous, and that God gives at least one such miraculous gift to each of his children, and they are taught to see tongues-speaking as a miraculous gift from God available to them. But behind this chain of thinking lies a seriously faulty exegesis of Scripture: on the one hand, the misinterpretation of the nature of biblical "speaking in tongues", and on the other, the narrow defining of "spiritual gifts" so as to exclude natural abilities.

Thus many people have gone seeking a "spiritual gift" (and come to find this in speaking in tongues), because due to faulty teaching they have not recognized all their own various talents and abilities as coming down from the Father of Lights (James 1:17): talents and abilities which should now be enlisted in the Lord's service and which *are* spiritual gifts because the Spirit takes them and uses them and works through them.

The seeking after tongues has in practice *diverted* many devout Christians from valuing the talents and abilities that God has already given them, and from devoting themselves to developing them and using them for the Lord in the power of and under the direction of the Holy Spirit. All that we have and are is part of the Lord's equipping of us for his service.

Today God still confers the gift of tongues (i.e., the ability to communicate in a known human language) but it is not now an ability miraculously imparted. Instead, like a gift for teaching or music or administration or pastoring, it is an inner and innate ability which has to be deliberately trained and developed by study and practice.

Moreover, tongues-speaking is not a sign of "baptism in the Spirit" or of the infilling of the Spirit - and the teaching that it is, is not correct biblical teaching but a mistaken interpretation. The inner witness of the Spirit that I am a child of God is the seal upon my conversion (2 Corinthians 1:22, Ephesians 1:13,14, 4:30) and is all the witness that I need (Romans 8:15-16) to my baptism with the Spirit (i.e., at my conversion).

## 4. Resist Psychological Pressure

The answer to the psychological pressure which is often applied to encourage Christians to feel that they, too, should speak in tongues, is to recognize that the Charismatic interpretation of the biblical references to "baptism in the Spirit" and "speaking in tongues" is only *one possible* interpretation, and to note that from the Early Church Fathers to the giants of the Reformation and the Evangelical Awakening in Wesley's day, through to the great Evangelical and Reformed theologians of the nineteenth and twentieth centuries, a *different interpretation* has been held, as set forth in this Commentary.

Why should we feel obliged to turn from the view of these men of God down through history to the new interpretation being urged upon us these days?

## 5. What Should We Be Expecting?

To "speak in tongues" (in the sense in which this is being used today, of speaking unintelligible utterances) is something that can be induced by appropriate circumstances - a personal desire and expectation, the excitement and enthusiasm of a meeting where this experience is advocated and promised, an awareness that others are praying that you will have this experience. It is something that can be taught - and can be learnt - at a purely human level. When a person "speaks in tongues" today, it shows that they have responded to the teaching and encouraging given to them, and/or that they have had an internal and psychological response to what they were seeking, and/or that they are apt pupils of what they were being taught (about the nature of speaking in tongues, and about the way to have the experience).

Their experience of tongues does not attest or demonstrate that they have entered any new level of experience of the Holy Spirit. It certainly does not validate the teaching given to them about tongues. It is possible for them to be encouraged to seek the experience of speaking in tongues, and for them then to have this experience that they are taught to seek and expect (even though the teaching they are given is mistaken in asserting that this is the gift of tongues found in Acts and 1 Corinthians) - and without this being the work of the Spirit at all.

## 6. Acceptance/Conformity Can Confirm Our Wrong Views

There is much mutual reinforcement of views and beliefs in groups who practise and advocate speaking in tongues. Their members reassure and support each other in what they believe. They give positive affirmation to those in such a group who speak in tongues, and encourage others to do so. There is a very real sense of belonging, and those who have not spoken in tongues feel a strong desire to do so in order to obtain the affirmation of the group and be fully accepted by them.

Thus peer expectation, peer pressure, a need for acceptance, and a wish to conform, can all combine to play a significant part in helping an individual speak in tongues - much as similar factors can encourage a person in some other particular Christian fellowship to be baptized.

Whether there is any biblical reason for being baptized - or speaking in tongues - or indeed for any other teaching one is given - needs to be sought out independently, in Scripture. But all these other factors can lead a person to wish for and seek the "baptism of the Spirit" and tongues-speaking, according to the beliefs of the group, whether or not the group's understanding of these things is biblically correct.

## 7. Pleasure And Enjoyment Can Be
## Based Upon Human Factors and Mistaken Views

Tongues-speaking can give a sense of release and joy, which confirms the person in believing that this is God's gift.

Part of this can derive from a perfectly human satisfaction at a new accomplishment. Part of it comes from a shared enthusiasm - and has no more particularly Christian content than the enthusiasm of the crowd at a sporting fixture or a pop concert.

Part of it flows from the feeling of being part of "a miracle being wrought by the Spirit", and of using a gift from God. This feeling is the result of the particular interpretation held about this "gift". This does not demonstrate that one's belief is right or correct or accurate, or even specifically Christian.

## 8. What Is The True Measure of Effectiveness In Prayer?

Praying in tongues can bring a feeling of "getting through to God on a direct line".

But this can be simply due to a belief that one is more effective in this way than (for example) if one has to find out what someone's situation and needs are in order to pray for them properly.

As we noted earlier, when you "pray in tongues" you are turning away from the type of prayer that Jesus taught, and adopting a type of "prayer" which in its most significant features is similar to that of pagans, and was condemned by Jesus.

Actually, people "praying in a tongue" don't know what they are praying, and therefore don't really *know* that they are engaging in prayer at all. They *believe* that they are, but this is an act of faith. And faith can be misplaced.

We are entitled to ask whether the Word of God gives us a secure basis for confidence that this belief is well founded. For the *experience itself* tells us *nothing* about its meaning or its source.

If in fact this kind of speaking and praying in tongues is not what Scripture teaches, then the good feeling it brings, far from being God-given, is based on a mistaken grasp of Scripture: and time spent praying in tongues is time wasted.

Better by far to follow the example that Paul sets in every Epistle he writes, in which he speaks of praying for specific things that he is aware are needful for the prayed-for - and he always knows and can write down exactly what it was that he has been praying about.

## 9. Respect For The Interpretation Accepted By Others

It is a very divisive thing when one company of Christians believes that they have a teaching and experience which others lack. This is different from the difference that exists between a new-born Christian and the mature Christian, or a difference of interpretation over such matters as sacraments or church government. It is the denial by one group that other Christians can be truly mature or obedient Christians unless they accept the same teaching and have the same experience that they themselves have had.

This fosters a (sometimes unconscious) attitude that the one group consists of "Class A Christians", an elite, whereas all others are "Class B" because of lacking the experience.

This attitude is a great barrier to true Christian fellowship, and can lead those who hold it to have difficulty in accepting ministry from those whom they regard as lacking a crucial experience from God. A person's attitude to the "baptism of the Spirit" and "tongues" becomes the one true basis for fellowship, without regard to questions of doctrine or holiness or commitment to Christ. In fact *these* matters - which the Scripture puts forth as crucial - become subordinated to acceptance of a particular view about the Spirit, and a particular experience.

## 10. The Wrongness of Using "Spiritual Gifts" in a Power Struggle

It is possible - and indeed it happens, as noted above - that some Christians will use the prestige and spiritual status that they are accorded in some circles on account of "speaking in tongues" (or "prophesying" or having "an utterance of wisdom" or "an utterance of knowledge") to achieve positions of eminence or control. Thus they at times succeed in gaining the ascendancy in congregations or Christian organizations, and in persuading people to their interpretation of the Scriptures.

Samarin 1972:211 makes this insightful comment:

> No special power needs to take over a person's vocal organs; all of us are equipped with everything we need to produce glossolalia. But once it is acquired, glossolalic speech can achieve different psychological ends, some more and others less consciously manipulated.

Frequently there is little resistance offered to this happening: when people do object to the Charismatic invasion, they are usually silenced by accusations of resisting the Spirit, disobeying the Scriptures, and/or causing controversy. This is akin to you being accused of causing the trouble and disturbing the peace when you catch a thief stealing your car and you try to stop him instead of just letting him drive it away.

Should we simply allow the new Charismatics to take away from us the Evangelical and Reformed heritage which we have, with its sane and logical and legitimate interpretation of 1 Corinthians 12-14? By all means let us profit from the new emphasis upon the work of the Holy Spirit and the ministry of spiritual gifts in the church. Let us consider the insights of the new Charismatics, and examine them in the light of Scripture, and benefit from them when they encourage our enthusiasm for the Lord. But let us not hesitate to draw attention to the wrongness of using "spiritual gifts" (understood according to the Charismatic interpretation) as weapons in a power struggle to gain ascendancy for that interpretation.

If someone for example is going to pray or speak in our gathering in glossolalia, do we accept this as legitimate, and look for an "interpretation" of it? Or do we point out that this is heaping up meaningless words like the pagans do (Matthew 6:7), and call upon people, rather, to pray according to the pattern that Jesus taught to his followers: that is, in specific petitions in a known language?

We can acknowledge the views of the new Charismatics in this matter. Samarin 1972:231 reminds us,

> Glossolalia is a linguistic symbol of the sacred. So it is understandable that for the charismatic movement it is a sacred symbol, a precious possession, a divine gift.

But it is one thing to acknowledge their views, and another to bow to their seeking to impose their interpretation upon us when we (for good reason) consider it to be a mistaken exegesis of the Word of God.

## 11. Being Freed From Feeling Obliged To Engage In Glossolalia

Numbers of former tongues-speakers have testified to a feeling of liberation when, after beginning to view glossolalia differently, they came to the point of not feeling required to continue with it as an obligation to the Lord.

H. A. Ironside describes his spiritual experiences in *Holiness - The True And The False*. He writes of the circumstances in the early years of the Pentecostal movement at the beginning of last century, a time when numbers of Christians who professed "holiness doctrines" were just beginning to practise the use of the "gifts of the Spirit", including "tongues". Ironside came out of this holiness movement, describing the tongues movement as "disgusting" and characterized by "an unhealthy craving for new and thrilling religious sensations and emotional meetings of a most exciting character" [38]. He turned away from this background, preferring rather a Christianity which would "Let ... the truth of the indwelling Spirit be Scripturally taught".

In *Corinthian Catastrophe* [7] George Gardiner discusses his involvement in the Charismatic movement and poses the question, "What does the Bible say?" He continues [7-8],

> It was this question, following the disillusionment common to Charismatics, which drove me out of the movement and into the relief and freedom I enjoy today.
>
> It all began with nagging questions about the gulf between Charismatic practices and Scriptural statements - a very wide gulf! When such questions were asked, the questioner was looked upon with severe disapproval and even warned about the "sin against the Holy Ghost". Peer group pressure, plus hesitancy to challenge older leaders, is usually enough to silence the critic.
>
> It took a war and four years of isolation from other Christians and the former surroundings to produce a climate where I dared honestly to face the questions and doubts I had repressed. Alone, with no book but my Bible, I went back over the Scriptures again.

He describes his examination of the Scriptures, and concludes the Introduction to his book (published in 1974) with the comment [9-10],

> If someone had shown me the clear warnings, the logical pronouncements and the spiritual patterns in Paul's epistle when I was a young Christian, seeking to know and please my Lord, I could have been spared years of bondage, disillusionment and despair. I can only pray that God will use this writing to spare others the same."

C S Butler describes in *Test The Spirits* [124-131] his involvement in the Charismatic movement in the 1960's and 1970's, and what it was like in his experience. He found it brought him, he says, only "disillusionment". In 1979, having rejected the Charismatic movement, he entered into a fresh experience of Christ through the ministry of a friend, and came to adopt the position and teaching of Calvin. In concluding his testimony, he says [131],

> I realize as never before how good the Lord has been to me, in calling me out of the charismatic movement.

## CONCLUSION

We have examined evidence from the first-hand research into glossolalia undertaken by men of the caliber of Kildahl, Samarin, and Welmers. We have seen the information about the widespread practice of non-Christian glossolalia supplied by these men and others like Bunn. We have noted comments on glossolalia by those who reject it, those who practise and advocate it, and those who used to be involved with it and have abandoned it.

What conclusions should we draw?

There are numerous accounts of a miraculous speaking in an unlearnt human language - xenoglossia - as on the day of Pentecost, and some of these accounts say or imply that this xenoglossic language is the "tongue" normally spoken by the person concerned when he/she "speaks in tongues".

This indicates that such glossolalists can speak in xenoglossia at will. It is therefore all the more remarkable that no objective observer has been able to tape-record **even one single instance** of xenoglossia or in some other way verify that one has occurred. To say therefore that glossolalists sometimes miraculously speak in an unlearned human language is a statement of faith which remains unsubstantiated by impartial evidence. Rather, all such evidence indicates that xenoglossia does not occur. This is not to deny that God **could** perform such a miracle today if he chose. But we are dealing in **ascertainable facts**, what **does** happen, not **possibilities**, what **could** happen. And the evidence is that it does **not** happen.

Our investigation has also looked at the nature of glossolalia, and in particular whether it is a language. Two lines of evidence show that it is not.

**First of all**, there is no correspondence between sets of sounds and particular meanings (that is, a glossolalic utterance does not consist of words that convey meaning), nor is there any system of organized structure (grammar), nor does it have any of the other characteristic features of language.

**Secondly**, as the discussion of interpretation has shown, a given glossolalic utterance can have any interpretation at all or even several different interpretations, totally unconnected in meaning with each other and all of them considered equally valid. This is not true of an utterance in a language - it cannot just mean anything at all but has a specific meaning which is being communicated. Linguists cannot "break into" a glossolalic tongue and learn the meaning of an utterance, because there is no inherent meaning there. It is not language.

Furthermore, as there is a mass of evidence to indicate, different kinds of glossolalic utterance have been found in most of the religions of the ancient and modern world. If glossolalia is typical of pagan religion, it is difficult to see how Paul could have endorsed this practice for the Corinthians or described it - a common phenomenon amongst unbelievers - as being a sign to unbelievers on those occasions when Christians did it.

We have looked at the various factors which encourage Christians to want to speak in glossolalia, and which in fact can prompt them to do so. We have seen that many of these factors derive from particular beliefs about the interpretation of the meaning of "speaking in tongues" in the New Testament. It is possible to account for Christian glossolalia in completely human terms - it does not require a miraculous gift from God.

Where has this study brought us? There can be no question about the existence of two distinctly different ways of interpreting "speaking in tongues" in the New Testament, and these in turn are part of two wider schemes of interpretation:

There is the Traditional Charismatic approach, which holds that the miraculous element in the *charismata*, "grace gifts", was for the apostolic age *only*, and that these gifts today, while still given by God to equip his people, and being supernaturally empowered by the Holy Spirit to enable us to serve and minister as God intends, are capacities to be developed by study and training. The gift of tongues finds its place in this as a facility for language, something which is of immense practical value in foreign missionary work in particular. And the gift of interpretation or translation is the ability to act as interpreter from one language to another, and/or to engage in the translation of the Scriptures and Christian books.

Then on the other hand there is the New Charismatic interpretation, which believes that the miraculous gifts given to the apostolic church continue to be available to people today. This view regards modern glossolalia as being the same as the "speaking in tongues" which Paul endorsed for the Corinthians, a miraculous gift for the edification of the individual in prayer or (through interpretation, which itself is also a miraculous gift) of the church.

Each Christian will need to examine the evidence for himself/herself in deciding whether to accept the Traditional Charismatic view of "spiritual gifts" (including tongues), or the New Charismatic view.

It will be helpful for mutual understanding between Christians who hold these differing views if Traditional Charismatics recognize the nature of the interpretation adopted by modern Charismatics, and the importance to them of the experiences they have. And if also, on the other hand, modern Charismatics recognize that Traditional Charismatics do not reject the doctrine of the Holy Spirit or the baptism in and filling of the Holy Spirit, or the value and use of spiritual gifts: they just differ from modern Charismatics in their understanding of what the Bible teaches about these things.

As I write these words I am concerned lest I be misunderstood by anyone as criticizing enthusiasm for the Lord, endorsing apathy, advocating complacency, encouraging acceptance of and contentment with the low level of spiritual life which is the status quo for many churches and Christians today.

This is not at all my meaning nor my intention.

We desperately need to see the mighty movement of the Holy Spirit in our lives, and in our churches. All the people of God should be discovering, testing, developing, and using the gifts that the Lord is giving us. What we must do, however, is allow Scripture to instruct us concerning the nature of these gifts and how they are to be used in the church to equip the saints for the edification of the body of Christ and for ministry to a needy and lost world.

If modern glossolalia is not the biblical gift of tongues, that does not mean that there is no gift of tongues for us today. Rather, God has provided some of us with a gift of languages and a gift of translation: through learning to speak other languages, we are to use these gifts as the means by which the message of salvation in the Lord Jesus Christ is to be proclaimed to those of other nations, the church there to be built up, and the Scriptures to be provided for them in their own tongues.

May God grant that these, the true gifts of tongues and interpretation which he is providing in his church, may be recognized and used for the salvation of the lost and the sanctifying of his people!

# CHAPTER FIFTEEN

## SECTION 5:
## CONCERNING THE RESURRECTION (15:1-58E)

### 1. The Message Of The Gospel (15:1-11)

Already in this letter Paul has many times spoken about the gospel which the Lord Jesus Christ commissioned him to proclaim (1:17), and which he brought to the Corinthians (2:1-2). Here he sets out in brief compass the essential nature of that gospel.

Note that, as he says in verses 1 and 11, Paul is addressing those who believe the gospel. None of what he says in this chapter applies to non-Christians, unbelievers. It is no part of Paul's purpose to discuss them - and he doesn't.

### (a) A Gospel Of Salvation:
### To Be Received, Adopted, And Held Firmly (15:1-2)

**15:1-2** For fourteen chapters Paul has dealt with practical issues at Corinth, many of them (it would seem) raised by the Corinthians themselves in a letter to him, and several of them raised by Paul out of his concern as a result of reports that had reached him. He has initially (chapters one and two, and throughout) spoken of the centrality of the cross in the Christian faith, but the practical application of his teaching has been to the fore. Now he turns to a major doctrinal issue - indeed, the one that is the center of and crucial to the whole Christian faith. It is his climax for the whole carefully-thought-out Epistle, and it is written not in response (it would appear) to anything raised by the Corinthians but rather to reports that Paul himself had heard, about some of those at Corinth. That is, it seems clear that Paul is raising this topic entirely on his own initiative.

He is able to start off on common ground: the glorious gospel of salvation in and through Christ, which Paul himself had brought them, and they had received, and through which they stand. Paul says, first, that he is going to remind them of the gospel that he preached to them, and he describes the impact of this gospel. When he preached it, they received it, and took their stand upon it.

**15:1** The gospel is not a message to be believed in an abstract, impersonal way, but to be received into the inner being and fabric of our lives, so that it becomes part of us. Moreover, when we have received it, it is then the foundation for the whole of our lives - upon it we take our stand. The Corinthians - whatever else their shortcomings - have taken their stand upon the basic truth of the gospel message. In v.11 Paul repeats this affirmation: "This is what you believed."

Thus the preaching of the gospel demands our personal response, and the acceptance of the gospel requires our total involvement.

**15:2a** When we thus receive and stand upon the gospel, then by it we are saved. Notice the tense here. Paul does not say, "By this gospel you *were* saved", as of some event in the past which happened once and is now over. Rather he says (RSV, NIV), "are saved" - in fact, the Greek meaning is more forcefully brought out by the translation (ESV, NRSV) "*are being saved*". It is not a once-for-all event. It is an on-going dynamic process as the gospel continues to save us day by day. That is, the salvation from sin initiated at our conversion is to be an on-going, continuous experience of being saved from sin. (Cf. "you shall call his name Jesus, for he will save his people from their sins", Matthew 1:21.) That is, the verb here in v.2 is an anticipatory present: a present with a future component: there is more saving still to take place. It is happening now, but it is to be completed in the future.

**15:2b** For this to continue to be true in their experience, it was essential that they should continue to "hold fast to the word" that they had received. Again and again Scripture emphasizes in this way the necessity of "continuing" (e.g. John 8:31; 15:4; Acts 13:43; 14:22; Colossians 1:23). So also Psalm 119:11, "I have stored up your word in my heart, that I might not sin against you." Note: "unless you believed in vain." Faith that does not continue is no true faith at all, but "in vain" or empty faith. This verse holds a fine balance between the truth of the eternal security of the elect ("you are saved") and the requirement of the perseverance of the saints ("if you hold fast to the word").

"Empty faith" is possible (one thinks of Jesus's teaching about professing disciples, and his parable of the sower). But Paul is not affirming that there will be such at Corinth: he says very tentatively "except unless" (ἐκτὸς εἰ μη, *ektos ei mē*), making the point twice.

### (b) A Gospel That Centers in the Person of Jesus Christ (15:3-7)

**15:3-7** Verses 3 to 5 are a statement of the common tradition of the church - or this common tradition may continue (as I would believe) to v.7. Paul now states the nature of this gospel by which they have entered into salvation. Note the chain: "I received", "I delivered to you", "you received" (v.1). These are technical terms (παραδιδωμι, *paradidōmi*, and παραλαμβανω, *paralambanō*) used in the New Testament for the transmission and the reception of the Christian tradition.

Paul does not say *how* he received the tradition. Noting the parallel with 1 Corinthians 11:23, where these same two words are used, some commentators take this as Paul's claim to have received this through direct revelation from the Lord, especially in the light of Galatians 1:12. However, we should note that in chapter 11:23 he states that what he passed on to them he received directly "from the Lord"; he makes no such statement here. He must already have known quite a lot about Christians and what they believed before his Damascus Road experience; or his vendetta against Christians makes no sense.

The best understanding of Paul's meaning here would be that, while the *facts* of Christ's death and purported resurrection were common knowledge, it was through his encounter with the risen Christ and through the enlightenment of the Spirit that he came to know that these things were true and real, and to understand their *meaning*.

He preached the gospel to the Corinthians ἐν πρωτοις (*en protois*): either chronological, *as the first thing* he proclaimed to them; or qualitative, "I delivered to you *as of first importance*". Both would be true: this is well captured in the REB translation "first and foremost".

He now reminds them of the core of the gospel message. This is a brief summing-up of the essence of Christian belief, and it is widely regarded as a credal statement of the message proclaimed by all Christian preachers and accepted by hearers as the basis of faith. Paul taught them many things, but these are the things of first importance, and are the means of and the basis for their very salvation.

Garland 684 writes, "That Christ died and that he was resurrected on the third day are facts, but their meaning is interpreted by the Scriptures." The gospel Paul gives is a summary of facts, their interpretation, and their attestation. Each section comes logically and grammatically after "I delivered to you", and begins with "that" (ὅτι, *hoti*):

that Christ died (*fact*)
    for our sins (*interpretation*)
        in accordance with the Scriptures; (*attestation*)
that he was buried (*fact*)
that he was raised on the third day (*fact*)
        in accordance with the Scriptures; (*attestation*)

that he appeared to: Peter, the Twelve, 500 people, James (the brother
of Jesus), all the apostles. (*attestation*)

**15:3** Notice the twofold "in accordance with the Scriptures" in these
verses. Jesus had taught this: see for example John 20:9; Luke 24:25-27;
24:44-46; Acts 13:32-37; 26:22-23).

Beginning with the Pentateuch of Moses, and in the Psalms and all
the Prophets, Jesus "interpreted to them in all the Scriptures the things
concerning himself" (Luke 24:25-27; 24:44-46). Peter declared that
Jesus was "delivered up according to the definite plan and
foreknowledge of God" (Acts 2:23); and Paul boldly bore witness (Acts
26:22-23), "I stand here testifying both to small and great, saying nothing but what the prophets and Moses said would come to pass: that the
Christ must suffer and that, by being the first to rise from the dead, he
would proclaim light both to our people and to the Gentiles." Paul
proclaims his gospel of the righteous of God through faith in Jesus
Christ, as "the Law and the Prophets bear witness to it" (Romans 3:21).

So, the message of the gospel is "in accordance with the Scriptures".
But, in accordance with which Scriptures?

Isaiah 53 is a major passage which allows insight into the passion of
the Messiah. It is the passage that Philip expounded to the Ethiopian
treasurer (Acts 8:31-35); and the basis of Peter's teaching in 1 Peter
2:22-25. The teaching of Jesus concerning giving his life a ransom for
many (Matthew 20:28//Mark 10:45) is an allusion to Isaiah 53:11,12; so
also Matthew 26:28//Mark 14:24; and these verses from Isaiah and the
Gospels lie behind numerous passages in Paul (e.g. Galatians 1:4; 2:20;
Titus 2:14).

Another significant passage, about the suffering of the Messiah, is
Psalm 22.

In Psalm 16:8-11, Peter finds a prophecy fulfilled in Jesus (Acts 2:25-
31); and he then cites Psalm 110 (Acts 2:34-35). Paul, too, quotes Psalm
16 (Acts 13:35-37); and also cites Psalm 2 (Acts 13:33).

Hodge 313-314 comments generally on the teachings of the Old
Testament Scriptures about the death and resurrection of the Messiah:

> The prophetic Scriptures, however, are full of this doctrine; for on
> the one hand they predict the sufferings and death of the Messiah, and
> on the other hand his universal and perpetual dominion. It is only on the
> assumption that he was to rise from the dead that these two classes of
> prediction can be reconciled.

**15:4** "Was buried" indicates "was really dead".

The ESV, NRSV and NIV all translate in v.4 as, "was raised"; but after a string of Greek aorists, there is a change here and the verb form ἐγήγερται (*egēgertai*), is perfect tense, "has been raised". The difference is that this verb form does not merely refer to the *fact* of the resurrection having taken place, but the sense of the perfect indicates that Jesus remains alive.

**15:5-7** Paul is not here seeking to convince unbelievers of the resurrection, and he is not intending to refer to *all* the resurrection appearances. What he includes links with the evidence in the Gospels and Acts: that Jesus appeared to:

1. Peter (Luke 24:34)
2. the Twelve (John 20:19, 26)
3. 500 people (apparently Matthew 28:16-20)
4. James (not expressly stated elsewhere, but implied by Acts 1:14)
5. all the apostles (Acts 1:2-11)

MacArthur 403 says,

> In going to Peter first, Jesus emphasized his grace. Peter had forsaken the Lord, but the Lord had not forsaken him. Christ did not appear to Peter because Peter *deserved* to see him most, but perhaps because Peter *needed* to see him most. Peter was the Lord's spokesman at Pentecost, and was crucially used in the expansion of the church for several years. As such he was the prime witness to the resurrected Christ.

"The Twelve" refers to a specific group of people, not to a particular number. There were of course at this time - after the defection of Judas and before the enrollment of Matthias - in fact just eleven. When Jesus appeared to them immediately after the resurrection they are specifically referred to as "the eleven" (Luke 24:9,33 [//Mark 16:14]); also similarly Matthew 28:16; but otherwise they were *The Twelve*, no matter how many of them were present at a given time.

**15:6** Lenski 636f. argues the case that the appearance to the 500 corresponds with the appearance on a mountain in Galilee:

> There is no reason for the repeated and emphatic summons to distant Galilee and even to a specific mountain there, if only the eleven are concerned, whom Jesus had [already] met twice in Jerusalem, namely on the day of his resurrection and eight days later (Luke 24:36; John 20:26). All is clear when we think that the eleven together with all of the other disciples of Jesus assembled in Galilee for this especially appointed meeting with Jesus. ... The occasion fits the number assembled. It was for the purpose of the majestic announcement of the Great Commission. It was proper that this should be a public meeting which included the entire body of the Lord's brethren. Here, on a

mountaintop, this host came together at the appointed time. Word had been circulated among them. Removed from observation by outsiders, all of them assembled. The exact day is unknown. It must have been after the appearance at the Sea of Galilee (John 21:1ff.); it probably occurred towards the end of the forty-day period.

"James": There are several men named James in the New Testament, but there is really only one who could be introduced in a catalogue of witnesses without further details being given to identify him: James the brother of Jesus, who became president or chairman or bishop of the church in Jerusalem, as we see in Acts. He is amongst those believers in Acts 1:14 who gathered in the upper room after the ascension. But when we read of him in the Gospels it is as one of Jesus's family who were scoffing at Jesus (John 7:1-10), and who declared that he was mad, and went to Capernaum to take charge of him and bring him home (Mark 3:21, 31). Clearly, something happened to James between these events during Jesus's ministry and the time of the ascension, and this information here about the resurrected Jesus meeting privately with him fills a gap in our understanding which would otherwise have remained a puzzle.

### (c) A Gospel That Brings Christ in Transforming Grace to the Individual (15:8-11)

**15:8-9** Note that Paul's conversion was the result of meeting the resurrected Jesus. He was aware, of course, of what the Christian were saying, but he considered that their claims were ridiculous. And, moreover, what they were saying about Jesus was blasphemous. Jesus was a fake Messiah, a fraud, and his claims were false: not least, the claim that he rose from the dead. But then the Pharisee Saul, well versed in the Jewish Scriptures, met the risen Christ for himself. And all his thinking was turned totally upside down.

So, after giving his list of these other appearances, Paul adds himself, using the same word ὤφθη (*ōphthē*) in regard to Christ's appearing to him (v.8) as he had used in reference to the others he lists (verses 5, 6, and 7). He does not regard his Damascus Road experience as "seeing a vision" but as an encounter with Christ risen from the dead that was parallel with those of the other apostles and disciples.

He says in relation to himself, "last of all". This means, chronologically, that he was the last of the apostles to see the Lord; but it means more than this: for, with his call and appointment as an apostle, the list of apostles is completed. There are no others called to this special and unique role after him. He was called and appointed an apostle on a par (as he is often at pains to stress) with those who were appointed as apostles before him.

He calls himself the *least* of the apostles, because of his prior activity as an enemy of Jesus and the gospel.

There are numerous speculations as to what he means by referring to himself as "one untimely born", literally "a fetus stillborn, a miscarriage". Almost, "a monstrosity".

It is suggested that this term may be an insult thrown at him by his enemies at Corinth - and yes, he will accept the description. He knows, he acknowledges, he is not worthy to be called by the Lord as (or chosen as, or described as) an apostle. But while all this is totally true, nonetheless he *is* an apostle, by God's grace.

Thus the account is not yet complete at v.7: the gospel includes also the fact that Christ reached out and touched Paul and transformed him (v.8).

Note that the gospel centers in the person of Jesus Christ: the reality of his death upon the cross, his burial, and his resurrection (attested by those to whom he appeared).

**15:10** Historically, Paul is writing of a particular, unique encounter of his own with the risen Christ, so that "by the grace of God I am what I am, and his grace toward me was not in vain." Thus Paul became a dedicated worker for Christ. Grace is not a substitute for nor an alternative to hard work. Grace alone is the reason and the explanation for Paul: but it made him the hardest of hard workers. That is both the consequence and the outflow of God's grace. Grace (mentioned three times in this verse) was not "empty", "ineffectual", but led to abundant and productive labor. Unselfconsciously Paul mentions then he labored more and harder than anyone else - but it was the grace of God working in and through him.

**15:11** "This gospel is what we preach (whether I or they): this is God's message and we are all of one accord in our agreement upon it. And this is the message of the gospel that you believed."

This is the gospel, Paul repeats, and anything else and anything less is *not* the gospel. Whether it is Paul who preaches, or one of the others, the message is the same, for this is what is preached, and this is the saving message they had believed. All the apostles in their preaching focussed on the resurrection of Christ - we can see this evidenced in their sermons in Acts. Once again Paul makes the point that he knows he is writing to those who share this faith. The gospel that is preached consists of:

1. Christ died;
2. Christ was buried;
3. Christ was raised;
4. Christ appeared to these witnesses (named);
5. and I have had an encounter with him myself;
6. This has transformed me by his grace.

That is the center of all Paul's preaching, and that is the essence of what the gospel is. As Paul also declares in Romans 1, the gospel is the power of God demonstrated in the resurrection of Christ Jesus, showing him to be the Son of God (v.4), and accomplishing the salvation of everyone who believes (v.16). The gospel is rooted in history, and changes people. The preaching of the whole gospel says, "This is what Jesus did, and this is how it has transformed me."

The NIV is misleading in v.11a in saying "whether then it was I or they", and introducing here a past tense "was". This is not paralleled in the Greek, which is not speaking of *past* preaching but of *all* preaching (κηρυσσομεν, *kērussomen*, present tense) without past implications. The Corinthians believed this (this verb is past tense), and it is the basis of their present standing in Christ.

## 2. Centrality Of The Resurrection (15:12-34)

**15:12** After setting out the nature of the gospel, Paul now takes up one aspect of this gospel - the resurrection - for further comment. He does this because there are some at Corinth who say that there is no resurrection from the dead.

**15:13-19** First of all, he asserts the reality of Christ's resurrection, and its centrality in the gospel: "if Christ has not been raised, then our preaching is in vain and your faith is in vain. We are even found to be misrepresenting God ... if Christ has not been raised, your faith is futile and you are still in your sins" (verses 14-17).

There would be, moreover, no life beyond death then for us (v.18) and if we have hope in Christ only for this life, we are of all people most to be pitied (v.19).

**15:20-28** This statement of hopelessness leads into his second section, the ringing assertion that in fact Christ *has* been raised from the dead, and that through him we also shall rise - his resurrection is our proof of this. If we believe in the resurrection of Christ (as we must, because of the evidence, as presented) then we have total confidence about our own resurrection, for the one guarantees the other. Then death shall be destroyed, and all things shall be under Christ's authority.

**15:29** Next Paul evidences the resurrection by two lines of argument. *Firstly*, by the baptism for the dead. Some commentators regard this as a practice of "vicarious baptism", whereby a Christian who has been baptized is rebaptized as a substitute for someone who has died without baptism. Lenski:

> It is needless to say that the New Testament knows nothing about "Vicarious Baptism"; and that if Paul had discovered the beginnings of such a perversion in Corinth he would have opposed it in no uncertain terms.

What then does v.29 mean? The clue is in the context. Paul has just been speaking of the situation of those Christians who had died (15:12-19), and of how the resurrected Christ has destroyed death and thus the sting of death and therefore our fear of death (15:20-28). He is next going to speak of the danger of meeting death which faces every Christian (exemplifying this in himself) - which is pointless if the dead are not raised (15:30-32).

So, in v.29, if the dead are not raised, it is in vain they have lived and died for Christ. Why should others - by taking their place alongside Christ in the profession of baptism - follow in the path of those who had died?

But when it is recognized that these dead are to be raised in Christ at his triumphant Return, then it makes sense to be inspired by the example of the dead (ὑπερ νεκρων, *huper nekrōn*, "in view of the dead") and to be baptized, with all that that implied.

See Lenski 691.

**15:30-31** Then, *secondly*, because of his faithful ministry, Paul is always in danger, and for Christ's sake he may lose his life any day. How pointless this is, and how foolhardy he is, if death comes as the end of existence.

This is as valid today as it was in Paul's time: the labors of many missionaries around the world spending their lives toiling in the work of Christ; the steadfastness of many Christians suffering persecution and death for their faith - all this makes sense only on the basis of the conviction that this earthly life is just the beginning, and the fullness of life for us, eternal life, lies ahead beyond death.

**15:32** The sequence of thought is: If the dead are not raised, then this life is all there is. Furthermore, if death is the end of existence, so that indeed this life is all there is, then we may as well simply indulge ourselves to the full until we die. (And Paul quotes from Isaiah 22:13 for this sentiment, as the prophet inveighed against the behavior of those of his day.)

**15:33** And "Bad company ruins good morals." Others around you are pressuring you (he says) to abandon your standards and indulge yourself without restraint. How can your good character hold up? You are in danger of being corrupted, ruined, by this bad company. Thus Paul pinpoints the pernicious problem of peer pressure, and gives a very strong warning.

But do not yield: do not be led astray. There is a two-fold implication here: Do not be led astray from the way of righteousness by those who have this totally self-indulgent philosophy; and, do not be misled by the erroneous teaching that there is no resurrection. Paul's point of course is that wrong doctrine ("there is no resurrection") opens the way to moral laxity ("indulge yourself now - for your whole existence ends tomorrow").

**15:34** A sharp exhortation: "Sober up righteously! Pull yourself together! Come to your senses, as you ought!" We can translate Paul's words in these different ways.

He goes on: "And stop sinning": negating a present, durative, imperative. "For some have no knowledge of God. For shame! I say to you." Note that this latter sentence is identical with his exclamation in 6:5 (except there he uses λεγω, *legō*, for "I say", while he uses λαλεω, *laleō*, here).

"No knowledge of God" could mean, "are not real Christians, are not converted, have not genuinely received the gospel and been transformed by it" - a possible explanation of the attitudes and behavior of some at Corinth. Or it could mean, "Some do not know the nature of God and thus what we are to be like as his people" - that is, they need to hear and respond to teaching about these things. Or, it could mean both.

### 3. Nature Of Our Resurrection (15:35-58E)

### (a) The Resurrection Body (15:35-53)

**15:35-49** Paul reverts to the main issue under consideration, moving to the next part of his discussion: he returns to what "some" in the church are saying. The NIV has the subjunctive here: "someone *may* ask". But the Greek is future indicative, definite future, not just a possibility: so, as in our version, "someone *will* ask". This is a real, rather than a hypothetical, situation at Corinth.

We do not know how many the "some" may be (it is singular in the Greek, but may well reflect a group at Corinth with these doubts), but the danger of their influence and the tremendous importance of this doctrine are both reflected in the effort - and the space - that Paul puts into refuting their error in this chapter. Evidently the idea of the resurrection of the body was being strongly rejected because it was thought to mean the resuscitation of corpses, conceived as rising out of a grave - and this idea was found repellent.

So Paul now explains the nature of the resurrection body. Paul's explanation may be summed up: At the resurrection, God will give us a new body suited to our new environment in exactly the same way as in this life we have been given a body suited to life on earth.

Paul's analogy of the seed has its limitations as a parallel, but it makes one thing very clear: as between who and what we are now upon earth, and in our resurrection bodies, there will be both continuity and transformation.

This is called a "spiritual body", σωμα πνευματικον, *sōma pneumatikon*). Some people, misunderstanding this term here, have taken it to mean that our new "bodies" will hardly be real and actual bodies, but wispy things, ghostly, insubstantial. This is to fail to grasp the significance of "spiritual".

As our present body is stamped in the likeness of the man made of dust, Adam, so our resurrection body shall be in the likeness of "the man from heaven", Christ the Lord (v.49). His body was solid and substantial: he could say (Luke 24:39), "Touch me and see", inviting touching; he could eat a meal with them on the seashore (John 21:12). But not subject to the limitations of our earthy bodies: he could walk through the rock sealed in front of his tomb, and through the locked door of the upper room. Doubtless there will be a great many other differences. What then is the "spiritual body"?

Gordon Clark 300 writes,

> The best interpretation, therefore, seems to be that the spiritual body is a body such as the Holy Spirit designs to be suitable and competent for the functions of the future life. Incorruptibility is the characteristic emphasized here; but no one would claim that this is the only difference between our two states.

We can confidently expect that we will have a new body as suited for our new realm of existence as our present one is for this life.

**15:50-53** At the return of Christ our flesh-and-blood body (v.50) will be transformed into our imperishable, immortal body - that is, it shall no longer be subject to death or wearing out (whether we are alive at his coming or have already died).

**15:51** "We shall all be changed": A significant issue in relation to the resurrection is the question of identity. The person who is spoken of must be identical with the person who died, otherwise obviously it is not a resurrection if it is somebody else. But, identical in what ways? Obviously not physically: we will have left our mortal bodies behind some time ago, and they have disappeared, "dust to dust".

But yes, in some sense physically, too: there must be this continuity in the same sense that there is continuity physically between an acorn and the oak tree which sprang from it, or else Paul's "seed" analogy is misleading. The kind of continuity and transformation also between a caterpillar and a butterfly: they certainly look different, but you can say that *that* butterfly came from that caterpillar and in a real sense they are one and the same being. So we have to be able to say, "I know I look a bit different, but it's still really me." And also, there has to be spiritual continuity: I have to be all that I was on earth, spiritually, but something more, not something less. There has to be personal identity preserved and continued. Intellect. Personality. Memory. Paul explains: I will be changed. Transformed. But in the ways that count, I will still be me.

### (b) The Lordship of Christ (15:54-58E)

**15:54-56** Thus the lordship of Christ, which Paul has already alluded to, shall be fully demonstrated. Death is swallowed up in victory - death's victory over life is snatched away. The sting of death is sin (and it is the law which convicts of sin): but the final victory of Christ over sin is now complete, and the sting of death is fully removed; Christ's victory swallows up death completely.

**15:57-58E** Not only so, but we are made to share in this victory (over sin and death) through our Lord Jesus Christ (v.57). Knowing therefore the certainty of our ultimate triumph in the Lord, we can stand firm no matter what assaults may batter us. There is nothing that can make us move. Rather, we give ourselves fully to the Lord without fear and without reserve, for we know that our efforts in serving him will always be fruitful, and never in vain (v.58).

Thus Paul's statement of the gospel leads into a consideration of the resurrection, and climaxes in an emphasis upon the lordship of Jesus Christ, who is victorious over all things, including death itself.

So Paul ends his detailed doctrinal section (v.58) with a wake-up call: Get yourself firmly planted, solid and stable, so that you are not blown about. Now: get going, full steam ahead; get on with the job. There is a great deal that still remains to be done. Right doctrine will issue in decisive action. And we have the assurance that we won't be wasting our time and efforts, for we know "that in the Lord your labor is not in vain."

# SOME PRACTICAL AND PASTORAL REFLECTIONS

## The Presentation of the Gospel (15:8-10)

The gospel is a gospel of saving power, of transforming grace. For each individual, the gospel becomes the good news when that person can say, echoing Paul, "and last of all he appeared also to me". The conversion experience for ourselves is most unlikely to include anything even faintly parallel to the resurrection encounters of all these witnesses with Christ: but nonetheless its culmination is in our testifying to our own encounter with Christ. Our presentation of the gospel falls short of the whole gospel unless it brings us to our own testimony to his saving grace.

Thus we can see here that the gospel is three things: *firstly*, a fulfillment of all that God had promised in the Scriptures; *secondly*, a number of historic facts; and *thirdly*, an interpretation of those facts - it happened "for our sins", and this is the basis (and the only basis) upon which we can have forgiveness. But then the outcome of these truths - also part of our message, as it was of Paul's - must be our own personal experience of the risen Christ in our lives. And then these truths require that in proclaiming the gospel we call upon the hearers to respond in repentance and faith, and also encounter Christ.

This personal encounter with Christ is the heart of the conversion experience of any person. It will take a unique form in the life of each one of us, as Christ meets us in whatever way is appropriate to our individuality. But his risen power and transforming grace will produce the same result in our lives as in Paul's: see Paul's response in verses 10 and 11. Similarly we will accept Christ's authority as Lord and become his devoted servant.

## The Practical Problem of Peer Pressure (15:32,33)

For many people, the only significant factor that acts as a brake upon their totally giving way to their lower nature is their concern about what others may think of them. If then they find their peers accepting low standards of behavior and engaging in activities of a very dubious nature, the pressure upon a person's morals and character is almost irresistible. And then the attitude a person will adopt - and the rationale they may well give subsequently for their behavior - is likely to be, "But everybody is doing it." As Paul puts it so succinctly here, "Bad company ruins good morals."

We see this insidious pressure, both subtle and open, all around us today. Peer pressure to conform to the world in our language, our goals, our behavior. If there is no life but this present one, why shouldn't we?

But we will act differently if we believe that this earthly life is but a preparation for the life that is to come, and moreover that the choices we make in this life are decisive for the outcome in the next, seeing that (as Hebrews 9:27 puts it), "it is appointed for man to die once, and after that comes judgement", for "each of us will give an account of himself to God" (Romans 14:12). Thus when we live as those who will have to give an account to God, and say a firm "no" to ubiquitous peer pressure, we are demonstrating in our lives our confidence in the Lord, and his gospel, and the reality of life beyond this one.

Indeed, as Paul says, if the dead are not raised, why not simply indulge ourselves before we die? But if we believe in the resurrection then we will turn away from a life of indulgence and sin (v.34), we will not let peer pressure influence us, and instead we will live our lives as "steadfast, immovable, always abounding in the work of the Lord" (v.58).

## The Lordship of Christ in our Preaching (15:57,58)

The lordship of Christ is implicit throughout this letter. The identification of a Christian is the meaningful cry, "Jesus is Lord", which is the evidence of the Holy Spirit's work in him (12:3b). And as Paul adds, in his very clear statement in 2 Corinthians 4:5, "For we do not preach ourselves, but Jesus Christ as Lord."

Let this note then of Christ's victory, of Christ's authority, of Christ's lordship, be always and equally a part of our own presentation of the gospel. The Christ who died for our sins is the sovereign Lord of all. To receive his gospel is to accept his authority as Lord, to commit ourselves to his service and to become participants in his victory (verses 54-58). It may involve danger or death (verses 30-32); it will certainly involve hardship and hard work (verses 10, 58). But this is what it means to receive Christ.

When, by God's grace, we have the privilege of proclaiming the gospel, let us be sure that it is this whole gospel in all its fullness that we preach: and let us be sure, also, that this whole gospel is being fully demonstrated in our lives.

# CHAPTER SIXTEEN

## SECTION 6:
## FINAL MESSAGES AND GREETINGS (16:1-24E)

### 1. Concerning The Collection for The Jerusalem Saints (16:1-4)

**16:1** Paul was engaged in arranging a contribution from the churches with which he was associated, for the "saints" - the Christians in Jerusalem. They had sold off their houses and lands (Acts 4:34) and other possessions (Acts 2:45; 4:32) and brought the proceeds to the apostles, so that the funds could be used to meet cases of need (Acts 2:45; 4:35). This was widely practised amongst them (Acts 2:44-45; 4:32, 34), although it was completely voluntary (Acts 5:4a). Later, Agabus predicted a famine, which caused "the brothers living in Judea" to be in need of assistance, and so the disciples in Antioch sent help to them "by Barnabas and Saul [Paul]" (Acts 11:27-30E). The Jerusalem church's need for outside support continued in subsequent years, and is referred to in 1 Corinthians, 2 Corinthians, Romans, and Acts 24:17.

Hodge begins his commentary on chapter 16 with an air of puzzlement. He says [361],

> For some reason not now to be certainly ascertained, poverty prevailed in Jerusalem among the believers more than in any other part of the church."

I could point out a reason: they were living beyond their means. They were living on their capital. No individual, no family, can do this for very long before being in serious financial difficulty. Neither can a church - not even the mother church in Jerusalem. God promises to look after us, and take care of us, but this does not put us beyond the law of cause and effect. God does not promise to suspend the principles of common sense or of economic management for Christians if they are generous enough. A string of bankruptcies through the years of soft-hearted Christians demonstrates that this kind of economic behavior is not showing faith in an almighty God: it is improvident foolishness.

Hodge does consider this factor, but does not rate it highly - he goes on to say, "Whatever the cause ..."

Much of Paul's time and energy was devoted to his large-scale collection from his churches for the assistance of the poor in Jerusalem. This was a practical expression of the love of Christ in action through his people, and as such it had a valuable role in awakening mutual care and concern amongst the churches, and confirming their solidarity, and in particular demonstrating to the Jewish church in Jerusalem the one-ness of the Gentile churches with them. Numerous commentators have pointed out the importance of this. I do not question the good that came from Paul's collection. This is always the result when Christians band together and bond together in times of crisis and disaster. But does that make these crisis events a good thing? I wonder personally whether Paul's collection was a case of the Lord bringing good out of evil. Certainly Paul would have been relieved of one very practical and quite burdensome drag upon his evangelistic and church-planting ministry if he had not had need to be so much concerned for the plight of the poor in the Jerusalem church.

**16:2** The only valid reason for mentioning the first day of the week was that this was the day when Christians met together (thus replacing the Jewish Sabbath, the seventh day), and when the amounts set aside would be taken to the assembly and placed in the church treasury, so that (as Paul said) no collections would be necessary when he arrived. Gordon Clark 317 comments:

> [What Paul says in this verse about "store it up"] does not mean "at home", but simply "by himself"; in other words, let each take to himself what he intends to give. [And] θησαυριζων [*thēsaurizōn*] does not mean "save at home" - it means "put into the treasury". This strongly suggests the common treasury of the congregation. Further, if the money were to be saved at home, there would be no point in mentioning the first day of the week. Setting aside money at home could best be done on whatever day the money was received. The mention of the first day makes sense only if Paul had in mind a church service on the Lord's Day.

Hodge 364 has carefully made the same point.

This reference is thus one of only about half a dozen in the New Testament which point to Sunday as the day of Christian worship. The New Testament picture concerning Sunday is drawn clearly enough, though it is not mentioned often. Because they were Jews, the early Christians continued to attend the synagogue, meeting on the seventh day, Saturday. It would appear from the mention of the numbers of Jews who were converted (Acts 4:4; 5:28; 6:7; 21:20), that there would be synagogues where the members were also all Christians. They continued their synagogue services and activities as hitherto, but with this difference: they celebrated the fact that the Messiah had come.

But the practice grew that Christians also met amongst themselves on the first day, Sunday. This began with Christ's disciples gathered together in the upper room, where the risen Jesus himself met with them two Sundays running (John 20:19, 26). When the so-called Council of Jerusalem determined to what extent the Jewish law applied to Gentile converts (Acts 15:5), it is highly significant that the keeping of the Sabbath was *not* one of the requirements. Instead, we find the evidence surfacing that they were meeting on the first day of the week, Sunday. Thus at Troas (Acts 20:7) it was on the first day of the week that they came together. And this day became referred to as "the Lord's Day" (Revelation 1:10).

Thus 1 Corinthians 16:2 can be seen as part of this pattern in the New Testament. But I do not feel it is appropriate to refer, as Hodge 363 does, to Sunday as the "Christian Sabbath". This carries with it too many innuendoes, too many inaccurate implications about the proper Christian use of Sunday. For while Christian worship and Christian attitudes to Sunday have adopted (and validly so) much of the worship pattern of the synagogue, and much of the concept of one day in seven being "special for the Lord", there are many aspects of the Lord's Day which are noticeably and significantly different from the Sabbath. The greatest of these of course is its fundamental meaning. The Sabbath was a day of rest, instituted in Exodus 16 and reinforced by the pattern of the giving of the manna, commemorating God's day of rest after creation (Genesis 2:2-3; Exodus 20:11). The Lord's Day, by contrast, began with the appearances of the risen Jesus, and is a weekly celebration of the resurrection, and is a day of worship, instruction, and service.

The danger on the one hand - which some fall into - is of identifying too closely the Lord's Day with the Sabbath when it comes to Christian observance. These Christians are to be contrasted, on the other hand, with those who are "treating all days alike", citing perhaps Romans 14:5, Galatians 4:10, and Colossians 2:16, and thereby misunderstanding the point and thrust of these verses. By this these people have in effect abandoned the concept of there being a Lord's Day each week, and they thus have impoverished themselves of the benefit, physically and spiritually, that God has planned for us by teaching us to set this day apart as special.

These teachings are the directions, he says, which he gave, first to the churches of Galatia, and now to Corinth. Though these instructions applied to a particular project, the principles which Paul lays down provide a sound general guide from the apostle for financial practice in stewardship in the church for our day as well as his - see "Reflections", below.

**16:3-4** It is noteworthy to see the care that Paul takes in all his financial dealings to ensure that the handling of these is beyond reproach and that he gives his enemies no opportunity to accuse him, no opportunity to claim that he is gaining personal benefit from his ministry.

Thus the Corinthian church, like the others, is asked to appoint representatives who would accompany him to Jerusalem, carrying their church's contribution personally as members of his party. The church's representatives need to be formally "accredited by letter" (ESV and others). Paul does not even insist on accompanying the gifts himself - he is not seeking any personal praise from this. His wise and careful behavior in this matter sets an example for us in the handling of money in the church.

The fact that Paul is undertaking such a scheme (which carries through into his second Corinthian and his Roman letters) is strong evidence against the view that chapter 7 of this letter indicates Paul's expectation of the return of Christ in the immediate future (note my comments about "The Question of the Impending Distress", on 7:25ff.).

In 2 Corinthians, written while he was actually en route to visit them, he speaks again of this collection for the saints in Jerusalem (8:1-9:15E), telling them of the response in Macedonia and encouraging them to a similarly generous response to the collection. When he arrives in Corinth he writes from that city to the Romans, telling them that he is on his way "to Jerusalem bringing aid to the saints", and explaining about the collection (Romans 15:25-29). When arrested in Jerusalem and making his defence to Felix the governor (Acts 24:10), he refers to the delivery of this contribution as the reason for his coming to the city (Acts 24:17).

By means of this collection Paul was able to acknowledge in a practical way his debt and that of the Gentiles to the mother church in Jerusalem (Romans 15:27), and to act to demonstrate his unity (and that of the churches he had founded) with the Christian church amongst the Jews.

## SOME PRACTICAL AND PASTORAL REFLECTIONS

### Looking After the Finances (16:2)

What Paul says about the particular situation he was discussing - the collection for the saints in Jerusalem - contains some very wise and practical directions which provide a sound general guide from the apostle for financial practice in stewardship in the church for our day as well as his.

The principles he sets out are:

**(a)** "On the first day": This reference (with the others which we find in the New Testament) indicates that the Christians made a practice of meeting together on the first day of every week (i.e., on the Sunday). Their giving is thus to be systematic, not sporadic, and it is tied in with the regular Christian worship, which would provide an ongoing reminder and motivation and stimulus for such systematic giving.

**(b)** "Of every week": Their giving is not only to be systematic but regular, and not occasional, or a matter of whim or impulse. The carrying out of this instruction will require planning and preparation, and will mean the incorporation of this Christian stewardship within the framework of a household's regular outgoings.

**(c)** "Each of you is to put something aside": Everyone is to be committed to this program of giving. It is not just for those who feel like it, or who are richer than the rest, or who believe themselves called to be liberal, as if there are others who may consider themselves excused from participation. Whether the sum of money set aside is small or large, each of them is to be involved in this project. The responsibility of giving aid to the saints was an obligation which every one of the brothers in the churches is to acknowledge and accept. So also today the same principle applies: all the people of God have a responsibility of Christian stewardship and as stewards should set an amount aside on a systematic and regular basis.

**(d)** "As he may prosper": Their giving is to be proportional to their means. The principle of proportional giving goes back into the Old Testament, where people gave a tenth of their increase (the tithe) to God. This principle of tithing is confirmed in the New Testament. That Abraham paid tithes to Melchizedek is mentioned in Hebrews (7:2) in a context that indicates that this is viewed favourably. Their tithing is the only thing for which Jesus ever commended the Pharisees: "These you ought to have done", Jesus tells them, "without neglecting the other, weightier, matters of the law: justice and mercy and faithfulness" (Matthew 23:23, cf. ESV and others). The Jews in the church would recognize the tithe as their minimum obligation in giving to God's service under the Old Covenant, after which one could make an offering (Malachi 3:8), and they would not think that under the New Covenant they could please God by doing *less* as stewards of what he had given them. The New Testament exhortations to generosity only make sense if seen as exhorting Christians to do *more* than they would have done as the people of God under the Old Covenant. Proportional giving exemplifies in the material sphere the general principle that "Everyone to whom much was given, of him much will be required" (Luke 12:48).

**(e)** "So that there will be no collecting when I come": Paul's instructions will ensure that the matter is handled in the best possible way, so that the congregation's contributions will all be built up and put aside pending Paul's coming, rather than there being need for a quick unplanned and unprepared-for collection when he arrives. Translated into the circumstances of stewardship for today, this would indicate a putting aside on a regular basis of a suitable proportion of our income so that we have our tithe, our "Christian stewardship reserve", available to expend in whatever way in Christ's service the Spirit brings to our notice. Some part will indeed go on a weekly basis for the support of ministry in our usual congregation, and some in regular support of evangelism, outreach, and relief of need and missionary work around the world, and some will remain "set aside" against the "arrival" of some Christian need to which we can then apply what we have saved up for this purpose.

## 2. Plans, People And Exhortations (16:5-24E)

**16:5** Paul's immediate plan was to travel from Ephesus (where he was at the time of writing) through Macedonia and thence to Corinth. This represents a change of plan for him: his original plan (which he sets out in 2 Corinthians 1:15-23) was to travel direct to Corinth from Ephesus by ship, then to head north-east to Macedonia, then back to Corinth, before journeying to Judea with the collection; and thus he would visit the Corinthians twice, on his way to and his return from Macedonia. But in this letter he is telling them of the change of plans: he will come to them after passing through Macedonia, because, contrary to what he had previously told them, he is going through Macedonia first.

**16:6-7** There are several reasons for this change of plan. The first one is, it will make it possible for him to stay with them for a while, indeed even to spend winter with them, instead of making two briefer visits while just "passing through". And this he will do, "if the Lord permits": Paul is very conscious that his times are in God's hands: man proposes, and God disposes.

"So that you may help me on my journey": the verb is προπεμπω (*propempō*), and is used in the New Testament specifically of financing the next stage of a preacher's or a missionary's itinerant journeyings. Paul uses it again in the same way, and referring to the same situation, in 2 Corinthians 1:16; and also in this same chapter 16 in v.11 in relation to Timothy. Its meaning can be seen clearly from Titus 3:13: "Do your best to speed Zenas the lawyer and Apollos on their way; see that they lack nothing." Also 3 John 6: "You will do well to send them on their journey in a manner worthy of God." For similar use of this word see also Acts 15:3; Romans 15:24.

Often the representatives of the church thus "sending someone on their way" would accompany them during the first part (at least) of the next stage of their journey, partly out of fellowship, and partly for protection: see Acts 17:14-15; 20:38; 21:5. Garland 757 comments further about this:

> Although Paul did not receive support from a congregation while he was working among them, he did allow them to equip him for his travel to his next mission point.

"Wherever I go": Paul has expressed some uncertainty as to whether he should accompany the gift to Jerusalem or not (v.4); if he does not do this, he may go somewhere else - such as (for instance) Rome (Acts 19:21; 23:11).

**16:8-9** The second reason for his change of plan - and, one suspects, the one which weighed more heavily with Paul himself - was that he now finds he has in front of him in Ephesus at this time a great door of opportunity for effective work, and he intends to stay on in Ephesus for a while longer to seize this opportunity which had opened up there. Not only so, but there are many opponents. The NIV says, "there are many who oppose *me*" but "me" is an interpolation, and not in the Greek; it would seem that this is not simply personal opposition to Paul but opposition to the whole church and the whole work of Christian ministry in Ephesus, and Paul wants to stay on and stand with the church in this time of severe attack by its enemies.

Paul was not the one to cut and run when there was opposition or when he foresaw troubles ahead. I like MacArthur's comment (467) on this verse:

> When we are looking for a place to serve the Lord, we should look for a place with problems, for a church that is discouraged, for a group in our own congregation that needs to have a better understanding of God's Word, for people who have never heard God's Word or have heard it only in a perverted or unbalanced form. That is where the Lord can truly use us.

Yes! That captures the essence of Paul's spirit, and the kind of dedicated, committed Christian disciple needed in the Lord's service.

But there was, it would seem, a further reason for staying longer in Ephesus: to allow time for Timothy to return from visiting them, as Paul goes on now to mention. But Paul's intentions about his next visit to Corinth, announced here (v.5), did not work out quite as he planned, as we are now about to see.

The reference here to Pentecost (v.8) is intriguing. It may be simply a time-note - he would be staying in Ephesus till mid-Spring. Or it may (and more probably does) indicate that Pentecost was celebrated in the church's calendar, doubtless because of the significance of the Day of Pentecost as the occasion of the baptism with the Holy Spirit.

**16:10-11** The ESV commences, "When Timothy comes ..." - but the Greek is, "If Timothy comes ..." (as in the NRSV, NIV, etc.). Timothy and Silas had had a share in the ministry that founded the Corinthian church - as Paul specifically reminds them in 2 Corinthians 1:19 (see also Acts 18:5). Apparently Silas and Timothy (though not mentioned) continued accompanying Paul on the remainder of the Second Missionary Journey, from Corinth back to Jerusalem, where this Missionary Journey could be said to come to an end.

Subsequently Silas became an associate of Peter's, and his amanuensis for his First Epistle, as Peter tells us (1 Peter 5:12). But Timothy continued with Paul, as part of his team, and was thus with him in Ephesus when he wrote this Epistle to the Corinthians.

Luke tells us (Acts 19:22) that Paul sent Timothy and Erastus ahead of him to Macedonia in preparation for his visit. Subsequent references (Romans 16:23 and 2 Timothy 4:20 - if they both refer to the same Erastus) place Erastus in Corinth. From 1 Corinthians 4:17 we learn that Timothy is currently on his way to Corinth; the church is exhorted to welcome him warmly.

One wonders about Timothy's attitude in this situation. Paul writes here "*If* Timothy comes ..." (ἐαν, *ean*, with the subjunctive), as if Timothy's coming may be a matter of uncertainty. But most commentators (for example, Garland 758) prefer to take Paul's meaning as *whenever* Timothy comes, simply reflecting the uncertainty of the time taken in travelling in Paul's world. However, see also Hurd's alternative suggestion in his thoughtful comment, cited (above) in my Introduction, about Timothy's "if he comes" visit to Corinth.

Now, Timothy lacked Paul's incisive insight into issues, and of course Paul's apostolic authority. And doubtless being well aware of the troubles at Corinth, Timothy may possibly have been just a trifle reluctant to pay the Corinthians a visit. Certainly Paul's exhortation here - "see that you put him at ease among you" - may reflect this. Then (verses 10b and 11) Paul equates Timothy's work with his own, so there should be no one at Corinth who looks down on him or is reluctant to accept him. An alternative approach: Garland 760 quotes Hutson, who sees this verse, rather, as emphasizing Timothy's fearlessness, rendering 16:10 as "If Timothy comes, recognize that he is fearless towards you; for he is doing the work of the Lord, as I am." Garland warms to this interpretation, which is a possible rendering.

Then the Corinthians are to see to it that they "help him on his way in peace" when he leaves to return to Paul. I have just discussed the meaning of "sending a person on their way" (v.6). Paul indicates he is expecting Timothy's return: the implication here is that Timothy will report to Paul on how this letter is received.

So, what did Timothy tell Paul about the situation in Corinth upon his return? Actually, as we learn from 2 Corinthians, things did not go at all well.

Garland 757 explains what Paul did next:

> We learn from 2 Corinthians that these initial plans changed, and he [Paul] made an emergency voyage to Corinth that proved to be disastrous and disheartening. A nasty confrontation with an unknown individual caused him to beat a hasty retreat and to fire off the letter of tears (2 Cor 2:1-4). But he appears to have followed the route proposed here [in 16:5] at a later date when he travelled to Macedonia and then to Corinth.

Fee 822f. says about the situation:

> One is left to wonder how this visit by Timothy turned out, since there is no further mention of it in Paul's letter. In any case, two things are certain. First, shortly after this letter [i.e. 1 Corinthians] Paul goes absolutely contrary to the plans here laid out, and pays a sudden, unexpected visit to Corinth. Why he did so is a matter of conjecture, but that he should so radically alter his plans suggests that perhaps the return of Timothy gave him reason for even greater alarm with regard to this church. The fact that the visit [to Corinth by Paul] turned out to be such a blow-up, apparently under the leadership of one person in particular, seems to give this suggestion some merit. Second, what Paul did do was to send Titus back to Corinth instead of either himself or Timothy (2 Corinthians 2:13; 7:6-7). For the present, neither of them is a *persona grata* to the community; it also means that Titus must have been a person of extraordinary grace. This, at least, is one viable attempt to make some sense of these very fragmentary pieces of historic data.

Barrett (*2 Corinthians* 7-8) describes slightly differently the situation after Timothy returns to Paul. On Barrett's view, Paul explains in 2 Corinthians 1 and 2 what happened. Paul changed his original plans (as they had been outlined in 1 Corinthians 16) in order to pay a double visit to Corinth (2 Corinthians 1:15-16): he now planned to cross by sea directly to Corinth, then travel to Macedonia, and then "come back to you from Macedonia and have you send me on my way to Judea." According to Barrett, Paul carried out the first part of this revised plan, but when he got to Corinth he found a group of "false apostles" established there, who, led by one man in particular, denounced him and insulted him to his face, and sought to stir up the Corinthians against him. Hurt and confused, Paul continued on to Macedonia, but - in the light of the reception he had received - he abandoned the second leg of his plan, and instead of returning to Corinth as he had told them he would, he returned to Ephesus. Barrett says that this scrapping of the return half of his plan is what Paul is referring to in 2 Corinthians 2:1, "So I made up my mind not to pay you another painful visit." He then wrote to them, from Ephesus, the "severe letter" (Corinthians C), which he sent to them per Titus.

While there are thus differences between scholars in how they understand the exact details of what happened, there is no question that Paul did change his initial travel plans affecting Corinth. Twice, apparently.

The Corinthians antagonistic to Paul were quick to seize upon any opportunity to attack him, and in 2 Corinthians we learn how they criticized him over his changes of plan. For Paul refers to the criticism they levelled against him - they now accused him of fickleness and of having no real regard for the Corinthians despite his pretence that he did. It seems they went further: their charge against Paul was that his word was not reliable: when it suited him he told them lies (he would say one thing - "yes" - and actually do another - "no"). We can see his response to this accusation in 2 Corinthians 1:15-19, especially 17-19.

This is hardly a fair accusation, seeing that he has here told them clearly of the change of plan and the reasons for it, because the situation at Ephesus made a recasting of his original plan a good idea. Now, his original plan was a good idea, too. And then his change of mind was a good idea, and for good reason. And even now, to his revised plan he adds, "If the Lord permits" - in this uncertain world even the new plan is not beyond the possibility of change. And in the event his plans did change again.

We must learn from this for our own day: it is right to plan ahead, as Paul did, but also, significantly, we should hold to our plans lightly, and be willing to change them as the Lord may change our circumstances. But if we do, we should be careful to fully inform others who are affected by this, and explain ourselves to them. Paul's example is a wise one, and the right course for us to follow.

However (notwithstanding his unexpected second visit to Corinth), the information Paul gives us here, plus 2 Corinthians, taken with what Luke tells us in Acts, enables us to get quite a good picture of Paul's movements and their timing. Paul plans now to stay in Ephesus until Pentecost, after which he will travel to Macedonia, and then Corinth, where he hopes to spend the winter.

In any case, after returning to Ephesus from this "painful visit", Paul wrote them this "severe letter", which is referred to as Corinthians C and is no longer extant. (Corinthians A is the letter mentioned in 1 Corinthians 5:9, also now non-extant; Corinthians B is our canonical 1 Corinthians.) This severe letter, which Paul refers to in 2 Corinthians 2:3 and 7:8, was apparently taken to Corinth by Titus, who then began his return journey to Paul with news of its reception.

After sending off Titus to Corinth, Paul had sought to continue his ministry at Ephesus, but could not settle to it. Paul's situation was further complicated by the fact that this was the moment chosen by Demetrius the pagan silversmith to stir up a riot in Ephesus against the Christians there (Acts 19:23f.). After this was resolved, Paul left Ephesus and travelled to Troas to meet Titus on his return journey - obviously a prior arrangement.

But Titus was not there, so Paul continued travelling towards Corinth (whether by road or sea is not known) and met with Titus in Macedonia (2 Corinthians 2:12-13). Paul then sat down in Macedonia, and wrote Corinthians D (our canonical 2 Corinthians) to this church. Then, as he announced in 2 Corinthians 12:14 that he would, he travelled south-west to pay them his third visit.

Acts 19:21a outlines Paul's plan to travel onwards to Jerusalem after first making a circuit through Macedonia and Achaia (including Corinth). Acts 20:1-3 describes this journey, during which he stayed in Greece three months, and then - because of a Jewish plot - travelled back to Macedonia. After the Feast of Unleavened Bread he and his companions sailed from Philippi to Troas, heading onwards for Jerusalem (Acts 20:4-6). He deliberately by-passed Ephesus in order to be able to reach Jerusalem before Pentecost (Acts 20:16). Lenski (*Commentary on Acts*, 835) carefully calculates the time involved in each stage of this journey to show that Paul would have landed in Caesarea with fourteen days available in which to complete the final leg to Jerusalem - which should allow him to arrive there with some days to spare.

**16:12** Paul now moves on to his next topic. From the περι δε (*peri de*) with which this verse commences, it could be taken that Paul is responding to another matter raised in their letter to him - and quite a few commentators do take it thus; that is, that in their letter to him, the Corinthians were extending an invitation to Apollos to return. Other commentators, however, think that this is not necessarily so, and prefer to leave the matter open.

In any case, Paul states emphatically that he has warmly encouraged Apollos to pay them a further visit; but Apollos has absolutely refused to visit the Corinthians again at this time. Apollos had ministered in Corinth on at least one earlier occasion (see Acts 18:27-19:1), and some of the Corinthians had formed a faction around his name (1:12; 3:4).

Paul strongly urged him, "Go!" Apollos flatly replied, "No!" Paul writes, "He was not at all willing to go there now", indicating quite a strong refusal.

Some commentators (like MacArthur) are confident that Apollos had good and proper reasons - such as commitments to some other ministry - for not going just at this time. This may well be so, of course. Or, it could be that when Apollos learnt of the troubles at Corinth, including the existence of a faction there that was invoking his name, he decided that this was not the best of times to visit Corinth. Especially as Paul was already writing them a letter to seek to straighten them out. His comment that he would get around to visiting them when he had a favourable opportunity strikes me to be of the "don't call me - I'll call you" variety. We know of Paul's continued contact with and commitment to Corinth: we do not know whether Apollos ever paid them another visit.

**16:13-14** In moving towards the close of his letter, Paul now gives a series of short exhortations. The exhortation "Be watchful: stand firm in the faith" is a succinct reminder that we are all engaged in a warfare against both apathy and the wiles of the devil. For the devil would, by false teaching, divert us from the truth if he can, and we must take a firm stand upon the deposit of truth we have received, and contend for it earnestly. One is reminded of Jude 3. This thus will make the highest demands upon us; and require our most ardent efforts. Paul here echoes the commission in Joshua 1:6-9: "You must be strong, and very courageous."

And this task, this challenge, will require the full use of our resources - Paul has said much about the resources, in the Spirit, with which God has equipped his people. Then in v. 14, in five short words, he reiterates what he has spent chapter 13 in emphasizing: that all things must be done in love.

**16:15-18** He now acknowledges the men, Stephanas, Fortunatus and Achaicus, who have visited him from Corinth - apparently an official or semi-official delegation from the church, who most likely brought him the letter written by the church (see 7:1). These visitors would also be one of Paul's principal sources for the detailed knowledge of the affairs of the church at Corinth which he displays all the way through his letter. His commendation of these men, coupled with the demand that they be accorded due recognition, reads as being part of Paul's initiative for improving the situation at Corinth. It indicates that Paul has discussed this situation with his visitors, and the Corinthians are now to pay heed to these men and to their other leaders (v.16). These men, Paul acknowledges, have ministered to him on behalf of the Corinthians (v.17): now the Corinthians must accept their ministry also. There is a very high probability that these men carried this Epistle back to Corinth with them as they returned.

**16:19-20** Paul sends closing greetings from "the churches [in the province] of Asia" (of which Ephesus is the major center) - he is frequently at pains to encourage mutual recognition, in the bonds of fellowship, between the different churches: for example, also in this Epistle, in 11:16; 14:33; 14:36; 16:1. Then he mentions in particular "Aquila and Priscilla [Prisca]", who came to Ephesus from Corinth and whom Paul had first met there.

As mentioned in the Introduction, it is not known when and in what circumstances this couple became Christians. We learn from Acts 18:2 that they had previously been residents of Rome, but had been forced to leave when the Emperor Claudius expelled the Jews, and they relocated in Corinth. Luke tells us that Paul went to see them, and then resided with them while he worked with them, as they were all tentmakers. Doubtless Paul's initial contact with them came through the synagogue, and Luke describes them as "Jews" - not as "believers" or similar. It would seem clear, then, that they were not Christians when Paul came to stay and work with them. So it appears highly likely that they were converted during his ministry in Corinth.

If this is indeed the case, it throws new light upon the apparent disaster of their expulsion from Rome, for this relocation led to their meeting with Paul and all that followed: the circumstances of their being thrown out of Rome were all part of a larger plan of God.

When Paul left Corinth, Priscilla and Aquila accompanied him to Ephesus, and remained there while he continued his journey to Jerusalem (Acts 18:18-19). In Ephesus they helped Apollos with his understanding of the Christian faith (Acts 18:26). As we see from this present verse, they are still in Ephesus when Paul returns there, and the church meets in their house; subsequently they returned to Rome, where Paul sends his greetings to them and to the church there that meets in their house (Romans 16:3-5). In his final letter, to Timothy, Paul again sends them his greetings (2 Timothy 4:19). At some point they risked their lives for Paul (Romans 16:4) - we do not have the details, but it may well have been during this period when Paul was at Ephesus, as he seems to have been in danger there (1 Corinthians 15:32).

**16:21** It is Paul's practice to have an amanuensis write down his letters for him, and then to close each letter with a personal note of greeting in his own handwriting. He does this deliberately as the authentication of all his letters. In 2 Thessalonians 3:17-18, he tells us, "I, Paul, write this

greeting with my own hand. This is the sign of genuineness in every letter of mine; it is the way I write." This personal ending, which he wrote
then in his own handwriting, can be identified more or less clearly at the
conclusion of each of his letters.

**16:22** This verse sounds unusually sharp, and pulls us up with a jolt:
which doubtless is Paul's intention. Those who do not love the Lord are
indeed under the curse of God. Note that the verb is εἰμι (*eimi*, "is"), not
γινομαι (*ginomai*, "become"). Perhaps we can take it then as not so much
***pronouncing*** a curse upon them as saying in effect: "As for those who
do not love the Lord: let them ***continue*** under God's curse."

This he follows with a brief prayer in Aramaic: "Come, O Lord." The
explanation of this cry, and the fact that it is in Aramaic, may have its
origin in the Jewish church, as a result of the angels' promise at the
Ascension in Acts 1:11, that Jesus will return. "Maranatha!" It makes a
great catch-cry, combining a fervent prayer for our Lord's return with a
reminder to ourselves that ***that*** is the consummation of all things, to
which we all look forward.

**16:23-24E** As Paul commenced this Epistle with a prayer for grace
upon them from the Lord Jesus Christ (1 Corinthians 1:3), so he now
closes it with a prayer for grace upon them from the Lord Jesus Christ.
This is significant: may all that he has written in between these greetings
be imbued with the grace of the Lord, and be accepted by the
Corinthians by the grace of the Lord.

And Paul's final words are a reminder of what he has sought to
emphasize all the way through: his teachings, especially his criticisms of
them, are to be read in the light of his deep love for them. Criticism is
easier to take, and to heed, when it comes from someone who loves us,
and who speaks in love, for our good.

On this note Paul brings to a close a letter in which he has had need
to correct them rather straightly, but which he has written thus because
he longs that he can change what he has had to say to them in chapter
3:1, and could view them henceforth as spiritual men and women. "Ah!"
I can imagine him saying, as after writing his final greetings in his own
hand, he puts down his pen, "if only! If only!"

# BIBLIOGRAPHY

## COMMENTARIES, MONOGRAPHS AND
## EARLY FATHERS, ON 1 CORINTHIANS

Alford Henry, 1860, edn 1968: *The Greek Testament* [Chicago: Moody Press]
Ambrose: in Kovacs
Ambrosiaster: in Kovacs
Augustine: in Kovacs
Barnett Paul, 2000: *1 Corinthians* [Focus on the Bible, Ross-shire Christian Focus]
Barrett C K, 1968, [2]1971: *The First Epistle to the Corinthians* [London: Black]
Basil of Caesarea: in Kovacs
Blomberg Craig, 1994: *1 Corinthians* [NIVAC ; Grand Rapids: Zondervan]
Bruce F F, 1971: *1 and 2 Corinthians* [New Century Bible; London: Oliphants]
Calvin J, 1546/1834/1960: *First Epistle to the Corinthians* [Edinburgh: St Andrew]
Carson D A, 1988: *Showing the Spirit: 1 Corinthians 12-14* [Sydney: Anzea]
Chrysostom John: in Kovacs
Clark G, 1975: *1 Corinthians: A Contemporary Commentary* [New Jersey: P & R]
Clarke Adam, 1831: *Commentary on the New Testament* [Nashville: Abingdon]
Clement of Alexandria: in Kovacs
Clement of Rome: 1 Clement
Conzelmann H, 1969/1975: *First Epistle to the Corinthians* [Philadelphia: Fortress]
Cyril of Alexandria: in Kovacs
Edwards T C, 1885/1979: *A Commentary on The First Epistle to the Corinthians*
    [Minneapolis: Klock & Klock]
Ellingworth Paul & Hatton Howard, 1985/1994: *A Handbook on Paul's First Letter
    to the Corinthians* [New York: United Bible Societies]
Fee G, 1987: *The First Epistle to the Corinthians* [NIC; Grand Rapids: Eerdmans]
Findlay G, 1900: *The First Epistle to the Corinthians* [Expositor's; London: Hodder]
Ganz R, 2003: *20 Controversies That Almost Killed A Church* [Phillipsburg: P&R]
Gardiner George, 1974/1992: *The Corinthian Catastrophe* [Grand Rapids: Kregel]
Garland David, 2003: *1 Corinthians* [Grand Rapids: Baker]
Godet F, ET 1886/1971: *First Epistle to the Corinthians* [Grand Rapids: Zondervan]
Goudge H L, 1903, [3]1911: *The First Epistle to the Corinthians* [London: Methuen]
Grant F, 1962: *Nelson's Commentary V. 7: Romans-Revelation* [New York: Nelson]
Green Michael, 1982: *To Corinth With Love* [London: Hodder]
Gromacki Robert G, 1977: *Called to be Saints: Exposition of 1 Corinthians*
    [Grand Rapids: Baker ]
Grosheide F, 1953: *First Epistle to the Corinthians* [NIC; Grand Rapids: Eerdmans]
Grudem W 1982 *The Gift of Prophecy in 1 Corinthians* [Lanham: UP of America]
Hillyer Norman, 1970: *1 Corinthians* [New Bible Commentary; Leicester: IVP]
Hodge C, 1857/1972: *An Exposition of First Corinthians* [Grand Rapids: Eerdmans]
Hurd John C, 1965: *The Origin of 1 Corinthians* [London: SPCK]
Irenaeus: in Kovacs
Ironside H, 1938/1973: *Addresses on First Corinthians* [Neptune: Loiseaux]

Jerome: in Kovacs
Johnson Alan F., 2004: *1 Corinthians* [IVP NT Commentary; Downers Grove: IVP]
Jovinian: in Kovacs
Justin Martyr AD 150: in Kovacs, and cited in Edwards
Keener Craig, 2005: *1-2 Corinthians* [Cambridge Bible Commentary; CUP]
Kistemaker Simon J., 1993: *1 Corinthians* [Grand Rapids: Baker]
Kovacs Judith (ed & trans), 2005: *1 Corinthians Interpreted by Early Christian Commentators* [Grand Rapids: Eerdmans]
Lenski R. C, 1937: *Interpretation of I & II Corinthians* [Minneapolis: Augsburg]
Macarthur J, 1984: *1 Corinthians* [MacArthur NT Commentary; Chicago: Moody]
Morris Leon, 1958/1963: *The First Epistle to the Corinthians* [London:Tyndale]
Murphy-O'Connor Jerome, 1979: *1 Corinthians: NT Message 10* [Dublin: Veritas]
Naylor P, 1996: *Welwyn Commentary on 1 Corinthians* [Darlington: Evangelical]
Oecumenius: in Kovacs
Origen: in Kovacs
Orr W & Walther J , 1976: *1 Corinthians* [Anchor Bible, New York: Doubleday]
Prior D, 1985: *Message of 1 Corinthians* [The Bible Speaks Today; Leicester: IVP]
Ramsey William, 1900-1; 1996: *Historical Commentary on First Corinthians* (Ed: M. Wilson; Grand Rapids: Kregel]
Robertson Archibald & Plummer Alfred, 1911: *First Epistle to the Corinthians* [ICC, Edinburgh: T & T Clark]
Ruef J, 1971: *Paul's First Letter to Corinth* [Pelican Commentary; London: SCM]
Stanley A P., 1858/1981 *Epistles of St Paul to the Corinthians* [Minneapolis: Klock]
Tertullian: in Kovacs
Theodoret: in Kovacs
Thiselton A C, 2000: *The First Epistle to the Corinthians* [Grand Rapids: Eerdmans]
Vines Jerry, 1979: *God Speaks Today: A Study of 1 Corinthians* [Grand Rapids: Zondervan]
Wesley John, 1754: *Explanatory Notes Upon the New Testament* [London: Kelly]
Willis W L, 1985: *Idol Meat in Corinth* [Dissertation Series; Chico, California: Scholars]
Wilson G, 1978: *1 Corinthians:Digest of Reformed Comment* [Edinburgh: Banner]

## OTHER BOOKS AND JOURNALS

Agrimson J E (ed), 1974: *Gifts of the Spirit and the Body of Christ* [Minneapolis: Augsburg]
Anderson Scott C.A., 1930: *New Testament Ethics* [Cambridge: Cambridge UP]
Bacchiocchi Sam, 2001: *Wine in the Bible* [Berrien Springs: Biblical Perspectives]
BAG: Bauer, Walter, Arndt W., Gingrich F. W., Danker F. W.: *A Greek-English Lexicon of the New Testament and Other Early Christian Literature.* Edited by Frederick William Danker. 3rd edition. Based on previous English editions by W. F. Arndt, F. W. Gingrich, and F. W. Danker.
Barrett C K 1973: *The Second Epistle to the Corinthians* [London: A & C Black]
Basham D W, 1969: *A Handbook on Holy Spirit Baptism* [Monroeville: Whitaker]
Basham D W., 1971: *A Handbook on Tongues & Prophecy* [Monroeville: Whitaker]

Basham D W., 1976: *Spiritual Power* [Springdale: Whitaker]

Berding Ken, 2006: *What Are Spiritual Gifts?* [Grand Rapids: Kregel]

Bilezikian Gilbert, 1985: *Beyond Sex Roles* [Grand Rapids: Baker]

Bridges Donald & Phypers D, 1973: *Spiritual Gifts and the Church* [Leicester: IVP]

Bromiley Geoffrey (Ed), 1988: ISB Encyclopedia [Grand Rapids: Eerdmans]

Bunn John T., 1973: "Glossolalia in Historical Perspective": in MILLS ·

Burdick Donald W., 1969: *Tongues: To Speak or Not To Speak* [Chicago: Moody]

Butler C. S., 1985: *Test The Spirits: An Examination of the Charismatic Movement*
        [Welwyn, UK: Evangelical Press]

Campbell Bob, 1973: *Baptism in the Holy Spirit* [Monroeville: Whitaker House]

Cassidy Michael, 1983: *Bursting the Wineskins* [London: Hodder & Stoughton]

Christenson Larry, 1968/1972: *Speaking In Tongues* [Minneapolis: Dimension]

Crawford D 1974: *Baptised with the Holy Spirit, Spiritual Gifts* [Sydney: Printatone]

Danker Frederick William , 1999, 2000: Editor of 3rd edition of BAG

Dillow J 1975: *Speaking in Tongues: Crucial Questions* [Grand Rapids: Zondervan]

Douglas  J. D. (ed.), 1962: *New IVF Bible Dictionary*: "'To break bread'"
        [Leicester: IVP]

Dyer Luther B (Ed), 1971/1972: *Tongues* [Jefferson City: Le Roi Publishers]

Edersheim A, 1883/1950: *The Life and Times of Jesus the Messiah*
        [Grand Rapids: Eerdmans]

Field L. C. *Oinos: A Discussion of the Bible Wine Question*: cited Bacchiocchi

Friesen Garry 1980: *Decision Making and the Will of God* [Portland: Multnomah]

Fryer Peter, 1966: *The Birth Controllers* [New York: Stein and Day]

Garratt T.S., 1963: *Christian Worship* [Oxford: Oxford UP]

Gehman H S, 1944: *The Westminster Dictionary of the Bible* [New York: Collins]

Glover John, 1971: "Summary Analysis and Conclusions": in Dyer.

Green Michael, 1975; 2nd Edn1985: *I Believe in the Holy Spirit* [London: Hodder]

Grenz Stanley & Kjesbo D, 1995: *Women In The Church* [Downers Grove: IVP]

Griffiths Michael, 1978: *Cinderella's Betrothal Gifts* [Sevenoaks: OMF Books]

Gromacki R, 1967/72: *The Modern Tongues Movement* [Grand Rapids: Baker]

Grudem Wayne, [2]2000: *The Gift of Prophecy in the New Testament and Today*
        [Wheaton: Crossway]

Gundry Robert H 1966, Vol.17,  pages 299 to 307, "Ecstatic Utterance (NEB)?",
        *Journal of Theological Studies*

Harper Michael, 1976: *This Is The Day* [London: Hodder & Stoughton]

Harris R L, (ed), 1980: *Theological Wordbook of the OT* [Chicago: Moody]

Hillis Don W (Ed), 1974: *Is The Whole Body A Tongue?* [Grand Rapids: Baker]

Howard J Keir , 1983 January: *The Evangelical Quarterly*

Hummel Charles E, 1978: *Fire In The Fireplace* [Downers Grove: IVP]

Hurley James, 1981: *Man and Woman in Biblical Perspective* [Leicester: IVP]

Hymnal Committee (ed), 1937: Book Of Common Praise [Melbourne: OUP]

Ironside H 1912/1980: *Holiness - The True And The False* [Neptune: Loiseaux]

Jeremias Joachim, ET [3]1966 , *The Eucharistic Words of Jesus* [London: SCM]

Kelsey Morton T., 1964: *Tongues Speaking* [London: Hodder & Stoughton]

Kildahl J P, 1972: *The Psychology of Speaking in Tongues* [New York: Harper]

Kildahl John P., 1974: "Six Behavioral Observations About Speaking In
        Tongues": in Agrimson

Kittel Gerhard (ed), 1933; ET 1964: *Theological Dictionary of the New Testament* [Grand Rapids: Eerdmans]

Knowling R, 1900: *The Acts of the Apostles* [Expositor's Gk; London: Hodder]

Lattimore R, 1996: *The New Testament: A New Translation* [London: J M Dent]

Lietzmann Hans, [English Trans] 1953: *Mass and Lord's Supper* [Leiden: Brill]

Lightfoot John, 1859/1989: *Commentary on the New Testament from the Talmud and Hebraica* [Peabody: Hendrickson]

Macarthur John, 1978: *The Charismatics* [Grand Rapids: Zondervan]

Macdonald A. B., 1934: *Christian Worship in the Primitive Church* [Edinburgh: T. & T Clark]

Martin Ralph P., 1975: *Worship in the Early Church* [Grand Rapids: Eerdmans]

Maxwell William, [8]1960: *Outline of Christian Worship* [London: Oxford UP]

May L. Carlyle 1956 February: "A Survey of Glossolalia and Related Phenomena in Non-Christian Religions" [*American Anthropologist* LVIII]

Mayers Marvin K 1973: "The Behavior of Tongues": in Mills.

McGowan Andrew, 1999: *Ascetic Eucharists* [Oxford University Press]

Meier Dick 1974: "Is The Charismatic Movement of God?": in Hillis.

Mickelsen A (ed), 1986: *Women, Authority, & the Bible* [Downers Grove: IVP]

Mills W E (ed) 1973: *Speaking in Tongues: Let's Talk About It* [Waco: Word].

Morris Leon 1959: *The Epistles to the Thessalonians* [Grand Rapids: Eerdmans]

Moule C.F.D., 1961: *Worship in the New Testament* [London: Lutterworth]

Newman B, 1971: *Concise Greek-English Dictionary of the NT* [London: UBS]

Nicole Roger 1986: "Biblical Authority and Feminist Asperations": in Mickelsen

Noonan John T. Jr., 1965: *Contraception* [Cambridge MA, U.S.A.: Harvard UP]

Pack Frank 1972: *Tongues & the Holy Spirit* [Abilene: Biblical Research]

Packer J. I., 1984: *Keep in Step With the Spirit* [Leicester: IVP]

Payne Philip, 2008: *Man and Woman: One In Christ* [Grand Rap: Zondervan]

Phillips J. B., 1972 Edn; *The NT in Modern English* [London: HarperCollins]

Powers B. Ward, 1987: *Marriage & Divorce* [Sydney: Family Life Movement]

Powers B. Ward, 1996: *Ministry of Women in the Church* [Adelaide: SPCKA]

Richardson Peter 1983 January: 37ff. *Novum Testamentum*

Rosner Brian S. 1999: *Paul, Scripture, & Ethics* [Grand Rapids: Baker]

Samarin William J. 1972: *Tongues of Men and Angels* [New York: Macmillan]

Samarin William J. 1973: "Glossolalia As A Vocal Phenomenon": in Mills.

Smail Thomas, 1980: *The Forgotten Father* [London: Hodder & Stoughton]

Schweitzer Albert ET 1910: *Quest for the Historical Jesus* [London. Black]

Stott John R. W. 1964; [2]1975: *Baptism and Fullness* [Leicester: IVP).

Svendsen Eric, 2001: *Who Is My Mother? The Role and Status of the Mother of Jesus* [Amityville: Calvary Press]

Trueblood Elton, 1964: *The Humor of Christ* [New York: Harper]

Wagner C P , 1979: *Your Spiritual Gifts Can Help Your Church Grow* [Glendale: Regal]

Warfield B. B. 1918/1972: *Counterfeit Miracles* [Edinburgh: Banner of Truth]

Welmers William E., 1963 November 8: *Christianity Today* VII 1963, 127.

Winter B. W., 1978 September-December: *The Reformed Theological Review*

# GENERAL INDEX

Plurals, participles etc are included in the simple/singular reference; capitalization is ignored unless significant; f (ff) indicates a reference also on the following page(s).

abstain: 117-126, 179, 181f, 215, 219
Achaia: 13, 14, 15, 16, 27, 467
Achaicus: 12, 17, 115, 118, 468
Adam: 67, 226, 228, 229, 274, 353, 453
Adams: 164
adulterer/-ess: 95, 96, 113, 137, 227
adultery: 119, 133, 138, 149
Agabus: 300, 457
agamos: 129-140, 147, 151f, 165f, 194
alcohol: 97, 261-270
Alexander: 72
Alexandria: 10, 49, 115, 123, 132, 146, 167, 190, 352
Alford: 125, 243, 258, 334, 352, 354
altar: 171f, 212f, 232, 250
amanuensis: 23, 464, 469
Ambrose: 115
Ambrosiaster: 23
Ananias: 73, 98, 300, 303
annul: 149
Antioch: 13, 17, 317, 457
aorist: 30, 98, 99, 125, 131, 346, 447
Aphrodite: 15, 96
Apollos: 17, 26, 33, 43, 45, 53, 54, 57, 63-66, 194, 462, 467-469
apostleship: 169, 189, 321, 340
Aquila: 13, 16, 17, 469
Aquinas: 266, 352
ascension: 47, 193, 236, 307, 448, 470
ascetic: 34, 115, 119-122, 269
Asia: 14, 26, 57, 351, 391, 412, 469
Athanasius: 115
Athens: 13, 16, 35, 36, 39, 200
Augustine: 53, 104, 123f, 151, 180, 352
authoritative: 42, 48, 79, 83, 163, 169, 204, 223, 243
autohypnosis: 395, 418f
babble: 373, 385, 387, 413
Bacchiocchi: 262, 264, 265, 266, 267
Bachmann: 226
BAG: 96, 139, 369, 387
baptism: -ize 11, 26ff, 98f, 134, 190, 208, 306-311, 315, 325, 374, 395f, 411, 415f, 420, 424-437, 441, 451, 464
Barclay: 131, 155, 164
Barnabas: 13, 35, 65, 147, 194f, 305, 319, 379, 457
Barnes: 352
Barnett: 156, 182
Barrett: 43, 55, 56, 74, 226, 247, 275, 278, 335, 383, 465, 466

Basham: 374, 399, 400, 411, 420, 425, 432
Basil: 166
Beck: 103, 131, 142, 224, 229, 414
Berding: 323
Berea: 13, 16, 382
betrothal: 155f, 162, 164, 325, 329
Bilezikian: 384
Bittlinger: 295, 325
Blomberg: 182-185, 198, 201, 203
Braga: 268
break: 69f, 78, 132, 138, 142f, 149, 212, 232-237, 249, 253-256
Bridges: 294, 295
Bromily: 267
Bruce: 209
Bunn: 412, 413, 415, 439
Burdick: 351, 356, 413, 423
Burrus: 14
Butler: 415, 439
Caesar: 15
Caesarea: 14, 166, 467
Calvin: 9, 111, 334, 352, 362, 377, 392, 439
Campbell: 365, 411, 415, 432
Canaanite: 96, 412
canon: 76, 268, 292, 297ff, 319ff, 342-346, 380, 467
Capernaum: 193, 448
Cappadocia: 351, 391
Carson: 284, 334, 338, 342, 343
Cassidy: 425
catamite: 95ff
catastrophe: 325, 439
Catholic: 134, 223, 248, 415
celibate: 115, 124, 128-133, 146, 149-152, 161ff, 167, 169, 194
Celsus: 293
Cenchreae: 15
Cephas: 26, 33, 53, 55, 63, 194
cessationist: 292
charisma: 24, 129, 275f, 280-287, 291ff, 296, 301f, 304, 317- 322, 328, 359f, 425, 426, 441
charismatic: 295, 365, 396-404, 409-415, 418, 420f, 423, 425- 431, 434, 437ff, 441f
child, -ren, -ish: 52, 123f, 142, 146, 191ff, 371f, 419f, 433f
Chloe: 17, 26, 118
Christenson: 364, 365, 416, 432

# GREEK INDEX